PAOLO BOZZI'S EXPERIMENTAL PHENOMENOLOGY

This anthology translates eighteen papers by Italian philosopher and experimental psychologist Paolo Bozzi (1930–2003), bringing his distinctive and influential ideas to an English-speaking audience for the first time. The papers cover a range of methodological and experimental questions concerning the phenomenology of perception and their theoretical implications, with each one followed by commentary from leading international experts.

In his laboratory work, Bozzi investigated visual and auditory perception, such as our responses to pendular motion and bodies in freefall, afterimages, transparency effects, and grouping effects in dot lattices and among sounds (musical notes). Reflecting on the results of his enquiries against the background of traditional approaches to experimentation in these fields, Bozzi took a unique realist stance that challenges accepted approaches to perception, arguing that Experimental Phenomenology is neither a science of the perceptual process nor a science of the appearances; it is a science of how things are.

The writings collected here offer an important resource for psychologists of perception and philosophers, as well as for researchers in cognitive science.

Ivana Bianchi was a close collaborator of Paolo Bozzi in his last years and is Associate Professor of General Psychology, University of Macerata, Italy.

Richard Davies teaches theoretical philosophy at the University of Bergamo, Italy. He previously held positions at Trinity College, University of Cambridge, UK.

PAOLO BOZZI'S EXPERIMENTAL PHENOMENOLOGY

Edited by
Ivana Bianchi and
Richard Davies

Routledge
Taylor & Francis Group

LONDON AND NEW YORK

First published 2019
by Routledge
2 Park Square, Milton Park, Abingdon, Oxon OX14 4RN

and by Routledge
711 Third Avenue, New York, NY 10017

Routledge is an imprint of the Taylor & Francis Group, an informa business

British Library Cataloguing-in-Publication Data
A catalogue record for this book is available from the British Library

Library of Congress Cataloging-in-Publication Data
Names: Bianchi, Ivana, editor. | Davies, Richard (Professor of theoretical philosophy) editor.
Title: Paolo Bozzi's experimental phenomenology / edited by Ivana Bianchi and Richard Davies.
Description: 1 Edition. | New York : Routledge, 2019. | Includes bibliographical references and index.
Identifiers: LCCN 2018015394| ISBN 9780815378457 (hardback : alk. paper) | ISBN 9780815378464 (pbk. : alk. paper) | ISBN 9781351232319 (ebook)
Subjects: LCSH: Bozzi, Paolo. | Phenomenology. | Psychology, Experimental.
Classification: LCC B829.5 .P345 2019 | DDC 142/.7--dc23
LC record available at https://lccn.loc.gov/2018015394

ISBN: 978-0-8153-7845-7 (hbk)
ISBN: 978-0-8153-7846-4 (pbk)
ISBN: 978-1-351-23231-9 (ebk)

Typeset in Bembo and Stone Sans
by Florence Production Ltd, Stoodleigh, Devon, UK

CONTENTS

ACKNOWLEDGEMENTS

The editors are deeply grateful to all the members of the team who have brought this anthology to completion, translating and commenting with the enthusiasm and commitment that Paolo Bozzi's work deserves. Paolo himself would have been enormously touched by this joint effort.

We would also like to thank the Department of Humanities of the University of Macerata and the Department of Letters, Philosophy, Communication of the University of Bergamo for putting at our disposal funds to cover the permissions fees charged by the original publishers of the papers that first appeared in English. Among those who have given us particular support and guidance in the process of finding an appropriate home for Bozzi's work, we would like to recall our gratitude to Lothar Spillmann, Gerhard Stemberger, Benedetto Scimemi, Alan Costall, Tim Crane, Douglas Hofstadter and Linden Ball. Special thanks go to Margarethe Braitenberg Bozzi for many reasons, not least for her charming trust in us.

—*IB*
—*RD*

SOURCE TEXTS AND CHAPTER ACKNOWLEDGEMENTS

Chapter 1

'Fenomenologia sperimentale', *Teorie e modelli*, n.s., VII, 2–3, (2002) pp. 13–48.
Ivana Bianchi thanks Hilary Wilson for her stylistic suggestions.

Chapter 2

'On some paradoxes of current perceptual theories' in S. Masin, (ed.). *Foundations of Perceptual Theory*, North-Holland, Amsterdam, NL, 1993, pp.183–196; re-elaborated by I. Bianchi and R. Davies; republished by permission of North-Holland. Sergei Gepshtein thanks Paolo Portoghesi for permission to reprint Figure 1 in his commentary (originally in R. Arnheim, *The Dynamics of Architectural Form*, University of California Press, 1971).

Chapter 3

'Esperienza fenomenica, esperienza epistemica ed esperienza psicologica. Appunti per l'epistemologia del metodo fenomenologico sperimentale', in G. Siri (ed.). *Problemi epistemologici della psicologia*, Vita e pensiero, Milan, Italy, 1976. pp. 73–87; subsequently entitled 'Appunti per una discussione con gli epistemologi', in Bozzi's *Fenomenologia sperimentale*, Il Mulino, Bologna, Italy, 1989, pp. 155–173.

Chapter 4

'"La corrente della coscienza" ossia gli eventi sotto osservazione', *Teorie e modelli*, 2 (1) (1985), 5–38; reprinted in Bozzi's *Fenomenologia sperimentale*, Il Mulino, Bologna, Italy, 1989, pp. 235–273.

Chapter 5

'Considerazioni inattuali sul rapporto "io-non io"', *Rivista di psicologia*, n.s., LXXVI, 1–2, (1991) pp.19–33.

Chapter 6

'Analisi logica dello schema psicofisico (S-D)'. *Teorie e modelli*, 2 (2), (1985), pp. 3–31; reprinted in Bozzi's *Fenomenologia sperimentale*, Il Mulino, Bologna, Italy, 1989, pp. 297–330.
Francesco Orilia and Michele Paolini Paoletti thank Richard Davies for his stylistic suggestions.

Chapter 7

'Cinque varietà di errore dello stimolo', *Rivista di Psicologia*, LXVI (3/4), (1972) pp. 131–141. Reprinted in Bozzi's *Experimenta in visu. Ricerche sulla percezione*, Guerini, Milan, Italy, 1993, pp. 165–76; and in U. Savardi, I. Bianchi (Eds) *Gli errori dello stimolo*, Cierre, Verona Italy, 1999, pp. 59–69.
Casati's work is supported by grants ANR-10-LABX-0087 IEC; ANR-10-IDEX-0001-02 PSL.

Chapter 8

Excerpted from *Vedere come. Commenti ai §§ 1–29 delle Osservazioni sulla filosofia della psicologia di Wittgenstein*, Guerini, Milan, Italy, 1996, pp. 13–23.

Some slight structural adjustments have been made for its present collocation as a free-standing essay. The illustrations have been re-elaborated from Bozzi's own hand drawings. The editors are grateful to Luisa Zecchinelli and Paolo Pachera for the transcriptions of the musical scores. Kevin Mulligan thanks Paolo Bonardi, Damiano Costa and Michele Ombrato for their help with the translation.

Chapter 9

'Descrizioni fenomenologiche e descrizioni fisico-geometriche'. *Rivista di Psicologia*, *55*, (1961) pp. 277–289; reprinted in *Atti del XIII Congresso degli Psicologi Italiani (Palermo)*, 1962, pp. 29–41; and in Bozzi's, *Fenomenologia sperimentale*, Il Mulino, Bologna, Italy, 1989, pp. pp. 65–81.

Chapter 10

'L'interosservazione come metodo per la fenomenologia sperimentale', *Giornale Italiano di Psicologia*, 5, (1978) pp. 229–239.

Chapter 11

Part A: 'Analisi fenomenologica del moto pendolare armonico'. *Rivista di Psicologia*, *52* (4), (1958) pp. 281–302.
Part B: 'Le condizioni del movimento "naturale" lungo i piani inclinati'. *Rivista di Psicologia*, *LIII* (II), (1959) pp. 337–352; reprinted in Bozzi's, *Experimenta in visu. Ricerche sulla percezione*, Guerini, Milan, Italy, 1993, pp. 51–67.

Chapter 12

'Direzionalità e organizzazione interna della figura', *Memorie della Accademia Patavina di Scienze Lettere ed Arti*, 81, (1969) 135–170; reprinted (with a re-written Section 1) in Bozzi's *Fenomenologia sperimentale*, Il Mulino, Bologna, Italy, 1989, pp. 123–153.

Chapter 13

(in collaboration with G.B. Vicario) 'Due fattori di unificazione fra note musicali: la vicinanza temporale e la vicinanza tonale', *Rivista di Psicologia*, *LIV* (4), (1960) pp. 235–258.
Luisa Zecchinelli thanks Paolo Pachera, a colleague at the Music Conservatory of Verona, for his precious help with the graphics of transcribing the musical examples.

Chapter 14

'Osservazioni su alcuni casi di trasparenza fenomenica realizzabili con figure a tratto', in G.B. D'Arcais (ed.), *Studies in Perception: Festschrift for Fabio Metelli*, Martello-Giunti, Milano, Italy, 1975, pp. 88–110; reprinted in Bozzi's *Experimenta in visu. Ricerche sulla percezione*, Guerini, Milan, Italy, 1993, pp. 177–197.

Chapter 15

'Osservazioni inedite su certe peculiarità delle immagini consecutive' in A. Garau (ed.), *Pensiero e visione in Rudolf Arnheim*, Franco Angeli, Milan, Italy, 1989, pp. 28–37; reprinted in Bozzi's *Experimenta in visu. Ricerche sulla percezione*, Guerini, Milan, Italy, 1993, pp 221–230.

Chapter 16

'Qualità terziarie' excerpted from P. Bozzi, *Fisica ingenua*, Garzanti, Milan, Italy. 1990, pp. 88–117

Chapter 17

Originally in L. Albertazzi (ed.), *Shapes of Forms*, Kluwer Academic Publishers Dordrecht, NL. 1999, pp. 19–50; the text has been revised and amended by the editors; republished by permission of Kluwer.

Chapter 18

The present text is a version substantially revised by the editors of an earlier translation of Bozzi's oral presentation at the Palazzo dei Papi, Viterbo 1991 and published as 'What is still living and what has died of the Gestalt approach to the analysis of perception' in S. Levialdi and C.E. Bernardelli, (Eds), *Representation: Relationship Between Language and Image*, World Scientific, Singapore, 1994, pp. 25–31; republished by permission of World Scientific.

CONTRIBUTORS

Tiziano Agostini is Professor of General Psychology at the University of Trieste, Italy, and he is coordinator of the PhD program in neuroscience and cognitive science. His research interests are in the fields of visual and auditory perception, multisensory integration, perception and action, and applied psychology.

Marco Bertamini heads the Visual Perception Lab at the University of Liverpool, UK, where he investigates a broad range of questions in perception and cognition, in particular perception of symmetry, solid shape and part structure, and factors that affect visual preference (see www.bertamini.org/lab/).

Ivana Bianchi is Associate Professor of General Psychology at the University of Macerata, Italy. Besides a general interest in methodological and epistemological themes concerning the experimental hhenomenology of perception, her main interests are in specific issues concerning the perception of opposition among various kinds of stimuli (from ecological environments to mirror reflections).

Paola Bressan is a research scientist at the University of Padua, Italy. The topics she has published on include visual perception (lightness, colour, motion, depth), inattentional blindness, time estimation, evolutionary psychology of altruism, kin recognition and mate choice.

Luigi Burigana is Professor of Psychometrics in the Department of General Psychology at the University of Padua, Italy. His fields of expertise include discrete mathematical modelling, combinatorial data analysis, psychophysical experiments on spatial vision and intuitive physics.

Roberto Casati is Directeur de Recherche at the French National Centre for Scientific Research (CNRS). He is the director of Institut Jean Nicod (Ecole Normale Supérieure and École des Hautes Études en Sciences Sociales, France). He is currently working with the neuropsychologist Patrick Cavanagh on a book about shadow perception.

Alan Costall is Professor of Theoretical Psychology at the University of Portsmouth, UK. His research takes a broadly ecological approach to the human sciences, but also draws upon the European tradition of Experimental Phenomenology. He is coeditor of *Michotte's Experimental Phenomenology of Perception* (London: Routledge, 2014).

Richard Davies studied and taught philosophy at Trinity College, Cambridge, UK. Since transferring to Italy, he has taught History of Philosophy and Theoretical Philosophy at the University of Bergamo, Italy. His research interests include the work of René Descartes, on whom he has written two books and numerous articles, as well as metaphysics, logic and ethics.

Maurizio Ferraris is Professor of Philosophy and Pro-Vice-Chancellor for Humanities Research at the University of Turin, Italy, where he is also Director of the LabOnt (Laboratory for Ontology) and of the Centre for Theoretical and Applied Ontology (CTAO). His research interests are in the fields of aesthetics, hermeneutics, social ontology and New Realism.

Carlo M. Fossaluzza received his PhD in Philosophy with a specialization in aesthetics and theory of arts from the University of Palermo, Italy in 2015. His main field of research focuses on the theory of the image and the psychology of art, especially in regard to photography and cinema, in the attempt to match a philosophical (both analytical and continental) with a psychological approach.

Alessandra Galmonte is Assistant Professor at the Department of Medical, Surgical and Health Sciences at the University of Trieste, Italy. Her main interests range from basic research in the domains of colour perception, perceptual organisation, and movement learning to methodology and psychophysics, and to applied domains such as psychology of sport, cognitive ergonomics, and usability.

Paolo Gaudiano is CEO of Aleria and Executive Director of the Center for Quantitative Studies of Diversity and Inclusion at CUNY (NY). He began his career at Boston University, MA, where he was a tenured Associate Professor of Cognitive and Neural Systems. He is a serial entrepreneur and has been the founder or key member of six technology-based start-ups.

Sergei Gepshtein is a scientist at the Salk Institute for Biological Studies in La Jolla, CA, where he investigates visual perception and visually-guided behaviour using tools of sensorimotor psychophysics, mathematical psychology, and computational neuroscience.

Robert Kelly is a PhD candidate in philosophy at the University at Buffalo, SUNY, NY. His research focuses on free will and moral responsibility, especially issues surrounding the phenomenon of addiction.

Michael Kubovy is Professor of Psychology at the University of Charlottesville, VA. He has conducted extensive research into visual and auditory perception, as well as the psychology of art from the point of view of Gestalt theory and phenomenology. Among his current projects is an investigation into the structure of lives.

Alessio Moretti is a philosopher and logician. He defended a PhD on 'The geometry of logical opposition' at the University of Neuchâtel, Switzerland in 2009. In his subsequent writings, he has inquired into the overall, complex history of the concept of opposition; the mathematics of the emerging new theory of opposition ('oppositional geometry', which is not reducible to logic); and its applications to fields where oppositions are in play, including various approaches to mind and cognition.

Kevin Mulligan held the Chair of Analytic Philosophy in the Department of Philosophy at the University of Geneva, Switzerland from 1986 to 2016. He has published extensively on analytic metaphysics, the philosophy of mind and Austrian thought from Bolzano to Wittgenstein and Musil.

Francesco Orilia is Professor of Philosophy in the Department of Humanities at the University of Macerata, Italy. His main research interests are in the philosophy of language, the philosophy of mind, the philosophy of time, ontology and logic.

Michele Paolini Paoletti is Adjunct Professor at the University of Macerata, Italy. His research is focused on metaphysics and philosophy of mind broadly conceived, including the nature of properties and relations, different conceptions of existence, fictional objects, the mind–body relationship and ontological emergence.

Ugo Savardi is Professor of General Psychology at the University of Verona, Italy. From his previous investigations of spatial perception, he has more recently moved on to the study of the theoretical bases of Experimental Phenomenology and the historical bases as well as the potential experimental implementations of a modern phenomenological theory of contraries.

Barry Smith is Julian Park Distinguished Professor of Philosophy and Adjunct Professor of Biomedical Informatics, Computer Science, and Neurology at the University of Buffalo, NY. He is also Research Scientist in the New York State Center of Excellence in Bioinformatics and Life Sciences. From 2002 to 2006 Smith served as founding Director of the Institute for Formal Ontology and Medical Information Science (IFOMIS). Smith's primary research focus is ontology and its applications, especially in biomedical informatics.

Achille Varzi is Professor of Philosophy at Columbia University, NY where he works mostly on logic and metaphysics, with a focus on the interaction between these two fields.

Ian Verstegen is Associate Director of Visual Studies at the University of Pennsylvania, PA and received his PhD in art history from Temple University. He has published books and papers on early modern and modern art history, theory and historiography.

Johan Wagemans is Professor in Experimental Psychology and head of the Department of Brain and Cognition at the University of Leuven, Belgium. His current research interests are mainly in perceptual grouping, figure–ground organization, depth and shape perception, including applications in autism, arts and sports (see www.gestaltrevision.be).

Daniele Zavagno is Associate Professor of General Psychology at the University of Milan-Bicocca, Italy. He specialises in the psychology of perception and its applications to the psychology of art.

Luisa Zecchinelli is Chair of Piano and teacher in the Psychology of Music and Vocal Chamber Music at the Conservatory 'E.F.Dall'Abaco' in Verona, Italy. She graduated in philosophy from the University of Bologna with a thesis in psychology of music on perceptual principles of musical organization in simultaneous melodies.

INTRODUCTION

Ivana Bianchi and Richard Davies

Paolo Bozzi (1930–2003) was one of the most fully-rounded and subtle thinkers in Italian experimental psychology, who, in addition to his laboratory work, was a philosopher, a violinist, a musical composer and an essayist.

After graduating in philosophy from the University of Trieste, Paolo Bozzi began as an assistant to the leading Italian Gestalt psychologist Gaetano Kanizsa (1913–1993) in the Institute of Psychology at Trieste, around which his academic career was centred (though he also taught for brief periods at Padua and Trento), where he occupied the Chair of Methodology of the Behavioural Sciences, from which he retired in 1990. Throughout his career, he kept close ties with the laboratory at Trieste in a series of experiments that were the first outings in what later came to be known as "naïve physics" beginning in the late 1950s, with studies of the perception of pendular motion and of bodies in free fall. In collaboration with his friend and colleague Giovanni Bruno Vicario (1932–), Bozzi published a seminal paper in 1960 on auditory streaming and on factors for the unification of musical notes. In the early 1960s, he isolated the function of directionality as a factor in the unification of visual events. In the 1970s, he proposed and defended the method of interobservation as an experimental approach to the study of vision, and in the following decades, he continued to bring to light interesting perceptual behaviours, such as achromatic transparency using simple lines and the dynamic behaviour of coloured after-images.

In parallel with this rich range of experimental discoveries concerning sight and hearing, of which we reproduce some of the leading results in Part IV, Bozzi was continuously engaged in elaborating a theoretical programme for his research. The resulting anti-metaphysical and anti-psychophysical stance underpinned an Experimental Phenomenology *iuxta propria principia* ("by means of its own principles"). As a point of methodology, his approach was to view his experimentation as an ethology of objects and events, and, as a point of epistemology, he regarded his results as a branch of natural science, of a piece with and a foundation for a naturalistic conception of knowledge. In what we might think of as an extreme version of Bozzi's view, for all that it is balanced and thoroughly argued for, Experimental Phenomenology is neither a science of the perceptual process nor indeed a science of the appearances, but is rather a science of how things are.

In Bozzi's writings, descriptions of phenomena are intertwined with descriptions of methodological matters and with theoretical elaborations of those very descriptions. Likewise, the observations that he made "in the laboratory" are intertwined with the observations that he made in the natural laboratory that is the world outside the laboratory, for Paolo Bozzi was an experimental phenomenologist in life as lived outside the walls of academe. As we gather from his writings, he was an acute observer of the passing scene, an attentive reader of the classics and a day-to-day experimenter so that a characteristic move in his writing and in his theoretical thought is a recurrent back-and-forth between laboratory observations and observations of everyday life.

The reciprocity between experimentation and reflection is perhaps the architectonic feature of Bozzi's approach to his chosen field of study. Just as he loved to manipulate the look of the facts under observation ("I change this here, to see what will happen there."), with the same pleasure and sense of need that a musician varies the ways of plucking the strings of a violin, with the fingers or with the bow, so as to hear what difference it makes, so he always kept before his mind the motto that "experiments are bits of reasoning". And these reasonings and reflections, binding together his experimental procedures, are of interest not only to the vision scientist who is seeking to manipulate the structure of the facts so as to bring out the perceptual structure or to the cognitive psychologist who is looking for the perceptual grounding of various cognitive phenomena concerning imagination, language, memory and thinking, but also to the thinker who is seeking a theoretical understanding of the reality of the perceived world. They are likewise of interest to philosophers of perception who are concerned with teasing apart (theoretically and methodologically) cognitive and phenomenal dimensions in visual experience, with the role of introspective reports, understood as descriptions of direct experience of the world in contemporary vision science as well as to anyone committed (for theoretical or practical reasons) to bringing out the structural isomorphism between any given conceptual field and what is often these days rather vaguely known as "common sense".

Out of Bozzi's output of about 100 articles, book chapters and monographs, the present anthology presents a selection of 18 items aimed at giving a taste of the complexity and richness of his thought. Only three of the papers have previously appeared in English, and are here presented in slightly revised form. Some of the others have appeared in various versions in Italian, in journals and in anthologies, or as re-worked by Bozzi himself in his most accessibile and wide-ranging statement of his overall position in *Fisica ingenua* [Naïve Physics] (Garzanti, Milan, 1990), a work that brings together, as its subtitle says, "studies in the psychology of perception", with many more personal musings on Bozzi's practical and theoretical engagements with music as well as with the questions that he already posed for himself as a child about the relation between words and things, between meaning and value, between sounds and objects, between observation and deduction, and between perception and imagination.

In his lifetime, Bozzi was reluctant about having his works translated out of the supple and trenchant Italian that is so noteworthy a feature of his performances – and so rare a feature of academic writing, not only in Italian. In collaboration with the translators, the editors have reviewed and revised all the texts singularly and as a whole, with a view to ensuring not only closeness to Bozzi's originals but also a certain degree of stylistic and terminological consistency from one chapter to the next. Despite the inevitable loss of some literary merit, we trust that our efforts will be redeemed by making his thought accessible to a wider readership. By "a wider readership", we mean not only the larger Anglophone world to which the name of Bozzi may be little known, but also a disciplinary broadening beyond the confines of the specialist publications in which many of the items first appeared, primarily dedicated to technicalities of the psychology of vision science. For those working in that field, many of these contributions to Experimental Phenomenology will suggest fresh theoretical ideas and methodological insights that call out to be integrated with the theories of perception of Gestalt and neo-Gestalt psychology (for a review, see Wagemans, Elder et al. 2012; Wagemans, Feldman et al. 2012), of Michotte (1946; see also Wagemans, van Lier and Scholl, 2006) and Gibson (1950 1968, 1979), as well as to be brought into dialogue with the more recent debates about the possible profiles for a science of experience that are also reflected in the current renewal of interest in Experimental Phenomenology as evidenced, for instance, by the reprint of the invaluable volume first edited in 1990 by Thiné, Costall and Butterworth, *Michotte's Experimental Phenomenology of Perception* (2014), by Albertazzi's *Handbook of Experimental Phenomenology* (2013), by the new edition of Don Ihde's *Experimental Phenomenology: Multistabilities* (2012) and by Niveleau and Métraux's *The Bounds of Naturalism: Experimental Constraints and Phenomenological Requiredness*. Bozzi's Experimental Phenomenology can contribute to investigating the structures and functions of mental simulation, commonly understood as "the re-enactment of perceptual motor, and introspective states, acquired during experience with the world, body and mind" (Barsalou, 2008, p. 618, 2010). In particular it can contribute to exploring the distinctiveness and at the same time "derivative" relationship between perception and imagination, perception and language (discussed, for example, in Gallagher and Zahavi, 2008; Thompson, 2007a, b; Bloomberg, and Zlatev, 2014; and empirically addressed in Pecher and Zwaan, 2005, but also in most of the psychological literature on naïve physics or naïve optics). It offers a useful perspective for those engaged in the development of experiential view in cognitive semantics and in promoting a cross-fertilisation between cognitive linguistics and phenomenology (e.g. Bloomberg, and Zlatev, 2014; Zlatev, 2010; Woelert, 2011). Moreover Bozzi's approach may be a source of stimulus in neighbouring research projects, such as those into visual and auditory scene analysis of complex environments or into robotics that use naïve-physics models rather than AI. Further afield, researchers with other interests in naïve observers' experiences, will find much that favours a realist theory of experience and a realist ontology, as well as providing thought-provoking insights into experimental philosophy and experimental epistemology.

The scheme of the present anthology aims at giving pride of place to Bozzi's own words and thus to open a free dialogue between the author and the reader in the hope of stimulating fresh thoughts and new ways of understanding whole sets of questions – or reinforcing reasons for dissent from the views that Bozzi put forward. The team of experimental psychologists and philosophers who collaborated on the anthology offered brief comments on the texts, in many cases continuing discussions that they had been carrying forward with Bozzi himself. The approaches taken in these comments have been left entirely up to the single scholars, so as to reflect the very different ways one might "dive into" these writings and come up with new observations, reflections and ideas for further research work. The hope is that these *intermezzi* will help the reader to get a feel for the debates to which the papers are still vibrant contributions.

The lead editor, Ivana Bianchi, is responsible for the selection and structuring of the material here presented, which is articulated into four parts plus a section of "afterthoughts".

The basis for this choice of the core themes derives from suggestions that Bozzi made in the course of a cycle of discussions held with a select group of friends and collaborators at the University of Verona in 2001 (two years before his death) focusing in each session on one or other of the writings that Bozzi had chosen to be commented on by and with him. It may be helpful to summarise the underlying architecture and some of the many interconnections that hold the parts together as follows.

The three papers that open the volume in Part I delineate an overall picture of Bozzi's standpoint. They set out the framework for the writings that follow and that go more deeply into one or another issue. Experimental phenomenology (Chapter 1) is one of Bozzi's last writings, to which the Verona discussions we have just mentioned were a spur. It is certainly *the* paper in which he presents an overview of his Experimental Phenomenology of Perception (henceforth, EPhP). If Chapter 1 defines what Bozzi expects EPhP to do, in Chapter 2, On some paradoxes of current perceptual theories, he highlights the drawbacks of alternative perceptual theories. He does this by discussing the paradoxes that are embedded in these alternative theoretical positions. Once the programme of Bozzi's EPhP has been clarified, one still needs to understand what "phenomenal experience" means for him. In Chapter 3, Phenomenal experience, epistemic experience and psychological experience. Notes towards an epistemology of the phenomenological experimental method, he sets out the differences among phenomenal experience (i.e. direct experience or "reality"), epistemic experience (i.e. the kind of experience described by means of operations or measurements, which is the object of a specific discipline) and psychological experience (i.e. the biological and psychological processes occurring in the brain).

One of the main conclusions reached at the end of Part I is that the contents of EPhP are "what is directly under observation" (i.e. "phenomenal experience" or "reality"). The next chapters in Part II define what is "under observation" according to Bozzi. Chapter 4, The stream of consciousness, or the events under observation, answers the question: what is "under observation" in temporal terms? This is a brilliant discussion of the temporal edges of the phenomenal present full of interesting references and observations. Chapter 5, Untimely meditations on the relation between self and non-self, clarifies what is "under observation" in spatial terms. Is it just what is strictly speaking "visible" (meaning the portion of space that occupies my visual field right now, given the position of my head and my eyes)? Or does it extend to the space which is not in front of my body but is behind me or out in the corridor which is just beyond the door of the room where I'm sitting and so on? The relation between these facts and the psychophysical chain, which is apparently the necessary framework for any analysis of the perceptual process, is addressed in chapter 6, Logical analysis of the psychophysical (L-R) scheme. In discussing the independence of the phenomenal world from the underlying mechanical processes, Bozzi adds a strong argument in support of his idea of an EPhP *iuxta propria principia* and at the same time provides a strong logical argument to avoid any type of physical reductionism or neuro-reductionism.

Related to the idea of EphP *iuxta propria principia* are the two warnings that he gives in the next two chapters: Do not confuse what we see (phenomenal experience) with the "stimulus" (Chapter 7) and do not confuse seeing with interpreting (Chapter 8). In Chapter 7, Five varieties of stimulus error, five variants of the stimulus error are presented and discussed. As often happens with Bozzi's writings, this paper highlights both the methodological implications for the experimental researcher of what is being pointed at and the epistemological implications of the issue discussed for a theory of perception. Chapter 8, Seeing As, presents

Bozzi's discussion of one of the descriptions Wittgenstein gives in *Remarks on the Philosophy of Psychology I* §1–29. The distinction between what we see and what we know about what we see is a key point in Bozzi's definitions of "phenomenal reality", i.e. the world that we interobserve and inter-subjectively share, over against the "cognitive integrations" or interpretations of it (which might indeed be subjective) that we apply to it.

Once Parts I and II have clarified what "phenomenal experience" (the subject of EPhP) is, according to Bozzi and what it must not be confused with, we can take a step further and define the basic tools to be used in order to produce an uncontaminated analysis of phenomenal experience. This is what is developed in Part III. Chapter 9, Phenomenological descriptions and physical-geometrical descriptions, defines the minimum criterion to be applied in describing the characteristics of the phenomenal world. The discussion focuses on the basic geometry of the phenomenal world, but the issues addressed here lead to a more general question concerning the relation between formalisms, technical constructs and vocabularies in the EPhP. Since the phenomenal world is not one's private world, it can be interobserved. In Chapter 10, Interobservation as a method for Experimental Phenomenology, Bozzi puts forward a new experimental approach, which he calls "interobservation", as an alternative to the classic experimental method adopted in psychology prescribing reports from independent subjects. He discusses the bases of this method, its advantages and the conditions under which its use is recommended.

With all these premises and tools in hand, which define the theoretical and methodological background of Bozzi's EPhP, we follow him into the laboratory in Part IV and consider some specific phenomena that he brought into focus.

Chapter 11, Phenomenological analysis of pendular harmonic motion and the conditions for "natural" motion along inclined planes presents two studies of the phenomenology of motion which are two inaugural works in what, twenty years later, came to be called Naïve (or Intuitive) Physics (McCloskey 1983; McCloskey, Caramazza and Green, 1980). Chapter 12, A new factor of perceptual grouping: demonstration in terms of pure Experimental Phenomenology, is an excellent discussion that adds a new law of unification to the list of factors initially identified by Wertheimer (1923/1938). The structure of its arguments emphasises the role of perception of couplings (i.e. direct relationships) in EPhP demonstrations. If the foregoing chapter represents an example of how Bozzi contributed to the development of Wertheimer's laws of organisation in vision, Chapter 13, Two factors of unification for musical notes: closeness in time and closeness in tone, shows an innovative development of these laws in the field of acoustics. Here Bozzi analyses two factors separately and in conflicting conditions: proximity in time and proximity in tone.

In Chapter 14, Observations on some cases of phenomenal transparency obtained with line drawings, in the tradition of Metelli's transparency law (Metelli 1974, 1985), Bozzi draws attention to another way of conveying the perception of transparency that derives from outlines rather than grey surfaces. Besides providing an opportunity to demonstrate the spectacular behaviour of chromatic after-effects (which led Bozzi to talk of a "hydraulic model"), Chapter 15, Original observations on certain characteristics of afterimages, shows EPhP at work on observations that lie at the boundary of the genuinely phenomenal distinctions between what appears to be subjective and what appears to be objective. This is a descriptive distinction in Bozzi's view.

In Chapter 16, Tertiary qualities, Bozzi addresses two questions. The first is: What is the place of tertiary qualities (or expressive qualities) in phenomenal experience? Drawing on

Gibson's account of affordances (1979), Bozzi suggests that these qualities cut across the traditional subjective-objective divide. The second: Do they share the same factual identity of what we mean by "reality"? Bozzi's answer is "yes".

The last section, Afterthoughts, is aimed at those readers who, having got to the end of the book, might be wondering how Bozzi located himself relative to the traditions of experimental psychology of which he was undoubtedly an heir. In Chapter 17, Experimental Phenomenology: a historical profile, Bozzi presents a look backwards over his discipline, tracing its philosophical roots in post- (and, in some key moments, anti-) Kantian philosophy as well as stressing the wealth of laboratory results on which the experimental programme was based; and Chapter 18, What is still living and what has died of the Gestalt approach to the analysis of perception, clarifies his relationship with key theoretical presuppositions of classical Gestalt psychology and at the same time as relaunching its methodological approach as a contribution to new trends.

References

Albertazzi, L. (ed.) (2013). *Handbook of Experimental Phenomenology. Visual Perception of Shape, Space and Appearance*. Chichester, UK: Wiley Blackwell.

Barsalou, L.W. (2008). Grounded cognition. *Annual Review of Psychology, 54*, 617–645.

Barsalou, L.W. (2010). Grounded cognition: past, present, and future. *Topics in Cognitive Science, 2*(4), 716–724.

Blomberg, J. & Zlatev, J. (2014). Actual and non-actual motion: why experientialist semantics needs phenomenology (and vice versa). *Phenomenology and the Cognitive Sciences, 13*, 395–418.

Gallagher, S. & Zahavi, D. (2008). *The Phenomenological Mind: An Introduction to Philosophy of Mind and Cognitive Science*. London: Routledge.

Gibson, J. J. (1950). *The Perception of the Visual World*. Cambridge, MA: Riverside Press.

Gibson, J. J. (1968). *The Senses Considered as Perceptual Systems*. Boston: HoughtonMifflin.

Gibson, J. J. (1979). *The Ecological Approach to Visual Perception*. Boston: Houghton Mifflin.

Hatfield, G., & Sarah, A. (2014). *Visual Experience. Sensation, Cognition and Constancy*. Oxford: Oxford University Press.

Ihde, D. (2012). *Experimental Phenomenology: Multistabilities*, 2nd edn. New York: SUNY Press.

McCloskey, M. (1983). Intuitive physics. *Scientific American, 248*, 122–130.

McCloskey, M., A. Caramazza, & B. Green. (1980). Curvilinear motion in the absence of external forces: naive beliefs about the motion of objects. *Science, 210*, 1139–1141.

Metelli, F. (1974). The perception of transparency. *Scientific American, 230*, 90–98.

Metelli, F. (1985). Stimulation and perception of transparency. *Psychological Research, 47*, 185–202.

Michotte, A. (1946). *La Perception de la Causalité*. Paris: Vrin.

Niveleau, C. E. & Métraux, A. (2015). (Eds.). The bounds of naturalism: experimental constraints and phenomenological requiredness. *Philosophia Scientiae*,

Special Issue, *19* (3).

Pecher, D. & Zwaan, R.A. (2005). The role of perception and action in memory, language and thinking. In D. Pecher & R.A. Zwaan (Eds.). *Grounding Cognition: the Role of Perception and Action in Memory, Language, and Thinking*, pp. 1–8. Cambridge, UK: Cambridge University Press.

Thinès, G., Costall, A., & Butterworth G. (Eds.) (2014). *Michotte's Experimental Phenomenology of Perception*, 2nd edn. New York: Routledge.

Thompson, E. (2007a). Look again: phenomenology and mental imagery. *Phenomenology and the Cognitive Sciences, 6*, 137–170.

Thompson, E. (2007b). *Mind in Life: Biology, Phenomenology, and the Sciences of Mind*. London: Belkarp Press.

Wagemans, J., Elder, J., Kubovy, M., Palmer, S., Peterson, M., Singh, M., & von der Heydt, R. (2012). A century of Gestalt psychology in visual perception: I. Perceptual grouping and figure-ground organization. *Psychological Bulletin, 138* (6), 1172–1217.

Wagemans, J., Feldman, J., Gepshtein, S., Kimchi, R., Pomerantz, J., van der Helm, P., & van Leeuwen, C. (2012). A century of Gestalt psychology in visual perception. II. Conceptual and theoretical foundations. *Psychological Bulletin, 138* (6), 1218–1252.

Wagemans, J., van Lier, R., & Scholl, B. J. (2006). Introduction to Michotte's heritage in perception and cognition research. *Acta Psychologica, 123*, 1–19.

Wertheimer, M. (1938). Laws of organization in perceptual forms. In W. D. Ellis (ed.). *A Sourcebook of Gestalt Psychology*, pp. 71–88. London: Routledge & Kegan Paul. (Reprinted from *Psychologische Forschung, 4* (1923), 301–350.

Woelert, P. (2011). Human cognition, space, and the sedimentation of meaning. *Phenomenology and the Cognitive Sciences, 10* (1), 113–137.

Zlatev, J. (2010). Phenomenology and cognitive linguistics. In D. Schmicking, & S. Gallagher (Eds.) *Handbook of Phenomenology and Cognitive Science*, pp. 415–446, Dordrecht, Germany: Springer.

PART I

1

EXPERIMENTAL PHENOMENOLOGY

Translated by Ivana Bianchi

The following pages represent a written version of the Keynote Address that I presented in opening the Padua conference on Experimental Phenomenology[1]. Speaking on that occasion, and more to the point, after I had finished speaking, I could not shake off the impression that the public – made up as it was of academic colleagues specialising in research more or less close to mine, and almost all of them indeed old friends of mine – were listening to what I was saying as if it were yet another of my nuggets of scientific autobiography, conjuring up old times and personalities of the past, a granddad's tale of scientific practice in bygone days, for sure interesting in patches and perhaps even relevant to today in their own way. This misapprehension was to a great extent my fault because I had not taken fully into account the amount of time that I had available to me; but, to a lesser extent, it was also due to my listeners' attitude, which habitually takes for granted that what I have to say and what I write is no longer up to date, and which contextualises my every idea in a historic limbo that is rather alien to the terminology, the theorems, the conceptual practices and the scientific stereotypes of today.

To try to get round this sort of misapprehension, in place of merely repeating the Address, I shall try to offer an anatomy of it, summarising certain phases of it that seem to me to be important, and offering some brief and radical theoretical comments on these short summaries. In this way I hope to boil the talk down to a sequence of propositions, if need be paradoxical or hard to swallow, that make up the main points of an ideal scheme that is wholly coherent, even if nobody cares. To help this procedure to work, I should begin by pointing out two introductory things about my subject matter. One is a fiction, the other is a warning.

The fiction

Not long ago, Professor Mazzocco reminded me that, in the early Sixties, I used to introduce my psychology courses in general psychology (always taking problems of perception as the key questions) by commenting in detail on a passage of Descartes where the philosopher speaks about the epistemological and metaphysical fiction of an evil demon. This demon is capable of generating in us all sorts of sensory impressions at whim, leading those of us involved in this kind of virtual reality to false beliefs concerning the world, thus providing the empirical basis for methodical doubt to be extended in every direction beginning with the senses.

Mazzocco remembered how, from this introduction, I drew a moral for the benefit of my students, who were all students in philosophy, since at that time the Faculty of Psychology did not exist. This moral, which Descartes himself had incidentally illustrated in a passage of the *Objections and Replies*, was: let the evil demon deceive us as he will, but regarding the virtual world which he has ingeniously constructed we can build an unimaginably large number of true propositions about what are improperly called the "appearances" as well as a great deal of coherent theory, given that the demon's virtual project is admirably consistent. In order to discover the regularities within these diabolical deceptions, we must observe and carry out experiments, systematically varying the mischievous devices created with evil intent. At this point I would then begin with experimental demonstrations, as my classroom was relatively well equipped. This, then, was Descartes' fiction.

But no. It is only the starting point. How could we doubt the entire unobservable realm that science describes as the external support, the basic condition of perceptual experience but that is beyond the boundaries of that experience? I say, how could *we* doubt, *we* who are nourished by *Scientific American*, university textbooks, interdisciplinary studies straddling physics, biology, physiology and AI, and by representations of the world offered by P. Angela and Son[2] and by the colleague who provides us with a philosophy suitable for connecting everything and anything? Come on! The fiction of Descartes is too far-fetched. I feel I must propose a slightly updated version.

Since I believe in what science says – albeit with some reservations and if only to save myself the trouble of doubting and to be able to trust what I am told by my doctors, some of them good ophthalmologists – I propose a meta-pretence based on the classic pretence.

Let's pretend to doubt. We can pretend to have doubts even about things that we blindly believe, things that are absolutely certain and regarding which an exercise in scepticism would soon lead to madness. We can pretend to doubt quite easily the conceptual artefacts we use daily in our profession, such as lateral inhibition or 2½-D sketch. And sometimes we really do doubt. Thus, we can pretend to doubt about stimuli (whatever that word means), and also about the response of certain measuring devices applied to the object of our observation. So I can, for example, pretend to doubt that Müller-Lyer parallel lines are of equal length even though I'm comparing them with the aid of a pair of compasses, repeatedly applying them to one and then to the other and noticing that, to do so, I do not have to vary the angle of aperture – and this is *one* possible definition of the phrase "equal length". Similarly I can pretend to doubt that the grey of the two samples that I cut from the same cloth and then placed one on white paper the other on a blackboard, is the same. But what do I mean when I say that when I observe them I doubt that I see them as different (or that I see a difference in length in Müller-Lyer lines)? In the very middle of observing, I say to myself "now I'll pretend to doubt what I see; here I go, I'm doubting, I really do not know anymore". If one really tries to do this, not merely to imagine it, and one forces oneself to doubt what one is observing, one quickly learns that this act does not make any sense. It is the verb "to doubt" which empties itself and vaporises, while nothing happens to the scene in front of one's eyes. When we pretend to have doubts about our retina and what is happening to it, or about the wave and corpuscular theories of light, or about the fact that, whatever they are made of, electromagnetic waves reach our eyes, or about 2½-D sketch, or about anything that Descartes regarded as doubtful, the expression of these doubts boils down to a sophistical group of propositions that are false with the regard to scientific objects, such as: "I doubt that this surface reflects light rays onto my eyes", "I doubt that this exists",

"I doubt that I have neural processes in the visual areas of my brain", and so on. But when I say I have doubts about what I'm observing, I am talking pure nonsense. Pretending to doubt is a game with the experience of nonsense.

This is the deep nature of the *explanandum* that is perception. You cannot pretend to doubt, just as you cannot believe that you believe.

The warning

If someone, at this point, thinks that such a conception of perception may be for sure philosophical, but that it falls outside the logical space of the natural sciences, to which experimental psychology is related by historical tradition and by its nature, that person needs to be reminded that this is not true. Experimental phenomenology is a branch of natural sciences and a part of a naturalistic conception of a theory of knowledge. I believe that it is the bedrock of a naturalistic conception of knowledge.

It is quite wrong to think that a naturalistic conception of perception must be the result of an assemblage of fragments of notions deriving from the natural sciences, if by that we mean an encyclopaedia of facts and concepts arising in biology, physiology, physics, chemistry, artificial intelligence, information theory and the like. For it is not by putting together, however ingeniously, pieces of knowledge acquired elsewhere that we can give substance to a theory of observable experience (visual, acoustic, tactile, proprioceptive and so on), which is to say to a theory or a way of thinking that brings coherence and, most of all, leads to the discovery of new facts about perception.

Rather, a natural science of perception – Experimental Phenomenology – can be achieved by adopting the investigative procedures that have been valuable in natural sciences, by multiplying observations and perfecting them in experimental environments, by reducing them to situations that can be observed in controlled conditions and then tracking the logical routes that bring them back from the lab to everyday observable reality and to the ecological dimension. It is a little embarrassing for me to suggest comparisons that are too obvious to my esteemed colleagues and co-researchers, but one already has the right system of coordinates to see Experimental Phenomenology as a naturalistic approach to the study of perception if one has understood how ethology arose and developed, and how it has revolutionised biology. It took shape from very many observations, directly scrutinising animal behaviour and inventing tricks to modify it, clearing animal psychology laboratories of those stereotyped farcical settings such as mazes, and replacing them with more ecological environmental con-ditions, including interwoven relationships, even those where the experimenter is a decisive element in the research. The work done by Rubin and Wertheimer, by Michotte and by Johansson and by Kanizsa and by others you are familiar with, is not different in terms of method, procedures, reasoning and arguments from the ethological way of working that we learned from Tinbergen and Lorenz, with the exception that instead of animals and their niches, there were colours and spaces, shadows and transparencies, the motion of objects and their figural conditions, a naïve physics, the sounds of things, their bulk and their weight. And this is naturalism, in terms of the methods, aims and results, that is, in terms of the discoveries it led to – in terms of the fact that, after a certain point, we realised that there were new observable facts in the world, which had previously gone unnoticed.

Of course later on, but only later on, what the other natural sciences have to say comes in useful, but only on specific occasions when the internal logic of an investigation demands or merely suggests it. The journey is always from here to there, from Experimental Phenomenology to different fields of knowledge, never vice versa.

1. The event under observation

In the past, I have likened learning to work on perception with Kanizsa to doing an apprenticeship with a Renaissance painter, as Vasari so well described it. Talk about theories was kept to a minimum; you immediately got to grips with facts, in the first instance those that were being studied there in Trieste. And when we spoke of the results of Michotte, Metzger or Fraisse, we first had to set up their experiments right next to ours, then we had to observe them for a long time, and only after that could we speak about them. The apprentice was invited to take the initiative, to make trials, to change the facts under the observers' eyes, to draw conclusions from these changes, taking care to check that what was in play had not already been found and observed by others – hence the need for a well-stocked library, especially with journals. Anyone who began posing new problems was invited to show the facts to be investigated, reducing descriptive and speculative aspects to the minimum in order to make room immediately for observation. These observations were repeated over and over again (the eye must never tire of observing), with the observers taking turns and trying to alter this or that aspect of the electrifying event. I remember well how silent and absorbed we were before someone burst out with comments to provoke new attempts and new inventions: Tampieri's rotating pyramid, Petter's transparencies, Bosinelli and Canestrari's trajectories, Minguzzi's animations, and Vicario's acoustic tunnels.

But this is just reminiscence.

The perceptual event, the focus of Experimental Phenomenology, only exists at the moment of observation, and this observation takes place in a time period which is the event's "real duration" (a good expression of Bergson's to stress that the reality of the event's occurring in a lapse of time), and which Stern likewise very appropriately called the "time of presence". A future perception is something that we can imagine, but it does not yet exist: it is the image of a potential future perception. Similarly, a past perception does not exist either: there is, so to speak, the memory of some past perception which again is an image if we evoke it and not simply talk about it. But, whatever people may say, there is no past perception in the sense that a memory of a perception that we had a moment ago absolutely cannot be a perceptual experience that is, as I shall say, "under way"[3]. "Past perceptual experience" is bad grammar on a linguistic level and it is also a contradiction on a logical level. If I want to study the "tunnel effect" in vision, I need to look at it until I am sated because its properties – whether they be salient or irrelevant I cannot yet tell – are there and can be verified (and lead to true scientific propositions), only so long as the experience of something passing behind a screen is under way. And in order to understand if one aspect of what is being observed is relevant or not, the changes I make must also be under observation because that is where things are decided.

During the course of an observation whole myths fall apart. There is the philosophical myth – also alas widely believed in the sciences – that the immediate experience of perceptual reality is continually changing so that it is elusive, ineffable and fugitive, and hence cannot be an object of science and still less an object to be systematically controlled. It is unique. It all flows like a river. All this can be argued while talking or with the (paradoxical) aid of diagrams on a blackboard. But if you are taught to observe persistently and insistently (and observation is where reality is studied and experimentally assessed) this immediately leads to the discovery that Heraclitus' maxim is false and rhetorical, a *fumus imaginationis*. Observable events under way have a remarkable stability at the time that they are being observed. They have well defined contours, unambiguous localisations and their transformations are themselves observable and verifiable. Suffice to say that every possible scientific measuring and observation device is applied right there. This stability of events under observation is the necessary condition for there to be precise points where measuring tools (from compasses to lasers) can be accurately applied. In Experimental Phenomenology, the act of observation is in no way disturbed by the thought of an infinitely smooth flow of internal changes in either perceived objects or their surroundings.

Furthermore, the immediate experience of perceptual reality is repeatable: indeed, it is probably the only place in the world where absolute repeatability is guaranteed. The equipment you use to achieve a good tunnel effect, considered as a physical piece of apparatus down to its smallest detail – even those of minuscule magnitude which are only detectable using very precise instrumentation – probably behaves in a slightly different way at each new presentation; that is each cycle is not precisely the same as the previous one. But all this happens below the absolute thresholds, which are the boundaries of Experimental Phenomenology. You of course are working well above these thresholds. The unrepeatability that can be ascribed to the physical states that ideally we use as "stimuli" cannot apply to the observable counterparts of these stimuli. Repeatability is thus guaranteed and unquestionable. If you do not see a difference there is no difference. A musical trill is literally a repetition of two alternating notes: the fact that its notes are in theory associated with different instants of time does not in any way affect its perceptual nature. Or take a pendulum: each swing is such that even the most finicky observer fails to notice any perceptible difference. Its oscillations, therefore, are absolute repetitions since any differences that might be detected with instruments on the level of kinetic microstructure are largely below any imaginable threshold, and thus simply do not exist. Repeatability is not only possible in Experimental Phenomenology, it is even quite common.

Another myth is that of "subjectivity". According to this myth, the phenomenal world is, by nature, subjective, both in the sense that it varies from subject to subject, from person to person, and in the sense that even when there are no imaginable differences it belongs in any case to each individual observer as part of the furniture of their private world which cannot be perceived by those who do not live in it.

This latter aspect will be discussed in the next section under the heading of inter-observation. The first issue is addressed here. Köhler liked to distinguish between "genetically subjective" and "phenomenally subjective". The first, a pseudo-concept in my opinion, is a mere allusion to the fact that all that can be experienced and all that is phenomenally explicit depends (within a certain theoretical framework) on processes occurring in the brain. Thus wherever I cast my glance[4], I find things that are generated by the precise activity that is taking place in my brain inside my skull. In this sense "everything is subjective": thoughts, images, memories, emotions and certainly the outside world of colours, tastes, smells, tactile resistance, movements, sounds, weight and so forth. In this way the skull is taken to constitute the three-dimensional border of subjectivity (and this in any case would be a hybrid concept) and a long inventory of events which we can pretend to have doubts about (and sometimes really do doubt) is assumed to be the foundation for a universe of events which it is impossible to pretend to have doubts about.

What is of interest for Experimental Phenomenology is, of course, the "phenomenally subjective". There are several observable facts that evidently bear these characteristics of subjectivity: afterimages, ringing in the ears and scotomas (if one has them) observed on a TV screen when it produces white noise and so-called snow. These things are clearly distinguishable in the stable phenomenal environment we move in while observing and which we also often observe while standing still. The fact that there are these two categories of observables with all their specific properties which Experimental Phenomenology aims to investigate either in the laboratory or "in the wild", makes the expression "the perceived world is subjective" a mere stereotype. In this stereotype all sorts of things, even things that are very different from each other, would belong together though in most cases they have nothing in common and, in fact, they appear to observers as specimens of different – and, after Savardi and Bianchi's book (1997), I might even say *contrary* – species. The world that we normally observe has nothing subjective apart from the odd facts or events here and there, and it is these singularities (characterised by an immediate and obvious dependence on the observer and what he/she does) that makes the adjective "objective" suitable for everything else.

2. Interobservation

And so we come to the issue of interobservation. The coercive phenomenal objectivity of events under observation always make sense of any invitation to others to come and see what we are looking at, with us fully believing that, if they do, they will experience as we do what is there to be seen or heard, possibly even dissenting with our description and helping us with their corrections to notice new aspects. This raises no difficulties either in theory or in practice.

Let me mention here a small autobiographical note. In the laboratory in Trieste where I was an apprentice, when someone discovered a new fact (and I invite my colleagues to consider that most of these discoveries today have a place in textbooks, encyclopaedias and treatises on perception even printed at the throne of the gods, from Blackwell to MIT Press), there was a lot of calling out from one room to another since it was necessary for this new event to be observed together accompanied by a rich counterpoint of comments. This happened both when the event under observation was static, unmoving on a cardboard support or on a blackboard, and when it was dynamic – obviously repeatable in the sense mentioned above and developing in its "time of presence", under direct observation. Directly observed by whom? By those who were there, three or four intrigued scholars with reactions between sceptical and fascinated, perhaps with a secret desire to be able to say "I do not see anything" or at least "anything interesting", but not in the position to say this because you cannot pretend to doubt what is evident, especially if it is observed at the same time by others who themselves feel they are fellow observers. Before this new "effect" underwent rigorous experimentation with all the trimmings, it was necessary to consult others, looking or listening together, paying attention to their opinions and descriptions, and trying several times to "shake up" the facts, changing lights, viewing angles, times and visual fixation points. Once all this bustle seemed to be coming to an end having nearly exhausted all the perceptual possibilities (other types of possibilities are almost infinite, but we study perception) the research was de facto done. Subsequent experimental rituals never betrayed and "data" functioned correctly, except for data related to subjects who had decided to drown the truth of their responses in the indisputability of protocols. Interobservation comes before experimentation and its related computation, and it has been like this since time immemorial: an unknowing but perfect method of investigation.

And indeed, looking closely at things – this time in terms of a logical and epistemological analysis – the problem of other people's perception, if put in the usual terms, is an authentic pseudo-problem: "Who knows what he/she is seeing now?"; "I wonder how this is seen by savages or depressed people or by others belonging to different categories or stereotypes?". I am not going to summarise here those wonderful neo-positivist demonstrations (in particular Carnap's) concerning the non-sense of the perception of others. I believe it's enough to say that none of my colleagues would agree with the affirmation that if one connects one's brain accurately to the kindly lent eye of a friend, one will see his/her private visual perception. Neither would this happen in any other way we might imagine doing this. And in fact I invite my interlocutor to describe whatever method – even impossible to realise but ideally coherent, imaginatively disciplined and understandable to the listener – that might enable us to say, "I perceive other people's perception". If there is no way, even extremely abstract, which would allow us to say this in at least one case, then this is a sign that we are facing an exquisite non-sense in the strictly technical sense of the expression. (Then, the fact that people who are convinced about this, and perhaps even make claims about it in class, are the same as those who end up asking me "But how many people have seen it this way and how many in a different way?" this is typical of the daily paralogistics of psychology and superficial philosophies.)

So everything is wrong, everything is solipsistic? Does the issue of methodological treatment of the so-called "subjects" simply not exist? Does the epistemological criterion of using many observers fall apart?

Never say this. If in everyday life we call other people to see what is happening somewhere, if we invite our friends to see a painting full of vibrating colours and lights, if we go to a concert together (with the aim then of dissecting the musicians' interpretations) and during the execution of the compositions we exchange meaningful looks just in certain moments and not in others, how can we believe that other people's perception is not an issue? Of course it is. But it is not at all a nonsensical issue concerning what the other person sees in their private and metaphysically unreachable world . . . (assuming that this means something). It is rather a question of the exploration of a phenomenal object in the public space of observable things carried out by two or more observers who interact and enrich the phenomenological analysis with strategies, pieces of advice and corrections; they show each other the salient points of exploration; they are as far away from puzzling about other people's perception as they are from wondering about black holes and they speak and act as if the shared object was exactly what you also might see if you joined them. And in all respects it is in fact exactly like this and is not a hypothetical transcription in terms of physics of the elements (stimulus) or an object pulled out of a hat in an inaccessible space just as the abstract space of others' perception is. The real perception of other people is manifested in shared interobservation, obviously "shared" during the act of perceiving. I emphasise this because if we loosen our grip on facts under observation and begin to discuss interobservation and the number of observers "in front of the blackboard" using concepts and pseudo-concepts, speaking about monads without windows, and about facts that have to be replaced by data to be further digested in the gastric juices of quantitative methods (which, in this way, instead of being useful and employable tools replace the facts that they are supposed to explore) – if we let all this happen, then we are in trouble.

I have described elsewhere[5], and very minutely, what happens during interobservation sessions, listing the strategies implemented by participants, the semantic games embedded in what they say to each other, and demonstrating experimentally the progressive convergence of descriptions which were initially different. Interobservational groups (usually consisting of three members) produce very stable versions of events under observation. This means that any discrepancies noted between individual observers (standard procedure in laboratory experiments) are much more diverse than discrepancies emerging between end-of-session versions of interobservational groups: the protocols agreed by several independent groups are indeed pretty much the same. This ensures the repeatability of experimental data collected interobservationally, just as dialectics between interobservers guarantees the necessity for more than one observer as mentioned above.

A corrective mechanism at the heart of interobservational activities is evidently at work guiding the formation of protocols: while individual observers in standard experimental procedure can produce superficial, approximate or intentionally misleading responses – trusting the indisputability of their responses – interobservers, simply because they see other attentive observers near them who are also perhaps in some way rivals, are careful not to risk descriptive statements which are too far away from plausibility (and this of course applies to all three if there are three of them). An interobservational group is small enough for there to be no suspicion of an Asch effect and in any case there is no possibility for participants to establish prior agreements. There is only reciprocal supervised control between them (which gradually increases during the session) concerning how the object under study should be observed, e.g. from close up or from the side and with changes in perspectives and other variously invented constraints. However these controls mainly concern the quality and refinement of the descriptive language. Of course it is obvious that these experimental conditions are not suitable for carrying out traditional psychophysics. In these conditions, however, one can do excellent Experimental Phenomenology; and one can do it across-the-board and one can do it particularly well when the object under investigation is characterised by a high degree of complexity.

3. Observables and language

I started my apprenticeship with Kanizsa after graduating in philosophy with a dissertation on Italian pragmatism, but after a full immersion on the idealism of Croce and Gentile during my four-year university degree course. The impenetrability of idealistic jargon was well-dealt with in a thousand pages written by Giovanni Vailati, first of all in his essay "Language as a Cause of Error"[6]. But in any case this turned out to be not enough for my laboratory work: except for about 30 technical terms that were necessary to allow us (Tampieri, Petter and myself) to understand each other while we were working away on our experiments, any form of refined language (not only philosophical but also that typical of experimental psychology, even Gestalt psychology) was frowned upon provoking harsh reproaches and accusations of vagueness. Even using the language of Köhler was considered to constitute philosophy; the border between the theoretical language of psychology and that of philosophy had shifted much closer. Simply speaking in terms of Piaget's epistemology was already taken to be open philosophising. This was the limitation of my school which had been scorched by the corrosive aversion of idealism – and therefore of Philosophical Faculties – to psychology. The consequence of this was that the technical vocabulary of our research was daily modelled on the events being studied and the techniques being invented. It was characterised by the abundant use of everyday language. There is a well-known expression in Trieste, a city which has frequently suffered in history but which remains essentially optimistic: "No xe un mal che no sia anca un ben" [corresponding to "every cloud has a silver lining"]. In effect, this invention of a technical jargon based on what we were observing and doing led to clarity (after a bit of practice) and above all cleared our minds of ambiguous habits − such as, for example, the habit of attributing what one sees in a given situation to the relative "set" of stimuli or to "habituation". It also cleared our minds of a tendency to acquiesce to expressions like "the subject judges the two lines to be of different length" (where in reality this is what is seen while judging is something very different) or "I think I see" (when in effect this is what one sees but one knows that measuring with an instrument would give a different outcome) and eliminated the habit of invoking the "adaptation level" as a last explanatory resort instead of chopping the problem into its phenomenally controllable components.

Please, check everything I have written and tell me how many times you find the word "Gestalt" to mean something other than the well-known school of thought . . . The language of psychologists was viewed with suspicion, as the importer of unwanted theoretical fragments − and if, à la Piaget, there was also a whiff of philosophy, addio! an outburst was guaranteed.

Dealing with language in this uncomfortable way, one was forced to be extremely clear and practical. But that's not the point. The point is that abandoning jargon and its stereotypes, one discovers that in the course of the investigation, it is the facts themselves that suggest the words and determine their meanings. Experimental phenomenology has its own technical glossary, which comes directly from common language, exempt from arcane, false theoreticisms (such as "unnoticed sensations", "unconscious thinking", "past experiences" − which are however present since they still have an effect − and other, usually convenient, contradictions of this sort). Common language is the mathematics of perception. The common use of words − once undergone a technically sophisticated check − reflects the states being observed, and their geometry in fact imitates the skeleton of the functional connections linking them.

The operating base of the language of Experimental Phenomenology is ostensive definition. It is useless to appeal to the famous myth of the ambiguity of ostensive definitions, since this is fallacious. Ostensive definitions are said to be ambiguous − and therefore unable to connect something observable to a group of phonemes − because if one points in a certain direction a hypothetical extension of the pointing finger may cover many things, namely the set of features the object indicated can be partitioned into. So a person seeing the gesture would not be sure: is he/she pointing at the colour, the shape or the size or at a portion of the surrounding space? This criticism, widespread among philosophers and linguists, is without foundation in the literal sense of the term "foundation". It lacks any phenomenological analysis since in the act of observation, no object appears as a sum or conglomeration of properties: it appears rather as an integrated unit of discernible features. Each of these features can be separately indicated with appropriate ostensive operations and without any use of words. It is easy on a computer screen to show a video with highlights successively display-ing the details of a complex object while at the same time articulated sounds are being emitted which allow us to build even short phrases entirely based on ostensive definitions. In any case, it is taken for granted that when the object is presented as a whole accompanied by a random group of phonemes, before the video highlights begin, this unambiguously results in the name of the object, and its clear that its individual features are subordinate.

Indicate Uncle Joseph to a child for the first time, calling him by his name and then check to see if the child thinks "Joseph" refers to Uncle Joseph's tie or the sleeve of his coat!

In phenomenological analyses carried out in laboratories, the technical language of perception is created by means of an interplay of ostensive definitions, explicit or masked, which takes place in the ordinary course of interactions between observers. The structure of the event under observation flows into the container represented by a word, changing its stereotypical meaning enough to make it fit the class of events that are isomorphic to what is being observed. In Michotte's causal paradigms (e.g. the launching effect), what happens between A and B at the precise instant when A reaches B is in fact a *hit*. And what the term *hit* indicates in this case – even though it can be used in hundreds of other different circumstances – is the visible moment when the impetus of an active motion instantly produces a passive motion. In this way *hit* becomes part of the technical vocabulary referring to the phenomenology of motion (naïve mechanics) and will thus be used appropriately in other circumstances that exhibit characteristics of a certain type, but not for events that are similar but that lack a certain group of conditions (e.g. dead times, the alignment of trajectories, etc.). It should be emphasised that the syntax of the sentence "A hits B", namely the presence of a subject on one side and a direct object on the other side of the verb "hit", rests on the observable characteristics of an "active motion" (related to A) and a "passive motion" (related to B). The dynamics noticed in the act of observation (or interobservation) are the *ultima Thule*[7] of the meaning of this sentence, either spoken or written; similarly pointing to something *red* is the *ultima Thule* of the word "red", as far as the meaning of this word is concerned. This is how the formation of minimal vocabularies takes place – i.e. based on acts of observation accompanied by a verbal introduction – as I pointed out in the introduction to my book *Experimental Phenomenology* (1989). There is no need to restate the fairly technical arguments discussed then.

I only want to add that the intrusion of technical terms belonging to one or another area of traditional psychophysics or other theories of perceptual facts risks contaminating the neatness of the descriptive level of Experimental Phenomenology – such as when, on observing a given fact, one might say "I see a perception of mine" or "I see a case of lateral inhibition" or "I'm watching certain stimuli in motion", etc. Not only this, but there is also a risk of contaminating the first layers which form the basis of its theoretical structure. "The association of sensations underlying perception", "optical effects", "correct information generating an illusory feature" are all routine verbal intrusions and jargon that right from the start prevent a harmonious design matching real observable facts and suitable linguistic formulations. All this has effects on how logically robust will be the theory's development.

4. The so-called stimuli

In my Keynote Address I mentioned how, in the laboratory-workshop where I gained my research experience and developed the ideas that make up my epistemology, so to speak, we took an attitude to psychophysics that was none too fine-grained; today if one wants to do research in psychophysics which isn't superfluous, a very different type of precision is necessary. We created movements with Michotte's discs and the spirals drawn on them. The pendulums I used to form the experimental foundations for what later became known as Naïve Physics were rectangles of cardboard attached to a shaft that was set in motion by an alternately rotating axle – with an inevitable but well-hidden recoil at each reversal of the rotation. Kanizsa's figures, which were sometimes of excellent quality, were well designed and carefully drawn or painted but were nevertheless graphic creations and colours on cardboard created by the painter Rapuzzi. The superstitious accuracy inspired by an ideal *De Imitatione Scientiarum* was not a feature of our apparatus. Unfortunately this ideal was all the rage elsewhere: one was discouraged from venturing into philosophical waters, as I have already mentioned, and there was a certain affected Gestaltist habit of appealing to physics – as if we were experts! – by way of mere analogies or improper associations.

This (obviously very controlled) negligence in setting up so-called stimuli caused me to reflect on a theoretically important point. What is hypothetically below absolute or differential thresholds is irrelevant to Experimental Phenomenology – provided that it is well below them to avoid risks. Moreover, it is perfectly indifferent how you obtained a certain bit of experience as long as its observable conditions are all there and explicitly traceable.

As to the first point, let's try for a moment to think in caricature. Suppose that we want to observe the uniform motion of a small circular object. A 3–4 cm disk is shown on a screen positioned vertically in front of us. The disk whose starting position is slightly to the left, starts moving at a speed that, from the first instant, allows us to follow exactly a trajectory without any positive or negative acceleration. With how much precision should the movement be presented? What tests should be applied to its trajectory to check whether there are microvariations in its speed? And with how much detail? It is clear that we do not need any physics laboratory equipment (and none of our colleagues in the visual sciences have ever mentioned in their articles that they have felt the need to use them when working with uniform motions – however these were obtained). It is sufficient that any irregularities (which would be guaranteed to be seen in a meticulous test or a close check) remain impossible to see. In Experimental Phenomenology a uniform motion is such if it appears as such. A square is a square if it appears as such, graphic imperfections aside. A thousand different physical states in the macroscopic world (in any case out of our reach) can make up the event underlying any given percept: there is always a one – many correspondence; and by "many" I mean very many. The very concept of a differential threshold is itself based on this. In experiments on the phenomenology of motion, it will be the way a movement or movements appear that will determine the conditions and the effects. It is with this logic that the Brown effect, for example, is analysed: the two rows of differently sized objects proceed with different speeds despite their being attached to the same background; what does it matter how fast the background is moving and how precisely the speed can be determined? Rough elementary operations persuade us that the distance covered and the time taken – from the point of view of the ruler and the clock – is more or less the same for both rows and that's it. These more or less fine-grained operations give us information about the state of motion of a given object in a physicist's ideal space and time and this state can be thought of in relation to what we are actually observing. Yet the operations are not part of the event to which they are – so to speak – merely applied.

An abstraction is never an ingredient of the phenomenology of an observable event – even if, in another area of Experimental Phenomenology, namely the psychology of thought, this is the specific object of investigation on its own account.

Starting from these considerations, a few simple logical steps lead us to the basic idea that it is perfectly indifferent what material is used to set up an observable event. What is important is that it is exactly as we wanted, with those specific visible elements necessary to satisfy the demands of experimental manipulation, independently of the nature of the device used. I need a small grey disk on a red background. I can get it from a Munsell Colour Sheet, just as I could also make a circular hole in a red surface and put a rapidly rotating black and white Maxwell disc behind it, since it looks grey and something is grey if it appears grey, and if it appears grey it really is grey. This word "appear", along with its derivatives, is ambiguous and unwieldy in Experimental Phenomenology, but for the obstinate, we could well say "is insofar as it appears" and "appears insofar as it is" (I will deal with appearing as such later on, that is with objects that have observable features of appearance or unreality).

Do we want to show someone a good example of Michotte's "launching effect"? We devise an object A that moves fast towards an object B that is stationary. B suddenly starts to move with a slower motion along a trajectory that extends A's trajectory. But instead of an object A actually in motion, the movement of A can be equally well replaced by stroboscopic motion since the stroboscopic movement of A is exactly the same as the non-stroboscopic movement of A. That is, A moves at a certain speed and that's that. As Vicario (2001) reminds us, a description of the stimuli employed is useful as a kind of recipe addressed to a colleague who wants to reproduce a certain experiment. And he/she should start from the same operative precepts that guided the original set up, subsequently changing them at will, so long as these changes do not affect the visual structure of the fact under examination.

Now, the "stimuli" constantly mentioned in laboratory jargon are nothing more than operations carried out in order to set up a specific observable event and to produce in it the observable changes that we want, on the basis of certain assumptions, or even just of our instinct as expert observers. It is believed that stimuli are packages of electromagnetic frequencies, compression waves in the ears, changes of state in some sensory receptors, objects and events in the space and time of physics, which are presented to the observer . . . To the observer? But if we are taught that observers only have to do with the very last effects of complicated chains of processes at the end of which are perceptions, feelings, impressions and the rest of the jargonistic repertoire. Who has ever seen electromagnetic waves? Who has ever heard compression waves? Who has ever experienced a change of status in their peripheral receptors? How wonderful Mozart would be made up simply of vibrations in the ears (the last four words come from Descartes). The conceptual equipment of "stimuli" is, alas, conceptual. It is made up of abstractions devised in the best possible way since to put them together it took that enormous amount of work, which in the end is the history of science. But to do this masses of visible and tangible operations were needed, applied to the interobservable material that populates direct experiences everywhere – because experience is entirely reducible to that material. If I start rewriting here the immortal pages of Bridgman I risk unwanted verbosity, but none of the ingredients of the stimulus package are anything other than operations, and the stimuli themselves are operations (formal, manual and instrumental) carried out on observable events underway. You will all tell me that, for contemporary physicists, Bridgman was not the only operationalist, though the school he headed lived and died with him. And this is obvious, because you are thinking of your physicist colleagues who deal with quantum mechanics and its "paradoxes", or with particles, or in any case plumbing the depths of subatomic nature. But we are talking of the mesoscopic world, which is the world identified by Gibson as the subject of the ecological approach to perception – which is not necessarily his but that is what the subject is about. And in this world Bridgman's analyses fit in perfectly: if you try to explain the concept of "stimulus" without referring to the jargonistic use of this word, but in respectably scientific terms, you will find yourself describing operations exactly in the manner of Bridgman; if you try to manipulate the conditions of presentation of your perceptual objects ("stimuli" if you want), you will find yourself performing operations and describing operations – operations carried out on the interobservable events you're dealing with. Stimuli are not beyond the events under observation. They are operations on them, and they are in turn observable, ontologically coplanar to the "Bezold Effect" or "Purkinije's Phenomenon". Everyday experimentation in perception should eliminate any thoughts of dualism of the "physical-perceptual" or "phenomenal-transphenomenal" sort – if there weren't a fossilised and contradictory laboratory jargon that maintained intact the ineffable intuition about a psyche and matter.

5. The independence of systems

In the eyes of other scholars, we seemed to be Gestaltists, and in the early years of my apprenticeship, there were clear orders regarding membership of this group. "Gestalt theory is here to stay"[8] Kanizsa used to say sometimes meaning that it was untouchable. Except that in the eyes of other scholars the Gestalt school was conceived of according to rather simplistic clichés. To give you an idea, first of all – according to these others – a Gestaltist had to claim that everything is in everything and everything depends on everything. If you change something here, necessarily a change is produced everywhere because the context functionally links each perception with every other etc. In our laboratory, woe betide anyone saying things like that.

The saying "the whole is greater than the sum of its parts" was dismissed as inaccurate and somewhat foolish while the other saying "the whole determines how the parts appear" was taken with extreme experimental caution, because it is evident that the whole sometimes determines something and sometimes not, or that it determines something in certain parts but not in others. This latter saying was pointless, since only one possible meaning could be implied: "go and see whether changing something here or there makes something else happen elsewhere, and, if so, see how this something affects something else". The word "Gestalt" was never used as an explanation of the internal architecture of an observable event.

Something that needs to be said first is this: in a universe where everything depended on everything else, experiments would be impossible – because by modifying any given particular every other particular would be modified. And therefore if we wanted to say that a particular has changed due to a modification, we could never say so because any other particular could be likewise suspected of having caused the change. In a universe of this kind, dependent variables could never be distinguished from independent variables.

One might then assert that observable events underway are indeed all linked together, some with strong links, others with weak links and others with links so tenuous that they may be considered negligible. In an ideal world ruled by a sort of ubiquitous Coulomb's law, all the masses that populate this world attract each other in a general balance of movements, but those bodies with larger masses and those that are closer to each other attract each other more strongly. Thus some attractions turn out to be totally negligible for practical purposes and functional connections are described only between certain bodies and not others. In this way, establishing whether there is or not a relationship between certain bodies would depend on the instruments of measurement that are available to us: a less accurate tool will reveal functional connections between certain bodies, but a more refined instrument will also reveal functional connections that went unnoticed before. And as instruments of detection continue to be improved further new relationships will be found. Only a perfect instrument would be able to really shed light on a system of "ubiquitous relations" *à la* W. James. (I'm totally ignoring the problem of inevitable interference of instruments with the structure of this ideal world since I'm assuming this interference amounts to nothing.) Whether there are or not relationships between A and B in a universe of this sort depends on the sensitivity of the measuring instruments. Beyond that sensitivity, so to speak, there are connections too small to be noticed and effects too weak to stimulate the sensitivity of the instrument chosen.

In Psychology we have always talked about sensations that are too small to be noticed or in any case of such a nature that they never appear on an explicit phenomenal level in the observable experience. This is a convenient concept, although it has the air of a contradiction in terms. Indeed, in the first phase of contemporary Experimental Phenomenology, Köhler, in his essay on unnoticed sensations and unconscious judgments (another contradiction in terms), did not simply highlight the antonymic nature of these theoretical ingredients of the psychology of his times, which are of course still with us. He rather insisted on pointing out that by combining unnoticed sensations with unconscious judgments (in today's terms: ratiomorphic elaborations of unconscious cognition), one could explain any perceptual phenomenon or any "effect", however paradoxical, unexpected or incompatible with the theory. And thus the theory turns out to be unfalsifiable, which is a death sentence for the theory, as Köhler clearly saw well before Popper did. In addition he also pointed out that the unfalsifiability obtained by skillfully playing with unconscious judgments and unnoticed sensations makes work on perception tedious and dries up the pleasure of research.

In Experimental Phenomenology we have independent systems of objects, events and in general observable facts; they are systems that can be considered as isolated in absolute terms and not as the result of relationships that are so weak that it is possible to ignore them. The independence of the events that populate our everyday experiences – which, considered on their own, would never suggest the crazy idea that everything depends on everything (even if *Scientific American* assures us that, according to certain algorithms, the flapping of butterfly's wings in Brazil produces an earthquake in Crete) – is guaranteed twelve thousand times a day by the ordered traffic occurring between us, our hands and the tools they wield, and the hurly-burly of the external world. Imagine what an enterprise it would be to drive a car in a world of perceptions linked by ubiquitous influences! The pieces of experience we deal with, the segments of reality encountered in the phenomenal world, are independent of each other no matter how things work in the world of physics and related sciences.

There is a grey area on a blue background; the grey is a small square, the blue background is also a square but it is quite a bit larger than the grey one. The blue induces on the grey a hint of yellow, which is clearly visible (especially if observed through a fine-grained filter). Now let us gradually increase the area of the grey square at the center of the blue square. At a certain point the yellow disappears. There are two possible lines of thought: 1) since the intensity of the induced colour depends on the ratio between the inducing area (inducer) and the induced area, at a certain moment the impression of yellow becomes too tenuous to be noticed. The induction of the blue on the grey is still there, but it cannot be seen; 2) the induction at a certain moment ceases to exist, even if the inducing area – which has at that point been reduced to a mere frame – is still just present.

Assertion number 1) has only the advantage that it is somehow possible to postpone, *pro bono pacis*, the break with a sensationalistic prejudice that everyone more or less rejects at least verbally (while thinking otherwise). According to this prejudice, sensations that are below the threshold will keep diminishing according to a function that is similar to that ruling their decrement above the threshold, i.e. in the world of perceivable data. Of course this is if the modification develops gradually and visibly in the same direction. The inducing action exists and it depends on the ratio between the inducing and induced areas; as this ratio gets smaller, it does not have enough strength to produce a visible impression of yellow and thus produces an invisible yellow (please note: an apparent but invisible yellow).

But what I want to stress is that this inducing relationship does not exist. It is a manner of speaking that we invented after having noticed that, in such and such circumstances, the famous line of yellow appears. Properly speaking, the inducing action exists only when one sees something that does something to something. Otherwise, it's just talk. Between two squares, one inside the other, there is no visible action. By changing the ratio between their areas, a sequence of observable states and facts occur, and nothing more. Claims about "action" or "influence" or any other relationship will here have the same meaning as that which we ascribe to these words when referring to objects described by physics or related sciences, that is, objects we can deal with only operationally, *à la* Bridgman, with more and more sensitive instruments. But it is here that we ought not to yield to the temptation to make analogies between disciplines. In our case, once the effect – which is the only indication of an "action" or "influence" which we can tolerate as *flatus vocis* – has ceased, there is no reason to believe that an inducing action should still lead its own life. The induction we talk about is essentially a synonym of "seen yellow" and once the yellow has disappeared the verbal constructs that we have attached to the yellow cease to have any support.

This manner of speaking (here referring to "inducing actions" but the same holds for any other "behindology" concerning perception, from "stimuli" to "lateral inhibition") originates more or less in this way: one sees that by varying the ratio of the areas, the visibility of the induced colour varies, ending in its disappearance. Then one says: the ratio between the two areas causes – in the sense of the Aristotelian efficient causes – the induced colour. But as long as the ratio between these areas is not zero, the cause exists and since there is no cause without effect, and if the yellow is the effect, then the yellow must also still exist. However, this conflicts with the facts, so that there are just two options. Either we come up with the story of a colour that was already a ghost but that is now too weak to be noticed, or we say that the action exists because the cause exists, except that nothing happens. In this way we make the acquaintance of a non-fact, whose determining cause is known to us.

Once these subliminal bonds that legend says hold between observable events are untied, we find ourselves in a world of clearly independent facts, in which slogans such as "everything depends on everything", "everything affects everything" and badly digested holisms or Gestaltisms of this sort should be taken for what they are. Thanks to this guaranteed independence, interobservable events then manifest several aspects which are linked by functional dependencies and finding these, discovering how they work and writing formulas to describe them is the task of Experimental Phenomenology.

6. Behindological fantasies

In my school the notion of "isomorphism" was familiar, although the section of Köhler's book *The Place of Values in a World of Facts* dealing with it was judged too philosophical, and I can tell you for sure that we never discussed it. I personally liked the idea of isomorphism because it was explicitly presented by Köhler as a postulate and also because I was convinced that it could be used if it were given enough elbow room. The scientific physiology of those times – pursued by real physiologists seriously studying the brain by means of their own instruments, concepts and ever-new excogitations – showed that nothing seemed to agree with the physiology imagined by Gestaltists. So I was led to think two things: first that the postulate basically meant that: if here (in experimental phenomenological analyses) we find that a phenomenon depends on four phenomenally explicit conditions working in this way, then we assume that in the brain something is going on which depends on (at least) four conditions, that might turn out to be chemical, electrical, osmotic or something else. And, in the second place, we had to keep an eye on the fact that certain perceptual singularities have visible analogies with electromagnetic fields; analogies, I supposed, which are the farthest thing one could imagine from a correct definition of "isomorphism". When in an unfortunate book I tried to put forward a theory of Gestalt with no reference to the postulate of isomorphism, and in which stimuli were presented as operational procedures, I was hounded by my teachers and by every other Gestaltist around.[9]

But this was simply a matter of ideology, of *esprit de corps*. In fact we spoke very little about isomorphism and its potential conceptual derivations have been never used in research by anyone I know of. Yet it was a banner and woe betide anyone speaking ill of it.

In the lab where I did my apprenticeship, the study of perception made little reference overall to the physiology of the senses or of the brain, mainly because we knew very little about it and had only the amateurish knowledge of readers of popular science. And we were well aware of what an amateurish knowledge is since we were masters of indisputable professionalism in our field that of the psychology of perception and Experimental Phenomenology. One who knows what "being able to do something" means, does not venture where they only have secondhand expertise. At least, that was how it was at that time.

What I want to say, however, is of a different flavour. I mean that if an observer (a scientist) is observing, even using the most technologically advanced instruments imaginable, some process in the tissues of the central nervous system that he/she considers to be connected to a given perceptual event, he/she metaphysically is unable to observe that perceptual event as well. And if a scientist, an observer, likewise as ideally equipped, is observing a perceptual event (such as for example a chromatic contrast or the Frazer illusion), he/she metaphysically is unable to observe the underlying processes as well. It is true that this impossibility as a matter of principle is worked around in many ways and with thousands of methodological strategies. And thanks to these ways of working around it, many good things can be done and many interesting relationships between the states of the brain and the ostensible facts that form a perceptual scene can be found. But these circumventions make the relationships between the ostensible facts and the measurements taken extremely indirect; so much so that, among the cognitive integrations called for to conceive of these relationships, a good deal of faith, which is to say mere belief, is also required. We believe that we know how a particular physical state of the cortex is a colour or determines (but where?) the onset of a colour. We believe that we know what the properties of a segment linking a point in physical space with a visible point on a sheet of paper are. And we believe that the things that we indirectly record by means of instruments are made exactly as we describe and depict them. Circumventions need to be made: science survives due to their cleverness and tomorrow we will know more than today. But we must be fully aware of their nature and not hide ourselves behind them, ignoring the crucial fact in the case, namely that if an ideal observer, ideally well equipped, observes a process (local or distributed) occurring in someone's central nervous system, he/she cannot also observe the percept; similarly, if an observer is observing a percept, he/she cannot at the same time observe the brain states that are deemed to be the direct physiological basis of that percept.

And this is not due to technical limitations nor imperfect instrumentation nor undeveloped theories, nor yet is it due to any kind of lack that might be hindering us until an ideally perfect future comes along, but from the given that nothing can both be and not be.[10]

A similar incompatibility of measurements (Heisenberg's) shook Physics to its foundations. But Psychology is never shaken.

7. Seeing and thinking

Every now and then a dreaded and unpleasant voice insinuated itself through the laboratory, saying (and I can still hear the sound of those voices): "stimulus error!" Someone had made a stimulus error and a transgression such as this particularly deserved to be pilloried. One day someone feared that in 1928 J. F. Brown had committed a stimulus error and panic exploded in the Institute. Then it was discovered that Brown was completely innocent of the crime and the improvident accuser was given a hard time.

Apparently the stimulus error is a very easy sin to avoid. In Köhler's version – the one we were familiar with – it consists of "the danger of confusing our understanding of the physical conditions of our sensory experience with the experience as such". However the matter is not so simple and often naïve observers (and not infrequently expert observers) consider as part of an observed scene things that they *know* have been used to set it up (i.e. what one might discover if one looked behind the scenes), or things they *know* concerning the nature of the material, or things they *know* concerning the formal structure. In other words, whatever can come to mind concerning the scene but that is from a phenomenal point of view not open to direct observation.

I've written a long essay about the perplexities I had at the time and I still have about the stimulus error, which is wholly true in its simplest formulation, but is slippery and ambiguous in its other applications. Here I want to recall how, in our daily business, the ghost of the stimulus error took shape, and to comment on the theoretical and epistemological consequences that I believe we are dealing with from a practical point of view.

It is clear that also the so-called proximal stimulation is involved in the stimulus error. Saying that the Müller-Lyer lines are equal is a *prima facie* stimulus error, for when we compare them visually they are different and we know that that's the way it is. But beyond this superficial version, there is another one, just slightly more sophisticated and appropriate: on the retina (if we look at the Müller-Lyer in foveal vision) the lines are the same; it's further along the pathway that something happens to make them different. (Nevertheless it is remarkable that if we look just a bit below or above the two lines – if they are positioned horizontally – their phenomenal inequality remains intact in spite of the contractions and expansions of the lines in the retina due to the rules of projection on a hemispherical concavity.) If we *know* all these things and say them as if they described what is actually *seen*, we commit the stimulus error – we could say "the proximal stimulus error" – just as Descartes does when he tells us that when we listen to music we hear nothing but vibrations in the ear.

However it is worth focusing here on the less sophisticated version of the stimulus error mentioned above since it contains an important and in a sense decisive lesson in order to arrive at a coherent theory of Experimental Phenomenology.

One of the quirks of the group where I did my apprenticeship was a taste for paradox, sometimes carried to extremes. On more than one occasion I argued forcefully against this since a perceptual discovery was really appreciated only when it was presented to participants in a way that surprised them. Musatti provided a very refined justification for this taste for paradox, comparing demonstrations in Experimental Phenomenology to the *consequentia mirabilis* in logic: if you want to convince someone that the fact of seeing a square moving closer or further away from the observer is merely a function of an increase or decrease in the length of its sides, you will first show him/her a square that is physically moved in space back and forth, then a similar square on a screen at a fixed distance from the observer which gets smaller and larger according to a given function. In both cases the observer will see a square moving back and forth and will remain persuaded that the cause of what he/she sees is the change of magnitude and nothing else. Thus there is a logic to the trick set up in the laboratory.

Things don't go very differently in other circumstances. Arrange a "tunnel effect" *à la* Burke in which there is an occluding screen in front of the observer, opaque and rectangular, with its longer side positioned horizontally. To the left of the screen there is a small object of a different colour. This object starts moving to the right and (this is how the apparatus is set up) immediately after it has slid behind the screen it stops moving. But hidden behind the right edge of our screen there is another small object, similar to the first, which comes out after a few moments travelling at the same speed as the first object along an imaginary prolongation of its trajectory. Everyone knows perfectly well that what one actually sees and – let's say it using an old expression in the study of perception – what one is coerced to see with full evidence of reality is a small object passing intact behind the screen, even when (due to the time interval between entrance and exit) it had to slow down a bit or to slightly deviate its course. The "correct" interval produces a flowing and smooth movement that remains present in the part of the trajectory where the object is momentarily invisible. And this is what happens in everyday life where if the tunnel effect did not work we would be in trouble.

Why do I dwell upon such details? Because in my apprenticeship the "wheeze"[11] consisted first of all of showing participants the back of the apparatus built to run the experiment in order to allow them to see that there were two objects behind the screen and to observe how they were mechanically controlled to move one after the other with an interval of absolute stillness in between. Thus, now aware of the deception, they returned to their place and saw exactly what they had seen before. And it never happened that they saw what they, at that point, knew. Every experiment was treated like that – from stroboscopic movement to causal effects, from studies on perceptual constancies to Tampieri's pyramid.

Every experiment, to put it simply, repeatedly demonstrated with evidence that when the balance between the factors involved is designed as it should be, the fact of "knowing" what happens "in reality" does not change one jot the evidence of the ostensible facts. But wait a minute, "reality"? There are at least ten different ways to produce the same phenomenally explicit conditions "in reality" thanks to whoever or whatever is responsible for this, including the laws of biological evolution. The important lesson here was this: knowing how things are, does not affect in any way the direct evidence of what is observed and therefore no cognitive process is powerful enough to be able to affect an event under observation when it has a clear and cogent structure.

This is what Ferraris means with his concept regarding the "unemendability" of the outside world and also what, at least in part, Vittorio Mathieu meant half a century ago with his concept of "inescapability". No conviction in the world can make one see (or hear, or touch. . .) the dance of the facts and the event on the stage of the observables under way in any way other than how the rules of the scenic design require. And even when one looks more closely at those facts (such as bi-stability or multi-stability) that seem to change in line with one's way of thinking, or rather in line with one's other commitments (whatever that might mean), one soon discovers that it's not really like that. Even these apparent exceptions are subject to the rules of the scenic design of the observable world, whatever a rather stupid epistemology (which was nevertheless long fashionable) might say about the observables being freighted with theory.

The first rules pertaining to how the observable world is set up are, of course, Wertheimer's laws; these are the building blocks of our experience of the outside world (and with many adaptations also of the internal world, that is, thoughts, memories, reasoning and various other ephemeral things). Then there are a number of prefabricated modules such as for example the tunnel effect, stroboscopic motion, static and kinetic three-dimensionality, chromatic configurations etc. (a long and rich catalogue), up to those which are less articulate but no less respectable consisting of "effects": Brown, Purkinije, Benary, Gelb, Liebmann, Rosenbach, Fuchs, Duncker, Emmert, Aubert-Fleischel, Morinaga, Pulfrich, Ames, Mach and many others – I throw these names out at random just so the reader can have fun seeing how many of them he/she really knows . . .

Now, if a dent in the behaviour of a phenomenological module cannot be in any way made by convictions obtained by means of observation and aided by many years of knowledge of elementary physics, by its logical consistency, by customary repeated practice with the world of manageable and usable objects and perhaps also by some innate logical and neuronal principle,[12] if all this cannot affect a phenomenological module, what should I think when people tell me that I see those modules on the basis of unconscious ratiomorphic processes that I unknowingly harbour in my head in order to set up exactly that theatre? A theatre that I can observe and study as if I were a botanist or an ethologist.

The "wheeze" mentioned above has an extraordinary theoretical depth since from time to time and from person to person it confirms the impossibility for there being a noetic (and let us say, cognitive) structure to act upon what is being observed. (While it can certainly act upon observable facts once they are remembered, imagined or are anyway outside our field of observation.) Furthermore, that wheeze blocks the start of a vicious circle in which unconscious ratiomorphic activities would produce observable facts placed in the outside world, which are intelligible thanks to other ratiomorphic activities but this time not unconscious at all – and indeed we do intelligent and decisive experiments, requiring lots of good reasoning to deal with those facts. If it really was like this, Nature – in her wise economy – might well have spared us this futile stage of creating an observable external world.

Furthermore, in this vicious circle there would be another obscure point that harks back to what we already discussed above with reference to the epigenesis of a perceptual event from a process occurring in the neuronal tissues. Here, instead, the problem is how we should imagine the formation of a colour from a logical operation involving chromatic judgments, a kind of ratiomorphic ideography that generates painting; or how we should imagine the formation of perceived movements or smiling faces full of analysable details which one then tries to analyse (and to some extent successfully does) using those undoubtedly ratiomorphic procedures that constitute the genuine reasoning one needs to do research.

And your colleague next door is sorry if he/she feels that his/her conscious ratiomorph does not coincide with his/her unconscious ratiomorph that, according to him/her, keeps the object of his/her momentary scientific interest alive. But (while he/she trusts this) he/she still rummages around in his/her house looking for objects that are in any case where he/she originally put them.

You may wonder why I am insistent about the problem of *imagining* the epigenesis of objects in the external world resulting from an event's taking place in the skein of neurons or from unconscious ratiomorphic processes. But what should I do if not imagine it? Should I reason? But that's the same thing . . . Should I rely on an intuition, an act of faith? But believing, as has been said, is the opposite of thinking . . .

8. Explaining things away

The intolerance of my masters as regards theories was a serious obstacle to getting the results of our research introduced into the rapidly developing panorama of contemporary scientific psychology – and the same was true for the contributions of the Gestaltists, as well as for those of Michotte, Rubin and the Japanese school, and often also for the experimental work being carried out in Uppsala. I used to state that every generation has to rethink from the beginning their own theories, but this statement was taken merely as philosophical vain ambition, as a kind of devious historicism and sometimes even as a heresy. (Metelli, joking about the book I wrote that never saw the light, said it was treason against Gestaltism.) But, as I already mentioned, "no xè un mal che non sia anca un ben" (i.e. every cloud has a silver lining).[13] And in fact there was a very positive consequence to that attitude: the fact that it was better to be cautious about what is theoretically already known.

The "already known" is a kind of believing that is not in itself harmful, but which has the potential to blind us to new facts and new ideas. This is familiar to those of us who while showing something interesting to a colleague hears them immediately point out that the explanation is this and that and that it's all a question of attention or lateral inhibition, masking, generalisation, habituation and so on . . . Or rather that "this is a sensation while that is a perception" or "this is processed in parallel while that is processed serially" (it's obvious!) or invoking theorems such as the one which says that when an instantaneous sensation (imagined in terms of local stimuli) has ceased, all that remains is memory and optical illusion. Kanizsa used to say that this way of theorising (or classifying) is a way of "explaining away" what in reality is still an issue worthy of careful exploration, observation, experimentation, conjecture and confutation.

The thoroughbred researcher in Experimental Phenomenology approaches phenomena in a kind of theoretical vacuum, of suspension of judgment. Of course he/she knows a lot of things and could explain away the phenomenon in five minutes with a flashy display of terminology and pseudo-concepts, referring to other notions belonging to the field of psychology (psychophysiological or computational).

This is how new and interesting facts pass unnoticed under the eyes of academics and remain hidden, although glimpsed and perhaps also for a moment regarded with curiosity. I will give here only one example of a widely used theoretical explanation, that of "past experience". This is indeed a low-level form of "explaining away", called exactly that, "past experience", for many decades and now often disguised under apparently more respectable terminology: we see something like this and like that because we are used to it.

I will not linger over the fact (see Höffding) that if now we see something like this and like that because many times in the past we saw it like this and like that, it still remains to be explained why in the past we saw it like this and like that. I will simply restrict myself to pointing out that a wide variety of circumstances can fall under the expression "past experience". They range from very short term "after effects" to events lasting an entire lifetime, passing through various unlikely circumstances. Examples of these "improbable" circumstances might be those proposed in Gray's manual according to which we see the Müller-Lyer illusion because when looking out of our windows we are used to seeing road repair signs, some upright and others flipped over. Or what about Usnadze's laboratory where you can see two small discs (black on a white background) of slightly different diameters positioned side by side which appear and disappear every four or five seconds a dozen times, followed by two other very similar discs which however have the same diameter? These last two discs appear to be different, albeit with the position of the larger and smaller discs reversed with respect to the fist two discs. And this is said to be due to "past experience" – i.e. more or less one minute before.

Being acquainted with some scientific generalisations originating from precise experiments but then frozen into theorems or having accepted some current theoretical generalities is a serious obstacle to discovery. This, I think, explains why many scholars of perception who write excellent books updating existing material or who conduct meticulous experiments to check facts discovered by others are unable to find anything new throughout their academic life. In contrast, other scholars of perception discover genuinely new facts (on which others will then work with patient skill) by virtue of an innate ethological talent in observing and finding new things. But not only that. I have had the chance to notice, as I have been close to some of these talented discoverers, that it is also thanks to an uninhibited scepticism towards accredited knowledge and in particular towards the attitude of *De imitatione Scientiarum* that often characterises the profession of Psychology.

9. The incompleteness of the *explanandum* and the function of discovery

It's worth dedicating a section to this last point because here lies one of the most important meanings of Experimental Phenomenology. If the purpose of theories of perception, whatever their nature, consists of "explaining" (in any of its many meanings) perceptual facts, the completeness of this catalogue of facts is ideally an essential prerequisite for establishing the plausibility of these theories – and ultimately for their scientific verification.

It should to be said at the outset that this catalogue will never be complete. But that's exactly what allows us to conceive of an epistemological plan coherent with the empirical research typical of Experimental Phenomenology. Let us imagine a logical space in which all the possible theoretical structures that can be imagined as *explanans* of the universe of perceptual facts are put in order, from the first principles down to more specific laws, local models and ranges of experimental hypotheses. The lower levels are linked to the higher by way of deductions. The deductive routes are those that in practice are, to simplify matters, tracked backwards by inductions. At the base, at the lower level, there are descriptive protocols, i.e. those describing the facts of perception, the raw material of Experimental Phenomenology.

Now if everything works properly, every observable fact, as such, falsifies a certain number of possible propositions. Whenever a perception scientist discovers a new fact (even by chance or serendipity, without theoretical planning), some part of that logical edifice made up of theories collapses; a part that perhaps had never been thought of by anyone, but that by definition already existed. Well-conducted experimental research is implicitly designed to prevent us from saying certain things, even if it apparently aims at confirming something else. This is exactly what testing a hypothesis means, as everyone knows: this can easily be seen in the pleasure exhibited by someone who accuses a colleague of making a mistake. Facts discovered by means of ingenious games of *a priori* hypotheses are welcome if, in the end, they are authentic and interobservable facts. But collapses also occur with new facts discovered independently of hypothetical planning based on theories – facts that, by whatever means they have been revealed, raise problems that had never been thought of before. And these collapses isolate systems of theoretical propositions that previously were potentially true but then turn out to be only plausible. Michelangelo taught that a statue is made by removing stone from a rock and liberating the figure that was imprisoned inside it. Something similar happens with knowledge by dint of large amounts of research. Naturally we cannot hope to come out with a definitive book – and indeed real, readable books show traces of this process of dismantling revealing underneath solid reliable parts that will lead to yet more research. We should bear in mind that we cannot hope for a definitive book because we know barely twenty percent of the universe of observable facts. How can we prove this? Of course we cannot. But the fact is that many researchers round off their careers without ever having found any new and unexpected facts, while others have found dozens of them and do not have time to study them in depth because at every step of their reasoning they stumble into something new that is just around the corner. This leads us to think that St. Patrick's Well is still quite full[14] and nothing it contains, so long as it remains hidden there, can contribute to completing the map of facts, whose completeness is essential to the invulnerability of theoretical edifices. The discovery of "perceptual effects", which is so despised today, has little to do with the logic of butterfly collecting and much to do with the constructive power of potential falsifiers of theories.

Of course this brings to light the disturbing idea of unending research. But this is not anyone's fault or if it is anyone's it's the Almighty's. This might also lead one to say: when we know all about perception, that is, all the bricks and modules that hold together the complicated, repeatable and shareable world of observable facts, then appropriate use of logic will allow us to design a theory. It's like waiting for Godot. Yet it is not too lamentable a position; I do not know how many dozen times in recent years I've read that once we possess a perfectly complete and accurate knowledge of physiology (as the undeniable increase in knowledge in this field allows us to hope) we will have solved every problem. And many theorists indeed tell me that already today physiology resolves everything. Therefore, everything is dissolved into physiology because, even if some pieces are momentarily missing, the debt will in the end be paid off. But by then the game will be over.

10. Realism

I often say to my younger friends working on perception in the spirit of Experimental Phenomenology, that in our research the phenomenological method is imperative and realism is optional. It's possible to be masters of the phenomenological method and be dualistic: on the one hand there is consciousness or the psyche or the phenomenal on which we work directly; on the other there is objective reality – which is what sometimes prompts us to say "in reality" to contrast certain scientific ideas with "appearances". This "reality" is often thought of in terms of operations carried out on phenomena, but is then frozen in an almost metaphysical stability.

Thus I'm not going to try to convert others to a monistic and realistic conception of the universe of observable events under way, i.e. what is taking place here and now for us, inter-observers, and what constitutes the starting-point for any scientific journey. I will only explain the reasons why I describe myself as a realist, indeed as a naïve realist, born that way like all of us – I think – and ever more persuaded of this blasphemous conviction as the years have passed and my research experience has continued to grow.

By studying perceptual phenomena experimentally I am contributing to the creation of a science of the external world and not a chapter of Psychology. Academic tradition would call me a psychologist and peer pressure – of the sort that psychologists exert – would like me to speak of the "phenomena" of "perception". (It is worth mentioning that Wertheimer once said: "My work has nothing to do with psychology apart from the use of the experimental method.") Indeed, in my whole life I have never encountered a single "perception" except, sometimes a slight ringing in the ears or a tiny creaking behind me that I wasn't totally sure I had heard. The facts, objects and events that fill my everyday life are for the most part so objective that they don't deserve at all the name of "phenomena" – if that word carries an overtone of "seeming" or "appearing", to the point of "illusion".

When my carpenter grandfather introduced me for the first time to some optical-geometric illusions I played with them for days using rulers and compasses. But it never crossed my mind to suspect that they were subjective. Try playing with them yourself and you will understand what I mean. (I also played with coils of wire attached to a rough battery I had made myself using coal and zinc in salt water inside glass tomato sauce jars to see how the position of the compass needle changed, and this was the same as observing what happens in so-called optical illusions.) Later when I was at high school they enlightened me about the subjectivity of reality while commenting on Berkeley, whose arguments I was already familar with thanks to a curious book, an introduction to philosophy by Cyril Joad. None of these arguments convinced me, least of all those that aimed to demonstrate the subjectivity of sensations. I cannot summarise my counterarguments here, but I am preparing a text to present them, all updated thanks to my experiences as a professor of psychology.

When later on I attended Kanizsa's lectures and the numerous experimental demonstrations set up in front of us to show what he was talking about, I never for a moment suspected that I was observing some sort of psychic activity or that those observable facts were taking place in my mind or that they depended on my subjectivity – resistant as those facts are to any solipsistic hankerings. Kanizsa sometimes said: "We are the real physicists" and I agreed. Nevertheless I was slowly adapting to the type of subjectivising and psychicalising language that is the jargon of psychology laboratories. So I found myself summing up my thoughts with words like "phenomenal", "stimuli" and "apparent" or with totally indigestible expressions such as "how do you experience that movement, that colour" or "the impression of reality" and so on. In other words the subjectiveness or psychic nature of observables under way was nothing more or less than a linguistic habit, one that was hard to correct in the given environment; they were manners of speaking that had been hardened by linguistic uses that worked well for philosophical puzzles.

Now, it is not that we lack examples in our world of observables that have an air of appearance, an aroma of subjectivity, a clear functional connection with our strategies of observation, a visible dependence on things that happen close to our eyes and ears or perceptibly within them. Rather, this is the real starting point. A categorisation of the subjective aspects of the experience of the external world has yet to be made. But we have all had the experience of after-images and phosphenes, of ringings in the ears and blurring of the eyes (clearly distinguishable from an external mist, which is one of the things out there). A good classification might perhaps lead to the discovery that the phenotypes of objects can be ranked from the most subjective to the indubitably objective. This is one of many as yet unwritten chapters of Experimental Phenomenology. There are useful strategies for separating subjectivity from solid external contexts: Gibson's theorising about the central status of an observer moving among rigid objects, provides us with an excellent paradigm for distinguishing the features that belong to the external world from those that belong to the moving perspective of the observer. An accurate and complete phenomenological analysis would allow us to cover the whole range from the scientific observation of the state of things in the outside world to individual introspection of the sequence of one's own thoughts *à la* Würzburg.

Precisely so: in this way the objectivity of the external world turns out to be perfectly delimitable. Of course, as we shall see in a moment, I'm not speaking about the world described by the physics of elementary particles, but the real, inescapably external world which is interobservable, shared with friends and animals, with enemies and other beasts. And it is so solid, detailed and precise in its features (colours, shapes, movements, solidity, space and time which are wrongly described as "phenomenal" but well handled in books on the psychology of perception), it is so stable and calibrated in its transformations that it is the only place in the universe where instruments for measuring and tools for checking can be directly applied – i.e. the so-called sensors that allow one to do science, in the first instance elementary physics. The innermost recesses, the most delicate microstructures of the external world – wrongly described as phenomenal – are our point of entry to observe and take measurements, even the most indirect, and of course also those that allow our scientific imagination to go far beyond classical physics, into the realm of numbers with very long positive or negative exponents.

This conceptual reduplication of the external world, which is based on the findings of measuring equipment and indirect observation, comes about by means of operations (in the manner of Bridgman as I said at the beginning), that define objects which are neither visible nor audible, and that make possible an original and different phenomenology of those objects. This use of operations is epistemologically important and in any case clearly evident in terms of common sense.

Restricting our attention to those operations that allow us to do mesoscopic physics (more or less the physics we learned in high school) we are forced to recognise that what in today's science of perception are called stimuli are ultimately concepts derived from operations. And our sensory apparatus, when considered from a physiological point of view, is a system of concepts derived from operations. And thus also the action of the stimuli on sensory apparatus is a system of concepts derived from operations (whether they be material, conceptual or mathematical).

However the concept of a billiard cue has never set a billiard ball – a real observable billiard ball – in motion. One consequence of this seems inescapable: we could easily get rid of terms such as "objective", "real", or "existing" or expressions such as "external world", imbued as they are with every imaginable ambiguity; or one could apply them at will and that's indeed what often happens. Semantic mobility becomes an advantage when there are no obvious links between words, on the one hand, and facts and concepts scattered about the world and in encyclopaedias, on the other.

A dualistic colleague will tend to associate these types of words with the world of stimuli, processes or any other entity in the current scientific imagination: according to this view stimuli are real, objective and are in a world "out there", whereas on this side there is appearance and phenomenon, the psychological counterpart of what is out there.

But the stimuli are not in a world "out there": outside what? Can one cut a strip à la Fontana out of the observable world under way so as to look behind the canvas and see what's there? Magnetic and compression waves, and chemical structures (tastes) are either pre-scientific intuitions or are concepts, formulas or algorithms. And the same holds for sensory processes: they are *entia rationis*, thoughts or demonstrations on a blackboard. The blackboard is for sure in the external interobservable world and is visibly objective and – everyone would say – real. Likewise the chalked marks on the blackboard, but not their meanings, which are in our heads. And by talking of "stimuli", "processes", "peripheral conditions" etc., we are alluding to meanings not to ostensible things; we are alluding to meanings that live in our heads and are made up of thoughts and therefore they are not the external world. Thus the set of directly perceivable facts, the immediate experience of the Gestaltists, or the observable events under way (in my preferred way of talking), is the range of ostensible facts that attract the words we have referred to and give them a sense. That's where lies what is "real", "objective", "external", independent of the observer, what appears to us to be a continuation of the past, appears to emerge from it and enter the future. And this is independent of whether this or that intention or theory is in the observer's head.

Bertrand Russell used to say that in a system like Kant's, if you take away the *noumenon* – which immediately after Kant seemed to be necessary – you are left with the world of phenomena as the only reality; and, it should be noted, you can no longer say that it is transcendental or empirical subjectivity because you have eliminated the element of contrast that made it such (i.e. the noumenon). The subjectivity of the phenomenal world bursts like a bubble at the instant the noumenon disappears. And in the same way the idea of "perception" as subjective, psychic, a mere epiphenomenon, a mental event disappears as soon as we recognise the radically operational nature of the stimuli and processes, which are by nature logical constructs. This is indeed what clearly emerges when dealing with "stimuli" in the ordinary course of laboratory work and also what becomes evident in the formal models that underpin the discourses (words) of the perceptual scientist at work.

Far from being the origin and basis of the perceived world, these *entia rationis* recover their scientific legitimacy solely in the rational manipulation of facts that are directly interobservable. And the guarantee of the primary reality of interobservable events all rests on the fact that not a single step towards the physics of elementary particles or psychophysiology would be possible without the objectivity of the points where we take measurements, which are the origin of any subsequent abstractions.

Experimental Phenomenology is the empirical science of reality *tout court* and subjectivity is only one paragraph – for all that it is important and as yet little explored. This is why the label "phenomenology" leaves something to be desired because it harks back to phenomena as appearances rather than beings, as deceptions and as epiphenomena of something else. But it is by now difficult to get rid of this label, and already many others need to be abandoned but the glue is so strong that they cannot be unstuck.

On the other hand there is Plato's "*Sòzein tà phainòmena*" which means "saving the facts" and this is exactly what the task of Experimental Phenomenology is. But the fact that the object of *my* studies is in no uncertain terms simply reality, within a realistic and externalistic philosophy, is optional.

Notes

1 Translator's note: "The Foundations of Experimental Phenomenology" conference held at the University of Padua, Italy in 2002.

2 Translator's note: Piero Angela and his son, Alberto Angela, are well-known on Italian television for presenting programmes of popular science.

3 Translator's note: Bozzi's phrase, which we render here and elsewhere with "under way" is "*in atto*", which he uses almost as a technical term to indicate not merely a relation of simultaneity but also a realisation or actualisation that might be contrasted with mere potentiality.

4 Translator's note: Bozzi uses here the expression "*Dovunque il guardo io giro*", a famous line from an aria by poet and librettist Metastasio (1698 –1782).

5 Bozzi, P., and Martinuzzi, L. (1989). *Un esperimento di interosservazione. Rivista di Psicologia, LXXIV*, 11–46.

6 Translator's note: Bozzi's degree dissertation was on Giovanni Vailati.

7 Translator's note: Roman poet Virgil (70BCE-19BCE) coined the term "*Ultima Thule*" (*Georgics*, 1. 30) to mean "the northernmost land"; Bozzi uses it here to mean an unattainable goal or "omega point" in the process of definition.

8 Translator's note: Bozzi quotes his mentor's words in the dialect of Trieste: "*La teoria della Gestalt la xè là*"

9 Translator's note: as it turned out, this book was never published because of a veto expressed by Bozzi's professors against its publication.

10 Translator's note: Bozzi cites from Dante Alighieri*'s Divine Comedy* (Inferno, XXVII, 118–120): "*Per la contraddizion che nol consente*".

11 Bozzi uses the Trieste dialect term "*viz*" which is derived from the German "*Witz*" meaning a joke; we have sought to go some way to preserving the sound as well as the register of the original.

12 E.g. a rotating spiral gets larger but does not expand, gets smaller but does not shrink – and this *a priori* rests on the principle of non-contradiction. [Translator's note: originally in parentheses in the main text; the principle is rendered earlier as "nothing can both be and not be".]

13 Translator's note: more Trieste dialect.

14 Translator's note: The reference is to a very deep well built at Orvieto by Pope Clement VII and associated with the legend of St Patrick's access to Purgatory.★

References

I list here (section by section) the writings where the topics briefly touched upon in this paper are more extensively developed.

Section 1

Bozzi, P. (1985). La 'corrente della coscienza' ossia gli eventi sotto osservazione [The stream of consciousness, or the events under observation]. In P. Bozzi (1989), *Fenomenologia sperimentale* [Experimental Phenomenology] (pp. 235–273). Bologna, Italy: il Mulino [translation in this anthology, chapter 4].

Section 2

Bozzi, P. (1978). L'interosservazione come metodo per la fenomenologia sperimentale [Interobservation as a method for Experimental Phenomenology]. In P. Bozzi (1989), *Fenomenologia sperimentale* [*Experimental Phenomenology*], (pp. 235–273). Bologna, Italy: il Mulino [translation in this anthology, chapter 10].

Bozzi, P. (1989). Un esperimento di interosservazione [An experiment in interobservation]. In P. Bozzi (1993), *Experimenta in visu. Ricerche sulla percezione. [Experiments in Vision: Inquiries into Perception*], (pp. 231–272). Milano, Italy: Guerini e Associati.

Section 3

Bozzi, P. (1989). Introduzione [Introduction]. In P. Bozzi (1989), *Fenomenologia sperimentale* [*Experimental Phenomenology*], (pp. 11–64). Bologna, Italy: il Mulino.

Bozzi, P. (1991). Parlare di ciò che si vede [Speaking about what one sees]. *Versus, 59/60*, 107–119.

Bozzi, P. (1991). Sulle descrizioni di eventi percettivi sotto osservazione [On the descriptions of perceptual evens under observation], *Intersezioni, XI* (1), *75–85.*

Section 4

Bozzi, P. (1961). Descrizioni fenomenologiche e descrizioni fisico-geometriche [Phenomenological descriptions and physical-geometrical descriptions]. In P. Bozzi (1989), *Fenomenologia sperimentale* [*Experimental Phenomenology*], (pp. 65–81). Bologna, Italy: il Mulino [translation in this anthology, Chapter 9].

Section 5

Bozzi, P. (1989). Introduzione [Introduction]. In P. Bozzi (1989), *Fenomenologia sperimentale* [*Experimental Phenomenology*], (pp. 11–64). Bologna, Italy: il Mulino.

Bozzi, P. (1999). Tempo e ripetibilità degli eventi sotto osservazione [Time and repeatability of events under observation], in *Atti del Convegno Francesco de Sarlo e il laboratorio fiorentino di Psicologia* [*Proceedings of the conference Francesco de Sarlo and the laboratory of Psychology in Florence*]. Bari, Italy: Giuseppe Laterza Editore.

Section 6

Bozzi, P. (1985). Analisi logica dello schema psicofisico (S-D) [Logical analysis of the psychophysical (L-R) scheme]. In P. Bozzi (1989), *Fenomenologia sperimentale*, [*Experimental Phenomenology*], (pp. 297–330). Bologna, Italy: il Mulino [translation in this anthology, Chapter 6].

Bozzi, P. (1993). On some paradoxes of current perceptual theories. In S. C. Masin (1993), *Foundations of Perceptual Theory* (pp. 183–196). Amsterdam: North-Holland (re-elaborated by I. Bianchi and R. Davies, and reproduced in this anthology by kind permission of the original publishers, Chapter 2).

Section 7

Bozzi, P. (1990). Considerazioni eccentriche sull'errore dello stimolo [Eccentric considerations on the stimulus error]. *Giornale italiano di Psicologia, 25* (2), 239–252.

Bozzi, P. (1991). Considerazioni inattuali sul rapporto "io non-io" [Untimely meditations on the relation between self and non-self]. *Rivista di Psicologia, 76*, 19–33 [translation in this anthology, Chapter 5].

Section 8

Bozzi, P. (1987). Senso e controsenso del "giudizio inconscio" [Sense and counter-sense of "unconscious judgement"]. In P. Bozzi (1989), *Fenomenologia sperimentale* [*Experimental Phenomenology*], (pp. 175–202). Bologna, Italy: il Mulino.

Bozzi, P. (1985). Falsificatori potenziali e teoria della Gestalt [Potential falsifiers and Gestalt Theory]. In P. Bozzi (1989), *Fenomenologia sperimentale* [*Experimental Phenomenology*], (pp. 217–233). Bologna, Italy: il Mulino.

Section 9

Bozzi, P. (1974). Appunti per una discussione con gli epistemologi [Notes for a discussion with epistemologists]. In P. Bozzi (1989), *Fenomenologia sperimentale* [*Experimental Phenomenology*], (pp. 155–173). Bologna, Italy: il Mulino.

Section 10

Bozzi, P. (2000). Idee nuove di un secolo fa [New ideas from a century ago]. *Discipline Filosofiche*, *10* (2), 93–105.

COMMENTS ON EXPERIMENTAL PHENOMENOLOGY

Ivana Bianchi

Every time I re-read this paper I have the feeling of how precious and very special it is. Not only is it the last paper Bozzi ever wrote[1], but it is also the only paper where in a few pages he sketches an overall picture of what Experimental Phenomenology is in his view. Of course, one can get a sense of his global view (and appreciate the subtlety of his thoughts and analyses) from wide reading of all his books and papers, where he focuses in detail on one or other of the aspects regarding what he had in mind about the objects and methods, and about the epistemological setting, of Experimental Phenomenology. Indeed, I hope that the papers selected in this anthology provide a taste of what this wider reading would yield. However, I think too that this last comprehensive paper of his is to be taken very seriously. This is where Bozzi was called on to draw together the threads of his work, and we can tell that this was certainly the result of a well-meditated and long-lasting process involving a re-analysis of all his studies. It was written on the occasion of a conference held in Padua entitled "The Foundations of Experimental Phenomenology", where Bozzi was invited to give the keynote address to open the conference. This paper thus condenses what he considered worth mentioning in a main lecture on Experimental Phenomenology. But it is not only for this reason that we must take the paper seriously. It is the culmination of a process that had kept Bozzi busy in 2001, when he accepted the invitation of a group of colleagues and friends in Verona (among which I had the pleasure to number myself) to identify and discuss a list of topics and corresponding papers which – retrospectively – he considered to be central to the ideas around which his perspective on Experimental Phenomenology developed. While he resisted insistent attempts, by the same group of colleagues and friends, to convince him to write a final compendium of his thoughts, he more than once thanked us for this opportunity which had stimulated him to systematically re-read his works and reorganise the thoughts he had developed in hundreds of writings. Why am I mentioning this? Because it provides a further guarantee that the article in hand, written in 2002, i.e. the year after these Verona seminars, is certainly not a hurried synthesis but is the result of a process of exhaustive revision.

According to Bozzi's synthesis, ten main points and some premises (which correspond to the sections that make up the paper) are the indispensable attributes of his Experimental

Phenomenology. I'm not going to go through them all. What I aim to suggest in the following notes are some focal themes to be found in Bozzi's text that come into view if we take in hand a magnifying glass trained on two orders of problems. On the one hand, there are those to which I have been sensitised in my role as a teacher and experimenter in psychology with deep roots in Bozzi's theoretical experimental procedures, in light also of various other perspectives encountered in psychology journals and conferences. On the other hand, and thanks also to the introductions that Bozzi himself gave me to distinguished philosophers (some of whom collaborate in this volume), there is the philosophical context to which his methodological programme is so signal a contribution. In these two directions, I wish to point our magnifying glass at some passages (that I quote at some length, and that it is worth going back to locate) that throw a sidelight on the paper under consideration.

A first question is whether realism is an indispensable feature of Experimental Phenomenology. As clearly emerges from Bozzi's words, the answer is *no*, if we consider Experimental Phenomenology as a method to be used in psychology, but the answer is *yes* if we consider Bozzi's personal idea of what he was contributing by studying Experimental Phenomenology. These two passages are very clear. The last section, entitled "Realism", starts with this clarification: "I often say to my younger friends working on perception in the spirit of Experimental Phenomenology, that in our research the phenomenological method is imperative and realism is optional. It's possible to be masters of the phenomenological method and be dualistic: on the one hand there is consciousness or the psyche or the phenomenal on which we work directly; on the other there is objective reality – which is what sometimes prompts us to say 'in reality' to contrast certain scientific ideas with 'appearances'. This 'reality' is often thought of in terms of operations carried out on phenomena, but is then frozen in an almost metaphysical stability". He closes the same section (and the paper) with a similar clarification: "saving the facts (. . .) is exactly what the task of Experimental Phenomenology is. But the fact that the object of my studies is in no uncertain terms simply reality, within a realistic and externalistic philosophy, is optional". However, realism is surely a mark of *his* Experimental Phenomenology as he emphasises explicitly in the last passage just cited and as emerges throughout the paper (e.g. "I'm not going to try to convert others to a monistic and realistic conception of the universe of observable events under way, (. . .). I will only explain the reasons why I describe myself as a realist, indeed as a naïve realist, born that way like all of us – I think – and ever more persuaded of this blasphemous conviction as the years have passed and my research experience has continued to grow."; "By studying perceptual phenomena experimentally I am contributing to the creation of a science of the external world and not a chapter of Psychology"; "Kanizsa sometimes said: 'We are the real physicists' and I agreed.").

And here a second question arises. How might one be a master in the study of perception using the methods of Experimental Phenomenology? In other words, can we extract from this paper a core of "rules" characterising being a master in Experimental Phenomenology? It was not in Bozzi's style to prescribe rules. The paper contains however several autobiographical pictures of the practices that Bozzi absorbed during his apprenticeship (as he calls it) in Kanizsa's laboratory and that he transformed into the building bricks of his own epistemological perspective. If one puts them all together it seems to me that what appears is an outline of the "rules" (in the sense of guidelines or points to be borne in mind while actually conducting laboratory work) for using the Experimental Phenomenology method. Let's collect these traces distributed here and there in the paper.

First:

- "Talk about theories were kept to a minimum; you immediately got to grips with fact . . ."
- "(. . .) when we spoke of the studies [of others] (. . .), we first had to set up their experiments right next to ours, and then we had to observe them for a long time, and only after that could we speak about them".
- "(. . .) observations were repeated over and over again (the eye must never tire of observing), with the observers taking turns and trying to alter this or that aspect of the electrifying event".
- "The apprentice was invited to take the initiative, to make trials, to change the facts under the observers' eye, to draw conclusions from these changes (. . .)".

We can draw from here what I will call the first rule: everything you say about observable events/perceived facts must fit in with what one sees under way. One cannot speak about perceptual facts in theory, neither can one reason about perception involving past or future perceptions which do not exist as such: these would be memories of past perceptions or images of potential future perceptions.

Second:

- "(. . .) when someone discovered a new fact (. . .) there was a lot of calling out from one room to another since it was necessary for this new event to be observed together (. . .)";
- "Interobservation comes before experimentation and its related computation, and it has been like this since time immemorial: an unknowing but perfect method of investigation".

The second rule: "phenomena" can and should be interobserved. Interobservation guarantees the refinement of the descriptions and ensures a close link between the description and the relative observable features, without contamination from non-observable constructs or beliefs.

Third:

- "(. . .) the technical vocabulary of our research was daily modelled on the events being studied and the techniques being invented. It was characterised by the abundant use of everyday language".
- "The language of psychologists was viewed with suspicion, as the importer of unwanted theoretical fragments (. . .)";
- "(. . .) any form of refined language (not only philosophical but also that typical of experimental psychology, even Gestalt psychology) was frowned upon provoking harsh reproaches and accusations of vagueness".
- "The operating base of the language of Experimental Phenomenology is ostensive definition".

The third rule: "Experimental Phenomenology has its own technical glossary, which comes directly from common language, exempt from arcane, false theoreticisms (such as 'unnoticed sensations', 'unconscious thinking', 'past experiences' (. . .). The common use of words (. . .) reflects the states being observed and their geometry in fact imitates the skeleton of the functional connections linking them".

Fourth:

- "In our laboratory, woe betide anyone saying things like (. . .) everything is in everything and everything depends on everything. If you change something here, necessarily a change is produced everywhere (. . .)";
- "(. . .) saying 'the whole determines how the parts appear' was taken with extreme experimental caution, because it is evident that the whole sometimes determines something and sometimes not (. . .)".

The fourth rule: "In Experimental Phenomenology we have independent systems of objects, events and in general observable facts (. . .)". Some events manifest "aspects which are linked by functional dependencies and finding these, discovering how they work and writing formulas to describe them is the task of Experimental Phenomenology".

Fifth:

- "(. . .) in the laboratory-workshop where I gained my research experience and developed the ideas that make up my epistemology (. . .) we took an attitude to psychophysics that was none too fine-grained (. . .): We created movements with Michotte's discs and the spirals drawn on them. The pendulums I used to form the experimental foundations for what later became known as Naïve physics were rectangles of cardboard attached to a shaft that was set in motion by an alternately rotating axle − with an inevitable but well hidden recoil at each reversal of the rotation".
- "(. . .) we do not need any Physics laboratory equipment (. . .). It is sufficient that any irregularities (. . .) remain impossible to see. In Experimental Phenomenology a uniform motion is such if it appears as such. A square is a square if it appears as such, graphic imperfections aside".

The fifth rule: "What is hypothetically below absolute or differential thresholds is irrelevant to Experimental Phenomenology".

Sixth:

- "(. . .) it will be the way (. . .) [something] appears that will determine the conditions and the effects".
- "it is perfectly indifferent what material is used to set up an observable event. What is important is that it is exactly as we wanted, with those specific visible elements necessary to satisfy the demands of experimental manipulation, independently of the nature of the device used. I need a small grey disk on a red background. I can get it from one a Munsell Colour Sheet, just as I could also make a circular hole in a red surface and put a rapidly rotating black and white Maxwell disc behind it since it looks grey and something is grey if it appears grey".

The sixth rule: in Experimental Phenomenology independent variables and dependent variables are both defined on a perceptual level. The relationships we look for are not between a psyche and a physical entity, but between one phenomenal entity and another phenomenal entity. Quite how this resonates with Kubovy and Gepsthein's idea of a phenomenological psychophysics (Kubovy 2003; Kubovy & Gepshtein 2003) and Epstein's discussion of percept percept coupling (Kubovy, 1982; Epstein & Rogers, 2003; see also Hochberg, 1974; Savardi & Bianchi, 2012) are two obvious points of discussion.

Seventh:

- "Every now and then a dreaded and unpleasant voice insinuated itself through the laboratory saying (. . .): 'stimulus error!'. Someone had made a stimulus error and a transgression such as this particularly deserved to be pilloried. (. . .) the stimulus error consists of (. . .) considering as part of an observed scene things that they *know* have been used to set it up (. . .)".
- "One of the quirks of the group where I did my apprenticeship was a taste for paradox (. . .) Musatti provided a very refined justification for this taste for paradox, comparing demonstrations in Experimental Phenomenology to the *consequentia mirabilis* in logic. A classic procedure consisted in showing participants the back of the apparatus built to run the experiment in order to allow them to see how what they were looking at was 'in reality'. Thus, now aware of the deception, they returned to their place and saw exactly what they had seen before. And it never happened that they saw what they, at that point, knew".

The seventh rule: what one *knows* about the facts under observation must not be confused with what one sees. This goes together with the ontological (and ontogenetic) primacy of the phenomenal world (which is "reality" in Bozzi's perspective) with respect to any other kind of description of the world derived from the applications of instruments (as opposed to ordinary sensorial endowment) or from technical constructs or meta–empirical notions (theory–driven definitions as opposed to definitions based on directly perceived entities).

Eight:

- "In the lab where I did my apprenticeship, the study of perception made little reference overall to the physiology of the senses or of the brain (. . .)";
- "It is quite wrong to think that a naturalistic conception of perception must be the result of an assemblage of fragments of notions deriving from the natural sciences, if by that we mean an encyclopedia of facts and concepts arising in biology, physiology, physics, chemistry, artificial intelligence, information theory and the like".
- "Of course later on, but only later on, what other natural sciences have to say comes in useful, but only on specific occasions when the internal logic of an investigation demands or merely suggests it. The journey is always from here to there, from Experimental Phenomenology to different fields of knowledge, never vice versa".

The eighth rule: remaining within the boundaries of what one perceives (features, objects/events and relations) is the necessary absolute starting point for Experimental

Phenomenology, and in general also its endpoint. This has a direct impact in terms of how experiments are conceived and designed, and in terms of how explanations are formulated and eliminates from the outset any form of epistemological reductionism. Points six to eight constitute, operationally, the essence of Bozzi's idea of the Experimental Phenomenology of perception as an approach *iuxta propria principia*.

Ninth:

- "There are several observable facts that evidently bear these characteristics of subjectivity: afterimages, ringing in the ears and scotomas (if one has them) observed on a TV screen when it produces white noise and so-called snow. These things are clearly distinguishable in the stable phenomenal environment we move in while observing and which we also often observe while standing still. The fact that there are these two categories of observables with all their specific properties which Experimental Phenomenology aims to investigate either in the laboratory or 'in the wild', makes the expression 'the perceived world is subjective' a mere stereotype. In this stereotype all sorts of things, even things that are very different from each other, would belong together though in most cases they have nothing in common (. . .)".
- "The world that we normally observe has nothing subjective apart from the odd fact or events here and there and it is these singularities (characterised by an immediate and obvious dependence on the observer and what he/she does) that makes the adjective 'objective' suitable for everything else".

The ninth rule: the distinction between "subjective" and "objective" is a central distinction in Experimental Phenomenology but merely on a phenomenal level. It identifies two different classes of experiences (and gradations between them) that are all potential subjects for experimental phenomenological investigations. It is well worth adding that Bozzi himself saw ample space for a phenomenology of thought processes. Indeed, two of the eleven chapters that make up his overview work on Experimental Phenomenology (Bozzi 1989) concern such matters: chapter two discusses some necessary conditions of the experimental study of the phenomenology of thought; and it is followed by an account of Wertheimer's approach to these questions. The connections that Bozzi points out also elsewhere (e.g. in Bozzi 1990) among perception and imagination, reasoning, and language offer resources for a fruitful dialogue between Experimental Phenomenology and the debates that have since grown up regarding the grounding of cognition in perception and action (e.g. Barsalou, 2008, 2010; Pecher, & Zwaan, 2005; Thompson, 2007; Zlatev, 2010).

Which of the points in this suggested manifesto can be accepted by all cognitive scientists who claim to be developing an experimental phenomenological approach to the study of perception, and which not, helps to pinpoint their distinctive features. I've suggested these considerations in the hope that they might suggest useful points for future debates to compare Bozzi's perspective with various profiles of Experimental Phenomenology that have been emerging from current parallel debates within cognitive sciences marrying phenomenology with psychophysics, computer science, or cognitive linguistics (e.g. Albertazzi, 2013; Bloomberg and Zlatev, 2014; Ihde, 2012; Zlatev, 2010) and with other well-known phenomenological perspectives developed within a philosophical, rather than experimental, tradition (from Husserl and Merleau-Ponty on).

TABLE 1.1 Suggested outline of the Experimental Phenomenology of Perception (EPhP) as a method

1. Everything that EPhP says about "observable events"/"perceived facts" has to fit with what one is observing.
2. "Observables events" can and should be interobserved.
3. The language of EPhP is based on ostensive definition; its technical glossary comes directly from everyday language.
4. EPhP's task is to discover – in a world of observable independencies between aspects, facts and events – those aspects that are linked by functional dependencies, and to express formulas to describe them.
5. Only what is above absolute or differential thresholds is relevant to EPhP.
6. Both independent and dependent variables are defined on a perceptual level.
7. What one *knows* about the facts under observation must not to be confused with what one sees.
8. The journey is always from the Experimental Phenomenology to different fields of knowledge, never the reverse.
9. The distinction between "subjective" and "objective" is central, defined solely on a phenomenal level: it identifies two different classes of experiences/objects of investigation in EPhP.

To conclude, I would like go back to the initial statement: according to Bozzi, one can be a master in Experimental Phenomenology (following all the rules) without being a realist, but *for him* the framework was realism. Philosophers might discuss better than me the nuances of Bozzi's realism, but *as a psychologist*, I find a few sentences in his text very radical and enlightening:

> "Experimental phenomenology is a branch of natural sciences and a part of a naturalistic conception of a theory of knowledge. I believe that it is the bedrock of a naturalistic conception of knowledge".

> "By studying perceptual phenomena experimentally I am contributing to the creation of a science of the external world and not a chapter of Psychology. Academic tradition would call me a psychologist and peer pressure (. . .) would like me to speak of the 'phenomena' of 'perception'. (. . .) Indeed, in my whole life I have never encountered a single 'perception' except, sometimes a slight ringing in the ears or a tiny creaking behind me that I wasn't totally sure I had heard".

> "The subjectivity of the phenomenal world bursts like a bubble at the instant the noumenon disappears. And in the same way the idea of 'perception' as subjective, psychic, a mere epiphenomenon, a mental event disappears as soon as we recognise the radically operational nature of the stimuli and processes, which are by nature logical constructs. This is indeed what clearly emerges when dealing with 'stimuli' in the ordinary course of laboratory work (. . .). Far from being the origin and basis of the perceived world, these *entia rationis* recover their scientific legitimacy solely in the rational manipulation of facts that are directly interobservable. And the guarantee of the primary reality of interobservable events all rests on the fact that not a single step towards the physics of elementary particles or psychophysiology would be possible without the objectivity of the points where we take measurements, which are the origin of any subsequent abstractions".

"The discovery of 'perceptual effects' (. . .) has little to do with the logic of butterfly collecting and much to do with the constructive power of potential falsifiers of theories. (. . .) Whenever a perception scientist discovers a new fact (even by chance or serendipity, without theoretical planning), some part of that logical edifice made up of theories collapses; a part that perhaps had never been thought of by anyone, but that by definition already existed".

This intimate confidence, i.e. that Experimental Phenomenology has to do with discovering facts and not with butterfly collecting, is perhaps what has kept Experimental Phenomenology of perception alive, despite the impetuous waves of more up-to-date and rewarding approaches in Psychology. Bozzi had not only the ability to put it so well into words, but also to turn it into epistemology and ontology.

Note

1 While "Experimental Phenomenology" (2002) represents Bozzi's fully worked-up thoughts, he submitted some "Notes on my education, my scientific experiences and the views I currently hold" that overlap as regards content to the journal *Gestalt Theory*; these appeared in 2003 under the title "*Anmerkungen zur Praxis und Theorie der experimentellen Phanomenologie*" (*Gestalt Theory* 25(3), 191–198) and may, on that account, be regarded as his last publication.

References

Albertazzi, L. (ed.) (2013). Handbook of Experimental Phenomenology. Visual Perception of Shape, Space and Appearance. Chichester: Wiley Blackwell.

Bozzi, P. (1989). *Fenomenologia sperimentale* [*Experimental Phenomenology*]. Bologna, Italy: il Mulino.

Bloomberg, J. & Zlatev, J. (2014). Actual and non-actual motion: why experientialist semantics needs phenomenology (and vice versa). *Phenomenology and the Cognitive Sciences*, 13(3), 395–418.

Epstein, W. (1982). Percept-percept couplings. *Perception*, 11, 75–83.

Epstein, W. & Rogers, S. (2003). Percept-percept Couplings Revisited. In U. Savardi & A. Mazzocco (Eds). *Figura e sfondo. Temi e variazioni per Paolo Bozzi* [Figure and ground. Themes and variations in honour of Paolo Bozzi] (pp. 93–106). Padova, Italy: Cleup.

Hochberg, J. (1974). Higher-order stimuli and inter-response coupling in the perception of the visual World. In R. B. MacLeod & H.L. Pick (Eds). *Perception: Essays in Honor of J. J. Gibson* (pp. 17–39). Ithaca, New York: Cornell University Press.

Ihde, D. (2012). *Experimental Phenomenology: Multistabilities*, 2nd edn. New York: SUNY Press.

Kubovy, M. (2003). Phenomenology, psychological. In L. Nadel (ed.): *Encyclopedia of Cognitive Science* (pp. 579–586). Basingstoke, Hampshire, UK: Nature Publishing Group.

Kubovy, M. & Gepshtein, S. (2003). Grouping in space and in space-time: An exercise in phenomenological psychophysics. In R. Kimchi, M. Behrmann, & C. R. Olson (Eds). *Perceptual Organization in Vision: Behavioral and Neural Perspectives* (pp. 45–86). Mahwah, NJ, USA: Erlbaum.

Savardi, U. & Bianchi, I. (2012). Coupling Epstein's and Bozzi's percept-percept coupling. *Gestalt Theory*, 34(2), 191–200.

Zlatev, J. (2010). Phenomenology and cognitive linguistics. In S. Gallagher (ed.) *Handbook of Phenomenology and Cognitive Science* (pp. 415–446). Dordrecht, NL: Springer.

2

ON SOME PARADOXES OF CURRENT PERCEPTUAL THEORIES

P. Bozzi

Researchers in the field of perception make frequent reference to epistemology. When we discuss research in progress, new models, or theoretical innovations, we always assume a shared philosophy. However, our assumptions are seldom made explicit so that they may be challenged.

My claim is that in our conceptions sometimes one hears a sort of false note. Although understanding the cause of this impression is no easy matter, its implications are fairly clear: one has probably the feeling that serious discussion of these assumptions might reveal ideas in clashing contrast or plain contradiction. It is my deep conviction that in the "epistemological subconscious" of most scientists of perception there dwell a number of paradoxes. In this essay, I intend to bring some of them to light and to elucidate their logical structure.

By way of introduction, I shall first briefly overview six assumptions that are often implicit in psychological or philosophical discussions.

1. Consider all objects and events that we experience when we look at a landscape, listen to music, walk in the street, or when we rummage through our papers for some lost memo jotted down some time ago. These objects and events may be called *observables*. For the perceptual scientist it is obvious to assume that any observable O corresponds to a specific brain state S. Of S we can have little knowledge, good knowledge, or unreliable knowledge, but we can nonetheless distinguish it theoretically from other states S', S'', . . . that are related to the observables O', O'' . . . and perceived at the same time by an observer.

2. All human beings have a functioning brain. Therefore, in the course of their lives they are constantly aware of a number of observables associated to some specific brain states. We can certainly say this of their daily lives, and in a way we can also say it in relation to those observables that they dream of when they are asleep. Here, we ought to point out an important aspect of this assumption. A brain, considered as a physical system, or as an information-processing device, must be studied in the framework of physical space-time, just as one would study other devices such as a watch or a calculator. On the other hand, observables must be studied in the framework of psychological space-time,

dimensions that are prone to well-known contractions, expansions, and distortions that are not easily translated into corresponding physical parameters. Thus, for each observer there is one perceptual world, just as there is one brain for each observer.

3.   The following assumption is common in the philosophy of knowledge. As there is no physically direct path connecting one brain to another, so there is no access – for any of us – to the observables O', O'' . . . associated to the brain states S', S''. . . . in someone else's brain. Thus, we cannot see or touch or in any way experience the perceptions of other people.

4.   The fourth assumption derives indirectly from the three assumptions above. It says that observables are always private. By definition they are introspective data. Now, if we take a methodological stance, we have to recognize that introspective methods are subject to fatal objections. Perceptual science must be founded on reliable findings, and these cannot come from introspection. Data derived from introspection are only accessible by single subjects, whereas a science of perception needs data that can be shared by the scientific community. Data that can be shared are called protocols, and in this context protocols are appropriately recorded observable behaviours, measurements, multiple choices, possible descriptions, and so on.

5.   The following assumption capitalizes on a number of concepts that have been developed in the field of information science over recent decades. The common sense of perceptual research assumes that brain states and the observables associated with them are enclosed within a metaphorical black box. We describe its output in terms of interpretable protocols. What happens inside the black box is the object of logically organized speculations, based on our knowledge of its input and output, and on appropriately conceived rules.

      It is important to stress that protocols, when interpretable without ambiguity, have to be considered as unquestionable evidence. In the common sense approach of perceptual researchers, protocols of any kind are prototypical factual data.

6.   The last assumption reads as follows. By simulating the processes that take place in the black box in some coherent way, with appropriate logical rules, and by means of appropriate devices, we can obtain an explanation or a description of the causal preconditions of phenomena. We can understand what is described in protocols. In the best cases, we can even understand the process that maps the class of input elements onto output elements. In short, we can reach a scientific understanding of perception.

Perceptual Paradoxes

1. "Sudden healing"

The first paradox is something one not infrequently encounters in perceptual laboratories. I propose to call it the paradox of "sudden healing".

   Consider a prototypical laboratory situation. An observer is asked to cooperate with the experimenter, but somehow refuses to provide the expected response. For example, the observer might not see the effect, or the response might be inconsistent with a theory. Of course, there are many possible reasons for this outcome. The experiment might be irrelevant, or not properly carried out. The experiment might lack some small detail that seemed irrelevant but turned out to be crucial. In the worst case, it may even be that one knows there is not much to be found within one's experimental setup, but in one way or another one hopes that, with the help of some more or less indirect suggestion, the observer will say or do just what the theory wants. In some rare cases, the feature being studied may not even be seen, such as when chromatic stimuli are presented to a colour-blind observer.

The paradox also arises in another case. After thirty years of experience in all sorts of experiments on perception, I can bear witness that observers quite often just want to show that their beliefs are all fibs and yarns. For example, observers may be convinced that perception is a faithful representation of stimuli. Thus they insist on denying any observation that does not correspond to what they know about visual stimuli. Such observers lie about a detail that they consider negligible, and they do so to maintain a theory-based faith in the five senses as witnesses of the physical world. They may lie in the name of an ideology that regards psychological experiments as manifestations of pseudoscientific gibberish. They know that experimenters will have to report their lies. Usually, subjects are university students who know that protocols are unquestionable and that respect for protocols is the hallmark of scientific research.

Suppose we want to show an observer a good example of apparent motion. In dim illumination, two small lights not too far from each other are turned on and off in turn, in accordance with well-known rules. In these conditions, everybody sees one single luminous spot moving back and forth.

The observer, after looking carefully, may say: "I see two lights turning on and off in alternation, in two fixed positions". The report cannot be questioned. Where is the experimenter who would dare not to take it into account?

Obviously, adding the latter result to the list of protocols will make this a probabilistic phenomenon. The experimenter will have to say: "about this many times out of the total, one sees . . .". He will have to conclude that optimal apparent motion is seen very often, but not always. Thus, one deontological rule turns into one that hinders the search for truth.

Perhaps at this point we should doubt the rules of laboratory procedures. Before recording our result on a data sheet, we should check what happens to our observer when not in the laboratory. Does the observer go to the movies? Watch television? See the multifarious motions of many-coloured lights suspended over the booths of a fair? Generally speaking, we should ask whether the observer realizes that daily life is replete with apparent motions between all sorts of lights, both during the day and at night. If we establish that the observer sees the scenes of a movie just as we do, then we can safely conclude that in the laboratory we had recorded a lie. Unless we believe that some people fall ill as soon as they enter a laboratory, that they become prey of a peculiarly fleeting disease that affects their visual systems and from which they are suddenly healed as soon as they go out of the door.

Similarly, consider an experiment on size constancy: a visible object gets progressively more distant from an observer and thus projects a retinal image that becomes progressively smaller. This object should look like an object that moves away from the observer, not like an object that shrinks. Suppose the observers are shown a variety of objects, for example surfaces with variously complicated linear structures, shrinking or expanding. If the observers claim that they just see the objects shrinking, and if they insist that they do so while remaining at the same distance from them, then on the basis of this report their driving licenses should be withdrawn.

One might say that the stimuli presented in the laboratory were oversimplified and out of context. In the laboratory, the great regularities of daily life are based on the efficacy of those very mechanisms that are reproduced in the laboratory. We should also note that almost everyone is willing to drive risky night trips on streets and highways. In these conditions, the outside world is summarized by luminous spots and illuminated stripes on the terrain that look just like the simplified stimuli presented in the lab. Yet, people drive at night. The twenty or thirty visual effects that exhaust the visual world of a night driver surely are effective, otherwise their failure would be fatal.

Given that scientific work aims at universal conclusions, theories of perception should be based much more on what people do normally than on a narrow range of data (even if motivated by rules of scientific method), because such data are just a small subset of all the reactions one could observe in similar conditions.

There is only one reasonable conclusion to be drawn: protocols are questionable.

If we believe that the rules of scientific method must still be trusted, for the sake of good relations between colleagues or for love the of reputation of science as a "rigorous" endeavour, then we must be aware of the consequences that follow. We are forced to admit that there are sudden failures in the functioning of observers, and these failures are followed by equally sudden healings.

The last, logical, consequence of this line of reasoning seems to be the following: the perception laboratory is the least suitable place for studying perceptual phenomena.

At this point, either we get rid of the unquestionability of protocols, which are falsely "objective" products of laboratory research, or we must believe that the laboratory has an unhealthy influence on observers.

2. Descriptions

I shall discuss now another paradox concerning protocols, one that arises when protocols take the form of "descriptions" of perceptual patterns. Of course, I am aware of the current trend in perceptual research of using non-descriptive responses in place of verbal descriptions. By designing methods for collecting responses that can be described by quantitative parameters, such as motor performance or the outcomes of comparisons or selections, perceptual researchers hope to eliminate the difficulties of dealing with the linguistic ability of various observers. Although non-descriptive responses are useful, it remains nonetheless true that the really important discoveries – the phenomena that open up new horizons for research – need in the first instance a verbal description. Finer-grained quantitative methods can play their role only after we have a description.

I need to recall here a fact of epistemology. Although it is commonplace in epistemological theorizing, this fact is all too often forgotten. In various fields of scientific research, observation is based on facts that are not the direct object of scientific interest. Usually, researchers are not interested in the modes of appearance of manometers, thermometers, or Geiger counters. Rather, they are interested in something that they believe is measured by these instruments, either at the time of observation or, in case of recordings, at some earlier time. Using the old terminology of Viennese Neopositivism – old but still appropriate and effective – we should always distinguish empirical statements from protocols.

In perception, however, empirical statements and protocols coincide. The object of scientific interest corresponds exactly to what the observer sees during an observation. Both for the experimental psychologist and for the observer, the observable is not a cue to something else, and above all it is not a representation of something else. The observed event is in a very precise sense a self-representation, a displaying of itself.

Of course, in practice any experimenter will ask a certain number of other observers or subjects or participants to witness the facts under observation in order to collect reliable data and to compute appropriate statistics. The involvement of a number of subjects seems to imply the general claim that the observables of our direct experience are questionable. Otherwise, there would be no justification for calling so many people to witness a perceptual event momentarily under investigation.

What is the job of observers in this context? Their job is to provide a protocol by means of a description, a classification, a choice, or a motor response. That is, by means of any form of behaviour that can be considered as an observable event. Now suppose the above thesis that all observables are questionable is sound. Then all protocols obtained from observer descriptions, being observables as well, are also questionable. If we assume that questionability can be dispelled by multiplying the observations, as we did initially, then we must call other subjects and ask them to observe the protocols previously obtained. And so on. In practice, we can put an end to this sort of infinite regress by leaping epistemologically from one side to the other of the theory. In practice, protocols are assumed to be "obviously" unquestionable. But we well know that practical convenience has nothing to do with methodological rigor. Quite to the contrary, the former is the negation of the latter.

If we go along with accepted practice, then the appearance of all objects within reach of our sight can be doubted, except for those objects that we mean to define as protocols. Naturally, the opportunities for doubt are very limited when protocols take the form of numbers or of other conventional signs; they are limited to the point of being a theoretical pretext (but philosophically sound all the same). Quite often the inspection of a perceptual event requires a gesture or a verbal description. What about the protocols that take this form?

Suppose that a subject is performing a careful inspection of two samples of photometrically equal red colours. One sample is a rectangle a few centimetres wide and with sharply cut edges. The other has approximately the same size and shape, but its edges are serrated like in a stamp. As Kanizsa found,[1] the colours of two surfaces do not look the same. The colour of the serrated surface, compared to the other, looks faded, veiled, and blurred.

Suppose the subject compares the two red samples and says: "this red sample has a more veiled, blurred, and softer colour than the other sample". If other subjects say more or less the same, it seems safe to suppose that among our observers there are individuals who have a mastery of the English language in all subtleties.

Since descriptive terms such as "veiled" or "blurred" suffer from a certain degree of semantic indeterminacy, we might wonder what the observer actually means. There is a way to disambiguate the description. One can ask our observer to indicate which surface looks veiled. At this point, after appropriate comparisons, one "sees" what those adjectives mean in that circumstance.

Perceptual researchers almost invariably adopt this tautological procedure in their pilot observations, when the discovery is still "fresh". It is through these procedures that one finds new and interesting elements that are successively subjected to codified experimental procedures.

At this point, two alternative conclusions may be drawn: either we admit that protocols based on observables are themselves observables of a new species and therefore that they require other protocols, and so on to infinity (that is, unless we apply an arbitrary, dogmatic cut by saying: "up to here, observations are questionable, but from there on, they are not") or we interpret observers' protocols by ostension, that is, by referring back to the observed objects that originated them; thus reducing the meaning of protocols to a fact.

Thus, we have either a regression to infinity or a vicious circle.

3. Inaccessibility

Along with a great number of philosophers, most students of perception agree on a thesis that was presented clearly by the epistemologist Evandro Agazzi.[2] The thesis reads: "*a nessuno consta il constare altrui*" which may be pretty literally translated as: "no one ascertains someone else's ascertaining". It is taken for granted that any human or animal observer has a private perceptual world that is, as Leibniz would have it, impenetrable and accessible only to its owner.

If the above thesis is true, and if it can be ascertained that somebody ascertains or does not ascertain something (as common sense seems to require), we should then write: "nobody can ascertain that 'no one ascertains someone else's ascertaining' ".

Let us consider the situation more closely. First of all, let us try to "enter" the environment of a solipsist. Suppose that into this environment, where the solipsist ascertains himself, there wander two ghosts A and B.

By definition, in the heads of A and B there is no private world in which percepts are ascertained or observed that the solipsist does not know. Nevertheless, they look just like two sound and refined individuals talking to each other in the presence of the solipsist. They may talk, for example, about the way they perceive a red sample on a blue background, or a tonic chord following a seventh dominant chord. In such a case the solipsist knows perfectly that, whatever they discuss, A will never ascertain how B perceives two colours or a group of notes. In the same way, B will never ascertain what A perceives. As a matter of fact, by definition, no private perceptual world is available to either A or B.

But let us move out of this "nightmare" and into another "theatre", the real common worlds of our daily experience. We just accept the existence of private perceptual worlds as an open question (they may exist or not, or exist in a thousand different ways like the possible worlds of epistemology). After all, we always do this in our ecological niche because it is very convenient to avoid intractable dogmatisms.

In this theatre, the subject is not a solipsist. The subject, called P, does not have any particular belief. At a certain point, P immediately applies this principle. Immediately, P finds out that on the basis of this principle it is impossible to say that A cannot ascertain what B ascertains, or say that B cannot have access to the perceptions of A. It would not be possible to demonstrate the contrary, even if A and B tried their best to explain, even with logical demonstrations that they actually do not have mutual access to their respective private perceptual worlds. P cannot ascertain if they are telling the truth.

The least that can be said at this point is that a perceptual researcher should never allude to the inaccessibility of someone else's perceptions for strictly logical reasons.

4. Black box

Increasingly over the past thirty years, the most widely employed metaphor for the inaccessibility of perceptions in other minds has come to be that of the black box. As cognitive psychology imported the jargon of information theory into experimental psychology, the metaphor of the black box was probably adopted in part because it seemed to dissipate or dispel the subtlest and most inconvenient philosophical problems concerning other minds.

To simplify as much as possible, this metaphor applies to the head of any person we have ever met in our daily life: it is sealed like a black box. It is not possible to see what its inside is like or what circuits it contains. It is not possible to say whether the clever devices hidden in it are electronic, mechanical, analogic, or digital. All we can do is to measure its input and output. Heads do not merely hide thoughts, fantasies, memories, and unconscious computations from our sight. They also hide those perceptions of the external world that all owners of a head have, and that let us share the world around us, at least as long as we are in the same environment.

As a scientific observer, what I can do is keep under observation external things as they obviously strike the sense organs of each owner of a head. At the same time I can observe the corresponding behaviours, either motor or verbal. But what happens inside the heads is purely conjectural, as far as an actual black box is concerned. The behavioural scientist can only record and classify actions, gestures, and words, sometimes as input and sometimes as output, for each black box or head observed from time to time.

Show me a head and I will show you a black box. We are all boxes . . . But hold on, not all of us are. For example, surely I am not a black box. True, I can observe directly all the facts and events of the surrounding world that I would consider either as input or output for a black box, including mine. However, in the world of my observation there is much more: there is, interestingly, all the material that another observer would swear is securely locked inside "my" black box. In other words, I can see perfectly well what another observer would consider as my motor or verbal output, and I can see those events of the eternal world that the same observer would classify as input for my action. But these facts are only part of a much wider collection of observables that includes a large number of things that are neither input or output, things that my colleague would consider as private processes of my mind to be approximated only by means of conjecture. Nonetheless, these things are definitely present in the large class of my observables. Thus, if we accept the definition given above, then surely I am not a black box.

Suppose then that I ask some people – some black boxes – about being black boxes. They would certainly give an "irrevocable" answer. Irrevocable and peremptory, precisely in the sense that I defined above in the introduction. They would say that they are not black boxes, and they would give the same reasons I myself give when I assert that I am not a black box.

After all, none of us believes that our shared observable world, the furnishing of the scene where both of us are acting, could depend on an analysis of our input. And even less do we believe that it depends on some conjectural interpretation of our behaviour, defined in terms of output (as our colleague's view would require).

It is particularly odd that our cognitivist colleague can nonetheless point to those things that at this moment he or she considers as input for my black box, and distinguishes them clearly from those locked inside the box. The latter are, of course, private psychic processes to be discovered by means of clever conjectural procedures but, at least in some cases, our colleague could very well point to those as well.

Consider the following case. Our colleague shows me the Michotte "launching effect". In this effect, a mobile object hits another object that was stationary before being hit. Having received the hit, this object starts moving, just like a billiard ball when hit by another.

The colleague will teach me that the two objects are the visual input for my black box, and so is their motion (speed, direction, type of trajectory). According to this colleague, however, the perception of the *collision* and the apparent causal dependence of the motion of the second object on the motion of the first are due to some input processing inside my black box. And this in spite of the fact that the colleague could witness these things, the collision and the causality, by pointing his or her finger. The very same finger the colleague uses to determine the length of the range of action of the passive motion of the second object and to measure it.

In this case, there is an odd reciprocal penetration of black boxes. After all, if we ask other people about their being black boxes, they will truthfully state that others might be, but they certainly are not.

We could conclude with the following limerick, which contains the moral of the story:

> If that oft-told old story of the black box
> really were true (not only as a paradox)
> then you could tell no story
> right or wrong (not even as a paradox)
> about that oft-told story of the black box.

5. Simulation

Finally, there is the paradox of the perfect Golem. In the cognitive approach to perceptual science, one finds the widespread belief that computer simulations provide a method for studying and explaining what is perceived. Simulations are thus said to explain precisely the facts that have been discovered, isolated, investigated, related to theories, and coordinated in general laws by the work of thousands of men and women in the last 150 years, men and women with diverse backgrounds ranging from philosophy to physics, not to mention biology and many other domains of organised knowledge.

Computer simulations are models for the processes that cause perceptual appearances. When they are successful, simulations reproduce the processes that underlie perception, that is to say, the chain of occurrences (physical, physiological, neurological) that lead to seeing, hearing, tasting, and touching things in the world, as they are defined intuitively by most people.

However, a simple fact about simulation must be borne in mind. Simulations are not literal reproductions. When constructing a simulation, one does not attempt to replicate the very occurrences described by some theory of perception or those that were conceived by God. If one goes out and buys copper cables and tin foil, assembles small magnets, and manufactures a small device to carry sounds over the cables, certainly one does not have a simulation of a telephone. What one has is an actual telephone, albeit a technologically primitive one. In contrast, if one builds an apparatus for carrying coherent light over long distances, and does it so that the light can vary in intensity as a function of certain mechanical oscillations induced by a voice, and if that light after several reflections ends up impinging on a magnetic head that will leave a trace on a tape, and if that trace, after adequate analysis, can be converted into a graph that can then be fed into a computer to reconstruct the oscillations and finally convert them into the original pressure waves, then one has a simulation of a telephone.

Note that all the various steps of the simulating process can be replaced by other equivalent steps. The causal chain can be stretched or shrunk. Teams of engineers can compete at inventing yet further steps, and certainly each will come up with a different simulation of a telephone at the end of the operation. But all that the simulations will guarantee is that if one says a word here, someone else may hear it elsewhere.

Now suppose that I have built a perfect Golem. The Golem is not to be a perfect copy of myself. If this were the case, then the Golem would be a reproduction, not a simulation. Thus, Golem hardware is completely different from physiology of actual men, but the result is a perfect simulation. The Golem will argue with me, he will tell me about Golem predilections in music or in poetry, about curiosities in the facts of perception. Eventually, the Golem will manifest an interest in a general theory of perception.

Thus, the Golem and I will start collaborating at the development of such a theory. I will show him all known optical tricks. The Golem will see them, and we will enjoy discussing them, for the Golem is perfect – as a simulation, not as a measuring device (in its imperfection as a measuring device lies its perfection as a simulation). We will observe the phenomena of perceptual constancy, discuss the fundamental properties of colour, and puzzle over apparent motion.

Being very intelligent and creative, soon enough the Golem will discover new visual and auditory effects, new problems for our theory. Every day the Golem will call me and take me to the laboratory, and show me new things, facts that I did not already know and that were not in the literature. I shall delight in taking part in the experiments designed by the Golem. We shall share observations, conceive new conditions, perform other experiments.

But the Golem knows perfectly well about simulations. I know that my perceptual system is different from the perceptual system I put into the Golem. And of course the Golem knows that too. In conclusion, we both know that the processes underlying Golem perception and complicated simulations of other processes, namely those that that underlie my own perception.

True, the Golem will start arguing that it is my perceptual processes that are simulations of the Golem perception. To this I cannot reply. At this point things have become very difficult.

Being perfect by definition, the Golem perceives the world just as I do, sharing my perceptual experience with characteristic nonchalance. And yet it is clear to both of us, again by definition, that the Golem's perceptual machinery does not resemble mine. Taken together, these two points create a certain difficulty for any attempt to explain human or animal perception by means of computer simulations.

Notes

1 Kanizsa, G. (1960). Randform und Erscheinungsweise von Oberflächen. *Psychologische Beiträge*, 5, 93–101. Translated by M. Riegle in G. Kanizsa (1979). *Organisation in Vision: Essays on Gestalt Perception* (pp.135–142). New York, NY: Praeger.
2 Agazzi, E. (1976). *Psicologia ed epistemologia* [*Psychology and Epistemology*]. Milan, Italy: Vita e Pensiero.

COMMENTS ON SOME PARADOXES OF CURRENT PERCEPTUAL THEORIES

Sergei Gepshtein

Situating Experimental Phenomenology

Paolo Bozzi's "On some paradoxes of perceptual theories" is an exposition of conceptual and theoretical difficulties of Experimental Phenomenology by one of its most brilliant exponents. To appreciate implications of these difficulties, I would like to begin by situating Experimental Phenomenology.

Let us recall that the *philosophical* discipline of phenomenology and the *scientific* discipline of Experimental Phenomenology have a common origin. This origin is the descriptive psychology introduced by Franz Brentano and promulgated by the "Brentano circle" (Jacquette, 2004) to the threshold of a new approach in the philosophy of mind and a new approach in empirical psychology. The aspiration of descriptive psychology was to develop a "science of mental phenomena." This aspiration became figurative in philosophical phenomenology and literal in Experimental Phenomenology, but the common origin left its mark on both disciplines. From the outset, their common goal was to investigate the human mind from an adamantly first-person perspective.

Let us also recall that the scientific study of the mind was the goal of another discipline that made no commitment to the first-person perspective. This discipline is sensory psychophysics, conceived just before Brentano's descriptive psychology and dedicated to investigating mental phenomena from the third-person perspective of natural science.[1]

These distinctions are important to keep in mind today as boundaries between the original commitments are being eroded by naturalization of the sciences of mind. Researchers interested in the first-person perspective of Experimental Phenomenology increasingly turn to third-person methods of natural science, as is often the case in cognitive science and cognitive neuroscience. By turning away from the first-person commitment, one is turning away from an opportunity to address one of the most urgent demands of our time, which has been articulated most vividly by adherents of philosophical phenomenology. Here speaks the Czech phenomenological philosopher Jan Patočka (Patočka, 2016), a student of Husserl:

> Modern man has no unified worldview. He lives in a double world, at once in his own naturally given environment and in a world created for him by modern natural

science, based on the principle of mathematical laws governing nature. The disunion that has thus pervaded the whole of human life is the true source of our present spiritual crisis. It is understandable that thinkers and philosophers have often attempted somehow to overcome it, yet they have generally gone about this in a way generally meant to eliminate one of the two terms, to logically reduce one to the other, to present one – usually on the basis of causal argument – as a consequence and a component of the other. (p. 3)

The concern voiced by Patočka was also voiced by other preeminent phenomenologists, most notably by Husserl and Merleau-Ponty, to whom we return below. It appears that the mentioned naturalization of the sciences of mind amounts to exactly the elimination of what Patočka called the "naturally given" phenomenal environment observed from the first-person perspective and replacing it by the environment described in terms of the third-person natural science.

In this light, our ability to resolve paradoxes of Experimental Phenomenology acquires exceptional significance. Indeed, because of its commitment to both first-person perspective and the scientific method, Experimental Phenomenology occupies a unique position at the juncture of first-person and third-person perspectives. Attempts to resolve these paradoxes can take several forms. In the conservative mode, one will aspire to improve techniques of Experimental Phenomenology, which is to devise new kinds of experimental "protocols" that involve new sensory stimuli and new tasks respecting the first-person commitment. And in the heterodox mode, one will attempt to elucidate limitations of Experimental Phenomenology and investigate how its practice can be supplemented by, and entwined with, methods that stand outside of Experimental Phenomenology, all in the effort to derive a comprehensive account of the first-person world.

The nature of the paradoxes of Experimental Phenomenology described by Bozzi raises the questions of whether it is the latter, heterodox approach that is more likely to produce a comprehensive "science of mental phenomena." In other words, it appears that only by deploying both first-person and third-person methods will we be able to paint a complete picture of the first-person world. To illustrate this position, I will describe how a fundamentally first-person challenge can be met using a decidedly third-person method. Our goal is to develop a conception of space as it is experienced from the first-person perspective (the space of experience), in place of the third-person conception of physical space (the space of physics).

Experience of space

Echoing Patočka and Husserl, the phenomenologist Maurice Merleau-Ponty had the following to say in his 1948 lectures on French radio (Merleau-Ponty, 2004):

The world of perception, or in other words the world which is revealed to us by our senses and in everyday life, seems at first sight to be the one we know best of all. For we need neither to measure nor to calculate in order to gain access to this world and it would seem that we can fathom it simply by opening our eyes and getting on with our lives. Yet this is a delusion.

. . . the world of perception is, to a great extent, unknown territory as long as we remain in the practical or utilitarian attitude. . . . I shall suggest that much time and effort, as well as culture, have been needed in order to lay this world bare and that one of the great achievements of modern art and philosophy (that is, the art and philosophy of the last fifty to seventy years) has been to allow us to rediscover the world in which we live, yet which we are always prone to forget. (p. 39)

Space was Merleau-Ponty's prime example of how the "world of perception" remained an unknown territory. He made the distinction between the "space of classical science," which is:

> the uniform medium in which things are arranged in three dimensions and in which they remain the same regardless of the position they occupy, (. . .) a medium of simultaneous objects capable of being apprehended by an absolute observer who is equally close to them all, a medium without point of view, without body and without spatial position — in sum, the medium of pure intellect. (p. 50)

and the space of experience, where

> (. . .) our relationship to space is not that of a pure disembodied subject to a distant object but rather that of a being which dwells in space relating to its natural habitat. (p. 55)

One realization of this relationship between the subject and its habitat was advanced by Rudolf Arnheim (Arnheim, 1977) in his study of architectural experience from a perspective derived from the Gestalt school of Experimental Phenomenology. Arnheim used a drawing by the architect Paolo Portoghesi to illustrate this relationship (Figure 2.1) and to develop the following description of the experience of a built environment:

> In perceptual experience, the spaces surrounding buildings and similar structures cannot be considered empty. Instead these spaces are pervaded by visual forces generated by the architectural structures and determined in their particular properties by the size and the shape of their generators. Visual forces are not isolated vectors, but must be understood as components of perceptual fields that surround buildings.
> Visual forces (. . .) must be understood as components of perceptual fields that surround buildings. (. . .) a field of visual forces expands from the center and propagates its wave front as far into the (. . .) environment as its strength permits. (p. 28)

This is a first-person account of architectural experience taking advantage of the concept of "field" that was central to Gestalt theory. But the concept of "visual force" deployed by Arnheim is unclear. One is prompted to ask whether the visual force is real in the same sense as the forces of gravitational attraction or electrical attraction are real. Or maybe this "force" is metaphorical? Or does it constitute a unique first-person concept that has no third-person counterpart? Similar questions arise about the notions that the field has a "wave front" and that its "propagation" is dictated by the "strength" of the force. Below I consider a third-person framework from which ideas similar to Arnheim's arise, but which does not prompt one to doubt the reality of the ensuing picture.

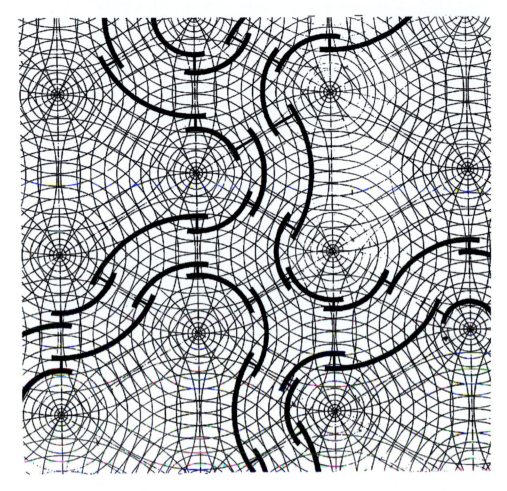

FIGURE 2.1 A hypothetical "perceptual field" of an architectural environment. The thick lines represent walls in plan view. Each set of concentric curves represents the potential effect of the corresponding wall on the viewer. Jointly, the overlapping sets of concentric curves form the "perceptual field." The drawing is by Paolo Portoghesi, reproduced from Arnheim (1977, p. 30).

Solid field of visibility

Visual scenes present the perceiver with a variety of entities: objects, surfaces, and events. Let us call them "features" of the environment. The features appear at different distances from the perceiver. Because of the selectivity of the visual system, the perceiver can experience only some features from any given location. We can reverse this argument and say that every feature can be seen from a limited set of locations even when it is not occluded by other features. The sum of such locations will make a pocket of solid space. Every visible feature of interest will have such a "chamber" of visibility attached to it. (Notice that I use the word "chamber" only as a linguistic shortcut.) The boundaries of such chambers of visibility are not visible themselves, but they are real in the sense that the perceiver will be able to see the feature of interest when inside the chamber and not see the feature when outside of the chamber.

Let us suppose that features of the environment are stationary and the perceiver is mobile. As the perceiver is moving through the environment, she will be crossing boundaries of the chambers of visibility. Since different chambers will afford visual access to different features, the perceiver will have a sequence of different visual experiences. We could predict the sequence of experiences if we knew the perceiver's trajectory and the locations of chamber boundaries.

Because many properties of visual selectivity are known from the third-person perspective, we can derive the boundaries of the chambers of visibility and from that predict the sequence of experiences (a first-person process) for any trajectory of the perceiver in the environment.

Notice that the boundaries of visibility in a stationary environment are stationary under the simplifying assumption that the perceiver's characteristics do not change as she traverses the environment. One can therefore think of the environment as partitioned in terms of potential experiences. A planar section of the environment – for example a horizontal section at the level of the floor or at the level of the perceiver's eyes – will produce a two-dimensional map of potential experiences.

Suppose we derive such a map using the contrast sensitivity function, following a procedure described in the Appendix. Contrast sensitivity is a characteristic of visual perception derived by third-person tasks, such as the aforementioned detection or discrimination. On this definition, feature visibility is a continuous function of viewing distance.

A boundary between those locations where the feature is visible and those where it is invisible can be defined several ways. An absolute boundary is found where visibility approaches zero. It is however common in psychophysics to define the boundary at some other value, called the *threshold of visibility* – for example, where the perceiver will be able to report the feature correctly 75 percent of the time. One can also entertain a third possibility, in addition to the absolute boundary and the boundary at the threshold of visibility. The boundary could be replaced by a transitional interval between low and high visibility. The transitional interval could be defined between the locations where the perceiver reports the feature correctly 75 percent of the time or more, on one side, the locations where the perceiver reports the feature correctly 25 percent of the time or less, on the other side. Now the perceiver would take some time traveling through the zone between visibility and non-visibility.

On any definition of the boundary of visibility, we have the space of the environment divided to parts. We can summarize this notion by saying that visibility of features of the environment constitutes a continuous solid field, which we partition for practical reasons. In a stationary environment, the field and its partitions constitute an objective structure of the environment: its objective spatial organization, given a visual characteristic of the perceiver derived by the third-person method of sensory psychophysics.

In the case considered here, visibility is derived from the perceiver's contrast sensitivity, which is a readily measured objective characteristic of every individual. For a perceiver with a different contrast sensitivity, or the same perceiver whose contrast sensitivity has changed, the spatial organization of the environment will be different, but it will be objective and knowable.

In general, every part of the environment can be characterized by more than one feature. For example, a person can be described in terms of her overall appearance (such as the silhouette) and in terms of her facial features. The silhouette and the face will be visible from different solid regions, which can overlap or nest in one another. What is more, the different solid regions will have different orientations relative to the person because the silhouette will be visible under angles different from those for the face. Such nuances can be readily taken into account by making the map of visibility more nuanced than in the simplified case illustrated in the Appendix (Figure 2.3), i.e., using a more refined third-person procedure.

Further generalizations of the above picture will include dynamics other than movement of the perceiver. In particular, the environment can be dynamic, when parts of the environments move or contain moving images. Perceiver's characteristics can also change, for example, because of changes of the overall illumination of the scene (sun light vs artificial light) or because of attentional fluctuations. In our illustration, where visibility is defined in terms of contrast sensitivity, the changes of visibility induced by varying illumination (or varying attention) are known, at least in part, allowing one to make testable hypotheses about the dynamics of the solid field of visibility and its partitioning.

The resulting conception allows one to predict certain aspects of the experience of architecture in first-person terms. But this conception is derived using a third-person method: measurement of contrast sensitivity. Just as in the account of Arnheim and Portoghesi (Figure 2.1), our conception concerns the impact of the environment on the person at different distances between the person and parts of the environment. But our conception only concerns boundaries of experience. The content of experience can be studied using traditional tools of Experimental Phenomenology. This way, we have developed a framework in which a complete picture of experience of space can be attained by combining first-person and third-person methods.

Note

1   Since the distinction between first-person and third-person tasks can be subtle, for the purpose of our discussion we can separate the two in terms of whether the task has a correct answer. Psychophysical tasks involve judgements of stimuli presented in two or more states known to the experimenter. For example, the stimulus can be present or absent (detection task), or the stimulus can move in one of several directions (discrimination task). Typical tasks of Experimental Phenomenology do not have a correct answer, such as in studies of perceptual grouping (where a number of tokens may *appear* to form one or another shape) or in studies of phenomenal identity (where a dot *appears* to move alone in one direction or as a part of dot collective moving in another direction).

References

Arnheim, R. (1977). *The Dynamics of Architectural Form*. Berkeley, CA: University of California Press.
Cornsweet, T. N. (1970). *Visual Perception*. New York, NY: Academic Press.
Jacquette, D. (2004). *The Cambridge Companion to Brentano*. Cambridge, UK: Cambridge University Press.
Merleau-Ponty, M. (2004). *The World of Perception*. Abingdon, UK: Routledge.
Patočka, J. (2016). *The Natural World as a Philosophical Problem*. Evanston, IL: Northwestern University Press.

Appendix

In retinal images of visual scenes, the density of detail and the magnitude of luminance contrast correlate with viewing distance. Objects located farther from the eye are projected at higher levels of pictorial detail (called "spatial frequency" of detail) and at lower contrast than nearer objects.

Figure 2.2, panel A, contains the Campbell-Robson chart (Cornsweet, 1970) of visual contrast sensitivity. Here the amount of detail (spatial frequency) increases from left to right while luminance contrast increases top to bottom. This chart makes it clear that visibility of patterns depends on the amount of detail. The boundary of visibility varies from left to right, represented schematically by the continuous curved line. This boundary is the contrast sensitivity function. (Sensitivity is defined as $1/c$, where c is the amount of contrast that makes the luminance pattern just visible: the lower the contrast the higher the sensitivity.)

In panel B, an image with a fixed density of detail (fixed spatial frequency) is shown at three viewing distances. Increasing the distance will lead to increasing the density of detail projected to the eye even as the amount of detail in the image is the same. The arrows from panel B to panel A indicate how increasing the projected amount of detail is expected to correlate with visibility, illustrated in panels C-D.

In panel C, the solid curved line traces the boundary between the visible and invisible elements of the image, as in panel A. The solid horizontal line marks a fixed low contrast at which the range of visible spatial frequencies is confined to an interval marked as the "window of visibility." In panel D, the image with a fixed density of detail has a lower

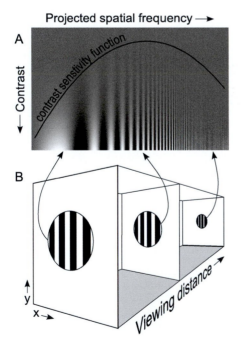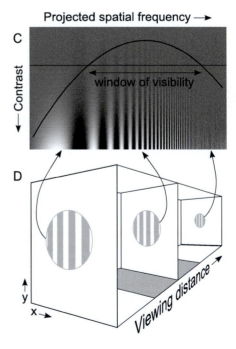

FIGURE 2.2 Pattern visibility over distance.

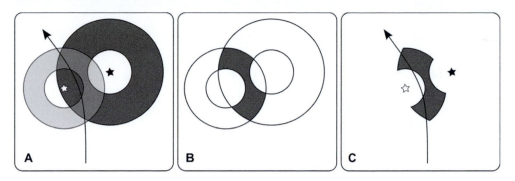

FIGURE 2.3 A map of joint visibility of two objects in plan view.

contrast than in panel B, corresponding to the contrast represented by the horizontal line in panel C. According to the "window of visibility," the image will be visible within a range of viewing distances represented by the grey area on the bottom of the panel. This limited range of viewing distances is represented in Figure 2.3 as annuli.

Panel A in Figure 2.3 contains a plan view of an area that contains two elementary objects represented by the black and white stars. The grey annuli represent the regions from which the two objects are visible as predicted in Figure 2.2D: the white object is visible from within the bright annulus and the black object is visible from within the dark annulus. The curved arrow stands for the trajectory of a mobile observer. In panel B. the dark shape represents the region of joint visibility: the intersection of the annuli from panel A. In panel C, the mobile observer on the trajectory represented by the curved arrow will intermittently enter the region of joint visibility, where the arrow overlaps with the dark shape.

3

PHENOMENAL EXPERIENCE, EPISTEMIC EXPERIENCE AND PSYCHOLOGICAL EXPERIENCE

Notes towards an epistemology of the phenomenological experimental method

Translated by Richard Davies

1. During the meetings running up to the encounter between psychologists and epistemologists that then came off in Varese in 1975, Professor Agazzi laid a certain stress on two ideas that I shall begin by trying to summarise.

(a) In everyday life, we have to do with "things". These are the "things" of common sense that have not been subject to scientific conceptualisations. They are the "things" that we can touch, buy, sell, enjoy and use, or even that are obstacles to our activity, that are means to do something, that are sources of aesthetic enjoyment and so on. In science these "things" are then divided up into "objects", and thus become the only entities that our system of conceptualisation can define and handle. Thus, a watch will be either an article of exchange (for economics) or a measuring instrument (for physics) or a historical witness (for the antiquarian) or an example of the laws (for mechanics). In these ways it is no longer a "thing", in which are all these specifications are inextricably intertwined, but rather an "object" defined within a network of logical relations.

(b) "No-one ascertains another's ascertaining": it is not possible for me to perceive what another person is perceiving at this moment, and it is quite beyond our means even to imagine how I could have access to how things seem to him; direct experience is thus private and falls outside the purview of the sciences.

After listening to the thesis set out at point (a), Professor Kanizsa claimed that he thought that Professor Agazzi's "things" rather than his "objects" were the stuff on which Kanizsa carried out his work as a scientist. I agree with him and shall try to defend his assertion.

As to point (b), I am convinced that "no-one ascertains that 'no-one ascertains another's ascertaining'", because of the contradiction that it harbours; for this reason, the epistemologists' assertion should be set to one side because it cries out for clarification. In the meantime, it is possible, by way of logical and phenomenological analysis, to study the act of observing together, which is to say the concrete sharing of the same "things" of experience that are to be found between more than one observer.

The discussion of these two points calls for us to distinguish among three ways of understanding the word "experience": as phenomenal experience, as epistemic experience and as psychological experience. The distinction will emerge as we proceed with our discussion.

2.   I should admit at the outset that what I have to say to justify Kanizsa's assertions can hardly hope to be universally accepted, and that, for all I know, some of it may not even be accepted by Kanizsa himself. My justifications may seem too philosophical to my psychologist colleagues, especially when compared with the precise methods of control that they normally employ, while to the epistemologists, the little philosophy I set out may appear presumptuous, a set of theses taken out of various contexts, which perhaps I should have discussed. I run these risks because I have not been able to find an alternative route to justify a position that, despite all the hazards, seems right to me. In a nutshell, it seems to me impossible that a whole branch of research in which, by means of certain logical tools and employing to the full the experimental method, discoveries are often made (and not only discoveries of laws, but also of new facts that had never been noted before and that are of a certain weight for the theory) should not be founded on a sufficiently robust logic so as to be able to reply to the questions of philosophers of science and epistemologists. But, to bring this point home, we need to make a slight adjustment to the commonly held views on the matter.

I ought also to set out three other premises. First, all my observations hold good only for the phenomenology of perception and not for psychology as a whole; many do not hold good (or only with adjustments) even for neighbouring regions of the study of perception, such as psychophysics. Second, we shall not even touch on the problem of the relations between Experimental Phenomenology and the phenomenology of Husserl or his disciples; because of the wealth of themes that it would give rise to, this is a matter that will have to be faced sooner or later, but by psychologists and philosophers together and not from just one of those angles. Third, we shall have to leave to another occasion any effort to trace the history of the method (Stumpf, Brentano, Hering, Gurswitsch, Gestalt theory, Strauss, McLeod etc.); there is no text that clearly sets out the lines of this development and we would have to try to pick out those lines by reading these authors.

Had I had time, I could have recounted a couple of research projects to show what happens in an informal way before the official phase of experimentation gets under way on a newly-discovered phenomenon. This unofficial phase is, in my view, eloquent about an implicit epistemology, which is different from, though in the end not incompatible with, the requirements set out in Professor Agazzi's contribution to the discussion.

The drastic dichotomy between "objects" and "things" can be set in a different light if we make a different use in talking about this of what I want to call the "Leibnizian model". As soon as anyone starts to think about psychology, they adopt this model as an implicit premise. In the first place each of us is the owner of a world of absolutely private experience, from which there is no way out so that I can in no way ascertain another's ascertaining. Every observable is within a psychism, and the act of observing is in this sense always an introspective act. From which there follow all the well-known objections.

Now, to get a little clearer about the problem of "things" as against "objects", I would like to propose, not so much to banish the Leibnizian model altogether and forever; there are problems with the model, but it can at a certain point become very useful, as I shall try to show later on; but I would like to propose introducing it a little later on in this talk, not right at the beginning or even before the beginning. This approach is, in a certain sense, unusual for a psychologist; after all, many people come to psychology precisely with the hope of breaking the shells of the monads and making windows in them; rather my approach indicates an antipsychologistic starting point: let us consider the things themselves, without distracting ourselves with the thought that every token of every one of them is reproduced within various observers, and so on.

It is true that this proposal comes from theoreticians of knowledge (C.S. Peirce, the physicist W. Heitler), but it is explicitly accepted in various places by psychologists such as Tolman, Koffka, McLeod and Gibson. They almost all agree that we can take things themselves and not a transcription of them as the object of enquiry, and I would hazard that they all agree in attributing to things determinate properties that allow the application of a certain logic. Thus, though he was opposed to the idea of considering psychology in terms of Experimental Phenomenology, and I choose to cite him for just this reason, Tolman says, "immediate experience, as initially given, is not my private world or your private world (. . .). It is the only tangible real that we have"; furthermore, he says, "there are (. . .) immediate colors, feels, shapes, images etc. in and of themselves. No misconceptions, errors or illusions about these sense data are possible. They are what they are".[1] (The former of these claims stakes out a viewpoint as far from that of Husserl as it is from that of the early Wittgenstein, who said "The world is *my* world").[2]

If we introduce the Leibnizian model from the start, we risk excluding from the enquiry a world of events that is full of interesting problems on the mere ground that we know that we have some difficulties communicating; and, in any case, we come to know about this latter fact precisely by analysing what goes on in the world of events.

3.   Let us look more closely at the non-Leibnizian point of departure. The claim made by Tolman and the others suggests that we should return for a moment to the fiction of Descartes' "evil demon",[3] which is helpful to bring out two levels of questions: (a) the one that leads us to put in doubt the transphenomenal objects that "go beyond" the observable facts in such a way that all these facts become deceptive (deceptive about those objects); and (b) the one that leads us to recognise that the phenomenological objects, vice versa, are not deceptive, and that it is possible to construct true descriptive propositions on the basis of them. Among these latter we find feelings and imaginations, which we cannot doubt that we are having when we have them, as well as perceptual data and even their physiological correlates(!).

The things about which Tolman says we cannot have illusions or fall into error, which is to say the things about which we cannot doubt that they appear as they appear, make up the field of application of the descriptive propositions about which, even in his moments of deepest sceptical discouragement, Descartes could not doubt on the grounds that he himself had proposed. For ease of reference, we may call these propositions "Cartesian propositions", and the things that are to be found within the field of the application of Cartesian propositions cannot ever "seem" or "appear": they "are what they are" (Tolman). They can be regarded as false images or deceptive seemings only in relation to the transcendent objects with which they are put in a one-to-one relation. For sure, we can use words like "seeming", "appearance", "image" and so on; but we cannot apply them to any of the observables that make up the field of application of Cartesian propositions. We can say of after-images that they are not experienced as *things* but rather as *images*; or we can say "it seems to me . . ." when the thing is close to the absolute threshold, and I am not sure whether I am experiencing it or not.

Whenever we proffer a Cartesian proposition, that proposition itself, considered as proffered, becomes part of the field of application of Cartesian propositions. I can say "I see a triangle" and straightaway say "I said: I see a triangle". On these grounds, the field contains both verbal facts and non-verbal facts, both things and (true or false) descriptions of things, which in turn can be taken to be things. Setting aside their internal peculiarities (a table may be made of wood or metal, a proposition may be meaningful or not, and so on) both of these subsets of things have the same standing as observables, as elements within or as segments of the present field of experience, whose totality I propose to indicate with the siglum E_1 (phenomenal experience).

Cartesian propositions are not protocols or protocol propositions in the technical sense, but they may become such under certain conditions. What is important to stress here is that they can never be confused with what they are about, just as, more generally the things to be found in this field cannot be confused with each other. No one muddles what they have in front of them with what they say about it.

Given a field of application, there are uncountably many (but not infinite) possible Cartesian propositions. Their potential existence consists in the fact that the things that make up the field appear as they appear. Hence, in virtue of what we said earlier about appearances, "they are what they are".

Of course, we are not always called on to be truthful in this strict sense. When faced with a triangle, we can say, "I see a circle"; looking at the Müller-Lyer trick, we can say, "the two horizontal lines are the same length"; before a random splash of colour, we can say "I see two verses of the Bible clearly printed". I can produce unsatisfactory or cursory descriptions; I can intentionally deceive with my description of what is in front of me, especially when my audience is a psychologist who is trying to verify some hypothesis of his.

But it can also happen that, at the same time, I become aware that the description I am producing does not fit the bill, that it is impoverished, that it is lacking something needed to make it clear to another person. I can be aware of this too, as well as – while I am misrepresenting – being perfectly aware that that is what I am doing. Let us leave this last case to one side and return to the other one. The perfectibility of a description is a very important matter from a number of points of view. In the first place, we improve our descriptions as if there were, in the end, some ultimate description. Some have appealed to this fact to claim that we are completely immersed in a universe made of language: we go on improving our descriptions of a given fact in the direction of an absolute description that is not there, and in the meantime, we remain in the realm of propositions. But one might as well think that the meaning of an assertion like "there is no such thing as the absolute description" is precisely tantamount to saying that no description, however elaborate it may be, can be put on the same level as the thing of which it is a description. Just so, Borges' map, for all that it covered the whole territory that it depicted by way of a one-to-one correspondence to places, was still a map and not the territory. We can pay attention to either the one or the other. And things can be studied as well as propositions can. In the second place, the improvements we can make to a description proceed differently according to whether the thing is present or absent. If it is present, then the process is guided precisely by the thing by means of a system of inescapable relations that tie the description to the thing (which is itself the aim of the operation rather than a perfect description, which does not exist). Things have all the rights relative to descriptions; and descriptions have all the duties relative to things. In the third place, the process of correction is much helped by the presence of other observers who produce other descriptions in their turn, which correct ours and supply us with expressions that are better suited to the case and at the same time help us to notice features of the thing that we would not have otherwise brought to the fore. An important phase of this process of interobservation is ostensive definition. And, lastly, ostensive definition can be put to work precisely because we can generally make descriptions less ambiguous by appeal to well-defined details of the thing and by showing them so as get across what is meant by a certain word or a certain expression. I would like to stress that, in this last case, it is the thing itself that improves the meaning and the understanding of the "protocol".

I would also like to stress another fact: in the work of interobservation, of collaboration aimed both at improving the description and, by so doing, at perceiving new visible features of the thing, the plurality of those present by no means implies the introduction of the Leibnizian model. In practice, there is a very wide margin for agreement without any pressing need to raise the question "but what does he or she see, in reality, in his or her private world?". This is what happens in practice. What it means in theory is not only that experience of the surrounding world (the world surrounding *me*) is not felt as *mine* because we spontaneously and successfully ascertain certain parts of it as public, but also that a goodly portion of the relations we have with others is carried out within the field of application of Cartesian propositions.

The model is invented or discovered when we are already to grips with experience and already have at our disposal uncountable true propositions arrived at in collaboration with others. This is roughly the outline of what I mean by phenomenal experience E_1.

4.   Let us turn now to sketch epistemic experience or E_2.

The obvious point of departure to get there is from E_1. When we are faced with things, we do not merely observe them and describe what we observe, for we also act on them bringing about transformations in them which are in turn observable. We take note that certain transformations bring about other transformations elsewhere, in more or less distant other parts of the field and regarding various features of the thing in question. Subsequently, and in line with a well-thought-out plan of hypotheses, we apply such transformations to the various things, sometimes repeating the tests, and bringing to light the phenomenal modifications that we have obtained. In this way, we can tie down the Cartesian propositions within logical structures. Let p and q be two Cartesian propositions: we may discover some relation between them such that "p R q" is not merely an inference constructed on the various observations made, but constitutes itself a Cartesian proposition in its own right. Sometimes, with a well-defined variation in p, not only will a variation in q be visible, but also the dependence in the variation in q on the variation in p. In such cases, "$q = f(p)$" will be a Cartesian proposition. Of course, this schematisation hides situations that are much more complicated.

What I want to draw attention to is that none of this imposes a rigid requirement to introduce the Leibnizian model. We are still within E_1, and so are some of the more articulated actions of observing and describing that we may call "operations". The accusations of solipsism that some commentators levelled at Bridgman are well enough known; but what Bridgman really meant with his insistence on "first person discourse", with his analysis in terms of activities that put the figure of the observer at the forefront, and with his unfortunate claim that we cannot go outside of ourselves, was that the basic operations come about at the level of E_1. "Operations" that go beyond pure observation imply assumptions whose evidence is different from that of phenomenology, even though that evidence is just as weighty and unavoidable.

I take a ruler and measure the length of the horizontal lines of a Müller-Lyer illusion; I see that the ends line up with the same notches on the ruler exactly as I see that the two lines are of different lengths. I have two incompatible beliefs (they are the same length and they are different lengths), each founded on an observation, one of which is aided by an operation with the ruler. But I assume that the ruler has not changed its length – a whole load of operations on the ruler show that it has not changed length, and in the first place it is not insignificant that, for all that I was watching carefully, it neither expanded nor contracted as I moved it from one line to the other.

I observe two red discs whose circumferences have different structures – Kanizsa's "marginal gradients" – and I see two different reds (which is what we all see). Then I place a screen in front of them so as to inspect the two reds through peepholes, and they are the same. I have two incompatible beliefs, and I might later say that they are two incompatible "Cartesian propositions"; the reds are the same and they are different. In this sort of case, the assumption that I have introduced is that the red surfaces have not changed their chromatic properties from one moment to the next.

By mechanical means, such as a revolving switch whose angular velocity I can regulate at will, I switch on and off in turn each of two light sources placed near each other. As I vary the angular velocity, I see either (i) two simultaneous flashings; (ii) a point moving along a trajectory between the places previously occupied (roughly) by the flashing points; or (iii) two alternating flashings. The three facts correspond to three bands of speed at which the switch revolves. I say that this depends on the timing of the intervals between switching on and off. Timing? Indeed. I inevitably graft certain assumptions onto the operation of varying the angular velocity: in particular, I assume a relation among the speed of rotation, the spaces covered by a certain point and the magnitude of the temporal intervals.

It is interesting to consider whether all this can be set out in terms of "Cartesian propositions". I think it can, given the phenomenal nature of the elementary material operations, and the unavoidable nature of certain logical transformations or of the axioms on which they are founded.

More complicated examples could be offered. For instance an Archimedean spiral traced on a disc that is turning slowly about its centre brings it about that what we directly observe is a continuous expansion (or contraction according to the direction of rotation) of the disc at the same time as the fact that the disc is not changing size. The incompatibility is phenomenally co-present: its elements are to be found at the self-same level, at the very place where the two opposed "Cartesian propositions" are applied. There is a whole set of operations that support the latter of them, and these operations will have certain assumptions built into them. Epistemic experience E_2 corresponds to a world of thing-objects (to mix up the terms proposed by Agazzi) that we imagine giving less weight to the phenomenal features than the things possess, though we do not remove them altogether.

We cannot be much more precise that this. Epistemic experience is the realm of facts as it is imagined by a scientist or an epistemologist, someone who is little familiar with the results of the psychology of perception, but who naturally and spontaneously adapts what he or she sees to a scheme that is promoted at one and the same time by common sense and by an elementary grasp of the physics of medium-sized objects.

5.   If we wanted to be just a little more precise, we might say that E_2 comes about as follows.

1.   By the elimination of the various incompatibilities, when they arise, between what is observed and what is measured. This will generally be in favour of what is measured or the upshot of an operation, or, when there are various facts in conflict, it will be in favour of what is closest to being measurable.
2.   By the postulate of the greatest invariance in the salient features of objects (as in the examples just given), such as permanence, identity, constancy of shape, size and colour, and so on.
3.   By the adoption of an assumption that embodies the greatest parallel between observable properties and measurable properties either in the objects or in their projective properties relative to the observer.
4.   By not denying to this world the basic phenomenal properties such colour, temperature and so on.
5.   Lastly, by the admission that here and there we run into obtrusive, not so say aberrant, "illusions" such as the bent-stick-in-water, the Müller-Lyer, the Moon illusion, hallucinations and so on.

By means of idealisations aimed at ensuring logical coherence, Musatti managed in a clear-cut way to extract this E_2 out of E_1 in a chapter written many years ago but still insufficiently studied for all that it is a *unicum* in the psychological literature. Musatti calls E_2 "empirical reality".[4]

Epistemic experience is what we refer to every time we need to talk about a reading arrived at by way of instruments or of accurate observations, directly on the facts for purposes other than those of psychology but rather to construct objects for science. Geodetic observations should be made "obviously" correcting for factors producing illusions; likewise astronomic observations carried out by optical means or other observations that are corrected for illusions: we often read, "obviously eliminating all the distorting factors, and especially those due to the imperfections of the human senses".

E_2 is generally taken to be the realm of the only facts that are truly real. The contrasts between E_1 and E_2 often risk being presented as an ontological contrast. In any case, the language of the laboratory creates an almost incredible confusion in psychology. "Real situation", "apparent", "real and apparent movements", "one seems to see", "the rat sees the stimulus" and so on. The crudest concepts that pass under the name of "stimuli" are in general bits of E_2; some more refined concepts that are labelled in the same way are bits of E_2 that have been stripped of all phenomenal properties, subtracting in the imagination all their secondary properties. However much they have been stripped down, these bits are all placed "beyond" the observables; since they must all be measured in terms of SI units, they are placed in the space and time of basic physics. Hence, there is a space and a time of physics "beyond" the space and time in which "Cartesian propositions" are applied.

I think that the epistemological incredibility of much psychology of perception does not depend so much on a failure to respond to Agazzi's sophisticated questions as on this conceptual confusion that Wittgenstein pointed out so incisively in the final section of the *Philosophical Investigations*. In this context, it is also postulated that those objects of E_2 that correspond one-to-one with certain things in E_1 can resemble the things in E_1 to a greater or lesser degree. For this reason, we sometimes hear it said that the observed object (the percept or perception) is no different from the constellation of stimuli, or that it differs from that very constellation of stimuli in this way or that. If "we see what is there", any problems arising are not of a psychological nature but are to be dealt with by the physicist and so on. If, on the other hand, "we see what is not there" or "we do not see what is there", then the problem is the business of the psychologist.

6.   All this comes about because, if we introduce E_2 and place it "beyond" E_1, we are accepting a way of viewing things that many English-speaking philosophers call "the causal theory of perception". For myself, I do not share this way of viewing things. In my view, we create trouble for ourselves if we reify the results of "operations": in that case, of necessity objects end up "beyond". In point of fact, the operations are carried out on the thing, the place where the object is to be found just is the place occupied by the thing, and objects are the logical unpacking of the properties of the thing. Yet we should admit that, if it is taken in a certain way, the causal theory yields a range of extremely productive hypotheses for the interdisciplinary connections among neurophysiology, psychophysics and Experimental Phenomenology. According also to this theory, epistemic experience (more or less completely stripped of its phenomenological features, even to the point of being identifiable with the realm of physical events) causes E_1. It makes up an immense and complex class of independent variables, of which E_1 is, from one moment to the next, the dependent variable. The physical world, from atoms to heavens, makes up the class of independent variables of which the reality that surrounds us is the dependent variable. Causal chains depart from objects and, by way of a certain number of events, produce the world of experience. This world of experience is, of necessity, not unique (it is not experience) because it is the final or terminal result of every causal chain that connects an object with a working brain.

If E_2 is conceived of as a world of "thing-objects", endowed with many qualitative features, then we are faced with a duplication of things: out there, there is an E_2-thing, and the observers around it each have a "mind" within which there is a corresponding experienced thing. If, on the other hand, E_2 is conceived of in its stripped-down and non-qualitative guise, then there are many causal chains belonging to the realm of physics that link objects to brains and from which the qualitative features are excluded (the process in the striate area that corresponds to red is not itself red, and the frequencies of the electromagnetic waves are not red). These causal chains have as their last member a sudden leap from quantity to quality. The psychism of each of us, which can be thought of by analogy with experience, in this case becomes "my experience". Let us call experiences understood in this way E_3, which is individuals' psychological experience. As regards the unascertainable content of these experiences, everyone can entertain any sort of scepticism, given that no one can ascertain another's ascertaining: here we have introduced the Leibnizian model.

The Leibnizian model has an advantage that we shall come back to. What should be noted for now is that, if we accept this way of viewing things, we can only and exclusively adopt a behaviourist methodology, whether or not behaviourism in fact arose out of different presuppositions. In this sense, I can credit only the data and not the facts, and I can assume as the only universe that is real for science the one made up of protocol propositions furnished by subjects or based on behaviours executed by subjects in measurable conditions. Things and their properties are left to philosophy. A psychologist who persisted in mixing up a bit of this and a bit of that would run into serious incoherence.

These three senses of the term "experience" – which are often muddled in psychologists, talk though they are perfectly distinguishable by conceptual analysis – give rise to many problems of method.

7.   Experimental phenomenology is founded on E_1, where things and the possibility of operations on things are at the disposal of every observer in a way that is broadly (phenomenally) independent of him or her, and where the formulation of laws is based on the description of these two sorts of facts, given that in every formula there is at least one symbol that stands for an operation. This phenomenology cannot put the things in brackets and treat the realm of protocols as the basis for its conceptual constructions. Ideally, protocols ought to be Cartesian propositions, as we learn from the stimulus error. In reality, either they are Cartesian propositions reached by a process of interobservation, or they are propositions proffered by subjects in aseptic conditions, in which case we must give them credit and register them without further question.

Thus we have to do with things and thing-protocols. These two classes of things can be accepted wholeheartedly or with some reservation or again with scepticism. But this holds both for the former and for the latter without privilege. The privileges of the protocols depend entirely on our accepting the Leibnizian model from the outset. If I have reason for doubt about the visible properties of things, I have equal reason for doubt about the protocols. Do I want to abandon immediate experience in favour of measurements and operations? I want to see where you go to perform the operation or to make the measurement.

I can subject both classes of facts to the most rigorous sceptical doubt. I can also do without that drastic position, but in that case I must not do so favouring only the protocols. We should stress here that, even if the privilege of protocols derives directly from the acceptance of the Leibnizian model, it is precisely as a consequence of that acceptance that the protocol (whether it be a description of behaviour or a description proffered by a subject) becomes more doubtful than ever. We allow three stages within others' minds: there is the "other's" thing, there are the "other's" words, and there is the meaning of those words. There may be a gap between things and meanings or between meanings and words. To put the point in Lockeian fashion: I can understand other men's words only when they designate things that I myself have experienced, otherwise the discourse is confused.

Moreover, a presumed "certainty" of the protocols – in the sense in which one might speak of a "legal certainty" – not only derives from but presupposes a large number of "Cartesian certainties" which are in turn founded on the tacit but tenacious acceptance of the properties of the commonly shared phenomenal world.

All the doubtfulness of the protocols can come to light only by thinking of what commonly happens in laboratories:

a. a subject wilfully describes a situation in misleading terms because the phenomenon is disconcerting and he or she wants to trick the experimenter;

b. the overview of many protocols calls for the formulation of laws in probabilistic terms even if what is at stake is a plainly deterministic phenomenon; and, once the only realm accepted as factual is that of the "data", there is irremediably no way to construct an underlying language that distinguishes deterministic observable sequences from those that are merely probable. In private, we know that certain phenomenal functional connections are as rigid as those of classical mechanics, because we have worked on them directly; but the protocols always make us say "eighteen subjects out of twenty. . ."

c. the very same state of affairs always prevents us from ever saying that two phenomena are independent of each other, except in terms of a relative independence based on the measuring instruments used or on the chosen statistics; yet it is a plainly visible fact that, unlike the world of physics or the like that might be constructed, in phenomenal experience certain properties of things are completely unconnected with certain other properties. If it were necessary, I could spell this claim out in detail; but the very concept of "differential threshold" says it all.

We ought thus to continually re-check the protocols against the things and grant to the things full rights and to the protocols only duties. A descriptive protocol offered by a subjects acquires its sense (perhaps) only when, trying to make it ours *in the face of the situation*, we ascertain what the philosopher J.L. Austin called *fitting the bill*, or the appropriateness of what is said about the thing.

When there is radical conflict, which does not boil down to subjects' cheating or to communication breakdown in giving the instructions (errors that are sometimes ineliminable), the most fruitful hypothesis is that the experimental set up, the structure of the unit of analysis, has been chosen ineptly, that is has been constructed so as to allow that the conditions determining the fact that we want to study are in conflict with other conditions in such a way that the fact under study shows a certain instability. When the situation has not been well chosen, the whole business of interobservation becomes more complex ("how's that? don't you see that. . . ." – "rather I see . . ."), and the corresponding subjects' protocols, even when they have been examined with aseptic procedures, get us nowhere.

8. The experimenter's skill lies in turning these unstable situations into situations in which the conditions for the desired phenomenon are at work without obstacles. Indeed, he or she needs to presuppose – again a point that needs to be discussed – that when certain conditions obtain in the field then a certain fact connected to them will always obtain. Repeatability is the repeatability of the conditions. If the fact changes its features, it is only because of other incidental conditions. It is no use interrogating a thousand subjects; what you have to do is make the situation reliable.

The Leibnizian model comes in very handy in this conceptual operation. I am greatly helped to imagine what I have to vary in order to get the descriptions to converge, if I imagine many worlds with different private experiences, which are extremely free in their articulation but bound (albeit mysteriously) to a given thing that I control and inspect. The question "who knows what he is seeing at the moment?" does not permit operationally valid answers, but it does encourage us to imagine new ways of seeing a thing.

No-one believes that, in the face of a red square, another person sees a green triangle. It would be simply dishonest to accept a protocol of that sort. A short-sighted person without their glasses on sees the objects out of focus; but this is just one operationally verifiable and correctable condition in E_1. The condition that has to be corrected is close to the observer we have next to us; it may be close to my "I", in which case it is I who have to put my glasses on or have my visual system fixed, if possible. But often the condition is in the thing itself, as in the case of multi-stable images, where it can take very little to come to one solution rather than another. Or we might think of simultaneous comparisons, where there is never absolute identity and the uncertainty seems, in the course of the comparison, to lie precisely in the things. "It is hard to say that . . ."; but then you look and discover the reason why it is hard to say is right there in the thing. Examples are legion.

It is worth adding that when the situation is well structured and happily chosen, there is no avoiding the independence of its properties relative to the observer, the mode of observation and the manner in which one might approach it; this is a feature of the ecosystem, a feature of the polarity as between observer and thing considered as a whole. The unanimity of the protocol descriptions is a reflection of this phenomenal independence, and should be understood in the light of it. Furthermore, within the field of application of Cartesian propositions, the proofs in favour of this independence are so many operative criteria that can be used to support the assertion of it. For all that I set myself to doing so and for all the efforts I make, I cannot bring myself to see this cube "as" a tetrahedron, nor Michotte's launch effect as a sequence of independent movements, nor the lines of the Müller-Lyer as equal in length. The description of a broader field of facts – the set of the various phenomenally explicit rations holding between the observer and the thing – provides the guarantee for the stability of the thing's properties. In this sense, there is no denying that objectification is directly related to the objectuality-objectivity that we encounter when we inspect the thing.

So why do we publish research findings in which the results are aligned and treated just like those produced by the behaviourists? Answer: so that a colleague in Tokyo or Pensacola can reproduce the same situation. And it will count as the same if he or she is careful to repeat the important conditions, since a given complex of important conditions may be wholly uninfluenced by other things present in the situation. And we do so so that the colleague can pursue the analysis, consulting other observers and comparing the data obtained from them with those we have furnished, as well as comparing the data with the situation he or she is faced with and is working on. In my view, in Experimental Phenomenology, the data, which is to say what we have at the level of protocols, make up an *external support for the internal consistency* of the theory. The direct exploration of the properties of things allows us to construct interobservational descriptions expressed in ordinary language. The use of ordinary language cannot be eliminated given that we find ourselves in possession of a ready-made language. And these descriptions are supported from without by the protocols obtained from subjects in aseptic conditions. In these descriptive contexts functional connections can be traced, and these connections are already in part expressible in a formalised language. Sufficiently large sets of semi-formalised functional connections can give rise to a consistent model, which may be formalised to such an extent that we do not need to say which properties of things can be inserted into the propositional functions at the level of the facts.

Examples can be drawn from various fields: constancies of shape or of size, or chromatic constancies. A single coherent model can work on such varied facts, and allow predictions to be made and hypotheses to be developed. In my view, the power of the model derives much more from the fact that it is coherent and applies to three sharply distinguished zones of experience than from the agreement among the protocols in the narrow sense. The model is at its most powerful when it can be applied virtually unmodified to other sensory modalities. For instance, there are phenomena of closeness and similarity both in the visual field and in the acoustic field. Obviously, when they move from one aspect to another or from one modality of experience to another, the models have to be retouched. But the retouchings do not affect their inner logic; and for the time being, they work. We would have to find some glaring new fact for them to be invalidated.

Notes

1   Tolman, E.C. (1961). *Behavior and Psychological Man*, p. 96. Berkeley, CA: University of California Press.
2   Wittgenstein, L. (1921). *Tractatus Logico-Philosophicus* (trans. D. Pears & B. McGuinness), par. 5.62. London: Routledge & Kegan Paul, 1962.
3   Descartes, R. (1641). *Meditationes de Prima Philosophia*. In *Œuvres de Descartes* C. Adam & P. Tannery (Eds), (1887–1913), vol. VII, p. 22. Paris: Vrin.
4   Musatti, C. (1964). Analisi del concetto di realtà empirica [Analysis of the concept of empirical reality]. In *Condizione dell'Esperienza e Fondazione della Psicologia* [*The Conditions of Experience and the Foundation of Psychology*]. Florence, Italy: Giunti-Barbera.

COMMENTS ON PHENOMENAL EXPERIENCE, EPISTEMIC EXPERIENCE AND PSYCHOLOGICAL EXPERIENCE

Notes towards an epistemology of the phenomenological experimental method

Maurizio Ferraris

At the time that Bozzi was writing this paper, few philosophers would have regarded perception as a particularly philosophical topic. The "linguistic turn" was then still in full swing. This is no longer the case. Suffice it to say that, the last book on which Hilary Putnam was working before his death in 2016 focused on perception (and he claimed that, unless one understands that, one cannot understand anything in philosophy), or that the title of the most recent book by John Searle, *Seeing Things as They Are*[1] could have appeared half a century ago from Paolo Bozzi's pen, so innovative was he as to seem out of joint with his times. The thesis against which Bozzi builds his argument is that "no-one ascertains another's ascertaining", which means that each of us is put in the position of a Descartes or a Leibniz as a unextended and hence incorporeal point or monad, which surveys the world from its own irreducible perspective. Underlying this assumption, there is a radical separation between mind and body, with which Bozzi took issue from the outset, insisting on interobservation and the ban on conducting experiments with a static observer. And this in turn has come to the fore of late in the idea of the embodied or extended mind.[2]

We can explain why twentieth-century philosophy has been so obsessed with mind and language, supposing that perception is none of its business, in light of this radical mind-body separation, where the former two are properly philosophical topics, while the latter is delegated *in toto* to other disciplines. With this assumption, philosophy inherited an older superstition, one that dates back at least to Descartes and Leibniz, to the classical empiricists and was taken over by Kant. This was the conviction that we are not in touch with the world "out there", but only with our ideas, or at most with the world "for us". Thus there came to be bodied forth what David Stove dubbed "The Worst Argument in the World"[3] and that Searle toned down, in the book cited earlier, to "The Bad Argument". For instance, if I eat a plate of oysters, it is I who am doing the eating so that those are not oysters "in themselves", but only "oysters for me".

Put this way, the argument is patently absurd, but we should not forget how many philosophers have maintained, that "the subject and the object do not exist, but only the subject–object relation". Now these philosophers are saying that the oysters don't exist and nor do they themselves, but only an "eating of oysters". *Bon appétit*. But the mystery remains of why it is these philosophers and not, for instance, the oysters who have to foot the bill. Seeing things as they are is not a matter of the mind, but of the world. This was what, more than half a century ago, Paolo Bozzi was reminding us of: perception gives us access not to our ideas or our images of things, but to the world. While what gets called "direct realism" and is dismissed as naïve, there is nothing more naïve than to think that we have access only to our images of things. For this claim has a devastating ontological twin, namely the claim that either things exist only if we think of or perceive them, as George Berkeley and Giovanni Gentile supposed, or they are not knowable as such and are just an obscure and amorphous something that lurks behind the phenomena, the things "for us", whether they be oysters or anything else, as was supposed by Kant and his legion followers.

But, as Bozzi observes in another essay[4] if it were really the case that to be is to be perceived, then someone who said that he usually goes shopping on a Wednesday wouldn't be telling the truth, given that there is only the given moment in which I hear his voice, while the recurring action that I do not perceive is quite another matter. And if perceiving meant only perceiving the image of something then, as was pointed out by J.L. Austin (Bozzi's only peer in the years that they were at work, though Austin had the great advantage of teaching at Oxford and Harvard rather than in the backwater of *Mitteleuropa* that was Trieste), dreaming of being received by the Pope or visiting the Taj Mahal would be the same thing as being received by the Pope or visiting the Taj Mahal, or contrariwise, the right answer to the question "Do you see Sirius?" would be "No, I see the fourteenth mirror of the telescope".[5]

One author whom Bozzi esteemed highly, Thomas Reid, had already pointed to the grim paradoxes that arise in a world that is made up only of representations: not only the sun and the stars but also our kith and kin become mere images in our consciousness, images that, following through the logic of the situation, we cannot pass on to other beings like ourselves precisely because there is no ascertaining of another's ascertaining. These are paradoxes that crash down on us in a landscape that even more uninhabited than that of the most despairing of the existentialists, and that in the end evacuate everything of all meaning because (as Locke observed), if someone were so obstinate as to suppose that there is no difference between dreaming of being in a fire and really being in a fire, then it really would be the case that nothing in the world, which is the cockpit both for realists and for antirealists, has any value whatsoever.

It might be said that that no-one has ever maintained this sort of pantomime antirealism. Yet this is what we find. Even in respectable company, quite above suspicion, we find the sneaking appeal of the worst argument in the world and its variants. Some, such as those I have named, present it in its most brazen forms, others slide it in apparently more moderate guises, such as those who say that we know only the phenomena but we do not have access to the *ding an sich*. This way of seeing things comes in many flavours, some of which apparently commit us to relatively little, such as the view that the world is like a sort of pastry waiting to be cut up into biscuits, a gunk that receives form only from our concepts. But even the most basic of these moves runs into a problem. Paolo Bozzi taught us this when he observed that his cat worked with the tunnel effect. If he threw a ball behind the settee, the cat was ready looking for it on the other side. This was enough to show that, for all the differences in perceptual apparatus and conceptual schemes the cat not only was able to interact with Paolo, but was looking for regularities in the world. A world that is not formless, but gritty, resistant and already formed (not to say often lumpy), but that also presents itself as the ground on which we have everything to play for, beginning with our happiness or our misery.

Notes

1   Searle, J. (2015).
2   e.g. Clark A. & Chalmers D. (1998) and Noë, A. (2004).
3   Stove, D.C. (1995).
4   Bozzi, P. (1991).
5   Austin, J.L. (1962), pp. 48–49 and 99.

References

Austin, J.L. (1962). *Sense and Sensibilia*. Oxford: Oxford University Press.
Bozzi, P. (1991). Parlare di ciò che si vede [Speaking of what one sees]. *Versus, Quaderni di Studi Semiotici*, *59/60*, 107–119. Reprinted in L. Taddio (ed.). *Paolo Bozzi: Scritti sul realismo* [Paolo Bozzi: Writings on Realism] (pp. 83–96). Milan, Italy: Mimesis.
Clark A. & Chalmers D. (1998). The extended mind. *Analysis*, *58*, 7–19.
Noë, A. (2004). *Action in Perception*. Cambridge, MA: MIT Press.
Searle, J. (2015). *Seeing Things as They Are*. Oxford: Oxford University Press.
Stove, D.C. (1995). Judge's report on the competition to find the worst argument in the world. In D.C. Stove (ed.), *Cricket versus Republicanism* (pp. 66 –67). Sydney, Australia: Quakers Hill Press.

PART II

4

THE STREAM OF CONSCIOUSNESS, OR THE EVENTS UNDER OBSERVATION

Translated by Achille Varzi

We ought to speak about
the world that we experience and
not about a world made of paper

(Galileo)

1.   Some problems, in psychology and perhaps also in other sciences, have a curious destiny: we have known for decades that they are perfectly legitimate, i.e., they are not mere plays on words; several good studies have been devoted to them from a variety of theoretical perspectives (to be discussed and reconsidered, perhaps, but precisely for this reason of considerable interest); some general statements concerning them are fairly uncontroversial, over and above local divergences, and we would all accept them in spite of the different frameworks that may guide our work. And yet no one draws the conclusions that follow from such knowledge, from that amount of agreement, from what has been established with a good degree of certainty. In the sciences, however (as physics has been telling us for over three hundred years), the most interesting game is precisely that of drawing the furthest consequences of such propositions as we take to be true – the furthest consequences that follow by the judicious application of appropriate logical tools.

2.   In this paper I consider the problem of the *specious present*[1] or – since Bergson played no lesser role in this matter – the *durée réelle*[2], trying to show that a discussion of the properties attributed to this phenomenon, back then as in some recent studies, along with a more thorough analysis of its epistemological role in the general theory of perception and of cognitive processes, leads to the conclusion that one can never speak with linguistic and theoretical propriety of observed facts (the "observables" of epistemology) unless we take them as they are really under observation, i.e., actual perceptual states; and that the world of perception should never be ascribed properties that cannot be found through observation, nor denied properties that are observationally present, as long as the goal is to build a theory of perception that is empirically grounded, which is to say naturalistically respectful of the events that it takes as its proper subject.

There are, strictly speaking, no observable facts except when we are observing them. The logical and hypothetical ingredients that inevitably show up in the theory must be carefully distinguished from the factual material to which they are connected. The descriptions themselves, which must have a decisive role in the theory, must always be considered as subordinate to the facts, no matter how they are obtained – and as dubious when the facts are absent.

3.   Some years ago, in a much-quoted essay, M.T. Turvey listed seven radical differences between iconic memory and schematic memory, the two very first phases in which the internal representation – as it is called today – of an instantaneous stimulus, exerted by some portion of the external world on the visual organ of some living creature, seems to articulate itself moment by moment. In the current improper and stereotyped laboratory jargon, "internal representation" means exactly what we see outside when we look at something.

The phrase "iconic memory" was introduced by U. Neisser in the course of a famous comment he made concerning certain experiments by Sperling. Sperling's subjects had the task of detecting alphabetic letters that had just been removed from their sight. As Neisser writes:

> Sperling's subjects reported that the letters appeared to be visually present and legible [. . .] even when the stimulus had actually been off for 150msec. That is, although performance was based on "memory" from the experimenter's point of view, it was "perceptual" as far as the experience of the observers was concerned. What should such a process be called? The subjects say they are looking at something, and it needs a name (. . .). There seems no alternative but to introduce a new term for the transient visual memory in question. I will call it "the icon" or "iconic memory".[3]

The label introduced by Neisser has been so successful as to become the hallmark of any form of visibility in time, including that of after-images. Initially, i.e., in Sperling's mind[4], this had nothing to do with the facts he was interested in, but later Neisser himself said that perhaps there was a kinship between the two, and Julesz ended up writing that iconic memory is "merely an after-image".[5]

The entanglement among the various forms of visual duration that can be analysed separately in the lab (with methods that run the gamut from simultaneity judgments and the measurement of reaction times to the stroboscopic illumination of moving stimuli,[6] the integration of form parts,[7] stereoscopic persistence, to the analysis of long-lasting persistences such as after-images) eventually led Coltheart to attempt an ordered systematization of the various phenomena that share the property of staying in the visual world of the observers, regardless of the stimuli employed and the theoretical perspectives of the experimenter.[8] The systematization is feasible, and the more the various aspects of the visual persistence are kept distinct, the more one can discover interesting relations, analogies, and functional dependencies among them. But what emerges clearly from Coltheart's essay, striking the imagination of a reader interested in theoretical issues, is the fact that besides the classificatory order there is the chaos of numbers, the jumble of the temporal magnitudes of the various effects and, obviously, of the conditions measured on the stimuli. Beginning with 150msec, the sampling offers persistences of all lengths, up to the minute and beyond, if we wish to include normal after-images in the catalogue.

As for "schematic memory", this is a label for what is left to be expressed in a visual language immediately after the extinction of the visual fact proper; independently of the destiny that will follow, through the network of retention and processing all the way to the final storage in long-term memory. It should be seen as the tail of iconic memory, in the sense in which one speaks of the tail of a comet, or – if we wish to say that the specious present has a bow and a stern, following William James[9] – as the wake of the rudder in the sea right under the stern. Those who acted as subjects in experiments in which situations like Sperling's are presented know very well that it is one thing to still be seeing, and quite another to still be finding, immediately thereafter, cognitive traces of what has already been seen.

According to Turvey's analysis,[10] this schematic memory differs from iconic memory in seven ways and his list is the best definition of the label, if not the only possible one. First, the object of iconic memory is strictly visible, but the schematic representation is not a visible datum. Second, the icon is literally what it is and does not stand for something else (it is not "symbolic"), while the schematic memory is abstract and refers to what has just been seen as a symbol refers to its object. Third, regardless of its specific value, the temporal magnitude of iconic memory is considerably less than that of schematic memory. Fourth, the icon can be masked, that is, perceptual events that are temporally proximate or that overlap it can – if properly selected – render the icon invisible, while this does not happen with schematic memory, where we can superimpose in thought whatever we want to onto the previously seen object without affecting it. Fifth, the persistence of an event in iconic memory does not depend on the complexity of the stimulus, unlike what happens in schematic memory. Sixth, the iconic representation seems to be broadly bound to the original coordinates of the stimulus, whereas the schematic representation is free. Seventh, iconic persistence turns out to be indifferent to the restrictions on processing capacity, while schematic memory, at least in its early stages, is quite sensitive to such limits.

Every visible event, then, resolves into a fact (a mental fact, if we wish) that can be clearly distinguished from it and that is characterized by the differentiating properties listed above. This new fact, which is not itself visible, as per Turvey's first distinction, is directly attached to the extinction of the iconic presence proper. This can be confirmed in appropriate situations set up in the lab, where we can even measure, case by case, the temporal magnitude of the iconic presence in the narrow sense. But we know that these temporal magnitudes may differ (according to the nature of the stimulus applied to the visual organ of the subjects, provided we wish to stay within this logic), and may differ considerably, even by an order of magnitude. That this happens in the lab involves no theoretical difficulty; on the contrary, it gives rise to a host of theories. But in the lab, each of the stimuli described by Coltheart is presented by itself, in isolation from the others, and that is how one can obtain accurate measurements. Outside the lab – where a theory of perception, or a fragment thereof, must still find some confirmation – difficulties may arise, at least if we wish to remain consistent with what we said earlier.

Suppose the natural environment is in a given moment filled with such events as to constitute, for a specific observer, a corresponding number of stimuli of the sort described by Coltheart. I realize that I am postulating a scenario that is very unlikely, if we wish to take things literally, but I don't know how distant such an unlikely scenario is from those we normally experience, if we wish to assess in a balanced way the theoretical weight of the critique I am about to sketch. Let us suppose that such "stimuli" are of different types: A, B, C, etc., where A produces a long-lasting consecutive image, B a very short iconic persistence, C a persistence of medium duration, etc. (the measures reported in Coltheart's essay offer all the examples we may want). Let us suppose, further, that all such stimuli stop at the same instant. The persistences thereby activated would start simultaneously and each one would have a different duration, depending on the relevant stimulus. In this way, we would have a certain number of local iconic memories, more or less long-lasting, each of which will be replaced, at the moment of its extinction – by (what shall we say?) the corresponding local schematic memory?

In point of fact, the iconic memory has one location and the schematic memory another. The event located in the iconic memory is in front of the observer, and its life has the same duration as the possibility to observe it: it is an event under observation. The event in the schematic memory is not located there, where its original is located: no one would mistake the location of the icon with that of the scheme, as the latter is in the head of the observer, who may – with suitable rehearsal acts – re-vitalize it at will. All of that happens in the location of intentions, thoughts, and images, i.e., the location that may rightly be called the theater of "internal representations" – in short, in the mind.

To be faithful to linguistic usage, we shall have to say: the icon is not an internal representation while the object of schematic memory is a good example of internal representation. In the world of events under observation, the icons – the examples of iconic memory – occupy a definite place in the visible space; different examples may occupy different places at the same time. The location of schematic memory is just one, and it is quite difficult for it to be occupied by two schematic representations – perhaps both subject to rehearsal – at the same time. One can check that schematic memory supersedes iconic memory only in cases when the subject is confronted with an isolated event. I have never felt any aversion to laboratory research, but this is a typical example of a result that does not carry over from the lab to the experience of the world as normally presented to our sight.

4.   The truth is that, in visual experience that does not match the cases mentioned in the psychological literature, there is no schematic memory that intervenes at each instant to replace all those events that cease to be visually present, or that undergo transformations. The visual world is filled with fleeting events whose theoretical importance for a psychology of perception was already stressed by Alexius Meinong.[11] However, only those events among them that are for a moment the object of our attention possess a mnestic tail in some way comparable to "schematic memory": if I see a hare pass between two tree trunks, it is quite possible that I tell myself, right afterwards, "Well, a hare went between those two trunks". I might even be able to reconstruct that short path. Meanwhile, however, countless other fleeting events will have happened without any process of "schematic memory" being activated.

On the other hand, iconic memory itself is seldom present – as *memory* – in the present. Neisser himself, in the passage quoted at the beginning of this article, says that the performance of Sperling's subjects was based on memory "from the experimenter's point of view", while from their own point of view it was a matter of seeing something. Why is it that looking at something "from the experimenter's point of view" is "memory"? Only because the experimenter knows that the stimulus has been removed at time t_0 and the subjects have performed a reading on something *after* t_0; and, moreover, because the experimenter presumes that everything that happens after the suppression of a stimulus is "memory". This last assumption depends on the acceptance (probably unconscious) of Augustine of Hippo's theory to the effect that the present is an unextended point that divides a line into two half-lines, one of which is the past (that does not exist because it no longer exists) and the other the future (that does not exist because it does not yet exist): a non-existing boundary between two non-existents. But perhaps we just have to be a little tolerant about the improper use of a word. One speaks of "memory" to mean, generally, "observable presence". Such a convention is acceptable. However, according to the literature on this topic, it is also necessary to accept that iconic memory consists in what is observable after the moment in which a stimulus has been removed; additionally, it is necessary to accept that the obliteration of the stimulus be instantaneous: all the cases illustrated by Coltheart are characterized by the instantaneous appearing or disappearing of something. We never hear about experiments that consider an object's progressive appearance or progressive disappearance.

From this point of view, the events upon which the concepts of "iconic memory", "primary memory", etc., were constructed may only be classified as rare events in the stream of current experience. Normally, the appearing and disappearing of objects is progressive: automobiles that come out of a side street or turn into an alley, people who enter and exit closed environments, a dog running among the trees, the appearing of a portion of landscape as one takes a turn on a mountain path. Even so-called instantaneous events are rarely such: the "gamma" movement – the motion of seeming expansion that comes with the sudden appearance of a sufficiently large visual object – makes it the case that even illuminating a room by turning on an electric light manifests itself as a progressive deployment of visibility, which reveals the pre-existence of the objects and of the furniture contained in it. And the progressive transformation of visible events, even when it characterizes the progress of an appearing or of a disappearing, does not give rise to noticeable after effects. As many studies from Helmholtz on attest, in a world of (more or less rapid) progressive transformations, such as the visual world as it is available every day to all sighted people, it so happens that even after-images are seldom noticed by its inhabitants.

My remarks so far converge strongly towards the conclusions that Turvey himself – a theorist of continuous transformations in the actual optical flux – had to draw from the analysis of models grounded on the hypostatization of moments into which the visual present might be broken down, and I propose what I have been saying as a natural integration of Turvey's views. He suggests (a) rejecting those explanations of dynamic perceptual transformations of events that rest on the supposition that both the iconic memory and the schematic memory are static, even if they are capable of mutual integration; (b) rejecting the hypothesis of ratiomorphic or quasi-conceptual mediations applied to discrete samples taken from the continuity of the optical flux for the purpose of explaining the various modules of continuous change in visual facts; and (c) assuming that we directly see the transformations in the events under observation, since we are in direct contact with the dynamic properties of the external world, even though a long tradition from Helmholtz to the cognitivists has accustomed us to think along quite different lines.

5.   A further step was taken by Gibson in 1979, and it is through Gibson that we shall arrive at our next topics. In his last book there is a section called "The false dichotomy between present and past experience".[12] I will proceed by citations and comments. Gibson says:

> The division between present experience and past experience may seem to be self-evident. How could anyone deny it? Yet it is denied in supposing that we can experience both change and nonchange. The difference between present and past blurs, and the clarity of the distinction slips away.

Soon there will be a school of scholiasts of this book by Gibson, which seems easy but is difficult and deep (I think the imminence of his death occasionally made him summarise his thought in the form of broad suggestions). Let me try to act as one of them: in the presence of dynamic events, we see the whole duration of the event, and there is a moment – that of its extinction – when we can say that we do not see it any more and we have instead some more or less good memory of how it unfolded. Even a lengthy transformation, a dynamic event lasting several seconds, permits this sort of consideration: as I am seeing this episode of overall transformation, I remember how it started and I can attach a mnestic tail to what I am currently seeing. But let us consider the protracted observation of a static event (Bergson's preferred example in *L'évolution créatrice*): something that is stably in front of me, and that I am not necessarily observing in a state of immobility or of laboratory constriction. In cases of this sort, as I continue to look at the object it is hard to say how it was a few moments ago; any attempt to remember how it was is useless. For the effort to recover the image of this object as I was seeing it then has no substance, it seems like obvious nonsense, somewhat like the attempt to imagine what I am seeing. How can we remember precisely what we have right in front of our eyes?

The presence of static pieces in the environment means that we cannot always grasp the limit that would separate what is under observation now from what was earlier under observation. The static pieces of the environment underwrite a persistence that is not limited backwards by memory, and constitute a frame of reference for the fleeting events that take place amidst them. Gibson continues:

> The stream of experience does not consist of an instantaneous present and a linear past receding into the distance; it is not a "traveling razor's edge" dividing the past from the future. Perhaps the present has a certain duration. If so, it should be possible to find out when perceiving stops and remembering begins. But it has not been possible.

(Gibson says "perhaps". If we wait to decide that the present has a duration only after having obtained temporal measurements at the point of contact between perception and memory, we cannot truly speak of durations; "perhaps", however, the duration possesses a direct phenomenological evidence, independently of any measurements, or in spite of any measurements.)

There have been attempts to talk about a "conscious" present, or a "specious" present, or a "span" of present perception or a span of "immediate memory", but they all founder on the simple fact that there is no dividing line between the present and the past, between perceiving and remembering.

Let me recall a point I already made in the third paragraph. I supposed there to be a world of stimuli capable of giving rise to after effects of various duration, arranged in space one next to another, and I supposed all those to stimuli stop at the same moment. If there were a dividing line between perception and memory, it would be a zigzag line (in space-time): for a certain event, memory would come after 150msec, for another after 330msec, for another still after 600msec, etc. Yet nothing of this sort happens, precisely because very few events present themselves as things that can be remembered immediately after their extinction. We have experience of a memory replacing a fact, but such an experience always takes place in a perceptual world articulated more broadly – as a frame of reference for such a replacement to occur – that in turn lacks the property at issue, i.e., never resolves into an all-encompassing mnestic tail.

Gibson continues thus:

> A special sense impression clearly ceases when the sensory excitation ends, but a perception does not. It does not become a memory after a certain length of time. A perception, in fact, does not *have* an end. Perceiving goes on.

The first three sentences are open to a variety of misunderstandings unless we consider the last one as a cornerstone of the argument. This is how Gibson writes when he wants to get a whole idea across in one stroke. It would not make much sense to distinguish between a sense impression and a perception, and it would be false to say that a sense impression (according to the current use of the term) ceases when the sensory excitation ends. We must, I think, read "sense impression" as "perceptual event" and "a perception" as "perception", or rather – as the last sentence suggests – "perceiving".

Thus, many perceptual events here and there in our current field of direct observation cease to exist, for evidently they may be extinguished. This is part of their lives as facts, but the perceptual environment to which they belong, and within which they make sense, never ends: "perceiving goes on".[13] The observable presence of a world in a given moment – or, rather, in "this moment" – is not subject to those incidents measurable in certain laboratory effects. The experiments on persistences (I mean, those of Coltheart's article, which Gibson certainly had in mind when writing some of the lines I have quoted) do not say anything about perceiving in general: they only exemplify modes of extinction of particular events *within* the perceptual world. They don't say anything about the totality of the environment directly given, which for them is rather a frame of reference.

"This is not to deny that reminiscence, expectation, imagination, fantasy, and dreaming actually occur", says Gibson a bit later. "It is only to deny that they have an essential role to play in perceiving". They inhabit our heads – I would add – at the same time as the external world continues to unfold, and moment by moment, in various guises, they dovetail with parts of it. Sometimes, the memory of an event begins as soon as the event is over, and perhaps that is the only thing one can say with certainty regarding schematic memory and its role. Other times, many times, different memories with different contents latch onto the facts in front of us as cognitive integrations.

6.   The duration of observation, as it emerges from Gibson's theory, i.e., cleaned up of all the internal mechanisms of mediation that the thousand and one experimental endeavors on short-term iconic memory had led to imagine, is simply the fact that we are observing, no matter how we may then put things; this fact is presupposed by every model and every persuasion and obtains on its own, regardless of the partial metaphysics that we get from our good readings in experimental psychology or artificial intelligence; it is a fact that, as such, is perfectly clear, even in the myriad of details that compose it, to anyone who wants to pay attention to the act of observing, as long as one is serious and not merely trying to imagine how observation works or to erect bits of a theory concerning the subject-object relationship.

Normally, this reference to observation underway gives rise to various objections. One of them warns against the danger of introspectionism; another against the mystical vacuousness of fixing an object that is ineffable because precategorial, or transcategorial; a third takes the ground away from under our feet highlighting the intrinsic fleetingness of the here and now, because the moment is ephemeral; and so on. One must beware of such objections, even though they have a long and accredited tradition, or perhaps precisely because they have one. On pain of subscribing to an extreme and irredeemable form of subjectivism, paying attention to things that are in front of our eyes is not an introspective act but, evidently, an extrospective act. The whole universe of past and repeatable observations on which humans erect their knowledge – the flimsy as well as the solid – makes sense to us and we accept it precisely because, implicitly or otherwise, we admit that it can be put again under observation, in the strict sense that we are here trying to illustrate. We admit that, no matter how long and complex and decisive the labyrinth of reasoning by which we finally arrive in front of the facts in a given case (such as a microscope slide, an exposed film, an acoustic signal, a coupling of insects, a papyrus fragment with some signs on it, a needle next to a number on a graded scale, the position of a leaf, a faint colour), once we get to this point, there is observation, exactly as the reader is now observing the page of this book (or can do so, if she wants), or as I am following the movements of my fingers on the keyboard of the typewriter, the forming of words on the paper, and the play of the type hammers that hit the paper exactly where the words are forming. To suppose that this is introspection amounts to removing from the scene the universe of observables, or to reducing it to an idealization that we never encounter in actual instances of observing. It is true that in the bulk of philosophical and scientific discourse, the observer and the observed are merely signs on a blackboard, echoes of fugitive words; but it is also true that sometimes speaking of what is being observed and actually looking at it come about at the same time, and that is a good opportunity to appreciate the primacy of presence over representation. In moments such as these, one feels more than ever the vacuousness of "everything is subjective", and of slogans bandied in the scientific community, such as "the perceptual event is an internal representation". The presence of the facts under observation is a genuine challenge to such subjectivist temptations, and the use of the word "introspection" – while I am looking through a lens at an ant carrying a small breadcrumb – sounds embarrassing to say the least, because it does not fit with what is really happening.

It is natural that within the act of observing, considered not *sub specie imaginationis* but taken from reality, there are subjective components and even internal factors that play specific roles: the saccades of the eyes that follow the scene; the limits of the visual field overcome with movements of the head; the possible sight defects that force us to look at things more closely, or from further away, or to choose the right glasses; the wrong perspective that gets corrected through suitable adjustments; and so on. Or – and these are conditions that are clearly "internal", introspectively accessible – the intention to look in a different way, the sudden doubt that forces us to repeat the observation, a distracting idea. But none of this can be mistaken for the facts under observation any more than a coffee cup can be mistaken for a fountain pen, when both are on the table next to each other. The continuous disentangling of the subjective components of observation, so that they do not interfere with what we care to discern, is the best proof of the *extrospective* and not *introspective* nature of this peculiar circumstance; to say that the object thus examined is itself an introspective datum is not good epistemology, as we are often led to believe, but bad metaphysics.

As for the idea that executing observations on the events involves something mystical, this stems from the assumption that whatever is non-verbal, and more generally non-categorial, is mystical. Suppose we were to say here that the events under observation were always tightly intertwined with reasonings, presuppositions, categorisations to be accepted, rejected, or tested, theorisations, hypotheses, prejudices to be extirpated, syntactic and logical structures and so on, And suppose we were to add that the observed material is not just tied to all this – which it certainly is – but also dependent on it, in the sense that its appearing as a fact is governed by all such cognitive arsenals in open or mysterious ways, or simply not yet ascertained, to the point of becoming its pale projection into a somewhat different dimension. In such a case, the objection would not be raised, for our interlocutor would be convinced that we agree with him/her on a fundamental point, namely that the facts exist insofar as they are theorised, or spoken of. Treating them as existing is already a linguistic fact – or so we would be invited to conclude – which gives them a specific function in the discourse. In one way or another, it is the discourse that becomes the fact, within the facts.

Those who look at the world around them suspending all cognitive functions – avoiding all sorts of thinking, which can be done with some exercise – find themselves in a mystical condition. Thus, to allow the facts under observation to possess features that can be ascertained independently of the logico-linguistic web in which they may be harnessed is a form of mysticism. That's the objection. But here we mean to hold exactly the opposite: that the facts stand on their own feet, and without sliding even an inch towards mysticism. The observable facts, considered as events under way, are independent of our cognitive make-up; they are premises for it, and in the vast majority of cases they are premises for our very intervention as observers.

7.   It is clear that if I speak of facts without placing them within an observation under way, they are no more that parts of discourse, or fragments of the imagination hanging from the logico-linguistic structures in question. In this sense, they depend on the observer (who, from this point of view, is also a logico-linguistic structure) to the extent that the logic of discourse requires it. In this moment, i.e., in these lines, the "facts", the "events under observation" (with inverted commas) that we are talking about, are of that nature. And it is for this reason that we do not mistake them for the open page full of words, or for the glass or the inkpot in front of us. But in this moment, provided you are looking at them, that glass and that inkpot (without inverted commas) are events under way in the sense that counts for our discussion. It is obvious that a cognitive psychologist can say that the objects of perception are constructed by the observer: she speaks of objects, of the mind, and has a "constructivist" theory. But I would really like to understand in what sense she can use the verb "construct" when, from the consideration of an abstract scheme in which a concep-tualized observer and a conceptualized object figure as moments, she can move on to the correct description of the concrete observing of things while they are happening.

We should never forget that, while we debate about subjects or objects represented on the blackboard by schemes and symbols, we are the genuine subjects, and the room with the blackboard is the class of facts under observation, the world of objects. From this perspective, the objects are the premises of our observation because, as they gradually enter the focus of our attention, and even field of vision, they appear to be inescapably pre-existent relative to any contact with our natural means of exploration. Symmetrically, when they leave our field of observation, they do not dissolve into nothingness as they cease to be seen (the instantaneous annihilation of soap bubbles, or of the small objects that happen to fall into the area of a blindspot, are special cases and must be studied as such). On the contrary, it is evident that they preserve, at the perceptual level, the availability to be reached again and re-actualised in observation. When they enter and exit the field of observability, they already have and preserve, respectively, the characteristics of their constitution; so little do they depend on the fact that we are meanwhile entertaining some private cognitive process. It is of decisive theoretical importance that such characteristics are already entirely present at the moment when the operations of observation begin, and that they continue unaltered through the unfolding of such operations. For the conditions under which this may not happen are well enough known, for instance when the object does not appear but is created, or when it is annihilated instead of exiting the field, or when the subjective concomitants of the observer change the properties of the object in a specific way, as with multistable figures or Rorschach blots.

In fact, pre-existence – or *parte ante* persistence, as it is sometimes called – shows that the characteristics of the object under observation do not derive from a pre-cognition, from some quasi-conceptual or categorial constructive act that presides over the object's birth. Theories that predict a cognitive intervention in the genesis of the properties of facts also predict, consistently, that a certain amount of time should be spent in their formation, or in the setting of their properties. But if the observable event presents itself as *already* constituted, what are we to say? Should we speak of negative times, just to stick to those theories? Moreover, setting aside the case of perceptual multistability (where the mechanical reversability that comes with the passing of time is often attended by a phenomenically explicit cause-effect relationship between what is cognitively intentioned and what happens to the object under observation), in normal circumstances every solipsistic impetus of the observer aimed at changing the things in front of him is bound to fail and appears to be pointless, not even fully imaginable, when one really tries to bring it about.

Let us now consider the three things together: (a) it is possible for there to be events under observation, with all the details into which they would be cognitively decomposable (and perhaps even more), suspending in every way the stream of thoughts, images, memories, associations (verbal or otherwise), etc.; (b) such events may enter the perceptual field wholly formed, indeed endowed with their entire constitution already a moment before they come under observation; (c) finally, such a constitution remains unaltered throughout the deployment of our cognitive processes under way, visibly obeying only its own dynamics, the autonomous destiny of the perceived events. There is nothing mystical about considering the universe of observables in this light. It simply amounts to attributing to it an autonomy of the subject that in recent decades much epistemological romanticism has denied, and that a few centuries of idealism has contributed to smother over.

Every corroborating operation on the observables, from the least troublesome to the most complex, can be analysed from the three perspectives mentioned above: a streetcar going through a traffic light, the visual control of several dials or lights, an ethological detection alongside a pack of wolves, the observation of the trajectory of something moving on a homogeneous field (in a physics or a perceptology lab: it's the same). Whether I go and check how things stand, or go and check that an idea I am entertaining is correct and whether and how the course of facts tally with it: sometimes it will happen that I am thinking about something else, and that the event continues to unfold on its own (this is necessarily so when we follow more than one fact simultaneously, as when we check our instruments). It will also happen that a new object or event enters my observation field, so that I will take into account the fact that was already there. It will happen that I expect something and that, no matter how strongly I desire it, it does not occur, or it occurs in a different way despite my intense will (as with horse races, so I am told). Finally, I will be completely inattentive, and things will continue to unfold of their own accord in front of my eyes. It is true that sometimes I am the one who deliberately provoked the circumstances about which I focus my observation, planning them and acting on the premises in a suitable way; but once I am there, once that counts as the present, the independence of the observables can only be ascertained and accepted.

In conclusion: if controlling things by keeping them in view and following their internal logic is mysticism, so be it. It would mean that we have adopted a pompous word to point out the obvious independence of the external facts from the mental processes of someone who occasionally looks at them.

Then there is the accusation of *flüchtige Augenblick*, the precariousness of the uncatchable instant in which everything becomes unsayable because it changes faster than thought. Here, too, we must take a closer look at the details. It is true that in our experience as normal observers we are sometimes exposed to what I have called, following Meinong, "fleeting events", which may not last long enough to allow a good observation, and which it would be pointless to try to chase once they have hidden somewhere in the past, with all the reservations deriving from our reading of Gibson. When we are talking about observation, fleeting events are of considerable theoretical importance and we shall come back to them time and again. Here we should repeat that they normally take place in an observational context that is stable, or relatively stable, whether we encounter them in normal everyday occurrences or we produce them in the lab, in line with some hypothesis concerning brain processes. It would be interesting to set up a whole experiential environment consisting exclusively of fleeting events: every zone of the visual, acoustic, and tactile world (odours and flavors would not lend themselves to the treatment) would turn into something else instantly, by swift substitutions and disappearances. In such a pointillist chaos, however, dynamic structures would form that are wider than the single fleeting events, which would appear as parts or moments of those structures, given the laws of formal organization of gestaltic memory or similar laws yet to be found. The single notes (fleeting events) in a musical composition such as Webern's *Trio Op. posth.* for violin, viola, and cello are just instantaneous transition loci of a wider, compact structure that extends in time far beyond the temporal duration of the individually discernible sound events, and it is a wonderful fact that the overall shape of a musical composition provides the frame of reference for the smaller events, thereby preceding them and to some extent making them what they are.

It is the events themselves that are on occasion fleeting, not the moment, if by a moment we mean the normal being here and now. A very rapid event under observation does not lend itself to being well described, but that is a trivial technical restriction. We could slow the event down, if that does not damage its important characteristics; or we could use suitable instruments to fix many moments within it, between its beginning and its end. Once we run out of imagination and we lack any further analytic methods adapted to the purposes of knowledge-gathering that guide us, we can only cry over a contradiction: for there is no way to slow down the unfolding of an event while making it retain its original swiftness, if that is really what we want.

8. The fleeting moment, taken as it is and not as a poetic image, is precisely the locus where we erect, correct, and revolutionise science as an empirically grounded logico-linguistic construction. Rather than label it with the words of Faust (or James, or Bergson), in the

following discussion I shall call it the "factual present". We shall argue that the factual present has a central role in the construction of scientific theories of perception.

Normally, we speak about perception in a lab discussion, during a class lecture, in academic meetings and conferences; and almost always we speak about it with a blackboard to hand. On the board, perception becomes a group of signs, typically next to other signs which stand for non-perceptions: psychological processes of various sorts (thoughts, memories, images, concepts, symbolic activities), peripheral and central physiological processes, or "intervening" logical constructs (buffer, parallel perceptual coding, attentional selector, control, etc.). Everyone is willing to admit that such signs are used because they stand for something, things that can be exemplified but that do not coincide with the signs themselves. Thus, the signs that stand for a certain thought process are not that very process (say, an operation of addition, or an operation such as "if . . ." and "if not . . . then . . .") and those that stand for physiological events are not themselves physiological events, which can rather be shown and reconstructed in the lab, however indirect the demonstrative procedures may be. As for the intervening constructs, sometimes they are strictly nothing but what you see on the board, hence they are their own referents; but sometimes they can be symbolic summaries of more complex constructs, in which case their referent is the whole, fully developed scheme. The signs that stand for perceptual properties likewise have a referent or a field of referents. We must see what it is.

I can write on the board a sign indicating a perception of mine that took place two minutes ago, a stroboscopic movement that everybody has seen, and they have seen that I have seen it. That sign will have a clear meaning for everyone and also for me; but it must be obvious that it does not stand for a perceptual fact. A perception of two minutes ago is not a perceptual fact: it can be a memory, possibly a vivid one, or it can be a scheme representing a complex of properties and containing a temporal indicator, or it can be something referring generically, through an indication that sounds concrete and autobiographic, to a class of facts of which one could give similar examples. It can even be the absence of a memory, which others are trying to remind me of with their words. Each of these things is an interesting fact in its own way, but none of them is the perceptual event we are talking about. Suppose two minutes ago we took some notes or some measures concomitantly with the observed fact: in a way, for the scientific community such notes and measures *are* that fact. Indeed, a behaviourist colleague will assure me that they constitute the only fact that matters for us scientists: protocolling is the researcher's empirical reality. But the careful description of that (true) fact does not resemble the things traced on the notebook or printed on paper by the computer. No one would be able to recognize the "facts", if the only clue we gave them were the description of the "data". Surely they are two different things, and for better or worse they must be kept distinct.

I may also speak of my perception two minutes from now. The fact that I can speak of it meaningfully and with epistemological propriety (I might be tinkering with a malfunctioning device that I am about to fix, and I might be certain that in two minutes I shall be seeing a certain stroboscopic effect) does not in the least imply that it is a fact, i.e., what it must be: a perceptual fact, not a transcription of one.

Let's take the example of the perception of an animal with a visual system radically different from ours, such as a dragonfly or a housefly. Perception here stands for a logical construct based on the anatomo-physiological analysis of the animal under consideration, and possibly on the interpretation of data regarding its behaviour. In this sense, von Uexküll[14] reconstructed the perceptions and the visual worlds relative to specific systems. But it is obvious that these are never perceptions in the proper sense of the term, that is, data that are observable and, in the more fortunate case, that can be pointed to.

9.   Special difficulties arise in connection with the perception of others, for the problem (which is very complex, as we know from John Wisdom's classic book,[15] though *not* from even the most recent psychological literature) becomes very different depending on whether the other subject is taken to be present here or located elsewhere. If an observer is elsewhere, it is clear that his perception of something is not an observable fact, even though we can speak of it meaningfully, for on top of the already ambiguous problem of "the perception of others" we have the problem of distance, which turns the situation into a question of messages. The problem gets complicated in an amusing way if we put it as follow: the perception of *others*, *elsewhere*, *now* (i.e., at this very moment). If the "other" observer is present here and now, and participates in the same scene in which the problem is set and from which the examples and the references needed to discuss it are taken, things are different.

I suppose some will find it completely implausible to distinguish the problem of the perception of others-*elsewhere* from that of the perception of others-*here*; but such a position obviously underlies the hypothesis that in both cases, and to the same degree, the perception of others is completely subtracted from and irredeemably negated for any form of attestation or direct observation. "No-one ascertains another's ascertaining", an epistemologist has written.[16] But since, precisely because of this assumption, no one has ever been able to ascertain that someone's ascertaining is not someone else's ascertaining, we have to dismiss this opinion, so popular among the scientists. For it is contradictory, insofar as it is egocentric,[17] and it *a priori* blocks the possibility of going to see what really happens when two observers are together and are visibly surrounded by the same things.

More directly, it should be said that, if by "perception of others" one means a colourful, three-dimensional image, small enough to fit inside a normal human head (for this is a requisite on which few have insisted), located there where I see the head of my interlocutor and present to me, or to someone else, just as clearly and directly so that I can freely and happily apply my Cartesian doubt to it; if this is the "perception of others", the problem should be rejected straight off and without appeal. And the same must be done with the way in which the problem is somehow derived from, or reduced to, the one I have just described. It is one of those typical games I was referring to a few pages above: one defines a certain state of affairs so that there is no way out, and then cries over the impossibility of getting out of it. One carefully shows to me that everything is determined, and then cries over the lost freedom. Let it be clear that not even the proof of functional identities at the physiological level can say anything, if the problem is put this way. But sometimes philosophers mention the eye itself so as to convince their interlocutors of the irredeemable subjectivity of perceptions.

10.   Turning now to more concrete universes, the problem of the perception of others *here and now* is certainly a complex one, but also a productive one.

Once we have got rid of the small theatre in the head of others, it is clear that, even if we confine ourselves to visual perception, those of us who are sighted see that the other sees, that the other looks, in which mood (or in which paraded absence of a mood) the other looks, that we are looked at, and that we are seen (sometimes, even without looking, we feel that we are looked at or seen). We also see where the other is looking, and even at which object behind our back the other, sitting in front of us, is looking, as Attneave has elegantly demonstrated.[18] There is a whole psychological literature devoted to each of these points, and it is incontrovertible that there are many empirically meaningful aspects of the problem of directly perceiving the perception of others, in the factual present.

If we look carefully, there even exist situations in which – no matter how hopelessly we put the problem: "Can I be certain that the other . . ." etc. – it really seems that there is little room for doubting. Try to give the following task to a person near you: "Pretend to observe attentively the features of this object"; and as you say so, put something rather complex in front of him, perhaps put it into his hand, inviting him to put it close to his eyes to see it better. You are giving an impossible task. It is impossible to pretend to see something attentively. Some may come up with the example of a blind person who pretends to be looking at something attentively; but there is nothing more unrealistic than that.

As a matter of fact, if we imagine two abstract subjects who are jointly observing something, we can invent lots of good logical problems that turn out to be false empirical problems. The analysis of the internal structure of the factual present, in cases when we find ourselves observing together a course of events or some set of properties of the world in front of us, reduces the number or purely logical problems and increases the number of empirically grounded problems.[19]

Considerable experience with interobservation built up over recent years at the Institute of Psychology of the University of Trieste by myself and my collaborators highlights some curious aspects of this sort of activity, among which the fact that in situations of inter-observation the problem of the perception of others (as classically understood – and all the interobservers were excellent philosophy students!) never surfaces, while everyone tries to show the others different aspects of the object under observation, or tries to step into their place to see how the others were seeing, or goes closer or further away from the object in Gibsonian fashion.

If the problem of perceiving together is actualised, i.e., embedded into a factual present, the perception of others becomes an interesting mesh of widely shared findings having as their object and frame of reference exactly what is in front of the observers – the only thing that we can rightfully subsume under the label "perceptual fact", namely, the event under observation. As soon as the situation ceases to be in the factual present, differences of opinion become deep, justifying the purely logical model of subjects isolated like monads, each carrying within it a distorted image of the event now only ideally under observation. One is inclined to think that the proponents of monad theory have never been exposed to situations of real interaction, modelled on the here and now, but only to what one imagines afterwards, when one writes.

Let us also consider for a moment the status of an "average" perception that many colleagues talk about, even though they may not call it that. There are infinitely many cases, namely all those cases in which, given the varying evaluative opinions of the subjects (since the material is collected among many subjects taken one by one), one arrives at a description of the object under inquiry that is based on a certain elaboration of such differing opinions. That, too, is a legitimate logical construct, but it is not a perception understood as a datum, i.e., it is not a fact. Often one cannot do any better, and let he that is without sin among us cast the first stone. But let us keep in mind that there might not be examples of a given "average" perception.

All the analyses outlined up to this point ought to be developed much more fully: each is a topic for further study. But as we wait for the inevitable objections that I have been unable to foresee, and that might debunk the premises of my story, what we can say on the basis of what has been said so far is that the facts of perception exist as facts only when they are under way. I believe that this is a justification of the phenomenological method in psychology.

The perception of others (classically understood), the perception of animals very different from us, the perception elsewhere, the perception of a minute ago, a future perception, perception as an average of the answers of the subjects, etc., all these things are mere logico-linguistic constructs that we assimilate through ordinary language and technical jargon, through symbols and sketches on the board to which we can try to give perceptual body – if we are unable to reproduce the situations in the factual present – at best in our imagination, as when we picture the phenomenon being described instead of representing it in a quasi-linguistic schematic form. Let us linger on this point for a moment.

Imagination in the strict sense, i.e., the attempt to see with our eyes closed or almost closed within a spatial location in front of us, is sometimes remarkably akin to the event under observation, for it palely preserves certain qualities in a qualitative way (apologies for the pun). The imagined "red" is not a word or an electromagnetic frequency: in the imagination, it is qualitatively red, even though we do not *see* any colour. But that is not the important point. Anyone who has taught experimental psychology of perception for years knows that sometimes we have to illustrate a certain phenomenon and yet we lack the instruments to do so. In such cases, there is no other option but to describe the phenomenon, and it is good practice to describe first the instruments that are necessary to its presentation and then what one sees, or hears. In such cases, perhaps, he or she may have found that when the audience understands correctly the experimental setting, even if untutored or completely unacquainted with that particular branch of perceptology under discussion, the audience will be able to imagine the perceptual solution in a way that is very close to the truth, which is to say the structure of the event under observation, as if it were being brought about in the factual present. It is better to stop at the description of the instruments brought into play and to ask the audience to imagine "what they see", closing their eyes and making an effort. Of course, this sort of experiment should be controlled more systematically; as far as I am concerned, I can guarantee that numerous generations of students have been able to imagine very well.

This, however, is the best we can get to approximate the properties of an event under way when the event is not under way. The poorest level is that of the data (a beautifully ordered table of data offers awfully poor information regarding the phenomenon under observation: no one would be able to trace the phenomenon from the numbers in one or more tables in an ideal Museum of Science); the level of phenomenological description is less poor, but it becomes richer when it is transliterated by way of an act of the imagination.

The hearer cannot listen to the phenomenological description, when it is accurate and truly filled out with details, without spontaneously forming fragments of images; nor can the description be reproduced, in the absence of the object, without the hearer resorting willy nilly to his or her imagination. Try to provide an accurate description of your fountain pen to the person in front of you, and you will easily see how heavily the appropriateness of your description depends on the pressures of the imagination.

11.   As to the pressures of the event under observation, if you are about to describe it while it happens, they are decisive in orienting the descriptive activity.

During the interobservation sessions I mentioned above, the subjects had the task of comparing certain greys, certain whites, and certain blacks that from the point of view of reflectance measurements were identical, though in each case they matched with one another in different ways. (The details of the experiments do not matter here.) At the beginning, the language of the observers consisted of "lighter", "darker", "same"; but since they did not fully agree in the evaluation of these relationships, they began to discuss. And by doing so they discovered that, in the world of greys from white to black matched in various ways, there is "dirtier but lighter", "milky", "*fumée*", "more black but more luminous", "sooty", "whitish", "opaque": a universe of qualifications on which it is much easier to agree, in the description, than on the rough use of "white", "black", "same", and "different". From the way the exchange of views evolved among the subjects, it became apparent to the experimenters that, in enriching their vocabulary, the subjects were being guided by the event under observation. The observers would trade places, they would go closer or further away from the objects, effectively modifying the conditions of visibility of the material, and by doing so they would either challenge or agree with one another. Had they participated in the experiment as traditional observers, providing the classical answers, which are so useful to quantification, "lighter", "same", etc., and had we asked them on the next day to further analyse those matchings of achromatic colours in a more fine-grained way, we would have obtained very little. Actually, other observers had previously been involved in a traditional experiment on the same material: they came one at a time, were given a clear task on the same materials and gave clear answers. It is not worth going through the whole research here. Suffice it to say that these honest fellows gave a great number of "same" answers, evidently in order not to commit themselves too much, imagining that the blacks must be the same as the blacks, the whites as the whites, the greys as the greys, given that psychology is built on tricks and it is good not to fall into the traps of appearances. During the interobservation sessions, if anybody said "same", he or she would be immediately challenged by the others, who would urge them to look harder; and when everybody agreed on "same", the result was not reached easily, but by dint of subtle balancing.[20]

When, many years ago, I was studying the motion of harmonic pendular motion, the observers exhibited great confidence in finding – in my altered pendulums – oscillations that were correct, too fast, or too slow, basing their tripartition on frequency variations produced under observation. Had we asked various people on the street, "What frequencies are too fast or too slow for such and such a pendulum?", I suppose our question would have been met with incomprehension, or might have received the answer, "The ones that differ from those dictated by physics". But the same persons, placed before a homogeneous screen in front of which a bar of a certain length oscillates, pivoting about its top end – as with the pendulums of old clocks – and having the possibility of modifying the period of the pendulum at will, would never answer our question with such a cognitive-linguistic subterfuge. For the observers, it is immediately apparent that the pendular motion in front of them "is not" right, natural, and they know how it must be modified in order to make sure the period is "neither fast nor slow".[21] The adjective does not fit, it doesn't find a place for being applying correctly, and the search for the "right" frequency proceeds with confidence, without the interference of any preconceived theory and without any temptation to offer a linguistic-cognitive solution of the problem like the one mentioned above. The problem is in the phenomenological datum. When, starting with oscillations that are too slow, a progressive increase in the frequency of the pendular motion takes one close to the period that will then appear as natural (after all, this expression belongs to ancient physics and was used by physicists for two thousand years, from Aristotle to Galileo, to designate a concept evident in itself), it is the internal properties of the observed motion that quickly reveal the fitness that the adjective "natural" (= "right" = "neither fast nor slow") will acquire in relation to the observed event. The transformation of the frequency is controlled by the observers on the grounds that they know which adjectival regions it applies to. In this way, everyday language is the strictly technical language in which the perceptual phenomenon is adequately expressed.

The world is not capable of imposing anything upon the phenomenon; it depends on the phenomenon, insofar as this is the event under observation. That an adjective of motion quantity becomes "appropriate" depends on what is happening before the eyes: the factor that licenses the categorisation is the play of affordances pertaining to the movement of the object. The meaning of the adjective boils down entirely to the properties of the event: it's not that first there is the word, then an abstract meaning (slow, fast, natural in absolute terms, though with a certain flexibility in the possible applications), and finally the application of that meaning to that sort of motion. The appropriateness of the qualification is rooted in the fact here and now, that either offers no room for doubting or, if there is such room, it also offers a clear indication of the necessary corrections.

It must be stressed, here, that within a non-phenomenological theoretical frame, borrowed from elementary physics, the three adjectives in question mean nothing. In mechanics, it makes no sense to speak of slow or fast movements, even less of natural ones. This why people who are asked the question without having the facts in front of them produce an evasive and physicalistic answer. But if we asked someone to close his eyes and to imagine a lamp hanging from a cord a few meters long, to make it swing in his imagination, and finally to indicate its rhythm with a hand – the rhythm it has when thus seen – we would already put them in a position to understand that, besides the evasive answer, there is also an answer rooted in the universe of seen facts, even if here the seeing is still improper and saturated with subjective arbitrariness.

The reader who is familiar with the examples of mechanical causation studied by Michotte[22] will understand perfectly well what I mean when I speak of "passive movement", i.e., the mode of appearance of the displacement of a body set in motion by another body colliding with it. However, when I try to explain to an interlocutor what Michotte discovered without resorting to the presentation of observable cases, she would hardly understand me even if during his life she has already seen a thousand times how a body colliding with another displaces it, for instance on the surface of a billiard table. In the best case, he would be inclined to understand such passivity as a linguistic custom, which is appropriate to certain situations variously tied to sensations of kinesthetic passivity and figuratively transferred to objects such as billiard balls. That is, he would make it a question of words and concepts, not a problem of observable properties that depend directly on conditions equally observable, and variable within the observation under way.

The slippage towards answers that duck the phenomenological problem (which is to say the observational *tout-court*) by appealing directly to linguistic customs is absolutely natural outside the observation under way; such is the distraction away from the real properties of observable events that characterizes our normal cognitive activities. Try to ask someone how long is a long line, how long is a short line, and what is the length of a line that is neither long nor short. A network of spontaneous cognitive prejudices will make your question sound silly, at least funny. "Obviously, a long line is long" may be a logically reasonable answer, and within these limits a linguistically appropriate one. But Professor Mosconi taught me that if you combine your question with a sheet of paper on which you draw a segment in front of your interlocutor, the question will acquire a completely new meaning and the answer will become obvious. For the linguistic fitness no longer refers to the game of abstractions, but rather finds a binding frame of reference in the event under observation.[23]

This slippage is interesting because it is largely in line with the distinctions between properties of the iconic memory and properties of the schematic memory drawn by Turvey, and because it allows us to develop further, concluding, remarks about the way in which perceptual processes are imagined in the theories of perception currently most accredited within the academia – those of the "establishment", to use Gibson's irony.

12.   Let us go back for a moment to Turvey's distinctions. He speaks of iconic memory on the one hand, and schematic memory on the other, and his seven distinctions refer to the results of the work of the "establishment" (tachistoscopic and chronometric research on visual information processing with short stimuli) with which he, as we said at the beginning, disagrees. In the following, I shall be concerned rather with the distinctions between events "under observation" and events "out of the field" (mnestic entities, cognitive reconstructions, topographic representations, and thus – with the possible exception of the objects of visual imagination already discussed above – the "facts" insofar as they are *not* under observation).

First: visible, non-visible. The event under observation lies outside the subject (some acoustic events may take place in the head, but we shall set aside the discussion of sounds), in front of the location of his eyes, and normally has the characteristics of being objectivity and resistant, and features a more or less complex structure of qualities interacting among themselves, even if not totally. The events out of sight are not visible, nor explorable with the means of visual exploration; they may approximate visibility when we try to give them some form in the imagination, and that is the only case in which they may form in front of the subject; in all other cases, they are just in the head and their exploration is of a logico-linguistic nature.

Second: being a referent, having a referent. The events under observation are what they are and do not stand for something else, the exploration picks out an object, the ultimate limit of our semantics: they are the facts. Even when they are words or street signs and have a semantic function, insofar as they are facts they do not stand for anything else, for anyone who knows their semantic function will still see them as facts, exactly like someone who knows the relevant code. The events out of the field, by contrast, typically "stand for": they refer to what would be seen if the situation were made real.

Third: the event under observation possesses definite spatiotemporal boundaries as well as a manner of unfolding. In the internal representation (in the true sense of this expression), such boundaries and the manner itself may be prolonged at will, so much so that we may debate for hours on events that last 150msec.

Fourth: a given event under observation ceases to exist when new events are introduced into in the field of observation, and a new event takes its place without any particular feature of it being removed from the field. Following such treatment, we know that the field of observation contains the initial event, though really we find ourselves dealing with something different. The initial event is a cognitive integration of the new event. The events out of the field may preserve their characteristics irrespective of the compresence of other cognitive ingredients and thus, on a purely logico-linguistic level, we may say that the first event is still there, even after the masking. (Strictly speaking, in the field of objects under observation, masking never occurs; we only speak of masking to refer to one of their cognitive transcriptions.)

Fifth: the fact that an object persists at length under observation does not affect in any way its structural complexity: on the contrary, the unfolding of the observation simply brings to light the pre-existence of all the details involved in its objective structure (it does not create them and only rarely transforms them).[24] The object out of the field is always very impoverished with respect to the original and its complexity may increase or decrease during the logico-linguistic work done by the subject involved in, say, reconstructing a memory or constructing a description.

Sixth: the event under observation exists and unfolds within the observational context, where some details could affect its observable properties while others, also compresent, will in no way act on them (though often we do not know which ones, and that is why we do experimental research). The event out of the field can be handled in a sort of contextual vacuum, which is quite convenient – and often the source of error.

Seventh: the event under observation is characterized by properties that remain indifferent not only to our concomitant cognitive processes (I have discussed elsewhere[25] the special case of multistability), but also to the absence of mental processing. The event out of the field, besides the structural decay that characterizes it relative to the original, suffers from all sorts of modifications owing to the concomitant cognitive activities: so much so that often one is surprised in going back to the authenticity of the original, which can force radical corrections in the theoretical games played on its internal representation.

The event out of the field is a mental event, and it is obvious that it suffers from the restrictions imposed on mental processing. In particular, it is essentially a logico-linguistic event and it is perfectly natural that it suffers from the consequences of concomitant logico-linguistic processes *in fieri*, or from other crowding of the channel (so to speak), i.e., from the general configuration of the noetic process under way.

13. I have been proceeding by analogy. I don't suppose I have provided an interpretation of Turvey's distinctions; but it is interesting that there is an analogy between these observations about the factual present and its shadow, and the facts that Turvey took from research on iconic persistence. Evidently, already in the *microcosm* of fleeting events and their mnestic tails one finds the traces of the complex relationship between real facts, insofar as they are directly observable, and their representations in our minds.

At this point, what must be stressed is the idea that perceptual structures, when considered as events out of the field, are not facts but representations, and that in this sense they have the same ontological status as the so-called stimuli on which they are supposed to depend, and as the processes or elaborations we envisage to connect them – logically and linguistically, and more often only linguistically – to those stimuli.

We can do all this on the blackboard, to say it one more time, precisely because the perceptual event is not longer a fact under way but an event out of the field: the blackboard is the ontological plane on which stimuli, processes, and perceptions are coplanar, figurative schematizations of logico-linguistic structures. Stimuli and processes are never, as such, events under observation. This does not mean, of course, that such constructs lack an empirical base; indeed they have lots of empirical bases, and of quite different natures.

When this empirical base is an observed event, and an event that can be observed by several observers, it is not the stimulus and it is not the process nor the elaboration. It is, in each case, a measure taken in the proximity of something with all those precautions and provisos that fit the bill; a "spike" on a paper strip that rolls at a known speed and whose segments can be put in one-one correspondence with certain positions of the arm of a chronometer; a button pressed by someone; in short, an operation in Bridgman's sense[26] – and on a strictly factual level nothing more than this. At this level, operations are controllable and ostensible happenings, and it is to this level that we need to resort when the logical construct relative to some such happening is for some reason called into doubt. Operations are the extreme terms of empirical testability, and they are so insofar as they are events under observation.

Stimuli and elaborations are logical networks linked to those operations, networks that vary moreover over time according to the instruments, the measurement systems, the theories and the various assumptions adopted. They are everything but facts. That such logical networks should be reified is fine. (Prof. Melandri told me more than once: "Reify, reify, there is always time to clean up everything afterwards"; afterwards, i.e., when by dint of reification we have come up with good discoveries.) It is clear, though, that the reification of these ingredients is nothing but a new linguistic accessory capable of enhancing the schemes' solidity and of favoring the economy of their construction.

Among the facts under observation we never meet stimuli, processes, or elaborations. But there is no observed fact that does not admit of being thought of in terms of stimuli, or elaborations, or processes, even at the very same time as we are observing its unfolding. The events in the factual present provide the observer with countless loci onto which one can latch the most diverse cognitive integrations: I look at a cup and I know that in its thickness there is a huge number of silicon atoms variously combined with other atoms in more or less complex molecules; I look at a colourful poster and I know that it has been printed in Hungary; I look at a bystander and I know he has a heart beating inside him; I look at a triangle and I know that the sum of its inner angles equals two right angles; I look at this gem and I know that it is cheap glass, and its splendid mounting is pinchbeck. Cognitive integrations cannot be recovered from observation, that is, they are not real aspects of the event under observation.

Stimuli and elaborations belong to this class of cognitive structures: if I look at the Müller-Lyer illusion, I know that the two lines are equal (that is, I know that by using a ruler I would find that their ends correspond to the same points on it), I know that in the brain there is something that does something in such a way as to allow me to combine the opinion of the ruler and that of the evidence; if I move my head in order to better locate where a sound is coming from, I know that all that has something to do with wave slippages and differences in local intensities, depending on the frequency and the pressure that a suitable measurement system would assign to it: that is, I know that my brain must perform some sort of calculation, analogically or digitally, if I want a certain conceptual construct to hold water. But nothing more than that.

In the factual present, the event only exhibits itself. As soon as it leaves the field, it becomes a remnant of the same stuff as any cognitive integration, with the losses that are typical of the latter and that result from the seven points outlined above. In this sense, too, a perception of two minutes ago, the perception of the housefly, the perception of others elsewhere, the "average" perception – all cases discussed above – are cognitive integrations of facts that may be truly present in experience. When I look at an object I can certainly say "I see it as I saw it two minutes ago": a successive comparison is always the comparison between an event under way and a cognitive integration that refers to a moment of the conceptual structure of the past (the internal difficulties of such a procedure are well known and rest precisely on that). When I look at a housefly that buzzes around the room I can certainly say: "It moves that way because it perceives the light and the texture of surfaces in such and such a way"; but, of course, it is not really perception but rather a conceptual scheme, possibly very fine-grained, that I am attributing to the housefly by placing it inside its nervous system, equally conceptualized. Similar examples hold for the perception of others elsewhere, but not for the perception of others here and now, which in cases of observational interaction is a fully-fledged event under way.

Once actual perceptions are reduced to events out of the field, that is, to logico–linguistic figures (symbols and graphemes), the connection between them and the rest of the conceptual apparatus – i.e., the properties operationally grounded on stimuli and elaborations – becomes easy and non-problematic. We are in the realm of non-facts, of logical constructs, which together are thought of, imagined, and treated as facts; it becomes obvious, then, to find in those schemes all sorts of causal connections, logical transformations, calculations on numbers, message transmissions, information processing, times spent doing all this work. It becomes difficult, however, to find what is left, upon actuating such schemes, of the event under way and its inner logic. For then the properties of the event have been tacitly dismembered, some have been set aside, others have been dissolved in various parts of the model and identified with operations of a conjectural nature.

This business of the blackboard can come to an end in various ways. In the most fortunate one, it comes to an end with a return to the actuality of experience, holding in our hands new possibilities for exploration that are capable of letting the facts under observation speak once again in their own language. In this way, with some additional instruments, a new episode of phenomenological analysis opens up. In less fortunate cases, the game may become an end in itself, and returning to the evidence of the facts – to a new experiment – may come down to the mere search for those fragments of events that are best suited to fit into a scheme that has already been traced, or that are capable of dismantling the scheme built up by another colleague.

By proceeding this way – and today's specialized literature is packed with excellent examples, even illustrious ones – we still remain at a respectful distance from the reality of experience, which awaits patiently to be studied, understood, and to a great extent discovered. What would we say of the ethologist who cuts three centimetres from the tail of his subjects and, forgetting entirely about the mutilated animal, focuses his scientific attention on the piece of tail in his hand?

Notes

1 James (1890).
2 Bergson (1907, 1934).
3 Neisser (1967), pp. 18–20.
4 Sperling (1960).
5 Joulesz (1971), p. 103.

6 Allport (1970).
7 Eriksen & Collins (1967, 1968); Di Lollo (1977).
8 Coltheart (1980).
9 [*Translator's note*: See James (1890), p. 609: "The unit of composition of our perception of time is a duration, with a bow and stern, as it were – a rearward and a forward-looking end."]
10 Turvey (1978), p. 68.
11 [*Translator's note:* See Meinong (1899).]
12 Gibson (1979), pp. 253–255. All citations are from this section.
13 Interesting remarks on this point may be found in an unpublished article by Stuart Katz, whom I would like to thank for our numerous and pleasant discussions in Trieste and in Uppsala.
14 Uexküll (1909).
15 Wisdom, J. (1952).
16 [*Translator's note*: The reference is to Evandro Agazzi, who apparently made the remark in question ("*A nessuno consta il constare altrui*") in a meeting between psychologists and epistemologists held around 1975. See Bozzi (1976), Chapter 3 in the present anthology).]
17 The proposition is not contradictory if it is interpreted egocentrically: I, the others. It becomes contradictory as soon as one asks, correctly, whether that non-appraising is appraised by someone, that is, whether it is a fact concerning two observers other than the speaker. It is the least one could ask.
18 [*Translator's note*: Attneave, F. (1962). Perception and related areas. In S. Koch (ed.), *Psychology: A Study of a Science* (pp. 619–659). New York: McGraw-Hill.]
19 See Bozzi (1978). [Chapter 10 in the present anthology]
20 Bozzi & Martinuzzi (1989).
21 Bozzi (1989). [Editors' note: the pendulum experiment is as described in Chapter 11 below, though this is not the version to which Bozzi makes reference here.]
22 Michotte (1946).
23 Mosconi (1966).
24 See Bozzi (1978). [Chapter 10 in the present anthology]
25 Ibidem.
26 [*Translator's note:* See Bridgman (1927).]

References

Allport, D.A. (1970). Temporal summation and phenomenal simultaneity: Experiments with the radius display. *Quarterly Journal of Experimental Psychology, 22*, 686–701.

Attneave, F. (1962). Perception and related areas. In S. Koch (ed.), *Psychology: A Study of a Science* (pp. 619–659). New York: McGraw-Hill.

Bergson, H. (1907). *L'évolution créatrice*. Paris: PUF (Eng. trans. by A. Mitchell: *Creative Evolution*, New York: Henry Holt and Company, 1911).

Bergson, H. (1934). *La pensée et le mouvant. Essais et conférences*. Paris: Alcan (Eng. trans. by M. L. Andison: *The Creative Mind*, New York: Philosophical Library, 1946).

Bozzi, P. (1976). Esperienza fenomenica, esperienza epistemica ed esperienza psicologica. Appunti per l'epistemologia del metodo fenomenologico sperimentale. [Phenomenal experience, epistemic experience and psychological experience. Notes towards an epstemology of the method of experimental phenomenology] In G. Siri (ed.), *Problemi epistemologici della psicologia* [*Epistemological problems in psychology*] (pp. 73–87), Milan: Vita e Pensiero. Reprinted as: Appunti per una discussione con gli epistemologi [Notes for a discussion with the epistemologists], In P. Bozzi, *Fenomenologia sperimentale* [*Experimental phenomenology*] (pp. 155–173). Bologna, Italy: il Mulino, 1989.

Bozzi, P. (1978). L'interosservazione come metodo per la fenomenologia sperimentale. [Interobservation as a method for experimental phenomenology] *Giornale Italiano di Psicologia, 5*, 229–239.

Bozzi, P. (1989). Sulla preistoria della fisica ingenua [On the prehistory of naïve physics]. *Sistemi Intelligenti, 1*, 61–74.

Bozzi, P., and Martinuzzi, L. (1989). Un esperimento di interosservazione [An experiment in interobservation]. *Rivista di Psicologia, 1*, 11–46.

Bridgman, P. W. (1927). *The Logic of Modern Physics*. New York: Macmillan.

Coltheart, M. (1980). Iconic memory and visible persistence. *Perception and Psychophysics*, *27*, 183–228.

Di Lollo, V. (1977). Temporal characteristics of iconic memory. *Nature*, *267*, 241–243.

Eriksen, C.W., and Collins, J.F. (1967). Some temporal characteristics of visual pattern perception. *Journal of Experimental Psychology*, *74*, 476–484.

Eriksen, C.W., and Collins, J.F. (1968). Sensory traces versus the psychological moment in the temporal organization of form. *Journal of Experimental Psychology*, *77*, 376–382.

Gibson, J.J. (1979). *The Ecological Approach to Visual Perception*. Boston: Houghton Mifflin.

James, W. (1890). *The Principles of Psychology*. New York: Holt.

Joulesz, B. (1971). *Foundations of Cyclopean Perception*. Chicago: University of Chicago Press.

Meinong, A. (1899). Über Gegenstände höherer Ordnung und deren Verhältnis zur inneren Wahrnehmung. *Zeitschrift für Psychologie und Physiologie der Sinnesorgane*, *21*, 182–272.

Michotte, A. (1946). *La perception de la causalité*. Louvain, NL: Nauwelaerts (Eng. trans. by T.R. Miles and E. Miles: *The Perception of Causality*, London, UK: Methuen, 1963).

Mosconi, G. (1966). Ricerca sperimentale sullle qualità espressive. Impressioni di lunghezza e di cortezza con segmenti di retta. *Rivista di Psicologia*, *LX* (1), 35–53.

Neisser, U. (1967). *Cognitive Psychology*. New York: Appleton.

Sperling, G. (1960). The information available in brief visual presentations. *Psychological Monographs: General and Applied*, *74* (11), 1–29.

Turvey, M.T. (1978). Contrasting orientations to the theory of visual information processing. *Psychological Review*, *84*, 67–88.

Uexküll, von J. (1909). *Umwelt und Innenwelt der Tiere*. Berlin: Springer.

Wisdom, J. (1952). *Other Minds*. Oxford: Basil Blackwell (2nd edn, 1968).

COMMENTS ON THE STREAM OF CONSCIOUSNESS, OR THE EVENTS UNDER OBSERVATION

Richard Davies

Though it is not quite the longest of the essays included in this anthology, Bozzi's discussion of the events under observation is, in my estimate, the most complex and challenging. To name the two longest, it is less programmatic than his late exposition of "Experimental Phenomenology" (chapter 1); and it is less historico-didactictic than his profile of Gestalt psychology (chapter 17). But it exhibits perhaps the full range of his competences and modes of operation as brought to bear on the seemingly marginal question of how long the present lasts in experience. Rather than reconstruct the overall view that Bozzi proposes on this point, I wish to draw the reader's attention to some features of his procedures, each of which is perhaps more to the fore in one or other of the essays here presented, but that in the essay we are considering are closely intertwined to form a densely-argued analysis of what turns out to be a thornier question than it might at first have seemed.

Starting at the extremes of Bozzi's text, we may note two of his characteristic ploys, one at the very beginning, one at the very end.

In the title, there is the phrase "stream of consciousness"; and, in the original publication, this phrase was placed in quotation marks, or perhaps in scare quotes, as if to indicate that it is someone else's phrase or that there is something amiss with it. Though, in the body of the text, we do find phrases such as "stream of current experience" and "stream of thoughts", Bozzi does not anywhere directly address *under that description* the notion evoked in his title. Rather, his procedure is to go about describing the facts in the case in such a way that talk of a "stream of consciousness" simply loses its appeal when we are talking about experience. Of course there are occasions on which Bozzi is openly polemical with stated positions of other thinkers, especially as regards orthodoxies in epistemology (chapter 2) and psychophysics (chapter 6), but often enough his sly subversions are rather more oblique. In "The events under observation", he cites the book – William James' *Principles of Psychology* – in which the phrase "stream of consciousness" makes its entry into current usage among psychologists, and he was surely aware of the use of the phrase also for certain literary effects created, for instance, by the one-time Triestine James Joyce, not to mention Virginia Woolf and Marcel Proust. But, instead of attempting to refute the presuppositions of such usages, Bozzi advances secure in the understanding that putting a negation before a proposition that is muddled will only create another muddled proposition. It is not so much that talk of the "stream of consciousness" has no application, as that, if we do without it, we are less likely to get into a muddle ourselves.

Vice-versa, if there is a question mark hanging over the first part of the essay's title, the last piece of punctuation is itself a question mark, and it marks a rhetorical question about an imagined ethologist who studies only three centimetres cut off the tail of one of his/her subjects. If we know that an ethologist is supposed to study the behaviour and interactions of living organisms in their natural habitat, then the presupposed answer to the question about what we should think of such a procedure will have to be that this scientist does not know his/her job. In the preceding pages of the essay, Bozzi has made only one passing remark about an ethologist observing wolves (§7); and in other writings, he has a great deal to say about ethology; but, in this context, the analogy comes out of the blue. Yet there are several references to an event under observation as having a "mnestic tail", where the ruling analogy is with what streams out behind a comet.

One of the risks of a rhetorical question is that the hearer or reader will give an answer different from that presupposed by the posing of the question. And, in this case, one might wonder how Bozzi's reference to ethology bolsters his case for thinking that an adequate phenomenology of perception must take account of much more than what can be ticketed by the standard procedures of holding laboratory subjects (rather than "participants") in unnatural positions of stress (Bozzi used to say that they were "with bated breath") to answer artificial yes/no questions, and of drawing up diagrams on a blackboard. If the analogy between the tail-docking ethologist and the protocol-following psychologist of perception holds, then the rhetorical force of the closing question of "The events under observation" is the insinuation that the standard procedures of the lab and the lecture room miss the point of studying what is going on when we observe our environment.

What gets missed out is developed in some detail in Bozzi's essays on interobservation (Chapter 10) and on the left-right scheme for presenting the phases of a perceptual episode (Chapter 6), but it may be worth making one or two remarks about how they surface in the text we are considering.

As regards Bozzi's characteristic approach to gathering phenomenological data, perhaps a key point comes out when he says that "people who are asked the question [sc. about relative greys and whites (see also Chapter 7) or about pendular motion (see also Chapter 11)] without having the facts in front of them produce an evasive and physicalistic answer" (§11). Who is supposed to have the facts in front of them? One would expect it to be the participant in the investigation. But, as Bozzi notes in §3, Neisser's distinction between present perception and "iconic memory" is introduced to account not so much for what the participant is experiencing, as for what the experimenter (physicalistically) knows about the cessation of the stimulus provided by alphabetic letters. If this is how the distinction arises, then it might be objected that if the experimenter chooses to call an experience that lasts 150msec longer than the stimulus "memory", this choice does not do justice to the facts in front of the participant. What the participant has in front of him/her is perceptual access to letters, even though these letters are no longer part of his/her physical environment. In this way, the introduction of "iconic memory" presents itself as a way of evading the question of how the process involved is experienced by the participant: it is subdivided into phases that are more-or-less arbitrarily labelled so as to conform to what the experimenter has determined about the participant's environment.

To bring out the schematic – not to say "prejudicial" – nature of the distinction in hand, Bozzi performs one of his trademark manoeuvres. On the one hand, in §4, he makes a lightning reference to St Augustine's sophistical account of the present as an unextended boundary between the no-longer existing past and the not-yet existing future. Here, he, perhaps over-generously, assumes that his reader will catch the allusion, but he returns in the following section to quote Gibson's refusal of the idea that the present is a "traveling razor's edge", which sums up Augustine's picture and, in turn, is the motivation for saying that an experience that does not correspond to what is in the subject's current environment may be called a "memory". We might say that this is the philosophical claw of the pincer-movement that Bozzi is putting in the field. For the other claw is his appeal to the data collected by the very experimenters who are wanting to make the distinction between experience and memory. If *they* say that the lapses between what is in the participant's environment and the various phases of his/her experience can vary from 150msec to up to a minute, then they should be ready to admit not only an extended present, but one whose outline is "zig-zag" (§5).

Perhaps what is most stimulating and most unsettling about this kind of operation is that Bozzi is perfectly at ease with the idea that scientists can be enslaved by a philosophical model in such way as to skew "the facts in front of them": in this case, they have to say simultaneously that the present is dimensionless and that it is to some degree indeterminately extended in time. As with the phrase "stream of consciousness", the point may be that that other Jamesism, "the specious present", is rather the name for a problem than its solution.

But one might well ask whether there really is a problem here that calls for a solution, or whether, instead, "the facts in front of us" are quite sufficient to overcome the dichotomy of present and past as time zones across which are distributed different cognitive states. Though it is true that there is a deep difference between seeing, say, the second hand on a clock in movement, and seeing that the hour hand is now in a different position from that occupied last time I looked, it is far from obvious that this difference is going to be accounted for by saying that seeing motion requires us to have experiences that are extended in time. Even if the movement under observation is extended in time, why must the observation itself be likewise? For Bozzi, it makes more sense to allow that there is what he calls the "factual present" (§§8ff.), which may be invoked in constructing theories of perception, but about which it seems to be indifferent whether or not we say that it has duration. For, as he points out, the construction of theories is something we do on a blackboard: I may represent a perception of mine of two minutes ago by writing a sign for it on the board, but the sign is not itself the perception in question. If the perception occurred two minutes ago, it is no longer a perceptual fact, however we choose to construe the notion of the present as against the past.

Underlying this attitude we might detect an approach that emerges also in Bozzi's handlings of such disparate questions of the relation between self and non-self (in the next chapter) and on what he calls tertiary qualities, which are closely related to Gibson's affordances (Chapter 16). The starting point is some philosophical paradox, whether it is St Augustine on time, Hume on the elusiveness of the "I", or Democritus and Galileo on the mind-dependence of secondary qualities. And it should be stressed how canny a reader of these classics Bozzi shows himself to be, picking out textual cruces that represent temptations into which reflection on everyday conceptions can easily lead us. He then invites us to examine more attentively what our actual experience of the phenomena in question teaches us. In this phase, he draws on an empirically well-founded understanding of the configurations that structure that experience. In homing in on what is supposed to be present under observation, Bozzi has no qualms about saying "I look at a colourful poster and I know that it has been printed in Hungary" (§13). Is the place and time of printing part of what is presently observed? Even if we call it a "cognitive integration", it is something I know by seeing it. Likewise, if we are upset by Hume's doubts about the substantialness of the self, we can find the places it successively occupies by following where it is not as I walk up and down a room (Chapter 5 §5). Even if the philosophical paradox, in the cases cited of a generally idealist stamp, has not been, as the jargon has it, "refuted", it has at least been defused or debunked. Seeing the Hungarianness of the poster, locating myself, detecting the sittability of a chair or appreciating the deliciousness of some jam (Chapter 16) are so integral to our experience of them that it calls for a certain perversity of spirit to cede to the idealist temptations.

The temptations are still there, but they are just that bit less, well, tempting. Just so, the infantile temptations of candy do not entirely subside, but an adult will not be dragged about by them. To adapt Bacon's remark about atheism, a little philosophy inclineth man's mind to idealism, but depth in philosophy bringeth men's minds about to realism.

5

UNTIMELY MEDITATIONS ON THE RELATION BETWEEN SELF AND NON-SELF

Translated by Alessio Moretti

1. The relations between the external and internal worlds: notes on Hume

At first blush, the problem of the relations between the external world and the world that is felt to be internal – which in the end is a problem firmly anchored in Experimental Phenomenology – presents itself as the opposition between two extreme philosophical views. One carries with it the denial that the self exists, and is most eloquently expressed in the writings of Hume. The other leads to the theorisations of the ubiquity of the self or of the systems of relations that make up subjectivity.

This latter view has been set out by more than one psychologist, believed by more than one philosopher and is still tacitly accepted by many more. But, for present purposes, I shall not attribute it to anyone because I know that, in the radical version that I offer of it, no-one would accept it. Nevertheless, we need to talk about it.

David Hume presents two versions of his arguments against the existence, within experience, of anything that is a "self" or personal identity. The first of these is to be found towards the end of the first book of the first edition of the *Treatise* (1739: I, 4, vi). The claim is that the identity that we ascribe to our minds and to those of others is a fictional identity, by which he means that is not much more than a name we give to a certain manner of representing sensations to ourselves.

Philosophers of various stripes were telling that the identity of the mind resolves the plurality of different perceptions into a unity. Taking this claim at face value, Hume replied honestly that this was not how things could be, given that the events within experience do not lose their differences in it, and every distinct perception that enters the mind is really distinguishable and separable from every other at the same time or later.

What authorises us then to talk of unity or identity? In his discussion of causality earlier in the book, Hume had determined that this does not hold between immediate data nor does it mean anything from a purely logical point of view. Causality is as spontaneous an attitude as it is ungrounded, which is generated by the workings of habit and does not associate real impressions – which is to say the facts – but only those pale copies of them that are ideas or memories.

We may thus suppose that experience is made up of bits each of which is external to the others, as well as of the set of images we have of them. These latter are fairly distinct one from another, but not to such an extent that factors such as habit cannot link them together in fictional relations that are not founded on matters of experience, such as similarity (which does not hold among things, because either they are the same or they are different) and causality, understood to be faith or expectation. The human mind, Hume says, is really to be understood as a system of various elements linked together by the relation of cause and effect. This should not surprise us: all he needs is to have denied that causality is an immediate given, while it can perfectly well survive as an illusory link that unifies memories and imaginings. Thus for instance we can say that memory produces personal identity, linking and almost confusing the images of the things we have experienced; but then memory also unveils personal identity because, just as we can recall external facts, we can also recall images of those very facts, which had previously been melded together in the same memory. Sometimes, the fictional or merely verbal links that connect the various and distinct fragments together obey some regularity, and in that case, we can meaningfully raise the question, referring to the fiction (model) of this imaginary principle of unity. This is the way that Hume himself speaks. "Self" is the name of any of these kinds of events.

The destruction of the self is thus not completely radical. Hume probably had an inkling of having left a job only partly done. Three years later, when he came to publish the third volume of the *Treatise*, he added an interesting appendix to correct the earlier theories. It is interesting also because he confesses to finding himself "involved in a labyrinth" (p. 321, Selby Bigge) not knowing how to correct the view he has publish nor how to make them coherent. But, even if it is false, the view that he promotes in the appendix is much more lucid and radical. In science it is absolutely essential that the theses we construct be coherent and uncompromising, even when they are false; these are always to be preferred to those that are fairly true and more or less in harmony with all points of view.

Hume asserts that, if we are to talk meaningfully about the "self" or something of that sort, we have to have an idea of it. But every idea derives from an earlier impression. Now we do not have any impression or experience of the self as something distinct, simple or individual, as we do of redness or of a square for instance. Hence, we have no idea of the self.

There is nothing confused or incoherent about saying that there are objects that exist distinctly and independently without needing to postulate some simple substance whose role is to keep them united. When we turn our reflection on ourselves, the object we have to do with is a set of perceptions, and there is never anything other than them. Hence, "self" is the name of this set.

At this point Hume seems to notice that the reference to "turning our reflection on ourselves" could introduce the idea of personal identity. But of course this is a separate problem and he admits to not having discovered any theory that gives him "satisfaction on this head" (p. 323).

But Hume realises that there is another essential question for our purposes, namely that when we talk about things that are separate and distinct, as he understand perceptions that have real simplicity and identity, the problem represents itself of the very principle of connection that is so evasive but that ought to give an empirical foundation to the self. For what is it that holds together the perceptions when they are constituted as unitary? "Here", say Hume, "I am sensible that my account is very defective".

Indeed, only a theory that interprets the delimitation of the self relative to the surrounding world *in the same terms* as it interprets the delimitation of one object from another will be able to give an answer here. But for that to be possible, the perceptions and the objects must be real ones and not the points of light, patches of colour or isolated sounds that Hume himself thought of as the nature of impressions. If we insist on staring at a phantasmagoria of that sort, then we are never going to find the self.

To sum up: experience is a set of elementary and unrelated sensations; I can from time to time call some arbitrary aggregation of these sensations my "self", but nothing guarantees that there is continuity or anything in common among these aggregations. On the other hand, no element taken on its own can any more rightly be called the "self" than any other.

2. Now we come to the opposite view

I have to confess that I have always had trouble understanding what it could mean, from any coherently imaginable point of view, to say, "everything is myself"; and this trouble is at least as great when I have tried to understand what this phrase could mean when taken in an empirical sense.

Any claim that begins with "every" or "all" should be handled with care, unless it introduces a proposition that refers to a set of events that has a non-empty complementary set, such as "everyone in Vienna's high society was at the races" or "all the squadron marched past our grandstand". When the "all" is taken in the sense of Totality, and is given the role of the subject of the proposition, such as "everything is . . ." then things are rather different. Without raising subtle questions of logical analysis, but sticking without the limits that help out discussion of the theories in hand, I can imagine three ways of reading the expression "everything is X": (a) X is a wider set than that indicated by "everything" and includes it; (b) X is a narrower set and is included; and (c) X and "everything" are coextensive sets. Only reading (c) is non-contradictory. But, on this reading, whatever is put in the place of X will become simply a synonym of "everything". That is, "everything is X" will always mean the same as "everything is everything" whatever set X designates; otherwise it is a contradiction.

This is how it stands with "everything is myself". If a certain person points his finger at everything around him and says, "everything is myself", I will have to draw the same identity as a conclusion of what he says, but this time in empirical terms. He will be saying to me that, in his language "myself" means the ensemble of presently discernible experiences. But given that these are not changed if, in place of "myself", any other word is uttered, then any word that is uttered will, from this point of view, be equivalent, and there will be no way to adjudicate which is more right than any other.

In short, there are some things that, if we are to speak seriously, should never be said. I have made these two criticisms solely to show that, if the problem of the self is raised in this way, then the arguments will continue hopelessly well beyond the lives of all of us, which is too long. On the other hand, the problem of the self becomes interesting and productive, not to say phenomenologically meaningful, only when this self is taken to be circumscribed, thus raising the questions of how to fix its limits and of the relations it stands in to external structures.

Nevertheless, the claim has been made that the self is present in every imaginable place of experience; indeed, this is a widespread conviction and so we must try to understand it.

Some of the routes taken to make this conception accessible are well enough known and form a sort of philosophical stereotype. One such, the most basic, which is usually used to convince the beginner of the plausibility of a subjectivist image of experience, runs pretty much as follows: first someone lists some obviously subjective phenomena, such as hallucinations, dreams and so on. Then they recite some objects of awareness, such as colours and sounds, pointing out how these differ from the physical models that are given of electromagnetic or acoustic waves, or they point out how the material bodies of which we are aware differ from the models of aggregates of molecules and atoms, claiming that it is only these that are "real". And then the story is rounded off with "and so and so forth", which leaves dangling an inference from mere enumeration.

Another route appeals to the peripheral sense organs and says that they cause colours, sounds and all the rest; and from there the conclusion is drawn that everything is subjective because it depends on those organs, forgetting the while to observe that the argument works only because it presupposes something that is not produced by the sense organs, namely the organs themselves.

A scientifically fecund claim is rather the one made out by Köhler when he defines the notion of the "genetically subjective" meaning that the organisation of the events that impinge on the higher activities of the nervous system have to be regarded as an isomorphic projection of the organisation of the actual field of experience, if we want the data collected in psychological experimentation to yield hypotheses that are valid for a possible physiology. Of course, this claim should not be treated on a par with the others because it does not in the least induce us to think that the self is present throughout experience; rather, starting from the observation that this is not how things stand, it puts a brake on the facile identification of the self with the organism and, implicitly, on that of subjectivity with an abstract sketch of the nervous system.

There are other routes to the undesired conclusion, but only one other is of use to our discussion. This is the thesis that the existence of situations of experience in which the observer's attitude is a variable of the observed structure would allow us to say that, whenever there is an observable structure, there is also the variable to be observed as more of less operative.

There are indeed situations in which the observer's attitude can determine the observed structure, or at least bring about noticeable differences in it. Reversible figures are well known, from the elementary organisations of figure and background in which the factors are in unstable equilibrium, to the more complicated but equally unstable cases of the "wife-and-mother-in-law" or the "duck-rabbit". And then there are situations in which the transformation does not happen all at once but continuously and generally in small steps, as when we try to modify a geometrical optical illusion by close observation or even by adding merely imagined lines, which are nevertheless operative.

3. The relation of observer to observed

It is precisely these last forms of active observation that will come in useful in the course of our argument.

The psychophysicists of a century ago set off with the presupposition that the true distribution of sensations in the field of visual experience repeats point for point the distribution of the stimulations on the retina, and, bearing in mind that the visual field is not normally at all organised in that way, they introduced into psychological theory a new definition of subjectivity that has remained standing even after their viewpoint has been eclipsed. We should be clear about this: sensations were not in those days thought of as something non-subjective. Because they had perceivable characteristics, albeit in special conditions, they were undoubtedly the – in some way "subjective" – counterparts of the stimuli and hence something psychic. But another set of other, more specifically subjective, activities was superimposed on this subjective order of the faithful mirror of the spatial distribution of proximal stimuli. These other activities were those that were said to be higher, such as memory, judgment, experience, attention and so forth, which intervened to configure apperception and thus produce our normal relations with observables.

It is in precisely this sense that it was possible to speak of unnoticed psychic events: sensations are something psychic, but other psychic forces build out of them what in the end results in apperception, which is the concrete situation of observation. And this end product cancels the initial distribution and takes its place.

The relation of observer to observed in a given moment is thus a wholly subjective act: every element that makes it up is a product of subjectivity, in both of the two senses that we proceed to set out.

Köhler's criticism of "unnoticed sensations" and of "unconscious judgments" is well known and even today his arguments hold good[1]. Now let us pose this question: if attention, judgment, familiarity and memory existed only as kinds of factors that reorganise the distribution of perceptions, as, that is, the ingredients of "elaborations", would we then have any right to speak of them once Köhler's criticism is taken into account? Obviously not. Granting that the object of our awareness are ready-organised perceptions, and that the factors in this organisation can be retraced within the same perceptual field and expressed in terms of functionally connected variables, those concepts would be left without definable content.

All the same judgment, attention memory and so on still mean something. For, after all, attention exists and is a matter of which I am immediately aware: I can shift my attention at will at it can be directed at this or that point in my field of experience by the indications given by a friend standing next to me because he or she wants to show me this or that. Likewise, there is the tertiary characteristic of familiarity, which can be had by some object that I happen to see (even for the first time in case of *déjà vu*). Equally, there are memories and the effort to recall something. The familiarity of an object can spur me to rummage through my memory for the first time I saw it. Again, judgments exist and they do so insofar as they are thought to be such.

But this is not all: each of these encounterable features of the world, which often present themselves as relations holding between one event of experience within the self and one event present in front of me, can become a factor in the structure of the external event in a way of which we can be directly aware; thus we can reduce the "aberration" of optical illusions by practice and by directing our attention in certain ways. These are inner efforts directed to the outside and sometimes they make a little difference.

In short, the higher activities appear in the act of observation under two completely different guises: (1) as memory, effort of attention, judgment and so on in the full sense, as concomitant inner experiences while we are observing an object; and (2) as ingredients that are not noticed as such, but that in the meantime silently work the transformations of sensations into the data of outer experience.

Now, no-one can deny that attention, judgment and so on, when taken in the first sense, are something "subjective" and within the self.

But if we allow that these very aspects of experience operate as what we would nowadays call the stages of an elaboration in determining the structure of outer experience, then we are allowed to say that the external world is something subjective, in the sense that in every point of it, there is some essentially subjective factor at work: unaware attention, unnoticed memory, unconscious judgment, calculation.

When I manage to lessen the length difference between the lines in the Müller-Lyer, on the one hand I perceive that I have brought about a particular attitude in myself towards the picture I have in front of me and on the other I see that the effect has diminished. In this way, on the one hand a trick of judgment brings it about that there is the illusion (I unwarily judge the part to be bigger because I see the whole to be bigger); on the other, a thought-out judgment (the lines are equal) guides my attitude as an observer and opposes itself to the effect of the unwary judgment. The former is a (silent) organising factor; the latter a judgment in the full sense.

But situations of this sort, in which a phenomenally inner factor is felt as an agent on the outer structure, are fairly rare.

If we led to say that it is only in such cases that there is, in the thing observed, "something subjective", the old-school psychologist or his constructivist colleague would come back at us at once: *all* thinkable experiences are subjective, because the action of memory, unconscious judgment and attention constitute perception in every circumstance. And it is true that it is only sometimes that we manage to oppose the action of unconscious elaboration with that of conscious judgment, the action of an acquired habit of which we are no longer aware with that of an exercise set deliberately on foot, or the action of an automatic fixing of attention by means of a conscious effort of the same. But, in such situations, a state of affairs that is always and everywhere present just comes to the surface. Where efforts of attention and conscious judgments do not have the upper hand, the reduction screens do; by removing from an observable object all those features that would make it recognisable and, hence, that would set to work the higher faculties of subjectivity, we see what sensations really are; and this *proves* that those faculties are at work in structuring experience even where it is not possible to oppose them by turning them against themselves.

The psychic forces of the higher activities, of which the self is formed, are often invisible as such, but they are certainly operative everywhere. This is what the classical doctrine of perception used to say, and we come upon it, dressed up in a new language, in many cognitivist theses.

The refusal of unnoticed sensations and of unconscious judgments, which was a logical consequence of the acceptance of falsificationism, eliminated this realm of "subjective" but unobservable operations. In their place had to go observable factors with potentially observable consequences, actual features of experience that have effects on other actual features of experience. By so doing, the words "attention", "judgment" and so on are given back their genuine phenomenological meaning.

From this new point of view, it would follow not only that there is nothing subjective in the objects so long as their organisation is regulated by factors that belong within the field of experience, but also that, therefore, we may speak of subjective factors only when we have to do with some fairly explicit form of functional dependence holding between an experience had from within and a transformation observed externally. The relation in question has to have also an autonomous directionality, from the inner to the outer; for, otherwise, we would find ourselves in one of the many situations in which an event that happens on the outside acts on the region of the self, which is to say that what is happening to me depends on something that has happened outside me.

But this is not how it happens, or at least not always. The attribute "subjective" often remains in the vocabulary of the psychologist of perception to designate the organisation of external events. This is all well and good so long as we hold on to the thought that subjective matters like judgments and memories work *inside* the things perceived. And to this attribute there still adheres a hue of spiritualistic pluralism, the crowd of psychisms that plagued eighteenth-century introspectionist psychologies. For sure, no psychologist describes himself as a pluralist, still less as a spiritualist; but that does not mean much, because the technical term to designate the conception we have outlined is precisely that. Just as I can say that the picture I have in front of me is round or a triangle without changing anything about it, so, when we talk about this conception, we can call it by its own name or by another, and it remains what it is.

4. The self as an object in space

These slides towards metaphysics are not really inevitable, but they are all the easier every time we allow the meaning of the words of the psychological vocabulary to grow unkempt on the tradition. Psychology was once a branch of philosophy and later an appendix to physiology; the theory of perception is nowadays mature enough to be an autonomous science and indeed to be a science that is able to clarify in terms of experience many concepts that are used uncritically in epistemology, theory of knowledge and the philosophy of science. For this reason, it is all the more pressing that we should regard what comes from the tradition with ruthless caution. We should not say that a concept is empirically well founded if even part of its definition refers to a use that has been made of it, or to fragments of ideas that were once built on imponderables. The analysis of a term's use and the history of its meaning are essential phases of scientific research precisely because they have the job of dissecting it before our eyes and showing us how much of it is living and useable, and how much dead and superfluous.

Philosophers have accustomed us to seeing the self everywhere, and it is a pity that psychologists have followed them in this direction. To the extent that it was a science of sensations, late-nineteenth-century physiology still needed subjectivity to explain orders of facts before which a physiologism that had grown out of anatomy was incapable of handling. And so the omnipresence of subjectivity has been handed down more or less intact to this day, leading to the highly sophisticated forms of constructivism.

All this came about for many reason, which it would be interesting to enquire into; but among these was the fact that it seemed to the philosophers appalling to see the self as something spatial. The self seemed much more dignified if it was conceived, for instance, as the logical condition of experience rather than as part of it. Classical psychology did not decline of attribute *also* spatial characteristics to the self, thus attracting the scorn of many philosophers; nevertheless, these psychologists gave way on a key point by admitting that space is a product of subjectivity.

If you say that space is a product of subjectivity, you must then admit that, either wholly or partly, subjectivity is not spatial. The contrast between the empirical self and the absolute self that the idealists developed arises out of the way that sometimes subjectivity is conceived as a condition of experience and at others as a feature of experience. Just as they do not like to be called spiritualists, psychologists do not want to appear idealists; but, insofar as they theorise on the basis of similar schemes, they are idealists. It is no use claiming that the subjectivity that produces space is nothing but the activity of the organism's nervous activity: a physiological *a priori* is no better than a logical *a priori*. Both are conceptual constructions founded to some extent on the concrete experience of subjectivity, which itself really is an *a priori* relative to every construction, because it is an experience that is thus and so prior to being thought, imagined or conceptualised.

Rather, a well constructed model of the nervous activities related to the structure of experience would presuppose an exhaustive analysis of the configuration and the limits of the self as it really is for us observers; such a model is so little of an *a priori* of experience that we should expect to have already performed the analysis before trying to put the model together.

It is therefore wise to put the operation off and, in the meantime, to try to see if and how an approximate definition of subjectivity is possible at the level of experience. We should exploit the opportunity of finding definitions for the terms of our phenomenological vocabulary within the spatial limits of the things themselves. We may think of an imaginary three-dimensional grid in front, around and within us, and each thing that is extended within the grid can be the bearer of a name that is as fully attached to that thing alone as the values of the coordinates allow us to precisely define a point in space. Even allowing that the self does not have spatially well-defined limits and even before we have distinguished within the self its various and variously distributed features, the region of the self will fall within our grid. It will be hard to say where the self is at any given moment, but there will be a certain number of places that can easily be pointed out where it certainly is not.

K. Koffka recounts that Köhler was in the habit of stressing the spatiality of the self in the following way: "Another argument of Köhler's (. . .) starts with the behavioural environment: yonder is the wall of the room; in front of it is a desk; on that desk are various objects, nearer and nearer; there are other walls to the right and the left, and other objects between me and these walls; but space is not only in front and at the sides, space is also, though less articulated, less clearly defined, behind. . . . Now then, Köhler's argument continues, what is there between the last thing just in front and the behind? Is space absolutely empty there? The answer is: certainly not; here, between the 'in front' and the 'behind', is that part of the behavioural world which I call my ego. It has a very definite place in that world, and well-defined, if variable, boundaries"[2].

The self is an object in space on a par with other objects; within the self there come about those events that we feel immediately as subjective, which is to say that they *are* subjective. There is no contradiction whatsoever in saying that the self is an object like all the others and then to claim that much of what happens within its contours has the feature of being subjective: no more than there is in claiming that a given character in a cartoon is from moment to moment pushed by this or that intention, by fear or attraction, while it moves in its environment of coloured lines and patches. Even if this character is just a little red square or a blue circle[3].

In any case, among the things that happen in space and are divided up by spatial contours and distances, my self is not the only owner of subjectivity, a theatre of "subjective" events. The spatial definition of the self that Köhler gives is perfectly well suited not only to my person, or to the only region that contains my "inside": it holds equally well for the subjectivities of others. The others have a position in the field of experience in exactly the same sense for each of us. We can say this much without postulating absolutely anything about their metaphysical "inside" that the spiritualists hanker after; indeed, we can this much without even raising the epistemological issue of the methods for verifying what is happening in other minds; for, here, we are talking only about the structures of pure experience and we are not aiming to open up the more general question of the so-called interaction with other minds. Persons are in space and find objects in front, behind and around them, more or less close to them; these objects are constituted as they are commonly seen by me and by them in such a way that we can show them to each other by pointing our fingers in a given direction, and without putting our hands into the spiritual world of the others. I say this not merely to stress the physical location of bodies, mine and theirs, in a common space; they are thoughts directly concerning the relations between my subjectivity and things, between their subjectivity and those very same things, and between their subjectivity and mine. Each of us can see clearly the others who are seeing and also *how* they see, how they are looking and so on. The network of relations that connects me to my world in the here and now is closely isomorphic at the phenomenological level with the network that connects each of the others who are here and now with the same common world. For instance someone's attention to an object in front of him is not something that I represent to myself or imagine, nor it is something that happens in some part of his person: it is precisely in his eyes, just as it is immediately felt close to my eyes when I make an effort to observe something attentively. In other words, it is a structure of the situation that concerns each of us, transferred whole to another place in space and centring on a physical person similar to us. He too has things that he sees, that are in front of *him* more or less distant from the place of his expression that makes him an observer. The sameness of structure in these sets of relations (between myself and the things in the environment, between him and the things in the environment) is sometimes so marked as to amount to identity: as when *I* have an attack of vertigo when I see *him* leaning over the balcony of the eighth floor.

The subject of the activity of knowing, the subject of real experience in the here and now is thus not necessarily "just one", except for the case in which one of us is on his own in a certain place with no-one else in view. When there are other persons with us (and animals can count as other persons in their own way), then the objects that are present are not felt only by me, and there can at a given time be various ways of looking at them, appreciating them in relation to various – and equally real – "subjective" perspectives. Someone who, in the presence of others, believes himself to be in some way privileged, or to occupy a point of view that is absolute as opposed to the relative perspectives of the others, thereby shows unmistakable symptoms of neurosis. (And everyone notices.)

It is on this scheme that it becomes possible to carry out an empirically well-founded analysis of the presence of the self in the world of objects.

5. The relations between the self and the external world

When we replace ideal relations with relations whose terms occur in the field of what can be encountered, it becomes possible to make sense of propositions that affirm the existence of relations between modifications of the self and modifications of the external world. Occult relations, such as the one thanks to which subjectivity gives rise to a continuous creation of the reality around it, thus lose all credibility. It is only when, by modifying myself, such as my way of looking, so that I am aware that something happens outside me, that I can say that the self has brought about something in outer reality. But every time that the external objects appear to be constituted as systems independent of the modifications of which I am aware *within* the contours of the self, then the self has not performed any action on those objects, because there is no such trace. In any case, the fundamental relations that bond the self to the external world are much more felt in our everyday life as coming from external events that modify what is "within", than as relations running in the opposite direction. If we want to say that the self is the author of the external world, we have to show concretely how it is so, bearing in mind that a discernible feature of experience will only change if it is affected by a sensible transformation, as Wittgenstein showed from many points of view in the *Remarks on the Philosophy of Psychology*.

Once a view like this has been thoroughly grasped, it becomes possible to set out the following two theses in their narrowly phenomenological sense, and hence to leave no room for a critic schooled in idealism or in some form of constructivism to level the accusation of metaphysics:

a.   the objects that, in actual experience, are in front of us and outside of us (that is to say they are at some *distance* from us), are ordinarily *presupposed* in the act of awareness of them and all the more so in the act of thinking about them. After all, what is *presupposed* in the act of knowing, even if that is understood in the broadest sense compatible with correct language use?: everything that, in actual experience, is constituted as an ascertainable fact independently of the act of observing.

b.   The field of actual experience of the external world is *wider* than the set of objects and events that can be shown in the here and now. Thus, still in reference to the phenomenological structure of experience and not to a transcription of it in the terms of some logical model, many things are *really* present, but lie beyond the limits of what can be pointed to or discriminate perceptually.

It is my belief that a renewal of Gestalt theory in the light of the implicit logic of the phenomenological method will lead to realism.[4] To a realism, indeed, that it would be easy to call "naïve" were it not technically and epistemologically so shrewd. Perhaps this is the underground route that led J.J. Gibson – a former pupil of Koffka – to the formulation in the late 1970s of the basic claims of ecological optics. And it is a route that is logically cogent.

To get a full understanding of point (a), we should consider things with a certain caution, which should not be a great burden on anyone who is expert in research into the phenomenology of perception: in the first place, we need to be careful not to attribute to the observed objects transformations that concern rather our attitude as observers. If one finds oneself overmastered by the desire to claim that subjectivity is at work at every point in our experience, it is easy to give in to the temptation to find in every transformation noticed from without an example that is in reality caused from within. More generally, it can become uncomfortable to recognise that this or that transformation happening in the place where the object is, or between us and the object, *does not* directly concern the subject. When we walk up and down the room, our point of view on things is changing from moment to moment, and this might induce us to say that the things are so closely linked to the self that they change with its change of spatial position. This is just not so. The best proof that it is not so is that, even when we are walking up and down the room, if some object underwent a real change, we would immediately notice the fact. It might be replied that we simply know how to distinguish between changes due to our movements and those that come about by other causes or in some other way. But this is just the point: ordinary language describes the former as "the things in the environment are stationary and have not moved" and the later as "such and such a thing has moved or is changing". And the meaning of these sentences is in the structure of the situation: ordinarily, some things – ourselves included – move among the many things that are stationary, and this is what we see.

Lurking under the harsh and abstract language imposed by his theory, there are many passages in Kant's masterpiece that present very acute phenomenological analyses, among which the observation that the apprehension of multiplicity in appearances always comes about through successive moments. The representations of the parts of an object follow one after the other: but the "determination of whether they are successive also in the object is a second point of reflection, which is not contained in the first". Thus, the mere fact that sometimes the perception of the parts comes about in temporal succession does not mean that we should believe that the object itself is being constituted along with it; and not the object "over and above", the "thing in itself"; there is no question of the relation between the transcendental object and the perception of it, which is an "impossible" question: Kant never made that mistake. The object of successive observations that are articulated over time and that I am performing is in the world of observables, exactly like the various phases of my observation. Yet that object is distinct from the succession of the representations of its parts. "For instance, the apprehension of the manifold in the appearance of a house which stands before me is successive. The question then arises, whether the manifold of the house is also in itself successive. This, however, is what no one will grant"[5]. The mention of the manifold "in itself" might make the reader think that what is in question is the transcendental house, considered that is over and above any experience, but this is not what is at issue; Kant immediately adds that the house, even in this sense, is not a thing in itself but only an observable event like the successive acts of observation, whose object "over and above" is unknown. Except that "that which lies in the successive apprehension is here viewed as representation, while the appearance which is given to me notwithstanding that is nothing but the sum of these representations, is viewed as their object; and my concept, which I derive from the representations of apprehension, has to agree with it" (B326), "that appearance, in contradistinction to the representations of apprehension, can be represented as an object distinct from them only if it stands under a rule which distinguishes it from every other apprehension" (ibid.).

As I said, the language is harsh, but the concept is absolutely plain: against the dualistic scheme according to which perceptual activity has the task of grasping the objects in themselves, we oppose the fact that in the realm of representation itself, we can make the distinction between the act of being aware (even at successive times) and the object of which we are aware: this is not a metaphysical object, but a phenomenon, just the activity of observing is a phenomenon. It is thus a phenomenal object presupposed in the observation, which is constituted as a region of experience on its own. The use of the term "presupposition" is entirely justified by the structure of the situation under consideration: indeed, the house that I am observing bit by bit, sweeping my gaze across it and stopping over this or that detail of it, is there and does not (phenomenally) change while I am observing only some of its features at a time; and while I am looking at the door, after looking at the windows and other parts, it is not as if the door is created: it was already there (phenomenally) while I was looking at the windows. All this follows from the admission that the house remained identical with itself as an object while I moved my gaze from the windows to the door.

6. Some examples

To help this manner of thinking become familiar and the theory easier to understand, I beg the reader to reflect on the following examples, so as to see that they are much the same thing.

First, let us take a case of the classic theme of the constancy of brightness. I am taking a walk under a portico, looking at the pictures in a magazine, and, as I go, I pass from well-illuminated zones to zones that are in shadow. Of course, in passing from the light to the shade, I do not see the white of the paper becoming darker. In two successive moments, the paper reflects into my eyes, as a physicist would put it, different amounts of achromatic light: we can see this by thinking about what happens on my eye's retina (part of a physical system) as a result of the change in the illumination of the reflecting surface (physical illumination and surface); but we can see it even better in the laboratory, covering up the light source and varying its intensity and viewing a small area of the piece of paper through a slit cut in a screen.

As the psychophysicists of the old school would have said, this shows us the real change in a luminous sensation in a similar situation. But there is more: even just continuing our walk under the portico, but observing the situation less distractedly, we will notice that in the passage between light and shade the sheet goes grey in some way, as when we cast a shadow on it with our hand and we can distinguish the part in the light and the part in the shadow. Setting aside for present purposes the question of constancy, and the possible psychological interpretation of such phenomena, what we should stress is the following fact. In this situation, something happens to the white of the paper without making us see that whiteness as affected by a transformation. We could give cases of the white of the sheet as affected by a transformation, for instance by reducing the illumination quickly and by a lot, so as to plunge it almost into darkness. Or by bringing about a situation like that above, in which the edges of the illuminated zone coincide exactly with those of the paper, and keeping the light source covered. But when conditions of this sort do not obtain, the whiteness of the sheet is not really the subject of a change, but it remains the same white, just in the shadow.

As has been proved innumerable times, the change that comes about in the situation is felt as a change in the ambient illumination and, hence, *not* as a transformation of the white of the paper. The space in which we and the things are has its own illumination: the light in a room is not just the ensemble of brightnesses of objects, it is light that fills the space that is not occupied by them. When the illumination of the environment in which an object is to be found is lowered or raised in fixed proportions relative to the brightness of the objects, the brightness of the object remains, within certain limits, constant, and we are aware only of the change in illumination. This is what justifies our speaking of the object not seeming to be affected.

Second, suppose we are projecting onto a screen some slides that show objects with clear outlines, and suppose that they pictures were taken with care, with light and shadow very marked and in a perspective that retains the effect of the reality and stereometric solidity of the things depicted.

Let us now try to vary slightly the focus of the image, intervening on the projector's dioptric system: the outlines of the objects are not as clear as before, but still what we see is rather a progressive clouding up of the whole scene, and not a change affecting the objects we see. Repeating the trial several times, passing fairly rapidly from a sharp focus to slightly out of focus, the objects will be seen as coming into and going out of a light mist, which is like the *medium* through which we see them. If the focus is so far out as to make the objects unrecognisable, so that there are just coloured patches on the screen, then this impression is lost: with each small change in the focus, the coloured patches are themselves affected by a change, in the shape they present and the sort of chromatic gradient that makes up their outlines.

But, beginning with the presentation of objects in focus, even if their outlines undergo a slight but still visible transformation, we cannot say that, considered as objects, they are affected by it: what happens is rather a separation between the fogginess of the whole environment and the objects immersed in it. This is particularly evident when one part of the image on the screen is in focus and another is not: this latter presents itself like a veil behind which the things are visible without any change in their properties.

Third, if we observe the countryside through a window whose panes are streaked with rain, we do not generally have the impression that the visible deformations caused by the water running down the glass are deformations in the various things in the countryside. This can happen if we fix our attention on a particular point, where, for instance, a bigger drop is held up by something in its descent and it turns into something like a lens: if we look at the objects outside, especially those that have regular forms (such a house's window or a perfectly straight pole), through the drop that is gathering, we shall be able to see them affected by some deformation, as if they were made of rubber and subject to some inner tension or perhaps to some invisible outer force. But on the whole, this is not what happens: the continuous transformations that the overall picture undergoes while we are looking are phenomenal features that belong to the rivulets of water on the glass, and *not* to the country-side beyond it. On the contrary, the things outdoors remain unchanged and are seen to be unchanged thought the modifications of the transparent surface we have before us.

Fourth. And I want to say straight off that the fourth case is structurally identical to the other three, except that the division between the freestanding object (the phenomenal object as thing in itself) and its manner of appearance does not fall between two phenomenally external bits of the world (thing-medium), but between a bit that is wholly external, the real object, and a region of the self, which is the act of looking in a certain way.

Let us look closely at what we have in front of us, but slowly narrowing our eyes in the way that comes naturally when we suddenly find ourselves in front of too strong a light source. Closing our eyes almost fully, so that the upper and lower lashes are interleaved, we can sometimes see the things in front of us as deformed, and as gradually deforming when we change the direction in which we are looking or slowly move our head. But if we narrow our eyes just a little bit as I suggested, it is unlikely that anything of the sort will happen. For sure, there will be visible changes in the whole scene, but they are *not* changes that we fell to be coming about in the observed objects making up that scene. It is enough to narrow the eyes a little bit and the whole visual field is affected by some noticeable change: the *visual field* and not the objects seen.

Thus, when there occur transformations in the phenomenal world, before invoking changes in the objects as a result of some modification of the self, it behoves us to observe closely whether this is how things stand, or whether the transformations regard rather the self, and the self alone, in the peripheral region of it that is the place of sight, from which derives the visual field in Gibson's sense, inasmuch as it is distinguishable from the "visual world"[6].

If we narrow our eyes, or if they are smeared with tears, we can but be aware of something happening in our head that, so to say, constitutes our optic point of view; this is in the region of the bodily self, the observation point from which Dr Popper drew the illustration for Mach's book.

And this fact, that of being aware of a modification at the edge of the self at the very time when a transformation is taking place in that region that is the object of the act of observing, might be enough to make for a divide just like those described in the examples one, two and three. In exactly the same way and just the same sense: there are divides among the various regions of the external world and they have determinate effects; an identical divide between a region of the self and another in the external world does not carry with it any greater theoretical difficulty to be encompassed in our thoughts, because the laws of segregation are the same. Hence the same effects can follow from them.

The existence of objects phenomenally independent of the act of observation is thus no stranger than the existence of undeformed objects behind a veil of water in movement.

7. Phenomenal space

The observations we have made hitherto allow us now to comment briefly on the thesis (b). The field of actual experience of the external world, understood as a system of spatial relations and distances, is phenomenologically wider than the set of things that can be pointed to, reached with the gaze, with hearing and so on.

The proof of that the self is in space, as Koffka witnesses Köhler frequently presenting it, began with the recognition that there are the walls of a room around us and, then, bit by bit, all the objects that are closer to us. But, even if the walls are the most distant of the visible objects for someone in a room, they are surely not the phenomenally most distant objects. Beyond them there is not a vacuum any more than there is a vacuum between us and the nearest objects. The walls themselves have thickness: we do not see them as paper surfaces, though we could make them seem so; but on the whole, the explicit conditions of phenomenal visibility are such that the walls present themselves as thick and hard: as hard even before they have been touched.

The space outside the environment limited by the walls is a space that is just as directly ascertainable. If we are travelling in a completely sealed railway compartment without being able to see anything outside, that "outside" through which the train is travelling is an object of direct awareness. In this sense, acoustic inputs have a certain importance inasmuch as they are localised as external to the environment in which we are enclosed. They can even give shape to the space in which the carriage is moving: when we pass among houses or enter a tunnel, the echoes that suddenly come about "narrow" the free space in which the train is moving; the lack of an echo is an almost completely empty space, to such an extent that we might imagine that we are travelling suspended over a void until some sound or other impression tells us otherwise.

Again, suppose we are in a room with the door open which allows us to see a sequence of other rooms through a series of open doors. The impression of the space present to us is not just along the line of sight that extends in the direction of our gaze, as if the house stretched out only in that direction; more or less markedly, it is the very place of which the room we are in is part, which is vast. Thus, the panorama is never restricted by the limits of the windows through which we view it, not just in the sense that it extends beyond them, to some extent amodally, but also because the panorama is that of open countryside, all the space that is out there, even if it is not visible, is broad and open, while if directly in front of the window is a massive building, the rest of the external space appears occupied and cramped.

The very common action of "going and seeing what is going on over there" can, I think, be explained to a great extent by the existence of this space beyond the limits of what can be pointed at. For sure, sometimes what guides us out of the environment in which we happen to find ourselves is the "knowledge" that elsewhere there is something that might interest us, or the "thought" that we shall find something better there and so on. But this account does not explain all cases, and in particular, it does not explain why, for instance, dogs can sometimes suddenly run to the window to look at what is going on beyond it, or to squint through a hole that allows them to glimpse portions of the world of which, within the confines of what is here and now visible, there is no trace other than the hole itself.

It is worth stressing that the limits of this space, only part of whose spatial articulation is taken up with the objects that can be discerned at the moment, extends beyond that amodal space that would be enough to bring about the classical completion effects that have been studied in visual perception laboratories.

Suppose that we use a magic lantern to project onto the wall of our room a situation of the following sort. A white rectangle with its longer sides kept horizontal is moving at a moderate speed from left to right; at a certain point, it right-hand shorter side stops while the left-hand side continues to move at the same speed and the longer sides are progressively shortened, producing a rectangle that is less elongated, then a square, then a rectangle whose longer sides are vertical and then ever thinner. As has been demonstrated, it is not possible to see the situation in the "physico-geometrical" terms in which I have just described it. What se see is a rectangle coming from the left and going right that at a certain point slips into a slit that is somehow present on the background, in the wall, so that the visible part is no more present than the invisible, which has already entered the cut, just as when we put a newspaper in the pocket of our overcoat. In this latter case, no-one at all sees the newspaper gradually being annihilated as it enters the pocket: what we see is that the newspaper is inside the pocket, with the hidden part as real as the part that is sticking out. Fine: the invisible part of the rectangle that has slid into the slit is perceptually real: it is behind and hence occupies space, a part of "amodal" space. Being behind after all means occupying a space behind.

But if we fix our attention in this scenario on the wall on which the projection is made, supposing it to have a certain roughness with small but visible lumps, we will be able to ascertain that, for all that it goes behind the background, the rectangle does not enter the wall. The wall is felt to be of a certain thickness, like every phenomenally solid surface, but the rectangle does not penetrate this thickness. The phenomenon of amodal "passing behind" comes about in space, but the space that is in question is part of a deeper space (by how much deeper, is not the point), in which amodal completions take place. When we see a man pass behind a column, there is behind the column not just enough space to let the man pass, but generally speaking, there is much more.

All the perceptual phenomena related to the structure of the external world happen in space: bodies with their visible surfaces occupy part of it; a further expansion of it is due to amodal phenomena and to totalisations in general, as is proven in the perceptological literature. But once we have said all that, we still have not given a complete description of phenomenal space because both the visible bodies and the places of amodal beings are themselves located *in space* tout court in such a way that, taking any phenomenon present in some part of it, there is always a spatial margin outside the place of the phenomenon itself.

It is my belief that this fact has an important consequence. In any environment whatsoever, when we move in any direction whatsoever, we never come up against the limits of our phenomenal space, which is to say the limits of the space of empirical reality.

The visible things that are furthest away from us are not limits of phenomenal space because they are wholly contained within it, in all directions. The walls of the room limit the possibility of looking beyond them, but do not annul the spatial regions that border on them on the other side: the walls make those regions less clearly articulated, just as the environment behind our back is less articulated. This means that we can be pushed to go and see what those regions are like, so as the make their articulation more precise. But, as I said, in doing so, we do not come up against the limits of reality, but rather get around some more or less complex bodily obstacles so as to reach those other regions and get to know them.

It is of no importance to say just how big this total phenomenal space is or whether, at some greater or smaller distance, it has limits or even what they would be like, given that we never come up against them in whichever direction we move. In passing from one place to another, whether it be from one room of a house to another or speeding down the motorway in a car, there is always somewhere else to go; at worst, we may run into insurmountable barriers, but these are never Ultima Thule, beyond which there is nothing.

8. The self as the mould of unreality

This is how the world of human experiences is, and I see no method for getting out of it. For among the many possible itineraries, there is none that, beginning from any given here and now, leads, for instance, to the world described by physics or, more generally, to some world of constructs. It is not possible to think of the properties, whether they be physical, phenomenological or logical, of a line that connects a point in physicist's space to a point in real space.

For this reason, I am unsure whether it is right to teach psychology students that, when we leave a room and close the door, there is nothing in it that resembles the experiences we can have of it when we are in it. According to this fancy, without an observer, the room becomes just atoms, radiation and void or, rather, variously structured and distributed energy fields.

We can at best imagine this, and never ascertain it. It is a scene that at most we can fancy to ourselves, for all that I am afraid that I can present it to myself in a way that no physicist would accept. I even doubt that an expert in physics can represent such a situation so that every detail of it corresponds to the things that he has learnt in his research; and even if, by dint of an extraordinary feat of imagination managed such a thing, I believe he would not be ready to claim "that is the physical world".

Beyond the door there really is ascertainable space; some noise or the very shape of the environment in which we find ourselves can give a certain articulation to this space, perhaps creating a system of expectations about what we will find beyond. Then we open the door and we find everything as normal or, vice-versa, something surprisingly different from what we had noticed before. But the things that we find were certainly not created by the act of pushing the door, nor have they passed to being tangible objects from being fields of force. The fact of their pre-existence welds them without interruption to the set of events that we were aware of before the door was opened.

In this sense, the objects of the physicist are never presupposed in the act of knowing, because they derive from his way of organising it; after all, it was physicists who made physics. On the other hand, the objects of direct experience *are* presupposed in the act of ascertaining them, both in thinking of them and in knowing them. Indeed, they are there with some position in space and certain absolutely special conditions are called for if we are to see them coming into being and constituting themselves, or for us to have the sensation that we are producing them. And in this last case, as soon as the act of production has come about, we cannot avoid the impression of having to do with something illusory and in the end unreal, precisely because the things that are ascertainably real do not arise from the self.

The self – in the end – is the mould of unreality.

Notes

1   Bozzi, P. (1985). Falsificatori potenziali e teoria della Gestalt [Potential falsifiers and Gestalt theory]. In W. Gerbino (ed.), *Conoscenza e atruttura. Festschrift per Gaetano Kanizsa* [*Knowledge and Structure: Festschrift for Gaetano Kanizsa*] (pp. 119–132). Bologna, Italy: Il Mulino.
2   Koffka, K. (1935). *Principles of Gestalt Psychology*. New York: Harcourt Brace and Company, p. 322.
3   Bozzi, P. (1990). *Fisica ingenua* [*Naïve Physics*]. Milan, Italy: Garzanti, Chapter 5.
4   Bozzi, P. (1989). *Fenomenologia aperimentale* [*Experimental Phenomenology*]. Bologna, Italy: Il Mulino (Chapters 1 and 8–10).
5   Kant, I. *Critique of Pure Reason*, B235 (trans. Norman Kemp Smith).
6   Gibson, J.J. (1950). *The Perception of the Visual World*. Boston: Houghton Mifflin.

COMMENTS ON UNTIMELY MEDITATIONS ON THE RELATION BETWEEN SELF AND NON-SELF

Robert Kelly and Barry Smith

How is it possible, given the nature of our experience, that we can delimit what we take to be *our selves* from what we take to be *outside of* our selves? In his *Untimely Meditations on the Relations between Self and Non-Self*, Bozzi considers two popular approaches to answering this question – one rooted in the discussion of personal identity in Hume's *Treatise on Human Nature*, the other rooted in the psychological doctrines of constructivism. He uses these to set the stage for his own account, which is at the same time realist and also rooted in Experimental Phenomenology and Gestalt theory. He outlines the method he uses to establish, first, that – against at least one reading of Hume – there really is a self. And second that – against the extreme constructivist position – it (or rather, *we*, which means: each and every one of our selves) can be distinguished ontologically from the objects of the external world. For Bozzi, both self and non-self exist. And to deny the constructivist position that the latter exists only because we *create* it does not require that we somehow get "outside of ourselves" in any illicit way. Bozzi defends his position from within an analysis of experience. His realism is, thus, phenomenologically derived.

Hume, familiarly, contends that "self" is just the name we give to a unity we take to be present in the unfolding of experience, but which is in reality absent. For Hume, "All the perceptions of the human mind resolve themselves into two distinct kinds (. . .) IMPRESSIONS and IDEAS" (1739/2000: I.1.i). These amount to, roughly, sense perceptions (for example sights, sounds, smells), and thoughts about sense perceptions (for example memories, acts of reasoning). These are all we can know, and hence, to delimit the self it is with these that we must begin – so we must take up a phenomenological approach. But when we pay close attention to our perceptions, says Hume, we see no unifying self:

For from what impression could this idea be derived? This question it is impossible to answer without a manifest contradiction and absurdity (. . .) It must be some one impression, that gives rise to every real idea. But self or person is not any one impression, but that to which our several impressions and ideas are supposed to have a reference. If any impression gives rise to the idea of self, that impression must continue invariably the same, through the whole course of our lives (. . .) But there is no impression constant and invariable (. . .) It cannot, therefore, be from any of these impressions, or from any other, that the idea of self is derived; and consequently there is no such idea. (1739/2000: I.4.vi)

From the bundle of perceptions – colours, shapes, feelings of joy, ideas of distance, and so forth, each of which is supposed to be separable from all the others[1] – we come to the view that this bundle is ours, that we are constituted by some unifying nexus that is thought to maintain our sense of ownership over our changing perceptions. However, Hume contends that we are mistaken. The term "self" is a term without a referent. But we can resist this Humean rejection of the self by fully embracing his idea that all we come to know when we reflect on our experience is a bundle of perceptions. That is, we can embrace Hume's own phenomenological approach, starting from and then analysing subjective experience, while still leaving a place for the self. We can do this by viewing the self as the very totality of these perceptions: the self is the bundle; as the bundle changes, from one moment to the next, so also does the self change; but it remains the self-same self, from moment to moment.

As Bozzi notes, a view of this sort can be associated with an unfortunate further view to the effect that the external world would thereby drop out of the picture. For if all I have are my perceptions, and if I am identical with the present bundle of perceptions that is my experience, then, as Bozzi notes, it would follow from the perspective of the Humean that "everything is myself." The view in question would then lead us away from the unwelcome conclusion that I do not exist – but at too high a price; for it cannot be, surely, that I am everything.

There is, certainly, a sense in which it is right to say that subjectivity is all-encompassing. Independently of whether an object of experience becomes a candidate for being a part of the self or a part of the external world, it is (trivially) always given to us as just an object of experience[2]. What we need, and what Bozzi offers, is an account that can embrace the apparent ubiquity of subjectivity while still managing to demarcate the boundaries of the self, and in a way that gives due status to the realm of what lies beyond the self, namely as something independent.

As George Davie observes in his discussion of subjectivism and objectivism in Hume, this is no easy task. Davie draws here on Hume's near-contemporary Sir William Hamilton, whose views on Hume had made a considerable impression on Brentano and, Davie suggests, on Husserl himself. For Hamilton, as Davie puts it, whenever one gets down, in a professional way, to the reflective analysis of the facts of consciousness involved in the cognitive situation, [the] apparently clear contrast between the body observed and my observation of it becomes extraordinarily cloudy and difficult to draw.

But, even though we are able to make some kind of contrast between the subjective and the objective, the perceiving and the object perceived, nevertheless the distinction it draws (. . .) is incapable of endowing the object-pole with the *independence* of the subject-pole which is demanded by our common sense about the external world. (1987, pp. 257–58, emphasis added)

To fill this gap, but without allowing either the self or the external world to drop out of the picture, Bozzi proposes that we appeal to Gestalt theory as a means to fix the limits of the self in relation to what is external while all the while working from within the realm of subjective experience. Gestalt theory teaches us, for example through its principles of reification and multistability, that our perceptions of what is given in sensation are structured. We recognise this, for instance, when we notice how four cleverly positioned three-quarter-filled circles can produce the perception of a square even though no square is present; or when a seemingly disparate array of black smudges produces, in a flash, the image of a Dalmatian sniffing around a tree. This tells us that our basic sensations are distinct from the perceptual field that is configured out of them, and that in every experience we have a two-way relationship between the observer and the observed. What we must determine, then, if we are to discover the boundaries of the self, is the nature of this relationship.

As noted above, Bozzi wants neither to go the way of Hume, claiming that, in fact, all there is is the observed, nor the way of the extreme constructivists, who claim that the entirety of the observed is simply a creation of the observer, something like a dependent mirage. To understand his approach, we are to envision ourselves as embedded in a three-dimensional spatial grid that extends all around us. The objects of our experience can be seen as each occupying a distinct location within this grid, and each object might be given its own name. We begin to see immediately that there is a particular region of this grid that we are inclined to call "self". Its boundaries are not exact, but we know that it occupies a space in the grid just as the other objects of experience do. And while we cannot yet say where it *is* with any precision, we can say with certainty where it is *not*. I, for instance, am not over there in the dining room by the bookshelf. Moreover, Bozzi continues, we will find that there are subjective experiences taking place *within* the self – the hearing of sounds, the thinking of thoughts, and so on.

As we envision this structure of experience, two points are crucial. First that the observer-observed relation obviously holds between the self and the other objects within the grid. Second, we become aware that we are not the only "owner of subjectivity" that stands in the observer-observed relation. Just as I am here noticing objects around me, so, too, are those other observers, noticing objects around them. In fact, I and they can even stand in the observer-observed relation to *the very same object.* For instance, you and I can both observe the box on the table, point to it, describe where it is in relation to the glass and so forth. Hence, the observer-observed relation can be seen as a *type* of relation with many instances, both between the self and different objects of experience and between any given object of experience and different selves. From this, we can infer that the structure of experience consists in *subjective perspectives*, none of which is privileged. Understanding the self this way, as an object in the space of experience, now allows Bozzi to more clearly delimit its boundaries in relation to the observed objects – i.e. in relation to the external world.

Recall the lesson from Gestalt theory that our perceptual experiences are configured, or structured, out of but in a way that goes beyond what is given to us in basic sensation. This lesson fits nicely with Bozzi's analysis of experience and the subjective perspectives of the observer. In other words, there is a sense in which the self can bring about changes on the side of the objects, as when the appearance of the box on the table changes as we walk around it, or when one of us looks at a drawing and sees a duck, where another, looking at the same drawing, sees a rabbit. Such changes are brought about by changes in the subject.

But Bozzi makes clear that we also experience the object being observed as *unchanged* in some way. As we walk around the table, it is *the table itself* that appears to us now in this way now in that. When the light hits the table just so, its colour changes. We do not then have the experience that a new table has popped into existence; and the same applies when the box, as we move around it, seems to change its shape. We automatically distinguish *changes in appearance* of the object due to changes in the observer-observed relation, from *changes* in the object itself.

Importantly, this is all given to us in experience. That is, in addition to the succession of changing experiences of a given object, we also experience that object, the same object that is appearing to us now in this way, now in that way, as somehow "standing behind" this succession of changing appearances. Bozzi provides a number of examples of this phenomenon. For instance, we experience one and the same house even as we shift our focus from the doors to the windows. We do not take the rain on the window to have actually distorted the countryside behind it, even when we acknowledge that it has distorted our perceptions. In this way, Bozzi captures both the primacy of subjectivity in experience as well as the independence of the observed from the observer.

We might summarise the lessons to be drawn from Bozzi's remarks in the following way. The self is situated in a spatial grid, where the latter can be characterised as an array of relations, of which the relata include both observers and observed. We and other observers, the other selves, are those loci of subjective experiences that can be found standing in observer-observed relations with other objects within the grid. Those objects are distinguished from each other, and other selves are distinguishing from my own self, by constituting (in Davie's terms) distinct *poles* of the token observer-observed relations they always instantiate. Just as we can separate distinct regions of observation, as when we observe this table here and that bookshelf there, so we can separate the region of the self from other regions we experience as standing apart from us. To be sure, the ways in which the regions (and their objects) *appear to us* belong to the side of internal, subjective experiences and thus are in some sense to be located within the region of the self. But as Bozzi has argued, it is a necessary presupposition of such experiences that the regions and their objects are apprehended as something that we do not create.

A final point may prove illustrative. Towards the end of his discussion, Bozzi emphasises that we are already familiar with the experiences he has been analysing all along. It should not seem strange to us to posit more than what is initially thought to be strictly given to us in subjective experience. Bozzi writes, "The field of actual experience of the external world (. . .) is phenomenologically wider than the set of things that can be pointed to. . ." (§7). We apprehend that there is a world of objects beyond the edges of our acts of observation – that there is a pasture beyond the pitch black of night, that the newspaper persists behind the overcoat it is slipped into, and so on. And if we apprehend objects of the external world always only partially, while at the same time recognising their existence as enduring denizens of reality, so we might apprehend our self, too, only partially, while recognising its existence as being in the same way something that endures.

There are aspects of Buddhism (its views on the non-self, on non-attachment) that have been described by appeal to an analogy with the situation in which, in observing a wall-sized mirror (for example in a restaurant), you mistakenly take your observation to be of a whole set of objects out there in the world. The lesson is supposed to be that this is what experience is like all the time. We get attached to "worldly" objects of our experience, naming them, imbuing them with value, and so on, when we should really understand all of this as an experience-sized mirror illusion. The world, understood as independent existence, including the self, is empty. However, Bozzi's method for identifying the self and delimiting its independent existence from the external world has taught us just the opposite lesson. Reflection on the structure of experience can seem like the wall-sized mirror in a way – it *does* represent a world of objects beyond what is basically given (given to the senses). But for Bozzi this is informative rather than (as for Hume, and – in the opposite direction – for the Buddhist) illusory. We must *begin* with experience and work from there. Bozzi's self as an object with its location in the spatial grid, distinct from those stable objects apprehended as standing behind our subjective experiences of them, is derived precisely from the nature of experience. But there is then no need for skepticism about the self; or for total ubiquity of the self. The tools for a phenomenologically derived realism were present all along. Bozzi's project is to teach us how to use them, and to recognise that they allow a self to be situated in a world of objects.

Notes

1   See Davie (1987), against this supposition.
2   Against the temptation to draw overly ambitious conclusions from this triviality, see Franklin (2002).

References

Bozzi, P. (1991). Untimely meditations on the relation of self and non-self. *Rivista di Psicologia*, n.s., *LXXVI* (1–2), 19–33 [Chapter 5 in the present anthology].

Davie, G. (1987). Husserl and Reinach on Hume's "Treatise." In K. Mulligan (ed.), *Speech act and Sachverhalt: Reinach and the Foundations of Realist Phenomenology* (pp. 257–274). Dordrecht: Martinus Nijhoff Publishers.

Franklin, J. (2002). Stove's discovery of the worst argument in the world. *Philosophy*, 77 (2002), 615–24.

Norton, D. F. & Norton, M.J. (Eds.) (2000). *David Hume: A Treatise of Human Nature*. Oxford: Oxford University Press.

6

LOGICAL ANALYSIS OF THE PSYCHOPHYSICAL (L-R) SCHEME

Translated by Richard Davies

> The variety of truths leads to the invention,
> growth and establishment of disciplines,
> and not to their diminution or destruction.
>
> (Galileo)

1.   Several decades during which all sorts of interdisciplinary activities have been promoted, and have sometimes been promoted only because interdisciplinary, have overshadowed the advantages that flow from isolating a given field of enquiry, for all that it is connected in obvious and traditional ways to other fields, so as to look within it for its proper primitive concepts and autonomous rules, or even, in the most fortunate cases, for its specific logic that can fit that field of enquiry into its place in a coherent overall map of intellectual endeavour.

Of course interdisciplinariness is a good thing and it arises both out of the insufficiency of individual disciplines and out of the intellectual honesty of those who cultivate them. Scientific curiosity and sometimes contingent calls to find information require researchers to turn to their colleagues down the hall or on the floor below, and sometimes these encounters can lead to surprisingly interesting upshots. In this way, problems may appear in a fresh light, an alternative vocabulary may suggest an unconsidered theoretical grammar and, not the least of the gains, the sense of disciplinary corporatism (which is often nothing but a stupid presumption of disciplinary superiority) comes out of the encounter with a few dents. This wholesome practice can run into degenerations of various sorts. Within this variety, one that is particularly noticeable these days is the formation of corporations of researchers specialised in being interdisciplinary; these corporations are made up of individuals each of whom collects a fair smattering of diverse competencies and takes this to be the theoretical backbone of his or her knowledge.

Another way that things can go wrong is the widespread and noticeable lack of interest in creating closed conceptual architectures,[1] or at least such that are meant to be so by those who create them, which, as is obvious and necessary, have certain limitations but in any case, require great internal consistency, a severe clarification of the basic concepts, a transparency and sobriety in inventing developments. And these are operations that we rarely encounter and appreciate in scientific projects that are made up by piling up parts each individually well done − a little bit of this and a little bit of that, so long as they are well tried and tested, good normal science. As regards the study of perception, it should be said that the very nature of the subject matter suggests considerable opportunities for interdisciplinary work, and for this very reason the set of its problems is in danger of being identified with them.

In recent years those who present themselves as perceptologists not infrequently show themselves, as much in what they write as in what a few hours' conversation reveals, to incorporate in a single head a good amateur knowledge of computing, a good amateur knowledge of physiology, a good amateur knowledge of artificial intelligence, a good amateur knowledge of psychophysics (whether global or other), plus a good amateur knowledge of epistemology and statistics as well as up-to-date reading in psychology and the like. These are areas of knowledge that demand the powers of a genius, but that often appear as the sum of partial competences ranged in mutual defence, yet in the dark about the theoretical drama that is being played out over their foundations.

The connivance among the fragments of encyclopaedic knowledge makes it hard to catch sight of the possibility of an autonomous theory of perception that accounts for the objects of *observation* by appeal to nothing other than the very principles of observability *iuxta propria principia* ("by means of its own principles"). After all, what could ever be the practical importance of a theory of such a kind? None. Working independently of a piece of knowledge brought academic honours neither to Bolzano nor, in turn, to Frege. So much the less today.

Of course, arguments have been advanced in some quarters against the mere idea of a self-sufficient science of perceptual facts. Yet it is obvious that perception depends on what goes on in living creatures' brains, and so all the scientific ingredients needed to clarify the brain's workings are mixed up in the problem of perception. The programmatic amateurism referred to earlier is thus justified; and it is programmatic precisely because it is inevitable. And not just that: it is the fruit of a long tradition. Ever since the Presocratics, the problem has been treated in terms that are at once observational and conjectural. Sensations and perceptions have been handled as observable facts and conjectures have been made about the physical states – in the widest sense – that are hidden behind the observables and that yet are able to explain them. The models proposed by the Presocratics (especially the Atomists) and by Aristotle were splendid. The great models of today cannot be constructed without help from all the sciences we have already mentioned and then some. They are complex to a degree that makes them hard to master and occasionally they come close to the splendour of their ancient forerunners. Any effort to try to divorce the problem of the observables under way, which is to say the problem of perception, from this obvious and traditional background, and to look within it for its own specific principles, without importing anything external, may seem fanciful and silly.

2.   Nevertheless, it is worth discussing at least one illustrious example that points in this direction.

Everybody knows how much logic and the foundations of arithmetic gained in terms of clarity, consistency and potential for growth when they broke away from their natural, obvious and traditional context, which was that of thought processes. For centuries, logic had been considered a theory of thought.[2]

It does not occur to anyone to suppose that logic has nothing to do with the fact that humans think and make signs, or that it was not created, invented, constructed by the thought of certain men and that other men have taken advantage of it in various ways by means of acts of thought. Thought – what anyone can observe introspectively – made logic and sometimes applies it, and it is beyond doubt (in the sense of *obvious* as used above) that thought is a factual precondition of its employment and its construction. Only a bravely

Platonistic mathematician would claim that, in its beautiful timelessness, logic is altogether beyond thought. If we talk about or have to use logic, we are inescapably bound to think. Indeed, we have the impression that even the Platonistic mathematician does so when he tries to convince us of his ideas.

But in fact it is possible to know a great deal about thought processes and relatively little about logic and the foundations of arithmetic; vice versa, it is possible to master the universes of formal discourse in a creative way while having only vague and slightly sceptical ideas about the psychology of thought. The psychology of thought provides absolutely nothing to extend logic or mathematics nor yet to help us better to understand their bases in a way that would satisfy an expert in these fields. Furthermore, we should take account of how, when the fashion for "non-formal logics with a formal logical structure",[3] in which cognitive problems were intertwined with problems of calculation and foundation, came to an end, it was just at that moment that the development of logic became unstoppable and the psychology of thought became a robust discipline.[4]

In 1884 Frege wrote that a description of the mental processes that precede the enunciation of a numerical judgment, even if that description is exact, can never take the place of a genuine determination of the concept of number. We shall never be able to call on it to demonstrate some theorem nor shall we learn from it any property of numbers. And indeed, number is not an object of psychology nor can it be regarded as a result of psychical processes.[5]

Some years later, while he was collaborating with Whitehead on the monumental *Principia Mathematica*, Russell wrote in his article on the "Axiom of Infinity", published in the Hibbert Journal, much the same thing, with an astringency that is in my view all the more admirable: "throughout logic and mathematics, the existence of the human or any other mind is totally irrelevant; mental processes are studied by means of logic, but the subject-matter of logic does not presupposes mental processes, and would be equally true if there were no mental processes".[6] It is *obvious* that, in writing these words or in talking to Whitehead, Russell was thinking. But there is in his claim a demand for hygiene that should be understood and respected and, where possible, emulated.

Let us take our own case, that of perception, which is to say the range of objects and events that are accessible to observation in a given instant;[7] let us now try to re-write Russell's drastic theorem applying it to this field and to other branches of knowledge that are accessory to it (such as neurophysiology, theory of information, physics of stimuli etc.). A transposition of it might run as follows:

In a theory of percepts and of the explicit phenomenal relations that intervene among them in a given instant, from whatever point of view we adopt on the problem, their dependence on other facts or processes (whether they be physical, merely model–theoretic or even metaphysical) that are not directly observable in that moment is totally irrelevant for the coherence and the heuristic power of the theory itself; the physics of stimuli, neurophysiology, artificial intelligence, informational models and every imaginable model-theory are constructed by using in various ways the percepts and their observable relations; but the arrangement of the percepts observable in a given instant do not of necessity presuppose any of this; rather everything in it would remain the same even if the facts of those sciences were wholly different or did not exist at all.

Of course I know in the *obvious* way that we have already referred to, that, while I was writing the words of the foregoing sentence, billions of events were taking place in the bundle of neurons inside my head, and thousands of things were going on between my fingers and the mechanism of my typewriter, and so forth. But this seeming paradox is no worse than Russell's, nor is it any more gratuitous. Rather, it is an adumbration of a programme of research, just as in the case of logic; and, as in that case, the paradoxicality is no more than a seeming.

3.   Let us make some of the necessary clarifications straightaway.

Wherever possible what is obvious should give way to criticism, and it has often happened that criticism has overturned the most obvious relations. At a later stage, we can continue to talk as we did before; indeed, an astronomer today assured me that the sun will rise tomorrow at 7:23. If a colleague wants to convince me that a model of his explains a certain perceptual event, he must first of all show me that event with all the necessary trappings, bringing it into the field of observables, and then, appealing to the appearances that can be ascertained in it and that can vary depending on certain conditions that he can control and (in order to convince me) that he lets me control, he will construct a model with words and symbols.[8] After which, to do him a kindness and to speak more efficiently with him, I too will say that the event is produced by the conjectures on which we have together found agreement. It is a convenient fiction, a convention to favour a quiet life. Examples are easy to find and we shall come back to them in due course. In the end "mental processes are studied by means of logic" as Russell put it; likewise the processes underlying perception are studied by means of perception, indeed, often by taking perception itself as the starting point.

A second clarification concerns the general possibility of constructing true or false propositions about perception independently of any assumption about anything else, especially about the underlying processes. Indeed, as was claimed for centuries, plausible talk about logic implies talk about thought, so also someone might think that it is impossible to construct claims about perception that do not imply reference to something that is non-perceptual.

I hope to clarify this point by appealing to Descartes' genial fiction near the end of the first *Meditation*:

> So I shall suppose [writes Descartes] that some malicious, powerful, cunning demon has done all he can to deceive me – rather than this being done by God, who is supremely good and the source of truth. I shall think that the sky, the air, the earth, colours, shapes, sounds and all external things are merely dreams that the demon has contrived as traps for my judgment. I shall consider myself as having no hands or eyes, or flesh, or blood or senses, but as having falsely believed that I had all these things. I shall stubbornly persist in this train of thought; and even if I can't learn any truth, I shall at least do what I can do, which is to be on my guard against accepting any falsehoods, so that the deceiver – however powerful and cunning he may be – will be unable to affect me in the slightest. [And he immediately adds] This will be hard work, though, and a kind of laziness pulls me back into my old ways.[9]

Indeed, it must be extremely hard work to doubt of all the factual propositions for which we have before us grounds either for or against. The demon will surely be malicious, powerful and cunning; nevertheless in the external world there are colours, shapes and sounds and all the rest, and there is little to be doubted about them (the doubt concerns, precisely, solely the "underlying" processes); Descartes can tell many truths about the lying world. Apart from the propositions about his thought, his thinking, he can also pronounce a thousand true propositions about what he takes to be the appearances – but which are not such – for all that the demon has at his disposal a convincing technology for producing illusions. In that world, Descartes can go as far as to perform experiments, to find regularity and to construct formulae such as $x = f(y)$ concerning "illusory" functional connections, namely those that can be ascertained by observation.

It is certain that Descartes never took this genial fiction seriously: in the *Replies* to the *Sixth Objections* (those addressed to him by Mersenne's learned friends), he explains that the immediate effects of sensation, which is to say the immediate experience of colours, shapes and sounds etc., are immune to any possible doubt because there can be no falsehood in them. In short, in the passage we have quoted, he is *pretending* to able to doubt, and he really could do no other.

The fiction of the malicious demon can be compared with a 0-level psychophysics; in it the perceptual arrangement of the world for a given observer in a given instant depends on the actions that are directly impressed by the wicked intentions of the demon who, given that he is very powerful (*potentissimum*),[10] controls every single, even minimal, part of that arrangement. If we want to know his will, we have only to observe what he projects onto Descartes. If, on the basis of observation, Descartes can construct formulae and laws, he knows that the demon has a plan of action or that his will is subject to laws etc. Even if this is a limited science, it is a science all the same. It is certain, it is empirically founded, and perhaps it is equipped with a strong internal logic (which depends on the demon, but also on Descartes' scientific skill).

4.   A similar type of knowledge has, after all, been proposed as a scientific programme. It appears in just these terms in the first chapter of Ernst Mach's *The Analysis of Sensations*,[11] where he sets out his famous anti-metaphysical preliminaries. That chapter is well known to anyone who studies the psychology of perception because the technical literature ever since is full of references to it; to grasp the way that the two proposals coincide, it is enough to bear in mind the relations: Mach's "A B C . . . complexes" are identical to Descartes' "the sky, the air, the earth, colours, shapes, sounds and all external things", while Mach's "K L M . . . complexes" are Descartes' "eyes, or flesh, or blood or senses". The systems of relations that hold between the members of these two orders of complexes allow us to construct, on the one hand, physics (when we remove all reference to the K L M . . . complexes from the constructive game), and, on the other, perceptual science (when the field of relations is taken as a whole).

This is Mach, professor of physics at the University of Vienna; but it is also a perfect fit for Descartes. I am aware that taking Descartes' fiction of the malicious demon as a starting point may make for misunderstanding: indeed, treating it as a case of 0-level psychophysics, there is the risk of introducing the idea of a subjective science founded on subjectivity, so strong is the stereotyped relation between the name of Descartes and metaphysical subjectivity. But we must take a distance from this historical stereotype: the fact that we can establish the two correspondences with Mach just mentioned undermine any possible subjectivist interpretation. Mach's complexes are simply the observables; in the passage from Descartes, the demon is obviously a fiction, without which what remains is just the world of facts as such.

Twenty years after Mach, this scientific programme was once more set out, this time by an author who cannot in any way be suspected of subjectivist tendencies. It is contained in some notes by Charles Sanders Peirce that is it worth quoting at length.

> Phaneroscopy [the ideal science hypothesized by Peirce] is the description of the *phaneron*; and by the *phaneron* I mean the collective total of all that is in any way or in any sense present to the mind, quite regardless of whether it corresponds to any real thing or not. If you ask present *when*, and to *whose* mind, I reply that I leave these questions unanswered, never having entertained a doubt that those features of the phaneron that I have found in my mind are present at all times and to all minds. (. . .) English philosophers have quite commonly used the word *idea* in a sense approaching to that which I give to *phaneron*. But in various ways they have restricted the meaning of it too much to cover my conception (if conception it can be called), besides giving a psychological connotation to their word which I am careful to exclude. (. . .) There is nothing so directly open to observation as phanerons; and since I shall have no need of referring to any but those facts which (or the like of which) are perfectly familiar to everybody, every reader can control the accuracy of what I am going to say about them. Indeed, he must actually repeat my observations and experiments for himself, or else I shall more utterly fail to convey my meaning to him than if I were to discourse of effects to chromatic decoration to a man congenitally blind. (. . .) It will be plain from what has been said that phaneroscopy has nothing at all to do with the question of how far the phanerons it studies correspond to any realities. It religiously abstains from all speculation as to any relation as between its categories and physiological facts, cerebral or other. (. . .) It does not undertake, but sedulously avoids hypothetical explanations of any sort. It simply scrutinizes the direct appearances, and endeavours to combine minute accuracy with the broadest possible generalisation. The student's great effort is not to be influenced by any tradition, any authority, any reasons for supposing that such and such ought to be the facts, or any fancies of any kind, and to confine himself to the honest single-minded observation to the appearances. The reader, upon his side, must repeat the author's observation for himself, and decide from his own observation whether the author's account of the appearances is correct or not.[12]

In this new guise, which I have carried almost in full because every line is worth a page, once it is set out explicitly, the scientific programme of a 0-level psychophysics remains above all suspicion and has no outstanding business with subjectivism. Peirce takes his distance from psychology (from psychologism) and three times stresses the interobservable nature of the *phaneron*. The range of facts to be brought into the theory after scrupulous observational tests may well include here and there some features of subjectivity (it will include for instance also consecutive images but it is not reducible to the "merely subjective", unless we take this latter adjective, or noun, with unseemly lightness in the face of grammar, logic and vocabulary. As to the two expressions (a) "religiously abstains from all speculation as to any relation as between its categories and physiological facts, cerebral or other" and (b) "sedulously avoids hypothetical explanations of any sort"; these are not hints at subjectivism, but are very clear indications in the direction of a theoretical position that is closed, methodologically self-sufficient and in line with its own specific principles (*iuxta propria principia* in the sense explained right from the outset of my book *Fenomenologia sperimentale* [1989]).

In support of a programme of this sort, we shall seek to offer some logical analysis of psychophysics of level $m > 0$.

5.   It is quite normal in the course of giving a lecture to go to the board and trace a scheme that starts on the left and proceeds towards the right in a few or many stages. This is how psychology of perception begins in introductory courses and also how it proceeds up to the level of international conferences.

Because of the direction in which it runs, I shall call this scheme "L-R".

On the left, we have a sketch of a physical object, which is the source of the stimulus. To its right there is room for the propagation of the physical effects of the object's presence in the surrounding space, which we suppose to be filled with some medium. Those effects will be compression waves if the object is a bell, electromagnetic waves of a certain frequency if it is a coloured cube. Further to the right there is a depiction of an eye, which may be more or less detailed according to the needs of the discussion. Then there is the optic nerve or rather both nerves to show the optic chiasm, then the lateral geniculate nucleus and finally other marks that lead towards area 17. (If a bell has been drawn to the left, there is an ear in the place of the eye and so on.)

The right half of the board tends to be very full of markings; indeed, in addition to the more or less anatomically inspired sketches, it will host, more or less in parallel with them, one or more flow diagrams. It is presupposed – whether knowingly or not – that "perception" is to be found beyond everything at the extreme right of the board, or that some fragment of it can be identified with some group of marks furthest to the right. This assumption is called for because, if the perceiver in the act of perceiving does not notice some of the events represented on the board, and yet we say that such events go to make up his percept, then they must have taken place before that final state that – in representation – portrays precisely his percept. If he does not notice any of them, and yet we suppose that they all go to make up his perception, then his perceiving must be found beyond the furthest rightward sign and so be further to the right.

At least in its general outlines, this L-R scheme derives rather from the experience of seeing someone in front of us who is looking at something than from the experience of ourselves looking at something. In this latter case, what we have in front of us are variously disposed objects and events, empty space or transparent media between us and them, and here, at bottom, the rather ill-defined limits of the visual field, to which we pay little attention and which vary in harmony with the movements of our head. This is a state of affairs that is depicted in the famous diagrams of Mach and Gibson and that is described by Wittgenstein when he says: "nothing *in the visual field* allows you to infer that it is seen by an eye".[13]

This theatre of Mach, Gibson and Wittgenstein is the one about which Descartes mistakenly believed he could be in doubt; it is the obvious referent to the word "perception" even though other words would really be more fitting. But the other case, in which among the things we are looking at there is, on the one hand, someone who is looking and, on the other, something he is looking at, with him on the right and it on the left of the scene, is completely different. The ideal line that joins the thing to the person can be subdivided into stages and can be extended beyond the person's eyes, which we can see, following pathways that we can imagine between those eyes and the more internal parts of his head, calling in aid our imagination and a neuroanatomical mapping. Once we have established certain criteria and accepted certain ideas, these pathways too can be subdivided into stages.

On the L-R scheme, pretty much all these things show up. I can also think that inside the head of the observer I am looking at there is a toy version – as Richard Gregory wrote to make fun of Gestalt theorists – that is similar to the thing that he is looking at; that toy thus becomes the final destination of the ideal pathway that leads to the right-hand edge of the board with which the sequence of processes represented to the left is brought to a close.

Irrespective of how the various stages into which it is subdivided are filled in by appealing to scientific knowledge, the L-R scheme is the visualisation of every causal theory of perception. It is a diagram that is articulated in vertices and edges by means of which we can represent psychophysics from level 0 to level $m > 0$, and it can be employed as a formal ingredient in a temporal logic as suggested by von Wright,[14] and in particular in the logic that he calls "causal analysis". This is done by assigning a direction to the edges so as to model an ideal flow of time. Thus the drawings adopted to portray the L-R scheme (and there can be as many as there are imaginable theories) will always have an orientation.

If we accept that to each point of the perceptual experience of Descartes as subject there corresponds an act of will on the part of the evil demon, we will put a vertex (demon's will), then a pointer that ends in a second vertex (Descartes' world). This is psychophysics of level 0.

If we adopt an idealised classical psychophysics then, to each point into which the perceived world can be dismantled (which is to say, to each sensation) there will correspond a place in the physical world (which is to say, a stimulus) whose physical effects in their rightward journey on the other side of the eye undergo a transformation (some sort of Weber-Fechner law). In this L-R scheme, the first vertex is the stimulus; the next, which is reached along an arrow, is the psychophysical transformation; and from this there derives a further arrow that leads to the vertex that is the sensation depending on the stimulus. This is a psychophysics of level 1.

Let us then suppose, following Helmholtz, that, before the subject is aware of it, every sensation has been manipulated by a higher faculty, such as unconscious judgment. The directional diagram will thus have in the first place on the left a vertex (the stimulus), then a new vertex (the law of psychophysical transformation), then yet another vertex (the point at which unconscious judgment comes in), and only after this a final vertex (the subject's perceptions); the four vertices are obviously connected by edges which are themselves directional in time order. Unconscious judgment is in a later position relative to that of the psychophysical transformation because it is only there, according to the Helmholtzian view, that it can be used to explain deviations from that law: it was invented to that end and so that must be its position. Here we have a psychophysics of level 2.

Sticking with Helmholtz, we may further suppose that, before it intervenes on the sensations in arrival, unconscious judgment must consult memory of previous experiences that are in some way connected to those sensations before determining the aspect of the perception. In this case, we have, in chronological order, a first vertex (the stimulus), a second vertex (the psychophysical transformation), a third vertex (the appeal to memory or similar states), a fourth vertex (the decision of unconscious judgment) and in the end the final vertex (the subject's perception). Indeed unconscious judgment must first look to memory and only then decide: this is the order. This is a psychophysics of level 3.

We can build to our heart's content. Ever since Fechner, we have witnessed a multiplication of vertices and edges in competition with loaves and fishes.[15]

I have cited Helmholtz because his theory lends itself fairly well without too much deformation to being presented in an oriented linear diagram. But it goes without saying that with this system we can extract networks of any degree of complexity, on the sole condition that the direction of time's arrow is respected. If we want to represent also retroactions of any given degree of complexity, we will have to make up an oriented diagram in three dimensions because – and it is well to be clear on the point – retroaction can take place in space but not in time. The standard flow diagrams that we find in psychology manuals are in this sense dangerously deceptive, where the danger is for the students, of course.

6.   We shall return shortly to von Wright-style causal analysis. For now, it is worth returning to the board and thinking about it in a less graphic and more intuitive way.

Suppose we have a red cube on the left. If we ask someone why the observer over there on the far right sees it as red (granted that he is not colour-blind), our random interlocutor might give us an answer of the following sort: "because the cube, or at least surfaces that are open to observation, are made of that certain chemical stuff that absorbs light of all wavelengths except for that narrow band within the visible spectrum that is rather approximately (after all, it is a fuzzy set) called red". We could straightaway make a small correction to this answer. It is not a matter of "that certain chemical stuff"; any chemical stuff with the same features of absorption and reflectance of the spectrum would do equally well. Strictly speaking, a wide range of materials with differing chemical make-ups have that same property. Our friend will immediately agree and will allow that whatever material it is has to be *such that* those frequencies of the packets of electromagnetic waves should be absorbed and the others reflected. That material there, in the contingent case, is a sufficient but not a necessary condition of seeing red:[16] indeed, many other chemically different materials would propagate in the surrounding environment frequencies of those dimensions so as to be picked up by instruments and to be visible.[17]

It would seem that, with this, the problem has been pushed to the right on the board. It is a problem concerning the properties of the radiation rather than those of the material.

But the problem is pushed further to the right as soon as we take into account Muller's principle of specific sensory energy, or rather the simple fact that suggested it to him. A colour does not arise in perception only thanks to the action of packets of electromagnetic waves on the retina's photoreceptors. To produce it, mechanical actions applied to the eye, or chemical or electrical stimulations suffice. For a colour to be seen, if we take into account only the eye and not what will happen further along the pathway, it will be sufficient to treat it in such a way that we bring about a modification in the bursts of electrical impulses that travel along the fibres of the optic nerve; the photochemical process of the photoreceptors is a sufficient condition for producing modifications in the electrical activity of the fibres and, in the current view of things, for producing signals; but it is not a necessary condition in relation to the electrical state of the fibres of the optic nerve.

Viewed abstractly, we could apply directly to them the action from a source whose functioning was perfectly calibrated both as regards the electrical parameters and as regards their distribution over time. It is theoretically possible to imagine so refined a prosthesis; and for the purposes of logical analysis what is theoretically possible is decisive.

If we had ideally complete knowledge of how the lateral geniculate nucleus works – which, after all, has been one of the stages in the visual system on which some of the most successful research has been done in recent years – then we could apply an analogous prosthesis also to the fibres of the optical radiations that carry impulses towards the cortex and that bear traces of the messages sent by the superior colliculus, the hypothalamus, the midbrain reticular formation and goodness knows what other messages that have been inserted into the train of electrical modifications that connects the eye to its cortical area.

We are about halfway across our board. From this point on the certain data of physiology become ever rarer (basically they are what can be obtained by means of evoked potentials, which is a technique that brings together our knowledge from the optic nerve as far as the cortex), while the psycho-physiological and cognitive models burgeon out of control.

The fiction of the ideal prostheses can be applied step by step, as we have ever more to do with moments of conduction or propagation; in the certainty that, if once we had complete knowledge, those prostheses could have perfectly definite material features. Indeed, so long as there is a direction of conduction, even considering only one electrical pathway isolated from everything else, then all the earlier states of the story can be bracketed, if, from a certain point onwards, the state of the system remains invariant; the preceding story is, strictly speaking, a sufficient and not a necessary condition of it.

Let us consider for a moment another way of putting the question, one that is, from the point of view of the logical schematisation, identical to what we have just set out.

If we look at the lessons on method in Braitenberg's most recent book, which is presented as introductory but isn't really, we find a playful account of a "law" which is that of "uphill analysis". It is harder to work out what are the inner mechanisms of a system that is observed to display behaviour of a certain degree of complexity than it is to construct an equally complex behaviour by means of an assemblage of mechanisms each of which is in itself simple, as Braitenberg does when he constructs his vehicles. "It is actually impossible in theory to determine exactly what the hidden mechanism is without opening the box, since there are always many different mechanisms with identical behaviour".[18] This assertion underlies the logic of the "law": indeed, the induction and the deductive approaches would be identical only if the system's setup were to include a postulate to the effect that the pieces and their connections cannot be replaced. Behaviour is an ambiguous semantics relative to the underlying mechanisms. This holds not only for the final behaviour, but for every state on which other states of the system depend. The story to be told further down the line is in any case open to replacements. There is nothing to stop us adding fifth wheels, or also substantially different alternative solutions, such as analogical as against digital ones, whole blocks of operations as against a simple and brilliantly thought-out solution.

Of course, the highly complex network of cortex-cortex connections that we encounter at the end of our journey from left to right across the board do not allow us to persist with our fictions of interchangeableness, even though it is true that each individual connection has a direction and can be thought of as a wire that carries a current. The state of the system now suggests analogies with states of dynamic self-distribution (in electrostatics, in hydraulics) that are arrived at by way of well-defined channels. It also suggests a self-referential situation: "the consequences of the system's operations are the system's operations".[19] Once the system is no longer sequential, the fictions of interchangeableness become hard to apply.

But it is exactly at this point, where physiology gives us only a secure topography of evoked potentials that the psycho-physiological models begin to do their work. Over certain stages, they proceed in parallel with the strictly physiological schemes, and the stages that physiology describes seem to be, as logicians say, the signs deployed in the model. Nevertheless, the data that can be obtained by means of typically psychological experimentation (reaction times, error counts, measure of apparent duration in relation to the length of stimuli, successive and simultaneous comparisons, deferred reactions, masking effects, recognitions strategies etc.) allow us to construct ordered sequences of unconscious mental events that, precisely because they are such, must *precede* the closure of the process of which they are stages, for that closure is what they contribute to determine.

7.   Two things should be stressed: first of all that that closure is the percept that is available to observation in the sense given by Descartes and Peirce, which is also the sense given by consistent Gestalists; if the closure is not the percept, then that means that the model is still short of one or more links before it arrives at what seems should be its obvious *explanandum*. In the second place, even here, each of the links connected by a "before" and "after" is a sufficient but not necessary condition of the one that follows.

In the models that are in use in laboratories that study cognitive processes, and especially after Miller, Galanter and Pribram's TOTE, the use of flow diagrams is widespread to represent conjectures about the sequences of unconscious mental states that determine – and hence precede – a given final state, a closure that may be the solution of a problem, but that may also be a perceptual event in the visual or acoustic field. In these diagrams, the moments are coordinated by "before-after" relations; the boxes condense "phenomena and function that in reality are often distributed and not easily localised"[20] and so should be viewed as moments in the elaboration of information, while the lines are transits along which information travels unaltered within the setup that has been assigned to them by the operations contained in the box from which they arise.

It is true that it is often necessary to represent certain passages of transmission and elaboration in parallel; but it is obvious that each individual passage reflects within it an articulation into "before" and "after" that may be as implicit as you like, but that is logically indispensable. It is also true that in flow diagrams we often find representations of primary or higher-order retroactions (that is to say, agents on retroactions), either simple or multiple (which is to say, agents on different boxes in the scheme). Their representation on the flat surface tends to make us underestimate, at a first glance, the system of "before-after" relations: only a three-dimensional representation does justice to the basically sequential tendency of every retroaction (such system can begin to oscillate because of this). Thus, even when there are retroactions in a flow diagram, it is a portrayal that is oriented in accordance with time's arrow, so much so that cognitive psychologists make predictions about the time lapses that they then measure looking precisely at the greater or lesser expenditure of time that is foreseen by the diagram. If those of the forerunners of the percept that cannot be easily referred to physiological facts are represented in this way we have two reasons for thinking that we are once more faced with chains of sufficient but not necessary conditions.

The first reason for thinking so is immediately visible in the form of the diagram: what will take place in a given box is determined, given its internal rules, only by the characteristics of the information that arrives at that box, namely, the characteristics that are conserved along the transit that carries the information to the box (the line). But these characteristics do not specify the kind of elaboration that took place in the preceding box or boxes: they are just the result of that elaboration. Other more or less complex elaborations or systems of elaboration can be imagined further up the line that could have produced just those characteristics at that point.

The second reason appears when we try to give a physical interpretation of the scheme. In that case, if the supposed elaborations are correlated with that level of physiological activity in which "the consequences of the system's operations are the system's operations" and, hence, in which "there is a simultaneous convergence or coherence of all the parts in play",[21] this means that we are presuming that there is a concealed sequence, one hidden in the network of interactions; if such there is, it is subject to the same decomposition into chains of sufficient but not necessary conditions on which the fiction of our ideal prostheses was founded.

Developing an idea of von Wright's, we may represent the history that connects a distal stimulus with a percept as follows:

On von Wright's account, the pointers that make up the horizontal axis, and the vertices that are connected by them represent the way the facts are really connected: they make up a "reality line". The space above and below the line is the "space of possibility" and the vertices within these spaces represent events that could have produced the event represented by that vertex on the reality line, and towards which those pointers converge.

We can come to an interesting conclusion by attentive reflection on a diagram of this sort. Obviously, it would have to be much more complex and ramified; and given the complexity of the facts that it refers to it would also have to be in three dimensions: one plane for the reality on which lies the complicated network of connections that really happen and two *semispaces* in which to put the merely possible events that are alternative cause of what is on the plane.

As a purely theoretical exercise, we could imagine without contradiction two observers whose perceptual worlds were identical from every point of view, but who were endowed with slightly or very different underlying mechanisms. Let us suppose that we are one or other of these observers. In such a case, I could find myself in the company of an absolutely perfect Braitenberg vehicle, endowed with a perceptual world just like mine, that he knows how to describe as well as or better than me and in which he moves as confidently as I do or even with greater skill, as I can gather by observing his behaviour and listening with astonishment to his words.

Now, this vehicle could have perceptological curiosities. In talking about these, we might decide to embark on a joint study of perception and, starting from the traditional bases of that science, he might show me a wide range of optical illusions (all those forming the classic repertoire), and I might show him some interesting effects, like that of chromatic contrast

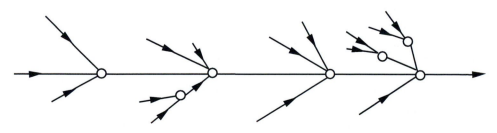

(6.1)

or of chromatic after-effects, seeking together to put some conceptual order into these phenomena. We might have two fairly different general philosophical orientations and different methodological problems. Indeed I come to think that he is rather brighter than me and more far-sighted in theoretical matters. But we must surely agree about the facts, at least as much as two or more human observers can agree about them. He is by definition a perfect Golem.

Once we leave the world of direct observation and of experimentation on the phenomena and proceed to experiment indirectly on our respective physiologies, we will discover to our delight that we are made differently, and the problems that should arise from this fact would feed into discussions of the philosophy of knowledge and of artificial intelligence: for him, I might be a fine specimen of artificial intelligence. And yet, despite those differences, we could still go a long way together in the study of perception, finding functional connections among events, empirical generalisations and laws.

Within the limits to which our collaboration might meet with success he and I would have set on foot a science that is independent of what he might have built around our respective "underlying" workings. Even if it is true that certain classes of modifications applied to those workings would make us disagree about some or all of the perceptual facts, the fact remains that other classes of modifications would not produce any disaccord between us.

In this narrow sense, it makes sense to talk of the logical independence of the problems of perception relative to the problems of what in general underlies it. This is the sense in which, indeed, we may talk of the independence of formalised logics relative to those acts of thought that nevertheless generate them, invent them, develop them and apply them.

8.   The independence in question has nothing to do with what Eccles points to.[22] After offering a fine description of Lake Como and of the villages that can be made out in the distance along its banks in the clear air, and after a hint at the pointillistic image that is formed in our eyes and at how the scene is elaborated in our brains, Eccles notes that the integration of all those signals in the splendid theatre that we living beings can admire will never be found at the neurophysiological level.

The best we can do in neurophysiology is the feature extraction performance observed in neurons of the inferotemporal lobe (. . .) Cell after cell can be discovered with selective response at this level of simple geometrical features. This performance is tremendously remote from the vivid picture that was impressed on our retina and which we experience at the end of all of this cerebral processing.[23]

David Hubel still says he feels that all the time we are learning more and more about feature extraction neurones and how they come to make more and more complex patterns but never does it get beyond the stage of showing us more than little flashes of simple geometrical fragments to which each cell is responding specifically. How the whole great picture comes to be represented in the brain is quite another matter[24].

On the contrary, it seems that it is not represented at all in the brain, if we want to take literally another passage in the same section: "It isn't assembled together by the brain and read out as a single unitary phenomenon of the mental experience by the self-conscious mind, but in our hypothesis the self-conscious mind is in fact doing all the putting together".[25] This claim sounds like a kind of demonstration of the existence of the soul, and in effect it figures as part of the arguments that Eccles uses in his popular lectures to convince his listeners of just that.

If we wanted to accept this line of thought, the move from the evoked potentials to the setting up of an experienced world, there would hold a rather weaker relation than one that holds between a sufficient but not necessary condition and its effect. If this relation were thus construed, it would seem to be rather an interruption, or "hiatus", than a connection.

On the one hand, there is the indication pure and simple of single characteristics that are both topologically and functionally independent of one another; on the other there is a complex system of interactions among classes of characteristics that are from time to time integrated to form objects and events in accordance with specific laws. The size of a surface makes a difference to the colour it displays, as does whether its edges are sharp or blurred; changes of shape become rigid rotations in space or even three-dimensional deformations of objects, with the specification of their elastoplastic properties; when colours are placed one next to the other they can produce transparent surfaces; combinations of movements present themselves as causal connections or even as intentional behaviours. And all this can be seen to happen in space and time; but here space and time are not those of the coordinates in which macroscopic physical systems can be inscribed. Rather this space and this time have their own anisotropies than can be as well brought out by laboratory experiments as by common observation of everyday life. Any standard – and modestly truthful – introduction to the psychology of perception will present a fair catalogue of such integrations between discernible aspects of objects and events, even though the examples will be less complex than those that are often hidden here and there in the world of things.

To give a scientific interpretation of this world – in which, after all, everything we do takes place – the response of neurons to its characteristics are much less than a sufficient condition. The hiatus that Eccles points to would be enough on its own to guarantee the epistemological and even metaphysical autonomy of a science of perception. But at what a price! It is far too high a price for anyone who nourishes a certain ideal of the unity of knowledge. Moreover, anyone who works everyday with the facts of perception has no sense whatever of handling anything like a self-aware mind.

It is in any case better to hope that neurophysiology has a great future ahead of it, in which even the complex task of assembling the world that can be experienced and shared will be understood and described not only in phenomenological terms but also in physical terms. Within that physiology, the complex system of signalling the presence of characteristics will come to make up a sufficient (but still not necessary) condition of successive states that are ever more complex and ever more approachable in the imagination to the order than can be made out among the facts under observation. Perhaps these new facts will resemble in some way the cognitivist conjectures regarding the elaboration of characteristics; but doubtless we shall have to find out something that is even further away if we want to get a convincing approximation to a picture of empirical reality *tout court*.

9.   The epistemological independence of the theory of perception has to be founded in a way that is at once more radical and less dogmatic.

On the one hand, we have to take account of the considerations presented in the foregoing section regarding the interchangeableness of the stages to the left relative to the "closure", which is the whole of what is observable. Which is to say, the story of the Golem. It is clear that any new discovery about the underlying functions, or any change of direction in the theories about them, or indeed further approximation to the observable, in the way that we all hope, over and above the limits set out by Eccles, cannot modify in any way whatever the truth value of the empirical propositions that concern the observable and shareable constitution of the percepts as such.

On the other hand, there remains the possibility of setting out a logic of this range of facts, which is not itself enslaved by reference to the underlying functions. This logic exhibits the constitutive form of the events under observation and of the observable or operationally attestable relations that hold among those events; its applicability takes its origin from the realm of description, but it can be developed to apply also to areas that admit of prediction and explanation.

By way of conclusion to this study, I shall try to outline the salient points of what seems to me some of the epistemologically most interesting fragments of this logical structure.

Let us once more consider the famous Wertheimer factors, which is to say that rather disorderly list of proximity, similarity, continuity of direction, closure and so on. From a reading of the manuals, we might think that they add up to a set of unconnected observations about typical cases of unity or "segregated events" that vary from time to time. In point of fact, however, they can be put in order thanks to a recursive logical structure whose applicability is completely independent of any assumptions about what we have heard Peirce calling "physiological facts, cerebral or other" as well as about what he calls "hypothetical explanations of any sort".

At the outset, let there be some elementary objects in a perfectly homogeneous universe, and let it be observed that certain relations (such as spatial proximity) that can be seen among them correspond to formations that are evidently segregated relative to examples of other elementary objects lying at visibly greater distances. (The distances between one object and another can be compared, given that they turn out to be such under direct inspection – and in any case, they can be measured; also the units turn out to be such under direct inspection – and every observer is able to say how many agglomerations of objects are to be seen in that universe.)

On the basis of these observations, we may suppose that the unitary formations are function of distances: not only will there be unitary formations where the distances are smaller, but further shortenings of those distances will make by so much more evident the unitariness of the formation. The hypothesis can be easily tested by direct observation and without introducing any new theoretical construction or any concept that is not already present in the realm of observation. We may thus write

$$\Phi\, u,u = f(F_1)$$

where there is a unitary formation ($\Phi\, u$), and it is such in virtue of a factor F_1, namely the visibly smaller distances. Now we may suppose that, in the whole visible universe, unities are formed only in virtue of this factor. Obviously it is enough to undermine this generalisation if we produce a single example in which a unitary formation comes about contrary to the expectations that form from the generalised assumption that $\Phi\, u,u = f(F_1)$.

Among Wertheimer's examples there is indeed a unitary formation that comes about contrary to the factor that we have already mentioned. There must then be another factor. We may then say that

$$\Phi\, u,u = f(F_1) \bullet (\overline{F}_1) \rightarrow F_2$$

to mean that, if a unitary formation is seen to come about when we already know a factor of unification, but it comes about not in accord with that factor, then there exists another factor that is able on its own to produce unitary formations. The existence of this factor is established even before we know its nature, and it depends wholly on the irreducibility of the example to the known cases.

As regards the nature of this extra factor, it will emerge from an inspection of the case adduced that counts as a counter-example to $\Phi\, u,u = f(F_1)$. This inspection can be broken down into three moments: (a) the construction of a list of all the properties directly noticeable in the counterexample, except those that have already been classified as factor F_1; (b) the assumption of each of the members of the list as a hypothesis about the nature of the new factor; (c) the systematic modification of the property corresponding to each of the list's members. Once it has been transformed, the visible property that gives rise to a visible modification in favour of the unification under examination or indeed to its disappearance is the new factor F_2.

We may now suppose that the whole visible universe is populated by unities produced by various combinations of the two factors F_1 and F_2. This generalisation may be expressed briefly as

$$\Phi\, u,\, u = f(F_1,\, F_2)$$

(By "various combinations of the two factors" we mean of course to include also cases in which F_1 and F_2 work together to form a certain unity, as is generally the case in "ecological" perception, in the direct registering of the complex objects that fill our experience; but in their synergic operation, the factors may be inextricable. The logical scheme we are suggesting here only works when we are in a position to produce oppositions by intervening operatively on the structures under observation.)

We may now write recursively

$$\Phi\, u,\, u = f(F_1,\, F_2) \bullet (\overline{F}_1,\, \overline{F}_2) \rightarrow F_3$$

If a case presents itself in which the unitary formation is not compatible with the expectations deriving from $\Phi\, u,\, u = f(F_1,\, F_2)$ then we have the demonstration of a factor

FIGURE 6.2 If we assume that the distance between the points is the sole factor that gives rise to the formation of a unity ($x = f(y) \equiv$ the greater the closeness, the more evident the unity $\equiv$ each point is associated with the one nearest to it) and we write the formula $\Phi\, u,u = f(F_1)$, in front of this figure, we are *not* in a position to explain how come we see one horizontal formation and one oblique formation: the two points that are visibly closest should bind together ($\Phi\, u,u = f(F_1)$, $(\overline{F}_1)$). Hence there exists another factor that cannot be reduced to the one that is already known: $\Phi\, u,u = f(F_1) \bullet (\overline{F}_1) \rightarrow F_2$.

FIGURE 6.3 If we assume that the unitary formations only come about as forms of the relations of distance and of directional continuity (as in Fig 6.1), and we are thus inclined to write Φu, $u = f(F_1, F_2)$, when we discover the figure on the right and see it in line with the scheme on the left, we should conclude Φu, $u = f(F_1, F_2) \bullet (\overline{F_1 \cdot F_2})$. The new factor is colour similarity. Indeed, for the F_1, we should be able to see a V in the upper part of the figure and, for the F_2, we should see a horizontal line of points in the lower part. Hence Φu, $u = f(F_1, F_2) \bullet (\overline{F_1}, \overline{F_2}) \rightarrow F_3$.

F_3. An inspection of the structure of this case – following the moments (a)–(c) noted above – will allow us to isolate the nature of the new factor.

The procedure is open-ended. Its application excludes the illusion that the unitariness of the objects of the empirical world can be reduced to a single principle, as would have pleased many philosophers (past experience and habit, as Hume would have had it, or the needs of man that are able to solidify into "things" the unceasing flux of sensations, as Bergson supposed, or again the transition from thinking thought to thought thought, as the idealists held). On the other hand, the number of factors, even if it is indefinite, is not very big: those that are already known are not more than about ten, and it is ever harder to find new factors.[26]

10.   In any case, if we wanted to carry on in the hunt for factors, the Golem and I could work efficiently together even though, under our shared outward appearance, the mechanisms are different in each case. If we agree to assume the formation of unities by proximity as the first link in the chain, he like me will be able to estimate greater and lesser distances among elementary objects, such as black points on a white paper. By definition, given that he is a perfect Golem, he will see the situation as do my students in class and I, and, given that he is intelligent, he will have no difficulty understanding that – in the case in hand – the amount of free space between the points is the "independent variable" on which we can work to obtain various grades of unitariness in the constellations that are formed from time to time. This unitariness has thus become a "dependent variable". Nor will he have difficulty classifying the various visible aspects of the situations we are examining – and that he will be able to check accurately with me as well as with others – under many various headings, each of which outlines a hypothesis about a new factor capable of producing a particular form of cohesion. Nor yet will he hesitate about the operations to be performed to work out whether a given aspect of the observed situation is itself a new factor to be added to Wertheimer's catalogue.

After a long period of enjoyable collaboration we will have a fair number of factual claims of the form $x = f(y)$, all appropriately interconnected in a fair complex but perfectly definite network. At that point, no-one can tell us that we have not been doing science just because we have (by definition) different "underlying processes" and we have not wanted to be bothered with them. We can hold on to our physiological and engineering peculiarities, while at the same time, we construct a logically coherent and factually correct bit of perceptology.

Furthermore, during our observations, as a result of the necessary multiplication of the facts to be observed, we will be compelled to register other phenomena: the articulation into figure and background with its curious paradoxes, the three-dimensional look of certain configurations despite their being constructed on a flat surface, the influence of certain colours on others, the properties of edges and so on. These are all problems that he and I can face up to at a later stage, inventing fresh logical networks and discovering other functions of the type $x = f(y, w, z \ldots)$, where the suspension marks stand for who knows what complex connections – all the while without abandoning our place as privileged-because-different observers. Of course it is also part of science to make a comparative study of the different ways we work; but whatever truths come out of that study, they cannot make any difference whatever to the truths that we are discovering in our game.

11.   At the root of this game, which is a genuine part of cognitive science, there lies the principle which we might call the "complanateness of variables", by which I mean that both dependent and independent variables, in all the complexity of their relations, all lie on the same plane of shared observableness.[27] This is what is shared by me and the perfect Golem, in the farfetched but instructive case that I am presenting, but it is also obviously shared by normal observers who, with or without spectacles, join in an exercise of this sort. Thus understood, the complanateness includes all those cases that Epstein gathers under the heading "percept-percept coupling"[28]: this comes about when a feature of the perceived event that is modified by some transformation performed on it, also modifies some other discernible feature of the same event. Thus, the whole relation $x = f(y)$ takes place under observation and if it is discovered that the dependent variable x can also come about in the absence of y, then we must say that the relation between the two variables is asymmetrical. In the case in hand, unitary formations can be obtained either by proximity or by similarity or by any of the well-known factors, and thus saying that a certain factor is present also means that a unitary formation is present; but the mere fact of a unitary formation does not allow us to tell which specific factor is at work. Epstein rightly notes that the logical form of these cases has the formal structure of material implication; and the present author has been in full agreement with him on the point ever since the 1970s.[29]

The only trouble is that Epstein is so concerned by the "underlying" (by how the Golem works) that he writes that "while it is obvious that a physical event can cause either a mental event or another physical event, the proposal that a mental event can interact causally with another is discomforting".[30] This seems to me a rather metaphysical concern; and, in any case – as I have tried to explain in the fourth section of this paper – there is no need to think of the facts under scrutiny as in themselves mental and so to contrast them programmatically with physical facts. Moreover, a purely mental event such as a sudden memory can easily and on the spot bring about (causally) another equally mental event such as a wave of emotion.

Furthermore, Epstein seems to locate the asymmetric relation of implication as between the terms of a percept-percept couple, with a rather strange orientation. His exact words are: "if under certain circumstances perceiving variations of X is causally related to perceiving variations of Y, and if X and Y had *not* been so related but circumstances were otherwise changed, the observer would still have been perceiving variations of X but not be perceiving variations of Y, then perceiving X is conditional and causally prior to perceiving Y".[31]

In fact, it would seem rather that in a situation as described, it is precisely Y that is the sufficient condition of X, on the supposition that X can occur if other conditions are met – as we illustrated in commenting on Wertheimer's principles.

But, apart from that, Epstein's argument seems to run as follows: if there is a percept-percept couple whose terms are connected by causality-implication, and that relation has not been extracted as information directly from the stimulus, there must have been some reason-like elaboration that imposed that relation on the percepts; hence the existence of percept-percept couplings is evidence against the theory of direct perception. But it is hard to imagine anything more directly given than any example whatever of percept-percept coupling.

What are we to say about this? Also in this case the recourse to the stimulus and, hence, to elaborations makes for a certain amount of conceptual confusion.

My Golem, when faced with the figure [12.19; see Chapter 12 in the present anthology], has learnt with pleasure that the white that appears between the points of the oblique band is brighter, in the zone where the horizontal band crosses, than the white that is to be found among the many other points on the same band; and then that the points that are in the zone next to the whiter channel seem further apart form one another than they do in the rest of the pattern; and finally that those very same points, understood as rows, divide that pattern in two by means of the lighter channel that runs between them.

On the one hand, if we go and measure the distances between the points, if, that is, we want to speak operationally of the stimuli, they turn out all to be the same distance from each other; indeed, they all belong to the same dot lattice. And if we go and see what happens in the tangle of elaborations, only the person who constructed the Golem would be able to tell us what is happening. On the other hand, in this example it seems precisely that a *seen* distance between the points determines a *visible* division between the two parts of the band. It must be said that our Golem is a very fine observer, and much more so than an amateur of zero-level psychophysics.

Notes

1 We may cite classical mechanics and Euclidean geometry as two grand examples that have had a great historical impact; but so did, in certain phases, some parts of chemistry; see C.S. Peirce, *Collected Papers*, 5 vols, C. Hartshorne and P. Weiss (Eds), Cambridge, MA: Harvard University Press, 1931–35, 2.488.

2 Henle, M. (1962). On the relation between logic and thinking, *Psychological Review, 69*(4), 366–378.

3 Scholz, H. (1959). *Abriss der Geschichte der Logik*. Freiburg, Germany: K. Alber.

4 Bozzi, P. (1973). Introduzione [Introduction] in P. Legrenzi and A. Marzocco, *Psicologia del pensiero [Psychology of Thought]*. Milan, Italy: Martello.

5 Frege, G. (1884). *Grundlagen der Aritmetik*, Breslau: Köbner. (trans J.L. Austin, *The Foundations of Arithmetic*, Oxford: Basil Blackwell, 1950).

6 Russell, B. (1904). The axiom of infinity. *Hibbert Journal*, II (4), 809–812.

7 Lewin, K. (1943). A definition of a "field at a given time". *Psychological Review, 50* (3), 292–310; Goodman, N. (1977). *The Structure of Appearance*. Boston: Reidel (last chapter). See also Bozzi, P. (1985). The stream of consciousness, or the events under observation [Chapter 4 in the present anthology].

8 See Bozzi, P. (1985). The stream of consciousness, or the events under observation, par. 13 [Chapter 4 in the present anthology]

9 Descartes, R. (1641). Meditationes de prima philosophia. In *Œuvres de Descartes Publiées par Charles Adam et Paul Tannery* (originally Paris, Léopold Cerf, 1897–1913) with corrections and additions by J. Beaude, P. Costabel et al., 12 vols, Vrin, Paris, 1964–76 (cited as AT VII, pp. 22–23).

10 *Ibid.* AT VII, p. 26.

11 Mach, E. (1886). *Die Analyse der Empfindungen under das Verhältnis des Physischen zum Psychischen, Jena: Fischer.* (trans. C.M. Willliams and S. Waterlow, *The Analysis of Sensations and the Relation of the Physical to the Psychical*, New York: Dover, 1959).

12 Ms of 1905 (The Principles of Phenomenology) in *Collected Papers*, cit., 1.284–7.

13 Wittgenstein, L. (1921). *Logisch-Philosophische Abhandlung* (originally in *Annalen der Naturphilosophie*). trans. D.F. Pears and B.F. McGuinness, London: Routledge, 1961, 5.633.

14 von Wright, G. H. (1971). *Explanation and Understanding*. New York: Cornell University Press.

15 Matt., 15, 32–8.

16 Nagel, E. (1965). Types of causal explanation. In D. Lernea (ed.), *Causal Explanation*. New York: Columbia University Press; von Wright, *Explanation and Understanding*, cit.

17 Sober, E. (1975). *Simplicity*. Oxford: Oxford University Press, pp. 95ff.

18 Braitenberg, V. (1984). *Vehicles: Experiments in Synthetic Psychology*, p. 20. Cambridge, MA: MIT Press.

19 Varela, F. J. (1985). Complexity of the brain and autonomy of the living. In G. Bocchi and M. Ceruti (Eds), *La Sfida della Complessità* [*The Challenge of Complexity*], pp.141–157. Milan, Italy: Feltrinelli.

20 Longo, G. O. (1980). *Teoria dell'informazione* [*Information Theory*]. Turin, Italy: Boringhieri.

21 Varela, F. J. (1985). Complexity of the brain and autonomy of the living, cit.

22 Popper, K. & Eccles, J. (1977). *The Self and its Brain*. Berlin: Springer.

23 Ibid., p. 534.

24 Ibid., pp. 533–534.

25 Ibid., p. 534.

26 See Bozzi, P. (1989). A new factor of perceptual grouping: Demonstration in the terms of pure experimental phenomenology [Chapter 12 in the present anthology].

27 See Bozzi, P. (1985). The stream of consciousness, or the events under observation [Chapter 4 in the present anthology]

28 Epstein, W. (1982). Percept-percept couplings. *Perception, 11*, 75–83.

29 See Bozzi, P. (1976). Phenomenal experience, epistemic experience and psychological experience. Notes towards an epistemology of the phenomenological experimental method, par. 4 [Chapter 3 in the present anthology].

30 Epstein, W. (1982). Percept-percept couplings, cit., p. 79.

31 Ibid., p. 79

COMMENTS ON LOGICAL ANALYSIS OF THE PSYCHOPHYSICAL (L-R) SCHEME

Francesco Orilia and Michele Paolini Paoletti

The main goal of Bozzi's paper is to ground the epistemological independence of "an autonomous theory of perception that accounts for the objects of *observation* in line with their specific principles (*iuxta propria principia*)" (p. 131), without worrying about whether these objects arise from the volitions of a Cartesian demon or from other more plausible sources, and thus along the lines suggested by Peirce's "phaneroscopy", and, we may add, Husserl's phenomenology. The goal, in other words, is to show the legitimacy of autonomously pursuing Experimental Phenomenology in the tradition of *Gestalt* psychology, thus hunting for intersubjective laws, such as Wertheimer's principles of perceptual grouping. The enterprise is "experimental", as these laws are grounded on experiments that manipulate parameters constituted by "percepts", with a methodology that Bozzi himself contributed to develop with his "interobservational" method (Bozzi, 2002; Vicario, 2001, Ch. 6). And it is autonomous, because it is in no way dependent on the study of the neurophysiological and psychological processes underlying perception. Bozzi offers by way of analogy the fact that the laws of logic can be investigated independently of whatever mental processes underlie our reasoning events, as Frege and others have argued in their criticism of psychologism about logic.

To reach his goal, Bozzi views percepts as entities in their own right with their own *observed* properties and relations, in sharp contrast with philosophical accounts of perceptions such as *adverbialism*, according to which, e.g., we do not see a red percept, but rather "see-redly" (Crane, 2011). Moreover, he appears to embrace a non-reductionist ontology of mind, according to which mental properties cannot be identified with physical properties in the way suggested by the so-called type identity theory (see below). Bozzi's non-reductionism must be quite different from the one stemming from Davidson's much-debated anomalous monism (Kim, 1998, p. 132). According to this doctrine, there are strict physical laws, but there cannot be strict psychological or psycho-physical laws, and this is why mental properties cannot be identified with physical properties and psychology be reduced to physics. But Bozzi could hardly agree with this line, as it appears to be in straightforward conflict with his acknowledging laws of perception. For these, we think, should be regarded as *psychological* laws, even though Bozzi (2002, par. 10) claims that, in doing Experimental Phenomenology, he contributes to a "science of the external world" (we see below how this idea may fit in Bozzi's view of the mind). But if not a Davidsonian one, what kind of non-reductionism can be attributed to Bozzi? Before trying to answer this question, let us briefly review some theoretical options currently discussed in the philosophy of mind and that are relevant here (for references and further details, see Kim, 1998).

As is well known, Descartes argued for a *substance dualism*, according to which minds are distinct immaterial entities exemplifying mental properties and causally interacting with material bodies exemplifying physical properties. This approach has still its own followers, including Eccles, discussed by Bozzi in his paper. The current *Zeitgeist* however favours a physicalist outlook, which shuns purely mental immaterial substances and presupposes the *causal closure* of the physical domain, i.e., that all effects must have physical causes. This is in tension with the intuition that a mental event can have a causal influence on the physical world. The tension arises in view of our inclination to accept an independently plausible assumption about causation, namely that there is, at least in typical cases, no causal over-determination. This rules out that an event with a physical cause may also have a mental cause.

At some point in the last century, the *reductive physicalism* proposed by Place (1956), Smart (1959) and others, also known as the *type identity theory*, dominated the scene in the philosophy of mind. A good deal of its success was due to the fact that it appeared to eliminate this tension, by claiming that any mental property is identical to a physical property. For example, it was typically asserted, feeling pain is nothing but having C-fibers firing. From this perspective, every mental event turns out to be a physical event and can thus be seen as a cause without infringing the principle of causal closure.

In spite of this success, reductive physicalism has fallen in disgrace, mainly because of the multiple realizability argument put forward by Putnam (1967) and others.[1] According to this argument, it is plausible to think that there may be creatures that are endowed with the mental properties that we humans possess (seeing red, feeling pain, etc.), but that simply do not have the physical properties that, according to the reductive physicalist, would be identical to the mental properties in question. Thus, for example, there could be a sophisticated robot or a Martian humanoid, made up of inorganic materials and thus devoid of C-fibers. Accordingly, they cannot have the property of having C-fibers firing and yet, for all the evidence we have, they could be in pain. Thus, feeling pain cannot be identical to having C-fibers firing. At most, it is some sort of "higher-level" property that can be "realised" by different "lower-level" physical properties in different creatures. In humans, the lower-level property may well be having C-fibers firing, whereas in the robot and the Martian it is, let us imagine, having R-fibers and M-fibers firing, respectively. Usually the higher-level properties are characterised as "causal" or "functional" roles and this kind of doctrine is accordingly called *functionalism*.

Reductive physicalism has thus increasingly lost consensus and a *non-reductivist physicalist* paradigm has come to the fore. This physicalism is non-reductive in that it accepts a *property dualism* according to which mental properties are not identical to physical properties (thereby making room for multiple realizability). But it is also physicalist in that it (i) still maintains the causal closure of the physical domain and (ii) typically holds that mental properties *supervene* on physical properties, in that, necessarily, for every organism x and mental property M of x, x has a physical property P such that, necessarily, whatever has P also has M.[2]

Bozzi explicitly acknowledges that a substance dualism such as the one defended by Eccles might be appealed to in order to ground the autonomous study of perception, but at the same time considers the ontological commitments of such a view as too high a price to pay. As an alternative, he offers two arguments, which we proceed to discuss.

1.   *The non-necessary conditions argument.* Bozzi grants that *our* percepts of such and such a kind are causally dependent on neurophysiological processes and (typically) distal physical stimuli of so and so a type, so that one can try and construct a "psycho-physical scheme" that provides a more or less plausible causal history of the path leading from the stimulus to the percept. Yet, he insists that the *physical* stimuli and processes involved are not necessary, but only sufficient conditions for the percepts: other physical stimuli and processes could do as well. A nice example (not used by Bozzi) at the level of the distal stimulus is provided by jade gemstones, which can be made of two quite different chemical substances, either jadeite or nephrite: there could in principle be two jade gemstones identical in colour and shape, although one is made of jadeite and the other of nephrite. Given of course the appropriate activation of the relevant neurophysiological processes, each gemstone is sufficient to produce in a normal human subject a visual percept of a certain type (in terms of perceived colour and shape). Nevertheless, since the other gemstone could perform analogously in spite of its quite different chemical composition, neither is necessary for that type of percept. Bozzi envisages other complicated ways in which the train of physical events ultimately leading to a percept of a certain kind could in principle vary while the percept remains of the same kind. For instance, mechanical, chemical or electrical stimulations of the eye could generate a photochemical reaction in the retina's photoreceptors of the same kind as the one produced by the normal impact on them of certain packets of electromagnetic waves. Or the electrical activity of the optic nerve's fibres that typically results from that photochemical reaction could be obtained by means of an appropriately calibrated prosthetic source of electrical signals. The electrical signals departing from the retina travel to the cortex through a complex path involving various components or areas of the brain, such as the hypothalamus and the mesencephalon, that somehow influence the signal. However, notes Bozzi, at each step of the path we can imagine a prosthetic device that artificially creates the same pattern of electrical signals that would have been normally generated by the activity of the relevant brain components. In the end, at any rate, as long as there are percepts, there must be a "closure of the process" and this closure "*is* the percept open to observation" (par. 7, p. 8; our emphasis). In sum, all the causal steps leading to the percept are (jointly) sufficient conditions for the percept, but none of them is necessary, for it could have been replaced by something else playing the same role.

This argument has been seen as a rejection of reductive physicalism, inasmuch as it has been taken to suggest that "no matter how much one searches among the physiological process in the central nervous system, one will never be able to find the last irreplaceable process identifiable with mental life" (Vicario, 2001, p. 186; our translation). But the argument cannot warrant this, because, correct as it might be, it tells us nothing about the "closure of the process" itself and its ultimate nature. It only tells us about the different ways in which the process could have been generated. The closure of the process is for Bozzi a percept, and thus, one can surmise, an object and not a property. Thus, at first, it might not be clear how to relate Bozzi's discussion to the debate between the reductive and non-reductive physicalist, framed in terms of mental *properties*. However, Bozzi might say, as long as there is a percept, there is the mental property of *seeing* that percept (assuming that the percept is visual) and nothing in the argument shows that such a property is not physical. To take a standard example of property reduction, consider a gas in a container reaching temperature T as a result of being exposed to sunlight on a sunny day for a certain amount of time. This exposure to sunlight is only a sufficient condition, for the same temperature could have been reached by exposure to an artificial source of heat. Yet, one might insist, the gas's having temperature T, whether it was brought about by sunlight or not, is nothing but its having a certain mean molecular motion. Similarly, if our friend Tom is seeing a red percept, the identity theorist could insist that this is nothing but, say, Tom's having certain neural pathways spiking with a frequency of 90 Hertz, even while conceding that this spiking could have had different causal routes from those it actually had, involving, e.g., a prosthesis in Tom's brain that generates appropriate electrical signals for the neural pathways in question. Such a claim of course rests on the assumption that at the closure of a process leading to the percept, there is a red percept if and only if there is also that kind of neural spiking. We might in principle find empirical evidence against this, but this is another matter. The point is that Bozzi's arguments speaks only about the causal antecedents of the closure not about the closure itself. This is enough however to establish what Bozzi wants to secure: how the percept was brought about is irrelevant for someone who can inspect the percept and wants to study *it*.

2.   *The Golem argument.* To further support this point, Bozzi goes on to consider the extreme case of an artificial agent, a "Golem" or "Braitenberg vehicle", presumably not made of organic matter and yet endowed with the same "perceptual world" (p. 17) as a typical human agent and capable of dissecting and verbally describing this world with the same perspicuity as Bozzi himself. The Golem and Bozzi would thus respond with a percept of the same type to the same distal stimulus (say, a jade gemstone at such and such a distance with lighting conditions of a certain kind, etc.) and both would report their observation with analogous words. Both would declare, for example, something like "I see a translucent and intensely green roundish object." Thus, and here we come to what is most important for Bozzi, the Golem and Bozzi could proficiently interact and, by appropriate experimentation and interobservation, come to realise that their perceptual worlds obey the same perceptual laws, e.g., they are both subject to the same Wertheimer principles. Yet, Bozzi and the Golem are endowed with "different underlying mechanisms" (par 10, p. 141). For example, let us suppose, the latter experiences red insofar as its inorganic "brain" has certain copper pathways that spike at a frequency of 90 Hertz (Churchland, 1988, p. 40), or perhaps at a different frequency.

It seems clear that Bozzi is here making the typical assumption of multiple realizability and thus one may be tempted to attribute to him the functionalist and non-reductive physicalist position that typically goes hand in hand with it, once substance dualism has been excluded. On the other hand, contrary to what the typical physicalist nowadays may perhaps be ready to grant, Bozzi seems to admit mental properties of a relational nature involving as relata percepts characterised by appeal to Mach, who is typically classified as a "neutral monist" (Stubenberg, 2010), because he views percepts as intrinsically neither mental nor physical: they are the latter or the former depending on whether we look at them from the point of view of the laws of psychology or of physics. Bozzi (2002) buys this idea (pp. 134, 143, 147) and presumably this is why he views phenomenology as a science of the external world.

In line with common sense, Bozzi decidedly grants mental causation (p. 20). Now, notoriously, the price that non-reductive physicalism risks paying is acquiescence in *epiphenomenalism*, the thesis that mental events as such are unable to cause other events, whether mental or physical (Kim, 1998, Ch. 9). A lot of contemporary discussion has focused on this problem and, among many theoretical options on offer, there is Chalmers' attempt (1996, Ch. 4, par. 4) to complement his non-reductionist and functionalist view with neutral monism, in a effort to avoid epiphenomenalism. We cannot explore here the complicated issue of whether this strategy ultimately works. Be this as it may, in the light of what we have noted about Bozzi's view of the mind, we may perhaps say that he to some extent anticipates Chalmers' combination of doctrines, and we may surmise that he might have been sympathetic with Chalmers' effort to proceed to a detailed exploration of it. But of course this is pure speculation for which we have no direct evidence.

Notes

1 See, e.g., Kim (1998, Chapter 3) for a discussion of reductive physicalism and multiple realizability and for further references to these topics.
2 It is worth noting that the kind of doctrine that emerges if one accepts the supervenience of mental properties may vary depending on how one understands the necessity invoked in the appeal to supervenience. Very roughly (see Chalmers, 1996, for a detailed analysis), if the necessity is logical-conceptual or metaphysical, one rules out altogether (metaphysically) possible worlds in which there are organisms with the relevant lower-level physical properties, but without the corresponding mental properties that in our world accompany those physical properties. This is the view typically espoused by functionalists (especially if the necessity is of the logical-conceptual kind), according to whom the supervenient mental property is a functional role that is realised by the corresponding subvenient physical property. If the necessity is merely nomic (causal, physical), one simply rules out possible worlds *compatible with the laws of nature* wherein there are organisms with the relevant lower-level physical properties, but without the corresponding mental properties. This is the "naturalistic dualism" famously defended by Chalmers (1996, p. 162), who is also a "non-reductive functionalist" (1996, p. 229) in that, according to him, the appropriate functional organization, even in the absence of organic matter, gives rise with physical necessity to mental (phenomenal) properties (which makes room for multiple realizability), although such properties should not be identified with functional roles.

References

Bozzi, P. (2002). Fenomenologia sperimentale [Experimental Phenomenology]. *Teorie & Modelli, 2–3*, 13–48 [Chapter 1 in the present anthology].
Chalmers, D. J. (1996). *The Conscious Mind*. Oxford: Oxford University Press.
Churchland, P. M. (1988). *Matter and Consciousness*. Cambridge, MA: the MIT Press.
Crane, T. (2011). The problems of perception. In E.N. Zalta (ed.), *The Stanford Encyclopedia of Philosophy*, Spring 2011 edition. http://plato.stanford.edu/archives/spr2011/entries/perception-problem/.
Kim, J. (1998). *Philosophy of Mind*. Boulder, CO: Westview Press.
Place, U.T. (1956). Is consciousness a brain process? *British Journal of Psychology, 47*, 44–50.
Putnam, H. (1967). Psychological predicates. In W.H. Capitan and D.D. Merrill, (Eds). *Art, Mind and Religion* (pp. 37–48). Pittsburgh: University of Pittsburgh Press. Reprinted as "The Nature of Mental States" in N. Block (ed.) (1980) *Readings in the Philosophy of Psychology*, vol. I, pp. 223–231. Cambridge, MA: Harvard University Press.
Smart, J.J.C. (1959). Sensations and brain processes. *Philosophical Review, 68*, 141–156.
Stubenberg, L. (2010). Neutral monism. In E.N. Zalta (ed.), *The Stanford Encyclopedia of Philosophy*, Spring 2011 Edition http://plato.stanford.edu/archives/spr2010/entries/neutral-monism/.
Vicario, G. B. (2001). *Psicologia Generale [General Psychology]*. Roma-Bari, Italy: Laterza.

7

FIVE VARIETIES OF STIMULUS ERROR[1]

Translated by Roberto Casati

1.   In this paper I aim to set out some of the developments of the concept of "stimulus error" derivable from the definition given to this notion by Köhler in the fifth chapter of his *Gestalt Psychology*.[1]

The definition runs as follows: "In psychology we have often been warned against the stimulus error, i.e., against the danger of confusing our knowledge about the physical conditions of sensory experience with this experience as such".

In pursuing the discussion, I shall stick closely to this definition, interpreting its literal meaning only by way of concepts explicitly theorized by Köhler and Koffka[2], or in the standard usage of these concepts in the context of experimental research by psychologists trained in the Gestalt tradition.

The need to be literal in accounting for the words in question follows from the fact that, within different theoretical settings, different versions of the concept of "stimulus error" have been given, and that these are so different from each other that one of them, among many reported by Boring in his essay on the topic,[3] says exactly the opposite of what Köhler meant with his own.[4]

As for the need to interpret expressions such as "physical conditions of sensory experience" or "experience as such" by appeal only to the concepts employed in the formulations of classical Gestalt theory, or, as the case may be, to the use we make of these expressions while designing or discussing experiments (that is, on occasions where these concepts are tools, rather than objects of criticism), this will come clear as we proceed.

In the discussion in the following pages, the task is to extract consequences that are already logically available in the premise, that is in the definition of the "stimulus error"; now, along the way, it will be necessary to turn expressions of quite broad meaning (such as "physical conditions of sensory experience" and "experience as such") into more specific statements into which Köhler's text can be analysed, by appeal to the premises on which the meaning of those expressions is implicitly grounded. It is clear, however, that these premises will always belong to the same system of concepts – lest we lose the validity and the meaningfulness of the operation.

This caveat is not as idle as it may appear. When he/she has finished reading these pages, the reader will easily see that the argument as a whole could not stand up had we included in the physical conditions of experience, say, the "proximal stimuli" in the sense given by Gibson[5] or the "physical objects" in the sense in which they are understood by Tolman;[6] as to the "experience as such", if we happened to believe, following Tolman,[7] that is a problem for philosophers or not a problem at all, it is clear that the whole discussion could not even get started.

In short, we will be happy to accept a certain number of concepts belonging to the doctrinal corpus of Gestalt theory without subjecting them to criticism, even if they may appear questionable in their formulation or in their substance.

2.   If we grant the foregoing conditions, the term "physical conditions of sensory experience" must be interpreted broadly: it has as its referent – as Köhler stressed time and again[8] – everything that happens in the space and time of physics and is in relation with a given perceptual experience: everything, starting from the physical source of energy, to the processes that we posit in the brain as the immediate physiological counterpart of that perception. The world of physiology is a world of events that take place in the space and time of physics and obey the fundamental laws of physics; it is therefore part of the physical conditions in question.

This very large class of facts can be so divided and ordered, in line with the treatises of Gestalt psychology:

a.   the source of energy, or "distal stimulus" (a vibrating bell, an object that reflects or emits light and, at the very least, the vibrating surface of a bell that determines the formation of the air compression waves, or the surfaces of an illuminated object, which thanks to their physico-chemical properties absorb certain wavelengths of the electromagnetic spectrum but reflect others, etc.);
b.   the propagation field of the energy in question, or at least a portion of it: the portion between the source and the peripheral sensory organ directly exposed to its action;
c.   the local effects produced by this energy on the parts of the peripheral organs that react to it, transforming it into other forms of energy; that is, according to Koffka, the "proximal stimulus": "the excitations to which the light rays (. . .) give rise";[9]
d.   the processes affecting the afferent pathways: i.e. the operation of the information channels that connect the peripheral organs to the centre;
e.   the "silent" organization, which – variously linked to the arrival of information from the outside – takes place in the nervous system without the subject having direct experience of it: without, that is, its being instantiated as "experience as such";
f.   the "manifest" processes, by definition isomorphic with the "experience as such", i.e. to the fact directly observed by the subject.

These are six moments or stages (whatever our reservations as to their demarcation or definition) that contribute to make up the physical conditions of the experience.

As to the "experience as such", it is formed by the set of all phenomenal objects considered at a given moment, and by all the phenomenally explicit relationships that hold among them. It is the world of "appearances" – if we are inclined to say so, albeit with great impropriety – that Descartes himself, in his moments of deepest methodological despair, could not cast into doubt. Of course, by definition, none of the events that take place in the space and time of physics can figure in the "experience as such".

Remember the little footnote written by Köhler in *The Place of Value in a World of Facts*: "A short time ago K. Lewin made the statement that the objects of physics are experienced no less directly than those of psychology" (*Principles of Topological Psychology*, 1936, p. 20). I hope that Professor Lewin will find an opportunity to explain by what argument he supports this opinion.[10]

The "physical conditions of sensory experience" and the "experience as such" occupy two mutually exclusive regions. The stimulus error consists in taking some part of direct experience for one or another of the items that make up – in the list above – its physical and physiological concomitants.

More precisely (given that in experimental research on the perception we have very often to do with observers' reports, that is, with the descriptions that they provide to the researcher): the "stimulus error" consists in taking a description of what is known or imagined about one or more constituent moments of the physical conditions of a given perceptual experience as if it were the phenomenological description of that very experience.

3.   At this point it will be clear that there are as many varieties of the stimulus error as there are different possible confusions between the describable properties of an object of experience and the properties related to any of the stages listed above.

Of course, not all the stages lend themselves equally easily to this sort of confusion. To rehearse an example that I have discussed elsewhere when dealing with this topic,[11] let us consider an extreme case. I show someone a glass, and ask him/her to describe what he/she sees, and I'm told "an immense aggregate of atoms" or "a bundle of light rays". This is certainly a way of committing the error we are talking about. My partner does not provide me with a phenomenological description, but he/she utters some things that he/she "knows" about the glass or about the type of information that his/her eyes receive from the glass. Nevertheless it is very rare to come across stimulus errors that are so subtly sophisticated. The two stages (inner structure of the "distal stimulus" and "wave propagation in the medium") are not likely to give rise to confusion. Others lend themselves much better to confusion.

In general, the possibility of mistaking the perceptual fact with the corresponding physical conditions holds only for some of the aspects of the perceptual fact, and only for some of the items listed in *a-f*.

Let me explain. Rightly or wrongly (but in my opinion much more wrongly than rightly), when discussing perceptual experiments we normally use language that suggests that it is possible to compare properties of phenomenal objects with properties of physical objects: we speak of a square "distal stimulus", and we then check if it can be seen, perceived as a square also in certain other conditions that we have already set up. This type of operation clearly reveals the presupposition that it is possible to relate and compare the squareness as a physical property of an object, a property which is purely operational, with perceived squareness. The everyday practice of research requires this approach and this language because it is extremely convenient and does not create theoretical difficulties in experimentation. Indeed, what we do is compare the results of some measurements carried out on the object (for example, with a ruler and compasses), the outcome of which is well summarized in the phrase "is square" as suitable for a certain phenomenal property, which can co-vary with certain conditions in the field. Already in his day Helmholtz had warned psychologists against believing that perceived objects are the *images* of the corresponding physical objects, and are *similar* to the latter. He suggested that they are rather *signs*, with no necessary resemblance to what they are signs of.[12] However, the language of the laboratory does not take this into account and allows you to say "it is square, but it is not seen as square" or "it is square, and it is seen as square".

In this, and the point is crucial, the language of the lab is in agreement with the language of the experimental subjects, that is with ordinary language, which is not constrained by highly elaborated scientific theories, but rather calls on a crude dualistic philosophy of reality that is extremely effective as a prerequisite for finding one's way in the world. "It seems so, but it is not", "in reality it must be so, but in this context it appears thus". And often, on the basis of this philosophy, the naïve subject (precisely in order not to be regarded as naïve) delivers reports that are affected by the stimulus error: suspecting that the experimenter is trying to deceive him/her, he/she tries to trace up from the object of phenomenological description to the "true" object, and sometimes he/she gives a description that is close to the one which can be made on the basis of the measurements performed on the material.

Thus, at the intersection of the laboratory language and ordinary language, it is possible and easy (despite the theoretical difficulties) to confuse some aspect of the experience as such with some aspects that are operationally attributable to one of items *a-f* of section 2; and in our example of the square, with a macroscopic property of the "distal stimulus".

It should be noted that this possibility of transferring attributes from one to the other of the two mutually exclusive regions – that of "experience as such" and that of "physical conditions of sensory experience" – is unlikely to affect all the attributes of an object of experience. It is probably limited to a narrow category of properties, including shape, size, speed, number etc. I have not tried to draw up a complete list of these properties, but I have tried, in the past, to analyse the reasons for this transferability.[13] In short, there are phenomenal properties of objects that – once expressed in appropriate linguistic form – may give rise to the construction of a more or less extended formal system suitable to represent models of relations that, with equally good approximation, can be referred both to phenomenal objects and to ideal objects, according to whose type we are led to imagine the transphenomenal facts.

Almost all the examples we shall discuss in paragraph 5 shall concern shape and size as properties transferred from phenomenal objects to some of the moments listed in *a-f*; but is not to be excluded that it is also possible to find other equally apt examples, for all that they are based on properties of different kinds.

All the examples I shall present will be drawn from the field of visual perception.

4.   We have seen that when committing a "stimulus error" it is possible to attribute a property of a perceived object, on the basis of what we know from the "distal stimulus" (section 2, point *a*). In what sense can we transfer an analogous property, for example squareness, to the events mentioned in point *b*? In the case of vision, this will be the case of the rays reflected by a surface: that is, that beam of rays that, once reflected, arrive at the lens and, refracted, end up – through the vitreous humour – producing photochemical reactions in the photosensitive histological units of the retina.

If it is reflected by a chromatically homogeneous surface of square form, such a bundle of rays does indeed give rise, after the deflection of the rays by the lens, to a geometrical locus determined by the class of all the foci (one for each point in which the reflective surface is ideally decomposable) which is "of square shape". If the eye is normal and the subject, when looking, focuses on the chromatically homogeneous square surface, this class of all the foci within the eye constitutes the final section of the bundle of rays carrying electromagnetic energy – indeed, it is there that this energy is converted into a photochemical process.

This does not in the least mean that the wave train carried the squareness to the eye. (The polemic of Gestalt psychologists against this temptation is well known, and there is no need to rehearse it here.) Instead, it simply means that: 1) if we reproduce the situation just described using a camera having, in place of film, a frosted glass, we see on this glass a chromatically homogeneous square 2) that elementary optics gives an exhaustive account of this fact 3) that from this point of view, the eye can be really compared with the camera.

A subject can master these notions and, instead of describing what he/she sees, can report – on the basis of them – what he/she thinks is happening to the rays of light in his/her eye. We may call this second step, which is a possible occasion for a "stimulus error", by the name "constellation of stimuli".

The "constellation of stimuli" should not be confused with the "proximal stimulus" (point c). In the case now under discussion it is the final section of a train of electromagnetic waves; the proximal stimulus – accepting, as we do, Koffka's definition – is the set of photochemical processes triggered by the arrival of waves at the retina, "the excitations to which the light rays (. . .) give rise". The set of these processes is the retinal image, which, although it can not be said to possess any kind of shape properties – as explained very well and very extensively by Köhler[14] – since it is constituted by a set of processes that are mutually isolated and independent, can nevertheless be thought of as a myriad of events, distributed within an area of square shape.

This is a further possible occasion for a "stimulus error". (It should be noted that in the case of the retinal image, we may even have the opportunity to commit two errors: 1) by attributing properties of the retinal image to the phenomenal fact, we commit the "stimulus error" 2) by attributing properties of the phenomenal fact to the retinal image we commit the "experience error".[15]

Point d hardly lends itself to the possibility of transferring properties to the phenomenal datum; it is difficult to imagine, for example, how the processes of nerve conduction in the optic nerve can be thought of as having shape, even if they are carrying information for the construction of a shape.

On point e there can be no confusion, if only because the silent organization is largely hypothetical. On point f there can be no confusion either, since by definition, in the logic of Gestaltists, according to the postulate of isomorphism, to each property of the phenomenal object there corresponds a phenomenal process, or a mode of a process, in the central nervous system.

In the light of these considerations, we now see that the temptation to attribute to the experience itself features that that we may consider as typical of the physical conditions connected to it originates mainly from three specific moments in which those conditions are articulated: the "distal stimulus", the "constellation of stimuli", the "proximal stimulus". We shall denote these three moments with the initials DS, CS and PS (the phenomenal object will be indicated as Φ) respectively.

5.   Before going further, it may be useful to summarise the points in the foregoing paragraphs as follows. Attributing properties of the phenomenal world to the world of physics is already a rather questionable procedure. But it does happen: it happens in the framework of common

sense and in the framework of the language used in laboratories. Thus, a further difficulty may arise: the physical events that are part the physical conditions of experience are imagined in phenomenal terms; are described as such; and then these descriptions are produced as phenomenological descriptions of that experience. Not all physical experiences lend themselves to this, but three particular items do: the "distal stimulus" (DS), the "constellation of stimuli" (CS) and the "proximal stimulus" (PS).

In a nutshell, it is indeed possible to say: "DS is square; given its position in front of me CS is a trapezoid and the same holds for PS, and I see ɸ square, tilted". Had I been unwise (as some philosophers have been in arguing that when I look at a coin in a position that is not straight on I "see an ellipse") I could have said "what matters is PS: therefore, I see a trapezoid". Or: "DS stays still but PS takes place in different places, at different times, on the retina (i.e., I move my eye); yet it stays still"; nevertheless I could say: "DS stays still, I know that CS causes PS in different places on the retina, at different times: hence Φ moves", etc.

How many combinations of this type can be found in experiments performed in psychology of perception? We shall try to give an overview here.

First of all let us draw up a table of the theoretical combinations. In this table, in the column under Φ we indicate the existence of a certain property belonging to the phenomenal datum with the "+" sign. In the other three columns, under PS, CS, DS, we shall denote by a "+" sign the assignment of one and the same property to one or another of the three moments indicated, and with the sign "−" the non-assignment of that property. As there are four terms at play, and as we do not take into account the cases of non-attribution of Φ given that they are symmetrical to the cases of attribution, there are eight combinations, thus arranged:

TABLE 7.1

	Φ	*PS*	*CS*	*DS*
1	+	+	+	+
2	+	+	+	−
3	+	+	−	−
4	+	−	−	−
5	+	−	−	+
6	+	−	+	+
7	+	+	−	+
8	+	−	+	−

If "the stimulus error" consists in mistaking the properties of one or more of the elements that constitute the physical conditions of a given experience for the properties of that experience as such, in principle there are seven varieties of stimulus error, given that the first line does not constitute a case of "error".

We come now to the examples.

Case 1 is trivial. Suppose we have before us, straight on, the usual chromatically homogeneous square, and that we take "squareness" as the critical property. Then we can say, in the above-discussed sense:

TABLE 7.2

$\Phi+$	$SP+$	$CS+$	$SD+$
Square	Square	Square	Square

(If we want to be through and through logical, here the stimulus error would be to say that Φ is square not because we see it as such, but because we know that in DS, or CS, or PS or in PS and CS or in DS and PS etc., it is a square. But as we are not in a position to judge the intentions of the subject, it is not an error.)

Case 2 can be presented with the following example: let us set in front of us a rotating Ames trapezoid, but let us keep it static and positioned so that, from where we are, it looks like a rectangle (thus taking care that all the cues to its inclination relative to the plane which is straight on to the observer are suppressed). In this situation:

TABLE 7.3

$F+$	$SP+$	$CS+$	$DS-$
Rectangle	Rectangle	Rectangle	Trapezoid

(Here the stimulus error would arise from saying, "I see a trapezoid" because I know that there's a trapezoid over there: this is the typical case.)

Case 3 can be exemplified as follows: let us set up in very simple form a case of permanence of the image on the retina by moving a lit cigarette in the dark, in front of the eyes of an observer; let the cigarette trace a circle at such a speed that allows the closing of the visible light trail (Talbot's law). The distal stimulus – the embers of the cigarette – is grossly punctiform, i.e. it is a small disk. Beyond the lens, in the eye of the observer, the rays emitted from the embers converge at one point, the focus. But the photochemical processes in the retina, having a certain inertia in switching off when PS no longer activates them, taken together form a practically stationary process, insofar as it is continuously reactivated, making a circular "picture", and we see a luminous circle. Thus:

TABLE 7.4

$\Phi+$	$SP+$	$CS-$	$SD-$
Stationary circle	Stationary circle	Moving point	Moving point

Case 4 is that of almost all optical-geometric illusions. We shall illustrate it with the illusion of Müller-Lyer: the two lines, to which are attached the well-known appendages, are measurably equal on the paper where they are drawn, are projectively equal as a constellation of stimuli, and they give rise – on the retina – to processes of equal size (so far as we know), but are seen as having different lengths. Thus:

TABLE 7.5

$\Phi+$	SP-	CS-	SD-
Of different length	Equal	Equal	Equal

Case 5 is represented generally by constancy phenomena. In front of me there is a square slanted in depth relative to the straight on plane, and indeed I see a slanted square, although I know that from the projective point of view and from the point of view of the retinal image they are trapezoidal areas:

TABLE 7.6

$\Phi+$	PS-	CS-	DS+
Square (slanted)	Trapezoid	Trapezoid	Square (slanted)

Case 6 can be illustrated as follows: suppose that we look with just one eye at a thin line drawn on a homogeneous background. Furthermore, suppose that a part of the line (excluding the ends) falls exactly on the blind spot; as is well known, we see the line unbroken. There is a line as distal stimulus, and there is a line from the projective point of view; but from the retinal point of view there are two segments of processes, for the area of the blind spot is inert. And we see a line. So:

TABLE 7.7

$\Phi+$	SP-	CS+	DS+
A line	Two segments	A line	A line

I have long sought for suitable examples to illustrate cases 7 and 8, but I have not found them – neither with regard to vision nor to other sensory modalities. I believe that this is largely due to my lack of imagination or to the fact that not all areas of research in the field of perception are equally familiar to me. I would beg the reader interested in this kind of problem to inform me of any situations suitable to fill the following two schemes so far left empty:

TABLE 7.8

Φ+	SP+	CS-	SD+
Φ+	SP-	CS+	SD-

So long as these lines are unfilled, we may count five logically distinguishable varieties of the stimulus error:

- Assigning to the phenomenal object properties belonging to the "distal stimulus";
- Assigning to the phenomenal object properties that can be said to belong to the "distal stimulus" and/or the "constellation of stimuli";
- Assigning to the phenomenal object properties that can be said to belong to the "distal stimulus" and/or the "constellation of stimuli" and/or the "proximal stimulus";
- Assigning to the phenomenal object properties belonging to the "constellation of stimuli" and/or the "proximal stimulus";
- Assigning to the phenomenal object properties that we know to belong to the "proximal stimulus".

It is important to stress that the varieties are really (not merely formally) different as a careful analysis of the examples can prove.

Of course, all this makes sense only under the conditions set out in the first sections of this work: in particular, it makes sense only if one agrees to subdivide the series of events "physical object (r) central processes" into the stages discussed above (of course there may be many other ways to cut the series at equally well-defined joints), and if one accepts – as do both the language of common sense and that used in the laboratory – that one can describe in the same terms both phenomenal objects and transphenomenal objects.

In any case, this much seems certain to me: that the distinctions among these different varieties of the "stimulus error" – taking into account the concepts fashioned by Köhler and Koffka so as to develop an interpretation of the transphenomenal, physical, world, in relation to the world of experience – came into being at the precise moment that Köhler wrote the definition given at the beginning, and they are entirely contained in it.

Finally we ought to stress a fact that is absolutely clear when we look at the matrix and consider line by line the examples discussed: despite the lack of examples for lines 7 and 8 (a lack that is perhaps provisional) the distribution matrix of cases suggests that – from a logical point of view – the phenomenal observables, the perceptual events, are *independent* both of the distal stimuli and of what takes place in the eye and on the retina.

Notes

1 Köhler, W. (1947). *Gestalt Psychology*, p. 162. New York: Liveright Publishing Corporation.
2 Koffka, K. (ed.) (1955). *Principles of Gestalt Psychology*, pp. 97–81, 96–98, 224–228. London: Routledge & Kegan Paul.
3 Boring, E. C. (1963). The stimulus error. In R.I. Watson and D.T. Campbell (Eds), *History, Psychology and Science. Selected Papers of Edwing G. Boring*, pp. 255–273. New York: Wiley.
4 Ibid., p. 256; according to Titchener, saying: "This package is heavier than this one" is to commit the stimulus error: you should say "this complex of organic sensations is more intense than that", everything else is interpretation, 'meaning' ".

5 Gibson, J. J. (1966). *The Senses Considered as Perceptual Systems*. Boston: Houghton Mifflin Company. See also Johansson, G. (1970). On theories for visual spatial perception. A letter to Gibson. *Scandinavian Journal of Psychology*, 67–79 (Gibson and response).

6 Tolman, E.C. (1951). Psychology versus immediate experience. In E. C. Tolman (ed.), *Collected Papers in Psychology*, pp. 95–114. Berkeley, CA: University of California Press.

7 Ibid.

8 Köhler, W. (1938). *The Place of Values in a World of Facts*. New York: Liveright.

9 Koffka, K., op. cit., p. 80.

10 Köhler, W., op. cit., p.143. See also Köhler, W. (1966). A task for philosophers. In P. K. Feyerabend and G. Maxwell (Eds). *Mind, Matter and Method: Essays in Philosophy of Science in Honour of Herbert Feigl*, pp.70–91. Minneapolis, MN: University of Minnesota Press.

11 Bozzi, P. (1969). *Unità, identità, causalità* [*Unity, Identity, Causality*]. Bologna, Italy: Cappelli, p. 83.

12 von Helmholtz, H. (1878). Die Thatsachen in der Wahrnehmung. In *Vorträge und Reden*, vol II, Braunschweig: Vieweg, 1896, p. 225.

13 Bozzi, P. (1989). Descrizioni fenomenologiche e descrizioni fisico-geometriche. [Phenomenological descriptions and physical-geometrical descriptions]. In *Fenomenologia sperimentale* [*Experimental Phenomenology*]. Bologna, Italy: il Mulino [Chapter 9 in the present anthology].

14 W. Köhler, *Gestalt Psychology*, cit., pp. 161–162, 180, 186, 237.

15 W. Köhler, op. cit., p. 162.

COMMENTS ON FIVE VARIETIES OF STIMULUS ERROR

Roberto Casati[1]

In the paper about the stimulus error Bozzi struggles with a net of exquisitely conceptual issues concerning perception and its objects. In a rather classical way, he highlights six steps in the causal pathway leading from the physical object to the experience thereof; the physical object itself, an event in the informational medium, the proximal stimulus, the flow of information in the brain, its processing, and the experience itself. A stimulus error occurs when a researcher attributes properties of any of these steps to the structure of the experience. Thus stated, of course, it is not completely clear what the exact import of the error is supposed to be. Say, we construe the physical object as square, and we mistakenly describe the experience thereof as square? This would be a category mistake – experiences are not square, they are as-of square objects. Or, to mention a possibility Bozzi himself discusses, I look at the glass in front of me and I utter the sentence: "I see an aggregate of atoms". This is according to him an error; however this utterance is not strictly speaking false, the glass is an aggregate of atoms, and if I see the glass, I do see an aggregate of atoms (only I do not see it *as* a bunch of atoms, or I do not have an experience as of a bunch of atoms); Bozzi just happened to write before people recognized the difference between epistemic and non-epistemic seeing. His main concern, however, is not ordinary parlance about perception. He might have agreed with Strawson (1979), who defended the *transparency* of perception, registered in the way we talk about it: we do say that we see tables and chairs, not the light, not our reaction to light, not our brain processes, and not our experiences. He might have agreed with Heider's solution to Meinong's problem (why do we have the impression of seeing objects, and say we see objects, rather than any other element of the causal chain leading to visual experience, even elements that are further back, such as the Sun, that does, after all, cause the object to be seen – see Casati, 2000): relevant structured co-variation is the key to explaining why we do not register media or any other intermediate step – they co-vary with experience, but not in a relevant way. He may have not disliked joining forces with phenomenologists who defended some variant of conceptual bracketing (*epoché*), methodologically necessary to provide candid descriptions of visual experience, without which there would be no usable *explananda* in psychological theory. But it looks as if his main concern was lab talk, the imprecise, biased descriptions of experiments. Although unregimented terms may be useful in communicating with colleagues, and may be innocent when recognized as provisional descriptive tools, they tend to stabilize their un-innocent ontological commitments, and disseminate confusions when they leak from the lab into larger theoretical enterprises, such as philosophical characterizations of the perceptual world. More poignantly, loose lab talk can bias the response of the subject, who may want to show off by introducing into her report some bits of knowledge, in a curious dialectic with the experimenters (who is fooling whom?).

Here is an illustration of the problems Bozzi addresses. Put a uniformly white sheet of paper in sunlight, and have an object cast a shadow on it. How do you describe the scene? The first description can be very rough. "There is an object, a sheet of paper, and a shadow." Now you, an experimenter, would like to know more. "How many colours is the paper?" You may want to elicit the answer that the paper is mono-chromatic, that the shadow is an accident, as you are after some aspects of colour constancy. The subject thinks she knows better, and says "two: here is a grey area, there a white area." She can even put a grey piece of cardboard in full light next to the shaded area, and claim that the two greys match. The subject-experimenter dialectic goes on. The experimenter retaliates by presenting the Adelson demonstration (Adelson, 2005), a *picture* of an object casting a shadow on a grey-and-white chessboard. This time the subject is dumbfounded: she may be completely unwilling to say that a white square in the shade matches a grey square in full light. Now is the experimenter's turn to convince her of the match, by juxtaposing an appropriate piece of cardboard to the image of the grey square in the light, and then to the image of the white square in the shade.

There is a lot of loose talk here in using the words "colour", "grey", "white", "square", especially as we are moving from ecological demonstrations to pictures of ambient scenes. When calling the shaded part of the sheet "grey" aren't we thinking of a picture of the sheet? thereby smuggling a property of the informational medium into the description of the experience. Indeed, more cautious experimenters would like to use concepts that disambiguate the description, to an extent: "grey" may characterize both *luminance* (a proximal or medial measurement) and *reflectance* (a distal measurement), but the question remains of why the normative use of "grey" in characterizing perceptual experience is set to reflectance and not to luminance – fastidious philosophers may even suspect some question-begging here. But there is no begging of the question. Not only we should not deprive ourselves of loose talk, if this has pragmatic virtues, we should always set for the big picture. We are not making a perceptual mistake if we do not see that the two squares are of the same colour; we are rather making an error of the stimulus. The conceptual power of the "stimulus tool" bears fruits: Adelson's "illusion" *is not an illusion*: the colours of the two different squares are seen as different, as they are. Shadow perception is in part a mechanism for discounting luminance differences that are caused by shadows, and for retrieving the relevant identities of reflectance. You will call it an illusion only if you construe your visual system as just measuring luminance. It is not: it computes reflectance. The appropriate normativity of "error" talk flows from a characterization of the performance of perceptual systems. Rather than uncovering question begging, it is reflective equilibrium that is summoned here, between untutored descriptions and theoretical characterizations. No one said the exercise was simple.

Note

1   Casati's work is supported by grants ANR-10-LABX-0087 IEC; ANR-10-IDEX-0001-02 PSL.

References

Adelson, E.H. (2005). Checkershadow illusion. http://persci.mit.edu/gallery/checkershadow Retrieved 15 Nov 2017.

Casati, R. (2000). Une note sur les milieu perceptifs. In P. Livet (ed.), *De la Perception à l'Action*, pp. 147–153. Paris: Vrin.

Strawson, P.F. (1979). Perception and its objects. In G.F. Macdonald (ed.), *Perception and Identity*, pp. 41–60. London: Palgrave.

8

SEEING AS

Translated by Kevin Mulligan

My present aim is not exegesis of Wittgenstein or his philosophy. Rather, I wish to look at some problems in the theory of perception that absorbed Wittgenstein's attention during one period of his life. More than anything else, it is a small part of a journey I have had the occasion to take with Wittgenstein, taking advantage of his reflections, which are closely connected with problems I have worked on over many decades as a student of visual and auditory perception in Experimental Psychology.

Sometimes the space in a laboratory turns out to be a little cramped to deal with all the theoretical questions which research raises or revives. It is not easy, in particular today, to find colleagues ready to discuss imaginatively and without prospect of return problems not belonging to any particular territory, at the borders between science, philosophy and other rather indistinct interests.

But it is precisely in the laboratory that doubts and aporiae come up about the relations between seeing and interpreting, about the expressive qualities rooted in visual and acoustic percepts, about the role these play – together with language – in communication between the experimenter and the subjects he/she works with, as well as in the everday practise of willed or casual interobservation.

I like to imagine having met this extraordinary observer and ingenious Socratic inquirer, having gone for a walk with him one day, to discuss and show each other sketches, figures and objects worthy of attentive scrutiny in good light, until the moment arrives when each of us makes his own way. From this imagined encounter, I have taken away for my own use a good number of very beautiful lessons.

Let us consider what is said about a phenomenon like this: seeing the figure now as an F, now as a mirror image of an F.

I want to ask: what constitutes seeing the figure now like this, now another way? – Do I really see something different every time? Or do I merely interpret what I see in a different way? – I am inclined to say the first. But why? Well, interpreting is an action. It may, for example, consist in somebody's saying "That's supposed to be an F"; or he doesn't say it, but when he copies the sign he replaces it by an F; or he considers: "What may that be?

It'll be an F that the writer slipped with". – Seeing isn't an action but a state. (A grammatical remark). And if I have never read the figure as anything but "F", never considered what it might be, we shall say that I see it as an F; if, that is, we know that it can also be seen differently.

For how have we arrived at the concept of "seeing this as that"? On what occasions does it get formed, is it felt as a need? (Very frequently, when we are talking about a work of art). Where, for example, what is in question is a phrasing by the eye or ear. We say: "You must hear these bars as an introduction", "You must hear it as in this key", "Once you have seen this figure as. . .it is difficult to see it otherwise", but also "I hear the French «ne. . . pas» as a negation with two parts to it, not as a step" etc. Now, is it a real case of seeing or hearing? Well, that's what we call it; we react with these words in particular situations. And in turn we react to these words in with particular actions.[1]

Perhaps it is worthwhile, before anything else, to free the page of written text in order to observe Wittgenstein's F without the constrictions that might interfere with the exploration of its figural properties:

Reducing the visibility of the double aspect suggested by our author risks, right from the start, preventing the reader from seeing the terms of the problem, which is not a problem of words but concerns the internal structure of the object *under observation*. I use the expression "under observation" in italics because the terms of the problem emerge from the black marks present on the page only during attentive observation. The question could not have been raised without the presence of the figure, for example by inviting the reader to imagine it or to think of it (what, at bottom, is the objection to saying: "imagine a capital F with its two horizontal bars sticking out left and right of an axis which is not quite vertical but somewhat inclined to the right"?); or by inviting the reader to construct an arbitrary representation and by trusting to his/her evident knowledge of the alphabet for the rest of the discussion. The theme has to be developed in the presence of the observable under discussion. The F here is not a demonstrative schema but what Goethe, at the beginning of the *Theory of Colours*, calls a "necessary instrument", referring to his coloured illustrations, which are not made in order to represent concepts but to be looked at, in so far as they are the ultimate aim of his inquiry.

Unfortunately Wittgenstein's F was not drawn felicitously and leaves more room to the imagination than to vision. I hope that my enlarged and slightly modified version, above all because it is isolated on a white page, succeeds in getting closer to the aim our author has in mind.

Now it is an F. But, if we look carefully, it is also a mirror image of F.

Well then: "Do I really see something different in the two cases? Or do I merely interpret what I see in a different way?". If the figure had been drawn very badly, if for example its horizontal bars had extended to the left only a little, then it would be necessary to "interpret" the statement alluding to the multistability of the figure in question. The fact that the drawing can be improved for our purposes already indicates that we have here a "seeing" rather than an "interpreting". We can project a series of F's in which the first one only allows itself with difficulty to be "interpreted" as facing left, and the last one presents itself equally well in both directions (except for that slight unnaturalness which comes from our custom of following written texts from left to right).

A specimen of writing in the style of Leonardo da Vinci may help us here:

Now that we are able to observe the phenomenon, and not merely to consider it in a distracted fashion as most readers do, we can read with profit the following assertions: "I am inclined to say the first . . . "interpreting is an action . . . seeing is not an action but a state" (*keine Handlung, sondern ein Zustand. (Grammatische Bemerkung)*).

The act of interpreting unfolds over time, perhaps a very brief time, and is organized in sentences which may also be very brief and fleeting. Usually, interpreting requires reflection and language; it is always a little like interpreting a text, the intentions of a speaker, a Latin inscription or an article of the penal code. The process need not last long, it may be a sudden intuition, more rapid than the sentence capable of expressing it. But it must be something that works on something else: in German *deuten*, to interpret, to explain, is closely related to *deuteln*, to quibble. Wittgenstein gives as examples of what goes along with interpretations: "it ought to be an F", with a margin of doubt, "what ever can that be?". But it is not necessary to say anything: the gesture of eliminating the sign and replacing it with a very clear F is the manifestation of a doubt followed by an interpretation and its expression. Of course, the psychologist or philosopher may say that when I see a horse I "interpret" that it is a horse, because there are really only sensations, *features* or *sense data*; but this way of talking – quite apart from being based on false presuppositions, some of which we shall meet in what follows – deviates in large measure from correct grammar, or better, it does not belong to the grammar of "interpret": it has its origins in the transfer of a verb which has an excellent use in everyday life to a suppositious niche in the activities of the mind, which no-one is in a position to verify nor, indeed, to imagine. In that dark hole anything can happen and many other verbs may be found appropriate so long as the corresponding actions are made completely unconscious. (It is the limbo of the unverifiable.)

But it is clear that with the verb "interpret" Wittgenstein is indicating actions extended over time which are both observable and identifiable. That this is so follows from the fact that he often contrasts the grammar of the word "interpret" and that of the word "state" (*Zustand*: state, also condition, in the sense in which one says "in good conditions", "in a condition of inferiority"; that is, again, "in a good state", "in a state of inferiority"). What this grammar is supposed to be can easily be seen from certain passages in Wittgenstein's *Remarks* in which he mentions "the different states of water – meaning thereby its temperature, the velocity with which it flows, its colour" (*RPP*, I, §130), or asks "why a law of nature should not correlate an initial and a final state of a system but hide the intermediate state?" (*RPP*, I, §909). That a system under observation may be considered a state in this sense, even if it is constituted by psychological ingredients, is shown by the section where we read: "when I get to know his mood it is as though I get to know the state of his body (his temperature, for example)" (*RPP*, I, §890).

It should also be noted that in this text, Wolfgang Köhler, along with Goethe and William James, is the author quoted most frequently; and that the chapters of Köhler's *Gestalt Psychology* most used by Wittgenstein refer in their bibliographies with polite insistence to another work by Köhler: *Die physischen Gestalten in Ruhe und in stationären Zustand*, published in 1919. It is unlikely that Wittgenstein did not notice this German title, in spite of his well-known indifference to bibliographical matters. Köhler's book deals with a variety of physical states and develops a point of view (the well-known postulate of isomorphism), according to which the objects of perception are systems present to consciousness in various "states", which are the observable face of correlated physical states of the brain. The chapters of Köhler's *Gestalt Psychology* that Wittgenstein studied most closely have a a great deal to say on this subject.

Thus whereas "interpretation" is an activity or action, seeing corresponds to having present an observable state in the field of direct experience. This is the totality of the features to be met with in the object in the course of observing it; it is neither more nor less than what is believed by all those who do not formulate philosophical problems, who are ignorant of the conjectures of psychologists of perception, and so who are not subject to the temptations which today we may call constructivist and which the day before yesterday were more or less idealist temptations.

Let us consider the following three drawings:

(a) is, once again, Wittgenstein's F; (b) is one of the most classical situations in which visual inversion of the figure–ground relation occurs, that is, a typical multistable figure; (c) is a sketch of something.

With a little exercise we have learnt to see the F (a) as facing right or facing left, now in one way, now in another. Prolonged observation of figure (b) leads inevitably to discovery of its multistability, an internal property of the system of edges that brings it about; the desire to see the cup or the profiles certainly helps the inversion to come about but it may also be of no help to obtain it; and sometimes the inversion occurs even the observer has no particular preference. Thus the intention to see is correlated only weakly with the phenomenon and is certainly not necessary. The same may be said about a suggestion made in the following sort of way: if someone suggests to you "the cup" or "the profiles", the mention of these objects may not make you glimpse this or that in the system under observation. But sometimes the suggestion seems to be decisive.

In (b) we have a change of state of a very pronounced type: the passage from one state to the other is characterised by an instantaneous flicker of something inside the figure, like a brief flash, and suddenly the other state is already present, as though it had always been there. In the case of the F there is also a change of state, but without our noticing the flash of the restructuring; the new direction of the F (indeed, given the tilt of the supporting line it is as if the letter, facing now to the right, now to the left, were slightly to lose its balance) appears evident, but it does not emerge from a crisis in the way it was seen before. The change of state in the two cases is evidence that seeing is a state. (Wittgenstein's starting point is well chosen, because the observation of a change of state that cannot be subsumed under a coarse physicalist interpretation, as the rapid substitution of one image for another might be, shows that "seeing" is a state and not the physical interpretation of what one sees. It is also well chosen because of its dramatic philosophical dimension: for, by choosing multistable figures as his specific object of inquiry, Wittgenstein must have noticed that, in that case, every detail of the world might be multistable, and hence that the whole world might be continuously on the verge of upheaval, whereas, as if by chance, the world is nearly completely stable, except for this upsetting black hole, which is well patrolled by a few laws of the science of perception.)

Finally, figure (c) allows us to understand properly what an interpretation is.

Look at it carefully: nothing happens in it, it does not change into another figure, nor does it display in its interior movements of any kind. But it could well be any of many different things: a coin, a *panforte* (cake) from Siena, a cigar, a flying saucer, a ham sandwich. Interpreting the figure in one way or the other you will find yourself appraising its particular details in different ways, sometimes even discerning them; but you never find yourself seeing one thing or the other, or catching a transformation in it, a change of relations or of figural equilibria. Here, too, it is necessary to play a little a fact of this sort, to keep and change interpretations, as though one were trying to catch the change that will not occur; as in the earlier cases, one must linger over the change of state for a little longer than is needed merely to understand what is presented and move on.

Indeed Wittgenstein writes as someone who has spent time observing figural inversions and inventing, with greater or lesser success, new ones.

Examples like the inversions of the F and the cup-profiles lend themselves well to introducing the famous problem of the use of "see" and of "see as". In fact, no one would say, while normally taking in with his/her eyes the lines on a printed page, following the sense of the words, that he/she sees an f as an f or a z as a z. Of Wittgenstein's F one can say that it is "seen" as an F "only if one knows that it can also be seen otherwise". Let us note here that it is not necessary to have really seen the letter in the two ways illustrated above; it is enough to know that somebody could see there, where I indicate the F, some other thing (not necessarily an F facing backwards). The cognitive context must include a possibility different from the one present to the observer as a state of the F if the expression "see as" may be used without clumsiness.

What it is important to note in this presentation of the problem[2] is that the claim that an alternative, although not necessarily the typical alternative of perceptual multistability, is a condition on the grammar of 'seeing as' immediately opens up a theoretical perspective on the second topic dealt with in the sections we are commenting on: the subject of expressive qualities. This subject is central to Gestalt psychology and in §334 of the second volume of the *Remarks* Wittgenstein refers directly to chapter 7 of Köhler's *Gestalt Psychology*, which deals with the relations between affective states and the expressiveness of perceptual structures, as well as with the affinities of expressiveness in different perceptual structures. Nowadays the labels "expressive quality" or "tertiary quality" are no longer fashionable amongst readers of psychology books; but given that nature and the world have not undergone any changes since these labels were employed, and given that some way of referring to these things is needed, what has popped up is the label "affordances", invented by J. J. Gibson, a pupil of Koffka. *Affordances* indicates in the first instance directly ascertainable dispositional properties of objects but also includes the physiognomic phenomenology of objects. It therefore suits us down to the ground. We shall use each label interchangeably.

How does the theoretical opening we alluded to above come about? In the world of expressive qualities multistability is quite at home, and it depends both on slight changes in detail of the object as well as on shifts of attention or more in general on the attitude of the observer faced with an object. There is thus a vast field of examples for "seeing as", which have in common the multistability of the expressive features of things and especially of the objects produced by art. But there is more. The reader should be warned now that, in Wittgenstein's hands in the following sections, tertiary qualities will be a scalpel for dealing with the problem of the perception of other persons, of their perceptual worlds, of seeing as a state for an interlocutor who is present or absent or merely imagined.

Here the prime examples are the following: "you have to hear these bars as an introduction" and "you must hear it as in this key".

You hear some bars of a musical composition. If you are uninitiated in music (not that this prevents you from hearing perfectly well, just like the others – it is just that you keep closed the shutters of the understanding, perhaps for covert polemical reasons), you may claim that they are sounds, that they form a melody, which at best pleases you or not, which is associated perhaps with certain words, or with a poet or with a cultural stereotype or something other than music. If you are used to playing music, you understand very well "you must hear these bars as an introduction", and you hear it not as though its referred to something external to the music but as referring to something that is within the music and that is its form. Consider the seven bars at the beginning of the fourth movement of Beethoven's *First Symphony*: perhaps it is a tuning exercise in the key of C for the first violins. But now I tell you: you must hear these fragments of scales as an introduction to the joyful explosion of the theme of the *Allegro molto e vivace*:

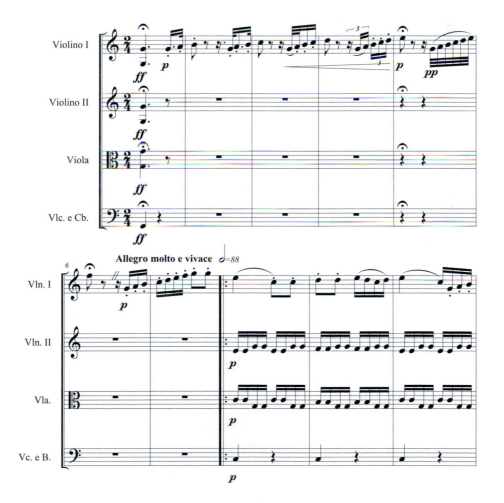

"Hear it as" has an absolutely clear sense, which lies completely in the sphere of what is heard, and the advice just given is immediately cancelled, to such an extent that it means nothing over and above the musical event under observation.

Or let us consider the beginning of the *Andante cantabile*, the third movement of Schumann's *Piano Quartet*, the violin phrase that played over a chord of the other instruments, which is a melodically autonomous fragment in its flexible expressiveness, is a phrase heard "as an introduction", although the theme to which it leads begins (cello) before its melodic curve is completed. Chronologically it does not introduce, does not prepare for something that comes later, as is the function of an introduction; but it is impossible not to hear it as an introduction in Wittgenstein's sense. Anyone who succeeds in abstracting from what comes later can hear the first four bars of the movement as a contrapuntal excerpt – and to such a person it does indeed make sense to say: "you must hear these bars as an introduction".

And thus: "You must hear it as in this key" or as this mode, major or minor. Suppose as a hypothesis that what is heard is the triad G–B–D; it may be the tonic of G major; but I may invite the listener – perhaps with the help of some other note, if he/she is not familiar with music – to hear the C major, so as to hear the triad as constructed on the dominant. And in this way the harmony become unstable, oblique and slightly interrogative, whilst when one hears the G major it is stable, closed and affirmative.

Or Wittgenstein's sentence may be understood in the following way, bearing in mind his preference for Schubert and his sensibility for quartets ("The last two bars of the *Death and the Maiden* theme; one is liable to think at first that this figure is conventional, commonplace – until one understands what it more profoundly expresses; i.e. until one understands that here the commonplace is filled with significance"):[3] listening to the *Quartet* op. 161 with a friend, at the last line of the first movement one may say to him/her, "you must listen out for the minor mode", in order to force him/her to fully grasp its absurd but quite logical irruption in the G major chord that promptly reappears for an instant, only to be flattened into the minor.

It will be objected that the case of "ne. . .pas" differs from the cases that emerge from the musical examples; I think the objection is a good one, at least as a point of psycholinguistics. But here every example is treated with an eye to the problem formulated at the end of the section: "is it a real case of seeing or hearing?"

If we bear in mind the fact that someone who knows and speaks French well will never entertain any trace of the idea of "a step" when he/she hears sentences containing "*ne . . . pas*", it is clear that everything is in order: we have to do with genuine hearing, with a genuine perception of sounds and, out of them, words as things organised over time.

Since to speak of a genuine seeing or genuine hearing may upset the ontological unconsciousness of many philosophers and psychologists, let us make do with following Wittgenstein on this point too: linguistic use is such, and in fact the grammar of hearing and seeing, unlike that of interpreting, is there in the things. We speak in this way when we want to call into question visual and auditive states, and we undertake appropriate actions when others speak appropriately of what one hears or sees.

Notes

1   Wittgenstein, L. (1980). *Remarks on the Philosophy of Psychology*, Vol. I (G. E. M. Anscombe, G. H. von Wright (Eds). Oxford: Basil Blackwell. (Translation slightly modified by KM).
2   This problem reappears many times in Wittgenstein's later writings; so often, in fact, that after Wittgenstein's death it was the subject of a meeting of the Aristotelian Society.
3   Wittgenstein, L. (1987). V*ermischte Bemerkungen – Eine Auswahl aus dem Nachlaß*, Georg Henrik von Wright (Hrsg.), Suhrkamp, Frankfurt am Main.

COMMENTS ON SEEING AS

Kevin Mulligan

Aspects

Wittgenstein's famous descriptions of what we see, and in particular of what has been called "aspect perception", take up puzzles and questions chewed over by earlier psychologists and philosophers writing in German, in particular the different members of the different traditions of Gestalt Psychology (GP).[1] Part of the interest of Paolo Bozzi's discussion of the descriptions Wittgenstein gives in *Remarks on the Philosophy of Psychology* I §1–29 derives from the fact that Bozzi was, like Gaetano Kanizsa, one of the last members of the last tradition of GP, the Austro-Italian tradition which goes back to Meinong, Witasek, Ameseder (Graz) and Benussi (Graz, Padua). Bozzi was steeped in the different traditions of GP and developed them in many directions. Wittgenstein, on the other hand, refers only to some of the views of the most influential representatives of Berlin GP, Koffka (Köhler). Since GP and the philosophies it grew out of and was influenced by are now unfamiliar, my remarks on Bozzi's chapter and the monograph of which it is a part are in part historical.

A good place to begin, if Wittgenstein is to believed, is language. Talk about perception comes in many shapes and sizes. We say that we see things, people, colours, shapes and events, that we see someone walk across the street but also *how* she moves and *that* someone is walking across the street. But we also say things of the form:

> x saw y/an N as an O
> x saw the figure
>
> $\mathcal{F}$
>
> as a mirror image of an F
> x saw the (drawing of the/a) duck as a (drawing of a) rabbit

The example of seeing a figure in different ways is the example from Wittgenstein with which Bozzi begins the present chapter. As Wittgenstein says about a similar example, "the eye distinguishes various aspects" (RPP I §22). Similarly, Wittgenstein points out, we say that we hear this or that as this or that:

You must hear these bars as an introduction.

There is a phrasing by the eye and by the ear (*RPP* I §1), there are visual and auditive aspects (cf. *PI*, II xi 206). As Meinong pointed out in 1906, when introducing the term *Aspekt* into the philosophy of perception, although the term comes from visual perception, we may employ it for other sensory modalities. Bozzi goes on to give a number of wonderful examples of visual and musical aspects and notes the importance in Wittgenstein's writings on aspects of what have been called "expressive qualities", "tertiary qualities" (Köhler) and "affordances" (Gibson). But contrary to what Bozzi suggests, these are all arguably very different things. Consider expressive qualities. Wittgenstein seems to suggest that there is a type of perceptual report appropriate to our perception of expression and of what it expresses. He writes:

> "I noticed that he was out of humour"
>
> Is this a report about his behaviour or his state of mind? . . .
>
> Both; not side-by-side, however, but about the one via (*durch*) the other (*PI*, II v 179)

Max Scheler had made a related but distinct claim: "I immediately see *in* and *through* (*durch sie hindurch*) these qualities, lines and forms [that present themselves to me] the 'joy . . .'"[2] In another formulation of his view, Scheler opts for "in" rather than "through" and "aware" rather than "see":

> For we certainly take ourselves to be directly *aware* of another person's joy *in* his laughter, of his suffering and pain *in* his tears, of his shame *in* his blushing, of his entreaty *in* his outstretched hands . . . of his rage *in* the gnashing of his teeth, of his threats *in* the clenching of his fist . . .[3]

Wittgenstein disagrees about both parts of "seeing in" in views like those suggested by Scheler's first formulation:

> It might be an incorrect use of language to say "I see fear in this face". We would be taught: a fearful face can be *seen*; but the fear in a face, or the similarity or dissimilarity between two faces, is *noticed*. (RPP II, § 552).

And here, as before, he says that we notice rather than see states of mind even when such noticing is made possible by what we see.[4]

"Tertiary qualities", as Köhler uses the term, are just values:

> *Charm* is a special value-quality; so is *loveliness* and *womanliness*. . . . That face looks *mean* – and I abhor it. *Dignity* I *hear in* those words which I have just heard Mr. X. speaking – and I respect him. Her gait is *clumsy* – and I prefer to look away. Everywhere *value-qualities* are found residing in such objects as characteristics of them.[5]

Our perceptual grasp of expression and of value are not, of course, always independent of one another. For example, the emotions we see or notice (like some of the qualities expressed by music) are themselves often the bearers of value-properties and, as Köhler suggests, reactions to the (apparent) exemplification of value-properties. And that is doubtless one reason why Bozzi refers indifferently to expressive and tertiary qualities.[6]

As we have seen, Wittgenstein likes to contrast *seeing* a person, a face or a colour and *noticing* aspects and relations such as similarity. If we say we see aspects or relations we are using "see" in a second sort of way. In a gnomic but apparently important formulation of his views, which is not to be found in the texts discussed by Bozzi, Wittgenstein says that "what I see in the dawning of an aspect is not a property of the object but an internal relation between it and other objects" (PI II xi 212). One type of internal relation is the similarity relation between qualities, as opposed to the external relation of similarity between two things or persons; the qualities, unlike the things or persons, cannot cease to stand in the relation of similarity. In the jargon of Graz GP, similarity is a higher-order object, not something which can be seen in the sense in which lower-order objects, such as the terms of the relation, can be seen but rather something which may be noticed. In the same tradition, and in early phenomenology (Brunswig, Scheler), the claim that one can be aware of relations of similarity between two objects even though one of the objects is not given is a common one.[7] A second type of internal relation is that of instantiating the same kind or essence. Another that between expressions and emotions. Detailed accounts of the way such internal relations relate to one another and may catch our attention, be noticed or attended to, are to be found in the work of Graz GP and of the early phenomenologists.[8]

Experiments

Bozzi's work on what we perceive and its description belongs to what he calls "Experimental Phenomenology".[9] The experiments peculiar to the latter, he thinks, differ in many respects from conventional experiments in psychology, the "experimental methods" Wittgenstein refers to in his *Philosophical Investigations* (PI, II, xiv). Phenomenological experiments may and perhaps should take place outside a laboratory; the participants are not kept in ignorance of what is going on, participate in fixing the goal of the experiment and may reconsider their responses.[10] The tradition to which Bozzi's Experimental Phenomenology belongs is an unfamiliar one. By this I do not merely mean that the different traditions of Gestalt psychology which inform Bozzi's writings are unknown. Rather, these traditions are themselves, in some cases, part of an approach to psychology which is unfamiliar since it is held by its proponents to differ from classical experimental psychology. The distinctive features of what was to be called Experimental Phenomenology were noted already in 1911 by Max Scheler:

> Not all experiments have or need to have an inductive sense, for example Galileo's experiments to demonstrate the principle of inertia. And in exactly the same way even a physiological experiment can serve the task of phenomenological clarification (*Aufhellung*). It then has a function analogous to that of so called illustrative experiments (*Veranschaulichungsexperimente*) in mathematics.[11]

One of Scheler's examples of experiments in the service of phenomenological clarification in early empirical psychology is the work of members of the Würzburg school such as Külpe and Bühler, the aim of which was to demonstrate that it is not essential to thinking that it be a sensory phenomenon, a claim which is also at the heart of Husserl's *Logical Investigations* (1900–01). The methodology of the Würzburg school was the object of severe criticism by

Wundt, criticism to which Bühler replied,[12] anticipating in some respects the position put forward by Scheler.

Scheler was indeed later to claim that a great deal of early experimental psychology – he mentions Katz on colours, Jaensch on visual space, Linke and Werthheimer on the perception of movement, Ach on the will, Mittenzwey on abstraction, Stumpf, Krüger and Köhler on auditory perception – in fact contains experiments the goal of which is not to establish inductive propositions but rather essential propositions or connections. But, he thinks, the psychologists mentioned (with the exception of Stumpf) were by no means clear about the difference between the two types of experiment. They often lacked

> a clear awareness of the unity of phenomeonological investigation, so that what is phenomenological in their investigations is nowhere sharply marked off from empirical observations (*Feststellungen*) and subsequent explanations; in addition, their phenomenological results often appear as the products of experiments with an inductive sense . . . But this by no means stands in the way of a reciprocal enrichment (*Befruchtung*) of the two parts of their inquiries.[13]

Scheler's own view about non-inductive, illustrative or phenomenological experiments is that they provide intuitions of general, essential connexions (which are *er-schaut*) between possible instances of essences or kinds whereas inductive experiments provide observations of singular empirical facts.[14] Whatever one thinks about this view and, for example, its relation to the distinction above between seeing things or qualities and noticing relations, in particular internal relations between perceived and merely possible items, or about its relation to the theory of *thought*-experiments, enough has perhaps been said to make it clear that the opposition on which Brentano, Husserl and Wittgenstein like to insist, between genetic, causal, experimental, empirical psychology, on the one hand, and the conceptual confusions of psychologists who have not listened carefully enough to the deliverances of Austrian philosophers, on the other hand,[15] can easily make us overlook the very possibility of an Experimental Phenomenology. Paolo Bozzi did not overlook this possibility. *Au contraire.* And his work should, I think, be the first port of call for anyone who wants to evaluate the descriptions of what we see given by Wittgenstein and Wittgenstein's understanding of description.

Notes

1 On these traditions, cf. Smith (1988).
2 Scheler (1911), pp. 146–147, emphases mine.
3 Scheler (1973), p. 254, emphases mine
4 Thanks to Richard Wollheim, it has become common in philosophy to talk of seeing things *in* pictures. cf. Wittgenstein, *RPP* II §444.
5 Köhler (1938), pp. 77–78.
6 Cf. Bozzi (2002), pp. 79, 90, 97, 103. What about affordances such as edibility or usefulness? Edibility, I suggest, is a deontic rather than an axiological property: to be edible is to be fit to be eaten, to be what may be eaten. Usefulness, on the other hand, is clearly an axiological property.
7 Cf. Ameseder 1904, p. 490.
8 Cf. Ameseder 1904. Cf. for example Ameseder 1904, at p. 498–499 and Wittgenstein *RPP*, I §1002 on the aspects presented by a chess-board.
9 Bozzi 2002, p. 35.
10 Cf. Bozzi 1989, ch. 7; Bozzi 2002, at 34–39, 63–71; Kubovy, 2002.

11 Scheler 1955, p. 286.
12 Cf. for example Wundt, 1907; Bühler, 1909.
13 Scheler (1957), p. 389.
14 Scheler (1957), p. 388.
15 Cf Mulligan (2012), Chapter 1.

References

Ameseder, R. (1904). Über Vorstellungsproduktion. In A. Meinong (ed.), *Untersuchungen zur Gegenstandstheorie und Psychologie* (pp. 481–508). Leipzig, Germany: Barth.

Bozzi, P. (1989). *Fenomenologia sperimentale* [*Experimental Phenomenology*]. Bologna, Italy: il Mulino.

Bozzi, P. (2002). *Vedere come* [*Seeing As*]. Milan, Italy: Guerini.

Bühler, K. (1909). Zur Kritik der Denkexperimente. *Zeitschrift für Psychologie, 51*, 108–118.

Köhler, W. (1938). *The Place of Value in a World of Facts*. New York: Liveright.

Kubovy, M. (2002). Phenomenology, cognitive. In L. Nadel (ed.), *Encyclopedia of Cognitive Science* (pp. 579–586). Houndmills, UK: Macmillan.

Mulligan, K. (2012). *Wittgenstein et la philosophie austro-allemande*. Paris: Vrin.

Scheler, M. (1911). Über Selbsttäuschungen. *Zeitschrift für Pathopsychologie*, 87–163.

Scheler, M. (1955). Die Idole der Selbsterkenntnis. In *Vom Umsturz der Werte* (pp. 213–292). Bern, Switzerland: Francke.

Scheler, M. (1957). Phänomenologie und Erkenntnistheorie. In *Schriften aus dem Nachlass. Band I. Zur Ethik und Erkenntnislehre* (pp. 377–430). Bern, Switzerland: Francke.

Scheler, M. (1973). *Wesen und Formen der Sympathie*. Bern, Switzerland: Francke.

Smith, B. (1988) (ed.). *Foundations of Gestalt Theory*. Munich, Germany: Philosophia.

Wittgenstein, L. (1953). *Philosophical Investigations*. Oxford: Blackwell.

Wittgenstein, L. (1980). *Remarks on the Philosophy of Psychology*, Vols. I, II (Eds. G.E.M. Anscombe, & G.H. von Wright). Oxford: Basil Blackwell.

Wundt, W. (1907). Über Ausfrageexperimente und über die Methoden zur Psychologie des Denkens. *Psychologische Studien, 3*, 301–360.

PART III

9

PHENOMENOLOGICAL DESCRIPTIONS AND PHYSICAL-GEOMETRICAL DESCRIPTIONS

Translated by Ugo Savardi

1. 1912, the year in which Wertheimer published *Experimentelle Studien über das Sehen von Bewegung*[1], the theoretical root of Gestalt phenomenology, is also the year when, according to Watson, behaviourism began "in overt form". Since then, many points of friction have emerged dividing the Gestalt method of direct observation from behaviouristic operationalism, in the realm of theory as well as in the application of experimental techniques. The two paradigms have undergone profound changes over the decades almost to the point of dissolution, and it is certainly not possible to say now, after so much work has been done, that the reasons for the conflict between them remain the same.

There is however one question that still pops up during discussions as it did in the past and it's a methodological question. It's a dilemma that is as old as the hills, inherited from a time when experimental psychology was still unthinkable and which in short can be summed up as follows: Is it or is it not possible to describe the immediate data of experience?

For a behaviourist, the immediate data of experience are not accessible by means of descriptions; the material on which scientific research has to be carried out is made up of the descriptions themselves, and these take on the form of a special kind of behavioural response, and so are considered as one of the terms of the "stimulus–response" relationship.

The facts directly under observation are excluded from scientific inquiry and remain nothing but good opportunities for poetry and metaphysics.[2] Behaviourism arose with the intention of eliminating introspection from among the tools used in scientific investigation. If we say that the directly ascertainable world is an object of introspection, that world ceases to be of importance as soon as the value of the introspective method is called into question.

2. On the other hand, if we want to study perceptual events as the units of analysis in a given context, that is, if we want to discover the laws of interconnection that regulate the perceptual structure of events being experienced here and now, then the object of investigation should be the observed events and their phenomenal characteristics (even though these are difficult to describe) rather than a group of "protocol propositions" linked to constellation of stimuli.

What should be of interest for the student of perception is the direct evidence of an event, which is itself always distinguishable from (and often largely independent of) the other facts that subsequently lead to the description of this event. The connection between an event and its description is, if anything, a different problem for psychologists to study.

It is true that I never see anything through another person's eyes (if this sentence even makes any sense) and I have to make do with what others tell me they see. But since there is no way I will confuse this sheet of paper in front of me with the description of this paper that I might give if asked, I'm not allowed to treat these two things as if they were one and the same.

If our task is to analyse the properties of perceptual events insofar as they cannot be confused with the properties of other concomitant psychological events (such as judgment formation or the search for an appropriate description), we must be allowed to consider the objects directly given to us as the starting point of a scientific investigation into the makeup of experience – regardless of the theoretical difficulties related to the concept of introspection.

3.   In the course of this chapter I will try to focus on some aspects of the problem raised by those who are in doubt about whether it is possible to describe direct experiences.

Not only orthodox behaviourist have denied that, because of their essentially qualitative nature, the phenomenal data can be expressed, but so too have representatives of various quite different philosophical schools of thought. Bergson's point of view, for instance, seemed to imply that descriptions formulated in the language of physics and geometry are necessarily unfaithful because of the inflexibility of the words used relative to the plasticity of the "immediate data of consciousness" – but I suspect that Bergson was overestimating this plasticity. For radically different reasons, some influential members of the Vienna Circle argued that elementary statements about the facts, i.e. "protocol propositions", are the ultimate data for scientific experience.

It should be noted that this assumption does not simply consist of claiming that many aspects of an immediate experience are difficult to express with the words that dictionaries put at our disposal, which is so true as to be little more than a banal remark. It rather consists of saying that there isn't even a single aspect of what we directly experience that we can describe in a univocal, unambiguous way.

4.   As regards univocality, according to this line of thought, language that describes objective things (as in physics) would constitute a much better basis. Indeed the language of physics can in all respects be made as precise as one wants it to be. The reason why it is possible to describe physical facts clearly is that they can be reduced to measurements and these measurements – which do not contain anything qualitative – can be connected to each other in relationships that are, in turn, univocally defined in terms of mathematical concepts. The concepts of mathematical physics have often been referred to as models of logical constructions that are capable of providing an interpretation of empirically ascertained facts and can at the same time describe their structure without ambiguity. Anyone who has sufficient mathematical training understands, for example, the formula that expresses the trajectory of a projectile in the same way as others with a similar training.

Since the beginning of psychophysics, students of the psychology of perception have often tried to express the results of their studies by means of formulas in which some of the symbols denote certain directly or indirectly ascertained facts and in which the symbols are connected to each other in well-defined relationships.

This use of formulas might go to show that students of psychology aspire to reach the same degree of clarity and univocality in the expression of the laws they have discovered as physicists do. However, if we try to analyse the meaning of any of these formulas, we will quickly discover that the interpretation of the symbols denoting some features of direct experience depends on our agreeing about the meaning of the symbols denoting the "objective" aspects. Leafing through the chapters on sensation and perception in any psychology textbook, all of the formulas we find contain at least one symbol which, rather than referring to a psychological event, refers to an operation applied to the stimuli.

5.   Let's take the simplest example, that is, psychophysical formulas.

These may be of greater or lesser complexity, but in the end they always consist of a one-many correlation between certain values on a physical scale of measurement and those on an empirically based evaluation scale, which is based on the limits of differential thresholds.

Now, although our knowledge about the physical world always stems from measurements carried out on directly accessed realities in the phenomenal world, it is in effect the values of these physical scales of measurement that teach us something about differential thresholds and not vice versa. There must be agreement on what a centimetre, a gram or a second is in order to understand the results of an enquiry that evaluates the length of something, measures the duration of the phenomenal present or compares two weights.

After all, physical scales of measurement are much more fine-grained than the human ability to discriminate, both in spatial and temporal quantities as well as weights, brightnesses, pressures, etc., in such a way that a single value on the "psychic" scale corresponds to many values on the physical scale, while a single value on the physical scale corresponds to one and only one on the psychic scale. This implies that subjective estimates provide ambiguous information about the values of a certain event which can be operationally determined whereas an operationally measured value gives us unambiguous information about the amplitude of a differential threshold (that is, about an estimate referring to one fact of direct experience).

6.   In phenomenological research the formulas used to represent systems of relationships are more complex, since the point here is not only to express a group of one–many relationships between changes affecting a simple distal stimulus and changes occurring in the domain of direct experience (as, for example, a "sensation" that has been purposely isolated from any functional context).

Relationships that appear in a formula summarising a phenomenological law are of either of two types: some of these relationships refer to the more or less complex characteristics of the constellation of stimuli, while others show how different characteristics of the perceived event are functions of each other.

Korte's laws[3] represent a good example of this. As is well known, they express the conditions for a stroboscopic movement to be perceived. If we analyse the structure of these laws, we realize that some symbols denote ratios concerning the "objective situation", or rather, the relative projective properties on a given plane that is ideally located at the observer's viewpoint. Here are few of these symbols:

s = spatial distance between stimuli
i = intensity of stimuli
e = exposure time of stimuli
d = differences in the intensity of the lights
t = inter–stimulus interval etc.

But others denote characteristics that refer exclusively to the phenomenal aspect, for example:

v = velocity of the movement
or the "opt" index which denotes the optimality of the conditions.

It should be noted though that some of these symbols are ambiguous. The intensity of the lights, for example, or differences in intensity, might be considered as much phenomenal as physical properties. According to Korte's study, it would seem that the author means the latter, i.e. physical. But this sounds a bit strange since it is the apparent intensity that is decisive in stroboscopic movement, and it is hard to believe that a change in the objective intensity, so long as it remains well below the differential threshold, could be responsible for a change in how one sees a stroboscopic movement.

A certain perplexity might arise from the consideration that Korte calculated the speed of a stroboscopic movement as one would for a physical object in motion; that is, as a function of the distance between the points of light which are alternately illuminated (the path) and the temporal interval between when the first light is switched off and the second light is switched on (time).

Leaving these rather obvious considerations aside, it is not difficult to see how the observations discussed above concerning psychophysical laws hold for phenomenological laws as well: also in this case, we need to agree on a certain number of concepts related to elementary physics to grasp the meaning of Korte's formulas. From a strictly phenomenological point of view, stroboscopic movement is a movement like any other. It is no less real than other movements which we call "real". It is our knowledge of the relationships between the phenomenal fact and some of the objective conditions that allows us to establish a system of functional interconnections among the phenomenal features of the event under examination.

7.   At this point, we need to attempt a definition – at least by way of an initial approximation – of what we mean by "objective conditions". Although many people are led to think otherwise, the issue of the connections between the structures of transphenomenal reality and direct reality is no less important for psychologists of perception than it is for epistem-ologists or philosophers of knowledge. If an understanding of phenomenological and psychophysical laws, set out by investigators into sensations or perceptual organization, depends on our agreement on the definition of the concepts that describe physical reality, then this problem is extremely important for psychology.

Obviously I do not intend to resolve this now. I just want to make one point that may be of some interest and which will hopefully simplify the concept of an "objective situation" rather than make it more complicated.

I think we need to keep in mind that when we talk of an "objective situation" or use similar expressions, we do not really mean to refer to the type of facts that we imagine when studying physics, but rather to a group of operations that we perform on the phenomenal world. Suppose that we want to study the Aubert-Fleischel phenomenon, i.e. the apparent change in velocity that affects an object moving with an objectively uniform motion; this change occurs when, after letting the object pass across our visual field, we suddenly follow it with our gaze, or conversely. To perform this experiment, we need an objectively constant motion. The technical devices at our disposal allow us to obtain uniform motion with varying degrees of approximation: it is clear enough that we will not be interested in the most perfect device that an Institute of Applied Mechanics might provide us with. A fair approximation of uniform motion suffices for our purposes since any irregularities in movement will be much smaller than we can detect. Beyond certain limits, which are actually quite wide, no attempt at greater precision will lead to any advantages: for the purposes of our experiments, we can already speak of an objectively constant motion that is guaranteed to be such by certain operations.

We are fully aware of the difficulties of measuring the exactly the wavelength of a ray reflected from a surface with certain chemical-physical characteristics. But we can still work on various problems concerning colour perception using relatively simple objective measurements, which might not satisfy a physicist interested in photometry. In this case too, beyond certain limits, greater precision would not lead to any significant advantage.

Similar observations could be made about the production of sounds in studies on the perception of acoustic events.

For these reasons, the language and concepts of classical mechanics and Euclidean geometry suffice for investigators of perception to be able to describe the objective and projective correlates of the experimental conditions they are examining. It would never occur to anyone to represent the movement of an object with respect to an observer in terms of relativistic mechanics. In other words, an "objective situation" is an abstraction or rather an idealization of a concrete fact that can be measured, more or less precisely, by means of physical devices and appropriate operations. The symbols that appear in our formulas and that refer to particular features of this objective situation denote precisely concepts or abstractions of this sort. And we can accept these formulas without elaborating on them too much because we all implicitly accept that the notions of elementary physics and the rules, axioms and definitions of Euclidean geometry are univocally definable.

8.   None of this, however, says anything for or against the impossibility of describing phenomenal data. I believe, in any case, that simply by bearing in mind what I have said so far, and by adding some further observations regarding the form of our experimental demonstrations, that we will be allowed to claim that some features of direct experience are genuinely describable, provided that it is admitted that we can understand those symbols that in our formulas denote the terms of the "objective situation". In short, I think that agreement on the meaning of these symbols (which basically means agreement on some concepts of elementary physics and the propositions of descriptive and projective geometry) implies also the describability of some salient features of direct experience.

Anyone who is familiar with research carried out in a laboratory will have noticed that experimental demonstrations frequently have a somewhat curious, even paradoxical, form. This pardoxicality may sometimes be emphasized, the experiment becomes a bit of a spectacle and those spectators who are not in the know are puzzled by the strangeness of what is happening to them. Those of us who work on perception are very familiar with the prejudices and resistances of individuals who are invited to take part in an experiment. They already imagine that they will see or hear something that "is not there" or something that nobody would expect.

There are actually some reasons for doing this. Since time immemorial the distinction between reality and appearance (even if this distinction is drawn in a way that would no longer satisfy anybody today) was based on appeal to cases where human observers had directly perceived something that subsequently – thanks to the application of some objective check (in the sense given above) – turned out to be different from what it initially seemed to be. Democritus and Aristotle emphasized the importance of "illusions of the senses" no less than the British empiricists or William James – even though they did not fully understand their importance. After all, the very distinction between reality and appearance seems to be possible thanks to the existence of these paradoxical situations: in a world where there were no "deception of the senses", a distinction between objects as described in the world of physics and objects as described in the world of psychology would appear artificial in theory and impossible from an operational point of view.

9.   It is worth remembering, at this point, that the air of paradoxicality that invests the experimental situations I'm referring to can be understood in at least two different ways. And it is important to keep these separate. One might want to call paradoxical situations those situations where both the terms of an antithesis belong to the level of immediate experience. A suitable example of this is the apparent dilation of a rotating spiral. This phenomenon is well known: if a spiral rotates with a constant angular velocity in the opposite direction to the one in which it is coiled, it seems to expand ever outwards. At one and the same time, an observer sees a) that the spiral continuously expands; and b) that the area containing the spiral (e.g. a disk) does not increase in size.

However, other much more common events are also said to be paradoxical, when the phenomenological description of a certain perceptual experience differs, more or less substantially, from the description of the corresponding constellation of stimuli. Or – to put it in Musatti's words – when "the phenomenal result obtained contrasts with the situation of the stimulus".

Musatti[4] analysed in detail these types of "paradox", claiming that their paradoxical character plays an essential role in rendering the experiments carried out in the phenomenology of perception a form of demonstration. Musatti's remarks seem to be of great importance and so I will linger for a moment to summarise them.

In logic and mathematics there is a demonstrative procedure similar to those known as *reductio ad absurdum*. These allow one to obtain by deduction the affirmation of a proposition starting from its negation. This was used by Euclid in the demonstration of the twelfth proposition of the ninth book of the *Elements*, and by Cardano (in a different form) in his demonstration of proposition 201 in his *De Proportionibus*. It was also used by Saccheri and Leibniz. It is not easy to explain the structure of this form of reasoning in a nutshell without analysing some examples in detail. For the sake of our discussion it is enough to know that, under certain conditions, it is possible to start from a negation $\sim p$ to obtain the affirmation p.

Musatti points out that a somewhat analogous demonstrative procedure is used in many experimental studies on perceptual structures, and he cites the classic ones on the perception of identity and perceptual constancies.

10.   It would be hard to convince a non-specialist interlocutor that the identity of an object is a question of the functional structures related to the phenomenal presence of that object, if we simply show him/her that an object, which remains materially the same while being subjected to some changes, continues to appear to be the same object. The interlocutor would react saying: "I see that it is the same because I know that it is the same".

For this reason, Musatti says, ever since the first studies on phenomenal identity, researchers have made use of stroboscopic movement or of other special conditions such as the tunnel effect. In these cases it cannot be said that the object is the "same" and thus it becomes clear that "sameness" (or "identity") is indeed a phenomenal property, which can be accounted for only in terms of perceptual organization.

He also mentions that perceptual constancies have been subjected to a similar technique: figural and kinetic transformations of physical objects and their projective properties do not correspond to the figural and kinetic transformations directly ascertained by the observer.

As happens with identity, in this way the structural nature of perceptual constancies becomes evident, and it is clear that these constancies cannot be interpreted by means of a complex system of one-one relationships holding between elementary physical events and "sensations", as it was tempting to imagine a century ago and as, in line with common sense, many are still tempted to imagine even today.

In common with Saccheri and Leibniz's logical procedure, this kind of experimental demonstration is characterized by the following pattern:

1)   an event is set up operationally excluding the properties x, y, z; and the result is precisely

2)   an event that observably possesses the properties x, y, z.

11.   The theoretical importance of the paradoxical form of these demonstrations is, in my opinion, not to be underestimated. Experiences set up in this way demonstrate two things at once. First, they show the particular laws governing the phenomena we are interested in; and second they prove that those laws cannot be reduced to a set of elementary stimulus-sensation relationships. We can take this second feature of these demonstrations for granted if we assume that in any case all the laws that we find are like this. And this is true. But it would be better not to assume this – we should derive it instead from the very form by which the laws of a given phenomenon are proved.

If an experience does not involve a paradox and, for example, we simply show someone that when a square moves away from their eyes what they see is in effect a square moving away, then we can always explain this by introducing a postulate such as, for instance, Lotze's postulate of "local signs".[5] This easy way out however becomes impossible when an observer sees a square moving away from them but knows that in reality it is shrinking on a plane that is not moving relative to them.

But the paradoxical situations studied by Musatti teach us yet another moral which is relevant to the topic of our discussion.

In these situations the paradoxicality that allows us to demonstrate not only the laws regarding the phenomenon but also the phenomenological nature of these laws is due to the fact that some geometrical or physical characteristics of the objective event are not present in the domain of direct experience or are present in a different form. That is to say that some systems of geometrical or dynamic relationships, when applied to the event understood as stimulus, lead to true propositions; but when applied to the direct ascertaining, they lead to false propositions; and vice-versa.

The paradox, in short, is due to the fact that the same language — that of elementary physical geometry — is used to describe the structure of an experimental situation both from an operational point of view (the distal constellation of the stimuli, its projective properties and the corresponding proximal stimulation) as well as from a phenomenological point of view.

As occurs with a description of the physical characteristics of an event, where we do not literally refer to what "really", "materially" exists (because a physical-geometrical representation is an idealized model of a concrete fact), likewise a phenomenological description of physical, dynamic and geometric features (its phenomenal weight, how it moves, its speed, its shape, its apparent centre of gravity etc.) is a reliable and univocal representation of some aspects of a directly perceived fact. This representation, of course, abstracts the selected characteristics from among the other complex phenomenological features — normally — belonging to the event.

But the important point here is this: when referring to a direct experience of mine, I say "I see a square moving away from me", I say it with the same meaning as I might write a similar sentence in a text on mechanics. Phenomenological language in such a case is no more blurred or imprecise or "poetic" than is geometric language when it is used to describe transphenomenal events. Protocol propositions of this kind are excellent for describing the nature of a visual experience and have the same intersubjective communicability that must be attributed to geometrical propositions used to refer — for instance — to the bodies that are the subject-matter of mechanics.

12.   There is a reason for all of this, and psychologists of perception should delve deeply into its nature.

In short: if we admit that we can understand each other about the meaning of the symbols that in our formulas refer to the physical conditions of the fact that is taken to be a stimulus (that is, if we accept some ideas from elementary geometry and physics), we cannot then say that we are unable to understand the meaning of the propositions that refer to the physical, geometrical and dynamic features of the objects around us, even if these features are accompanied by other less easily describable, because qualitative features.

As we have already seen, we do not need more elaborate geometry than Euclid's (or one based on a different axiomatic system). What we use in studies regarding psychology of perception is, in the final analysis, Euclid's geometry. Nor do we need more advanced dynamics or kinematics than those of Galileo and Newton in order to describe, for example, motion. But Euclidean geometry (the language of which is also used in elementary mechanics) is based on definitions — the *horoi* (definitions) of Euclid's *Elements* — which, despite being purely formal definitions, are also descriptions of how things appear immediately. I'm tempted to say that they are descriptions of how the "drawings" exemplifying the structures of elementary geometric entities appear. Right from the start, this geometry is a language based on phenomenal experiences.

Euclid[6] states that:

1. A point is that which has no part.
2. A line is a breadthless length.

6. The extremities of a surface are lines.

13. A boundary is that which is a limit of something.

14. A figure is that which is contained by a boundary or boundaries.

Although all more complex geometrical entities are derived deductively in accordance with certain rules from the simplest ones, these simple geometrical entities are sufficiently congruent with our visual experience of the corresponding graphic representations for us to be able to talk of the geometrical aspects of direct experience in a coherent geometrical language.

This might seem to many to be a bold claim. It has always been said that elementary geometrical entities do not correspond to experience because they are nothing but an audacious abstraction.

But I think that a few considerations will suffice to make us change our minds about this scholastic prejudice. With respect to points (understood as visible entities without parts), there is a passage in Hume which in effect constitutes an experiment in the phenomenology of perception:

> Put a spot of ink upon paper, fix your eye upon that spot, and retire to such a distance, that, at last you lose sight of it; it is plain, that the moment before it vanished the image or impression was perfectly indivisible. It is not for want of rays of light striking on our eyes, that the minute parts of distant bodies convey not any sensible impression; but because they are removed beyond that distance, at which their impressions were reduced to a minimum, and were incapable of any farther diminution. A microscope or telescope, which renders them visible, produces not any new rays of light, but only spreads those, which always flowed from them; and by that means both gives parts to impressions, which to the naked eye appear simple and uncompounded, and advances to a minimum, what was formerly imperceptible.[7]

The distinction between physical ingredients (rays of light) and visibility is very clear here and according to Hume's line of argument the fact that something may not have parts and yet exist in perception becomes self-evident. This analysis dates back to 1737 and in fact was contained in the first part of the *Treatise* – too old and stuffy to be useful in a discussion involving scientific psychologists.

But this argument as it stands was taken up again in 1921 by Rubin (the discoverer of figure-ground organization) in a little-known pamphlet called *Die Flechenfigur, die Kontur und der Strich*.[8] In this case it was applied to a line, which, according to Euclid, is a length without breadth. Draw a line on a piece of paper and then move the piece of paper away from you. Just before the line disappears you will discover that you can no longer distinguish the right hand edge from the left hand edge (if the line is vertical) or distinguish the upper edge from the lower edge (if the line is horizontal). If you look at it close up, the line actually has a thickness, but when it is far away it in fact appears to be a length without breadth.

The phenomenological basis of Euclid's definition number 13 can be found in the analyses of the properties of contours carried out by Gestalt psychologists, in particular by Koffka in the *Principles*. These properties relate to the unilateral function of a margin that separates an area from its background and the bilateral function of a margin that connects two shapes with a boundary in common.

If in the end the meaning of geometrical propositions is based on some specific features of direct experience, then it is clear that geometrical language (as well as being suitable for describing a constellation of stimuli) will also be suitable for the physical-geometrical features of directly experienced objects.

Thus, although some qualitative features of the perceived world are difficult to describe (such as, for instance, expressive qualities or the "meaning" of perceptions), it cannot be said that direct experience can never be a subject for description.

If the foregoing considerations are correct, I do not think we can endorse the view of orthodox behaviourists as being the only one that is acceptable and capable of satisfying the requirements of an unassailable research method.

Insofar as the objects that we experience directly possess geometrically and physically well-defined and stable characteristics they can be the starting point of our investigations without this implying that we will run into the spectre of introspectionism. The very language of geometry and physics allows us to talk about these experiences without ambiguity and so guarantees the intersubjective validity of our descriptions.

Notes

1 Wertheimer, M. (1912). Experimentelle Studien über das Sehen von Bewegung. *Zeitschrift für Psychologie*, Bd. 61, Heft 1 (1912), pp. 162-265.
2 Tolman, E. C. (1951). Psychology versus immediate experience. *Collected Papers*. Berkeley, CA: University Press.
3 Korte, A. (1915). Beiträge zur psychologie der Gestalt und Bewegungserlebnisse, *Zeitschrift für Psychologie*, 73, 193–296, at p. 277.
4 Musatti, C. (1958). Di alcune analogie fra problemi della percezione e problemi logico-matematici. *Rivista di Psicologia*, 52, 1–20; reprinted in Musatti, C. (ed.) (1964). *Condizioni dell'esperienza e fondazione della psicologia*. Firenze, Italy: Giunti-Barbera.
5 Translator's note: "The concept of a local sign is similar to that of 'positional information' in developmental biology. Rudolf Hermann Lotze (1817–1881) put forward the theory of local signs to explain how positional information was transmitted from the retina to the motor system. Under the influence of Kant, he thought that local signs could not, in themselves, be spatial. He therefore postulated that they were qualitative properties of the nerve fibres themselves. Later, he modified this theory in favour of the notion that local signs were related to the sense of effort associated with eye movements" (Morgan, M.J. (2002) Lotze and the theory of local signs. ECVP '02 Abstract: *Perception* Lecture, p. 3.)
6 Euclid, *Elements of Geometry*, Book I, Definitions.
7 Hume, D. (1737). *A Treatise of Human Nature*. D. Fate Norton and M.J. Norton (Eds). Book I, Part II § I. Oxford: Oxford University Press, 2000.
8 Rubin, E. (1921). *Die Flechenfigur, die Kontur und der Strich*. Copenhagen: Gyldendalske-Boghandel.

COMMENTS ON PHENOMENOLOGICAL DESCRIPTIONS AND PHYSICAL-GEOMETRICAL DESCRIPTIONS

Ugo Savardi

The thesis: the study of experience does not allow assumptions of inadmissibility

With the sensibility of the excellent musician and violinist that he was, Bozzi dedicates the overture of this argumentative score to exposing the fallacy behind the behaviourist assumption regarding the impossibility of using introspection in describing the immediate contents of experience:

> Psychology as the behaviourist views it is a purely objective experimental branch of natural science. Its theoretical goal is the prediction and control of behaviour. Introspection forms no essential part of its methods, nor is the scientific value of its data dependent upon the readiness with which they lend themselves to interpretation in terms of consciousness. (Watson, 1913)

The argument proceeds in an apparently dialectical spirit setting Watson's program against Max Wertheimer's dense account of the experimental study of motion (available in the English translation by his son Michael Wertheimer published in an important volume edited by Lothar Spillman, 2012). In Wertheimer's fifty pages, the subjects and the method of data gathering could not be better described with a view to marrying the necessary methodological correctness and respect for the priority of the experiential given:

> The two assistants at the institute, Dr. Wolfgang and Dr. Kurt Koffka, and later also Frau Dr. Klein-Koffka, were kind enough to make themselves available as regular observers.

> On a number of occasions, especially in slider experiments under comfortable observation conditions, I also used other observers, including some who were completely naïve with respect to psychological observations.

> The essential experiments were all made without observers knowing the purpose of the experiment, and the experimental results were always revealed to the observers only after they had each spontaneously reported their results.

It turned out that a large number of observers was not necessary since the characteristic phenomena were altogether unequivocal, spontaneous, and compelling. (Ed. 2012, p. 14)

Bozzi's stress on the temporal coincidence between the publication of Wertheimer's original text (*Experimentelle Studien über das Sehen von Bewegung*) and that of Watson's founding manifesto of Behaviourismi is one of the author's rhetorical ploys which neither determine nor condition the argumentative scheme, which develops independently of this coincidence but rather on grounds that concern psychology's epistemic and methodological standing. What was happening in European and American psychology at the turn of the last century is presented neither as a historical reconstruction nor to discuss its implications for subsequent developments in psychology. Nor again does the value of Bozzi's article reside in some allusion to or premonition of the complete collapse of Behaviourism, but rather in one of the keystones on which depends the possibility of exploring human experience:

> There is however one question that still pops up during discussions as it did in the past and it's a methodological question. It's a dilemma that is as old as the hills, inherited from a time when experimental psychology was still unthinkable and which in short can be summed up as follows: Is it or is it not possible to describe the immediate data of experience?

The setting out of this claim enables Bozzi to develop some of the hinge themes that constitute and articulate the formation of a phenomenological-experimental theory (see the first chapter of this book on Experimental Phenomenology). The point could be made as a purely methodological matter, and Bozzi himself held the chair in Methodology of the Behavioural Sciences until his retirement. Nevertheless, it is the same thesis that Wertheimer (1912) posits as a necessary condition of the perceptual study of motion and, we may go so far as to say, of the whole structure and program of Gestalt Theory:

> (. . .) to this end, one must above all avoid a certain definition of the word "illusions": One must not deal with this as an illusion concerning the actual physical situation. Rather, the investigation must strive to describe and study what is *psychologically given*. (Ed. 2012, p.7)

The "psychologically given" takes on an ontological significance in declaring that the object of psychology is defined by the recognition of the priority of experiential contents, of what they bear witness to. The physical description of the stimulus cannot be the standard against which every other description deviating from it is turned into an "illusion". It was not until Boring in 1921 that this serious epistemic "bias" was corrected: thereafter, if, instead of describing the "psychologically given", one were to furnish a physical description of the stimulus, one would be committing a "stimulus error". The consequences of disregarding the priority of the phenomenal datum in favor of the physical are well known (see Chapter 7 of this volume).

Historical context

The first publication of this article dates to 1961 and it was later placed at the head of the collection of writings that Bozzi himself organized under the title "Experimental

Phenomenology" (Bozzi, 1989). This further stresses the importance of the theses defended for the entire structure of his vision of phenomenology. Its appearance pre-dates by some years both the pathfinding work of Neisser (1967), which set out a coherent system of arguments that led to the birth of cognitivism, and Gibson's pioneering contributions (1966, 1979).

In those years, Vittorio Benussi's group at Padova and the Trieste school headed by Gaetano Kanizsa, Bozzi's teacher, were undertaking a profound work of methodological and experimental reflection on the themes of the psychology of perception in general and, in particular, on Gestalt Theory. At Padova, Fabio Metelli was formalizing the perception of transparency; Kanizsa was collecting observations and empirical data on some important phenomena in visual perception, such as anomalous figures and amodal completion; Bozzi and Giovanni Bruno Vicario were studying the perception of time; and Mario Zanforlin was engaged in studying animal perception, examining the mechanisms at work in flies' reactions to landing, and in pioneering studies of chicks' perception. In this atmosphere of deep commitment to experimentation, the community of psychologists in Trieste and Padua measured up both to the Gestalt tradition and to developments in Gibson's ecological psychology and the then-emerging cognitivism.

The conference that Metelli organized at Abano (Padua) in 1979, attended by European and American psychologists (and whose proceedings were enriched with other writings on the theme, *Organization and Representation in Perception*, edited by Jakob Beck, 1982), was an occasion for open debate on all the going concerns at the meeting point of Gestalt theses, cognitivist claims and Gibsonian ecologism, each of which was proposing its own approach to perception independently of the others. And it is in Gibson's 1950 book, *The Perception of the Visual World*, that we can find affinities with Bozzi's theoretical outlook, so much so that Bozzi, along with Riccardo Luccio, brought out the Italian edition of *The Ecological Approach to Visual Perception* in 1999 (Gibson, 1979/1999). One of the surest points of convergence between Bozzi and Gibson's thought, which was already explicit in *The Senses Considered as Perceptual Systems* (Gibson, 1966), is the radical refusal of the Aristotelian vision of the independence of the senses and the steadfast anchoring to the structuring of the world, to which human perception had to be able to have direct access.

Phenomenology between physical and geometrical descriptions

Among the other matters dealt with in this article, I think it is important to focus the attention on the central role that Bozzi gives to the relation between phenomenal description of experiential content and its transformation into measures. Once more, Bozzi handles the question as if the methodological feature belonged to the ontological nature of the experience itself and were not optional nor closely tied to the best result that can be obtained for reasons internal to the instrument employed. I earlier referred to chapter 7 of this book on the value to be given to respecting the relation between physical and phenomenal descriptions, where the latter has priority in conditioning the choice of the former with a view to providing a coherent transcription of the perceptual laws (see also on this point the debate on percept-percept coupling, e.g. Epstein, 1982).

It is in this direction that reflection points for the phenomenal foundations of the best geometry for the measurement of space. Bozzi was well aware of the adaptations and profound changes that research into the foundations of geometry had undergone since their first systematic formulation in Euclid's *Elements*. He was likewise aware raising the question of the usefulness of Euclidean geometry for the description of direct experience had to pass through a dismantling of the effort at abstraction from the empirical datum that we find in Euclid's definitions. In his notes to his Italian translation of the *Elements* (1565), mathematician Niccolò Fontana Tartaglia writes of the effort needed to pass from the forms left by nature or by a human trace on a sheet of paper, to the percept, to the barely-visible percept, right down to the absent percept so as to justify, by successive approximations, the presence "under observation" of that conceptual abstract residue that is a *point* or a *line*. This inevitable relation between the axiomatic-abstract forms and their experienced counterparts is recognisable in Euclid. Not that Euclid was unaware that there is a boundary between the contents of an experience of space, its forms and elements, and the result of abstraction. But there is certainly more than a mere trace of their relation in another book by Euclid, the *Optics*, in favour of an organization of perceptual space that can in the same way be described and formalized using the demonstrative instruments that are no less valid than those employed in the *Elements*. It is the pure phenomenal world that is systematized in the *Optics*, making it, to all intents and purposes, a treatise on the theory of vision.

Whether and how Euclidean geometry can be a formal reference system for the perception of space has been taken up by psychologists of various theoretical persuasions. For instance, Suppes 1977, sets out a clear and well-documented history of it down to that time, aware of some of the themes that Bozzi too had brought to the fore: "The development of Euclid's *Optics* is mathematical in character, but it is not axiomatic in the same way that the *Elements* are". Cutting and Vishton (1995) offer an orderly survey of the experimental work on depth perception analysing the reliability levels of psychophysical functions defined by the information sources in relation to possible geometries, among which the Euclidean is the primary reference point. In discussing the relations between experimental results that could support a phenomenological theory of geometry, Gogel (1990) cites the work of Foley:

> This result, together with that from a previous study (Foley, 1965) in which it was found that perceived visual angle usually exceeded physical visual angle by about only 10%, suggested that the intrinsic geometry of visual space was non-Euclidean. It was found, however, that subjective space became more Euclidean as distance information was increased (Foley, 1972).

Starting from different angles, the foundations of spatial perception have been investigated also by comparing human to animal perception, for instance in Spelke, Lee and Izard (2010):

> (. . .) studies of navigation provide evidence for a core system of geometric representation that guides navigation both in animals and in young children. The system is truly geometric in three respects. First, it captures shape relationships abstractly: animals navigate by the shape of a chamber whether or not the chamber is visible (Quirk, Muller, and Kubie, 1990) and over dramatic changes in the chamber's colour, texture, and material composition (Lever et al., 2002). Second, it preserves information for Euclidean distance and left-right direction: two fundamental properties of Euclidean geometry. Third, it supports inferences about the orientation of the self and the locations of objects and significant places. Nevertheless, the system fails to apply to the simplest and most prototypical objects of Euclidean geometry: two-dimensional surface

markings. Moreover, it fails to capture the central Euclidean property of angle. Thus, the core navigation system is not the complete system of "natural geometry" envisaged by Plato, Descartes, or Kant. (p. 869).

The bibliography on the psychophysics of space, and on how far available geometries may furnish useful descriptive tools for a theory of space, is obviously much richer than we can signal here. But it becomes an intriguing question whether and how Bozzi's observations may provide interesting and useful material for reflection. Likewise, it is worth wondering whether and how those same observations might open up a whole new field of enquiry into this aspect of the phenomenal foundations of the basic concepts from which geometry abstracts, while they also form the ground on which geometry stands.

References

Beck, J. (1982). *Organization and Representation in Perception*. Hillsdale, N.J: L. Erlbaum Associates.

Bozzi, P. (1989). *Fenomenologia sperimentale* [*Experimental Phenomenology*]. Bologna, Italy: il Mulino.

Cutting, J. E., and Vishton, M. (1995). Perceiving layout and knowing distances: The integration, relative potency, and contextual use of different information about depth. In W. Epstein and S. Rogers (Eds.) *Handbook of Perception and Cognition*, Vol. 5, *Perception of Space and Motion*, pp. 69–117. San Diego, CA: Academic Press.

Epstein, W. (1982). Percept-Percept Couplings. *Perception*, *11*(1), 75–83.

Euclide (trad. and ed. N. Tartaglia, 1565). *Euclide megarense acutissimo philosopho, solo introduttore delle scientie mathematice. Diligentemente rassettato, et alla integrita ridotto, per il degno professore di tal scientie Nicolo Tartalea brisciano. Secondo le due tradottioni. Con vna ampla espositione dello istesso tradottore di nuouo aggiunta*. Venetia: Appresso Curtio Troiano. http://www.liberliber.it/biblioteca/licenze/.

Foley, J. M. (1965). Visual space: A scale of perceived visual direction. *Proceedings of the 73rd Annual Convention of the American Psychological Association*, *1*, 49–50.

Foley, J. M. (1972). The Size-Distance Relation and Intrinsic Geometry of Visual Space: Implications for Processing. *Vision Research*, *12*, 323–332.

Gibson, J. J. (1950). *The Perception of the Visual World*. Boston: Houghton Mifflin.

Gibson, J. J. (1966). *The Senses Considered as Perceptual Systems*. Boston: Houghton Mifflin.

Gibson, J. J. (1979). *The Ecological Approach to Visual Perception*. Boston: Houghton Mifflin.

Gogel, W. (1990). A theory of phenomenal geometry and its applications. *Perception & Psychophysics*, *48* (2), 105–123.

Lever, C., Wills, T., Cacucci, F., Burgess, N., and O'Keefe, J. (2002). Long-term plasticity in hippocampal place-cell representation of environmental geometry. *Nature*, *416* (6876), 90–94.

Neisser, U. (1967). *Cognitive Psychology*. Englewood Cliffs: Prentice-Hall.

Quirk, G.J., Muller, R.U., and Kubie, J.L. (1990). The firing of hippocampal place cells in the dark depends on the rat's recent experience. *Journal of Neuroscience*, *10*(6), 2008–2017.

Spelke, E., Lee, S. A., and Izard, V. (2010) Beyond core knowledge: Natural geometry. *Cognitive Science*, *34*(5), 863–884.

Spillman, L. (2012) (ed.). *Max Wertheimer: On Perceived Motion and Figural Organization*. Cambridge, MA: MIT Press.

Suppes, P., (1977). Is visual space Euclidean? *Synthese*, *35*, 397–421.

Watson, J. B. (1913). Psychology as the behaviorist views it. *Psychological Review*, 20(2), 158–177.

Wertheimer, M. (1912). Experimentelle Studium uber das Sehen von Bewegung. *Zeitschrift fur Psychologie*, 61(3), 161–265.

10

INTEROBSERVATION AS A METHOD FOR EXPERIMENTAL PHENOMENOLOGY

Translated by Michael Kubovy

1.   I would not want the reflections and suggestions in this chapter to be read as yet another indictment of the experimental method in the context of scientific psychology. Quite to the contrary. Until now, at least as far as I can tell, experimentation – when combined with theoretical imagination – has been the natural source of discoveries. By experimentation I mean a knowledge-gathering activity through which one may, once in a while, find something new: by means of cleverly designed experiments, we may discover things – that may even have always been staring us in the face – and give them a form, a name, and a place in theory. The clever design of experiments is the creation of a logical space around the things under investigation.

   Since this, of course, does not happen very often, it should not surprise us that the experimental method is an appealing target to shoot at. Indeed, in the world of "normal" science, experimentation is a highly standardised and clearly marked practice, which relies on canons that indeed make the science normal. But when experiments are based on fresh discoveries or lead to them – and do not merely test hypotheses – they have the undoubted virtue of making life harder for theories, which in turn thrive on such challenges.

   Yet, confronted by the bulk of experiments that say little, I do not think it would be productive to embark on an anti-experimental crusade. It might instead be opportune, from time to time, to dismantle parts of the experimental method in order to reassemble them after they have been appropriately revised. This is the task I outline in the following pages.

2.   In some research on perception it is still important – in spite of the perfection achieved by other methods – to ask observers to accurately describe the fact under examination. I take it as a premise that when such a descriptions are generated by several observers working together under no constraints, the description will be more reliable and more valid than if it were produced by a single observer operating under constraints that seem irreproachable in conventional experimental practice. A similar approach has been proposed by Harré and Secord (1972)[1] for the analysis of the internal dynamics of small groups in social psychology; they call it an interpersonal "negotiation", which – the authors note – is common in "family psychotherapy session[s]" (p. 236). They define it as follows: "a negotiation consists in the pooling of viewpoints, and the subsequent correction of accounts" (p. 236).

It is obvious that not all perceptual research can be conducted in this way. I do not see how to use this approach, for example, to obtain psychophysical data from several subjects taken together, to measure reaction time, or to get button-press responses, etc.

Actually, I believe we can say more. The use of single observers under uncontaminated conditions is proper when one wants to study problems where the units of analysis have been arbitrarily carved out by experimenters who take it for granted they are studying the kind of topic for which very small units of analysis are appropriate. These units of analysis appear plausible to them in light of a theory or a set of hypotheses that they have in mind and not because they are the results of subjects' spontaneous segmentation of immediate experience. Thus, the early psychophysicists were right to study individuals one at a time, to give these individuals an extremely specific task, (sometimes) to ask for their first impression, and to require an unambiguously classifiable response. Contemporary psychophysicists have been highly sophisticated in developing all this – and they are well advised to do so because they are actually interested in the way the nervous system works, not in things to do with experience.

What is strange here is that despite the introduction of the phenomenological method, the rules of the ritual have remained unchanged. What must have happened may be what also happened to the criteria of repeatability and the need for multiple observers: physicists, for reasons of their own, canonised these criteria; the behaviourists then imported them wholesale into psychology (the eternal charm of *de imitatione scientiarum*), while phenomenologists paid no attention to all this – with the exceptions of Lewin and Metzger in relation to repeatability.

So one finds oneself having to ignore certain research problems because the facts upon which they rest have not been officially signed, sealed and delivered. Now, in the specific case of the experimental ritual, we may perhaps not end up excluding entire research problems, but paradoxically we may have trouble figuring out what the facts truly are.

3.   Thus, according to the experimental tradition:

a)   the materials of the study should be presented in an environment that is as barren and isolated as possible, away from noise, etc. (restrictions may vary from experiment to experiment);

b)   the observers should be naïve, uninformed about what you are looking for, and should not be prompted;

c)   the instructions should be inflexible, unambiguous, and should not contain any information that could bias the observer, whether explicitly or implicitly;

d)   often the first impression is the one that counts;

e)   often subjects may not retrace their steps in order to correct their responses or in order to see other alternatives, etc.

f)   the subjects' responses must be unambiguous, or at least they must pass through a grid that makes them uniquely classifiable.

I find it of great significance that it was under these or functionally analogous conditions that Rosenthal[2] and Orne[3] found their well-known demand characteristics. In contrast, demand characteristics never undermine Kanizsa's demonstrations where anomalous surfaces or masking of familiar figures were simply drawn with pen and paper, working with the most diverse subjects, tracing the design approximately, and often with considerable noise in the environment.

It is likely that each of the strictures just listed has more drawbacks than benefits and that taken together they are methodologically flawed. At the very least they are flawed under two conditions. The first is when one is interested in understanding a phenomenon that is theoretically important because it is a pillar of everyday experience. Among these phenomena are the tunnel effect, causal connectedness, intentional movement, formal masking, or pictorial depth cues, and so forth. The second condition is when one wants to experimentally investigate the internal relations of the phenomenon or the relations that bind the phenomenon to its context or the relations that make it independent of the context.

4.   Let's consider these points one by one.

First point (a). If you work on a phenomenon under uncontaminated conditions, you will never find out whether and how it depends on what surrounds it. In other words, you will never find out whether its internal properties also constitute the building blocks of what happens outside the laboratory and can be observed in everyday life. This means that you will never know whether the conditions that underlie perceptual identity in the lab also ensure the perceptual identity of two objects in the street. Nor will you be able to say whether the conditions that underlie the perception of causality are the same that lead us to perceive a collision between two cars. Nor will you be able to say whether the Brown effect explains why we perceive the motion of a Fiat 500 as "hurried" while that of a bus as "majestically calm". (But what is the point of phenomenology if not to guarantee this?) The characteristics of a phenomenon should be considered worthy of attention only when they are robust in the face of noise.

Second point (b). I find it amazing that those collaborators who are participants in our experiments should be kept in the dark about the very thing we want to understand in our work with them. After all, in order to collaborate they must clear their minds of a hundred of other things and focus only on certain specific aspects of the fact. Moreover, we need to tell them what to look for; they need prompts. If after all of this, they still report they cannot see the feature of interest, only then can we conclude that the phenomenon we wanted to explore was not robust enough. You need not worry that, under these conditions, participants might end up seeing whatever you want them to see, because the set of perceptual outcomes that we can imagine could be seen is much larger that the set of perceptual outcomes that could actually be seen.

Third point (c). Instead of being inflexible and unambiguous, instructions should be very rich and flexible in order to allow participants to take a variety of observational stances. In fact, an exhaustive exploration of the properties of something is the result of combining such a variety of observational stances. With respect to giving suggestions, see the second point (b).

Fourth point (d). A first impression counts as much as the others, since it too is a possible perceptual outcome. Such an impression might be less reliable than others because it came about before observers have had the time to understand the relation between the instructions and the object under observation; that is, fully to understand what the experimenter is looking for, which was explained when the problem was presented. Some evidence I have collected, and to which I shall return, has led me to acknowledge that first impressions may not be the most stable, but actually the most mediated, i.e., the least phenomenological.

Fifth point (e). Observers should be given the chance to backtrack. The observation of a percept gains subtlety when it is sufficiently prolonged, since one learns to look at it carefully. As we said earlier, observers will never end up seeing what cannot be seen – this is not a real threat. Instead they will see a variety of features that are real. Backtracking gives them an opportunity to compare the reliability of these features.

Sixth point (f). Observers should be allowed to respond, regardless of the classification of responses that the experimenter has in mind. That classification may be wrong; the task of the experimenter is to base the classification on what emerges from the experiments under way. If what they want to do is to confirm what they already thought, then it is likely that they will feel the need to have available a neat classification that fits their model. But if they want to construct a theory, then the theory will gradually emerge from the results of these careful observations and the understanding of these observations will emerge from the development of the theory.

These are my criticisms of the six points. Here I cannot refrain from repeating what I usually say at the outset when I address these issues: there is nothing new in what I have said; every good researcher implicitly knows it and applies it in practice. Indeed, before designing an experiment that follows traditional paradigms, a scientist usually discovers something – and I am happy to report that I have had the good fortune to be part of several such discoveries. On such occasions, very strange things happen from the methodological point of view. Those who find something new, have an immediate urge to interobserve it; not so much because they are afraid that they are taking one thing for another, but because sharing observations with others who are sufficiently informed and are trained to observe, and discussing it with such people, both leads them to a richer and more reliable observation of the fact and helps them identify ways to broaden the problem in new directions. In this phase of the research, all the rules that constrain standard experimentation are broken and, what is more, this is often done in order to design a better standard experiment. But at this stage, experimentation is absolutely pleonastic relative to the conclusion already reached. And furthermore, if the experiment is not well thought through, it may lead to a loss both of theoretical and of factual knowledge.

5.   Let us now turn the traditional rules upside down. This would roughly produce the following:

a)   It is a good thing to eliminate the laboratory atmosphere; any environment is fine as long as the fact under study is really a fact.

b)   Observers should be sufficiently informed about what we are looking for; they should be aware of the problems. Their naïveté should be given clues.

c)   Instructions should be broadly formulated. Indeed there might even not be any. Instead, observers should be given suggestions from time to time which they may accept, reject, or modify.

d)   The first impression should be surpassed and many others that follow it, to the point of saturation, are needed to have a command of the field of possible solutions.

e)   Observers should sometimes backtrack, to correct their responses, or to allow them to be corrected by others.

f)   A wide variety of responses, interconnected in many different ways should be allowed. Some of these responses might remain vague, but not to worry. We have plenty of time to subsequently revisit these responses as we develop an adequate system of classification based on hints gleaned from these very responses.

We must now make some theoretical, albeit parenthetical, remarks. The desire for a single response from observers (such as their "first impression") does not only have roots in the psychophysical tradition. I believe that it is also based on certain incomprehensible realistic assumptions, by which I mean the assumptions of an uncritical dualistic realism, which may be jettisoned after the ripening process of Experimental Phenomenology. According to these assumptions, each particular stimulus is associated with a single true perceptual outcome. This is why textbooks discuss multistable figures in a separate chapter and – in the best of the cases – treat them as a clue to how the perceptual system works; and – in the worst of the cases – treat them as effects aimed to inspire awe in the uninformed observer.

In a critical monistic realism – which I consider to be the proper theoretical basis for an Experimental Phenomenology – an object, or event, or phenomenal fact under observation is the logical sum of all possible configurations that can be perceived given a certain disposition of their discernible elements. To put it differently – using terms that do not sit well with me because they carry theoretical implications that I consider untenable – "a phenomenal datum is the class of all possible perceptual outcomes given a certain stimulus set-up".

Even those who study perception because they are interested in the processes that underlie it might find this definition advantageous. Indeed researchers will end up with learning a lot about the perceptual system if, given an input that remains constant or an input that is repeatedly presented under identical conditions, they consider the various possible transformations of an output. I also hazard that free observation contains much more information about what happens in the intermediate steps of the perceptual process than the yes-no answer implied, for example, by a task that requires a key-press (or some other similar response) obtained under very constrained conditions. The set of all possible perceptual solutions displays everything that a more or less hierarchically organised processing system can do, under given conditions; but most of all it reveals what the processing system cannot do. And this excludes of a large number of theoretically possible models. Metzger[4] magisterially shows that a certain distribution of elements in the visual field could – from a purely hypothetical point of view – give rise to a surprisingly large number of perceptual outcomes, whereas the number of phenomenally possible outcomes is not much greater than two. The set of configurations which are actually perceived obeys a law according to which certain elements can only combine only in this way or that and not in others.

It would be a mistake, however, to draw from this the conclusion that interobservation is a method of investigation applicable first and foremost to ambiguous structures.

6.   At this point we need to bring a new idea into focus. There exists a kind of ambiguity that is in fact no such thing and to which little attention has been paid since it does not have a large experimental payoff. Nevertheless, from a theoretical point of view, it is remarkably important.

It sometimes happens that we overlook a book we were looking for in a bookcase, but when we look again, we find it. In my opinion we cannot say that the second scan of the bookcase reorganises the elements that were present in the visual field during our first search.

For sure we cannot say that the book wasn't perceptually there at the first inspection, since its non-existence would have been revealed by the presence of a gap. At the moment when, during our second look, we saw the book among the others, it appeared with the manifest feature of pre-existing the moment of its discovery. This is what makes us say: "I didn't see it earlier". The term "see" here is semantically special; its semantics overlaps what happens at a phenomenological level: it means "it existed there" (I mean: it perceptually existed, not as a matter of physics) and not having seen it means that I did not pick it out rather than I did not, strictly speaking, *see* it.

Suppose that two people are looking for the book together and that one sees it and the other does not. The former draws the attention of the latter by uttering "ah, here it is". This is enough to make the second person *see* the book – as pre-existing, already looked at but not seen. This is to say that the cooperation between two observers improves the exploration of what is under observation even when the situation does not allow an internal re-organisation.

Something of this sort happens also, and even more readily, with tertiary qualities. I'm personally fairly blind to the figurative arts – perhaps with the only exception of architecture. But if someone points out something in the painting, I see it. And I do not see it materialising in that precise moment. It is not born under my eyes thanks to the power of suggestion. Pointing to it makes me discover it in the same way as when someone is pointed out in a crowded street.

Let's now connect this problem of multi-stability with that of an exploratory observation. If two people are looking at something together, they exchange information that helps the other see something, both when the thing appears at that moment before the eyes of one of them – because this person has been observing carefully – and when the thing was already there, previously unnoticed.

Now, in everyday experience multistability is very rare. And this fact has non-negligible theoretical consequences. When we measure thresholds or collect data under extremely simplified conditions[5] we almost always find a considerable variability in responses which is when the tools of statistics help us put things in their place – on paper. In point of fact, a problem remains and it is this: how can we reconcile so much variability found in data collected in experiments carried out in these simplified conditions with the confidence with which for example we drive a car in the traffic? When driving in traffic there are problems of size constancy, of relative and absolute speeds and accelerations of other objects (and Runeson[6] has shown, accelerations and decelerations are not perceived: in simplified experimental conditions, subjects perceive abrupt variations of speed). And there is the problem of one's own speed and acceleration. And there are probably other things that do not come to mind right now. If the uncertainty of drivers were what is found in the laboratory, where each of the mechanisms just mentioned is studied separately, the roads would be littered with wrecked automobiles. The truth is that each mechanism, when taken separately, works quite approximately but the joint work of many of them establishes a stable reality that it is hard to misinterpret.

The idea that each observer sees the world in their own way is of course very romantic and appealing, and responds to deep need for self-centredness so well represented by the philosophers of idealism and of various types of spiritualism. The findings of experiments carried out in simplified conditions further support this need: one might in fact easily end up thinking that since sensations vary so much from subject to subject, the multiplication of this variability by the various sensations experienced at a certain moment, will render enormous differences between the worlds concurrently seen by two people standing side by side. However, adding even a grain of evolutionary theory to the functioning of sensory systems suggests that an increase in the collaboration between different mechanisms should lead to exactly the opposite result.

Once while I was standing in front of the main door of our university building with an art historian, he tried to convince me that the two of us, when looking around, were seeing different things because of our different past experience and culture. I offered him a very simple test: if this thesis were true, then looking together around us with patient scrutiny, we would find things that he could see and I could not; things that I could see and he could not; and other things whose geometric shape, organoleptic properties, and other features describable in no uncertain terms, about which we were in strong disagreement. After spending a few minutes of trying, he lost patience. He ended up asserting that although such differences exist, they concern a certain class of properties, the so-called tertiary properties. This was enough for me, of course, and I could even partially agree with his last conclusion. But what was undoubtedly true, however, was that during the course of our uncontrolled interobservation session, he did show me things that I hadn't noticed and I also showed him other things that he hadn't noticed. Furthermore, even in the brief span of this inter-observation, we learnt to use our descriptive language in a more appropriate way and with greater agreement between us.

Naïve dualistic realism claims that for each stimulus there is one privileged perceptual solution. A critical monistic realism acknowledges that at a high enough level of complexity things are stable, objective, and largely independent of observers, who in the course of observing may discover in them new features as the observation proceeds.

To cut a long story short: some perceptual structures are characterised by multistability and in these cases interobservation helps draw our attention to all possible configurations. But every multistable object, if observed closely enough, ceases to be multistable. Instead, it becomes a perfectly intersubjective fact. When it does, interobservation reveals the object's features and the relationships among them.

It follows that interobservation as a method is not restricted to the discovery of characteristics of ambiguous figures; it allows us to obtain as much information regarding the structure of direct experience as possible.

7.   Now we are left with the task of describing what happens during a session of inter-observation.

One year, in a course I taught, I organised around twenty session of interobservation in order to observe interobservers at work. These interobservers were students in my course, working in groups of four or five; they were asked to discuss some of Kanizsa's figures – those where amodal completion is not "logical", would not be predicted by a confident Gestalt psychologist – and some other figures designed by Gerbino and myself in which multiple factors that affect perceptual grouping were combined and applied in a quite complex way.

Observers were invited to discuss the figures freely. The only thing that was clearly explained to them at the beginning of the sessions was that there is a big difference between what one actually sees and what one can imagine it represents. Other explanations were given during the session if question were raised – since according to the method of inter-observation, the experimenter is on the same level as the participants.

The following are, in my view, some important points to keep in mind:

a) Among the observers, a leader soon emerges. This is often the person who is most skilled at discovering perceptual solutions, and who is always the first to understand what the experiment is getting at. In the end, this leader is the one who, more than the others, corrects and interprets what the others are saying.

b) Various perceptual solutions emerge, one at a time, in an order that varies from session to session but that follows certain systematic sequences.

c) Participants comment upon and discuss their judgments about the obviousness of various perceptual solutions. It is not always the first solution that turns out to be the most obvious.

d) Participants also comment on the stability of various perceptual solutions. It is not always the first solution that turns out to be the most stable. Often, but not always, stability and obviousness match;

e) As the session proceeds, the group's use of phenomenological language becomes more refined. The presence of the object to which the participants attend leads them to use descriptive terms and sentences of increasing precision. Their terminology gradually converges as they realise the need to reach a good fit between the words they use and the structures they are describing.

f) The interobservers explain to each other how to reach certain perceptual solutions by varying their observational attitude, their viewpoint (getting closer to the object, tilting the head, occluding a specific part of the figure with a hand and so on) or what they should imagine in order to see that . . .

g) The final point is probably the most important; it deserves to be explained in greater detail. Hearing me present the ideas of this paper, colleagues have often asked me why I was not worried about the massive influence of the Asch Effect, which leads subjects to give, for one reason or another, non-perceptual solutions. Fine. Fortunately the discussion among the interobservers points to the opposite conclusion: as the session progresses, the distinction between what they are seeing and what they are imagining or thinking becomes more refined; this is a change that occurs *in experience* and not *in the abstract*. At the same time, observers become increasingly critical and more demanding before they accept the authenticity of descriptive solutions offered by other observers. The exchange of judgments and suggestions leads to fewer of the feared effects of suggestibility. The standard advice given in laboratories is "Never give instructions that might bias participants." This advice is fine and well, if there is no other way of correcting responses. But the critical presence of the others is a corrective because the exchange of suggestions leads precisely to the cancellation of suggestibility. In other words, groups behave in the way good researchers have always behaved in the pre-experimental phase of their studies, which – I insist – in almost all cases is nothing less than the research itself.

One might object that this way of proceeding cancels individual differences.

When, at Professor Giovanni Vicario's interview for promotion, one of the members of the board asked him whether he had tried to measure the acoustic tunnel effect with children, the elderly, with widows etc., Vicario replied "but I was interested in the tunnel effect, not in the elderly or children". Much good theory underlies this answer, which I cannot go into here. It is even possible that Vicario himself is unaware, at least in part, of this theory or would not approve of it[7]. But his answer goes to the heart of the problem.

There is little doubt that in the case of interobservation individual differences emerge in the descriptions generated at the beginning of a session. But the wonderful thing is to watch these differences evaporate – since they come to be recognised for what they really are, namely instances of defective communication and clumsy uses of language. As far as true individual differences go, it is immaterial whether the method of interobservation keeps us from noticing these individual differences or covers them up. The subject-matter of Experimental Phenomenology is things, not individual differences, or perhaps, an ideal brain which is not that of any individual participant in one study or other. The interaction between observers leads to an outcome which is most likely different from the average of the descriptions contained in data collected from individual participants; this could easily be tested. But I would question the claim that this outcome could be worse than a statistical summary. Rather, it is my impression that it generally contains more information, both in the technical sense of the word and in its common-sense meaning.

Notes

1   Harré, R. and Secord, P. F. (1972). *The Explanation of Social Behaviour*. Oxford: Blackwell.
2   Translator's note: Rosenthal, R. (1963). On the social psychology of the psychological experiment: The experimenter's hypothesis as unintended determinant of experimental results. *American Scientist*, *51*, 268–283. Also Rosenthal, R. (1966). *Experimenter Effects in Behavioral Research*. New York: Appleton-Century-Crofts.
3   Orne, M.T. (1969). Demand characteristics and the concept of quasi-controls. In R. Rosenthal and R. Rosnow (Eds), *Artifact in Behavioral Research*, pp. 143–179. New York: Academic Press.
4   Translator's note: Spillman, L. (2009) (ed. and trans.). *Wolfgang Metzger: Laws of Seeing*. Boston: the MIT Press. (or. title: *Gesetze des Sehens*. Gebundene Ausgabe – 1936).
5   Translator's note: Bozzi characterised such conditions as those in which the subject is forced to "hold his breath", meaning innatural conditions of partial sensory deprivation.
6   Runeson, S. (1974). Constant velocity – not perceived as such. *Psychological Research*, *37*, 3–23.
7   [Editors' note: Giovanni Vicario (b. 1932) was, with Bozzi, an assistant of Gaetano Kanizsa at the University of Trieste. Though he and Bozzi were close friends, and often conducted research together, Vicario always claimed that he had no bent for theory, which he left to Bozzi.]

COMMENTS ON INTEROBSERVATION AS A METHOD FOR EXPERIMENTAL PHENOMENOLOGY

Michael Kubovy

I plan to write personal comments on several thought-provoking sections of this paper. I have not chosen those that I consider to be the most interesting. Rather, I have chosen the ones to which I can most readily contribute a constructive sequel.

1.   Bozzi sets a high standard for experiments that lead to discoveries. Only experiments that do not "merely" test hypotheses meet this standard. Experiments that do not do more, are doomed to say nothing.

This is a bold and acute methodological observation, which – to my mind – applies to most papers published in psychological journals. Consider the first example that came up in a Google Scholar search I just did. Here is a summary of an experiment by Spears (2011):

> (. . .) subjects were randomly assigned to a smaller ("poor condition") or a larger ("rich condition") budget (Spears, 2011) and were then asked to make a series of "purchasing" decisions. Naturally, those with a smaller budget faced more difficult trade-offs because they could afford fewer of the desirable goods. Because decision-making under difficult trade-offs is likely to consume scarce cognitive resources, subjects with a small budget were hypothesized to be impaired in subsequent tasks that require willpower and executive control (Muraven & Baumeister, 2000). The study indeed found that previous decision-making in the poor condition – but not the rich condition – impaired behavioral control, as measured by the duration of time subjects were able to squeeze a hand-grip and their performance in a Stroop task. Thus, poverty appears to affect decision-making by rendering people susceptible to the willpower and self-control depleting effects of decision-making. (Haushofer and Fehr, 2014, 862)

You might ask, what is wrong with this study? There is no reason to believe that Spears's conclusion is wrong. But in itself it did not lead to a discovery. All it did was to demonstrate that it is possible to contrive a setting under which one can observe the hypothesised behaviour.

Under which circumstances, then, could such an experiment have led to a discovery? Only if it had carefully pit two or more plausible ideas (preferably mature theories) against each other, as recommended by certain methodologists (Chamberlin, 1965; Platt, 1964). But however much I tried, I have been unable to come up with a plausible theory that would predict that decision-making in the rich condition would impair subsequent behavioural control. In that sense this experiment was doomed to say little, i.e. that it is possible to contrive a setting under which one can observe the hypothesised behaviour. (I think Bozzi was a bit carried away when he said that such experiments are doomed to say *nothing*.)

2.   If I could talk to Bozzi today, I would ask him a question: Is it really the nature of the experimentation in psychology that is to blame? Could the culprit not be the weakness of our theories?

In physics, before a theory can be formulated, we must have a descriptive law. Take, for example, the ideal gas law (for a history, see Arsenjev, Lozovitski, and Sirik, 2003):

$$PV = nRT \tag{1}$$

where P is pressure, V is volume, n is the amount of gas (in moles), R is the ideal gas constant, and T is absolute temperature. Only after such a law was established, could the kinetic theory of gases come along to explain the ideal gas law. The theory assumed that a gas consists of a large number of perfectly elastic molecules of negligible size, moving rapidly and colliding with each other and the walls of the container. From these assumptions it became possible to deduce the ideal gas law.

In psychology such a two-stage process has not been thought to be possible, mainly because our observations do not lend themselves to mathematical formulations. And so what passes for theory in psychology may be more aptly treated as hunches, or conjectures about restricted phenomena. The ideas of Spears (2011), mentioned earlier, rely on three vaguely defined limitations, *limited attention, limited willpower*, and *limited cognition* (Figure 10.1).

Nevertheless, contrary to what it may seem, I'm not saying that psychology needs more mathematisation or even greater clarity or precision. Nor did Bozzi. Instead, I suspect that Bozzi implies here that psychology is poor in well-founded, systematic, consensually agreed-upon description. Biology (and physics) emerged from ambitious efforts to create natural histories, systematised collections of observational data (a long-standing precursor of science first practiced by Pliny the Elder, 2015, in 77–79 C.E.), culminating in the 1930s with development of ethology by Tinbergen, Lorenz, and von Frisch. With few exceptions, psychology seems to have pushed observation into the non-public context of discovery (Reichenbach, 1938, where he distinguished between the context of discovery and the context of justification), by staying within the chain of evidence offered by previous non-observational studies, as the example of Spears shows.

3.   Bozzi contrasts two methods for psychology. One the one hand, there is the conventional (and virtually universally followed) method that assigns to multiple observers the task of describing a perceptual experience or to perform a task that produces data, which the experimenter believes will uncover an experience or a mechanism. When this method is used, it is up to the researcher to collate and summarise what all the subject-by-subject data have in common. In contrast, there is Bozzi's approach, the *method of interobservation*.

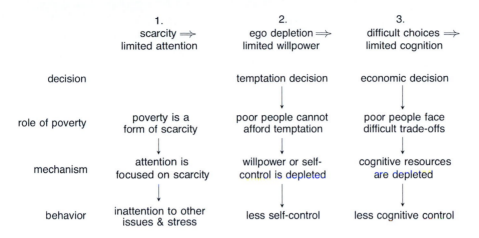

FIGURE 10.1 Three ways poverty can affect behaviour, according to Spears (2011).

The experimenter assigns a task to a group of observers who try to produce a consensual description. This means that certain kinds of experiments are out of reach (experiments that require the determination of thresholds or reaction times or correct and incorrect responses).

Interobservation is designed to overcome the idea that partial experiences of the world may be irreconcilable or at least hard to collate, as the parable of the blind men and the elephant[1] suggests. This is clear from his anecdote about his conversation with an art-historian colleague:

> (. . .) during the course of our uncontrolled interobservation session, he did show me things that I hadn't noticed and I also showed him other things that he hadn't noticed. Furthermore, even in the brief span of this interobservation, we learnt to use our descriptive language in a more appropriate way and with greater agreement between us.

In his description of what happens during a session of interobservation he comments on the group's meandering path through tentative descriptions of how they see what they are looking at:

> (. . .) groups behave in the way good researchers have always behaved in the pre-experimental phase of their studies, which – I insist – in almost all cases is nothing less than the research itself.

But how does one exercise the method of interobservation? I suspect that Bozzi would not disagree with the following: Start from careful and informed observation that is readily recognisable by one's audience as being correct. Take the following passage from Elias and Dunning (1986, pp. 86–87, which I quoted in Kubovy, 1999):

> It may not be easy to find a clear consensus with regard to the characteristics of plays or symphonies which provide a high and low degree of audience satisfaction, although the difficulties may not be insuperable even in the case of concerts in spite of the

greater complexity of the problems. With regard to sports–games such as football [soccer], the task is simple. If one follows the game regularly one can learn to see, at least in broad outline, what kind of game figuration provides the optimum enjoyment: it is a prolonged battle between teams that are matched in skill and strength. It is a game which a large crowd of spectators follows with mounting excitement, produced not only by the battle itself but also by the skill displayed by the players. It is a game which sways to and fro, in which the teams are so evenly matched that first one, then the other scores and the determination of each to score the decisive goal grows as time runs out. The tension of the play communicates itself visibly to the spectators. Their tension, their mounting excitement in turn communicates itself back to the players and so on until the tension reaches a point where it can just be borne and contained without getting out of hand. If, in this manner, the excitement approaches a climax, and if then suddenly one's own team scores the decisive goal so that the excitement resolves itself in the happiness of triumph and jubilation, that is a great game which one will remember and about which one will talk for a long time – a really enjoyable game.

What turns it into interobservation is two features: it (to paraphrase Bozzi) reveals things that one had not noticed, and at the same time seems to be unquestionably true, with the benefit that it provides us (in Bozzi's words) with a "more appropriate" "descriptive language."

Note

1   Attributed to Jainism, whose followers espouse the theory of the many-sided nature of reality (Matilal, 1981). This is inconsistent with the use to which the parable has been put in contemporary discussion of science, where it implies that without science we are like the blind men.

References

Arsenjev, S. L., Lozovitski, I. B., and Sirik, Y. P. (2003). The gas equation for stream. (Eprint: arXiv:physics/0303018).

Chamberlin, T. C. (1965). The method of multiple working hypotheses. *Science*, 148 (3671), 754–759. (Reprinted from *Science* (old series), 1890, 15, 92–96.).

Elias, N., and Dunning, E. (1986). *Quest for Excitement*. London: Blackwell.

Haushofer, J., and Fehr, E. (2014). On the psychology of poverty. *Science*, *344* (6186), 862–867.

Kubovy, M. (1999). On the pleasures of the mind. In D. Kahneman, E. Diener, and N. Schwarz (Eds), *Foundations of Hedonic Psychology: Scientific Perspectives on Enjoyment and Suffering*, pp. 134–154. New York: Russell Sage Foundation.

Matilal, B. K. (1981). *The Central Philosophy of Jainism (anekānta-vāda)*. Ahmedabad, India: L.D. Institute of Indology.

Muraven, M., and Baumeister, R. F. (2000). Self-regulation and depletion of limited resources: Does self-control resemble a muscle? *Psychological Bulletin*, 126 (2), 247–259.

Platt, J. R. (1964). Strong inference. *Science*, *146* (3642), 347–353.

Pliny the Elder (ed. 2015). *Complete Works*. Hastings, UK: Delphi Classics. (Translated in 1855 by J. Bostock and T. Riley).

Reichenbach, H. (1938). *Experience and Prediction: An Analysis of the Foundations and the Structure of Knowledge*. Chicago: University of Chicago Press.

Spears, D. (2011). Economic decision-making in poverty depletes behavioral control. *The B.E. Journal of Economic Analysis & Policy*, *11*(1), 1–44.

PART IV

11

PHENOMENOLOGICAL ANALYSIS OF PENDULAR HARMONIC MOTION AND THE CONDITIONS FOR "NATURAL" MOTION ALONG INCLINED PLANES

Translated by Paola Bressan and Paolo Gaudiano

(A) Phenomenological analysis of pendular harmonic motion

1. Preliminary considerations

This enquiry into the phenomenal organisation of the oscillations of pendulums was stimulated by two converging interests.

The first was that of studying the perceptual aspect of a motion that is often present among our visual experiences and characterised by great regularity: a motion, therefore, truly apt to shed light on the possible influence on the ways that it is actually "seen" exerted by extra-perceptual factors of an intellectual nature such as physical and mathematical ideas, or else by the familiarity due to the frequent recurrence of the experiences themselves.

The second reason was of a more complex type. I always found it not unreasonable to believe that certain errors of interpretation – those that can be found in the most elementary forms of scientific constructs, for instance – derive their plausibility from the immediate evidence of the facts as they appear.

Ancient science, in reality, was quite cautious about what was known as "the deception of the senses"; but in practice it is very difficult to fully take in the fact that *all* of our direct experience of the external world is regulated by the same laws that "the deceptions of the senses" obey.

The perplexities raised at the beginning of the seventeenth century by the Galileian laws indicated fairly clearly to me that the case of harmonic pendular motion could be a situation in which the hypothesis just suggested (about the validity of theorisations that are too faithful to immediately available evidence) might be tested experimentally. It is arguably the case that some other problems of the history of science – even if restricted and particular – may be approached in a similar manner, employing the data of phenomenological analyses. I realise that from a narrowly critical viewpoint there are many difficulties facing this type of approach, but some attempt along these lines will be perhaps not devoid of interest.

1a)   Galileo and the Aristotelians of his times. There is something curiously paradoxical in contrasts that separated Galileo from the Aristotelian physicists whom he represented, in his major dialogues, with the figure of Simplicio. This consists of the apparent agreement among the speakers on what should be the principles of a sound scientific investigation.

Indeed, both Galileo and the Aristotelians recognise that physical sciences must be a complex of descriptions faithful to the *facts present in experience*, and that, at least in principle, observation has every right to dictate theory, and theory every obligation to abide by observation.

Furthermore, since, as Aristotle had taught, scientific knowledge consists of a construction of concepts of general validity, whereas a science of individual facts is not possible, their agreement extends to the notion that observation must be systematic and logically organised starting from numerous particular cases.

Because of this ambiguous agreement of viewpoints, Galileo always leaned toward the belief that had Aristotle come back to life during Galileo's times, he would have been convinced by the new demonstrations; even though there was perhaps not a single Peripatetic thesis with which, in his mature years, he would have been disposed to agree.

In reality, there is no convergence of viewpoints; beneath the ambiguous statements with which it is supported, there remains a radical disagreement – over and above various points of detail – above all about what must be meant by *the facts of experience*.

To grasp the nature of this disagreement, it will suffice to remember the accusation of "abstractness" that – initially formulated by experimentalists of the Renaissance against the Peripatetics – these later turned against Galileo. In the words of E. Cassirer:

> Galileo is continuously accused of disregarding the single case in his distinction and determination, trying to comprehend nature under general laws and principles. The strength and character of the particular fail to be acknowledged if one wants to compress, as he does, in a single formula all of the possible instances of the motion of bodies, from the flight of birds to the swimming of fish and to the propulsion of "simple" bodies and "composite" bodies. The characteristic of (Peripatetic) physical investigation is that it cannot leave these differences to one side and remains forever entangled as a result of its first formulation of the problem. The true task of induction in physics, now insist the adversaries (of Galileo), consists of the faithful collection and analysis of the particular: it cannot be carried out by resolving nature – instead of following it in all its details – as a system of abstractions and mathematical relationships.[1]

It is not difficult to understand why, starting from such a point of view, it seemed illegitimate to neglect, in the study of the physical world, the immediate appearance of things, which is to say, the fact that they have various shapes, colours, sizes and expressive values, and that are spread out far and near in visible space, etc. It was incredible, for instance, to think that the sun is stationary and the earth revolves around it, when one can plainly *see* by observing the facts that the earth is stationary and the sun traces an arc in the sky. In the same way it was clear that one could not deny physical truths such as these: "the things on the earth are either large or small", "objects are either near or far", and so on; nor could one deny intuitive principles such as the laws of the fall of heavy bodies, according to which the more a body weighs the faster it falls: in fact, as soon as it is released, it accelerates more and more until it reaches its "velocity".

An examination of the actual differences between the way of thinking about experience and abstraction in pre-Galileian methods and in the new physics cannot be broached in this study; this theme is developed in a recent book by L. Geymonat, and particularly in its later parts, regarding the *Two New Sciences*.[2]

What must be underscored here is the particular type of plausibility invoked by the readers of Aristotle, namely that, all reasoning notwithstanding, people see things *thus-and-so*, and hence the search for generalisations capable of unifying in a single theory facts that are evidently various implies a progressive loss of sight of the reality of experience.

This way of presenting things appears frequently in the Simplicio of the Galileian dialogues, and from time to time allows us to sympathise with his point of view.

Among the most incredible (in this sense) discoveries made by Galileo in the course of his mechanical investigations, is that of the laws of the harmonic motion of the pendulum. One result of his experimentations was that the only factor acting upon the frequency of oscillation of a pendulum is the length of the pendulum itself. This fact indirectly demonstrated the exactness of the laws that had been found for bodies in free fall and generalised to inclined planes.

For pendular oscillations, as for free-falling bodies, the conditions of motion are independent of the mass or the weight of the body in question; in the case of the pendulum, additionally, if the length is unchanged, no external push can slow down or increase the frequency of the oscillations, which remain, with great approximation, isochronous for any amplitude of the arc traced by the pendulum.

All these observations, however, seem to be made only to conflict with common sense.

The physicist Guidobaldo del Monte, unconvinced by a first letter from Galileo in which he had been told of the laws of pendular harmonic motion, expressed his perplexities to Galileo, who replied apologising for his insistence "in trying to persuade you of truth of the proposition about motions that take place in equal times", and added that "having always appeared marvellous to me, now it appears even more so, as your Lordship deems it *impossible*" (Letter dated November, 1602).[3]

Guidobaldo's doubts reappear, later on, in the first day of the *Discourses*. Salviati at one point recounts the experiment that he carried out with two pendulums – one ball of lead and one of cork, hung by strings of equal length – which "repeating one hundred times (. . .) the forward and backward sweeps" maintained isochronous oscillations. The lead pendulum "neither in one hundred vibrations, nor in one thousand anticipates the time by a single moment"[4] – adds Salviati – as if it should have been obvious to expect such a thing; in addition he notes, as if to underline a curious fact, that the isochronous motion persist even when the cork pendulum travels along a minute arc, while the lead pendulum undergoes large oscillations.

A few pages later Sagredo mentions that he has several times observed "lamps hung in some churches by very long ropes": "but that I was about to learn" – he adds – "that the same mobile hung from a rope one hundred yards long, removed from the lowest point once by ninety degrees, and another time by only one degree, or a half, as much time would spend in tracing this smallest arc, as it would in tracing the widest. I certainly do not believe that I have ever witnessed a fact that still appears to have something of the impossible".[5]

These types of attitudes are undoubtedly of great interest for the history of thought, because they offer to the student, almost *in vitro*, fragments of physical views that are very simple and were popular for centuries, translated into peculiar and deep-rooted prejudices, so much so that they became part of the spontaneous way of thinking.

I think, on the other hand, that they can also present a considerable interest from the point of view of the exploration of the world as it is directly experienced. Witnesses such as those cited lead us – quite reasonably – to suppose that there are particular perceptual structures that favour a determinate way of seeing a fact, and, on this level, create an obstacle to the acceptance of physical laws that are in conflict with the evidence of the "data", as we see them.

1b)   An experiment by J. Piaget. For similar reasons, there is also great interest in the observations made by B. Inhelder and discussed by J. Piaget on the kinds of attempts made by children of various ages to find the variable acting on the frequency of oscillation of a pendulum very close to the mathematical one.[6]

The experiment was carried out with a view to studying how the ability to identify logically a causally effective variable among a set of irrelevant variables progresses between the ages of six and fifteen years. The variable to be isolated in this case was the length of a pendulum (a thin string stretched between the axis of oscillation and the oscillating body) whose modification was accompanied by a change in the frequency of the oscillations. The other variables – objectively non-operative, but this, of course, was a fact that the children were unaware of – were chosen among those factors that, without prompting, are considered responsible for the frequency of pendular oscillations. The children could thus make the pendulum heavier or lighter by replacing the oscillating body with others of different weights; they could give the pendulum a more or less energetic initial push; and they could reduce or increase the amplitude of oscillations, with the opportunity to repeat the operations until they had found a satisfactory solution.

The problem to be solved was the following: what must be done to make the pendulum swing more rapidly or more slowly? For the authors of this research, this is essentially a problem of logic, not one of how to read experience. The subjects' reports quoted in this study document the gradual increase in the power of abstraction, and the development of a capacity for ever more refined analysis of the factors involved. It appears that an erroneous reading of the experience should be interpreted as a result of the mistakes present in the logical reasoning: Piaget does not state this explicitly, but from his exposition as a whole one gets the impression that this is his point of view.

The fact still remains, however, that after they have manipulated irrelevant variables, the children *see* that the pendulums have increased or decreased their frequency of oscillation, or, at the very least, claim to see it and behave accordingly. The pendulums are seen as oscillating more slowly or more rapidly when the weight of the oscillating body has been changed (subjects: Jac; Bea; Cro; Jot; Ros; Lou; p. 63 ff.); or else when the amplitude of the oscillation is varied by pushing the pendulum more or less energetically, or when it is let go from a higher point in the pendulum's path (subjects: Hen; Jac; Per; Ros; same pages). After performing the operations these children used the following expressions: "this time it goes quickly", "it goes more quickly", "it is the slowest one", etc.

It is impossible to establish whether or not these expressions refer to what each child sees at that moment compared with what he or she had seen in the preceding situation, or if – in spite of the facts he or she sees – the child insists on maintaining an idea that had been formulated as a hypothesis prior to the operation. In any case, the constancy of these errors and their fixed direction (for example: oscillations along broader arcs are always seen as "faster") allows us to speculate that they may originate in causes of a perceptual nature.

1c)   The resistance of spontaneous physics. There is another fact worth mentioning here, which is also able to confirm the existence of psychological obstacles which make it difficult to accept the Galileian laws of pendular motion.

At the end of some of my experiments, I tried to question the subjects, all with diplomas from the classical high school, about their convictions on the physical motion of pendulums; I later broadened this inquiry to other university students who had not taken part in my experiments. The results may not be considered as reassuring for physics professors as they are for the purposes of the present research: none of the students remembered the laws of pendular motion, and, in an attempt to replace the forgotten physics with some theorisation that had some plausibility or that agreed with common sense, they would make up sentences of this type: "the greater the amplitude of oscillation is, the slower the pendulum will swing"; "the heavier the pendulum is, the slower it moves", or the opposite: "the more it weighs, the faster it moves" (in the first case, they claimed, it must be slower because it is more massive and thus encounters more resistance in the medium, etc.; in the second case its motion would be "faster because its weight makes it fall more rapidly"). In addition, some would find it reasonable that an initial push could increase the frequency of oscillations by virtue of its greater energy. Only one claimed that the frequency of oscillations increases with the length of the pendulum, and few others that all existing pendulums oscillate with the same frequency; the majority of the students realised that frequency diminishes with length, but almost invariably this relationship was seen as linear.

In the course of these conversations I noticed analogous errors about falling bodies, the same errors that led Galileo to perform the famous demonstration from the tower of Pisa.

1d)   Pendulums that are "too fast" and "too slow". Finally, there is one more thing to consider, more closely connected with my experiments. It is evident that objects oscillating at a great distance from the point to which they are attached have a period of oscillation that is notably long in relation to our way of perceiving an actual duration: a period, i.e., that cannot be contained entirely in the phenomenal present and is thus perceived as "too slow".

An oscillating lamp that hangs from a sixty-metre chain has a period of roughly 15 seconds. In all likelihood, if one tries to imagine the motion of such a body, one would imagine it to be less slow than it actually is.

The same thing comes about in the opposite situation: the oscillations of very small pendulums (e.g., 3–6 cm) have a much higher frequency than one would expect, and give the clear impression of being "too fast" for that oscillating body; that is, they are not "right", they are not "proper".

Starting from this observation, it is possible to set up a simple experience. Show someone a small pendulum, say, four centimetres long, and, while holding it still, ask that person to imagine with what rhythm it would swing, if it were released. After about ten seconds, release the pendulum to start its motion. It is highly probable that the observer will admit to have expected oscillations of a lower frequency.

If the cases of the Aristotelians, of Piaget's children and of my students, can legitimately be regarded as inexact operations and inadequate convictions that in the end are only interesting problems to do with the organisation of thought, the last observation reported above represents a very different case: it clearly indicates the involvement of factors acting upon the immediate organisation of the data of phenomenal experience, thus confirming the supposition that guides this paper.

2. The notion of "proper motion"

2a)   Proper velocity. In the last section we used a special term: that of phenomenally "proper" motion. In passing, we suggested interpreting this expression as indicative of the perceptual character of an oscillation that is neither "too slow" nor "too fast". This concept, however, calls for further discussion. From the point of view of physics, it is nonsense to speak of fast or slow motions, and it is particularly nonsensical to speak of motions that are *too* fast or *too* slow. Indeed, in physics there is no definition that allows them to be discriminated, even within a given frame of reference; it is clear that such a distinction would serve absolutely no purpose.

In any case, if an eccentric person wished to introduce such a distinction in order to group certain velocities in the class of "too slow", some others in the class of "just right", and the remaining ones in the class of "too fast" he should proceed approximately so:

a)   assume as stationary a certain frame of reference S;

b)   arbitrarily choose two other frames of reference that are moving relative to S, such that their velocities relative to S be unequal; name S' the one with slower velocity and S" the other;

c)   give to the class of velocities relative to S and ranging between the velocities of S' and S" the name of class of *right* velocities;

d)   and finally label the velocities ranging between S' and the state of rest (with respect to S), with the expression "too slow", and all velocities greater than S"with the expression "too fast".

Only by means of a set of irrelevant and artificial conventions such as this, is it possible to create – from a purely objective point of view – a tripartition of motions with respect to their velocities.

In general, nonetheless, everyone understands what is meant in everyday language by a reference to velocities that are *low* or *high*, even without explicit indication of a criterion for discrimination; and in the same manner, one understands what is meant by the expressions "too fast" and "too slow" even when their limits are not specified.

In this context too, after all, it is possible to confirm phenomenal experience in part with an example drawn from pre-Galilean physics. From Aristotle to Galileo physicists never doubted the legitimacy of the distinction between "violent" and "natural" motions. "First of all" – writes Aristotle in the *Physics* (IV, 8, 215al; and also: V, 6, 230a29–31) – "every motion is either violent or natural. Given that there is a violent motion there must also exist a natural motion: the violent one is against nature, and 'against nature' is the opposite of 'according to nature'."

Without doubt, this distinction must not be seen as a mere description of two phenomenal characteristics of motions: it also arises from the necessity of logical coherence, justifiable if one keeps in mind the overall organisation of Aristotelian physics, and in particular the theory of local motions in terrestrial and celestial mechanics. The tenacity of this mistake in two thousand years of the history of science, however, becomes easier to understand if one supposes that the subdivision of movements in this way is very spontaneous, precisely because it reflects our way of seeing reality. L. Geymonat talks, in this connection of a "genuine methodological courage demonstrated by Galileo, in combining two motions of almost opposite kinds, such as the 'natural' motion of falling objects and the 'violent' motion due to the explosion of gunpowder in a cannon: Aristotelian physics would never have allowed a unified scientific handling of two such different concepts."[7] Different, one could add, because they distinguish two categories of visual experiences "of almost opposite kinds".

2b)   Proper frequency. Bearing these distinctions in mind, let us now examine the motion of pendulums. From a physical point of view, it does make sense to speak of a *proper* motion as a way of saying each individual pendulum has a determined period of oscillation depending on its length, if we have a pendulum that is very close to the mathematical one, and on the distance between its centre of gravity and the axis of oscillation, if we have a composite pendulum.

We can thus say that the meaning of the expression "*proper* pendular motion" of a given pendulum – *in a physical sense* – consists of Galileo's formula (or, if greater accuracy is desired, Huyghens') appropriately applied to the individual case.

To define the meaning of the same expression on the phenomenological level, we must first take into consideration the observations reported in the paragraph *1d)* of the first part of this paper, where it emerged that, for the oscillatory motion of a pendulum there are at least two distinct expressive characteristics, that we can denote with the attributes "too slow" and "too fast".

Starting from this datum, and using an apparatus that will be described later, we can proceed as follows. We let a pendulum, for example 30 cm long, swing through the full range of frequencies between a very low number of oscillations per minute (e.g., 20), and a very high one (e.g., 90); it is then possible to see that at the onset of the demonstration the oscillations of the pendulum take place with an exasperatingly slow motion, and that at the end of the demonstration they become extremely fast. Between these two bands of frequencies there is an area where the motion of the pendulum appears neither restrained nor pushed by some external force, but instead *right* and – so to speak – well proportioned to its size, so that one would think that an identical pendulum, left to itself, would naturally oscillate in that manner.

Oscillations that are too slow can be described as those of a pendulum that oscillates within a dense and viscous medium; and those that are too fast can be described as the oscillations of a pendulum that is nervous and restless; if pushed to the limit they give rise to exaggerated deformations of the oscillating figure, along with a poor perception of its contours.

Similarly, we can also define as phenomenally *proper* or *right* the motion of a pendulum characterised by the absence of the phenomenal properties mentioned for slow and fast oscillations.

In reality, a definition of this concept cannot be other than an ostensive one. It is in fact not possible to communicate interpersonally descriptions of expressive properties of the perceived world only by means of linguistic signs. For the sake of correctness, then, we should then say that, for a given person, the concept of phenomenally proper motion of an observed pendulum is *defined by the operations of choice* that the person executes during the observation of that pendulum, whose frequency of oscillation is successively increased and decreased, starting from frequencies that are paradoxically slow or paradoxically fast.

From an epistemological perspective, this definition still cannot be considered quite satisfactory, but it is the best that can be done for the purposes of this enquiry.

It is obvious that a concept defined ostensively will present, moreover, a certain variability from person to person: what is important, though, is that this variability be maintained within an experimentally ascertainable range, and that it be subject to some criterion of measurability. In my experiments I made use of a method somewhat akin to that used by Ida Kohler in her research into "personal time"[8] and I was able to notice that, although the task presented to the subject was necessarily imprecise because of the imprecision of the terms used (slow, fast, etc.), they grasped it with great ease, and found the distinctions perfectly obvious.

In the course of the following exposition, the limits of the range of *proper* frequencies will be expressed with the number of oscillations per minute (preceded by the Greek letter η), so that an immediate comparison can be made between these values and those of the frequency of an identical pendulum that is oscillating spontaneously.

3. The Experiment

3a)   Experimental setup. The experiments that will be described in the coming pages were designed to ascertain the existence of well-defined relations between the perception of *proper* pendular motion and the presence of a number of factors that can act upon it.

The working hypotheses that guided my research are the following:

1)   The frequency of oscillation that for a given pendulum can be seen as *right* or *proper* is probably different from the frequency that the pendulum would exhibit if it were oscillating freely.
2)   This frequency may depend on more than one variable, not just one, as in the case of physical pendular motion ($T = f\sqrt{l}$).
3)   Furthermore, we should not expect the quantitative relationship between length and frequency that regulates physical motion to hold true on the phenomenal level as well.

In more general and exact terms, we can say that just as for the physical motion the relationship

$$T = f(x)$$

holds, where x is, in the simplified case, $\sqrt{l}$; thus, for the phenomenally *proper* motion of a pendulum the relationship

$$\Theta = \psi(\alpha, \beta, \gamma \dots)$$

must hold, where Θ is the *proper* frequency, and the Greek letters in parentheses indicate different variables, such as amplitude of oscillation, various length ratios, apparent mass and apparent centre of gravity, etc.

In order to isolate these variables to study them separately, each as a function of the phenomenally proper motion, we built an apparatus capable of transforming circular motion into harmonic pendular motion (Figure 11.1).

This apparatus consists of a variable speed transmission with conical gears, which allows continuous modulation of the angular velocity of disk A. This disk is oriented vertically, and has a protruding pin B fixed near its border. A thin belt C is attached to pin B and,

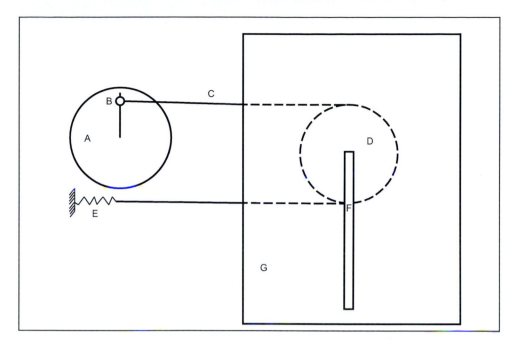

FIGURE 11.1 A: variable speed disk; B: protruding pin; C: thin belt; D: pulley; E: spring; F: pendulum; G: screen

about one and a half metres away, the belt is wrapped half way around a pulley D and circles back to where it is attached to a spring E. When the disk is rotating, pin B, with one end of belt C attached to it, describes a circle, and exerts tension on the belt through two quadrants, consequently turning pulley D through some arc. In the other two quadrants pin B releases tension, and the belt is pulled in the opposite direction by the spring E; thus the pulley D itself revolves in the opposite direction through the same arc. Attached to the axis of rotation of pulley D is the upper end of pendulum F. A screen G is located between the pendulum and the pulley to hide the mechanisms from the observer.

With this method the period of oscillation of the pendulum can be varied as desired by the experimenter, who controls it by acting on the transmission.

The range of frequencies that was used during the course of my experiments varies from a minimum of η17 (complete oscillations per minute) to a maximum of η95. In the vicinity of these two extremes the effects of *too slow* and *too fast* are so evident that the investigation of a broader range would be superfluous.

The pendulums used in the experiments were black, rectangular, 2.5 cm wide, and respectively 10, 20, 40 and 60 cm long. The screen behind them was rectangular, 1 metre wide and almost 2 metres high, of a light grey colour.

3b)   Action of the "oscillation amplitude" factor. The effect of oscillation amplitude on the "proper" frequency of the pendular motion was studied with a 40 cm pendulum. The observer was seated roughly 2.5 metres away from the screen,[9] which was illuminated from the front. The procedure followed the four phases as follows.

I) The black rectangle, placed on the screen in a vertical position, was suddenly animated by a pendular movement of η95, with an amplitude of 10°, while the observer was asked to describe the situation. If in the description there was no spontaneous mention of the excessive rapidity of the motion, the experimenter would pose the following question: "In your opinion, is this pendular motion 'just right', 'too fast', or 'too slow'?"[10] changing each time the order of these attributes, and without specifying more exactly what they might mean.

Very few subjects felt the need to ask for further clarification of "just right"; and the occasional additional explanations always remained equally ambiguous.

All the subjects considered the η95 frequency excessively fast.

By acting on the transmission, the frequency was then reduced, at a rate of approximately one oscillation per second; the subject was told to stop the experimenter by waving his/her hand when the oscillations no longer seemed "too fast."

The frequency first chosen by the subject could then be modified as many times as he/she wanted, in search of a motion deemed satisfactory for his perception of "just right" motion.

This motion was often described by the subjects as characterised by the impression that the pendulum "goes by itself", "moves freely", "moves in virtue of its own weight, left to its own weight", etc.

II) At this point the subject was asked to look away from the screen for a few seconds; at the beginning of the new observation, the pendulum still oscillated at the same frequency, but now sweeping arcs of 60° instead of 10°.

The experimenter then asked again if the oscillation was right, "too fast", or "too slow"; often it was unnecessary to pose the question because the subject had spontaneously voiced his observations.

III) The same operation was carried out starting from η17 with the 10° amplitude;

IV) This was then changed to 60°.

The four phases of the experiment were carried out in the above order with some of the subjects; with others, the order was varied as follows: III, IV, I, II; II, I, IV, III; IV, III, II, I.

The results obtained are summarised in Table 11.1.

Analysis of these data clearly indicates that the 60° oscillation is seen as "too fast" at the same frequency that is judged "just right" for the 10° oscillation.

In more general form, the result of these experiments can be expressed as follows:

1) *when the amplitude of oscillation is increased, the phenomenally "just right" motion of a pendulum is found at lower frequencies.*

From this proposition one can infer that:

1a) *a phenomenally greater velocity (or smaller velocity), for a given pendulum, is obtained by increasing (or decreasing) the amplitude of its oscillation.*

TABLE 11.1 Effect of amplitude of oscillation on the "just right" frequency (40 cm pendulum)

Participants	Objective frequency perceived as "just right" oscillation		Differences between 10° and 60° arcs
	Arc of oscillation: 10°	Arc of oscillation 60°	
A	↓58	↓39	−19
	↑47	↑40	−7
B	↓60	↓39	−21
	↑40	↑31	−9
C	↓60	↓60	0
	↑63	↑60	−3
D	↓54	↓36	−18
	↑43	↑34	−9
E	↓71	↓56	−15
	↑56	↑47	−9
F	↓70	↓70	0
	↑70	↑70	0
G	↓65	↓40	−25
	↑41	↑30	−11
H	↓55	↓42	−13
	↑36	↑36	0
I	↓41	↓35	−6
	↑31	↑29	−3
L	↓51	↓36	−15
	↑36	↑30	−6
M	↓41	↓30	−11
	↑29	↑26	−3
N	↓48	↓40	−8
	↑27	↑27	0
O	↓75	↓48	−27
	↑65	↑48	−17
P	↓80	↓68	−12
	↑48	↑38	−10

Note: The frequency is expressed in complete oscillations per minute.

The symbols ↑ and ↓ indicate that the value was determined, respectively, starting from "too slow" and "too fast" frequencies.

That is:

$$w = \frac{\lambda}{A}$$

where w is the objective frequency, λ is the phenomenal velocity of the motion, A is the amplitude of oscillation.

From which:

1b) *in order for a given frequency to remain phenomenally unaltered, it is necessary that the objective frequency be decreased (increased) to compensate for an increase (decrease) in the amplitude of oscillation.*

That is:

$$\lambda = A_w$$

The children of Piaget, therefore, were right to say "now it goes more quickly" after increasing the amplitude of oscillation by pushing the pendulum or by dropping it from a higher starting position. As a matter of fact, if their way of perceiving the motion was analogous to that of the subjects I examined, they were "seeing" the pendulum moving more rapidly (1a).

For the same reasons, however, also the doubts raised by the experiments of Galileo were in their way legitimate. Indeed (1b), because, for a given type of oscillation to remain phenomenally unchanged, the increase in amplitude must be accompanied by an increase in the time necessary for one oscillation. In other words: it is obvious to expect that a pendulum oscillating along greater arcs would take a longer time to sweep them.

Two subjects were exceptions to the general agreement of the data, but their results, nevertheless, obeyed a rule; evidently they found, in each of the presentations, a rhythm that was for them particularly recognisable or particularly good, perhaps leaving to one side the visual nature of the pendular motion. The frequencies, respectively $\eta 60$ and $\eta 70$, indicated by these subjects are moreover rather high compared with the average frequencies indicated by the others. These facts support the hypothesis that the "personal time" of the two subjects overruled the evaluation of the *proper* oscillations; indeed, according to the previously mentioned study by Ida Kohler, most people appear to have a personal time between 70 and 100 cycles per minute.

It is probable that even the intersubjective differences in evaluation that I often observed among my subjects can be explained as a function of their "personal time"; but only a comparative study on a sufficiently large number of people could allow us to assess the correctness of this thesis.

3c)   The "length of the pendulum" factor. The results of the experiment just presented demonstrate that the phenomenal frequency is affected with some regularity by a factor totally inactive from a physical point of view, namely, the amplitude of oscillation.

In the experiment that we now present, conversely, we examine the variable that actually affects the frequency of pendular harmonic motion, namely, the length of the pendulum.

We have already mentioned that the length of the pendulum, in physics, is defined as the distance of the oscillating body from the axis of oscillation in the case of a mathematical pendulum (which consists of a point-mass attached to an ideal wire), while for composite pendulums this value is determined on the basis of the distance of the centre of gravity of the oscillating body from the axis of oscillation.

In both cases, however, a simple relationship exists between the number of oscillations in a given time and the progressive increase in the length of the pendulum: if the pendulum has length 1 and duration of oscillation 1, then, increasing the length to 4, 9, 16, 25, . . . the duration of its oscillations will be 2, 3, 4, 5, . . . i.e. always the square root of the number representing its length.

Even before the start of the experiments it seemed fairly plausible that the relationship $f\sqrt{l}$ could not hold between the length of the pendulums and their phenomenally "just right" frequency. Indeed, we have already alluded to the fact that, among freely-oscillating objects, it is easy to find some whose motion is too slow, and others whose motion is too fast.

To ascertain the kind of difference holding between the physical situations and the perceptual situations – the latter evaluated in terms of the *proper* frequency – I used the apparatus described above, with pendulums 10, 20 and 40 cm long.

These pendulums (as I already mentioned, rectangular and 2.5 cm wide, so that they can be considered – from a physical point of view – as homogeneous bars hung from one end), when released to oscillate freely have the following frequencies:

> the 10 cm pendulum, η112 (complete oscillations in one minute), equal to a period of 5.357 tenths of a second;
> the 20 cm pendulum, η79, equal to a period of 7.594 tenths of a second;
> the 40 cm pendulum, η56, equal to a period of 1.0714 seconds.

The experimental setup is the same as in the preceding study. Once again each presentation starts with the request of a fairly detailed description, followed eventually by the request to classify the observed pendular motion in the tripartition "too slow", "just right", or "too fast".

The order of presentation of the three pendulums was appropriately varied in the course of the experiments. The results are given in Table 11.2.

The interpretation of these results becomes easier when the data from each of the subjects are compared. Indeed, if we trust to the mere numbers, the intersubjective differences are often rather large. The 10 cm pendulum, for example, was seen by a subject as oscillating

TABLE 11.2 Effect of length of the pendulum on the "proper" frequency

Participants	Frequencies perceived as "proper"		
	Pendulum length: 10cm	Pendulum length: 20cm	Pendulum length: 40cm
A	↓65 ↑55	↓56 ↑42	↓48 ↑41
B	↓46 ↑27	↓36 ↑26	↓34 ↑21
C	↓67 ↑41	↓48 ↑31	↓38 ↑30
D	↓60 ↑48	↓42 ↑39	↓31 ↑31
E	↓59 ↑42	↓45 ↑34	↓37 ↑30
F	↓56 ↑45	↓48 ↑34	↓48 ↑32
G	↓80 ↑64	↓56 ↑41	↓30 ↑28
H	↓70 ↑58	↓53 ↑42	↓40 ↑32
I	↓80 ↑60	↓65 ↑40	↓55 ↑37
L	↓75 ↑61	↓63 ↑57	↓54 ↑42
M	↓65 ↑53	↓55 ↑50	↓46 ↑40
N	↓60 ↑48	↓55 ↑46	↓40 ↑40
O	↓77 ↑45	↓61 ↑36	↓38 ↑28
P	↓80 ↑56	↓63 ↑50	↓45 ↑36

The frequency is expressed in complete oscillations per minute.

The symbols ↑ and ↓ indicate that the value was determined, respectively, starting from *too slow* and *too fast* frequencies.

"just right" at η80 (↓) and η60 (↑), by another at η56 (↓) and η45 (↑); the 20 cm pendulum in one case was seen moving "just right" at η65 (↓) and η40 (↑), in another case at η36 (↓) and η26 (↑); the 40 cm pendulum in one case at η55 (↓) and η37 (↑), in another case at η31 (↓) and η31 (↑).

When the "just right" frequencies for each subject are compared, however, the following three facts become clear:

1) *As the length of the pendulum is increased, the frequencies have lower values.* The amount of decrease is not constant (although it is typically greater between the 10 cm and 20 cm pendulums than between the 20 cm and 40 cm pendulums), nor is there regularity in the differences between (↓) and (↑) presentations for the three pendulum lengths (although the difference is generally smaller between the two values determined with the longer pendulum than with the shorter one).

2) *The phenomenally "just right" frequencies are always inferior to those that an identical pendulum would exhibit while swinging freely.*

3) *This difference decreases with an increase in the length of the pendulum.*

These three upshots, verifiable for every subject, can be represented schematically by averaging the results of the (↓) and (↑) presentations, respectively, for the 10, 20 and 40 cm pendulums, and using these values to construct a histogram that can be readily compared to the curve corresponding to the objective frequencies of identical pendulums (Figure 11.2).

The fact that the difference between the objective frequencies and the phenomenally ones for the same pendulums becomes increasingly smaller with the increase in pendulum length, suggests the existence of a point of convergence at which the subjective evaluation of the "just right" frequency spans a range of frequencies including the one that is correct from the physical point of view. It also seems likely that, beyond this point of convergence, the effect would be reversed: for progressively longer pendulums the frequencies should be represented by greater values than those of the physical frequencies of identical pendulums; until the "too slow" effect that is typical of lamps hanging from extremely high ceilings comes about.

Some tests that I carried out with a 60 cm pendulum seemed to confirm at least the first of these hypotheses. However, the investigation was suspended, for the moment, because of some technical difficulties encountered in trying to force longer pendulums to oscillate at all of the desired frequencies.

4. Conclusions

The two experimental analyses reported here clearly demonstrate, at least as regards the length and the amplitude of oscillation, that the structural laws of phenomenal pendular motion are far from those that regulate the same motion at the physical level. The immediate phenomenal organisation was found to be just as independent of factors external to the perceptual system, such as physical and mathematical notions, as of the familiarity gained with repeated experiences. On the other hand, since the effect of the "amplitude of oscillation" can be easily related to Piaget's protocols and to the quotations from Galileo reported above, my results support the hypothesis that the same phenomenal peculiarities of harmonic pendular motion may have played a role in hindering or delaying the discovery of the laws that determine such motion in the physical realm.

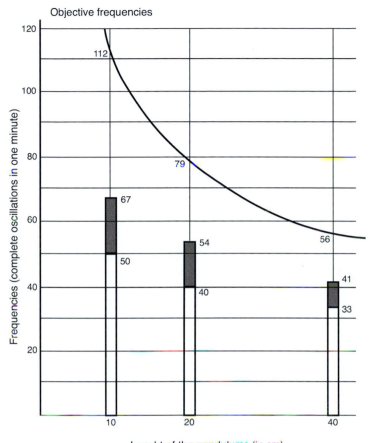

Objective frequencies

FIGURE 11.2 The curve, going from right to left, shows the increase of the physical oscillations for progressively smaller pendulums, from about 40 cm to about 10 cm. The grey areas on the bars indicate the range of frequencies within the averages (rounded to the nearest integer) that were experimentally determined starting from high and low frequencies, with the 10, 20, and 40 cm pendulum.

In order to complete this investigation it will be necessary to study experimentally – in addition to the possible correlation between the characteristics of "personal time" and those of "proper frequency" – at least two additional variables: apparent mass and apparent centre of gravity.

Also in relation to hints given by pre-Galileian mechanics, I hope to carry out some research on free fall and inertia, with a view to determining whether or not, also in these cases, perceptual data are able to justify – at least partially – the extraordinary vitality enjoyed by Aristotelian physics in the past.

Notes

1 Cassirer (1954), pp. 425–426.
2 Geymonat (1957), at p. 312 ff.; p. 320 ff.; p. 328 ff.; p. 339 ff.; p. 368 ff.

3 Galilei (1882), vol. I, at p. 23.
4 Galilei (1882), vol. I, at p. 128.
5 Galilei (1882), vol. I, at p. 133.
6 Inhelder and Piaget (1955), ch. IV, at p. 62.
7 Geymonat (1957), at p. 310.
8 Frischeisen-Köhler, I. (1933a), at p. 721 ff.
9 Some tests demonstrated that changes in the distance of the observer from the screen – at least those between 1 m and 5 m – do not affect the evaluation of frequencies.
10 Frischeisen-Köhler, I. (1933b), at p. 293.

References

Cassirer, E. (1954). *Storia della filosofia moderna* (*Das Erkenntnisproblem in der Philosophie und Wissenschaft der neueren Zeit*; 4 vol. 1906–54). Italian translation by A. Pasquinelli, 1954, Torino Italy: Pgreco

Duhem, P. (1958). *Le Système du Monde* (tome VIII). Paris: Hermann.

Frischeisen-Köhler I. (1933a). *Das Persönliche Tempo. Eine erbbiologische Untersuchung*. Leipzig, Germany: Thieme.

Frischeisen-Köhler I. (1933b). Feststellung des weder langsamen noch schnellen (mittelmässigen) tempos [Determination of the neither slow nor fast (medium) speed]. *Psychologische Forschung*, *18*, 291–298.

Galilei G. (1882). *I dialoghi sui massimi sistemi tolemaico e copernicano*, Milan, Italy: Sonzogno (the English text adopted by the original translators is that of Stillman Drake (1953), *Dialogue Concerning the Two Chief World Systems*. Berkeley, CA: University of California Press).

Geymonat L. (1957). *Galileo Galilei*. Turin, Italy: Einaudi.

Inhelder, B. and Piaget, J. (1955). *De la Logique de l'Enfant à la Logique de l'Adolescen*. Paris: Presses Universitaires de France.

Toulmin, S.E., and Baier, K. (1952). On Describing. *Mind*, LXI (251), 13–38.

Wertheimer, M. (1945). *Productive Thinking*. New York: Harper.

Whiteley C.H. (1956). Meaning and Ostensive Definition. *Mind*, LXV (259), 332–335.

(B) The conditions for "natural" motion along inclined planes

1. Preliminary considerations

In an earlier paper, experimental analyses had allowed me to point out the existence of a fairly well-defined relationship between the phenomenal structure of pendular oscillations and the type of objections raised by Aristotelian physicists against Galileo, when he published his findings on pendular harmonic motion.

Those analyses demonstrated that a particular qualitative feature of oscillating motion, which can be defined as "going neither too slow nor too fast" and which can be expressed in terms of objectively measured frequencies, is a variable that depends on the length of the observed pendulums and – for a pendulum of given dimension – on the amplitude of oscillation. This last point, in essence, indicates that the law of isochronic motion does not hold from the point of view of phenomenally "natural" (neither slow nor fast) oscillations. This was indeed the law that Galileo's opponents challenged.[1]

At that time I planned to perform a similar analysis on the structure of some other types of motion about which, at the dawn of modern physics, the views of the Peripatetics clashed with the results of experiments carried out in line with Galileian methodology; that is, experiments quantitively controlled and able to yield results that could be expressed in terms of physical geometry. Indeed, the qualitative nature indicated by the words "natural", "proper" and so on can be extended to motions other than periodic pendular oscillations. In this sense there may happen to be other cases in which, having experimentally found the best structure for a certain motion, it might then turn out that the description of this structure is isomorphic to the description that had been offered for the same motion by the Peripatetics, or by Aristotle himself.

One type of motion that may be of interest in this respect is that of a body in free fall. Many well-known controversies, based on Aristotelian treatises on dynamics, developed throughout the Middle Ages on the matter of free-falling bodies, and led Galileo to carry out some of his famous demonstrations. In point of fact, the discussions dwelt more upon the causes of the motion driving bodies that are allowed to fall freely, than on the description of the falling motion. It was believed (1) that the velocity of a falling body is directly proportional to its size, or to its weight (these two concepts were often confused); and (2) that a free-falling body at first undergoes an acceleration that takes it from rest to its "proper" velocity; from there on it proceeds with uniform motion until it finds an obstacle capable of stopping it. This second point, however, was never completely agreed upon because of the ambiguity of the Aristotelian writings; several commentators, beginning with Simplicius, half intuited that the motion of a free-falling body is a motion with constant acceleration, and this claim was later openly supported by other physicists, including Averroes, Roger Bacon, and Albert of Saxony.[2] The fact remains, however, that in his day Galileo had to demonstrate his theory on accelerated falling motion, often in the face of significant opposition, which allows us to suppose that the authors just mentioned did not exercise a long-lasting authority.

If one wanted to study the problem of free fall with the method I used for the phenomenological analysis of pendular oscillations, one might start by asking a very simple question: when is it that the downward motion of an object is seen as free fall? In fact, if the movement is too slow, it might be seen as a "glide" or a "restrained descent"; if it is too fast, it might be seen as the motion of a projectile that is shot downward. In all likelihood, there ought to be an intermediate velocity, neither fast nor slow, which is to say "natural", that gives the impression of free fall.

The experimental analysis of this problem, however, is complicated by the fact that an event such as free fall – if it takes place over too short an interval – happens very quickly, which makes it difficult to obtain a sufficiently accurate observation. Indeed, in order to examine accurately the motion of a falling body, one should be able to follow it for at least a few seconds, and hence over a distance of several tens of meters. Because it is necessary to be able to modify the speeds and the accelerations of the falling bodies, it is not at all simple to reproduce these conditions in a laboratory. I thought I could circumvent this difficulty satisfactorily by reducing the problem of free fall to that of motion along an inclined plane.

From a physical point of view, inclined planes simply represent a special case of free fall. The acceleration is given by the same constant g; the difference is that the distance covered in a time t decreases as the slope of the inclined plane is decreased, that is, as the angle of the inclined plane is increased as measured from vertical. When this angle reaches 90° the distance covered in time t is zero; we then have rest, or inertial motion.

We can formulate the phenomenological problem of motion along inclined planes as follows: what are the properties that the displacement of an object along an inclined plane must have in order to be seen as "natural" sliding, neither too fast (as if it had been pushed) nor too slow (without noticeable friction) along its entire path? Is there a change, and if so, of what kind, in the structure of such motion as a function of given variables, such as the slope of the inclined plane and the size of the object? Lastly, is it possible to infer from the analysis of the perceptual structure of this motion anything that relates to pre-Galileian laws of dynamics?

The results of the experiments that will be described in the next pages allow us, within some limits, to provide an answer to each of these questions.

2. A study by Max Wertheimer

2a)   The deduction of the concept of inertia from falling and descending motions. In Wertheimer's book, which collects a set of essays on productive thinking, there is a chapter dedicated to the origins of Galileo's logical unification of the phenomena of free fall, motion along an inclined plane, and inertial motion.[3] The acute analyses carried out by the author on the thought processes that led to such a unification were concerned only with the logical aspect of the problem. Yet, even though the object of Wertheimer's study are the inferential processes that allow the determination of the objective structure of those very motions that we shall examine from a phenomenological perspective, it will nevertheless still be useful to summarise some parts of his research; this will allow us to illustrate in which sense one can say that – in some cases – perceptual facts can make it difficult to accept the result of a correct inference.

Galileo's reflections on motion – according to Wertheimer – must have begun with a few isolated observations. The most elementary of these is the observation that, when released, objects will fall. (The ancient physicists would have said that they descend toward their natural place, the earth.) In addition, we are well aware that if we push an object along a horizontal surface, it will continue on its own over a greater or lesser distance according on the force with which we pushed it, and it will then come to rest.

Everyday experience further shows that movements are affected by other factors, such as the shape of the moving objects, whether or not there are obstacles in the way, etc. How is it possible to find a relatively simple logical scheme to frame these elementary observations in an orderly fashion? Galileo thought he could start looking for such a scheme by observing a motion that (a) takes place without the need of a push, such as free fall; but that also (b) takes place along a surface, such as inertial motion; descent down an inclined plane satisfies both conditions.

If we think of the entire range of inclined planes with greater and greater slope, from horizontal to vertical, it becomes evident that free fall is simply a special case of downward motion. In this way – because the lesser the slope of an inclined plane, the slower a body will descend down its length – Galileo was more easily able to study the nature of such a motion, discovering that it is continuously increased by a constant acceleration, and that there is a precise relationship between the distance covered by the moving object in a given time and the slope of the inclined plane in question. As a result of this kind of reasoning, it was easy – in the end – to discover the law of free fall.[4]

However, inclined planes between vertical and horizontal, taken together, define only one class of motions: those directed downward. It is possible to imagine a complementary class of motions: that of upward motions. This is probably what led Galileo to take up the analysis of projectile motion. His experiments indicated that there holds a perfect symmetry between the two classes of motions. As a matter of fact, an upward motion caused by a force is characterised by a constant negative acceleration of the same magnitude as the positive acceleration that is at work in free-falling bodies. In addition, if we push some objects upward along inclined planes of various slope, the dynamical laws in action turn out to be exactly symmetrical to those for the downward motion along the same inclined planes.

Let's now consider all these motions together, from upward motions to downward motions, with the various intermediate cases. "What happens" – wonders Wertheimer – "when the plane is horizontal, when the angle is zero, and the body is in motion? In all cases we may start with a given velocity. What *must* consistently happen in accordance with the structure [of the reasoning outlined above]? The positive acceleration below and the negative acceleration above decrease from the vertical case to . . . no positive or negative acceleration, that is . . . a constant movement?! If a body moves horizontally in a given direction, it will continue to move at constant velocity – for all eternity, if no external force changes its state of motion."[5]

This conclusion – adds Wertheimer – is in sharp contrast with the old belief, reinforced by everyday experience, according to which a body moving on a horizontal plane must come to rest sooner or later. Furthermore, this paradoxical claim can only be accepted because it follows consistently from some acceptable premises, but it can in no way be experimentally proven: the external forces that oppose inertial motion can in no circumstances be removed. In spite of this, it is in just this way that Galileo set out the bases of modern physics. Nowadays we are fairly familiar – says Wertheimer – with concepts of this type; but if we carefully consider the situation, it will not be difficult to see how implausible and paradoxical – relative to the common way of thinking – this concept really is.

2b)   Inertial laws and inertia as a phenomenal experience. The paradoxicality we have just brought to light is very instructive for those, such as ourselves, who are interested in the phenomenological analysis of motion. This paradoxicality does not derive only from the contrast with everyday observations – and with the authority of the ancients. That this is so is shown by Michotte's experiments on the "launch effect": when the motion of an object is experienced as being caused by a collision with some other object, the first portion of the motion clearly seems to depend on the "impressed force" on the object by the collision; later, however, the perception of this dependence vanishes. If the object moves even further away, its motion becomes an autonomous displacement bearing no relation to the collision that originally had given rise to the impression of a causal relationship.[6]

Hence, in the case just considered, it is easy to see that the logical-mathematical reasons that allow an understanding of inertial motion are in disagreement with the perceptual structure of phenomenal "inertia"; and nothing prevents us from believing that – even alongside everyday experience, and even alongside the authority of the ancients that sometimes survives in common ways of thinking – such a structural factor may play a significant role in reducing the credibility of the result of those Galilean inferences that Wertheimer tried to reconstruct.

From this perspective, the experiments that I will report in the following paragraph may be seen as an extension of the parallel that can be set up between phenomenal structures and physical-geometrical structures, illustrated in this paragraph with the case of inertial motion: on the one hand there is the perceptual fact – that is, the phenomenal inertia in Michotte's paradigm of causal launch – while on the other hand there is the logical necessity of admitting that inertial motion is constant and infinite, as emerges from the reasoning analysed by Wertheimer. This extension concerns the "intermediate cases" between inertial motion and free fall.

3. The Experiment

3a)   Procedure. In order to generate a downward motion along an inclined plane of perfectly known dynamical characteristics, I employed the method of tracing a spiral on disks rotating behind a slotted screen. This method, among other options, combines precision with ease of implementation.

The disks with the spiral appropriately calculated for the case under scrutiny were connected to a variable speed transmission fitted with a device for the readout of disc velocity during the experiment.

A variety of screens can be mounted in front of the disc. A roughly triangular figure is drawn on the centre of each screen, with one side representing the inclined plane: this side is 30 centimetres long; the slope of the inclined plane varies between figures. In the various experimental conditions I worked with slopes of 5°, 10°, 22°, 45°, 68°.

A slot is cut out of the screen along the side of the figure that represents the inclined plane, in order to transform the circular motion of the spiral into a linear motion of a small square. To study the motion of small objects, the slot on the screen and the thickness of the spiral are both 0.4 cm in size, so that the observer sees a roughly square moving body, with each side 0.4 cm long. In the situations set up to study the motion of large bodies the size of the spiral and of the slot are increased to 1.6 cm, so as to give the observer the impression of a body four times as large, along each side, as the one used in the previous case.

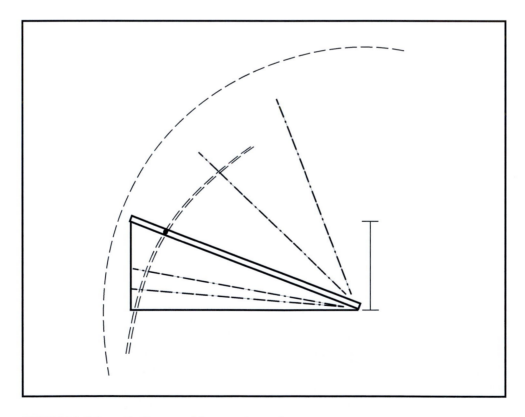

FIGURE 11.3 Schematic diagram of the experimental apparatus

By combining the various screens and the various discs it is possible obtain a large number of different situations. The variables examined in these situations are:

1)   the "form" of the motion (constant, naturally accelerated, uniformly accelerated, variably accelerated; and lastly, partly accelerated and partly constant);
2)   the size of the object (each side 0.4 cm and 1.6 cm long);
3)   the slopes of 5°, 10°, 22°, 45°, 68°.

During the presentations the observer was about three meters away from the screen. Some tests showed that the distance of the observer from the screen seems to have no influence on the judgments made.

3b)   The "form" of the motion. The following question was the first one to be experimentally approached: What must a motion along an inclined plane look like in order to be perceived as a sliding motion at every point along the entire path; so that, in other words, during the entire descent the object does not appear either "restrained" or "pushed"?

Our attempts began with the examination of two very simple motions: 1. uniform motion; 2. naturally accelerated motion (the true motion of free-falling bodies).

Beginning with the preliminary phase of the experiment, it became evident that neither of these types of motion was the desired one: the uniform motion of an object along an inclined plane is seen as too fast at the beginning, while naturally accelerated motion is seen as too fast at the end of the descent.

Bearing these observations in mind, we prepared some spirals corresponding to motions that are a combination of accelerated and constant motion. More precisely, two of these generated accelerated motion, but with the acceleration decreasing toward the end of the inclined plane; a third one was calculated to produce accelerated motion along the first part of the descent (the first quarter of the whole distance), and then constant motion – that is, with no acceleration or deceleration for the rest of the descent.

We will label A and B, respectively, uniform motion and naturally accelerated motion; we will label C and D the motions in which acceleration decreases toward the end, and E the motion that is accelerated at first and constant thereafter (Figure 11.4).

In the experiments carried out to determine which is the best sliding motion along an inclined plane, the slope of the inclined plane was 23°, and the object moved along a 30 cm path in just over one second. (This is a fairly good spatio-temporal ratio for a 23° inclined plane, as will be seen in the following experiments.)

The observers were asked to examine the situation carefully and as many times as they wished, in order then to be able to suggest which corrections would be necessary to make it a "natural sliding motion", a "good descent", as would be the motion of an object sliding down a frictionless inclined plane.

The task, when explained in this manner, might seem difficult and ambiguous. But by observing a movement such as the one we generated, it is simple for anyone to understand what these instructions mean. For example, the friction exerted by the object upon the inclined plane, when the motion is phenomenally too slow, can be seen as clearly as the shape of the object or its colour. Conversely, "excessive speed" is also a fact that can be seen very well. It is as if at that point the object were still set in motion by a previously imparted push: in other words, its motion is "pushed".

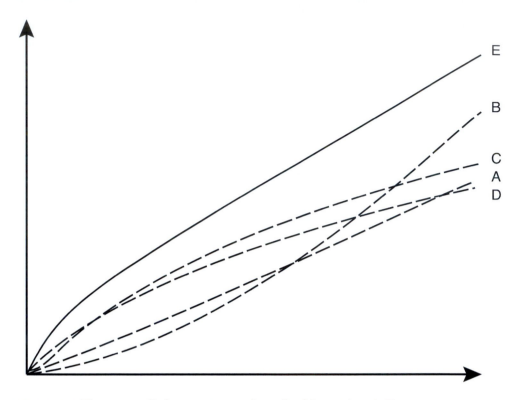

FIGURE 11.4 Time versus displacement curves for each of the motions A–E

By mentally subdividing the object's path into three or four parts, any observer is able to tell along which section the object goes too quickly, too slowly, or in a natural manner.

As the corrections were being suggested, other discs were shown until the subject declared that he saw a good motion, that is, a truly natural sliding motion. I examined in this way ten cases, and in nine of them the choice of the observer indicated as "best" the motion E, the one consisting of a brief section of accelerated motion followed by uniform motion.

I report here some of the exact words used to express the judgments that dictated the observers' choices:

Motion A (uniform): "it is fast at first, then it seems to slow down; it's like a car the starts going downhill at full speed, but then disengages the engine and proceeds naturally"; "initially it is quite fast; if anything, it is slow at the end"; "initially it jumps, then continues smoothly to the end"; "at first it is as if someone had pushed it. From just before half way to the end it is fine. There is a sense of a sudden decrease in speed (around the end of the first third of the path) that reduces the excessively fast motion to a correct level."

Motion B (naturally accelerated): "at first it is just a bit too slow; from half-way on it is way too fast"; "the beginning is fine, it is at the end that it is definitely too fast"; "first too slow and then too fast, because it accelerates around the middle"; "good initially: it is a sliding motion; then it goes too fast along the last part of the inclined plane."

Note: One of the subjects found this to be the correct motion: "Maybe it is slow at first, the last part is correct − (I corrected the motion to make it altogether faster) − now it looks good even at the beginning".

Motions C and D (with decreasing acceleration): "good situation; maybe a bit fast at the end"; "still too fast at the end of the inclined plane"; "fine . . . maybe slightly fast at the end".

Motion E: this was judged to be the best; the only defect that sometimes was mentioned was that of being slightly fast at the end (observation made by two subjects). It is described as: "overall very good"; "it is the best of all"; "it is really fine"; "very good . . . just a bit fast at the end".

The results of this experiment thus allow us to say that the motion of an object along an inclined plane, in order to be phenomenally a good motion, without portions that are too fast or too slow, or seen as the result of external factors (push or brake), *must be an accelerated motion at first, until a certain velocity is reached, and uniform from there on.*[7]

The experiments that followed were carried out bearing these results in mind, that is, employing a motion like the one just described (E); occasional questions to the observers showed that, even after changes in the other variables, the motion of an object according to this function remains satisfactory.

3c)   The size of the object and the slope of the inclined plane. The second question to be tested experimentally was the following: which is the downward movement that is neither too fast nor too slow, all in all, given an object of a certain size and an inclined plane of a certain slope?

It must be pointed out immediately that when we speak of a motion that is neither too fast nor too slow, i.e., neither restrained nor forced, we are referring to all parts of the motion at the same time, to the motion as a whole, and not, as in the previous experiment, to its individual parts.

Because the question reported above carries with it reference to the two variables of slope of the inclined plane and the size of the object, it could be rewritten as follows: is there, and if there is how does it make itself felt, an objectively noticeable difference between the downward motion that appears "natural" for a given object and a given slope, and the downward motion that appears "natural" for objects of different sizes sliding down inclined planes of different slopes?

In order to give an answer to this question I carried out a number of experiments with two different techniques, employing in all cases the spiral for movement E that, as we have seen, had shown itself to be the most appropriate.

A first group of subjects was given the task of determining, each time, the natural motion (neither forced nor restrained), starting from movements that were clearly "too fast" or "too slow". While the subject observed the situation, the speed of the event was gradually changed by means of the angular-speed transmission and reducing it if the starting motion was "too fast", or increasing it if it was "too slow". The subjects' task was to stop these changes when they thought appropriate, and they were given ample opportunity to correct the situation in order to make it more satisfactory.[8]

Given an object of a certain size (for example, the small square with a 4 mm side) and a given slope (for example forty-five degrees), the two determinations described above were made. Then the situation was changed, and so on for all the situations in the experimental design.

All in all there were six situations, three carried out with the small object and three with the object whose side was four times as long; the slopes used were 23°, 45°, 68°. In this experiment the other slopes were omitted to prevent sessions from lasting too long; they were already found to be long and fatiguing.

The results are summarised in Table 11.3. In addition to the values obtained for each condition the table presents the relationship between the average values for the various situations. Examination of this portion of the table shows that these relationships are consistently similar between subjects.

It was obvious to expect that, as the slope of the inclined plane decreased, the event had to last longer in order to be seen as a "natural" motion; this was indeed the case. However, examination of the effect of changes in slope gave results that do not allow safe generalisations: while in some cases there were large differences between the values obtained in the various conditions in other cases these differences were, contrary to all expectation, very small. Thus the slope of the inclined plane seems to be definitely important for some subjects, but less important or wholly negligible for others. For this reason, any attempt to turn this relationship into a precise law, on the basis of our results, would be difficult and probably arbitrary; all we are allowed to say is that if an inclined plane is steeper than another, then an object placed on it must move comparatively faster in order to appear to be sliding freely.

More interesting are the results related to the size of the object: the square whose side is 1.6 cm long requires a shorter sliding time for its motion to be seen as "natural", as compared to the time required by the smaller object.

The desire to establish this fact with greater clarity led me to carry out another experiment with a different group of subjects. This consisted essentially of a series of comparisons and subsequent corrections.

First of all, I asked the subjects to observe carefully the entire range of event durations that could be achieved with the angular-speed transmission, from the shortest to the longest and vice versa. In this way they could see – so to speak – the whole sample of possible motions along a given inclined plane. Then, starting from one or the other end of the range, I asked them to determine as accurately as possible the "natural" motion; the subjects were allowed to correct the situation as many times as they wished. Once the most satisfactory motion was found, the situation was altered in such a way that the object would have a different size from the object in the previous case (smaller if the original one was large, larger if the original one was small). The mechanism then started to move at the same velocity that had been previously selected by the subject.

At this point I asked the subjects to observe carefully this new downward motion, inviting them to tell me whether it was necessary to modify the speed of the present situation – in relation to the "natural" motion – and, if so, in what direction the change had to be made.

The results obtained in this manner are always the same: if the small object was presented first, followed by the large one, it was necessary to correct the situation by decreasing its overall duration; if the presentation of the small object followed that of the large one, the overall duration of the event had to be increased.

In order to be able to compare the results obtained with this method of comparisons and subsequent corrections to the relationships reported in Table 11.3, I continued the experiment leaving the size of the object used in the second situation unchanged, and modifying instead the slope of the inclined plane. At the same time the event duration previously selected by the observer remained the same: the new correction, therefore, was related to the variable representing the slope of the inclined plane.

Because of the greater ease and brevity of this type of experiment, I also examined some downward motions for inclined planes of gentler slopes (10° and 5°). The results are reported in Table 11.4. In this table, as in the previous one, the absolute values for each condition have little meaning; what counts instead is the fact that *all* the corrections were made in the same direction when similar situations were presented in the same order.

These new results confirm those discussed above. With both methods the relationship between the values obtained in the various situations is indeed basically the same; but, in the latter case, we also eliminate those doubts that – given the large variance – might arise in the interpretation of the results obtained with the first method. While, in the first experiment, these relationships emerge from the comparison of two independently formulated judgments, in the second, they arise from a direct comparison: having seen that the descent was good in a certain situation, the subjects saw that in the ensuing situation the new motion was no longer good, and corrected it in a certain way.

And it is precisely that that one typically wants to ascertain through phenomenological analyses: namely that a difference, or an identity, or a change be simply *observed*; that it appears, in other words, as a structural characteristic of immediate experience.

4. Conclusion

It is clear that the results of the first experiment allow us, once again, to compare an example of structural "goodness" in the perceptual realm with a typical prejudice rooted in pre-Galilean dynamics: downward motion is good when it consists of an initial acceleration that at a certain point decreases to zero, and is then followed by uniform motion. This acceleration is necessary to take the object from rest to its "proper" motion, characteristic of that object when it is falling: "One cannot doubt that the same object in the same medium must have a fixed, and naturally determined velocity, which cannot be increased without imparting a new impetus upon it, or decreased without the restraining action of some obstacle"[9] states Simplicio in the Galileian dialogues, acting as spokesman of the Peripatetic physicists of his own day.

In addition, "proper" motion would be directly linked to the weight (or the mass, or the size, all concepts that, as I have said, were often run together) of the falling object: the more an object weighs, the more rapidly it falls: as stated in "Aristotle's proposition, that the velocities of descending bodies retain among themselves the same relationship as their weight" writes Galileo; and shortly thereafter he adds that the objects in question are "differing in weight, not because of a difference in material, but solely because of a difference in size."[10]

There is also a clear connection between this "proposition" and the results of my second experiment; a similar conclusion could in any case be drawn indirectly from the research on the perception of velocity carried out by Brown in Berlin and at Yale.

After all, Galileo himself in at least two places (in his *Discourses concerning two new sciences* and in the *Postille* on Antonio Rocco) alludes, not without amazement, to the connections

TABLE 11.3 Duration of "natural" downward motion for large and small objects at various slopes

Slope (degrees)	Duration of the "natural" motion for the small object (seconds)	Duration of the "natural" motion for the large object (seconds)	Relationship between average values for the two objects at various slopes — small	large	Subject
22	↓1.40 ↑1.32	↑0.87 ↓0.74	1.36 <	0.81 —	A
45	↓1.07 ↑1.15	↑0.98 ↓0.98	∧ 1.11 <	∧ 0.98	
68	↓0.74 ↑0.91	↑0.74 ↓0.70	∧ 0.83 <	∧ 0.72	
22	↓1.36 ↑1.48	↑0.98 ↓0.91	1.43 <	0.95	B
45	↓0.98 ↑1.23	↑0.78 ↓0.97	∧ 1.10 <	∧ 0.88	
68	↓0.57 ↑0.70	↑0.61 ↓0.53	∧ 0.64 <	∧ 0.57	
22	↓0.84 ↑1.07	↑0.87 ↓0.66	0.96 <	0.77	C
45	↓0.71 ↑0.78	↑0.74 ↓0.58	∧ 0.75 <	∧ 0.66	
68	↓0.61 ↑0.74	↑0.62 ↓0.52	∧ 0.67 <	∧ 0.58	
22	↓1.32 ↑1.49	↑1.04 ↓0.78	1.41 <	0.91 —	D
45	↓1.07 ↑1.30	↑1.05 ↓0.97	∧ 1.14 <	∧ 1.01	
68	↓0.91 ↑1.04	↑0.78 ↓0.65	∧ 0.98 <	∧ 0.72	

Group E

Cond	↓	↑	↓	↑			
22	↓0.71	↑0.74	↓0.45	↑0.70	0.73	<	0.58
45	↓0.52	↑0.65	↓0.45	↑0.61	0.59	<	0.48
68	↓0.36	↑0.49	↓0.36	↑0.39	0.43	<	0.38

Group F

Cond	↓	↑	↓	↑			
22	↓0.78	↑0.85	↓0.66	↑0.78	0.82	<	0.72
45	↓0.70	↑0.78	↓0.65	↑0.78	0.74	<	0.72 (−)
68	↓0.57	↑0.61	↓0.45	↑0.61	0.59	<	0.68

Group G

Cond	↓	↑	↓	↑			
22	↓1.07	↑1.30	↓0.70	↑0.70	1.19	<	0.70
45	↓0.74	↑0.74	↓0.57	↑0.61	0.74	<	0.59
68	↓0.45	↑0.52	↓0.45	↑0.45	0.49	<	0.45

Group H

Cond	↓	↑	↓	↑			
22	↓1.05	↑1.42	↓0.74	↑0.78	1.19	<	0.74
45	↓0.91	↑0.97	↓0.65	↑0.78	0.94	<	0.70
68	↓0.65	↑0.87	↓0.58	↑0.65	0.76	<	0.62

Group I

Cond	↓	↑	↓	↑			
22	↓1.23	↑1.76	↓0.58	↑0.58	1.50	<	0.58 (−)
45	↓0.98	↑1.07	↓0.58	↑0.68	1.03	<	0.62
68	↓0.70	↑0.78	↓0.53	↑0.61	0.74	<	0.57

Note: Arrows indicate effected change (e.g., ↑ means starting velocity was too slow). Angle brackets (< etc.) indicate magnitude relationships between the average of each ↑ and ↓ in the same condition.

TABLE 11.4 Duration of downward motion for large and small objects with various slopes.

Subject	Object Size large (duration in seconds)	Δ	small	Slope (degrees)	Slope (degrees)	Object Size large (duration in seconds)	Δ	small	Subject
A	1.05 →	↓	<u>1.32</u>	22	45	<u>0.98</u>	↑	1.45 →	E
A	0.61	↑	0.74 →	68	10	1.75 →	↓	2.21	E
A	0.74 →	↓	0.91	45	5	2.08	↑	2.46 →	E
A	2.14	↑	2.35	5	68	0.40	↓	0.57	E
B	<u>1.82</u>	↑	1.57 →	5	22	<u>0.78</u>	↑	1.07	F
B	0.82	↓	1.23	22	68	0.57 →	↓	0.66	F
B	0.66 →	↑	0.78 →	45	10	1.23	↑	1.69 →	F
B	1.30	↓	1.40	10	45	0.74	↓	0.98	F
C	<u>1.06</u> →	↑	1.32 →	45	68	<u>0.39</u>	↑	0.57 →	G
C	1.50	↓	1.82	5	22	0.45	↓	0.71	G
C	1.42 →	↑	1.74 →	22	5	1.56	↑	1.79 →	G
C	1.49	↓	1.82	10	10	1.23	↓	1.48	G
D	0.32 →	↓	<u>0.40</u>	68	68	<u>0.58</u>	↑	0.74 →	H
D	1.23	↑	2.14 →	10	5	1.75 →	↓	2.28	H
D	2.14 →	↓	2.40	5	45	0.65	↑	0.93 →	H
D	0.87	↑	1.15	22	22	0.75	↓	1.17	H

Note: Underlined numbers indicate starting conditions. Arrows indicate effected change (e.g., → means large object was replaced by small one, etc.).

that can be found in Aristotelian writings between *experimenting on* and *seeing* the phenomena of motion. When Salviati – who in the *Dialogues* represents Galileo himself – observes: "I greatly doubt that Aristotle did not experiment how true it is that two stones, one ten times heavier than the other, dropped at the same instant from a height for example of one hundred yards, are so different in their speed that at the arrival of the larger one to earth, the other would find itself having barely descended ten yards", Simplicio replies: "One can see even from his words, that he made the experiment, because he says: 'We see the heavier object etc.'; now, that 'seeing' is a token that he had made the experiment".[11]

Notes

1 Aristotle (ed. 1926), p. 295
2 Duhem, P. (1958), pp. 231 ff. The description of free fall that is closest to the equation of Galileian dynamics is undoubtedly that formulated by Albert of Saxony in *Quæstiones in libros de Caelo et de Mundo*, Vol II, quaestio XIV: "*Secundum quod ipsum corpus naturale movetur diutius et diutius, secundum hoc sibi acquiritur major et major impetus, et secundum hoc moventur velocius et velocius; nisi tamen hoc impedietur per majorem crescentiam ipsius rcsistentiae quam esset impetus sic acquisitus.*"
3 Wertheimer, M. (1945), p. 205 ff.
4 Galilei, G. (ed. 1882), vol. 2, p. 195ff.
5 Wertheimer, M. (1945), p. 209.
6 Michotte, A. (1954), p. 40ff.
7 Editors' note: When Bozzi re-elaborated the present article in Chapter 8 of his *Fisica ingenua* [*Naïve Physics*] (Milan, Italy: Garzanti, 1990), he took account of a correction that had been brought to his attention, which we quote from pp. 307–308 of the book:

> The participants had rejected uniform change of place on the screen of one of my experimental situations with the inclined plane because it was 'too fast at the beginning'; they made me correct the experimental presentation so that this 'too fast beginning' disappeared; and as a result of the corrections, I had introduced the initial acceleration that put everything to rights. But it was precisely this initial acceleration, there on the screen, that was invisible to the observers, who in the end saw a uniform motion from beginning to end. And I myself saw it this way, but I insisted on saying and writing the wrong way of expressing it. It was only by withdrawing thc uniform motion that uniform motion became visible. Runeson immediately saw that I had not seen and published in *Psychological Research*, referring briefly to my researches and presenting all the details of the new phenomenon that he had discovered (Runeson, 1974).
>
> Working with objects in motion on a straight horizontal trajectory that was quite long (the one I saw in Uppsala in 1974 took place on a screen of more than a metre), Runeson had shown beyond all doubt that a uniform motion is always seen as having a start of much higher speed than what is seen in the rest of the journey. The start is like a jump, and it is only immediately afterwards that the objects adapts itself to proceeding in an orderly uniform motion. As a result, he had found that it is possible to correct this sort of jump and obtain a 'smooth start' by connecting the body's initial state of rest ot the speed that is called for in the rest of the passage by means of a more or less smooth acceleration. In these conditions, what the observers see is a genuine uniform motion from beginning to end.
>
> Thus, if all this is true (and it certainly is true, because Runeson has worked on this problem for years without ever running into evidence to the contrary), what my observers and I myself saw when we followed the natural descent along inclined planes, a motion produced by a connection between and initial acceleration and a uniform motion, was nothing other than a uniform motion from beginning to end. Which is just what Galileo's Simplicio says.
>
> I was very happy to receive that article of Runeson's, for up until then no non-Italian psychologist had shown that they had taken notice of my experiments in naïve physics. To tell the truth, no such discipline had yet come into being, and well we know that stray enquiries that are not embedded in a widely-recognised context tend to follow their own

rules. But I re-read my own writings a couple of times, astonished that I had been unable to see for myself the blunder I had made. Runeson drew my attention to them pointing out that 'unfortunately' the look of the thing had escaped me. But, with great good grace, he inserted my findings along with his own and thus I had the feeling that I had not, at the time, worked in vain.

8 In this experiment and the next, an outline of a little man, about 8 cm tall (about a quarter of the height of the descent) was attached next to the inclined plane. The purpose of this figure was to provide a stable spatial reference frame for the inclined plane and the object: indeed, if it is placed against a homogeneous background, the triangle upon which the object is sliding can equally well represent a short inclined plane of few centimetres in length located a few metres away, or the side of a hill half a kilometre away. And this, of course, results in an ambiguous interpretation of the subjects' descriptions of a "natural" motion; a motion that is natural for a small ball rolling down a short path cannot at the same time be natural for a bus that is driving downhill along a road tens of meters away from the observer. Indeed, preliminary trials showed that it is much more difficult to determine the "natural" downward motion when the figure is absent than when the figure is present on the screen. Without the figurine, many different situations may seem good.

On the other hand, we cannot say that the little man spatially anchors the inclined plane with such accuracy to allow us to establish a comparison between the objective duration of a downward motion along a seven-meter inclined plane, which would be the length of our inclined plane to scale, and the duration of the events that take place in our experiments. The figure was used only in order to make the subjects' decisions easier.

9 Galilei, G., op. cit., II, at p. 177.
10 Ibid.
11 Ibid. vol. I, at p. 121.

References

Duhem, P. (1958). *Le Système du Monde*, Vols. VII and VIII. Paris, FR: Hermann.

Galilei, G. (1882). *I Dialoghi sui Massimi Sistemi Tolemaico e Copernicano*, Milano Italy: Sonzogn (the English text adopted by the original translators is that of Stillman Drake (1953) *Dialogue Concerning the Two Chief World Systems*. Berkeley, CA: University of California Press)

Michotte, A. (1954). *La Perception de la Causalité*. Louvain, NL: Publications Universitaires.

Wertheimer, M. (1945). *Productive Thinking*. New York: Harper.

COMMENTS ON PHENOMENOLOGICAL ANALYSIS OF PENDULAR HARMONIC MOTION AND THE CONDITIONS FOR "NATURAL" MOTION ALONG INCLINED PLANES

Marco Bertamini

It is always a pleasure to read the writings of Paolo Bozzi. His studies of the phenomenology of motion using the pendulum and using the inclined planes are well known. This is one area of activity for which Bozzi has been relatively well known also outside Italy. Both articles appeared in 1989 in English translations by Paola Bressan and Paolo Gaudiano, and they are covered in some detail in the semi-autobiographical book entitled *Fisica ingenua* (*Naïve Physics*, 1990). The original work, however, dates to 1958 and 1959, and so preceded international interest in this area of research by a few decades.

Bozzi studied systematically the perception of natural motion, using the methods of Experimental Phenomenology, and made some fascinating discoveries. In "Phenomenological Analysis of Pendular Harmonic Motion" the pendulum is chosen as an ideal test of the idea that certain motions are perceived as natural or unnatural in a way that is not the same as what is physically possible. From the first page, Bozzi also explains that he had been fascinated by the possibility that certain theoretical errors present in the history of scientific thought could be related to the way the world appears to us. The Galilean dialogues feature prominently in the story not only because the work by Galileo on mechanics is relevant. Bozzi points out that in the original dialogues we can detect the tension between how things appear (perception) and what, as scientists, we have to accept because they follow from the principles that we have established as true. Moreover, the fact that much opposition was expressed to Galileo's ideas by his contemporaries suggested to Bozzi that this phenomenon was one well suited for the investigation of the perception of natural motion. In other words, Bozzi was crossing the boundaries of history of science, philosophy and cognitive science. As we know, this rounded approach is a key to the study of perception. The starting point for this work was in line with the work of the Gestalt school, especially in terms of the focus on phenomenology. Also of importance was the work by Michotte, who started from similar premises but focused on different aspects of motion.

Today these studies are known as part of a research area called intuitive or naïve physics. The term "naïve physics" was used by some psychologists as early as 1917 (in the writings of Köhler, see Smith and Casati, 1994), but it is interesting that Bozzi did not use the term, at least not in the sense of a field of research. He did use terms such as "spontaneous physics", and perhaps whether this is exactly the same as naïve physics is just an issue of terminology.

On the one hand, Bozzi was working within a Gestalt tradition that made his work possible. On the other hand, it is important to emphasise the pioneering nature of his studies. These are experiments carried out with extreme care and skill. From the building of the necessary apparatus, to the careful choice of the questions to be presented to the observers, to the tables of results, one can see that Bozzi was not a philosopher dabbling in a few empirical observations. These studies are beautiful examples of what we call Experimental Phenomenology.

Interest in the relationship between the history of science and how we perceived motion as natural or unnatural was revived in the 1970s, in particular in a paper in *Perception* in which Benny Shanon noted how "people do not conceive the world as physicists do", in part at least because of how they perceive the world (Shanon, 1976). Some naïve concepts appeared to coincide with what was believed by Aristotle (and his followers down the centuries), exactly as Bozzi had pointed out.

The presence of systematic mistakes in people beliefs about the world and in particular about motion, generated great interest and a series of important papers in the 1980s, for instance by Michael McCloskey (McCloskey, Caramazza, and Green, 1980) and Dennis Proffitt (Kaiser, Proffitt, and Anderson, 1985).

The literature on naïve physics in this period focused on mechanics. Bozzi was correct in seeing that this was an important aspect of the physical world because the changes in how science understood mechanics before and after Galileo shows how certain concepts are intuitively appealing. The idea is that concepts are built from and around what is seen as natural. It should be noted, however, that the story is not so simple. Some mistakes that people make originate from perception, but other may originate from models that people develop, as illustrated by studies with children (Kaiser, McCloskey, and Proffitt, 1986) and adults (Yates et al. 1988).

Although interest in naïve physics is not so strong today as it was in the 1980s, there have been important new developments. For example, some researchers have started to investigate other areas away from naïve mechanics, such as naïve optics (Bertamini, Spooner and Hecht, 2002; Croucher, Bertamini and Hecht, 2003). It is therefore important to make as much of Bozzi's work available in English as possible. As mentioned above, we can find in these studies a wonderful combination of theoretical insight and innovative experimental designs.

References

Bertamini, M., Spooner, A., and Hecht, H. (2003). Naive optics: Predicting and perceiving reflections in mirrors. *Journal of Experimental Psychology: Human Perception and Performance, 29*(5), 982–1002.

Croucher, C.J., Bertamini, M., and Hecht, H. (2002). Naive optics: Understanding the geometry of mirror reflections. *Journal of Experimental Psychology: Human Perception and Performance, 28*, 546–562.

Kaiser, M., McCloskey, M., and Proffitt, D. (1986). Development of intuitive theories of motion: curvilinear motion in the absence of external forces. *Developmental Psychology, 22*(1), 67–71.

Kaiser, M., Proffitt, D. R., and Anderson, K. (1985). Judgements of natural and anomalous trajectories in the presence and absence of motion. *Journal of Experimental Psychology: Learning, memory and cognition, 11*(4), 795–803.

McCloskey, M., Caramazza, A., and Green, B. (1980). Curvilinear motion in the absence of external forces: naive beliefs about the motion of objects. *Science, 210*(5), 1139–1141.

Shanon, B. (1976). Aristotelism, Newtonianism and the physics of the layman. *Perception, 5*, 241–243.

Smith, B., and Casati, R. (1994). Naïve physics: an essay in ontology. *Philosophical Psychology, 7*(2), 227–247.

Yates, J., Bessman, M., Dunne, M., Jertson, D., Sly, K., and Wendelboe, B. (1988). Are conceptions of motion based on a naïve theory or on prototypes? *Cognition, 29*, 251–275.

12

A NEW FACTOR OF PERCEPTUAL GROUPING

Demonstration in terms of pure Experimental Phenomenology

Translated by Luigi Burigana

1.   This paper presents an existence proof. Its subject is a factor of perceptual grouping to be added to the list produced by Wertheimer in his seminal article of 1923 (proximity, similarity, good continuation, closure, etc.). As it is usually presented in textbooks, the order of this list does not appear to descend by logical necessity from the system of direct experience; nor is such a derivation explicitly stated in Wertheimer but only gestured at. There is such a logic nevertheless, and it allows us to demonstrate the reality and function of any new factor in a rigorous manner, that is, to demonstrate that any new factor must take a definite place in the list, and to specify the role it plays relative to other previously discovered factors of perceptual grouping.

   The demonstration I develop in the following pages has a further distinctive epistem-ological feature: it entirely rests on non-psychophysical bases, and is carried out in purely *phenomenological* terms (except for one point; see the exposition in *Phenomenological description and physical-geometrical description*).[1] This means, for example, that in our theoretical argument and corresponding experiments, the "distance" between the points making up the figures is not necessarily the distance measured by a ruler, but rather the distance as we really see it; the "rows of dots" mentioned in our discussion and shown in examples obviously do not have any psychophysical counterpart; the "shapes" of sets of dots and their orientation relative to horizontal and vertical axes are conditional on the contingent appearance of the page containing them, that is, proximal and external reference frames depend on each other at the strictly phenomenal level, in the sense set out by Koffka (1935, pp. 184–185 [reported, in the present paper, in Figure 12.11]).

   The concepts that figure in our demonstrations emerge from each other through ostensive definitions and (except for one of them, relating to properties of the last figure) do not require operational definitions. The remodellings of the figures, based on the logic of demon-stration, generate step by step new observables which themselves are given by ostensive definitions; in ensuing steps they become the components of still other observables defined in the ostensive manner. This interplay of *percept-percept couplings* extends from the simple situation of equidistance between dots forming the nodes of an ideal square-meshed dot lattice, to encompass the construction of three-dimensional structures having an "in front of" and a "behind".

A special operation is needed if we want to demonstrate that the relevant "distance" is phenomenal and not metrical: the use of a pair of compasses or a ruler on Figure 12.19 shows that metric distance between corresponding points in the two oblique rows of dots is the same as between any two adjacent dots in the picture, while the space between those rows appears wider and lighter.

The demonstration makes use of a concept, that of "force", which in the present context is not fixable either in the ostensive or the operational manner. For example, in the course of our discussion, we make use of the notion of forces that work together in coordination or that are opposed one to the other. Expressions like these do not imply any reference to supposed underlying brain processes or other causal entities transcending the phenomenal data. In this context, the concept of "force" is a useful fiction without any direct or indirect referent. It is only used to illustrate the strategy followed in creating the figures, or at most to suggest – at the intuitive level – an imaginable mechanism generating the perceptual structures under observation. Lastly, the enquiry highlights the concept of "coplanarity" of variables. By this is meant variables that, whether be they dependent, independent, or mutually interconnected, all belong to the class of observables subject to direct visual exploration.

A technical note: when the patterns to be observed are shown as constellations of light points in the dark, then the effects are even more forceful, given the absence of the ineliminable spatial constraint represented by the page on which the dots appear.

2.   If we have a certain number of dots distributed on a homogeneous surface equidistant from one another like the nodes of a square-meshed net, and occupying a square region of the surface (Figure 12.1), then it is equally easy to see in the resulting pattern either a structure made of horizontal rows of dots, or one made of vertical rows of dots. It is less easy to see in it a structure made of oblique rows, that is, rows parallel to one or the other diagonal of the square; indeed, this configuration may last for a moment or so, and only involve the dots along the diagonals and those adjacent to them.

(12.1)

This fact is readily explained when we recall Wertheimer's first law (1923, p. 308): all else being equal, the groups of elementary phenomenal items that organize themselves as unities are those whose members' positions within the whole are closest to one another. In our case, the dots closest to one another are those lying on a horizontal or vertical row (assuming the whole figure is a square resting on a horizontal base); and it is in just this way that the two most spontaneous groupings come about.

If, instead of considering them in this ordering, we want to see them along the lines parallel to a diagonal, we find that the distance between one and the next is greater than that in the previous case by as much as the diagonal of a square is longer than its sides. As a consequence, this structure is harder to see and less stable, even when the subject sets him or herself to sustain it.

We find still greater distances if we try to group the dots in other theoretically possible ways. Such groupings cannot be seen at all – they exist only as a matter of geometry – because the distances between the dots in them are much greater than the shortest distance between the dots in the given situation, i.e. the distance that fixes the two most immediate and stable organizations.

3.   Now let us suppose that, in situations like these, the equal ease of the horizontal and vertical structures depends exclusively on the proximity factor. If this were so, then any cancellation of dots carried out in such a way that proximity relations between the remaining dots remained unchanged should not disturb the balance between the two easiest organizations (horizontal rows and vertical rows), so as to favour one over the other.[2]

The four instances in Figure 12.2, however, contradict a hypothesis of this sort. As regards each of these examples, if we apply only the proximity law, then we ought to expect an equally easy organization in (more or less long) rows of dots, as much in the horizontal as in the vertical axis. Indeed, as can easily be seen, each of the instances in Figure 12.2 derives from Figure 12.1 by subtracting a certain set of dots from it, while keeping unchanged the proximity relationships among the remaining dots. Thus, all these organizations are in principle present in Figure 12.1.

Yet the most spontaneous organization of Figure 12.2a is in vertical rows: that of Figure 12.2b in horizontal rows; in Figure 12.2c, which has the shape of a set square, the rows are partly vertical and partly horizontal; in Figure 12.2d the dots may also group to form a square, like ornaments along the sides of a picture frame.

In short, the rows of dots are differently organized in the four instances of Figure 12.2, and their various organizations seem to depend on this simple law: dots align so as to follow the direction of the constellation to which they belong (the vertical rectangle in Figure 12.2a, the horizontal rectangle in Figure 12.2b), or if the constellation is made up of articulations with different directions, then the dots align so as to follow these latter (Figure 12.2c and Figure 12.2d). In any case, we ought to conclude that, in situations like these, some other factor is at work along with the proximity, favouring from case to case one of the possible unifications into rows.

4.   In the present proof, we shall identify this factor with the feature of directionality possessed either by the whole of a given situation or by one of its visible articulations. We start with this definition, but without excluding the possibility of further reductions of this concept. For example, it may be reduced to a tendency to form the least number of rows compatible with the geometrical makeup of the given situation (e.g., only three vertical rows in Figure 12.2a, rather than 11 horizontal rows of only three dots each; three horizontal rows in Figure 12.2b, rather than 11 vertical rows of three dots each, etc.), or it may be reduced to a tendency to form rows with the largest possible number of dots, as if the link unifying dots by mutual proximity could be reinforced by repetition, etc.

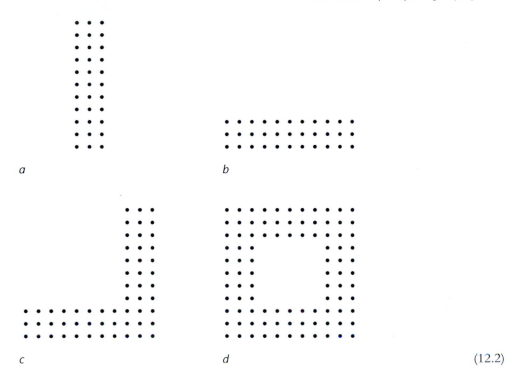

a b

c d (12.2)

Three important requirements should be borne in mind in defining a factor capable of acting in the way, in our case, directionality is acting. (1) Situations must be available in which organization takes place in a way not deducible from the factor (or factors) already known. (2) The new factor must be sought among the qualitative properties that are present in all these situations. (3) The factor must be identified with that feature that satisfies (at least) these conditions: (i) if the factor is changed, then the amount of unitariness present in the situation changes; and (ii) it should, in some instances, be able to conflict with the previously known factor, albeit weakly[3].

Examples like those in Figure 12.2 satisfy requirement (1). If proximity were the only factor at work, then both groupings in rows of dots (horizontal and vertical) should be equally spontaneous and easy to see, as happens when looking at Figure 12.1. Indeed, the examples in Figure 12.2 are produced by merely subtracting dots from Figure 12.1, while keeping unaltered all the spatial relations among the remaining dots. But this is not what happens: some rows in Figure 12.2 appear better connected than others, and this appearance is very similar to that of a structure obtainable from Figure 12.1 by weakening the proximity links between one dot and the next (along horizontal rows in Figure 12.3a, or along vertical rows in Figure 12.3b).

As regards requirement (2), all constellations in Figure 12.2 present (among others) the feature of directionality. It belongs to the constellation as a whole in Figure 12.2a and Figure 12.2b; it belongs to the parts into which the constellation is visibly articulated in Figures 12.2c and 12.2d. Wertheimer (1959, pp. 138–139) convincingly demonstrated that directionality may be viewed as an immediate feature or qualitative aspect of some wholes, in relation to sinusoidal curves, in a discussion on the phenomenology of graphical

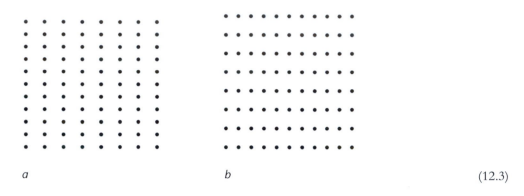

a   b   (12.3)

representation of mathematical functions. In a similar way, it is present in our figures. We find it difficult, however, to give the concept (in our phenomenological perspective) any definition other than an ostensive one.

Requirement (3) sets two conditions. The first condition (i) will be satisfied if we find that varying the evidence of the presumed grouping factor leads to a corresponding variation of the evidence of the grouping itself. In this regard it is useful to refer to examples *a-c* in Figure 12.4, as well as examples *d* and *e* in the same figure. In situations like these we can readily see that the evidence of perceptual grouping in rows of dots varies as a function of strengthening or weakening of the directionality feature of the whole or of its articulations.

In order to satisfy the second condition (ii) of requirement (3) we need to find visual situations in which the grouping into rows of dots takes place in conditions of rivalry with

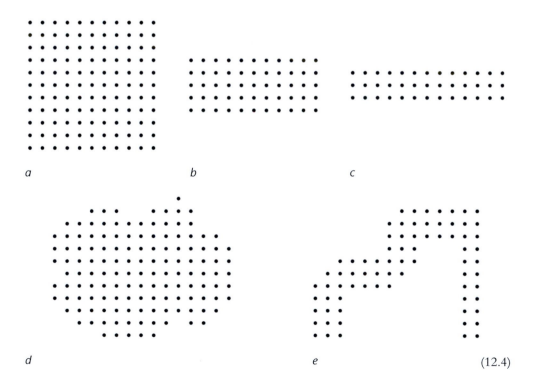

a   b   c

d   e   (12.4)

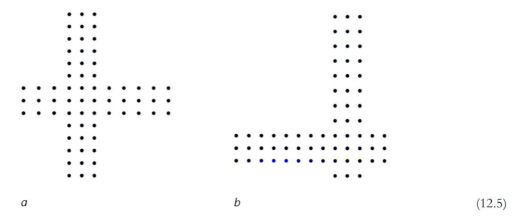

a   b   (12.5)

some other organizational factor whose mode of action is already known. For the kind of situation we are discussing, a well-known and always securely present factor is proximity.

To this end I organized the following experiment. The pictures in Figure 12.5 were shown to twenty participants in individual trials. The lattices were 70cm x 70cm and were presented on a frontal plane distant three metres from the observer. The task was to choose one sketch from *A*, *B*, *C*, and *D* as shown in Figure 12.6 which best matched the pattern in Figure 12.5*a*, and do the same for pattern in Figure 12.5*b*, by choosing one of sketches *A'*, *B'*, *C'*, and *D'*.

The eight sketches were defined by considering four theoretically possible organizations for each of the patterns in Figure 12.5. More precisely, four sketches (*A* and *B* for pattern 5*a*, *A'* and *B'* for pattern 5*b*) represent the organizations that should prevail if proximity were the only important factor in the presumed situations. The other four sketches (*C* and *D* for pattern 5*a*, *C'* and *D'* for pattern 5*b*) represent alternative perceptual solutions, which could apply if another organizational force (different from proximity) were in play running in the main direction of one of the two articulations. We drew the sketches by representing the possible grouping directions as dotted lines. In this way they trace in an almost caricatural fashion the overall look of the figures proposed to the observer, which indeed are – in the way they immediately appear – precisely the *shapes* made up of groups of dots.

Of course, it is to be supposed that the choices made by participants are based on a congruence between the dotted lines that make up the sketches, and the rows that, in the patterns, are more robustly organized. Although not explicitly proven, this supposition seems reasonable to us. Besides, whenever participants are involved in an experiment on perception and are charged with this or that task, there is lurking some unproven assumption of this kind.

Participants expressed their judgments having both patterns of Figure 12.5 (*a* and *b*) and all the sketches of Figure 12.6 (*A-D* and *A'-D'*), simultaneously in view.

Pattern in Figure 12.5*a* was seen to be best represented by sketch *A* in six cases, by sketch *B* in two cases, by *C* in one and by *D* in eleven. Pattern in Figure 12.5*b* was seen to be best represented by *A'* in four cases, by sketch *B'* in three, in one by *C'* and by *D'* in twelve. No participant refused to give the experimenter a judgment.

It will be noted that in all the patterns in Figure 12.6, both in the series *A-D* and in the series *A'-D'*, there are always two articulations, one horizontal and the other vertical. One of these articulations in each of the two series is made up of dots at equal distances both

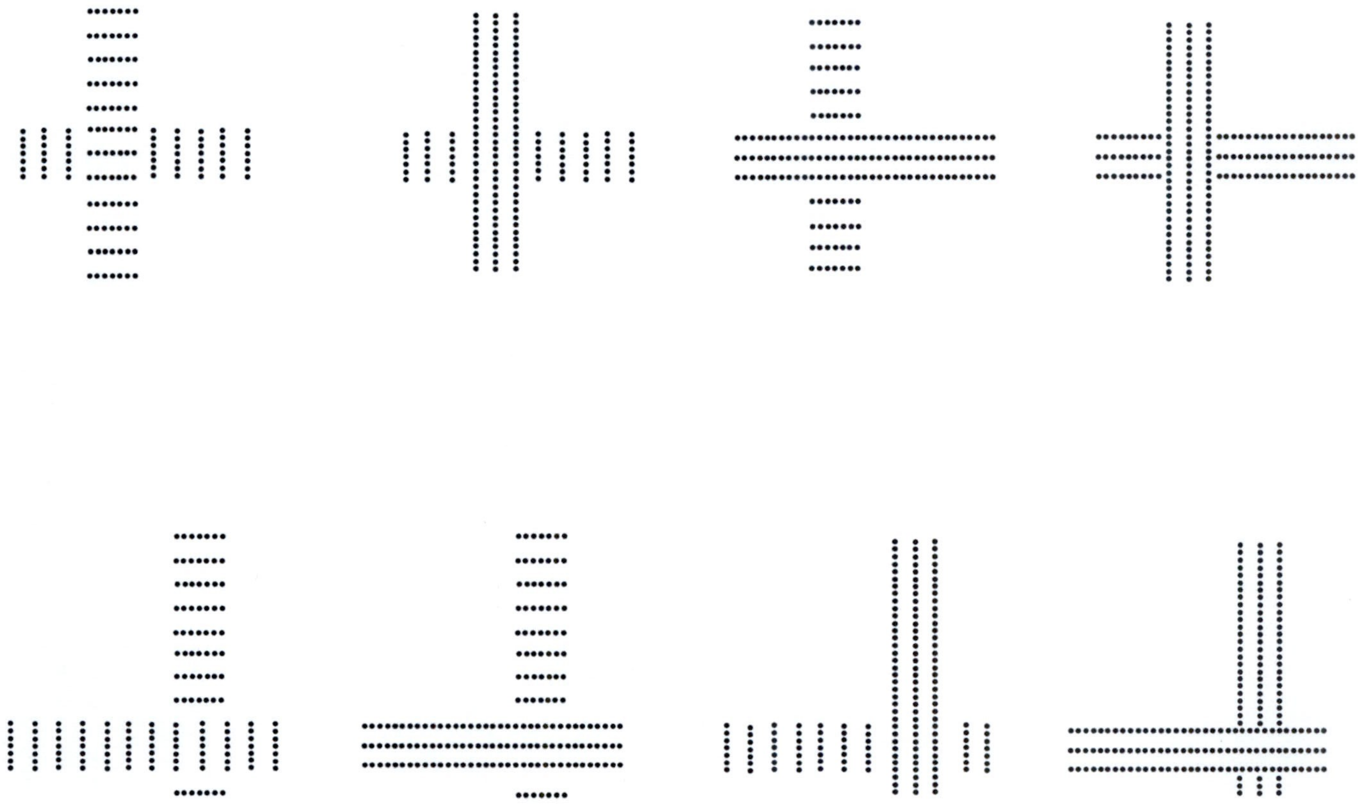

(12.6)

horizontally and vertically. In the other two, the distance is greater by 20% when we consider the dots aligned in sequences parallel to the directionality of the articulation to which they belong (in the figures shown in the experiment 4.8 cm as against 4 cm).

5.   Although they imply that all four organizations per pattern are possible, the results just given nevertheless show that sketch D for the pattern in Figure 12.5a and sketch D' for the pattern in Figure 12.5b come out as clearly the best. The chances of seeing the pattern in Figure 12.5a in accordance with sketch A, and that in Figure 12.5b in accordance with A', are also good. The remaining sketches (B, C, B', C') were rarely chosen presumably because in these sketches the structural heterogeneity as between the horizontal and vertical articulations is too marked. This heterogeneity does not appear when looking at one or the other pattern in Figure 12.5.

A similar supplementary experiment was carried out using the pattern shown in Figure 12.7 in which the relations of greater proximity among the dots are still arranged to act against the presumed directionality factor. The pattern too has two main articulations, one vertical and one horizontal. Within the former the dots are so arranged that proximity should favour alignments opposite to those favoured by directionality (5 cm against 6 cm). In constructing the latter component (the horizontal one) the same criterion was applied (7 cm against 6 cm).

Figure 12.7 reproduces a scaled-down version of the original figure presented to the 8 participants who gave us their judgments. In this case, they were experts in research on visual perception, and were aware of our problem. With them we did not use the method of choice among sketches. Rather, we simply asked them to express a judgment about the most spontaneous direction of grouping into rows. Six judgments were in favour of grouping in line with the directionality of the articulations. Two judgments were uncertain in that the two possibilities seemed more or less equivalent to the observers.

6.   The observations illustrated so far perhaps do not conclusively demonstrate the claim that "directionality" is a factor of unification in Wertheimer's sense (1923). But they make up a bunch of clues worthy of attention. At least they convincingly show that some necessary conditions for including directionality in the class of grouping factors are indeed satisfied. Even stronger evidence can be brought to light by considering more complex situations, in

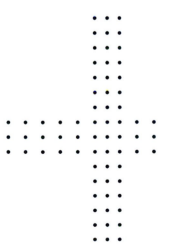

(12.7)

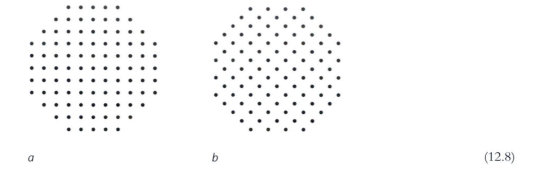

a   b   (12.8)

which groupings by directionality may take place at the expense of other more or less strong organizational forces acting among elementary objects like those so far considered.

In order to discuss these cases we need first to take a detour.

The American philosopher C.S. Peirce in his essay of 1878, which is generally regarded as the manifesto of pragmatism, drew attention to the substantial difference, from a phenomenological perspective, between the two patterns given here as parts *a* and *b* of Figure 12.8 (see Peirce in Buchler, 2000, p. 29). The difference is so big that many observers find it difficult to convince themselves that they are faced with the same geometrical structure only rotated by 45°.

Also considering this case, we ought to formulate the problem by posing the usual question: could this situation be explained by if the only factor connecting the dots were proximity? Obviously not. Moreover, for these patterns, it is useless to call on some factor of the kind illustrated on Figures 12.5 and 12.7, because there are evidently no privileged directionalities. The only difference lies in their position relative to the page on which they are printed, or, in the case of the observers we consulted, in their orientation relative to the spatial coordinates in the environment.

Probably, in this case we have a distribution of forces similar to that characterizing "Mach's square." In discussing symmetry in *The Analysis of Sensations*, Mach wrote: "Two figures may be geometrically congruent, but physiologically quite different, as is shown by the two adjoined squares, which could never be recognized as the same without mechanical and intellectual operations" (Mach, 1900, p. 77; 1959, p. 106).

One way of explaining this fact may be as follows. It is well known that an angle as a perceptual fact has a vector associated with it, which "points" in the direction of the vertex of the angle. This is not merely an aesthetic consideration, nor one of crude phenomenology. Von Schiller (1933, p. 194) showed that, in a situation of ambiguous stroboscopic movement, a crown of angles like that in Figure 12.10 rotates spontaneously in the direction indicated by the points of the angles. Wertheimer (1923, p. 318, footnote) similarly commented on how three non-aligned points are organized in the visual field. All the same, the properties of the horizontal and vertical main axes are well known, be they defined as the environmental coordinates, or as the coordinates of a specific frame of reference (Koffka, 1935, pp. 184–185). Now, in Figure 12.9*b* the vectors of the angles of the square coincide with the horizontal and vertical axes, whereas this is not the case with Figure 12.9*a*: in this part the base of the square "rests" on the horizontal axis and the vectors of the angles point in intermediate directions bisecting the angles formed by the vertical and horizontal axes.

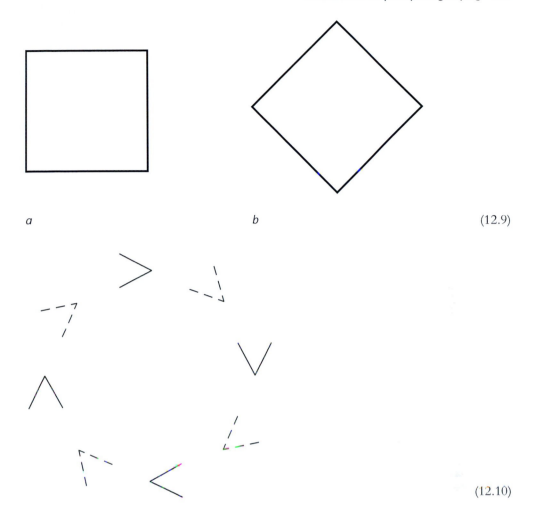

a   b   (12.9)

(12.10)

In Peirce's example we are obviously not dealing with angles. What, in Mach's case, are the oriented vectors of the angles here become the directions of unification by proximity. In Figure 12.8a those directions coincide with the horizontal and vertical axes, whereas in Figure 12.8b they extend along the lines bisecting the angles between those axes.

The difference between the two patterns of Figure 12.8 is very pronounced, and no effort to take a different view will make it vanish. From a phenomenological standpoint the difference may be described as follows: the pattern in Figure 12.8a is more "compact," is made of a well-organized texture, which is square meshed; the "rows" of dots are clearly visible, both in the horizontal and in the vertical directions, and the figure as a whole looks like a neatly defined octagon, having a reasonably precise contour. By contrast, the pattern in Figure 12.8b is definitely less compact and less strongly structured; it is made of a texture looser in organization, designed along the lines of a Roman quincunx, rather than square meshes; groupings by proximity are less stable, and the figure as a whole appears less clearly as an octagon; that is, the eight sides are visible, but the whole contour appears somewhat rounded.

We cannot be sure that the interpretation just suggested for Figure 12.8 (with the help of Mach's square) is right or is the only one conceivable. An inquiry could be carried out in this direction, and may yield interesting results, especially with a view to clarifying the possible modes of appearance of the microstructures. For now, and for the purposes of our present analysis, suffice it to remark this circumstance: within fairly large sets of dots arranged as the nodes of a square-meshed net, *ceteris paribus*, groupings by proximity turn out to be stronger if they run parallel to the horizontal or vertical axes than they appear if they are rotated by 45° relative to those axes.

7.   The circumstance noted in the preceding paragraph is not the only one to be considered in dealing with the problem of connections among dots. Above we mentioned the idea contributed by Koffka to interpreting a reference frame as an environment endowed with main axes. The argument developed by Koffka (1935, p. 185) is well known. The differences between Mach's squares can be made to vanish without intervening on their orientation relative to the page on which they are printed, or relative to the environmental coordinates. We only need to enclose each square in a proximal reference frame (for example, a rectangle, as shown in Figure 12.11), such that the other reference systems (page and environment) fall outside its boundary, and so located that the spatial relationships between the frames and the enclosed squares turn out to be suitably modified.

Now this operation can also be performed in our dot lattices, supposing that the meshes of the net on the nodes of which the points are fixed are connected to the overall figure by a relation similar to that which links Mach's square to the proximal frame of reference suggested by Koffka.

Let us develop this idea as follows. Patterns *a* and *b* of Figure 12.8 are regular octagons (they are copied as parts *a* and *b* of Figure 12.12, which also includes the other dot patterns explained below). Thus, the profile of their outline is such that four sides in each case are in

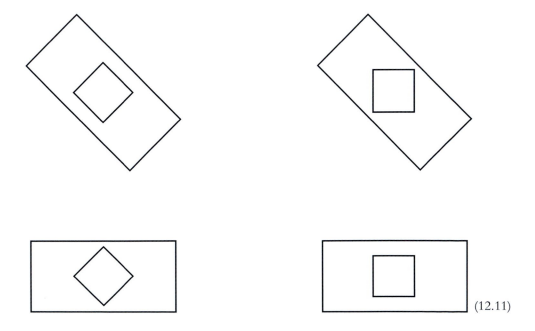

(12.11)

line with the fundamental horizontal and vertical axes, and the other four are in opposition, at 45° relative to them. If we take the octagonal outline as a proximal frame of reference in Koffka's sense, then it does not positively support either the horizontal-vertical grouping factor, or the proximity factor, whichever pattern is considered.

Now, if we want to transform both octagons into squares, by adding dots, we can do this in four different ways:

i)   Add dots to the pattern in Figure 12.12*a*, applying the same distribution rule, so as to transform it into a square whose sides are parallel to the horizontal and vertical directions (Figure 12.12*c*).

ii) Add dots to the same pattern in Figure 12.12*a* so as to transform it into a square whose sides are at 45° relative to the horizontal-vertical axes (Figure 12.12*d*).

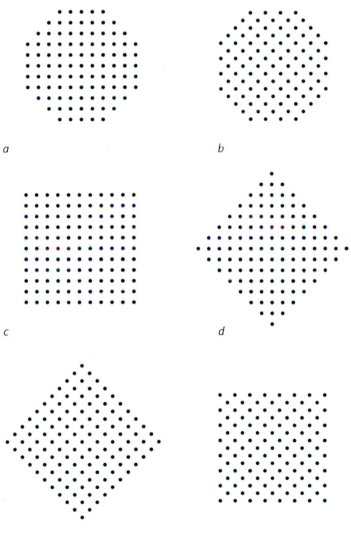

a

b

c

d

e

f

(12.12)

iii) Add dots to the pattern in Figure 12.12b, applying the same distribution rule so as to produce a square whose sides are at 45° relative to the horizontal and vertical directions, but are parallel to the grouping direction defined by proximity (Figure 12.12e).

iv) Lastly, add points to the pattern in Figure 12.12b in the same way so as to obtain a square whose sides are parallel to the horizontal and vertical directions (Figure 12.12f).

Each of these four squares c-f may be thought of as the proximal frame of reference for the lattice it encloses, in line with the hypothesis suggested earlier. Taken together, these four squares make up all the possible combinations of the orientations of the proximal reference frame (the contour), the orientations of the external reference frame (horizontal and vertical main directions), and the orientations of the grouping by proximity.

Once we have seen what happens with patterns a and b of Figure 12.12 we may proceed to reason as follows: the pattern in Figure 12.12b is less compact than the pattern in Figure 12.12a; and we know that in the latter the external frame of reference acts in favour of "proximity", whereas in the former it acts against this factor; in both patterns the proximal reference frame is neutral. If the lesser compactness of the pattern in Figure 12.12b depends on there being a force (the horizontal–vertical) that acts against the proximity factor, we may frame the following general hypothesis: "a dot pattern, of the kind discussed so far, appears less compact the more forces act against that of proximity."

If we suppose that the outlines of the squares c-f in Figure 12.12 can act as proximal reference frames in Koffka's sense on the texture of dots they enclose, then those outlines represent so many situations in which the proximal and external reference frames variously act for or against the proximity factor. In particular, in c both frames act in favour of "proximity"; in d the external frame cooperates with "proximity", but the proximal frame contrasts with it; in e the opposite is the case, i.e., "proximity" is reinforced by the proximal frame and contrasted by the external one; and in f both frames act in opposition to "proximity".

If our generalization is well founded, then we may draw the following supplementary hypotheses:

(1) of all the squares c-f in Figure 12.12, c should turn out to be the most compact;
(2) squares d and e should turn out to be less compact than c, but more compact than f.
(3) Furthermore, considering that in squares a and b the proximal reference frame is neutral (relative to "proximity"), we may reasonably expect:
(4) square c should appear more compact than a (because the proximal reference frame acts in favour of "proximity");
(5) square d should appear less compact than a (because the proximal reference frame acts in opposition to "proximity");
(6) square e should appear more compact than b;
(7) square f should appear less compact than b.

From what we can observe on Table 12.1, it is easy to see that the only one of these hypotheses that is not supported by the facts is the last of them, (6). Apart from that, we seem to be licensed to suppose that the more general hypothesis from which the others are derived is fairly well substantiated.

TABLE 12.1

Matched Figures (X–Y)	X>Y	X=Y	X<Y
a–b	40	0	6
a–c	11	13	22
a–d	23	11	12
a–e	11	8	27
a–f	37	4	5
b–c	5	3	38
b–e	9	5	32
b–d	12	5	29
b–f	10	24	12
c–e	28	11	7
c–d	41	3	2
c–f	39	2	5
e–f	38	2	6
e–d	19	0	25
d–f	41	2	3

The data presented in Table 12.1 emerged from a study carried out with 46 participants. The six patterns *a-f* of Figure 12.12 were printed on sheets of white cardboard (50 x 60 cm; dots were 1 cm in diameter and positioned to form a square lattice; the side of each square, and hence the distance between the dots, was 3 cm). The figures were presented pairwise in random order in all 15 possible comparisons of the six patterns *a-f*. Participants were asked to judge, for each pair, the compactness of the figures, choosing among three possible responses reported on a response sheet: $X>Y$, $X=Y$, or $X<Y$, meaning respectively that the pattern on the left (X) appeared more compact, equally compact, or less compact than the pattern on the right (Y).

The results confirmed hypothesis (1), as square *c* was judged more compact than *d* (*c>d*: 41; *c=d*: 3; *c<d*: 2), more compact than *e* (*c>e*: 28; *c=e*: 11; *c<e*: 7), and more compact than *f* (*c>f*: 39; *c=f*: 2; *c<f*: 5).

Hypothesis (2) was also confirmed, as square *d* was judged more compact than *f* (*d>f*: 41; *d=f*: 2; *d<f*: 3), and *e* turned out to be more compact than *f* (*e>f*: 38; *e=f*: 2; *e<f*: 6).

Hypothesis (3) was confirmed as well: square *c* was judged in general more compact than *a* (*c>a*: 22; *c=a*: 13; *c<a*: 11), whereas *a* was judged more compact than *d*, according to hypothesis (4) (*a>d*: 23; *a=d*: 11; *a<d*: 12).

In agreement with hypothesis (5), pattern *e* appeared more compact than *b* (*e>b*: 32; *e=b*: 5; *e<b*: 9).

Hypothesis (6) was the only one receiving no support from the data. Indeed, most participants judged squares *b* and *f* to be of equal compactness, and the remaining participants were almost equally divided between the other two opposite judgments (*b=f*: 24; *b>f*: 10; *b<f*: 12).

8. Certainly, the analysis developed in the two previous sections is far from exhaustive, and may be open to criticism in certain respects. Presumably there are still other forces acting on fields of elementary objects like those examined, and perhaps more fine-grained and more rigorous criteria might be thought up for classifying the various kinds of textures from a

(12.13)

phenomenological viewpoint. Thus the analysis developed above ought to be regarded as just an outline of a research project, which is relevant for present purposes because it allows us to be acquainted, by and large, with the sorts of forces the directionality factor will have to interact with in the situations presented in this section.

Figure 12.13 shows a constellation of dots very similar to that represented in Figure 12.12*f*, in which both reference frames act against unification by "proximity". Given however that this configuration has the shape of a rectangle rather than a square, we might conjecture that, if "directionality" has some weight, then it should act in favour of a grouping into horizontal rows of dots and thus together with one of the directions (the horizontal) of the frames of reference.

Here, all the forces in play act homogeneously, giving rise to a uniform "quincunx" organization. *We may therefore suppose that, if the groupings in one part of the field become stronger, as a consequence of some change, then these groupings will be due to the action of some factor other than those already present.* For example, the subjective attitude of the observer may act as an albeit fleeting grouping factor of this sort. Given, however, that fleetingness is an essential feature of subjective attitude, it is always a straightforward matter to establish whether we are dealing with organizations dependent on it.

In order to get the directionality factor to be active within fields of grouping forces such as those illustrated by Figure 12.13, we take advantage of the special properties of some configurations first noticed by Koffka (1935, p. 141), and then systematically studied by Petter (1956). These configurations can be described as follows: (i) they consist in definite chromatically homogeneous areas of the visual field; (ii) owing to the shape of their outline, they are seen as two or more partially overlapping objects (see Figure 12.14). In particular,

(12.14)

Petter explored the conditions that favour one of these objects' appearing – in the overlapping region – as placed "in front of" the other.

In our case, the areas making up the image won't be chromatically homogeneous. Rather, they will be made up of uniformly distributed dots as in the examples discussed so far. Nevertheless, to the extent that sets of discrete dots may represent continuous lines, the areas will be so determined as to reproduce the profile of the outlines that produce the scission effects studied by Koffka and Petter.

Let us apply this procedure to the area of Figure 12.13 in line with Figure 12.14. As it can easily be seen, Figure 12.15 (as compared with Figure 12.13) has two additional groups of dots, which are so arranged that they simulate the visible parts of the oblique bar in Figure 12.14, in so far as a picture made of dots makes it possible.

The unification of these additional groups of dots gives rise – as in Figure 12.14 – to the phenomenal existence of an elongated object endowed with a marked directionality. This object is made of rows of dots, exactly like the objects discussed above. Its rows of dots extend from one end to the other of the object, hence also within the area visible in Figure 12.13. This means that the dots in that area – which in Figure 12.13 are only subject to the play of forces examined in the previous sections – here (in Figure 12.15) are connected in a way which cannot be explained only by the action of those forces.

It should be noted that in Figure 12.15, the directionality factor acts on the dots in harmony with the proximity factor; in Figure 12.16, by contrast, "directionality" is left to work alone, against all the other forces in the field. In this case, the grouping of the rows linked by "directionality" is very weak though not impossible. Almost all observers we asked (eight out of ten) described this kind of organization as non–spontaneous, though attainable with the help of a suitable attitude. Conversely, the spontaneous organization is characterized by strong compactness of the texture included in the outline of the larger rectangle – within which, as we said earlier, proximal and external reference frames, proximity factor, and, if indeed it is a factor in these cases, a certain feature of horizontal directionality all act consistently with one another. This compactness of texture persists within the region of intersection with the oblique bar, which thus appears unified "behind" the texture, rather than "in front" of it, as is the case with Figure 12.15.

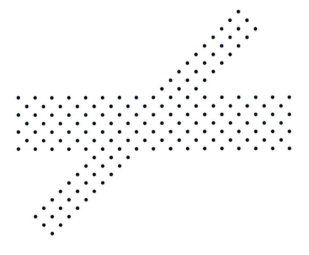

(12.15)

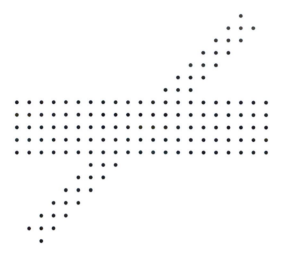

(12.16)

This fact is not without its importance from the theoretical point of view, as it allows us to draw a sharp distinction between the general phenomenon of grouping by good continuation and the special grouping phenomenon under discussion here. Indeed, Figure 12.16 illustrates that a perceptual organization is possible in which a grouping by good continuation does take place (the oblique bar passes behind the horizontal rectangle) without there being any grouping of compact rows from top to bottom along the whole length of the object. In other words, an articulation may be unified as a whole, without its elements (the dots) being linked in rows. This means that, in our examples, the dynamics of the unification of a whole may be distinguished from the dynamics of the formation of its parts (the rows).

In turn, the stated distinction is helpful for clarifying the dynamics of the entire process in question. (i) Thanks to good continuation, in Wertheimer's sense, the object (bar) comes into being as a unity (this effect takes place as in Figure 12.14, which is formed of colour homogeneously distributed in an area, rather than a constellation of discrete dots). (ii) As soon as it is unitary, and not before, that object has the feature of "directionality". (iii) If it is allowed by the other conditions regarding the relations among the dots, "directionality" brings about a grouping of dots into "rows".

Indeed, if the first unification did not take place, then the object could not take on so typical a quality of a whole as directionality is; nor could the directionality act in the manner we have seen emerging unless the relationships among the dots were governed by forces so balanced as to allow for such an effect.

9.   It is worth observing that, for all that they refer to modes of appearance of the overall objects very similar to those studied by Petter, the phrases "in front of" and "behind" regularly used by observers in describing what they see on Figures 12.15 and 12.16 signify structures hardly comparable with Petter's from the point of view of how perceptual organization comes about.

Studying situations like that in Figure 12.14, Petter found that when a chromatically homogeneous region of the visual field has its outline configured so as to give rise to a scission between two partially overlapping figures, and these figures are markedly different in size, then it usually happens that the larger of the units appears to stand "in front of" the other, in a clear and stable way. Petter suggested the following possible explanation of this result: should the larger figure appear behind the smaller, then much longer virtual edge would be called for to unify the smaller figure than those needed in the opposite solution, which is what actually happens (Petter, 1956, p. 218). Thus, the phenomenon would be ruled by a minimum principle.

The objects studied by Petter, however, are chromatically homogeneous surfaces, which may be conceived as sets of points only from the point of view of geometry. In their phenomenal appearance they reveal no discontinuities, and so there are no grouping forces at work among elementary components of which the dynamics described above has to take account: the only relevant question is the economy of the edges. In contrast, in our examples, the "in front of" and the "behind" are perceptual outcomes that arise from specific groupings that link one dot with another, giving rise to rows. And once these rows of dots are organized, then the whole of which they are part tends to appear as lying "in front of" simply because their compactness is not seen to be interrupted.

True, we might suppose that in Figure 12.15 the oblique bar appears "in front," whereas in Figure 12.16 it appears "behind," for reasons relating to the formation of the edges of the figures into which the constellation of dots splits. One might argue as follows. In Figure 12.15 the horizontal dotted rectangle should appear as standing in front of the oblique bar for the very reason suggested by Petter, as with this solution the required virtual edges would be shorter; but the edges of the oblique bar are favoured by closer proximity between dots; hence Petter's effect would not take place because of a number of unifications by proximity that are playing against that effect. In contrast, in Figure 12.16 the horizontal dotted rectangle should stand in front of the oblique bar both because of Petter's rule and because its edges are formed of dots closer to one another. Thus, in this figure both kinds of forces act together, and thus the result is precisely what we should expect. If the line of argument just set out were the correct account of the facts, then in Figure 12.17 the oblique bar should appear as lying "behind" the horizontal rectangle. Indeed, given that this time the constellation is constructed on a triangular meshed lattice (each mesh is a small equilateral triangle), the dots are equally distant from one another, both along the edges of the oblique bar, and along

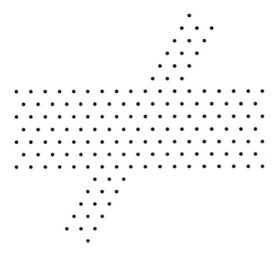

(12.17)

the upper and lower edges of the horizontal band. Under the rules just stated, because the proximity factor is now acting neither in favour nor in disfavour of either of the articulations, the minimum principle applied to the edges should be the deciding factor, just as is the case with continuous and chromatically uniform figures. That is, the oblique bar should appear to lie behind the horizontal rectangle. Which can be made to happen – as judged by almost all our observers – only with the aid of a suitable subjective attitude in observation: the most spontaneous structure is that in which the oblique bar appears in front. Thus, at least in this case, the perceived structure cannot be explained by referring to the minimum principle of edges, but, once more, to the greater robustness of the rows determined by the directionality factor.

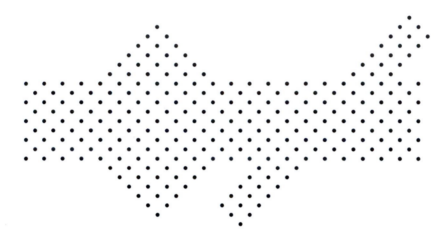

a

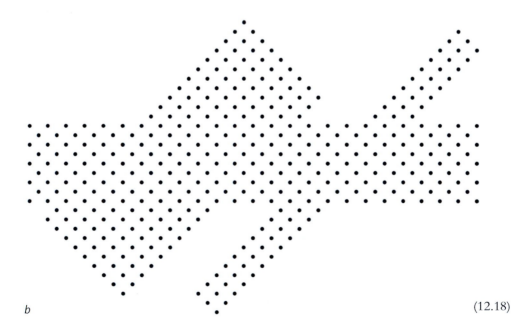

b

(12.18)

10.   A final observation is called for in this connection. Employing articulated situations like those just considered, we may take up under a fresh guise an issue we have already discussed. If directionality is, as suggested, a factor in aligning dots into rows, then the more marked the directionality of the constellation is, the more conspicuous the rows themselves will be. Patterns *a–c* of Figure 12.4 show how this happens with constellations of dots that are not articulated into different objects. Patterns *a* and *b* of Figure 12.18 show that objects endowed with stronger directionality unify dots into rows – in the zone of intersection with a band formed into quincunxes – and these rows are more compact than those that can be seen in the zone of intersection between the quincunx and other "stockier" objects, which is to say those that are less decidedly directional.

The 14 observers questioned about this all agreed with what we have just said. Moreover, six observers spontaneously noticed that the spaces between one "row" and the next in the oblique thin bar in both pictures are whiter and emptier than the other spaces, both within the horizontal dotted rectangle, as well as within the stockier figures intersecting it. This phenomenon becomes even more clearly visible when the "rows" making up the bar are reduced to only two in number, as shown in Figure 12.19. Rather, in this case, the two "rows" of dots in the bar appear to disrupt the continuity of the horizontal rectangle and, relative to the two parts into which it is divided, they almost take on the function of edges.

The empty space between the two oblique "rows" appears lighter than that between dots in other parts of the same figure, and the distance between corresponding dots in one and the other "row" is slightly greater than in the rest of the lattice. This last piece of evidence makes it certain that what really produces unification and segregation is not the metric distance but rather the observable distance regardless of operations of measurement.

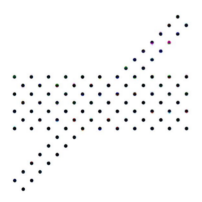

(12.19)

Notes

1   [Editors' note: see chapter 9 of the present anthology, sections 5 and following.]
2   Indeed, this should hold for any subtraction and any addition, so long as the change is effected on a figure with dots distributed according to our rule.
3   See *Logical analysis of the psychophysical (L-R) scheme* [chapter 6 in the present anthology].

References

Koffka, K. (1935). *Principles of Gestalt Psychology*. New York: Harcourt, Brace, & World.

Mach, E. (1886, 1900). *Die Analyse der Empfindungen und das Verhältniss des Physischen zum Psychischen*. Jena: Gustav Fischer. [English translation (by C.M. Williams): *The Analysis of Sensations and the Relation of the Physical to the Psychical*. New York: Dover Publications, 1959]

Peirce, C.S. (1878). How to make our ideas clear. *Popular Science Monthly, 12*, 286–302. [Reprinted in J. Buchler (ed.), *The Philosophy of Peirce* (pp. 23–41). London: Routledge, 2000].

Petter, G. (1956). Nuove ricerche sperimentali sulla totalizzazione percettiva. Fattori della apparentemente diversa dislocazione spaziale di figure cromaticamente omogenee vissute come parzialmente sovrapposte [New experimental inquiries into perceptual totalization. Factors in the apparently different spatial dislocation of chromatically homogeneous shapes experienced as partially overlapping]. *Rivista di Psicologia, 50*, 213–227.

von Schiller, P. (1933). Stroboskopische Alternativversuche. [Stroboscopic alternative experiments] *Psychologische Forschung, 17*, 179–214.

Wertheimer, M. (1923). Untersuchungen zur Lehre von der Gestalt. II. *Psychologische Forschung, 4*, 301–350. [Press English translation in W.D. Ellis (ed.) (1950). *A Source Book of Gestalt Psychology* (pp. 71–88). New York: The Humanities Press.] [English translation by L. Spillmann and M. Wertheimer (2012). *On Perceived Motion and Figural Organization*. Cambridge, MA: the MIT Press].

Wertheimer, M. (1959). *Productive Thinking*. New York: Harper & Brothers.

COMMENTS ON A NEW FACTOR OF PERCEPTUAL GROUPING

Demonstration in terms of pure Experimental Phenomenology

Luigi Burigana

Topics and method

The perceptual objects examined by Paolo Bozzi in this study are patterns of dots distributed over regions of the pictorial surface according to regular schemes, that is, regions covered by regular dotted textures. Relative to such patterns, he considers a set of dots O, which may be either the whole pattern (as in Figure 12.1), or a definite part of it (as in Figure 12.5). Then, regarding set O, he compares two kinds of properties. One kind (I denote it by A) includes properties of the global *shape* of set O, in particular properties of *directionality*, which may concern either the longitudinal axis of the shape or specific parts (margins) of its contour. As suggested in the first paragraph of Section 10, he conceives of directionality as a graded property; in particular, when the set O has the global shape of a rectangle, then its directionality is supposed to be the more conspicuous the more elongate the rectangle, that is, the greater its "aspect ratio". The other kind of properties (I denote it by B) relates to the apparent *grouping* of the dots belonging to set O into definite *rows of dots*. In the hierarchical organization of the pattern, such rows take a place intermediate between individual dots (which lie below in the hierarchy) and the set O (lying above).

The main thesis in his study is that properties in A are *influential* on properties in B, that is, the way in which dots in set O perceptually group together to form rows is influenced by properties of the global shape of O, in particular its directionality. So, the core of the discussion is a *dependence relationship* between properties residing in the same part of the visual field. The method used for substantiating this thesis consists in constructing and examining (in simple experiments) a variety of dot patterns, and showing that variations of properties in A are accompanied by variations of properties in B, and that the latter do not correspond to variations of other properties in the context (i.e., other properties known to be relevant for perceptual grouping). This method is formally stated in the second paragraph of Section 4 and consistently applied throughout the paper. Thus, other "grouping factors" – such as proximity, good continuation, proximal and external reference frames – are also taken into consideration in this study, and the specific effect of directionality is illustrated by comparing it with those of other such factors.

Considering all these characteristics, this study may properly be classified in that branch of vision psychology that deals with the *formation of perceptual unities*, that is, processes of "unification and segregation" of the visual field, as characterized by Koffka (1935, p. 126). This is a theory that finds its most authoritative source in Wertheimer's (1923) paper. Indeed, Bozzi's opening paragraph characterizes his contribution as defining a new unification factor to be added to Wertheimer's system. Furthermore, the method he uses in exploring the specific effect of the new factor is precisely in line with the method originally devised by Wertheimer, and referred to as a paradigm throughout the Gestalt tradition.

A topic distinct from that of perceptual grouping, but closely intertwined with it, is that addressed in Sections 8 and 9. It concerns *order in depth* between perceptual unities, that is, the case in which two (or more) perceptual unities appear to overlap with each other, and the question of which conditions may decide which unity will appear as standing in front of the others. Such phenomena are examples of "double representation" (Koffka, 1935, p. 178), that is, a region in the proximal stimulus may participate in forming two (or more) distinct unities in the perceptual scene. They belong to a class of phenomena that have inspired highly significant research in vision science, such as static and dynamic occlusion as a cue to depth (Gibson, 1979, pp. 76–86), amodal completion (Kanizsa, 1975), and perceptual transparency (Metelli, 1970).

A peculiarity of Bozzi's discussion of the order in depth is that he examines this property in *discrete* patterns of dots (rather than pictures made of topologically continuous and chromatically homogeneous regions). This choice leads him to conceive new hypotheses about the factors that may be influential on the order in depth. In particular, in the third and sixth paragraphs of Section 9 he hypothesizes that the *apparent compactness* of rows of dots plays a decisive role in favouring a set of dots to appear as standing in front of another set of dots belonging to the same pattern; the suggested principle is that more compact rows oppose firmer resistance to their interruption by superposition. Note that apparent compactness of rows of dots is a perceptual property (as the rows themselves are perceptual entities), and the apparent order in depth between perceptual unities is itself a perceptual relation. So, the hypothesis he advances is a case of "percept-percept coupling" (or intra-perceptual dependence), which is one of the key concepts he mentions in the introductory section.

Reasons for interest

Returning to the main topic (perceptual grouping), I note that there are at least two features of this study that make it noteworthy and instructive for researchers in perceptual psychology, especially those interested in the theoretical and methodological aspects of the discipline.

One feature is that the dependence studied by Bozzi goes from properties of a *whole* (directionalities implicit in the global shape of a dot set O) to properties of its *parts* (how dots inside the set O group together into rows of dots). True, this is not an absolute novelty of this paper, as the theory of vision includes several examples of phenomena showing that properties of parts may depend on properties of their wholes. Gestalt theorists, consistently with the emphasis they place on the salience and partial autonomy of wholes (Gestalten), were especially effective in discovering and analysing such examples. A peculiarity of Bozzi's case is that the properties of the parts he considers concern a grouping phenomenon (the emergence of rows of dots), viz., a kind of basic or primary phenomenon which one may presume depends only on properties of the elements involved, *not* on properties of perceptual entities located *higher* in the structural hierarchy of the perceived scene. In my view, demonstrations like those in the paper are especially significant, as they are symptomatic of the complexity of perceptual organization: as well as aspects in which smaller and simpler units link together to form larger and more complex units (for example, by proximity, similarity, or good continuation), there are aspects in which the action appears to go in the opposite direction, from properties of a whole to properties of the parts it includes.

The other feature I note is that Bozzi characterizes the dependence he explores as an *intra-perceptual* one, that is, a dependence of *perceptual* properties on *perceptual* properties. Actually, towards the end of Section 8 he emphasizes that the directionality he considers comes into being as soon as (and only if) the dot set O becomes a perceptual unity, endowed with a global shape, so that directionality is a perceptual property, and its hypothesized effect on the rows of dots inside O (which are themselves perceptual entities) is an intra-perceptual dependence. This character of the subject is pointed out by the author as a distinctive feature of his contribution, and leads him to a consistent choice of concepts and terms throughout the paper. For example: his reference to "percept-percept couplings" (a concept already present in Koffka, 1935, p. 229 and p. 265, and later re-examined by Hochberg, 1974, and Epstein, 1982); the concept of "coplanarity of variables" (meaning that *all* the main terms involved in his arguments are data of perceptual experience); expressions such as "elementary phenomenal items", "angles as perceptual entities", "visually observable distances", etc. (in which the adjectives "phenomenal", "perceptual", and "observable" signify that the basic terms considered are data in perceptual scenes); and the absence of the word "stimulus" throughout the paper (presumably because using this word would imply the dyad stimulus-percept, which is typical of the psychophysical approach in vision science, and this is *not* the approach taken by Bozzi in this study).

Still earlier and more conspicuously, this epistemological standpoint is set out by the expression "pure Experimental Phenomenology" in the title of the paper. Arguably, by this expression the author means a program of vision science which aims to find the reasons behind perceptual phenomena in factors and conditions which are themselves perceptual in nature; a program especially alternative to the prevailing psychophysical approach in vision science, this approach being focused on the dependences between optical stimuli and directly experienced percepts. In asserting this conception, Bozzi is in line with views previously expressed by other theorists, especially in the Gestalt tradition. For example: "covariations of intra-phenomenal coexisting data" and "regular relationships among data of direct experience" as privileged subjects of perceptual psychology (Witte, 1962, p. 455; Metzger, 1966, pp. 737–741); the idea of a "purely psychological theory of perception" (Bischof, 1966, p. 43); and a possible "theory of phenomenal geometry" (Gogel, 1990).

Open questions

With regard to the feature just highlighted – i.e., the dependence of local dot grouping on global directionality understood as an *intra-perceptual* rather than a psychophysical relationship – I wish to add three comments.

One is that, if we classify a dependence as "psychophysical" when in it a property of the percept (the psychological part) becomes related to properties of the stimulus (the physical part), then such classification necessarily depends on how we – as researchers into vision – conceive and represent the optical stimulus. The question is important, because the mode of representing optical stimuli within vision theories is *not unique* – Gordon (1989, p. 234) rightly notes that "stimulus definition is theory-dependent". More specifically, if we presume a "pointillistic representation" of stimuli – in the sense of a "mosaic of stimulation" of traditional theories, or an "image intensity function" of the contemporary computational approach – then a dot set O as meant above is *not directly* a datum in the stimulus (although it may be *derived* through computation from stimulus information), and its global properties (such as the "directionality" discussed by Bozzi) are *not directly* properties of the stimulus. The same may be said of the individual dots in the pattern considered, and the properties and relations (such as distance) of the dots. In these conditions, it is entirely legitimate to assert that the dot set O and its global properties belong to the class of *perceptual* data, and then maintain that the influence those properties exert on perceptual grouping of dots in O is an *intra-perceptual* (not a psychophysical) dependence. The legitimacy of this conclusion, however, depends (in principle) on how stimuli are represented in a theory of vision. For example, the conclusion could be different if a scientist presumes a stimulus representation which includes "higher order features" of the optical information from the environment – this is the case, for example, with the "ambient optic array" as understood in the "theory of direct perception" (Gibson, 1979, ch. 5; Rogers, Gillam, & Gregory, 2009).

As a second comment I note that arguments similar to that in the preceding paragraph (concerning directionality) can also be developed for other law-like dependences in vision, in particular those coded as "laws of perceptual unification" in Wertheimer's system. For example, let us consider the "proximity law," which is an elementary and rather strong principle of perceptual grouping. If a pointillistic representation of stimuli is presumed (in a vision theory), then it may well happen that the elements involved in a grouping by proximity are not directly present (as units) in that stimulus representation, so that their properties (in particular, their reciprocal distances) cannot properly be classified as properties of the stimulus. In such conditions, the suitable epistemological option would be to classify those elements and their properties as entities belonging to the category of perceptual data, and then consistently conclude that the proximity law expresses an intra-perceptual dependence, rather than a psychophysical one. This reading of the proximity law is suggested by Bozzi in the first and last sections of the present study. More generally, the view that Wertheimer's laws of perceptual unification may be interpreted as principles of intra-perceptual dependence, or results of "Experimental Phenomenology" of vision, is illustrated by Bozzi (1985, on pp. 23–27; see chapter 6 in this anthology).

My third comment is that, if we accept as legitimate the concept of "intra-perceptual dependence", then quite naturally we are led to hypothesize *chains* of such dependences, that is, sets of perceptual entities linked together by such dependences and arranged in definite orders of precedence. This consequence finds an example in the last two paragraphs of Section 8, where a "process" in three steps is outlined: formation of O as a perceptual unity, emergence of its directionality, action of that directionality on the dots inside O. It is well-known that Gestalt theory (Berlin School) is not inclined to argue about perceptual phenomena in terms of "processes" as sequences of steps taking place in real time; in other words, the theory is not sympathetic with the idea of "information processing" in algorithmic form. Consistently with this general stance, Bozzi keeps to a minimum the use of word "process" in his paper, has a preference for the word "dynamics" (which is less suggestive of a sense of a series), and reasons in terms of *simultaneous* "forces" that interact and balance with one another (a kind of "electromagnetic" modeling; Köhler, 1920). It is a fact, however, that accepting the concept of intra-perceptual dependence naturally entails accepting the concept of chains or nets of such dependences. In view of this, the following question may be raised: is there a sense in which arguing in terms of such chains or nets may be compatible with the typical stance of Gestalt theory, which is extraneous to the idea of multi-stage procedures in the genesis of perceptual phenomena? More specifically: is there a sense in which what Bozzi states at the end of Section 8, about a "process" in three steps, may be compatible with what he states in Section 1, concerning the absence from his analysis of substantial references to "underlying brain processes or other causal entities transcending the phenomenal data"?

My answer to the question is in the affirmative, and relies on the distinction between a "processing sense" and an "analytic sense" of a psychological hypothesis, a distinction defined, for example, by Davies (1989) in discussing connectionism and modularity. For example, the hypothesis of a chain of operations is in the *processing sense* when it is believed to represent a chain of events really going on in a real system – e.g., what really happens in the perceptual system of an *observer* during an act of vision. It is in the *analytic sense* when it is the expression of a theory constructed by a *scientist* about the observable rendering of a system – in this latter view the distinction of several steps and their arrangement in an order is a way of coming to terms, by means of analysis, with the complexity of the dynamics in the system. My interpretation is that Bozzi, in line with Gestalt theory, does not ascribe a processing sense to possible chains of intra-perceptual dependences. Nevertheless, he allows for chains of such dependences – the "interplay of percept-percept couplings" mentioned in Section 1 – as a legitimate way of theorising, in an analytic form, about the complex dynamics of vision.

With these comments, which arose from salient passages in the paper translated, I wish to indicate epistemological aspects of vision psychology which may appear complex, somewhat ambiguous, and perplexing to anyone who approaches this discipline with expectations of a clearly designed and soundly grounded system. I have reasons to believe that Bozzi was intellectually fascinated by those debatable and yet fundamental aspects.

References

Bischof, N. (1966). *Erkenntnistheoretische Grundlagenprobleme der Wahrnehmungspsychologie.* In W. Metzger (ed.), *Handbuch der Psychologie.* Band 1.1. *Allgemeine Psychologie: Der Aufbau des Erkennens (Wahrnehmung und Bewusstsein)* (pp. 21–78). Göttingen, Germany: Hogrefe.

Bozzi, P. (1985). Analisi logica dello schema psicofisico (S-D). *Teorie & Modelli,* II(2), 3–36.

Davies, M. (1989). Connectionism, modularity, and tacit knowledge. *British Journal for the Philosophy of Science, 40,* 541–555.

Epstein, W. (1982). Percept-percept couplings. *Perception, 11,* 75–83.

Gibson, J.J. (1979). *The Ecological Approach to Visual Perception.* Boston: Houghton Mifflin.

Gogel, W.C. (1990). A theory of phenomenal geometry and its applications. *Perception & Psychophysics, 48,* 105–123.

Gordon, I.E. (1989). *Theories of Visual Perception.* New York: Wiley.

Hochberg, J.E. (1974). Higher-order stimuli and inter-response coupling in the perception of the visual world. In R.B. MacLeod and H.L. Pick (Eds), *Perception: Essays in Honor of James J. Gibson* (pp. 17–39). Ithaca, NY: Cornell University Press.

Kanizsa, G. (1975). Amodal completion and phenomenal shrinkage of surface in the visual field. *Italian Journal of Psychology, 2,* 187–195.

Koffka, K. (1935). *Principles of Gestalt Psychology*. New York: Harcourt, Brace, & World.

Köhler, W. (1920). *Die physischen Gestalten in Ruhe und im stationären Zustand*. Braunschweig: Vieweg. [Abridged English translation in W.D. Ellis (ed.) (1950) *A Source Book of Gestalt Psychology* (pp. 17–54). New York: The Humanities Press].

Metelli, F. (1970). An algebraic development of the theory of perceptual transparency. *Ergonomics*, *13*, 59–66.

Metzger, W. (1966). Figural-Wahrnehmung. In W. Metzger (ed.), *Handbuch der Psychologie*. Band 1.1 *Allgemeine Psychologie: Der Aufbau des Erkennens (Wahrnehmung und Bewusstsein)* (pp. 693–744). Göttingen, Germany: Hogrefe.

Rogers, B.J., Gillam, B., and Gregory, R.L. (2009). Optic arrays and retinal images: Discussion. *Perception*, *38*, 159–163.

Wertheimer, M. (1923). Untersuchungen zur Lehre von der Gestalt. II. *Psychologische Forschung*, 4, 301–350. [Abridged English translation in W.D. Ellis (ed.) (1950). *A Source Book of Gestalt Psychology* (pp. 71–88). New York: The Humanities Press; English translation by L. Spillmann and M. Wertheimer (2012). *On Perceived Motion and Figural Organization*. Cambridge, MA: the MIT Press].

Witte, W. (1962). Zur Wissenschaftsstruktur der psychologischen Optik. *Psychologische Beiträge*, *6*, 451–462.

13

TWO FACTORS OF UNIFICATION FOR MUSICAL NOTES: CLOSENESS IN TIME AND CLOSENESS IN TONE

Translated by Luisa Zecchinelli and Richard Davies

1. Introduction

When a piece of music is played, what the listener hears is not really a large number of unconnected sounds, but rather an interweaving of melodic lines that are clearly separable and relatively independent one from the other within the musical context.

If we had to give a description of a piece of music in a narrowly analytic fashion – for instance in the terms of physics – listing separately each of the sound events in the sequence of instants, we would never get round to explaining the presence of organised structures such as phrases and melodies. These come to the fore at a different level of observation and can be grasped only by appeal to concepts that can hardly be reduced to those called for by "objective" descriptions such as those of physics.

When the question was raised of the unified organisation of visible objects, the situation was basically the same. Indeed, as a point of history, it was von Ehrenfels's observations on the phenomenal properties of melodies that introduced a new perspective that was able to show that there were problems concerning the organisation of directly given experience that were unthinkable within the empiricist and atomistic paradigm that dominated psychology at the end of the nineteenth century, foremost among which was the problem of the unity of perceived events.

If we grant the constancy hypothesis in the relations among physical, physiological and directly experienced events, and if we take some definitions of unitariness as holding of objects such as the "rigid body" accepted in mechanics, then we ought to expect an organisation of the field of actual experience that differs in many points from the way it in fact is. Wertheimer drew attention to an extremely fertile method when he formulated the laws of the unitary organisation of visible objects on the basis of the relations that hold at the level of direct experience, without being further analysable, and proceeded to adopt as a measure of their relative weight the perceived results obtained in situations where the factors conflict. This is the only way to pick out the rules that bring about the organisations of the field that are the objects of direct observation.

These laws do not easily reveal themselves to simple observation of the objects that fill our experience. They emerge more readily from a analysis of fairly elementary situations in which we can isolate the factors from the interaction of a large number of variables.

These variables should not be so broken up as to destroy the factors of unification that we are seeking. Because he was particularly interested in the visual field, Wertheimer took into account some extremely simple – obvious even – visual facts to this end. These are the facts that exemplify the well-known laws of organisation in the visual field: proximity, similarity, common fate etc.

We may employ a line of reasoning similar to Wertheimer's to try to explain some features of our tonal experience, looking at some case of unification among notes that are generated in very simple situations. These cases of unification are strongly similar to the first of the factors that Wertheimer listed, namely proximity.

Thanks to this factor, a sequence of dots that is presented on a uniform background as follows:

$$\bullet \; \bullet \qquad \bullet \; \bullet \qquad \bullet \; \bullet \qquad \bullet \; \bullet \qquad\qquad (13.1)$$

is normally seen as a sequence of pairs, with the first dot paired with the second, the third with the fourth and so on, and not the second with the third, the fourth with the fifth and so on.

There is a straightforward sense in which, when we talk of proximity as a factor of unification, we do not mean that there is some precise distance that has this power, but rather that in an overall situation two objects are closer to each other than either is to other. After all, in the following sequence:

$$\bullet \qquad \bullet \qquad\qquad\qquad \bullet \qquad \bullet \qquad\qquad (13.2)$$

the same distance that in (1) divided in (2) unites by way of "proximity".

We shall make use of this observation later.

2. Two meanings of "proximity" in music: temporal proximity and tonal proximity

Is it possible to carry this system of relations over into the field of tonal experience? Wertheimer had already at least implicitly floated this supposition when, among other cases of unification by proximity, he refers to a situation made up of sound elements: "That the principle [of proximity] holds also for auditory organisation can easily be observed by substituting tap-tap, pause, tap-tap, pause for (1) and likewise for the other cases".

Clearly, transpositions of this sort, from one sensory modality to another, can only be carried out so long as we do not require perfect fit between their terms. As Wertheimer applied it to acoustics the concept of proximity has some features that distinguish it from that of the dots. Because the sequence of taps and pauses are of necessity distributed in time, they do not generate a simultaneous representation of grouping, as the dots do, but a sequence of distinct rhythmic figures.

We may, therefore, speak of "proximity" in music in at least two ways.

To begin with, we have temporal proximity, as already described in the example given by Wertheimer. This can be compared quite easily with spatial proximity, especially if we avail ourselves of the usual spatial representations of time. In the first place, just as a sequence of equidistant dots does not give rise to salient groupings of the elements that make it up, so also a series of sound at regular intervals, as in Figure 13.3, does not lend itself to groupings that are other than subjective and fleeting rhythms. If, on the other hand, we make the succession discontinuous by introducing pauses, the notes that are not separated by these pauses will tend to unify, as we see in Figure 13.4:[1]

(13.3)

(13.4)

Furthermore, "proximity" also in acoustic situations is a relational property: when two events are separated by a certain amount of objectively measured time, will be "closer" than others that are separated by a longer lapse, as we have already noted. If we then project any temporal distribution of acoustic stimuli, as in Figure 13.4, into a shorter time span, then the "proximity" relations remain unchanged (Figures 13.5 and 13.6).

(13.5)

(13.6)

Of course these conditions hold only within certain temporal limits: if the stimuli come too quickly or too slowly, the relations lose their salience.

The other case of musical proximity is quite different. This is what we are calling "tonal proximity", which can be specified in terms of *intervals*, which is to say "distances" between tones on the musical scale.

Consider the following example:

(13.7)

Here we have a chromatic musical scale in which each element is at the same tonal distance from the next, namely by a semitone. At bottom, this situation is precisely the same as that in Figure 13.3, inasmuch as no privileged grouping imposes itself on us because the action of the new variable – tonal distance – is uniform from one note to the next. (In the chromatic scale, all the notes are a semitone apart.)

Let us now consider Figure 13.8:

(13.8)

Here, the notes do not stand in the same interval one to another; in some pairs it is smaller and in others bigger. From the point of view of perception, the situation does not present a series of notes, but a sequence of binary groups. This brings out the unifying function of a new factor: the notes that are tonally "close" are experienced as making up pairs, where the tonal interval is smaller.

This new kind of "proximity" can likewise be defined relationally: tonal proximity should be taken as a lesser distance relative to a greater. For this reason, the same interval that can be experienced as "divisive" in one situation can be experience as unifying in another. The following two examples clearly illustrate this concept: the first two notes in Figure 13.9 can be regarded as "close" while, by comparion, the second and the third are "distant". In Figure 13.10, the same interval that, in Figure 13.9, separated the third note from the second now unifies the first two notes. This fact becomes all the clearer if the notes are heard in rapid succession, as indicated in the second part of each example.[2]

(13.9)

(13.10)

3. Tonal proximity and identity

Let us now consider the following sequence of notes (Figure 13.11):

(13.11)

When we hear this succession of sounds, we notice that they are clearly grouped into pairs, as in Figure 13.8. Yet there is a big difference between the successions in the two cases: while in the former, the notes that make up pairs were tonally "very close" but different in the latter, they are the same. Thus, we have two radically different circumstances that produce the same effects.

Regarded abstractly, this would be easily explained by treating the case of "identity" as just a special case of tonal proximity, namely that in which the tonal distance is reduced to zero. Yet this solution cannot be accepted so easily because we have to take two important facts into account. The first is that the impression of sameness is quite different from that of nearness, however small the gap. The other is that there are notes that, in terms of tonal quality, are the same, namely those with the same name in different octaves (all the Cs, all the Ds, all the Es and so on), but that are further from each other than they are from the "different" notes that are nevertheless tonally close.

The first of these facts is very evident. Hearing a B followed by a C is a very different thing from hearing the same C twice over. In this case, the difference in pitch between the two notes is, from the musical point of view, the smallest that there can be, namely a semitone, but even reducing that difference to 4/9, 3/7 and so on, so as to bring the B as close as possible to the C as the threshold will allow, the impression of difference remains and indeed it may be said to increase.

To explore more fully what so elementary an experience means and to clarify the distinction between a case of proximity and one of identity, we may compare the three sequences of notes in the following examples:

(13.12)

(13.13)

(13.14)

If sameness really were just a special case of tonal proximity, there should be the same kind of phenomenal difference between, on the one hand, Figures 13.12 and 13.13 and, on the other 13.13 and 13.14. Indeed, Figure 13.14 is derived from 13.13 on the same principle that 13.13 is derived from Figure 13.12: in each case, a semitone has been subtracted from the fixed interval that separates the elements in each of the series. What actually happens, however, is that Figures 13.12 and 13.13 are very different from Figure 13.14. The former are clearly sequences of ever-lower notes, while the last can be described as the repetition of the same note.

The second fact is no less evident. In a situation like that of example Figure 13.15,

(13.15)

we have unification of the notes that are "close", and not those that are tonally "identical", which it might be better to call "corresponding". Now, the qualitative affinity among notes that have the same denomination is the most powerful that there can be; nevertheless, they are not experienced as unified in a pair. Rather, we find unification between notes whose affinity is reduced by the dissonant interval, but that are not separated by a great tonal distance.

There is, however, another way to get at the relation between the proximity factor and tonal identity. This is to replace, in situations that are structurally similar, an identity relation with a proximity relation, and thus to see whether there is a difference in the perceptual outputs in the situations under observation. Thus we should be able to see whether or not the two unification factors act in the same direction.

Let us examine the following examples:

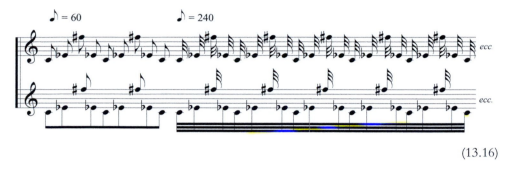

(13.16)

(*Continued* 13.16)

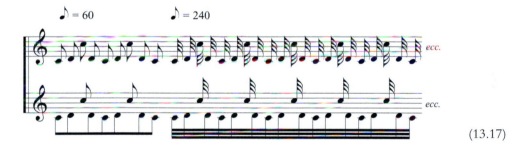

(13.17)

(13.18)

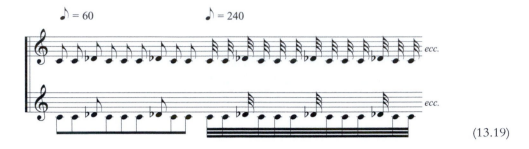

(13.19)

If we listen to these sequences in the first instance at the first of the given speeds (= 60), we can easily discern that the note separated from the others by a bigger interval appears phenomenally "isolated" within the piece as a whole. Moreover, if we increase the speed of the sequence, for instance to = 240 (the second speed indicated), the phenomenal isolation of the highest note reaches a point where it creates a sort of schism within the tonal field into two levels: on the upper one, there is felt repetition of the high note and on the lower we have an undulating and uninterrupted melodic line.[3] The important thing to bear in mind is that all these examples have the same overall perceived structure, but this is produced in the first three by a proximity relation among the lower notes, whereas in the fourth there is another factor that has to some extent taken the place of the greater relative proximity. In Figure 13.19, the note that is experienced as isolated is at the smallest possible tonal distance from the others, and the unification of the others cannot be due to anything other than their identity.

Thus, we have seen that, even when the separating interval between one note and the next is as small as can be, the only factor that can dominate over this segregation by proximity and break the grouping is note identity. This ought to happen all the more when the separating intervals are greater, as it is easy to imagine and as we have observed experimentally with sequences that fit the bill.

On these grounds we are not allowed to suppose that the sameness of two notes is just a special case of tonal proximity (that in which the distance is reduced to zero), but we are allowed to say that whenever a proximity relation is replaced by one of identity then we should get the same result, namely a unification of the sound elements involved.

4. Two factors at odds. The influence of speed of succession

So far we have taken tonal proximity and temporal proximity separately, trying to specify their essential characteristics using examples in which only or the other was the operative variable. Yet in real musical situations the two factors are always at work together, so that we must examine their relative weightings in structuring tonal forms. For this reason, we must look at how they behave when they are at odds with each other albeit at an elementary level.

One situation in which the two factors work in opposing directions is as follows:

(13.20)

Between each C below the line and each G above, there is a considerable interval, so that the tonal distance works as a separating factor. But these two notes are closer to each other in point of time than is each G above the line and each following A flat, so that the temporal distance would favour the unification of the first two notes. On the other hand, each G and each A flat are tonally very close, so that the tonal proximity works in favour of unification; but they are separated by a large time lapse relative to the first two notes, which has a separating effect. The same applies to the following notes, namely the C sharp and the C below the line, followed by a G above the line. And so on.

When we listen to a sequence of sound stimuli with this structure, we hear pairs of notes melodically rising and falling, separated by pauses: that is to say, the unification comes about as a result of the factor we have been calling temporal proximity. In such a case, tonal proximity is too weak to be noticed.

Yet we can make tonal proximity dominate without changing the temporal relations or the tonal intervals of Figure 13.20. It is enough *to increase the speed of the sequence of stimuli*. If we listen to Figure 13.20 at = 240, then we still hear pairs of notes, but they are made up of G and A flat and of C and C sharp, which is to say the notes that are tonally closest.

The same result can be got replacing the proximity factor with the identity factor, for the reasons given in the preceding section. Consider Figure 13.21: at = 60, we have unification among temporally close notes; but at = 240, the notes with the same name unify.

(13.21)

(*Continued* 13.20)

(*Continued* 13.21)

As we can see, they are made up of the fast versions of Figures 13.20 and 13.21. What marks them out is a musical notation that brings to the fore the overall structure of what we hear when we increase the speed of the presentations from which we began. At = 240, the process of unification between tonally close notes goes so far as to bring out two distinct sequences of sounds, each made up of pairs of notes. These two sequences are present together but separated into two sound levels, as we might find for instance in the high and low parts in a composition for two voices.

From what we have said, it is clear that whether unification by temporal proximity dominates over tonal proximity or vice versa depends on a further variable, which is the speed of the sequence. It is very hard to explain just how this variable acts on the two factors, because when we increase the speed of the presentation of the stimuli, we are not really modifying the temporal relations that hold objectively. It seems that the dominance of one unification factor over the other comes about according to whether the temporal relations discussed above fall or do not fall within certain absolute ranges.

5. Further observations on tonal proximity: the trill and the tremolo

In the resolution of conflicts between temporal and tonal proximity, this latter factor plays a more complex role than we have so far been able to bring out. Let us consider the following situations (Figures 13.22a–f):

(13.22a)

(13.22b)

(13.22c)

(13.22d)

(13.22e)

(13.22f)

When we listen to these situations at the indicated speeds one after another, it is easy to hear that the first two (Figures 13.22a and 13.22b) are radically different from the last two (Figures 13.22e and 13.22f). While the first two are perceived as a rapid alternation of two notes, that is to say as a trill, the last two are experienced as two series of repeated notes that are both present, as in the Figures 13.20a and 13.21a in the preceding section. For all that they closely resemble the two that follow them, the two intermediate situations (Figures 13.22a and 13.22d) present a lower level of unification by tonal identity.

This schism of the events with in the auditory field into two sharply distinct series is even more evident if we consider situations like these (Figures 13.23a–f):

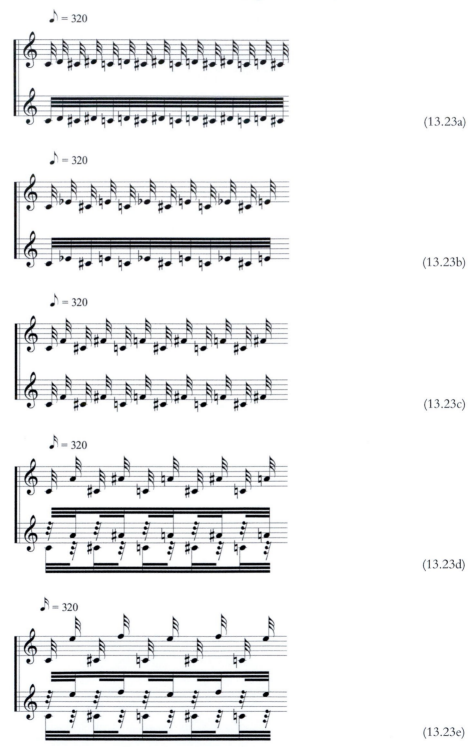

(13.23f)

When we listen to these six examples at the speeds indicated one after another, we notice an increasing differentiation of two melodic lines, each of which presents itself as a trill. These two trills are experienced as both present but as lying in different regions of the tonal space: the one "high" and the other "low". It goes without saying that situations of Figure 13.23 are basically similar to those of 13.22. In type 13.22 cases, the unification of the notes in the upper line and in the lower line comes about through identity, while in type 13.23, it comes about through tonal proximity. In these latter, however, the segregation between the two melodic lines is equally strong, because the unification between notes that are so tonally close generates a very significant structure: that of a trill (or, to be precise, a double trill made up of a "high" part and a "low" part).

It is worth pointing out that the first two situations in each of the two series differ from the last two in respect of a single variable, namely the tonal distance between the even-numbered notes and the odd-numbered ones. In all other respects each of these groups of examples is constructed in the same way.

Why should it be that the unifications come about differently in the extreme situations? If they are correctly applied, the considerations brought to light in the foregoing sections can be employed to explain the two perceptual effects that musicians call the trill and the tremolo.

As regards the Figure 13.22 cases, we may begin our explanation by appealing to a simpler case drawn from visual perception that is nevertheless closely similar to the one that interests us. If we have a certain number of dots arrayed on a uniform background thus:

i)

●　　　●　　　●　　　●　　　●　　　●

●　　　●　　　●　　　●　　　●　　　●　　　● (13.24)

they look to us like two rows of dots one above the other. If we arrange the dots in successive situations in which the rows appear progressively closer, we get to a point where there are no longer two rows, but just one that unifies the dots in a zigzag, thus:

ii)

●　　　●　　　●　　　●　　　●　　　●

●　　　●　　　●　　　●　　　●　　　●　　　● (13.25)

This is very easily explained. In the first example (Figure 13.24), the first four dots stand in the following proximity relations:

iii)

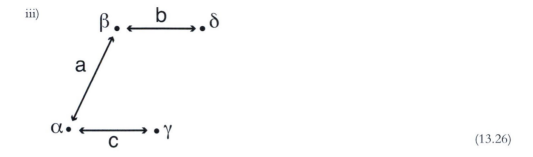

(13.26)

The relation *a* is metrically greater than the relation *c*; hence, the dot α is unified with dot γ. Dot β is separated from dot α because it is nearer to dot δ. Similar conditions are repeated for all the dots in the example.

In the following case (Figure 13.25), the proximity relations have changed to:

iv)

(13.27)

dot α is unified with dot β because it is metrically less distant from β than it is from γ, and so on.

In our musical cases, the transformation of a trill into a tremolo is due to a similar change in the structural relations that hold among the sound stimuli. Except that the explanation inevitably becomes more complex, because, alongside the variables corresponding to the relations of tonal proximity, there is also that of temporal proximity. Indeed, the dots are perceived all at once, while the sequence of sound stimuli is produced over time.

In a trill, the two tonally close sounds alternate to make up a series of temporally equidistant notes, and the trill presents to the listener as a rapid sequence of alternating notes, just like the zigzag in Figures 13.25 and 13.27.

In this case, unification by tonal proximity acts in concomitance with the relation of temporal proximity, which binds together all the notes in the sequence:

v)

t ------------------------------------>

(13.28)

The relation of tonal identity that connects all the even-numbered notes and all the odd-numbered notes does not produce a phenomenal unification because the two factors that are at odds with it are stronger than it: (1) the tonal proximity between the notes one, two, three and so on; in joint action with (2) temporal proximity, which binds each note equally to the one immediately before and the one immediately after it. In this case, the joint action of tonal proximity and temporal proximity mean that there is no unification among the notes that are the same as one another.

Naturally, we can produce different phenomenal organisations by varying the balance among these relations. In the last figures in the series under scrutiny (13.22), the action of the tonal proximity among the even-numbered notes and among the odd-numbered ones is no longer operative because the interval between one note and the next has been much increased, as in the visual situation (13.26). In this case, we find unification by tonal identity at the expense of temporal proximity, which no longer acts jointly with tonal proximity:

vi)

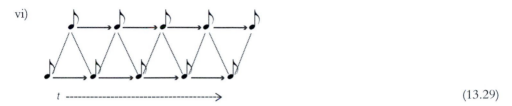

(13.29)

This new mix gives rise to the musical effect of the tremolo, which is a schism of the notes into two lines of sound events that are distinct and coexistent.

The case of the double trill, exemplified in the various cases of type 13.23 situations, can be analysed in the same way.

6. The question of tonal space

In discussing the experimental situations offered in this study, we have had occasion to speak of "tonal proximity", of a "schism of the tonal field into different levels" and of "regions of the tonal space". Considered as descriptions of what we hear when we listen to our musical examples, such expressions may be regarded as fairly clear; after all, they often recur in the talk of musicians and others who take an interest in music. Yet such usages might be regarded as incorrect insofar as they have been wrenched out of the vocabulary that we normally use to describe our experiences of sight and touch. If it were just a question of linguistic propriety or of expressive clarity, it would be hardly worth tarrying on the point: what is really at issue is whether we can properly speak of a tonal space in relation to musical notes in just the same way as we can speak of a visual space when it comes to visible objects, and, if so, what relations hold among the properties of each.

Geza Révész took the problem to be a matter of some importance and proposed that this sort of transposition of terms is not legitimate:

> (. . .) if we compare the tone sensations with the actual spatial impressions (optical and tactual), we soon find that there is not the slightest phenomenological similarity between the spatial and acoustical concepts of "height" and "distance", let alone ideational identity. The fact that the various tongues use spatial expressions (high and low) for the rising and falling aspects may well be interesting from a linguistic–psychological point of view. But one cannot deduce from this the extensity of the tone

sensations*. There is no doubt that her one has to do, not with spatial relations, but simply with analogies, exactly as with concepts tone "colour" and colour "tone".[4]

In his discussion of this view, Révész is led to distinguish between the "absolute height" and the "musical height" of sound events. The former may be due to the fact that certain acoustic frequencies resonate with parts of our bodies that are experienced as "high": "if we sing a high note, we localize it *high up*, in the head (head resonance)"; while other frequencies resonate with "lower" parts: "[t]he vibrational sensations engendered by the bass viols and the deeper notes of the cellos (if one is in the proximity of these instruments) are usually felt in the middle part of the chest.".

"Musical height" on the other hand, "should be understood as a well-defined characteristic of the sound sensation". This is a specifically musical property of notes in virtue of which they can be ordered in a series, at the ends of which we find sounds that are "acute" and "bass" or "bright" and "dark" and so on. In other words this is a property by which we can distinguish notes that have the same name but belong to different octaves.

Granting these two definitions, it follows that the terms referring to absolute height have to do with the common experience of "high" and "low", while "musical height" does not; on these grounds, it is improper to use the terminology of space to describe the musical properties of sounds.

Nevertheless, the problem cannot be raised and resolved so easily. It is not just a matter of finding out whether or not a given note can occupy a certain place "high up" or "low down". No-one would wonder whether there is a spatial relation between a certain bookshelf and the F sharp in the second octave; if we put it that way, the problem goes away on its own. The question is rather: can the laws that give unitary organisation to visual space be found also in the unitary constitution of sound objects? If so, then in the same way that we can speak of a "space" when we have to do with the relations among visible events, we may also speak of a tonal "space" to delineate the field of the relations among audible events.

Thus it is clear that we have talked about a "tonal space" only because we have been able to use the terminology of "proximity", "distance" and so on, with a view to picking out some of the relations among musical notes. It is worth pointing out that we could have used any old terms for these relations, without making any reference to the spatial characteristics of our visual and tactile experience. If we did not use arbitrary terms, it is because the words "proximity", "distance" and so on do not have a merely analogical sense as Révész urged, nor a wholly conventional and metaphorical sense as might seem from what we written so far. Rather, in our view, the generically spatial terms with which we have described the situations analysed in this study are used in all propriety, which is to say more than analogically and more than conventionally.

In the first place, we should point out that the expressions "high" and "low" are not a mere curiosity for psychologists of language. If, of all the theoretically possible adjectives, it was precisely these that were chosen to designate certain zones of the musical scale, there must be a reason. Even Révész, for all that he insists that there is nothing but vague analogy, cannot throw doubt on the degree of unanimity in the choice. But it is not our intention to argue the point.

What we do want to say is that the "proximity" that Wertheimer discusses acts on events in visual space in accordance with a rule that is that same as the one obeyed by the factor of unification that we have called "tonal proximity".

Some doubt might be raised, however, about the possibility that one of the other factors of unification that have already been elicited in the theory of forms has an equal right to be identified with the factor of unification that we have brought out in the course of our observations. At first sight, it might seem for instance that "similarity" could be relevantly cited.[5] That is one might say that sounds produced by frequencies belonging to a certain specified critical band or to some broader stretch of frequencies are heard as "similar" and are thus unified. Two sharp sounds surely resemble each other more than they do a deep sound, and this might explain the fact that they are heard "together".[6]

There are many reasons, however, to resist choosing "similarity" to explain the phenomena that we have interpreted in terms of the factor of "proximity".

In the first place, we should observe that, if we were to do so, that it would be hard to find another apter term to designate the perceptual salience of the interval of an octave: it is the notes that have the same name that are "similar" in the strict sense. Moreover there is widespread abuse of the notion of "similarity" in music: notes with the same timbre are said to be similar, likewise with those that have the same intensity or that have equal value (relative duration). In addition, the similarity relation also binds notes that have slightly different timbres.

In any case, there is no lesser variety of meanings of the term "similarity" in the visual field. The "similarity" that Wertheimer appeals to as a factor of unification is a kind of relation that binds two or more objects that are spread out in space but that are otherwise *identical*. It is thus a relation that holds among the members of a group insofar as they are all different from the members of another spatially nearby group. In common usage, however, the term "similarity" is employed to express a different kind of relation: two things are said to be similar when they are not identical, but the differences between them are slight. This is the usage respected in psychology to indicate those minimal differences among the features of two or more events that do indeed serve to distinguish them, but that are only just above the difference threshold. As regards colours, we say for instance that oranges resemble one another when they are due to the mixture of red and yellow in proportions that are not so different one from another.

This account of similarity has been used to construct a variety of "spatial models" for the main perceptual qualities of things. Colours have been organised by way of Ebbinghaus's double pyramid, which orders the similarities along different parameters of tonality, brightness and saturation (this was the taxonomy that Munsell later perfected); a simpler model is that of Hering's circle; the square of mixtures; the triangle that coordinates brightness with mixtures; and so on. Analogous geometrical mappings have been thought up to classify tastes and smells.

Révész himself constructed a geometrical model for musical notes. This must be a three-dimensional scheme, since "the note series is characterized not by one but by the synthesis of two characteristics, of which one progresses continuously and in a one-way direction (pitch) and the other progresses continuously and periodically (quality)".[7] In effect, we have a vertical cylinder on whose outer surface we can trace a rising spiral. "The continuity of direction of the pitch series is expressed by a continuous line from the starting point; the periodicity of the quality series by the dots corresponding to the notes of similar designation (within each octave) which lie on the spiral line vertically one above the other".[8]

Clearly, all the phenomenal "similarities" ordered by these spatial models can be described in terms of geometrical "proximity". But where in the cases of colours, tastes and smells, to speak of proximity is blatantly metaphorical, in the case of musical notes, we have something that is more than a mere analogy. From the practical point of view there really is a certain convenience to talking about colours being "close" or "distant" on a given axis: this allows us to indicate them and to recognise them relative to a standard classification, or to fix their position relative to a colour sample. Nevertheless, in speaking about colours in a non-technical way, we are inclined to use expressions that presuppose relations of similarity.

This does not happen with musical notes. We carry on speaking of "proximity", "height" and so on irrespective of Révész spatial model, which is not well known either among musicians or among lay commentators. Moreover, there are at least two cases in which it would be extremely awkward to introduce the notion of "similarity" while that of proximity is the only one that fits the bill.

If we agree to talk about the similarity between notes belonging to the same range of frequencies, this agreement will hold only so long as we attend to single notes produced one after another, with perhaps a brief rest between them. That is, only in situations of comparison is it possible to say that one note is more or less "similar" than another to a pre-chosen standard note. On the other hand, when we listen to a melody, no-one hears a sequence of similarity relations among the notes that make it up; we cannot say that some are more similar to each other and others less so (except in the cases of unison and the octave): they are all in certain sense different from each other. What we really hear is that the melody "moves", "rises" and "falls", and that within these movements, the distance between some notes and others sometimes sounds large and sometimes small. These relations define the "melodic profile".

In the second place, that vague impression of similarity that can arise out of hearing in isolation two or more sounds of much the same frequency, is completely erased when the musical notes are played simultaneously, as in chords or in contrapuntal structures. Chords can be "tight" or "broad", compact or sparse, and we cannot experience any relation of similarity among the notes that make them up. In counterpoint, we experience so vividly the relations of "proximity" and "distance" among the parts that we draw from it the impression of a genuine "space" with in which the various melodic lines are articulated.

For this reason, we seem to have to exclude the interpretation of the factor of unification that we have been analysing as "similarity" among the elements in play. Yet, as we have seen, appeal to "proximity", as Wertheimer described it, allows us to explain more naturally the acoustic situations on which we carried out our experiments.

In conclusion, what warrants our speaking of a tonal space is not so much a possible congruence between it and the visual space, as the fact, which we have sought to establish, that certain structuring conditions hold of the acoustic field that are identical to others that hold of the structuring of the visual field.

Notes

1   When our examples are made up of two lines one above the other, they are to be read as follows: the upper line represents the objective distribution of sound stimuli, so that the notes are written so that they are graphically isolated one from another; the lower line represents the groupings that are formed as a matter of phenomenology. In the latter case, thanks to a convention of musical notation, the notes are connected in accordance with the unification. The sound situations that are reproduced in writing in our examples and on which we carried out our observations were recorded on magnetic tape.

2   A third case of proximity might be this: among three sounds variously spread out in space and equally distributed over time, the two whose origin is experienced as closest will be unified. This

case raises a problem in the study of acoustic perception in general but is not very important for the psychology of music.

3   Someone with more than a smattering of music theory might object to these examples by recalling that the isolation of the upper note is mostly due to the fact that it is higher than the others, given that in musical compositions the higher notes play the role of figure (voice) relative to the others that are background (accompaniment). The objection is not, however, telling against our examples, because we also have the following case:

4   Révész, G. (1946). *Introduction to the Psychology of Music* (trans. G.I.C. de Courcy, Dover Reprints, Mineola, NY, 2001, p. 68). The asterisk in the original refers to Révész' own "Gibst es ein Hörraum?", *Acta Psychologica*, III, 1931, 137–192. The citations in the next paragraph are from *Introduction*, pp. 68–69.

5   In the discussion we have already cited, Wertheimer cites musical examples like ours to illustrate the "similarity" factor.

6   On this point, see Bozzi, P. (1959). Un aspetto della qualità armonica: la tendenza alla risoluzione [An aspect of harmonic quality: the tendency to resolution]. *Rivista di psicologia*, *LIII* (II), p. 159.

7   Révész, *Introduction*, cit., p. 67.

8   Loc. cit., and Figure 18.

COMMENTS ON TWO FACTORS OF UNIFICATION AMONG MUSICAL NOTES: CLOSENESS IN TIME AND CLOSENESS IN TONE

Luisa Zecchinelli

As well as being a perceptologist, philosopher and narrator, Paolo Bozzi cultivated an eclectic range of professional and artistic interests. But most of all, he was a musician, playing the violin and the viola after a rigorous training in Rodolfo Lipizer's famous school. He left an engrossing account, dedicated to his violin teacher, of the musical education that ran in parallel and overlapped with his studies in philosophy and psychology.[1]

He was so familiar with instrumental technique that he was enabled to explore the complex unfolding of the sound organisation of musical language "from within" as a theoretician, as a performer and as a composer. It was thus from this deep acquaintance with the language of the violin, worked on and enjoyed through daily practice as a learned professional performer, that grew his compositions for strings, with subtle attention to the "body" of sound and to phrasing in his unceasing search for musical gestures that would convey the expressive qualities of the instruments.[2] Phenomenology and musical "sensibility" therefore came together in his reflections on the functional characteristics of musical structures in way that was neither sporadic nor divorced from his scientific enquiries.

Within Gestalt psychology, which forms the background of Bozzi's study the organisation of perceptual events in line with Wertheimer's laws is widely recognised both for the visual field as well as for the acoustic, though in this second case, there are fewer systematic studies that isolate the individual factors of unification and segregation, and set them in contrast one with the other in relation to the phenomena under investigation.

Paolo Bozzi was among the first to apply the methodological considerations of the Gestalt theory to acoustics, and the experiments referred to in the article proposed in this collection arose out of his experience of playing. Here is how he described the initial intuition, dating to the 1960s and first published in collaboration with Giovanni Vicario:[3]

> We set up the experiment on "two factors of unification among musical notes" and found the phenomenon that, thanks to the work of Bregman and van Noorden,[4] would many years later come to be known as the "auditory stream". The work's staring point was a peculiar effect, this time typically musical, that composers often make use of to produce the effect of a melodic structure raised on a pedal as if with

monodic instruments such as the flute or with those that do not easily lend themselves to polyphony such as the violin, by alternating the notes of the former with a repeated note of the latter. Our fancy was much taken while playing by the phenomenon both because it stood out in a slightly paradoxical way and because of its evident kinship with the so-called Wertheimer's law of proximity.

Isolating the dependent and independent variables, the author started from this observation to a systematic perceptual analysis in line with the method of Experimental Phenomenology, linking together in a logically rigorous skeleton a sequence of melodic profiles, examining separately the notions of temporal proximity and tonal proximity, setting them in conflict with each other, adding in the factor of speed, clarifying the concepts of sameness, similarity and tonal space, thus producing situations in which (as he himself said of Kanizsa): "the phenomenon is clearly observable, with no need of indirect proofs, and whose causes can be seen with the same immediacy".[5]

The question raised at the outset finds its reply: Bozzi demonstrates the existence of a specific tonal space within which the unifying factor of tonal proximity is endowed with the same logical sense and cohesive force that proximity has in the visual field. Under certain conditions, tonal proximity has so strong an effect as to overcome the linear succession of notes that are unified by spatial proximity alternating one after the other, and it makes no difference whether the notes in the other sequence are higher or lower.

It is not by chance that, in the final section of the paper, Paolo Bozzi considers the theory of the "double component" set out by Révész, and emphasises the distinction between sameness and similarity of notes. In light of the spread of registers in which we perceive musical sounds, the importance of their cyclical nature is sometimes downplayed: the notes are distributed in a discrete succession separated by 12 semitones and they repeat a constant tonal "quality" that bears the same name at each repetition though the absolute pitch varies, as in a spiral running from the lower to the higher. The position of the notes is not neutral. The cyclical subdivision means that two notes that are a whole octave apart are the most "similar" to each other, so that they create the maximum perceptual fusion when they are superimposed (and, for some hearers, they are a single sound), while those that are closer together, separated by only one semitone, are the most "dissimilar", so that they make for a confused tremolo effect (trill) when they are played in quick succession and the strongest perceptual dissonance when played simultaneously. It might seem otiose to recall the succession of the octaves, which is normally taken for granted. In point of fact, is it by beginning with this features of the acoustic field and with the most elementary situations that we can reveal how much deductive cunning is need to account for such evident and conflicting phenomena.

When we listen to the sound profiles in the act of making music and observe them as they unfold in succession, we sometimes hear how the notes sensibly dispose themselves in a manifest "self-organisation", which derives from the dynamic structure of the situation.[6] The notes themselves override the metric streams and the bar divisions in a way that does not depend on the will of the composer who aims to use them in a programmatic "design" or of the performer who is trying to follow as closely as possible the written text.

In this way, there arise fecund ambiguities, whether willed or not. And what if the composer wanted to play with the "bricks" that make up the perceptual laws? To test this, we may take the thirteenth of Bozzi's examples, where tonal proximity is pitted against the octave difference and where what happens is just what we would not expect, which we might call with Kanizsa (1979)[7] an "expectation error". Tonal proximity does not pair the "same" notes, namely those that bear the same name and so count as similar, but rather the tonally closest notes in terms of interval distance, namely those adjacent to the right.

Let us now compare a little musical example – Figure 13.30 – from Alfredo Casella's *Valse diatonique (sui tasti bianchi)*.[8]

(13.30)

A first glance at the score proposes a very clear – banal even – segmentation of the triple rhythm visually coincident with the bar lines. It is a very simple alternation of the tonic and the dominant with the left hand, with a perfectly symmetrical and clear-cut structure of a rising-and-falling little theme on the five fingers of the right hand. Yet if we try to play it, the rhythm becomes unmistakably duple and stays that way. Even if we put a forced stress on the triple metre, we cannot make the accompaniment follow the set rhythm. The high G that fixes the shift of octave remains isolated, splitting off from the two lower notes in an identically repeated beat in counter-rhythm, while the two alternating lower notes unify in a fixed pairing at an interval of a fourth. In this way, a genuine tonal stream segregation is produced. Moreover, even in expert hands, with the duple phasing that dominates over the metric beat, the intervention of the right-hand figure further precludes our perceiving the set rhythm. The upshot is a perceived shift in metre generated at three levels, which disturbs both the movement of the hand and the soothing recollection of an innocent C major waltz. The triple metric stream is restored only when the inner notes of the accompaniment come closer together within the octave.

Another interesting example – Figure 13.31 – is provided by a passage of Goffredo Petrassi.[9] Here, the piano part makes us feel how the ear is able to perceive widely separated notes as connected or unified by an invisible thread in virtue of a tonal proximity that is coherent in unification by common fate.

This resembles the examples cited by Bozzi. The single melody is made up of two parallel lines of isorhythmic quavers in a stream of notes of the same name at three octaves distance. This simply reinforces the density of the timbre because the two melodic lines melt perfectly into each other in a single stream. The smallest temporal proximity unifies the falling notes, while the tonal proximity separates them into groups that start with the highest notes. We thus have a splitting of the stream into two branches in which the higher notes are separated and become the acoustic anchorage for the common fate of the rising branch, while the quantity of notes in the falling branch fixes the metrical variation of the segregations.

The splitting into two branches sets aside the written tempo indication and opens a gap for variable leaps in accordance with the inner unifications that arise one after the other:

first there is a distance of a third, then a fourth, then repetitions with minimal chromatic variations, and lastly the final passage with the segregation of the two streams that are perfectly bistable and that form pairings with inverted chromatic movements from the interval of a fourth, a fifth, a sixth and a seventh, until they reach the unison of the octave.

(13.31)

In terms of the theory of harmony, all this stimulating asymmetry is "atonal". But, in virtue of the tonal proximity, it creates an internal structural crescendo, a forward-pointing temporal enlargement or compression, and the pressure is greater when the interval is chromatic. This is presented as if it were an exemplary phenomenological experiment on the dynamics of the possible interactions between the intervals within the range of an octave, and it represents a higher grade of complexity than the classical analysis of Bachian melodic lines, where the stream splits into more than one branch but in a way that is metrically coordinated and harmonically coherent with the subdivision of the time signature.

Just as Bozzi shows in discussing the trill, the tremolo and the double trill (Figures 13.22 and 13.23), the interval distance within the third helps to keep the notes linked to each other forming bistable units on the basis of both temporal and tonal proximity, while with a distance of from a fourth to a seventh (and greater than the octave) the interval facilitates horizontal directionality among sharp and bass notes unifying them in two separate streams that are temporally dislocated and connected only by tonal proximity. The faster the speed of playing, the sharper becomes the splitting of the monody.

Both the foregoing Figures 13.30 and 13.31 obey the following condition: the interval of a fourth acts as a segregating factor in Figure 13.30 connecting tonally the first note to the third and breaking the unification of the octave; the same interval of a fourth in Figure 13.31 sets up the splitting of the stream into two parts unifying the tonally close parts in proportion to the number of the intermediate notes that are overcome in the present of perception. The faster the speed of playing, the stronger becomes the convergence effect by the law of the continuity of direction.

It is worth stressing that the functional property of tonal proximity, which is isomorphic with that in visual space, is not in the least influenced by the stylistic conventions of classical harmony, or those of other organisational systems, whether they be atonal, dodecaphonic, polytonal or aleatory. Rather, it is decisive in aiding the organisation of musical memory and in the processes of recognition of sound clusters in movement.

In his chapter on the factors of unification, masking and the performer's play.[10] Paolo Bozzi takes up the question of the relations of phenomenal equilibrium among notes that follow each other in a single melodic profile. Here, he speaks of a *Ludus Wertheimerianus*, referring to the ways and to which extents, in certain situations, musical performers can help the unification of a group of notes or, in others, cannot avoid the segregation of the notes. Or, in others again, they cannot bring them to the fore unless, by virtue of perceptual masking, the notes are enclosed in compact units, even when the performers make use of all the varied "fundamental palette of tertiary qualities in the acoustic field", such as rising or falling intensity, accents in phrasing, changes of timbre and variations in timing.

The "distribution of the notes in tonal space" affects the tertiary qualities of the "elementary clusters of sounds", which is to say the perception of their stability or instability, the specific amalgam of sounds thus becomes a "semantics of two-note chords",[11] considered as a perception of their distinct "harmonic quality".[12]

In his volume on "seeing as".[13] Bozzi cites musical phrases from Beethoven, Schubert and Brahms to gain some illuminating insights into the "expressive qualities" carried by musical structures with reference to "the grammar of hearing", to the sound gesture, to the "physiognomic characterisation" of a sensory object and to how an object "allows itself to be recognised" or changes its state "under our eyes" in certain conditions. This leads him to stress the difference between seeing (or in our case, hearing) and interpreting: "whereas 'interpretation' is an activity or an action, seeing corresponds to having present an observable state in the field direct experience".[14]

All this comes about in what Bozzi calls a perceptual present. To round off the reflection on the factors of unification and segregation in more complex musical phenomena, we cannot leave out a reference to the role of the structuring of "figure and ground in elementary musical episodes".[15] Here, recalling a Gibsonian optical ecology, Bozzi offers a swift description of the soundscape presented by an ideal acoustic ecology that he saw and heard on a trip to the Quiberon peninsula in Brittany, in which the acoustic form of the waves is sculpted in a natural amphitheatre, which arises out of the encounter between the ocean and the cliffs:

In that forest of sounds, the bass notes can clearly be heard as a constant and well-defined counter-bass pedal. In that low bourdon sometimes one can hear the typical grinding of the low frequencies of the large stringed instruments, and one sometimes feels that one is standing next to a large organ pipe. It is no use trying to distract the attention: the bass obstinately stresses the roar of the sea for all eternity, for it comes from an eternity.

But higher up, in the region of the violins, the flutes and the piccolos, there is an ongoing play of high frequencies, which is very variegated and uneven. Sometimes there are distinct but fleeting screeches, sometimes skitterings like small pearls skidding across a polished marble floor. But at other times, there arise huffings like a cat on the prowl or barely audible hissings of sound ghosts. Between these two bands, the one high and the other low, there is a counterpoint of sounds and noises, relatives of the clarinets, the violas, the horns and the trombones with their tricks of mutes and lip stops, or a rowdy crew of strings, all piled up in a hodge-podge of sounds (. . .) Directing the attention is a spatial operation; I can listen to the frenetic play of the high frequencies and put the low to some extent to one side; or I can concentrate on the unceasing rumble of the latter; or again follow some of the melodic darting in the middle band, the bangs, slides, sharp voices and little calls of the water and of the rock struck, the sudden presence of a well-placed trumpet. In this way, we enter into a game of back-and-forth like that of figure and ground in the multistable images of Rubin and the Gestalt psychologists (. . .) The deep bass can be the figure and so can the occasional outburst of wave showers. We can, so to say, sculpt the matter of the sounds by paying attention here or there. But we cannot create it: there is no getting away from that mass of sounds, like a mass of stone, and it contains all the voices that our attention can pick up. The subject's act of attention brings to the fore this or that note or this or that move in the score, but it cannot create sounds that are not there and it cannot destroy sounds that make up that chorus of voices.[16]

What underlies this great metaphorical description of the orchestration of nature, to which the ear lends the greatest attention, is the whole phenomenon of acoustic multistability, offering the opportunity to follow a complex polyphonic structure within which various elements coexist in simultaneous and discontinuous superimposition.

In order to understand how the ear can pass from one melodic line to another or can be open to more than one solution or to parallel streams without losing its perceptual integrity yet remaining aware to a lesser degree of the other elements present, Bozzi starts from the features of Rubin's "ambiguous images" (though in the visual case, only one profile can be seen at a time). To test the factors that make one line dominate as figure relative to the other that becomes the ground (in Gestalt terms) and the parameters that interfere with each other or that work together to produce an overall stable or bistable perception, he proposes an experimental design that confronts a range of possible movements between two superimposed melodic lines. I had the privilege of Bozzi's expert guidance in developing the theme of musical figure-ground variability for my graduation dissertation in Psychology at the University of Bologna in March 1994[17] and in presenting the results at the 3rd International Conference for Music Perception and Cognition, organised by ESCOM at the University of Liège in July of the same year.[18]

The subtle and precise interplay of the laws of Gestalt, with their related conditions of prevalence and conflict among the factors present in melodic profiles, is decisive of the relations of figure to ground, and is so especially given the complexity of twentieth-century music. For, in the evolution of this "new" harmonic language, the traditional reference points have been deliberately suppressed. The "emancipation of dissonance" has become the rule; pre-existing listening habits have been broken; the only degree of the ear's organisational freedom in listening to music is provided by the recognition of perceptual units by means of the factors of unification and segregation that, in their own way, guide the listener's attention.

Let us take as an example Arnold Schoenberg's *Präludium* from the *Suite for Piano op. 25*.[19] This was one of the first dodecaphonic works and it is impossible for the listener to pick out the theoretical construction imposed on the "series" of the twelve notes employed by the composer. This can only be done by looking at the score and laboriously deconstructing the scheme. Yet some sequences of aggregations form themselves out of rhythmic symmetries, and others out of continuity of direction in virtue of tonal proximity; moments of stability based on the repetition of the same immediately recognisable note alternate with moments of stream segregation in a continuous re-orientation that runs the full range of the registers of the keyboard. From the point of view of the harmonic "quality", there is clear dominance of two-note chords, chords and dissonant agglomerations and the rare consonances are happy exceptions.

If we look instead at the second study for piano in György Ligeti's *Cordes à vide*.[20] we hear a double stream segregation that has been set up from the start. There is a fourfold segregation of the sound stream, with a ragged double ramification guided by the tonal unification of the higher notes of the right hand, and a double ramification with long arpeggios of a falling fifth for the left hand, where the higher notes create a tonal unification that is out of synch with that of higher range. The only moment of acoustic rest in all this continuous fluctuation of sound, with the tempo marking "rubato molto tenero", is the "pianissimo" beat of the two-note chords of a fifth (which are precisely "open strings"), that occasionally run up and down from the high register to the low. The piece then develops in a much more complex and stratified way, which it would be hard to describe here without specific reference to the score. Also in this case, we are confronted with a perfect exercise in style, where the reference stimulus, namely the choice of an interval that recalls the tuning of a violin, provides a pretext for and become the occasion of an in-depth experimental variation on the given theme.

Similar examples can be found in the works of Bela Bartòk, John Cage, Luciano Berio, all composers who, as Bozzi says, knew exactly how to bring it about that the listener hears this rather than that, and hears it in the desired way. For this reason, they are cases that exploit the laws of an Experimental Phenomenology that has not yet been written, nor thought out nor yet of interest to such musicians, given that they know with instinctive confidence what they are about. [21]

Sometimes, it is precisely the spatial limitations imposed by the manual stretch of the performer in physiological contact with the instrument that become the stimulus to an insight, as a precious resource for the creative intelligence, for the composer/experimenter. Bozzi's scientific experimentation was often connected to his artistic production and unfurled along the boundaries of the daring and physical manuality of playing the violin and the viola, to which his *Der Psychophysische Bogen* is dedicated.[22] Written as a Capriccio, this piece was composed for the occasion of a conference in honour of Valentino Braitenberg held at the Max Planck Institute at Tübingen on 27th June 1986. Bozzi had been invited as a researcher into visual perception to talk about the psychophysical chain, which is to say the succession of events that occur between the physical object and a perception of it. Instead of presenting a paper like that on the "logical analysis of the L-R scheme" (see Chapter 6 above) he invented a transposition into musical terms of a fragment of the scientific imagination. The logical models of the luminous rays, the photo-chemical, photoelectric processes, bursts of neural impulses are rendered as a transcolouration of arpeggios, "double fluted notes", chromatic scales, trills, double tremoli, acoustic waves which spout, embedded in the harsh chords of the physical object, the "form or Gestalt of which is insistently evoked in all the phases of the process".[23]

We can identify stream segregation effects, highly dissonant stretchings produced by rubbing together sounds by a quartertone, which produces the so-called beat-effect within the range of the critical band, the varying games of the "harmonic quality" of two-note chords with their openings (in the wide position) and contraction (in the narrow position). The musical outcome is extraordinary not only for its evocative power but also for the technical virtuosity that it incorporates and whose execution demands that the performer master a daringly modern language.

The most characteristic, and most widely played, of Bozzi's musical compositions for the violin is, however, *Meta-Kitsch*,[24] whose very title announces the ludic aim of retrieving a style that was recognised as having crystallised into a cliché. This piece is an experiment in stylistic contamination that cunningly collects the tropes of violin technique gathered from the hand exercises set out in the classic manuals for learning the instrument (with fragments in the styles of Spohr, Vieuxtemps and Veniawski), which are then transformed as if they were an improvisation. These formulaic units intersect with and melt into more flexible and nostalgic phrases ("melémi", melodic phonemes) that the author himself recalls with explicit reference to Kaffeehausmusik for the violin and Italian popular songs of the Thirties. But how does this transformation of the sound object from "model" to stylistic "allusion" come about without its losing its own qualitative features? What modifications or alterations can a melodic pattern undergo to be recognised as such, and how can contrasting, but complementary, features come together in a solid formal construction without giving the effect of a medley? Let us take as an example the central passage of the piece – Figure 13.32 – where the indeterminate pulsation in quarter notes gives rise to a waltz rhythm:

(13.32)

Among the references made in the preface is the well-known song *Tea for two*, which is a leaping duple allegro motif, with the triple repetition of the pattern G–E–F#. One melody's relational structure is very solid in retaining "the meaningfulness of those three notes that emerge here and there with the force of a thematic cell",[25] yet we have only a vague sensation of the theme in question, dependent above all on the constancy of the rhythmic oscillation. As a matter of fact, the metre here has become triple and so undergoes a temporal dilatation that is emphasised by the two ironic pizzicato on the "fourth string". The intervals take a chromatic falling turn, in virtue of the tonal proximity added to the continuity of direction while holding stable the interval of a minor third. When the characteristic melodic pattern cited above can be picked up, it has by now lost its playful leaping quality: the thematic cell has become "slanted" and becomes further depressed in pursuing its fall to the point of hitting Eb without the final fling of the original.

Bozzi thus obtains a genuine perceptual masking in the sense of a figure that is "closed" by the law of the continuity of direction like Gottschaldt's figures,[26] in which also the expressive character is changed and has come to be uncertain and insecure (after having been so daring in the original), even though the fragment cited is literally identical. Only its evocative aroma is left intact.

Paolo Bozzi's own words are a helpful guide to what is going on:

> It is difficult to deny these pieces of music a touching and indestructible exhaustion of feeling, a yearning sense of delicate allusions, sometimes a hint of melancholy, which do not cease to move to tears in their own way even at the thousandth repetition, and which are intimately connected to the mystery of violin and to the roots of its language. Therefore I believe that this piece ought to be performed with irony, yet not without a touch of participative nostalgia.[27]

We may infer from all the examples we have given that the phenomenological approach to musical structure, building on the tradition of research founded by Wertheimer, is still vital and deserves further development in the analytic study of the art music not only in the West. Perhaps it is no accident that the composer James Tenney, theoretician, pianist, mathematician, student and performer of Cage, was so taken with the study of sound perception and made use of the Gestalt laws to analyse twentieth-century music. In particular, he employed the notion of "clang" as a perceptual unit of variable length in light of temporal Gestalts,[28] which was an intuition not so far from the phenomena examined in the chapter by Bozzi that we have been considering. Perhaps it is no less an accident that the first generation of Gestalt psychologists were also musicians, each with his own instrument: Köhler on viola, Metzger on violin and Wertheimer at the piano. And is it not perhaps the acuteness of the musical ear exercised in a tenacious confrontation with the primitive element, with the hard, inescapable concrete matter of sound and with its palpable expressive control in the changing evolution of timbre, that is the necessary and stimulating ingredient at the heart of phenomenological discovery? Bozzi himself confesses:

> There are not many people who will spend their time searching inside a musical instrument, almost tormenting it, to find a balance among a few elementary sound facts so that they can say what they must say. Someone might say, "but it is not music". But anyone who makes music knows perfectly well that it is indeed music.[29]

This is an important insight of his into the primacy of handiwork and represents an inheritance from which we should not avert our gaze in the world of phenomenological observation. We may surely say that the cluster of themes that the Master tackled in light of the Gestalt approach has not fallen away with the passing of time, but has kept its lively and logical analytical freshness. For he was always able to keep the attention unwaveringly on the real object of interobservation. And every time one re-reads his scientific, literary and musical works, one finds something new and one never runs out of things to learn from the subtlety of his scrutiny.

It is with thanks that I carry with me the memory and the "colour" of his illuminating conversation, the many hours spent together playing the works for violin or viola and piano from the early twentieth century, and discussing the psychology of perception. A highly refined observer and a poetic investigator, Paolo Bozzi was, as he said in his book on naïve physics "curious about the shining truths hidden in the details", a great artist of sound, of the word, of design and of all those nuances to which the study of perception, understood as a phenomenology of the objects under observation, is bound "*iuxta propria principia*".[30]

Paolo Bozzi's Musical Biography

Paolo Bozzi, began taking violin lessons in the 1930s and 40s with Rodolfo Lipizer, who had recently published his *Tecnica superiore del violino* [Advanced violin technique]. The memories of this apprenticeship are narrated in *Rodolfo Lipizer nei miei ricordi* [My Memories of Rodolfo Lipizer], by Paolo Bozzi, published by Studio Tesi, Pordenone in 1997. In 1944 he was awarded the Bruno Bruni scholarship from the Trieste Music School, but was not able to take up this opportunity.

After completing high school in Gorizia, he enrolled in the Philosophy Faculty at Trieste University and, after graduating, joined Gaetano Kanizsa's research group on experimental Psychology. At the same time, he resumed contact with Lipizer and, between 1955 and 1957, collaborated with him in organising Musical Saturdays in Gorizia's Civic Music School.

While pursuing his academic career (assistant at Trieste, assistant professor at Padova, full professor at Trento) he abandoned playing the violin and devoted himself to music only from a theoretical and musicological point of view.

In 1960, in collaboration with Giovanni Bruno Vicario, at the time an assistant in Psychology, he discovered the phenomenon now known as "auditory streaming" (see Bregman, *Auditory Stream Analysis*, MIT, 1999) which, in the psychology of musical perception, is the basis for the forming of melodies.

A sudden return to music and the violin, in the mid-1970s, at first led him towards "Pedrollo Orchestra" at Vicenza conducted by Sergio Chiereghin and in the following years he performed with chamber orchestras "Piccola Orchestra Giuliana" and "Piccola Orchestra Veneta" conducted by Nino Gardi.

As a member of instrumental groups of those orchestras Bozzi took part in a large number of chamber music concerts with programmes often dedicated to 20th century music.

Only in 1986–87, urged by his composer friend and companion of frequent private chamber music adventures, Fabio Nieder, did Paolo Bozzi decide to publish some compositions for violin, viola and violoncello (*Meta-Kitsch*, *Der Psychophysische Bogen*, *Romantika – Pizzicato*, Udine, 1987). From then on he continued to compose cycles of brief musical ideas for those same instruments, but without publishing them.

These compositions were performed on various occasions, separately or in groups: in 1992 at the Accademia Bartolomeo Cristofori-amici del Fortepiano in Florence, in concerts at the Schools of Music in Bolzano and Udine, by Ennio Francescato (cello), Paolo Rodda (violin) and Giuseppe Miglioli (violin). The same musicians performed the pieces in 1999 in conclusion of the Bozzi Fest-congress, organised by the University of Padua in the Archivio Antico at Palazzo del Bo.

At the 1995 festival and convention on twentieth and twenty-first century music and culture "Valentino Bucchi-Città di Roma", *Meta-Kitsch* was an obligatory piece in the violin competition. It was later broadcast several times by the Italian national radio with Dan Costescu on violin.

In autumn 2000, Paolo Bozzi held a series of 16 lessons on the philosophy of music at the Scuola Superiore di Formazione Umanistica at Bologna University, concluding the course with a performance of Bartòk's complete duets for two violins which he played with violinist Ika Reggiani.

He held courses and seminars in Psychology of music at the Music Academies of Parma, Verona, Trento and Udine.

Paolo Bozzi's musical compositions

For solo violin

Meta-Kitsch, Pizzicato edizioni, 1986;
Camargue, unpublished manuscript, 1987;
Momenti Musicali. Soundtrack for the reading of "Innsbrucker Augenklinik" by Giancarlo Mariani, unpublished manuscript, 1990.

For solo viola

Der psychophysische Bogen, Pizzicato edizioni, 1986;
Aforismi alle quattro corde vuote, unpublished manuscript, 1996;
Cinque Brevi Canzoni e una Brevissima coda, unpublished manuscript, 1999.

For solo cello

Romantika, Pizzicato edizioni, 1987;
Corale, unpublished manuscript, 1993;
Jodl, unpublished manuscript, 1997.

Duets

Skolastica, two canons for violin and cello, unpublished manuscript, 1992;
Alt-duet, for alto flute and viola, unpublished manuscript, 1991.

Notes

1 Bozzi, P. (1997). *Rodolfo Lipizer nei miei Ricordi* [*My Memories of Rodolfo Lipizer*]. Pordenone-Padua, Italy: Edizione Studio Tesi.
2 Zecchinelli, L. (2008). L'arco musicale di Paolo Bozzi, "ascoltare come": antropomorfismi, qualità espressive, eventi multistabili nelle osservazioni musicali di Paolo Bozzi [Paolo Bozzi's musical bow, "hearing as", anthropomorphisms, expressive qualites and multistable events in Paolo Bozzi's musical observations] (Translator's note: the word *"arco"* covers not just a violin bow and the act of bowing so as connects the notes in a musical phrase but also that with arrows as well as meaning a trajectory over time: Bozzi may well have been playing on these overlapping connotations)] *A tutto Arco*, *I*(2), 17–23. Comment on Paolo Bozzi's complete works for strings in the CD "*L'arco musicale di Paolo Bozzi*" (Live recording of performance at the international conference *Relations and Structures. Developments of Gestalt theory in Psychology and other related fields* held in Macerata (May 24–27, 2007), promoted by the *International Society for Gestalt Theory and its Applications* in collaboration with the University of Macerata [Performers: violin: Michela Dapretto; viola: Giuseppe Miglioli; cello: Ennio Francescato; soprano: Annunziata Lia Lantieri; piano: Luisa Zecchinelli]).
3 Bozzi, P. (1993). *Experimenta in Visu. Ricerche sulla percezione* [Experiments in Vision. Inquiries into Perception]. Milan, Italy: Guerini.
4 Bregman, A.S. (1990). *Auditory Scene Analysis*. Cambridge, MA: The MIT Press. In the second chapter, *Sequential Integration*, Bregman examines the sequential grouping of sounds and considers the rapid repeating sequence of high tone and low tones that form separate streams. This he calls "auditory stream segregation" or "streaming effect", and refers to research on this topic by Gestalt psychologists who focused on its use in music. As an example, he cites an abstract of the present study of acoustic demonstrations by Bozzi-Vicario created at University of Trieste, stressing the temporal separation and pitch separation of tonal elements, and that these same demonstrations brought home the relevance of Gestalt principles of grouping in explaining the phenomena in question. Furthermore, the Gestalt principles of visual organisation are the same as those applicable

to the auditory situation. In the 1970s, Bregman himself witnesses the interest in the splitting of auditory streams – citing his own earlier work with Campbell (1971) and Rudnicky (1975) – as well as van Noorden's (1975) and Warren (1972). Before 1990, all the references to auditory stream segregation in the Anglophone psychological literature (e.g. Deutsch, 1982; Sloboda, 1985; Tenney, 1980; Huron, 1989) are only to these early researches by Bregman. But, after the publication of *Auditory Scene Analysis*, this is the only reference point and there are no further references to the Bozzi-Vicario experiment on temporal proximity and tonal proximity.

5 Bozzi, P. (1993). *Experimenta in Visu*, cit.

6 Bozzi, P. (1969). *Unità, identità, causalità* [Unity, Identity, Causality]. Bologna, IT: Cappelli.

7 Kanizsa, G. (1979). Organization in Vision: Essays on Gestalt Perception. New York: Praeger.

8 Alfredo Casella, *11 Pezzi Infantili per Pianoforte* (Eleven Infantile Pieces for Piano), Universal Edition, 1929.

9 Goffredo Petrassi, *Invito all'Eràno* (Invitation to Eranos), in *Due liriche di Saffo* (*Two Lyrics by Sappho*), Edizioni Suvini Zerboni, Milan, 1942.

10 Bozzi, P. (1982). I fattori di unificazione, il mascheramento, il gioco dell'interprete [Factors of unification, masking and the performer's play]. In L. Pizzo Russo (ed.) *Estetica e Psicologia* [*Aesthetics and Psychology*] (pp. 211–220). Bologna, Italy: il Mulino. Also in Bozzi, P. (1993). *Experimenta in Visu. Ricerche sulla percezione* (pp. 69–91). Milano, Italy: Guerini.

11 Bozzi, P. (1985). La semantica dei Bicordi [The Semantics of Two-note chords]. In: G. Stefani & F. Ferrari (ed.), *La psicologia della musica in Europa e in Italia* [*Psychology of Music in Europe and in Italy*] (pp. 185–191). Bologna, Italy: Edizione CLUEB.

12 Bozzi, P. (1959). Un aspetto della qualità armonica: la tendenza alla risoluzione [An aspect of harmonic quality: the tendency to resolution]. *Rivista di Psicologia*, LIV (II), 153–172.

13 Bozzi, P. (1998), *Vedere come. Commenti ai § 1–29 delle Osservazioni sulla filosofia della psicologia* di Wittgenstein. Milano, Italy: Guerini e Associati [excerpted as Chapter 8 of the present anthology].

14 Ibidem

15 Bozzi, P. (1996). La figura e lo sfondo negli episodi musicali elementari [Figure-ground in elementary musical episodes]. In G. O. Longo and C. Magris (Eds). *Ambiguità* [Ambiguity] (pp. 611–626). Bergamo, Italy: Moretti e Vitali editore.

16 Ibidem

17 Zecchinelli, L. (a.a.1992–1993). *Figura-Sfondo: lo studio dei fondamenti percettivi dell'organizzazione acustica* [*Figure-Ground: A Study of the Perceptual Foundations of Acoustic Organisation*]. Unpublished thesis, Facoltà di Lettere e Filosofia, University of Bologna, supervised by Prof. Nicoletta Caramelli.

18 Bozzi, P., Caramelli, N., and Zecchinelli, L. (1994). Figure-ground: An experiment on principles of musical organization in simultaneous melodies, *Proceedings of the 3rd International Conference for Music Perception and Cognition* (pp. 233–236), ESCOM Université de Liège: Irène Deliège editor.

19 Arnold Schoenberg, *Praeludium*, Suite für Klavier op. 25, Universal Edition, 1925.

20 György Ligeti, *Cordes à vide, Étude pour piano, premier livre*, Schott Musik International, 1986.

21 Bozzi, P. (1996). *La figura e lo sfondo negli episodi musicali elementari*, cit.

22 Paolo Bozzi, *Der psychophysische Bogen per viola sola*, Pizzicato edizioni, 1986.

23 Ibidem.

24 Paolo Bozzi, *Meta-Kitsch per violino solo*, Pizzicato edizioni, 1986.

25 Bozzi, P. (1982). *I fattori di unificazione, il mascheramento, il gioco dell'interprete*, cit.

26 Ibidem.

27 Paolo Bozzi, *Meta-Kitsch, Prefazione dell'Autore*, cit.

28 Tenney, J. and Polansky, L. (1980) Temporal Gestalt perception in music. *Journal of Music Theory*, 24 (2), 205–241.

29 Bozzi, P. (1990). *Fisica Ingenua* [*Naïve Physics*]. Milano, Italy: Garzanti.

30 Bozzi, P. (1989). *Fenomenologia Sperimentale* [*Experimental Phenomenology*]. Bologna, Italy: il Mulino.

References

Bregman, A. S., and Campbell, J. (1971). Primary auditory stream segregation and perception of order in rapid sequences of tones. *Journal of Experimental Psychology*, 89(2), 244–249.

Bregman, A. S., and Rudnicky, A. I. (1975). Auditory segregation: Stream or streams? *Journal of Experimental Psychology: Human Perception and Performance*, 1(3), 263–267.

Deutsch, D. (ed.), *The Psychology of Music*, Academic Press, New York (*1982*).

Huron, D. (1989). Voice denumerability in polyphonic music of homogeneous timbres. *Music Perception*, 6 (4), 361–382.

Sloboda, J. A. (1985). *The Musical Mind: The Cognitive Psychology of Music.* New York: Oxford University Press.

Tenney, J. and Polansky, L. (1980). Temporal Gestalt Perception in Music. *Journal of Music Theory*, 24 (2), 205–241.

Van Noorden L. P. A. S. (1975). "Temporal coherence in the perception of tone sequences," Ph.D. thesis, Eindhoven University of Technology, Eindhoven, The Netherlands.

Warren, R.M., and Obusek, C.J. (1972). Identification of temporal order within auditory sequences. *Perception & Psychophysics*, 12(1), 86–90.

14

OBSERVATIONS ON SOME CASES OF PHENOMENAL TRANSPARENCY OBTAINED WITH LINE DRAWINGS

Translated by Richard Davies and Ivana Bianchi

Introduction

The observations reported in the following pages do not represent experimental research about new cases of phenomenal transparency, but rather form an albeit incomplete catalogue of figural situations that share the following two characteristics:

a) that they are obtained by employing only the means normally used in line drawing (lines and dots on chromatically homogeneous backgrounds),

b) that they are visually organized as layered pairs of perceptual objects in which one of the objects, the one that appears on top, is seen as a medium through which the other can be seen.

In the various situations that we are going to list, the medium lets us, in various ways, see the object through it.

In some cases one can say that these different modes in which the object shows through correspond to different phenomenal properties of the medium: higher or lower density, lucidity, granularity, curvature, thickness, etc.

The existence of these various properties seems to raise a problem: that of the matter of the transparent phenomenal media. Together with the fundamental dimensions "translucent-opaque" and "light-dark", which were investigated by Metelli and, thanks to his work, can be interpreted in terms of one of the most fully formalized theories that scientific psychology boasts today, one can say that there are other classes of characteristics typical of transparent media; and in particular that there are conditions – probably figural conditions rather than chromatic ones – that produce the material features of what the object that acts as a medium appears to be made of in a given situation.

Given that the present work is a catalogue of examples, containing no experimental analyses based on specific hypotheses and carried out on cases controlled from all points of view, it will not be possible to establish exhaustively the nature and the number of such conditions, nor to establish the bases of a taxonomy of them.

By mentioning examples I aim only to stress the fact that this problem exists and, at most, to suggest (as in the first case discussed) a path for setting up future investigations that will be genuinely experimental.

Milky opacity of the medium

a) Here is a first case of phenomenal transparency[1] obtained using only lines variously connected among them and located on a homogeneous background (Figure 14.1).

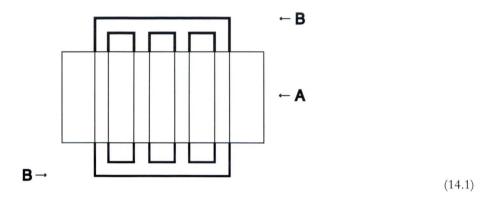

(14.1)

Here the marked characteristic of transparency, or rather of "partial opacity" (compare the milky white that occupies the area enclosed by the contours of the horizontal band A with the white of the rest of the page)[2] seems to depend on the sudden thinning of lines at the point where the lines that serve as margins of object B meet the contour of A. That is, since the vertical lines inside A are visibly thinner than those that – falling outside A – join to them by continuity of direction, join between the two lines of different thickness can reasonably be considered as a condition of the milky opacity of the area inside A.

Indeed, neither the presence of the thicker lines adjacent to A alone nor the presence of the thinner lines inside A alone are sufficient to produce this specific mode of appearance inside A, as can be seen in Figures 14.2 and 14.3:

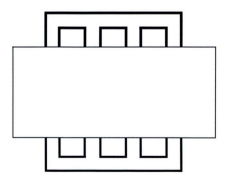

(14.2)

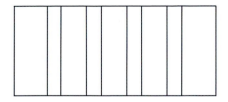

(14.3)

b) The difference between the lines that seems to be responsible for the phenomenon may be seen from two points of view: analytically, in which case it is a matter of thinner lines inside A drawn with the same colour as the rest of the situation; or phenomenally, in which case the difference in thickness of lines is also a difference in colour. Thus, we might say that the phenomenally different colour (lighter grey) of the vertical lines inside A determines the transparency of A according to a dynamics similar to that which regulates the cases of transparency obtained by putting chromatically different surfaces one next to the other. It could perhaps be tested experimentally whether the independent variable of the effect under consideration is the sudden thinning of the line or the sudden chromatic change following it. I have not been able to find a crucial situation to decide this question.

What is certain, however is that the different thickness of lines inside A (or the chromatic change that arises from the difference between the thickness of lines inside A and outside A) is not by itself a sufficient condition for the transparency visible in Figure 14.1 (or in Figure 14.24 in the appendix). What is necessary, as we shall see shortly, is the presence of at least one other factor in the situation.

c) Indeed, if the transparency of the area inside A in Figure 14.1 depended only and exclusively on the changed thickness of lines or on the associated change in colour, one would see transparency also in Figure 14.4, but this does not happen.

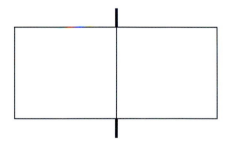

(14.4)

We presented the following five figural situations (Figure 14.5) to 120 observers in such a way that each of them would have to deal with only one figure of the series, and each figure of the series would be submitted to 24 observers. Their task was to give a free description of the figure, and the experimenter intervened during the survey only to encourage them to give details so that at the end the description would be fairly ample.

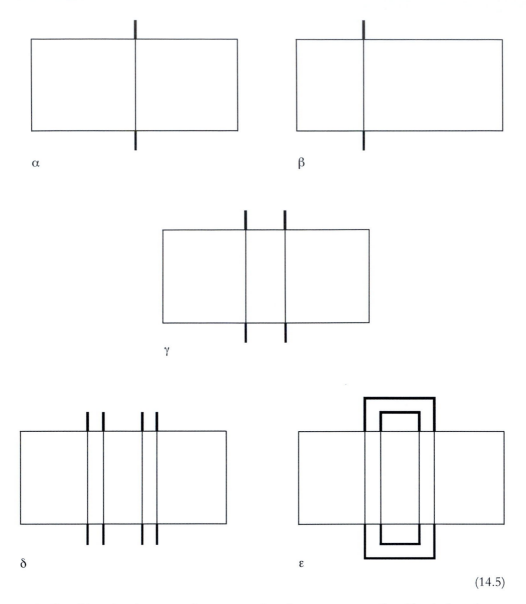

(14.5)

In describing situation α no observer mentioned transparency, and an identical result was obtained with situation β; two observers mentioned transparency in describing figure γ, and four in describing figure δ. In the case of situation ε, 21 observers spontaneously said they saw transparency, versus three who did not mention it.

Responses in favour of transparency were always very clear and immediate; often, also responses against transparency were such as to leave no doubt: the longer the description, the more frequently particulars emerged that were incompatible with a structuring of the figure capable of producing transparency (for example, in the case of situation β, "the two flaps are not continuous with the internal division line"; "two flaps that emerge from behind but are not part of the fold in front [that is, the thinner line];" in the case of situation α: "two adjacent rectangles"; "a rectangle divided in two by a central segment with two larger ends"; "like two pages of an open book"; describing the situation δ: "a rectangle plus some parallel lines that intersect it"; "a rectangle cut by two roads").

Thus the difference in thickness of the lines, or the difference in colour, is not enough to produce the effect. The tests carried out would suggest that an important condition for opaque transparency in situations like these would be the characteristic of representing "a thing", or "a solid object" (and hence not merely a line), as a property of the figure located behind the transparent medium.

The more the figure that is seen through has this characteristic (which is most present in Figure 14.1 and least in Figure 14.5 α), the more clearly the area of A exhibits a milky transparency.

d) The following series of figural situations (Figure 14.6) can make this last assertion even more plausible.

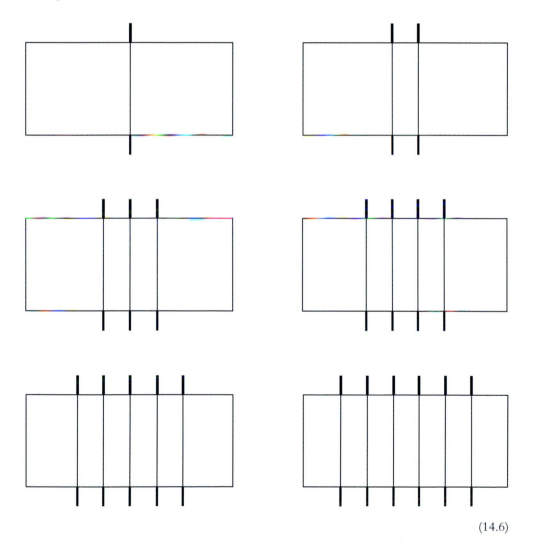

(14.6)

Of these six situations, the first reproduces that of Figure 14.4, about which no observer said they saw transparency, while the others were obtained by progressively adding each time a new vertical element with a sudden thinning of the line at the point where it passes from the outside to the inside of rectangle A; these elements (in the situations with more than two elements) are equidistant, parallel, and arranged so that the first and the last are in each situation equally distant from the vertical sides of rectangle A.

Faced with this series of figures – not presented in three rows of two, as on this page for typographical reasons, but in one single horizontal alignment – eight observers out of ten noticed that the characteristic of opaque transparency, within the rectangle, progressively became more marked starting from the second or third figures; while two said they saw only a weak effect of this kind in the last two, those with five or six vertical elements.

Let us now move to the six situations of Figure 14.7. They were obtained using the same construction rules used in the previous case, except for one: the role played in Figure 14.6 by the vertical elements is here taken by pairs of elements, identical to one another, produced by means of the factor of proximity.

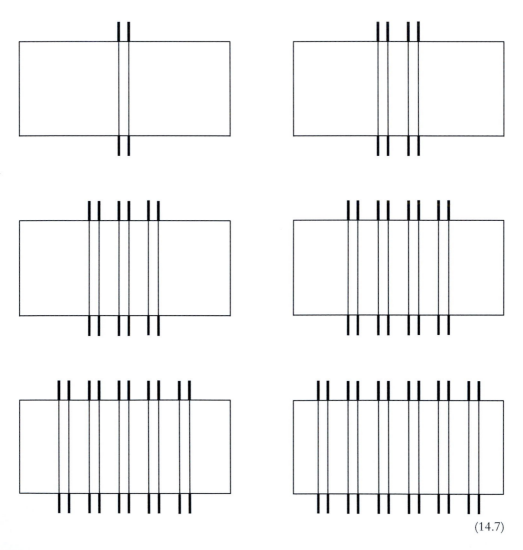

(14.7)

Faced with this series, ten observers – different from those who had collaborated with the discussion of the previous case – also noticed that the greater the number of vertical pairs of elements the more prominent was the opaque transparency of the area inside the rectangle: however, only two observers said they noticed the presence of the effect in all the figural situations; four observers indicated the presence of the effect in the third and following situation; four only in the situations from the fourth onward.

On the basis of the indications provided by these 20 observers we may say, as a general rule, that the more what is seen through the medium appears well-articulated as a whole and with the characteristic of being "a thing", i.e. not one or two lines, but, for instance, a grill or a fence, some structure of elements rhythmically arranged in space, the more marked is the effect under consideration.

Moreover, still on the basis of the same indications, we may say that the effect occurs with greater prominence when the vertical elements form pairwise couples unified by proximity.

The comparison of the two situations of Figure 14.8 (according to the judgment of seven out of ten observers) seems to confirm this last thesis.

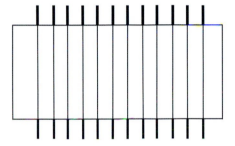 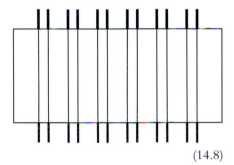

(14.8)

The effect of proximity perhaps is less felt (according to the judgment of five out of ten observers) when the unitariness of the articulated whole located behind the medium is already guaranteed by other factors – such as closure – which lend it the characteristic of being a thing, a genuine object: compare the two situations of Figure 14.9, which were submitted to the judgment of the ten observers, and synoptically compare the four situations of Figure 14.10.

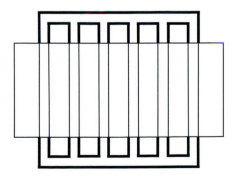 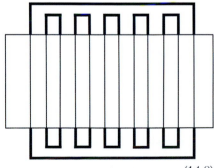

(14.9)

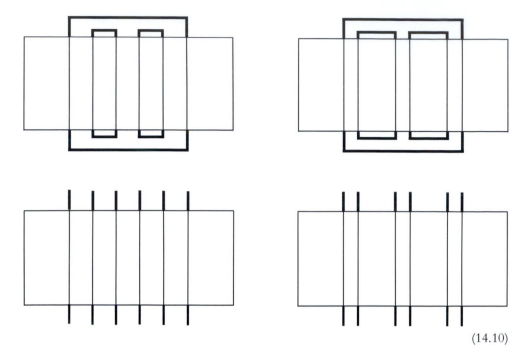

(14.10)

In conclusion, in cases such as those we have examined and for this particular case of milky transparency, we seem to be in a position to say that the thinning (or the chromatic change) of lines inside the margin delimiting the medium produces the effect under consideration only provided the structure seen through the medium has a sufficiently rich articulation; and that it produces it in a particularly marked manner when that richness of articulation carries with it the characteristic of thingness.

Magnification and clearness

By inverting the arrangement of the two types of lines, the thinner and the thicker, with respect to the border of region A in Figure 14.24 in the Appendix – that is, by drawing the articulations outside of A with the thinner line and those inside of A with the thicker line – we have a different mode of transparency, as can be seen in the first example of Figure 14.11.

Observers described this effect in various ways, while nevertheless agreeing in describing it as a sort of transparency. Some reports spoke of "magnification", others of "greater clarity" (probably in the sense of clearness); one observer said that it was "like looking through a smoked glass". For everyone, the effect was more prominent in the second situation of Figure 14.11, which makes one think that in this case, as in the previous ones, the richness of the articulation and the characteristic of the thingness of the object seen through the medium play an important role.

The deforming medium

a) Let us consider the two situations of Figure 14.12.

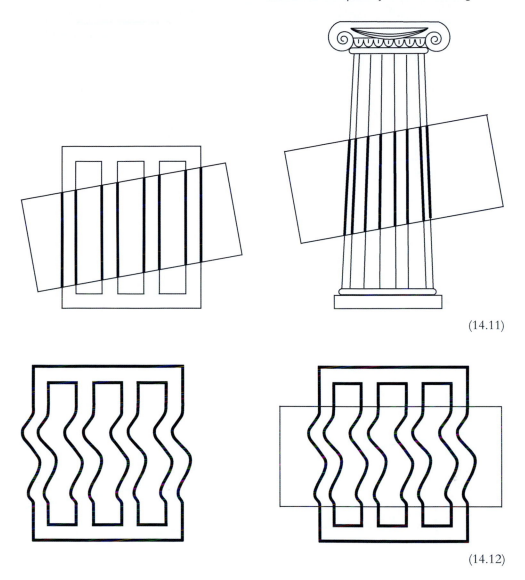

(14.11)

(14.12)

When we present the observers with either only the first or only the second of the situations and ask them to give a fairly ample free description of what they see, we obtain from the reports that in one case crookedness is a property of the vertical elements of the structure ("a grid with crooked bars"; "a railing made in a 'kneeling' fashion"; "a grid of folded, corrugated paper") while in the other this property is attributed to the transparent medium ("bars seen through a deforming glass"; "a window with a non-homogeneous sheet in front"; "a block of ice in front of a central heating radiator"). I questioned some of the observers in this second group about the "true" form of the object seen through the transparency and they showed some surprise at my question, because – as one of them said – it is "obvious that the object must be straight, even if one can also think that it is crooked just behind the area of the glass". This mode of transparency is perhaps better visible in the structures of Figure 14.13.

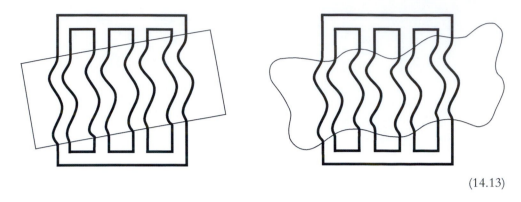

(14.13)

b) There are probably many properties of the medium that one can obtain in this way; that is, by joining by means of the continuity of direction the unities inside area A (where these unities are obtained with different trends of lines or with different graphical techniques inside A) to the articulations of the external structure that touch the margins of this area. The following example suffices: it can be imitated in many ways by varying what is included in the area covered by the medium, as long as there are visible units in it connected by continuity of direction to the elements of structure B (Figure 14.14). The medium, in this case, has a granular microstructure.

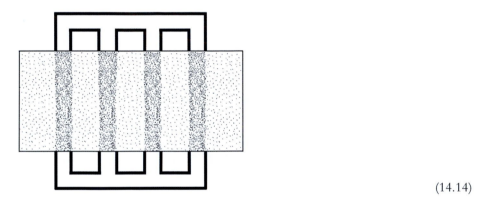

(14.14)

Thickness of the medium, its clean and smooth aspect

a) In these situations, the continuity of direction that ensures the unity of the elements seen in part through the medium is not a geometrical continuity, or a continuity that could be thought of in some sense at the level of the stimuli, but rather a distribution of signs that organizes itself phenomenally as a junction: it is a continuity of direction guaranteed at the phenomenological level. This is evident from the following examples (Figures 14.15 and 14.16).

Observers describe this kind of medium as a "lens", a "thick sheet", or "a big crystal", "a quite smooth and shiny shop window glass"; the two drawings in Figures 14.15 and 14.16 were shown separately to 30 persons (15 + 15) who had no relationship with psychological laboratories and no knowledge of problems of perception: however transparency was mentioned in all reports. The vertical lines inside rectangle A are in some way the continuation of the margins of the vertical elements belonging to structure B, external to A, if what we have said in relation to previous cases is true: that is, that area A becomes a medium so long as the elements contained in it join to this structure.

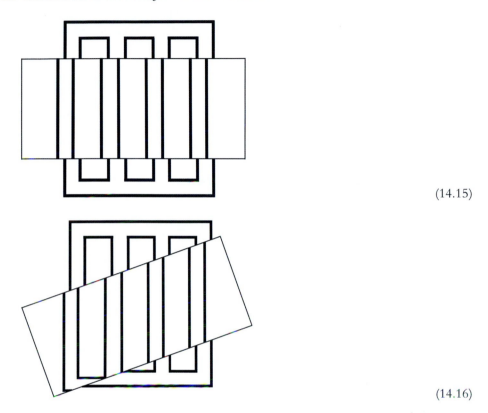

(14.15)

(14.16)

b) A similar effect (a medium described by observers as a sheet of "clear glass", "a rigid rectangle of plastic") is visible in Figure 14.17, in which the vertical elements inside of A lie on the ideal prolongation of the vertical elements belonging to structure B, without however any continuity of the lines.

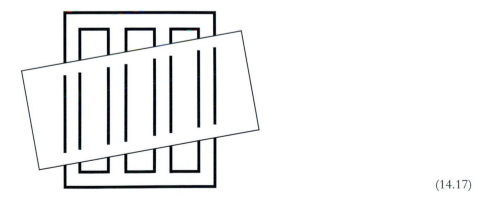

(14.17)

Transparency of the grid, deformation due to the grid

a) A particular case of transparency obtained by the technique of line drawing, which is different from those previously described because the object seen through the medium lies entirely behind the medium itself without sticking out at any point beyond its limits, is the following:[3]

(14.18)

Ten observers invited to give an exhaustive description of Figure 14.18 all mentioned transparency, some comparing this mode of transparency to that obtained with glasses marked by closely-spaced corrugations ("a glass crossed by many small undulations"), others comparing it to the vision through a grating, a "venetian blind", a "rolling shutter of tied reeds".

b) It should be noted that other attempts I made to obtain transparency without protrusion using means similar to that employed in Figure 14.18 – that is, by thickening the line in certain areas of a grating of fine lines or by thickening the marks as in Figure 14.19 so to form discernible perceptual units – had no success. In the case of Figure 14.19, only one out of ten observers described the situation as "a glass beyond which one sees the shadow of objects".

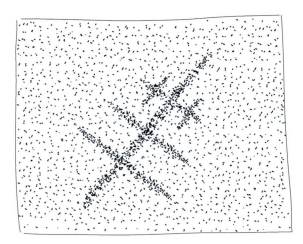

(14.19)

c) If the trend of the lines that constitute the medium is such as to produce the presence of a variously undulating non-flat medium and if by the technique employed in Figure 14.18 one builds an object whose structure is easily assimilable to that of a regular geometrical situation, this object, besides being seen though the medium, is also seen as being regular in itself but deformed in its appearance by the medium's lack of homogeneity (Figure 14.20), in a way similar to what occurs in the case of the situations in Figure 14.13.

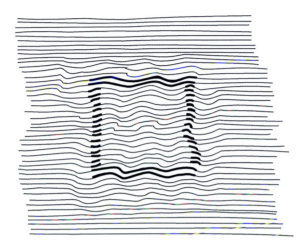

(14.20)

The cases of Figure 14.13 and Figure 14.20 perhaps allow one to speak of a figural *Spaltung*, that is, a phenomenal split – which may occur in given conditions – between a form experienced by the observer as belonging to an object in itself and the form effectively "seen" in a strict sense, having certain characteristics due to the interposition of a medium which is sensed as such. Perhaps it is also possible to say that – in cases similar to those mentioned before – a medium may be perceived as the *phenomenal cause* of the visible deformation.

A note on the problem of the window

a) A final case of transparency obtained without the use of different coloured surfaces, but only with means that are part of the practice of line drawing, is connected – in my opinion – to a discussion raised by Metelli (1967) in the last section of his article "On the analysis of the phenomenal appearances of transparency".[4] The discussion concerns phenomenal transparency in cases as that of a normal window where the theory of the four fields, set out by the author in the previous sections, cannot be applied since there are only two fields present (the wall and the window recess) and so there are not the conditions for obtaining a split based on the specific relationships between coloured areas expressed by Metelli's formulae.

According to this author, because the transparency of a window (whether the glass is coloured or not, so long as there are no reflections, and whether it consists of one or more panes) cannot be included in the cases explained by the theory of the four fields, it must, rather, be interpreted on the basis of the peripheral cues of three-dimensionality thanks to which the objects visible through the recess stand beyond the plane to which the window belongs. Besides these cues, however, other field conditions could also have a role. In a note[5] Metelli says: "one of these conditions seems to be the closure of the frame, and another the tendency to completion of those figures that happen to be cropped by the frame itself".

The example illustrated in Figure 14.21 and in the two situations of Figure 14.22 may be considered as a contribution to finding other conditions of this kind (pictorial depth cues) acting in the absence of peripheral determinants of three-dimensionality.

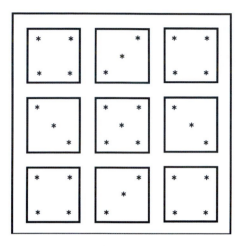

(14.21)

The situation of Figure 14.21, presented in isolation to twelve observers, was described by ten of them as nine squares "drawn inside", or "put on" a larger square, and marked with some asterisks arranged like the dots on a die; only two observers described a grid within the spaces of which there were asterisks.

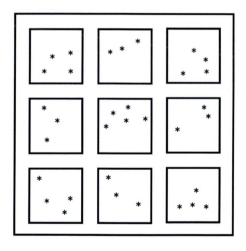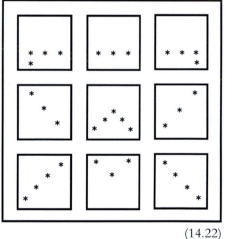

(14.22)

The situations of Figure 14.22, presented at a later time to the same twelve observers, were described by all as grids or windows beyond which constellations of asterisks were visible, arranged on a plane more or less distant from that to which the grid belonged, and behind it.

One of the observers wanted to make a three-way comparison, examining once again the situation of Figure 14.21 and comparing it with the other two; he claimed that if we set ourselves in front of Figure 14.21 so as to see the groups of asterisks as patterns on a die, then all the articulations of the configuration – asterisks included – lie more or less on the same plane; but if instead of subjectively grouping the asterisks as the dots on a die we try to see among them a more complex geometrical configuration arranged on an area larger than that of a single square, then the whole constellation "passes behind" the plane of the grid. Some of the other subjects agreed with this observation, which we refer here since it broadly suggests an explanatory hypothesis for the difference in stratification that seems to hold between the example of Figure 14.21 and the examples of Figure 14.22.

It is possible to hypothesize, indeed, that if the arrangement of asterisks in the nine squares obeys sufficiently simple geometrical rules, and we have an equally simple rule that connects the single groups of asterisks to each of the squares to which they belong by inclusion, then the asterisks are on the plane of the squares; while if the arrangement of the asterisks in the various squares is apparently random (that is, it obeys a complicated rule) or obeys a simple rule but has as a reference system other than the frames of the nine squares but rather the grid as a whole, then the asterisks are placed beyond the plane of the grid, and are seen behind it.

b) Even clearer results have emerged from other similar situations not made with line figures. I submitted the situations visible in Figure 14.23 (made on placards 70 × 70 cm) individually to 45 observers (15 + 15 +15) asking them to make a free description.

When no data useful for the problem under consideration emerged from the free description, they were asked one question only: "and where are the dots?"

All observers who described the situation *a* said that the dots were on the black squares; twelve out of the 15 observers who described the situation *b* said that the dots were behind the grid, or window, as "constellations of stars"; and all those who described the situation *c* also said that the constellation of dots was located beyond the plane of the grid.

In relation to the problem of the window, therefore, and at least for cases closely similar to these, it is possible to suppose that the arrangement of the objects in the squares – that is, the topography of the spatial relations that connect the objects one to another and to the reference system – is one of the conditions that contributes to forming a space included between the plane of the window and the place of the objects seen through it; it is, therefore, a factor for the perception of total transparency, without visible media in the way.

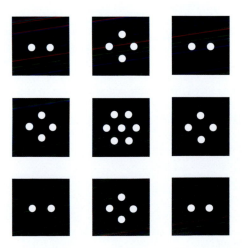

(14.23a)

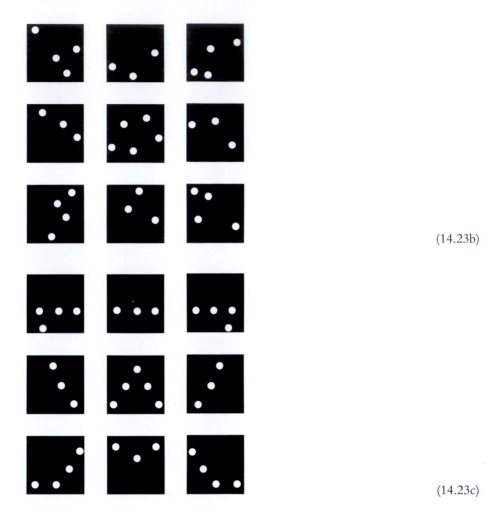

(14.23b)

(14.23c)

Notes

1 This particular effect was independently observed by Prof. Dolores Passi Tognazzo and myself, in the very same days and at the same Institute, while we were working on two completely different problems at the beginning of the academic year 1966–67.
2 See also the Figures in the appendix. [Editors' note: because the three figures take up space on the page in what was originally a footnote, we have moved them to the end of the essay to ensure their legibility.]
3 Effect observed together by Prof. Gaetano Kanizsa and myself during the academic year 1960–61.
4 Metelli (1967), p. 303.
5 Metelli (1967), p. 304

References

Metelli, F. (1967). Zur Analyse der phänomenalen Durchsichtigkeitserscheinungen. In R. Mühlher and J. Fischl (ed.), *Gestalt und Wirklichkeit*. Berlin: Duncker and Humboldt, pp. 285–304.

Appendix

The effect of phenomenal transparency is perhaps more visible in Figure 14.24 because of the relative inclination of the two structural elements definitely favours stratification into two planes, "above-below". That this kind of relative inclination between elements involves stratification in different planes is easily noticeable when observing the patterns in Figures 14.25 and 14.26, where the enclosed squares can easily be seen as the margins of a hole when their sides run parallel to the fundamental dimensions of the figures that contain them, but become margins of a superimposed square when this parallelism no longer occurs.

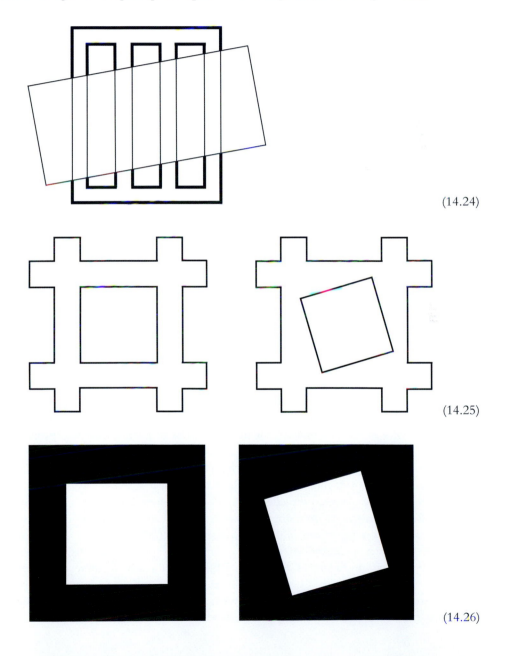

(14.24)

(14.25)

(14.26)

COMMENTS ON OBSERVATIONS ON SOME CASES OF PHENOMENAL TRANSPARENCY OBTAINED WITH LINE DRAWINGS

Daniele Zavagno

In his 1975 paper, Bozzi presented a sample of transparency effects obtained with achromatic line drawings, that is with drawings made only of black lines and dots. Commenting his work, I will follow the structure of his paper. Without the time to run appropriate experiments, and having shown the demos proposed in this work only to a few expert observers, whose descriptions are however consistent with my own impressions, when describing the effects I will rely on what *I* see, aware of the need for proper experiments to be carried out.

Milky opacities

Among the number of demos published in Bozzi's paper, those in which the transparent surface appears characterized by a somewhat milky opacity are those that, in my opinion, deliver the strongest impression of phenomenal transparency. The effect is obtained by using thinner lines for the part of the grid enclosed by the horizontal rectangle (see Bozzi's Figure 14.1). However, as Bozzi not only pointed out but also empirically verified, the difference in line thickness – which perceptually translates into a difference in *pronouncedness* (thinner lines tend to appear somewhat less *black* than thicker ones traced with the same ink)[1] – is not by itself a sufficient condition for the appearance of phenomenal transparency. In fact, what is required is something that we may call *articulated structure*: the structure to be seen through the "transparent" surface must be characterized by a certain degree of articulation[2] and be object-like, that is it should possess a characteristic of *thingness*.

As Bozzi wrote, he observed the effect in 1966–67 (see note 1 to Bozzi's paper), about ten years after Kanizsa's paper on transparency effects published in Italian (1955; an updated English version of the paper can be found in Kanizsa's 1979 book). The importance of Bozzi's paper is better understood if we briefly consider one of Kanizsa's demos, proposed in a simplified version in Figure 14.27. Whether Bozzi was directly or indirectly influenced by a similar demo will remain a mystery, as Bozzi makes no reference to Kanizsa's paper, and Kanizsa makes no reference to Bozzi's paper in his 1979 book. Curiously enough, Metzger in his 1975 edition of *Gesetze des Sehens* describes both Kanizsa's and Bozzi's works on transparency, but in different chapters, 9 and 13 respectively, in which he makes no link between the two. Nevertheless, when describing Kanizsa's demo (Figure 14.27a), Metzger writes that the transparency effect appears enhanced when the textured parts of the disks are all slightly modified in shape or shifted in position (Metzger, 1975, pp. 281–282). To understand what Metzger means, look at Figures 14.13, 14.15 and 14.16 in the translation of Bozzi's paper (or at Metzger, 1975, p. 414, Figure 435). Would Metzger have proposed such a consideration (yet without the aid of an illustration) if he had not had in mind Bozzi's demos when analysing Kanizsa's figure?

Whatever is hidden behind this lack of cross-references, Kanizsa's demo (Figure 14.27a) is in many ways a precursor of Bozzi's study with line drawings. Indeed, Kanizsa's demo is itself formally nothing but a line drawing. In his 1979 chapter on transparency, Kanizsa shows other two figures, simplified versions of which appear in Figures 14.27b-c. In Figure 14.27b the phenomenally transparent surface is an outlined vertical rectangle in which the central portion is coloured in a lighter shade of grey, while the bottom and top portions have the same reflectance as the square background, but they appear somewhat lighter than the background. Figure 14.27c shows a bi-stable configuration where one can see either a relatively large horizontal rectangle with irregular quadrilateral holes cut in it, under which lies a vertical rectangle (in this case the vertical rectangle is amodally completed behind the horizontal one), or a relatively large horizontal rectangle with irregular quadrilaterals on top of it, on top of which lies a vertical transparent rectangle (in this case the vertical rectangle is characterized by illusory contours). When the last is seen, the transparency effect resembles translucency, an effect that is somewhat similar to the milky opacities obtained by Bozzi.

Both Kanizsa's and Bozzi's demos bring out the crucial role of figural structure and perceptual organization in transparency phenomena. But this is exactly where Bozzi's demos pick up the ball and run with it. For the role played by figural structure is strongly underlined in Bozzi's demos by the fact that if we exclude differences in the thickness of the lines, there are no real achromatic differences in his displays. In Kanizsa's most graphic demo (Figure 14.27a), on the other hand, we must consider at least three achromatic colours: the colour of the paper, the colour of the contours, and the texture that fills the sectors included in the

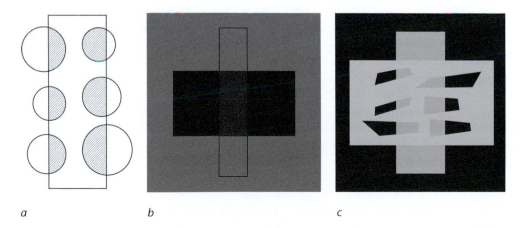

a   b   c

FIGURE 14.27 Demos modified from Kanizsa 1955 and 1979 (see text)

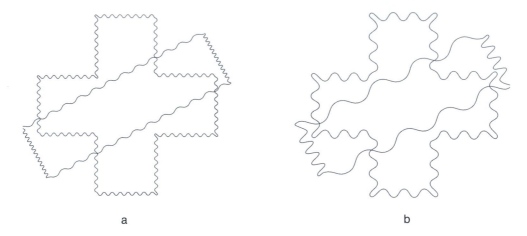

a   b

FIGURE 14.28 Modified from Metzger 1975 (see text)

vertical rectangle, which delivers an impression of light grey. In Bozzi's demo, paper reflectance is not a factor simply because it characterizes all the structures portrayed in the figure: the background, the solid grid, and the transparent layer.

One may be tempted to argue that the transparencies shown by Bozzi in his first set of demos are more cognitive than perceptual, that is that we "interpret" or "understand" those drawings to be representations of transparency effects, not that we actually see transparency. There are, however, two major facts that strongly oppose such an argument. The first is related to the role of articulated structure mentioned earlier: Bozzi demonstrates that in line drawings, given similar drawing rules (e.g. the thickness of the lines), the possibility of perceiving transparency increases in relation to both the articulation and the object-like characteristics of the set of lines to-be-seen-under the transparent layer.

The second relevant fact is that one actually sees translucency in Bozzi's Figure 14.1, Figure 14.24, and Figure 14.9. In other words, the transparent layer not only appears of a different white, but it appears of a different consistency. As it is not easy to put this difference into words, consider Figure 14.28, modified from Metzger (1975): neither in 14.28a nor in 14.28b does one necessarily see transparency, yet when we focus on the central portion of Figure 14.28a, delimited by the intersection of the wiggly figures, this appears of a somehow different white, more *pronounced* (see note 1). The effect of slight lightness differences is even stronger in Figure 14.28b, as each enclosed part can be also easily seen as juxtaposed independent shapes. As such, each portion retains its own lightness – though it would be hard to quantify the differences – while in Bozzi's demos the milky appearance is diffused over the shape that appears translucent. This "diffusion" effect somewhat recalls neon colour spreading (Van Tuijl, 1975; Varin, 1971) or the watercolour illusion (Pinna, Werner, & Spillmann, 2003).

As a final note to this section, I would like to show that Bozzi's milky transparencies can be also achieved with colours. For colour reproductions of the figures, please see the Plate Section. The aspect I will focus on is the colour of the transparent layer. For convenience, I will refer to the seen-as-transparent rectangle simply as *rectangle*, to the outlined larger rectangle with smaller vertical ones inside as *grid*, and to the *grid*'s lines included in the *rectangle* as *segments*. Figure 14.29a follows Bozzi's thickness rule but with lines in blue instead of black: the milky transparency is equivalent to Bozzi's, yet tinged blue. Figure 14.29b shows that if we don't follow Bozzi's thickness rule, we fail to achieve phenomenal transparency with monochromatic configurations (this is true even with a rectangle drawn with thicker lines). In Figure 14.29c, I made the rectangle and the segments yellow, and transparency seems to work. However, if we replace all the yellow lines with red ones, as in Figure 14.29d, then

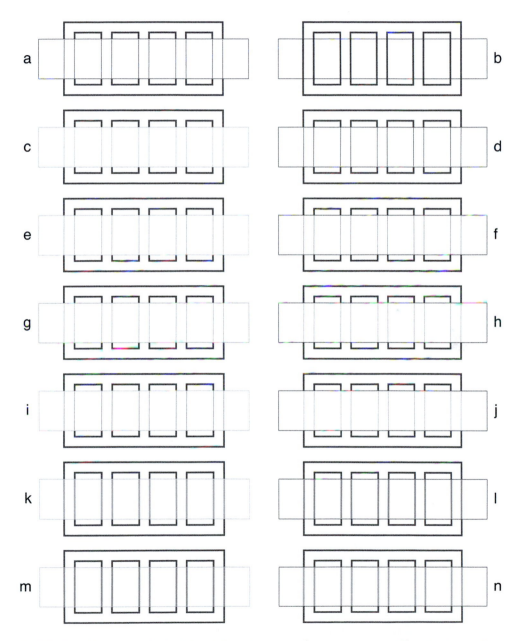

FIGURE 14.29 Colours applied to Bozzi's line drawing milky transparencies (Plate Section p. 1)

even though the figure complies with the thickness rule, transparency is more conceptual than a clear-cut perceptual outcome. I think that this demonstrates the role of pronouncedness in these effects, as red is chromatically more pronounced than yellow on white backgrounds.[3] If we keep the rectangle either yellow or red but we change the segments according to a suitable fusion colour, such as light green and light purple respectively, we will see more of a translucency effect, with filters tinged respectively in yellow and red (Figures 14.29e–f). If we were to stop here we could conclude that in order to see transparency in multicolour line drawings it is necessary for the segments not to be so pronounced in colour, or to be of a plausible fusion colour, i.e. the resulting colour of a subtractive colour combination of the grid and the rectangle; in turn, the nuance of the milky transparency appears to be driven by the outline colour of the rectangle, as it should if it were a full coloured transparent rectangle (da Pos, 1989). Figure 14.29g supports such arguments, as now, with a green outlined rectangle, the milky transparency is a greenish-grey.

There are, however, some problems with the aforementioned conclusions: Figures 14.29h–i still show transparency, though the segments are not appropriate fusion colours, as I swapped them. Why is it that we can still see phenomenal transparency? One possibility is that when lines are very thin their nuance tends towards grey, as Bozzi noticed in his achromatic displays. A translucent filter, in fact, would reduce not only the thickness of the lines, but also the pronouncedness of their nuances. Figures 14.29j supports such an argument, as the segments are grey while the rectangle is red and translucent (and it works just as well with a yellow rectangle). Are all the problems solved then? Not really: Figures 14.29k–l show that Bozzi's thickness rule is unnecessary if we use multicolour line patterns. What changes is how the colour of the segments contributes to the nuance of the filter, which appears greenish-yellow in 3k and violet-red in 3l. However, the real challenges are represented by Figures 14.29m–n, in which the coloured segments are swapped from green to purple and from purple to green, respectively. One still sees transparency though the segment colours are not affected by a greyish appearance. But what colours characterize the transparent filters? Confusing as it might be, I think they are best described respectively as violet-yellow (3m) and greenish-pink filters (3n): that is as more or less impossible colour filters. Of course all these considerations are very preliminary and ought to be followed up by appropriate experimental research.

Magnifying effects

Bozzi claims that if we invert the thickness ratio between the lines in his drawings we obtain a different kind of transparency effect, in which the filter shows a magnifying effect. I do not find his drawings all that convincing in this case. I applied colour to his ideas to have a closer look at the phenomenon. In Figures 14.30a, c, e rectangles are traced with thick lines, and in Figures 14.30b,d,f with thin ones: if anything, the impression of transparency is visually more convincing in the last group, meaning that in outline drawings transparency works better if the transparent layer (the *rectangle* in these drawings) is traced with thin lines.

Bozzi, however, pointed out that the magnifying effect is stronger with higher articulated configurations. Applying the Italian concept of articulation to the configurations in Figures 14.30g-j (see note 2), I simply rotated the rectangle and indeed the impression of transparency with a magnification effect is enhanced, even when the rectangle is outlined with thick lines (Figure 14.30i). However, in Figure 14.29i-j we basically see transparency with magnification, while in Figures 14.29g-h I see more a translucency effect with magnification.

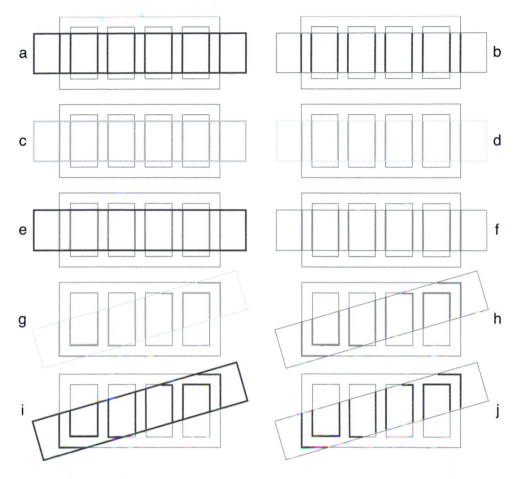

FIGURE 14.30 Magnifying effects with colour (see see Plate Section p. 2)

Deforming effects

While Bozzi's milky transparencies are the most convincing, his deforming transparencies are probably the most intriguing. I have already mentioned that I think Metzger paid a silent tribute to Bozzi's findings when describing Kanizsa's demo; I like to imagine that Kennedy too (1974) would have been thrilled by the possibility of showing deforming transparency effects in simple line drawings. Figure 14.31 shows those effects in colour. As noted above, when the rectangle is traced with thick lines, transparency is not a clear-cut outcome (Figure 14.31a), while when it is traced with thin lines the deforming transparent effect is seen in both monochromatic and multicolour patterns (Figures 14.31b-d), even when the segments are of an inappropriate fusion colour (Figure 14.31d). In Figures 14.31e-f I increased articulation by rotating the rectangle, showing also that deformation can be combined with the magnifying effect (Figures 14.31f).

With reference to Bozzi's Figure 14.14, while the effect is rather interesting I do not think it can be classified as a line drawing, due to the presence of a dense texture that not only defines the material quality of the rectangle, but directly introduces surface colour as a

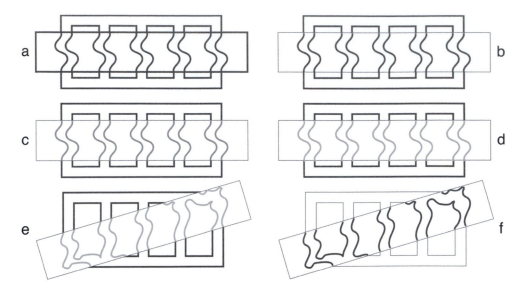

FIGURE 14.31 Applying colour to Bozzi's deforming transparencies effects (see Plate Section p. 2)

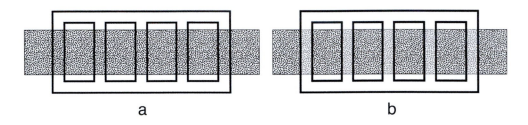

FIGURE 14.32 Bozzi's Figure 14 revised

variable, as in Kanizsa's demo (1955, see Figure 14.27a). In addition, the drawing is misleading because there is no reason why the parts of the grid under the texture should appear darker. In fact, correct renderings of Bozzi's idea would be Figures 14.32a-b, in which either the grid is seen through the textured rectangle, or the grid itself appears transparent, under which one sees the textured rectangle. Notice that in the last case the grid becomes somewhat greyish, as in Kanizsa's demo (Figure 14.27a). While Figure 14.32b is potentially interesting because of the apparent achromatic and surface quality modifications of the grid with respect to the background, Figure 14.32a does not constitute a major problem for perceptual sciences: the density of the transparent layer is already determined by the texture employed in the drawing, hence the visual system needs only to register what is already physically given.

Thickness or spatial distortion?

Bozzi also shows the possibility of generating an impression of thickness in the overlapping transparent filter. The effect is achieved by simply translating the segments in order to break-up good continuation. The effect, however, is more compelling in his Figure 14.16, in which

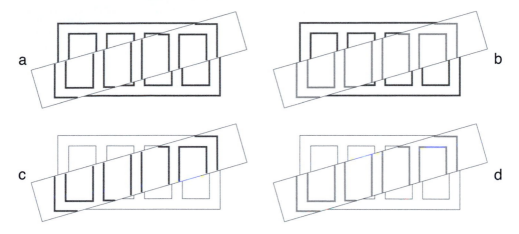

FIGURE 14.33 Bozzi's thickness effects in colour (see Plate Section p. 3)

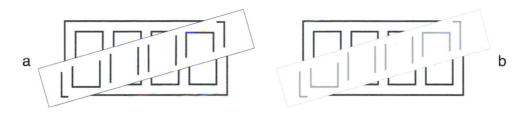

FIGURE 14.34 Bozzi's Figure 14.17 in colour (see Plate Section p. 3)

the rectangle intersects the grid obliquely, than when it intersects it horizontally, showing once more the crucial role of articulation. Figures 14.33a–b show a blue and a multicolour version of Bozzi's demo: while the demos seem to work, it is questionable whether one actually *sees* thicker rectangles in such displays with respect to the previous ones. Indeed, I see a transparency effect with a spatial distortion. Many *know* that most often such an impression is associated with a transparent surface having a certain thickness, but the relevant question is whether we actually *see* the thickness of the transparent layer. In my opinion, we see an effect that might be physically caused by the thickness of a transparent layer (a refraction effect), but we do not see thicker rectangles. I also tried to combine these spatial distortion effects with the magnifying effect (Figures 14.33c–d), and my impression is that the combination delivers a more compelling transparency impression in monochromatic drawings (Figure 14.33c).

Figure 14.34 shows instead a monochromatic and a multicolour version of Bozzi's Figure 14.17. Here I think the effect is particularly strong in the multicolour version, which delivers an impression of something close to frosted yellow glass.

Grid-like transparencies

In his investigation into the possibility of rendering transparency impressions with simple graphic elements, such as lines and dots, Bozzi also tried to achieve transparency effects in which the transparent layer covers completely the solid object behind it. His Figures 14.18 and 14.20 succeed in this attempt. On the other hand, Byzantine artists adopted similar graphic solutions more than a thousand years ago. Figure 14.35 shows the *Baptism of Jesus*, a mosaic in the Battistero degli Ariani in Ravenna (Fifth century), in which Jesus is represented in the waters of Jordan River by employing the same technique proposed by Bozzi, only in colour (Zavagno, 1996).

Concluding his paper on transparency effects achievable with line drawings, Bozzi addresses also the issue of seeing what lies behind a window. The topic is conceptually interesting, as it picks up a problem posed by Metelli (1967). However, I think that Bozzi's arguments in that last part of his paper have little to do with the possibility of showing transparency in line drawings. The originality of Bozzi's previous demos lies in the fact that he was the first to show the possibility of creating impressions of transparency simply by employing lines, modulating them in thickness (pronouncedness), shape, and spatial arrangement, while playing around with the Gestalt grouping law known as *good continuation*. By introducing colour to Bozzi's displays, I have tried to show how strong those effects are, as one gets to appreciate even more the colour modulations of the transparent layer connected to the transparency effects, determined solely by relative colour pronouncedness, figural structure, articulation and good continuation, the last three themes underlying Bozzi's arguments. In arguing why the last part of his paper is irrelevant to everything that goes before it, I will once more make use of coloured displays (Figure 14.36).

Because of the Gestalt laws of proximity and good continuation, the dots in Figure 14.36a are grouped in a wavy line; this allows for the grid structure to appear quite stable, meaning that the large horizontal rectangle and the smaller vertical ones perform different structural

FIGURE 14.35 *Baptism of Jesus*, Battistero degli Ariani, Ravenna, 5th century (see Plate Section p. 4)

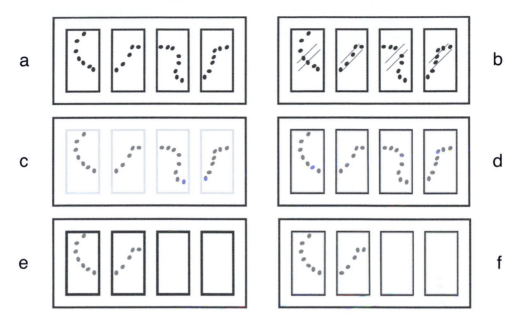

FIGURE 14.36 Transparent windows (see Plate Section p. 5)

functions: the former is a frame and the latter are apertures – or holes, or even windows, if one prefers – thanks to which we can see the dotted line amodally completed underneath the horizontal rectangle, which thus appears as a grid. But does one actually see transparency? In the end, the situation is formally similar to Figure 14.28a: two structures intersect, namely the grid and the line, but transparency is not a *necessary* outcome. In Figure 14.36b I introduced a graphic stratagem often used in comics to show transparent glass: two thin oblique lines that represent the reflective power of glass surfaces. In this connection, Kennedy (1974) states that reflections are used in line drawings to represent roundish smooth surfaces, such as balloons or bottles. I think however that it is possible to employ lines to create the impression of reflections even in line drawings portraying flat structures. Yet it is hard to say if one actually sees transparency in Figure 14.36b, or just a graphic convention useful for representing windowpanes, or maybe an effective visual metaphor (Kennedy, 1982) that can be used to represent glass-like material.

In Figure 14.36c, a multicolour configuration, the results are not better: even if the dotted line simulates the fusion colour achievable with the blue dots of Figure 14.36a covered by a 55 percent transparent yellow layer, it is still questionable whether transparency is an actual experience in such a configuration.

The point is that in order to see transparency, one needs to perceive also something that may be called the "material consistency" of the transparent layer, or its "surface-like nature": a specific perceptual quality of appearing as a surface, i.e. with a certain impression of *density* and *colour* that distinguishes it from the background. Edges alone do not guarantee this outcome (see Figure 14.28). One needs to employ Metelli's rules for transparency (1974), or to modulate in appropriate ways the spatial and colour proprieties of the elements of a configuration, as in Kanizsa's demos (1979; see Figure 14.27), or one must employ Bozzi's empirical rules for transparency effects in line drawings. All these possible ways have one point in common: the to-be-seen-as-transparent layer does not cover the entire surface that should be seen under it. Hence the window problem needs to find some other solution, a solution that can induce the perception of semi-opacity. In one way or another, the transparent layer must be seen if we are to speak about transparency. I tried to achieve this in the grid and dot patterns in Figures 14.36c–f by employing double coloured lines, as in the watercolour illusion. With this stratagem, rectangular grid holes appear yellowish or pinkish. The impression of transparency, however, does not come from the watercolour illusion per se, but from the combination of the illusion with the impression of structure delivered by the dots, which appear as a whole because of the synergic combination of the Gestalt laws of proximity and good continuation, as well as the phenomenon known as amodal completion. It is important to point out that the colour of the "windowpanes" is driven exclusively by the watercolour illusion, as Figures 14.36e–f demonstrate, in which the "underlying" structure, namely the line made of dots, has no influence on the colour of the windows (compare also the colour appearance of the *rectangle* in Figure 14.29n with the colour appearance of the windowpanes in Figure 14.36e). While the presence of the dotted structure is required to see transparency, it is still not a sufficient condition in grid-like configurations such as those employed by Bozzi and in Figure 14.36.

Bozzi's previous demos are important because when we see transparency in those line drawings, we actually see the transparent layer as such and not as a simple frame or wire-like figure (as in Figures 14.28a). Instead, looking at his Figure 14.21 what one eventually sees is a square with nine holes – i.e. a grid – under which there is a certain array of dots that because of proximity, good continuation, and amodal completion appear as a whole, that is as a structure and not just as a random distribution of dots inside small square surfaces. However, the important question is whether the grid is a window. Given the regular distribution of the smaller squares inside the big ones, Bozzi's Figure 14.21 could be the representation of an articulated window frame; yet the windowpanes are not *transparent*: they are simply *not visible*. Transparency and invisibility are not the same thing: a transparent surface exists in our phenomenal space, whereas an invisible surface does not; hence invisibility is dangerous, as we might run up against an invisible surface before recognizing that it is actually just very transparent. Hence the importance of Bozzi's demos, which show us that transparency is a phenomenal outcome actively pursued by the visual system, given the appropriate set of stimuli, even when these consist physically only of lines.

Notes

1 The word "pronouncedness" was introduced by Katz (1935) to describe a complex quality in the appearance of achromatic colours to which the word "brightness" does not render justice. For instance, we can see two surfaces both characterized as black, nevertheless one may appear as a better or "blacker" black. In this sense the term "pronouncedness" is meant to encompass the meaning of brightness, which usually describes the continuum dim-bright, yet confining it to a more limited range. Hence the accent shifts from the dim-bright continuum, which is a quantitative domain, to a qualitative one, in which, for instance, the best black is also more salient (on this issue see also Beck, 1972; Zavagno, Daneyko, and Sakurai, 2011).

2 In the Italian tradition, *articulation* is most often used to denote overall structural complexity, thus defined not only in terms of the number of elements or parts of a configuration, but also referring to the type and quality of relations between parts and other features such as symmetry, spatial organization, etc. In this sense, though structurally similar, Bozzi's Figure 14.24 (carried in this anthology, in the appendix to Chapter 14) is more articulated than his Figure 1.

3   In addition, I also changed the colour of the backgrounds; the appearance of the transparency effects with the same set of coloured lines as those used in Figure 14.29 are either enhanced or disappear completely, depending on how *pronounced* the colours of the lines are against the lightness of the background.

References

Beck, J. (1972). *Surface Color Perception*. Ithaca, NY: Cornell University Press.

da Pos, O. (1989). *Trasparenze* [Transparencies]. Padua, Italy: Icone Srl.

Kanizsa, G. (1955). Condizioni ed effetti della trasparenza fenomenica [Conditions and effects of perceptual transparency]. *Rivista di Psicologia 49*, 3–19.

Kanizsa, G. (1979). *Organization in Vision*. New York: Praeger.

Katz, D. (1935). *The World of Color*. London: Kegan Paul.

Kennedy, J.M. (1974). *A Psychology of Picture Perception*. San Francisco, CA: Jossey-Bass.

Kennedy, J.M. (1982). Metaphor in Pictures. *Perception, 11*, 588–605.

Loomis, J. M. (1972). The photopigment bleaching hypothesis of complementary after-images: A psychophysical test. *Vision Research, 12* (10), 1587–1594.

Metelli, F. (1967). Zur Analyse der phänomenalen Durchsichtigkeitserscheinungen. In R. Mühlher and J. Fischl (Eds), *Gestalt und Wirklichkeit* (pp. 258–304). Berlin: Duncker and Humblot.

Metelli, F. (1974). The perception of transparency. *Scientific American, 230*, 90–98.

Metzger, W. (1975). *Gesetze des Sehens*. Frankfurt am Main, Germany: Verlag Waldemar Kramer.

Pinna, B., Werner, J.S., and Spillmann, L. (2003). The watercolor effect: a new principle of grouping and figure-ground organization. *Vision Research, 43*, 43–52.

Van Tuijl, H.F.J.M. (1975). A new visual illusion: neonlike color spreading and complementary color induction between subjective contours. *Acta Psychologica, 39*, 441–445

Varin, D. (1971). Fenomeni di contrasto e di diffusione cromatica nell'organizzazione spaziale del campo percettivo [Contrast phenomena and chromatic diffusion in the spatial organisation of the perceptual field]. *Rivista di Psicologia, 65*, 101–108.

Zavagno, D. (1996). L'effetto trasparenza nella Lunetta di San Lorenzo nel Mausoleo di Galla Placidia in Ravenna [The transparency effect in the lunette of San Lorenzo in the mausoleum of Galla Placidia at Ravenna]. In L. Bortolatto and O. da Pos (Eds). *Effetto Trasparenza* (pp. 18–22). Treviso, Italy: Le Venezie.

Zavagno, D., Daneyko, O., and Sakurai, K. (2011). What can pictorial artifacts teach us about light and lightness? *Japanese Psychological Research, 53*, 448–462.

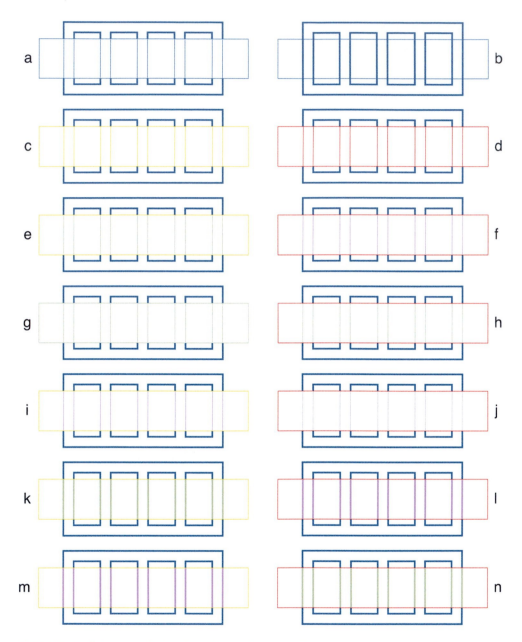

FIGURE 14.29 Colours applied to Bozzi's line drawing milky transparencies (see text)

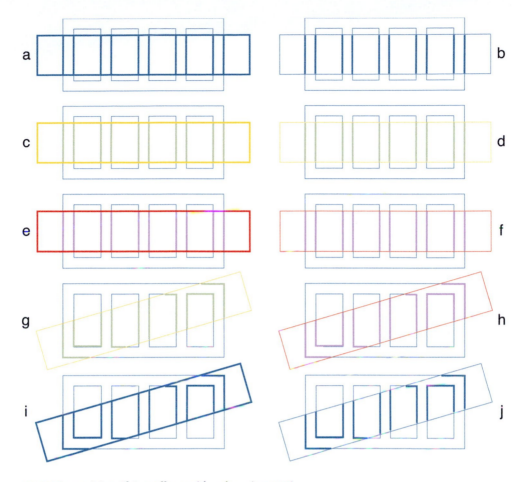

FIGURE 14.30 Magnifying effects with colour (see text)

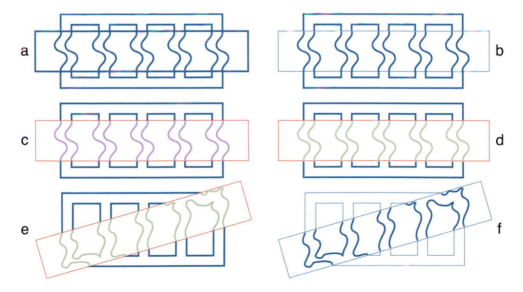

FIGURE 14.31 Applying colour to Bozzi's deforming transparencies effects (see text).

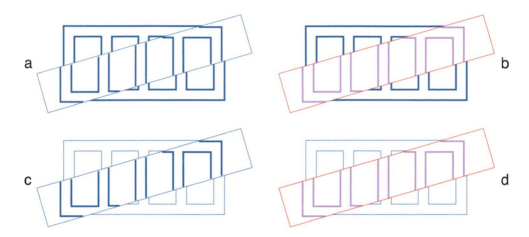

FIGURE 14.33 Bozzi's thickness effects in colour (see text)

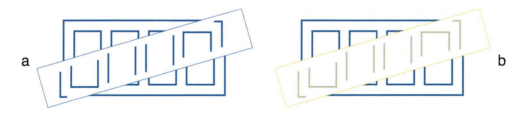

FIGURE 14.34 Bozzi's Figure 14.17 in colour (see text)

FIGURE 14.35 *Baptism of Jesus*, Battistero degli Ariani, Ravenna, 5th century

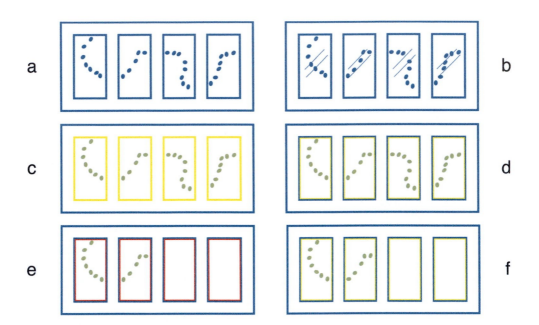

FIGURE 14.36 Transparent windows (see text)

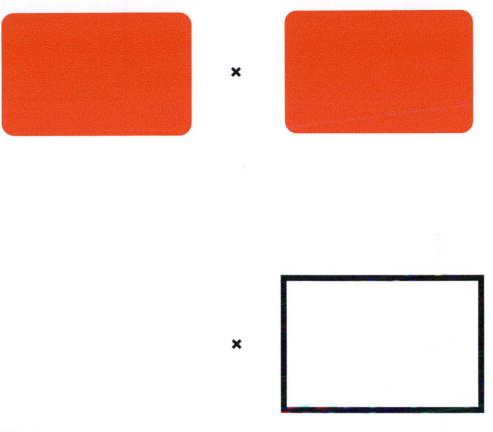

FIGURE 15.1

FIGURE 15.2

FIGURE 15.3

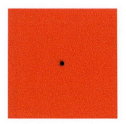

FIGURE 15.4

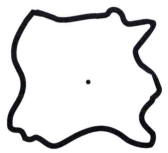

FIGURE 15.5

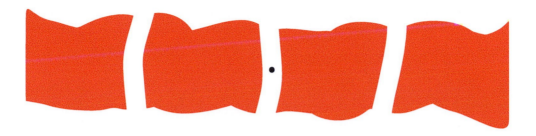

FIGURE 15.6

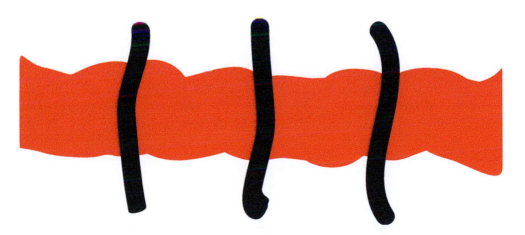

FIGURE 15.7

15

ORIGINAL OBSERVATIONS ON CERTAIN CHARACTERISTICS OF AFTERIMAGES

Translated by Tiziano Agostini

1. A "liquid" model for afterimage colours

Let us consider the simplest and best-known example of an afterimage. A single coloured shape (a square, a disc, a star) is placed on a homogeneous white or light grey surface. You stare at it for quite a long time, in good lighting, and then shift your gaze to a certain point on another homogeneous surface, similar to the first one. You hold your gaze still and immediately, or after a short delay, a very visible ghost of the shape just observed appears, with a different colour, according to the rule that we learnt from Goethe: red-green, blue-yellow, yellow-blue and green-red, though this is subject to variation, owing partially to factors involved in the observation, partially to strictly subjective elements.

This ghost image, the afterimage, is just that, a ghost, for all that it is visible and sometimes – at the beginning – very visible indeed. It is unlikely that someone should mistake this extra coloured shape for an object that can be grasped: as well as having the qualities of its shape and colour, it also has the quality of being an *appearance*. To avoid facile and predictable objections, we may say that it has "the appearance of appearance", the feature of being unreal. This unreality becomes more acute as the seconds pass, because the colour – of itself already diaphanous – tends to pale and seems to dissipate, while the outline, becoming uncertain as well as blurred, gives the image an instability that is not normally found in solid objects, but rather in certain reflections of light, or faint clouds. Moreover, the image comes and goes in unpredictable cycles.

Despite these ethereal properties, the afterimage is usually easy to describe. It may be hard to say what its colour is, both because our vocabulary for colours is impoverished, and because various factors affect it: transparency, background disturbance, the constantly shifting borders, a certain filminess, etc. But its shape and the way in which it changes can be described, as can its size in relation to other objects, how long it stays and for how long it is gone, what its position is in relation to the plane of observation, and so on.

What happens in the brief life of an afterimage can in part depend upon its surroundings. We should bear in mind that, from an abstract and model-building point of view, the image only exists in the eye and the brain. In actual fact, it is to be found among the objects that fill the field of our direct observations. Of course, everything can be referred back to those abstractions and models, but to do so, we should have to go and look at what happens in direct observation, when the image is made to interact with other visual events.

A first test can be made by enclosing an afterimage in a frame. The easiest way to make good observations of these things is as follows.

Place two coloured figures together on a homogeneous background, two red rectangles for example, one next to the other, marking a point or a cross exactly halfway between the two, halfway up (Figure 15.1). Then mark another cross under the first and, to its right (or left, of course), draw a black rectangle big enough for the afterimage of one of the red triangles to fit in exactly.

Holding the objects thus prepared at an appropriate distance, the observer places himself or herself straight on and in very good lighting, and starts to stare at the cross between the two rectangles, without ever shifting the gaze. This lasts as long as is necessary, between 30 and 40 seconds. Then they shift their gaze quite quickly to the cross drawn next to the empty frame, and begin staring at that. If everything has been done properly (for example, if the observer hasn't tilted his or her head when shifting the gaze from one point of reference to the other), the afterimage of the rectangle on the right will fall within the frame, while that of the rectangle on the left will remain free in the homogeneous area.

In these conditions, we can make some interesting observations. The afterimage without a frame develops over time, in line with what we already know, and loses and acquires its

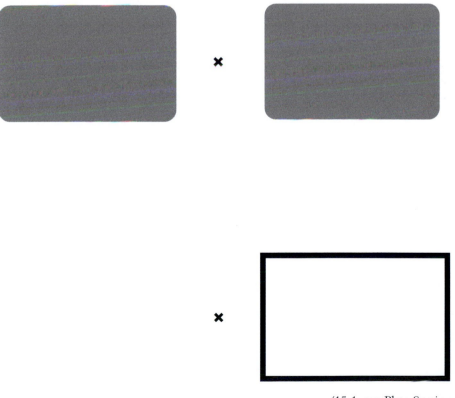

(15.1, see Plate Section p. 6)

characteristics as has already been noted. Meanwhile (and the advantage of experimenting with two images at the same time is that they can be compared moment by moment) the other image – the one inside the frame – appears darker, perfectly homogeneous in colour, and often without that feature of unreality mentioned earlier. Thus one might say that the space within the frame actually has that colour, as though it were painted: it is as though the colour appears to have dyed the material within the frame, rather than just being superimposed on the background, as it seems to be in the other case, because of the transparency of the afterimage colour.

Secondly, this colour is very stable over time. While the unframed afterimage comes and goes, fades and then revives, and becomes of uncertain outline, the colour within the frame undergoes a slow but constant deterioration, which is hardly visible in the initial stages. Conversely, once it has completely disappeared, it is unlikely to return.

What I now put to you is, of course, a metaphor, but it is difficult to avoid the idea that the colour in the frame is "contained" within it, like a liquid in a container, whose sides limit the possibility of its spilling out. The fraying at the edges of the unframed image, on the other hand, can be compared to what happens to the edges of a splash of liquid on a porous surface, which tends to spread a bit, and is absorbed a bit here and there by what it is lying on.

A similar thing happens when, using the same method, we compare an unframed image with one which falls within the borders of an anomalous surface: the almost perceptual edges have the ability to hold in the colour like those of a frame (further proof of the fact that an anomalous surface doesn't just look like an object but effectively behaves likes an object).

If we make a non-continuous frame, but with dashes, so that there is much less total black compared with the previous case and the frame has numerous gaps, once again the colour within it is very stable. Here too, the colour is darker than the unframed image, and lasts noticeably longer. (Only by comparing the two afterimages, one placed in the continuous frame and the other in the frame with dashes, can we see that the latter is slightly lighter, maybe simply because there is less induction of black.)[1]

This changes, however, if we place the afterimage colour in a frame with the same amount of black as in the previous case, but this time marking only the corners of the frame, with large, continuous strokes, rather than using dashes. The afterimage colour, briefly staying within the outline of the square, starts to fill and then overflow from the lateral openings. As the colour spills out towards the exterior, it fades, and often the image quickly disappears (Figure 15.2).

Some observers assert that, if the image doesn't disappear, the spreading of colour stops when it meets other edges possible in this arrangement. Indeed, if we look at the square formed by the four corners without positioning any afterimage inside, it is not difficult to see another square, this time anomalous, resting on it and rotated through 45 degrees.

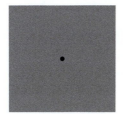

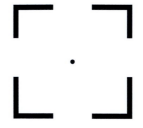

(15.2, see Plate Section p. 6)

The anomalous square, if it is seen, covers a certain section of each side of the frame (the frame is amodally continuous behind it). This establishes itself as the place for the afterimage, which falls within it. To go back to the liquid analogy, in this case the anomalous square is the container for the afterimage colour.

The analogy with a liquid might inspire us further, still based on what we have seen in the two previous situations, and lead us to consider that the afterimage colour, for all that it behaves as a fluid, behaves as a fairly viscous fluid. It is unable to pass between the dashes, which are too close together, like thick oil in a container with small holes. But it is easily able to pass through larger openings, like those in the last example.

The analogy can be taken further: in cases in which the image pours out, it quickly loses its colour. If we compare the density of the colour with the level of liquid at the bottom of a container, the leaking of the liquid through some hole corresponds to a lowering of its level.

If we place a large drop of quite thick oil on the bottom of a square container, it will momentarily form a disc, or rather a circular blob of a certain thickness. However, almost immediately its edges will move towards those of the container and at the same time it will become flatter: eventually there will be a square of oily matter, less deep than the blob we started with.

Let us see how the analogy works with afterimage colours. Stare at a red disc of a certain diameter for a sufficient amount of time, looking at its centre, without moving your eyes. When the afterimage has formed, move your gaze to the inside of a black, square frame, whose sides are the same length as the diameter of the disc. For a few moments, the afterimage colour has the form of the disc previously observed, and then it starts to spread inside the frame, until it reaches it at all points, all the while losing its colour. The colour, like a liquid, expands, and thus its level decreases.

The same thing happens, of course, if we put a square afterimage inside a circular frame with the same diameter as its diagonal.

The best way to observe how colour settles in the frame is as follows. Draw a coloured patch with an irregular outline, which can fit entirely within the square frame, but which touches it in several places, with some parts protruding from its edges (Figure 15.3).

(15.3, see Plate Section p. 7)

Alternatively, construct a sample of a square of colour and a frame with uneven, irregular sides, able to contain the whole afterimage of the square, and in places touching its sides (Figure 15.4).

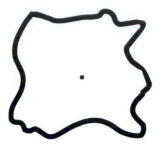

(15.4, see Plate Section p. 7)

(15.5, see Plate Section p. 7)

In these cases, even though the eye is forced to stare at the central point within the frame (marked by a cross or dot), it is easy to follow where the colour penetrates the empty spaces, in some sections spreading quickly, in others more slowly, and meanwhile fading.

Lastly, I will describe a situation that doesn't always work, and indeed that never works for some subjects. But it does sometime work and when it does, it is easy to see. This too can be explained using the liquid analogy already referred to.

Let the primary stimulus – that is, the object to be stared at to obtain the afterimage – be a red square. Its afterimage will then be directed onto a homogeneous surface, covering a quite large section of it; in the area covered by green, two frames are drawn as in the previous cases, but small enough so that the green doesn't just fill them but also surrounds them to a certain extent (Figure 15.5).

Gradually, the image fades, but often it is possible to note that it fades less inside the frame, so that when the image has disappeared, some colour remains inside the frame, while on the rest of the screen there is no trace left of it. This chromatic difference, which can also appear as a difference in the degree of darkness (the internal areas are darker), persists for a few seconds. This happens more easily if the primary stimulus is a bright colour, or, better still, slightly phosphorescent.

2. A "metaphysical" model for afterimage objects

Bishop Berkeley, who confused perception with what happens at the back of the eye, consistently denied that we could perceive the third dimension of visual space: all perceived objects (and *esse est percipi! – to be is to be perceived*) are in the same plane. Just as consistently, he concluded that we only see what has colour. Hume, who fully understood Berkeley's theories, discussing the case of a person partially hidden by a fence or a table, explained to his readers that we "imagine" the legs or other parts of that person which are not visible, or we think of them, or postulate them on the basis of our past experiences of similar cases. If *esse est percipi*, on the basis of this theory, a man who is on the other side of the fence has no legs.

Much very good experimental research and a profound readjustment of the basic concepts have relegated this fallacy to narrow circles of pure psychophysicists, or the depths of the minds of a few philosophers.

There is genuine perception of the hidden parts of objects that are not wholly visible because of some obstacle placed between us and them. The properties of the parts perceived as existing behind the obstacle can be empirically determined, and follow rather strict autonomous rules.

However, even if we are convinced that the actually perceived world consists in large measure of the layerings among things that lie behind other things, and that in turn hide parts of other backgrounds, and for all that we accept that we are able to perceive as present and real those parts of objects whose colour does not reach our eyes, it is very difficult to believe that there can be afterimages of "what has no colour", which is to say, afterimages of these parts.

Yet, at least in certain conditions, which psychologists will have the task of exploring further, it is possible to find examples of afterimages in which the non-exposed parts of a partially hidden object are also represented, which is to say those parts that can be perceived as real on the other side of some obstacle that happens to block them, and whose existence guarantees the integrity of the object.

Let us take four red patches, arranged one next to the other (Figure 15.6). If we stare at a fairly central point of this configuration we obtain an afterimage of four patches in the opposite colour: if they are red in the primary stimulus, the afterimage will then be green.

Now, however, we position in the spaces that separate one patch from another in the primary stimulus, three vertical black sticks that are wide enough to completely cover those spaces (Figure 15.7). Here, in the primary stimulus, we have all the conditions for an amodal completion (as the jargon has it), and indeed no-one fails to see a horizontal strip of a certain width and colour (red) running behind three vertical shapes (black), which prevent some small sections of it being seen.

Having obtained the afterimage of such a structure, it is often possible to perceive the presence of a horizontal, coloured strip presented *as a whole*, which now and again disappears

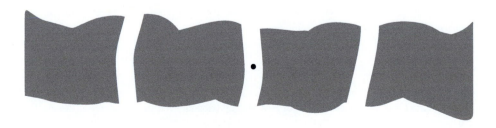

(15.6, see Plate Section p. 8)

(15.7, see Plate Section p. 8)

to be replaced by three vague vertical lines, or by a whole strip in front of which three uncertain light and transparent ghost images hover, or sometimes by a whole strip and nothing else. Very rarely can we see our patches divided from each other, with or without vertical lines.[2]

To take the situation to the extreme (at least in terms of certain hypotheses on retinal processes), green vertical lines can be used – if the four patches are red. By these means, the aim is presumably to excite within the eye an opposite process in the retinal areas corresponding to the intervals between one red patch and the next, and in those corresponding to the red patches themselves. In these conditions and following the logic of retinal processes, the chances of seeing a single horizontal bar should be hindered.

But the experiments carried out with opposing colours give the same results as those carried out with colours that are not opposites of each other, including achromatic black and white. In fact, what have here are afterimages that cannot be interpreted in peripheral terms, but only – possibly – central terms. Which means, in the current state of play, that we must remain vague on the matter.

What can be said in all seriousness is that, after all, the afterimage is an image of what is effectively seen, perceived as existing, phenomenologically real, and not of what falls on the eye or what a photo-sensitive instrument could operationally verify. In the world of direct experience there is something that has that shape, and when only the afterimage of it remains – exactly as in the case of the remembered visual image – it is that form that is preserved. Not what the eye has seen, but what, objectively, has been in front the observer in the act of observation, mother of all things.

Notes

1   The patient experimentation in many of the situations described in this first section is thanks to the skill of Dr. Maria Luisa Vidotto, who also carried out the necessary statistical analyses of the results.
2   Dr. Nicola Bruno, Dr. Cristina Giorgi, Dr. Lidia Martinuzzi, and Dr. Paola Paliaga helped me with these experiments.

COMMENTS ON ORIGINAL OBSERVATIONS ON CERTAIN CHARACTERISTICS OF AFTERIMAGES

Tiziano Agostini and Alessandra Galmonte

The present translation reports one of Paolo Bozzi's enquiries that, in our opinion, is perhaps the one that allows us most fully to appreciate his peculiar approach to the study of visual phenomena, in this case afterimages. Indeed, a sequence of observations highlights his brilliant way of detecting and bringing out the features of this phenomenon, of explaining it in terms of the hydraulic model, and of demonstrating unequivocally, without the aid of sophisticated equipment or statistics, which seems to be essential and inevitable in so much recent research, that afterimages cannot simply be attributed to a low-level explanation, as many visual perception manuals still insist.

The best way to describe afterimages is probably to use the very words used by Paolo Bozzi himself. In the present note to the translation, we make use of direct citation of his original work, because we are convinced that in this way we can grasp his manner of reasoning more clearly. This is why we have decided to speak through his words and, so, through his eyes.

Talking about afterimages, Paolo Bozzi says in Section 1: "This ghost image, the afterimage, is just that, a ghost, for all that it is visible and sometimes – at the beginning – very visible indeed. It is unlikely that someone should mistake this extra coloured shape for an object that can be grasped: as well as having the qualities of its shape and colour, it also has the quality of being an *appearance* (. . .) we may say that it has "the appearance of appearance", the feature of being unreal. This unreality becomes more acute as the seconds pass, because the colour – of itself already diaphanous – tends to pale and seems to dissipate, while the outline (. . .) [becomes] uncertain as well as blurred (. . .) Despite these ethereal properties, the afterimage is usually easy to describe. (. . .) its shape and the way in which it changes can be described, as can its size in relation to other objects, how long it stays and for how long it is gone, what its position is in relation to the plane of observation, and so on."

Da Pos (1996) states that the few occasions that reveal to lay persons the existence of afterimages are those in which, after intense visual stimulation, such as staring at the sun or other particularly strong light sources, persistent bright or dark spots come into view. Ordinary people probably consider afterimages as a perceptual effect of no particular interest, if not an inconvenience; let's simply think of the common phenomenon of visual disturbance that arises after fixating on the sun for a little while: as a result, for some seconds, a small dark dot will appear superimposed on our visual environment and will follow our gaze. On the contrary, they have been receiving the specific attention of vision scientists for centuries.

The first attempts to study afterimages systematically were made by eminent scientists such Mueller (1842), Fechner (1840), Helmholtz (1866, 1924), to name but a few. Richard Gregory (1987) offers a definition of afterimage that, with variations, it is quite common to find in psychology manuals: "An image seen immediately after the intense stimulation of the eye by light has ceased. For about a second, the afterimage is 'positive', and then it turns to 'negative', often with fleeting colours. The positive phase is due to after-discharge of the receptors of the eye; the negative phase is caused by loss of sensitivity of the receptors as a result of bleaching of the photo-pigments by the intense light" (p. 13).

However, this definition is oversimplified. In the first place, it mentions only one of the many possible ways in which we can experience afterimages; that is, the situation that commonly occurs in the immediate aftermath of seeing a bright light such as the sun, or a camera flash. But it is possible to perceive afterimages also after staring for some time at an ordinarily illuminated object, as is clearly shown in all Bozzi's illustrations in the present article.

Moreover, in subjects with strong visual imaginations, afterimages can be evoked by merely imagining stimuli (James, 1890; Weiskrantz, 1950; Oswald, 1957), or also following vivid dreams (Gruithuisen, 1812; Alexander, 1904; Oswald, 1957), therefore in absence of light stimulation.

And, maybe most important, the "locus of the processes that give rise to afterimages has been the subject of an entertaining controversy for a very long time" (Kolehmainen and Tuomisaar, 1969). Afterimages are usually explained by reference to the fact that when the eyes' photoreceptors adapt to overstimulation they lose sensitivity. Normally, the images are constantly moved to a fresh area of the retina with small eye movements. But, if the eye remains too steady, the photoreceptors that are constantly exposed to the same stimulus will eventually exhaust their supply of photopigment, resulting in a decrease in their signal to the brain. Afterimages are of the complementary hue of the adapting stimulus. The opponent-process theory maintains that the human visual system interprets colour information by processing signals from photoreceptors in an antagonistic manner. The opponent colour theory suggests that there are three opponent channels: red vs green, blue vs yellow, and black vs white. Responses to one colour of an opponent channel are antagonistic to those to the other colour. Therefore, a green image will produce a magenta afterimage. The green colour fatigues the green photoreceptors, so they produce a weaker signal; i.e., anything resulting in less green is interpreted as its paired primary colour, which is magenta.

There is growing substantial evidence in the literature that afterimages cannot be accounted for solely as a photochemical process (e.g., Craik, 1940; Brindley 1962). Even if, of course, at least in certain cases, neural adaptation in the retina constitutes an essential part of the process (e.g., Loomis, 1972; Virsu and Laurinen, 1977), a number of more recent findings show a significant cortical involvement in the formation of afterimages (e.g., Shimojo et al., 2001; Suzuki and Grabowecky, 2003; Gilroy and Blake, 2005). These findings bear on the issues below since, as we argue, many sensationalists implicitly cleave to an out-dated, purely photochemical conception of afterimages.

It is then especially remarkable and right and proper to notice that, in this 1989 essay here translated, Paolo Bozzi already said: "In fact, what have here are afterimages that cannot be interpreted in peripheral terms, but only – possibly – central terms. Which means, in the current state of play, that we must remain vague on the matter." (p. 340 in the present anthology).

At this stage, a reasonable question that could arise is why study afterimages, especially from the viewpoint of a vision scientist. The answer is quite simple, Paolo Bozzi would probably say; that is, because, being visual facts, they can help us to understand how the visual system works. Afterimages are, de facto, illusory phenomena, and illusions are certainly important for theories about perception, since they help us to understand the normal functioning of the perceptual system. Indeed, cases in which there is no correspondence between perceptual reality and physical reality are more informative for discovering the laws of normal perception processes. Baldwin (1895) asserted that the study of illusions is as important for the understanding of normal perception as the study of pathologies is for the comprehension of the body's normal functioning in medicine. Moreover, illusions are useful tools for testing existing theories, comparing different theories, suggesting new experiments and new explanations, and finally for finding new illusions.

But, we might ask ourselves, why did afterimages become an object of interest for Paolo Bozzi? Reading his works carefully, we might reasonably suppose that his intrinsic curiosity, which shines through all his texts, was stimulated by the idea of making an *"appearance"* interact with *"the appearance of appearance"*. Coming back again to his words: "What happens in the brief life of an afterimage can in part depend upon its surroundings. We should bear in mind that, from an abstract and model-building point of view, the image only exists in the eye and the brain. In actual fact, it is to be found among the objects that fill the field of our direct observations. Of course, everything can be referred back to those abstractions and models, but to do so, we should have to go and look at what happens in direct observation, when the image is made to interact with other visual events." (p. 335 in the present anthology).

Overall then, what emerges from Paolo Bozzi's observations reported in this article, is that "the afterimage is an image of what is effectively seen, perceived as existing, phenomeno-logically real, and not of what falls on the eye or what a photo-sensitive instrument could operationally verify. (. . .) [the afterimage] – exactly as in the case of the remembered visual image – (. . .) [is] Not what the eye has seen, but what, objectively, has been in front the observer in the act of observation, mother of all things." (p. 340 in the present anthology).

Paolo Bozzi's experimental journey through afterimages represents, then, a path that leads us, by way of the shrewd observations and experimental configurations that he proposed, not only to catch very relevant insights about the nature of this phenomenon, but also to precious information about his way of arguing over perceptual facts.

References

Alexander, H.B. (1904). Some observations on visual imagery. *Psychological Review, 11,* 319–37.

Baldwin, J.M. (1895). The effect of size–contrast upon judgements of position in the retinal field. *Psychological Review, 2,* 244–259.

Bozzi, P. (1989). Osservazioni inedite su certe peculiarità delle immagini consecutive. In A. Garau, Pensiero e visione in Rudolf Arnheim (pp. 28–37), Milan, Italy: Franco Angeli. Re-published in Bozzi, P. (1993). *Experimenta in Visu. Ricerche sulla percezione [Experimenta in visu: Inquiries into Perception]* (pp. 221–230). Milan: Italy: Guerini e Associati. [Chapter 15 in the present anthology]

Brindley, G.S. (1962). Two new properties of foveal after-images and a photochemical hypothesis to explain them. *Journal of Physiology, 164*, 168–179.

Craik, W. J.K. (1940). Origin of afterimages. *Nature, 148*, 512.

Da Pos, O. (1996). I colori e le loro immagini postume. In P. Boscolo, F. Cristante, A. Dellantonio, and S. Soresi (Eds). *Aspetti Qualitativi e Quantitativi nella Ricerca Psicologica* (pp. 237–251). Padua, Italy: Il Poligrafo.

Fechner, G.T. (1840). Ueber die subjectiven Nachbilder und Nebenbilder. *Annalen der Physik und Chemie, 40*, 193–221.

Gilroy, L.A. and Blake, R. (2005). The interaction between binocular rivalry and negative afterimages. *Current Biology, 15*, 1740–1744.

Gregory, R.L. (1987). *The Oxford Companion to The Mind*. Oxford: Oxford University Press.

Gruithuisen, F.V.P. (1812). *Beytraege zur Physiognosie und Eautongnosie, fuer Freunde der Naturforshung auf dem Erfahrungswege*. Munich, Germany: I. J. Lentner.

Helmholtz, H. von (1866). Concerning the perceptions in general. In *Treatise on Physiological Optics*, vol. III, 3rd edn. (trans. J. P. C. Southall, 1925, *Optical Society of America*. Section 26, reprinted New York: Dover, 1962).

Helmholtz, H. von (1924). Mechanism of accommodation. In J.P.C. Southall (ed.). *Helmholtz's Treatise on Physiological Optics* (pp. 143–173). New York: The Optical Society of America (trans. from the 3rd German edition, 1909).

James, W. (1890). *The Principles of Psychology*. Cambridge, MA: Harvard University Press.

Kolehmainen, K. and Tuomisaari, R. (1969). The locus of visual afterimages. *Scandinavian Journal of Psychology, 10*, 45–48.

Mueller, J. (1842). *Elements of Physiology*. London: Taylor & Walton.

Oswald, I. (1957). After-images from retina and brain. *Quarterly Journal of Experimental Psychology, 9*, 88–100.

Shimojo, S., Kamitani, Y., and Nishida, S. (2001). Afterimage of perceptually filled-in surface. *Science, 293*, 1677–1680.

Suzuki, S., and Grabowecky, M. (2003). Attention during adaptation weakens negative afterimages. *Journal of Experimental Psychology: Human Perception & Performance, 29*, 793–807.

Virsu, V. and Laurinen, P. (1977). Long-lasting afterimages caused by neural adaptation. *Vision Research, 17*, 853–860.

Weiskrantz, L. (1950). An unusual case of after-imagery following fixation of an "imaginary" visual pattern. *Quarterly Journal of Experimental Psychology, 2*, 170–175.

16

TERTIARY QUALITIES

Translated by Ian Verstegen and Carlo Maria Fossaluzza

Anyone who has attended a good high school knows the distinction made by philosophers, first in antiquity by the atomists but then proposed with new arguments by Galileo and finely dissected by the English empiricists to the point of disintegration, between the primary and the secondary qualities present in that objects that populate our world.

On the one hand there is the real object, that which exists indifferent to the gaze of an observer and the same as itself even when no-one is looking at it. The properties that it possesses have to do with solidity, extension, weight, form, size, motion. These are *primary* qualities.

On the other hand there is the object's appearance, as it is often and even today improperly called, made up of attributes that derive from the relationship between a complex of primary qualities and an observer, such as a fly or a man, equipped with some sensory apparatus. The qualities of appearance are *secondary*, not least because they vary with the variation of the states of the possessor of the perceptual apparatus but also because they are placed within it and not in the space that contains real objects, and therefore only primary qualities. Nothing could be clearer.

The ancients were even more radical. "We know nothing accurately in reality, but (only) as it changes according to our bodily condition, and the constitution of those things that flow upon (the body) and impinge upon it", writes Democritus.[1] The objective world, stable and eternal, on the other hand is in fact only atoms in movement in a void. Galen comments: "People think of things as being white and black and sweet and bitter and all the other qualities of that kind, but in truth 'thing' and 'nothing' is all there is. That too is something [Democritus] himself said, 'thing' being his name for the atoms and 'nothing' for the void. All the atoms are small bodies without qualities, and the void is a space in which all these bodies move up and down forever" and adds "none of them becomes hot or cold, or dry or wet, much less turns black or white or suffers any qualitative change of any kind."[2] Aristotle reports that they can have only a given form or shape, a certain position in respect to the spatial coordinates and a certain order in the connections that associate them.[3] They are constituted exclusively by primary qualities, and are subject to motions that continually agitate them in empty space.

On this point it is worth reading Galileo. Allow me to quote a long section from *The Assayer* because, if it is Democritus' merit to have seen the problem with scientific lucidity for the first time, framing it in a form that not even today can be circumvented in spite of the growth of the physical sciences and of the psychology of perception, it is no less Galileo's merit to have expressed it in a very effective literary manner with prose that in places approaches the Leopardi of the *Operette morali*. And in real science the quality of expression goes hand in hand with the quality of thought. Galileo writes then,

I say that whenever I conceive any material or corporeal substance, I immediately feel the need to think of it as bounded, and as having this or that shape; as being large or small in relation to other things, and in some specific place at any given time; as being in motion or at rest; as touching or not touching some other body; and as being one in number, or few, or many. From these conditions I cannot separate such a substance by any stretch of my imagination. But that it must be white or red, bitter or sweet, noisy or silent, and of sweet or foul odour, my mind does not feel compelled to bring in as necessary accompaniments. Without the senses as our guides, reason or imagination unaided would probably never arrive at qualities like these. Hence I think that tastes, odours, colours, and so on are no more than mere names so far as the object in which we place them is concerned, and that they reside only in the consciousness. Hence if the living creature were removed, all these qualities would be wiped away and annihilated (. . .) A body which is solid and, so to speak, quite material, when moved in contact with any part of my person produces in me the sensation we call touch. This, though it exists over my entire body, seems to reside principally in the palms of the hands and in the finger tips, by whose means we sense the most minute differences in texture that are not easily distinguished by other parts of our bodies. Some of these sensations are more pleasant to us than others. (. . .) The sense of touch is more material than the other senses; and, as it arises from the solidity of matter, it seems to be related to the earthly element. Perhaps the origin of two other senses lies in the fact that there are bodies which constantly dissolve into minute particles, some of which are heavier than air and descend, while others are lighter and rise up. The former may strike upon a certain part of our bodies that is much more sensitive than the skin, which does not feel the invasion of such subtle matter. This is the upper surface of the tongue; here the tiny particles are received, and mixing with and penetrating its moisture, they give rise to tastes, which are sweet or unsavory according to the various shapes, numbers, and speeds of the particles. And those minute particles which rise up may enter by our nostrils and strike upon some small protuberances which are the instrument of smelling; here likewise their touch and passage is received to our like or dislike according as they have this or that shape, are fast or slow, and are numerous or few (. . .). Then there remains the air itself, an element available for sounds, which come to us indifferently from below, above, and all sides – for we reside in the air and its movements displace it equally in all directions. The location of the ear is most fittingly accommodated to all positions in space. Sounds are made and heard by us when the air without any special property of "sonority" or "transonority" – is ruffled by a rapid tremor into very minute waves and moves certain cartilages of a tympanum in our ear. External means capable of thus ruffling the air are very numerous, but for the most part they may be reduced to the trembling of some body which pushes the air and disturbs it. Waves are propagated very rapidly in this way, and high tones are produced by frequent waves and low tones by sparse ones. To excite in us tastes, odours, and sounds I believe that nothing is required in external bodies except shapes, numbers, and slow or rapid movements. I think that if ears, tongues, and noses were removed, shapes and numbers and motions would remain, but not odours or tastes or sounds. The latter, I believe, are nothing more than names when separated from living beings, just as tickling and titillation are nothing but names in the absence of such things as noses and armpits.[4]

The sharp cut made between primary and secondary qualities is an operation of the highest surgery. It has to be made with severity and expertise because it cleanses many of the pollutants that normally obstruct the recognition of where the realm of direct observation ends and that of theorization, of conceptual schemes, of conjectures and imagination begins. And it must be repeated in each new age of science because facts and conjectures multiply from one paradigm to the next as knowledge advances.

Each time, this cut must be followed by an operation of reconstruction so that half of the world will not end up cut off from the other and wandering off as an unrecoverable *noumenon*. We do not want to be left on this side, with our sensations and impressions, while the atoms with their shapes, sizes and connections are lost in the void. Science needs to keep its hands on the whole of reality, even when it is making the most radical cuts on it.

It is worth saying that already Theophrastus, disciple of Aristotle and an original scientific thinker (even if he passes for a doxographer, as if his job were to preserve for posterity the opinions of others) sewed the first stitches. He found it strange that if each sensation is explained in terms of a special kind of atom (spiky atomic shapes produce an acid taste; sweet is made up of roundish particles, not too small, etc.), one could then say that sensations are false and merely apparent because different creatures sense the same atoms in different ways. He found problematic the fact that "Even if the same object doesn't produce in all the people the same sensation of sweet or bitter, it is sure that all the people conceive in the same way the nature of the sweet and of the bitter" (Diels–Kranz 1985, 68A135). And he asked in the end whether good logic doesn't want either to deny objective reality to all objects or to concede it also to all sensible qualities given that those like these – as is admitted – are states of matter and on a par with it. Not decisive objections perhaps, but interesting and full of consequences.

The reader will not have failed to notice the kind of vocabulary that Galileo employs in introducing his arguments. He says, "whenever I *conceive* any material or corporeal substance, I immediately feel the need to *think* of it as bounded, and as having this or that shape."[5] "Conceive" a corporeal substance: not observe it but think of it (perhaps imagine it); this is working with logic upon an idea. In fact, he says, "I immediately feel the need to think of it", that type of need that obliges us to conclude something from something, because that need is enclosed in the conceptual representation like the mechanism of an ingenious toy, and requires the play of our imagination and fantasy. Galileo does not find primary qualities in the realm of physical things, nor the bonds that connect them so as to generate secondary qualities: he obviously lives like the rest of us in the midst of observed things, and hence in the context of the secondary qualities.

He lives there so successfully – the reader will notice – that he sometimes forgets the severity of his dichotomy to the point of admitting distractedly (or not?) that real objects are here among us despite the deception of the senses. In a footnote annotation to the *Dianoia Astronomica, Optica, Physica* of his opponent, Franciscus Sitius, Galileo writes, "Hasn't experience perhaps already taught us that vision is not fooled at close distances, when getting closer to objects, we know that they are truly as they appear?" There is a mass of vital tissue that the delicate surgery has not succeeded in removing even when the scalpel goes deep.

Something similar happens also in Berkeley's *Three Dialogues between Hylas and Philonous* as well as in the pages of Locke. Hume is perfectly aware of this when he writes:

It is universally allowed by modern enquirers, that all the sensible qualities of objects, such as hard, soft, hot, cold, white, black, etc. are merely secondary, and exist not in the objects themselves, but are perceptions of the mind, without any external archetype or model, which they represent. If this be allowed, with regard to secondary qualities, it must also follow, with regard to the supposed primary qualities of extension and solidity; nor can the latter be any more entitled to that denomination than the former. The idea of extension is entirely acquired from the senses of sight and feeling; and if all the qualities, perceived by the senses, be in the mind, not in the object, the same conclusion must reach the idea of extension, which is wholly dependent on the sensible ideas or the ideas of secondary qualities. Nothing can save us from this conclusion, but the asserting, that the ideas of those primary qualities are attained by *Abstraction*, an opinion, which, if we examine it accurately, we shall find to be unintelligible, and even absurd. An extension, that is neither tangible nor visible, cannot possibly be conceived: and a tangible or visible extension, which is neither hard nor soft, black nor white, is equally beyond the reach of human conception.[6]

Relative to Galileo and the Atomists, Hume's way of putting things, with his usual flat and unadorned style, as if, instead of setting off a revolution, he was merely recounting a curious anecdote (he nevertheless in a note at the end of this paragraph acknowledges his debts to Berkeley), executes two conceptual inversions.

The first inversion consists in inverting, across the entire problem, the position of the "explanans" relative to the "explanandum". In Democritus and in Galileo, the complexes of primary qualities are what give rise to the secondary properties; in the new version, the primary qualities derive from the secondary qualities; indeed, because they too are secondary in the full sense, they form part of that totality of observables from which we obtain both the notion of primary quality and that of secondary quality.

The second inversion is the following: once we have recognized that the hardness, the weight, the shape and the position of objects are not less empirically given than their colour, taste and smell, we discover that the former class of properties is inextricable from the latter: the triangularity of an object completely stripped of other tactile or visual attributes is unimaginable; nor is its position in space imaginable without a bunch of secondary qualities suitable to let us discriminate it in some way from the surrounding environment. In such attempts it is possible to reach a high level of abstraction, but any primary quality that is picked out in this way becomes a progressively more abstract affair, and so less concrete, despite the Democritean requirement that makes only atoms (with their shapes and positions) and void real. The primary qualities in a strict sense are pure abstractions.

These two inversions carry a very high price for Hume's theoretical proposal and for that of the classical empiricists in general: the whole universe reduces itself to the subjectivity of the sensing subject. The indiscriminate use of the English word "idea", applied both to the events of the actual observables and to the representations in imagination and in thought, leads to this unavoidable slide toward the nothingness of the empirical subject (of which, nevertheless, many readers approve; we should not hide from ourselves the fact that subjective idealism of the most common sort – and maybe even other sorts – satisfies certain yearnings for total egocentricity). We must make an effort to extract Hume's argument from the ideological quagmire into which it sinks at the end of that slide.

That effort would need to be set out in many arduous pages, probably of a whole book. Instead of recounting the complicated rescue of objective reality along with the secondary qualities, we offer the reader three theoretical possibilities, according to taste.

Readers disposed to solipsism may assume that in their world of sensations there's enough to have an idea both of primary qualities and of secondary: for them it is a classification carried out on materials to hand, which doesn't imply the existence of two ontological spaces, and that on occasion may even work well, without cracking open the solitude of its users.

Incorrigibly realist readers (like the present author) may assume that the incredibly rich world of observables, omnipresent and under everybody's eyes precisely because it can be seen from innumerable perspectives, and quite independent of the solipsistic urges of more neurotic subjects, has a finite but extremely vast number of ascertainable features, running from the most fugitive and shadowy aspects of perceptual experience to the more solid and stable supporting structures, which are "perceptions" only out of bad linguistic habit, but are rather unquestionable and hard facts. They are quite independent of anyone who knocks into them, and are fully explorable when they are placed under observation.

Dualist readers will enjoy the maximum of benefits with the only expense of two worlds for the price of one. On the one hand, there is the universe of primary qualities, which for the contemporary man is nothing but the world described by physics and by the sciences which refer to it in one way or another: within it there is everything that can be described using the language of physics and of those other sciences, including the brain of anyone who holds the dualistic belief, as well as that of everyone who adopts the other possible theses. On the other hand, there is the universe of direct ascertainings, which, in this case can be unashamedly called the "psychic world", which contains perceptions such as thoughts, memories and imaginings and, in short, everything that ascertainably happens.

Irrespective of the chosen assumption, however, it will be possible to find a convincing interpretation of the empiricist argument, and at the same time to give a well-defined sense to the distinction that separates the primary qualities from the secondary. The convincing interpretation of the empiricist argument can be found in the laboratory. If somebody believes that, unlike the primary qualities, the secondary qualities (colour, taste, sound, etc.) are subject – insofar as they are features directly observable in reality – to "illusions" or to interferences with the observational activities of the subject, and that the primary qualities are not so subject, s/he's wrong.

A single colour (a colour, that is, that displays constant properties in terms of appropriate physical measurements) appears lighter on dark backgrounds and darker on light backgrounds, more milky if its contours are hazy, and variously transformed if the observer has just been looking for a long time at another colour. As for tastes, everybody knows how they change because of other tastes, or because of spoilt mouth. A sound just heard in a particular melodic or harmonic context can now not appear as such, for instance after a modulation; and a sound well localized in front of us thanks to a suitable stereo can, with few turns of the control knob, be localized even in the centre of our head.

If these circumstances, which are just a little bit out of the ordinary relative to the expectations of common sense, cast a shadow of relativity on the secondary qualities, other circumstances will show us that primary qualities are subject to the same vagaries of conditions.

Let's take motion, indeed, the particular case of velocity. If in front of your eyes a movable object travels in a constant speed along a rectilinear horizontal trajectory perpendicular to the direction of your gaze, as long as you follow it with your eyes it will appear to you to travel at a certain speed, but as soon as you fixate on a stationary point and allow the object to cross your field of vision, it suddenly will go much faster. Another example of a primary quality subject, so to speak, to "illusion", a primary quality that comes to depend on how observers uses their eyes, is represented by the Brown effect. If spectators are allowed to modify the speed of one of two processions of disks until it appears to them equal to that of the other, they will discover that the equivalence of the two seen speeds is in direct relation to the diameters of the disks (Brown 1931, p. 199 ff.).

Motion itself, in any case, is a terribly secondary "appearance", considered in itself and for itself: one need only switch on and off alternately two small sources of light placed at a short distance one from the other and perfectly stationary, to have under one's eyes a good motion of coming and going, provided that certain onset times in relation with the intensity of the sources are respected.

Regarding position, understood as a system of relations between points in the space – which is the sense that underlies Democritus' atomistic account – it is sufficient merely to look briefly at the Necker cube to discover that the ways that observers set themselves to look can upset the relations existing between the vertices of the cube and the corresponding points in the surrounding space, and therefore the arrangement of the cube relative to the observer. (It is even better to look at a luminescent Necker cube in the dark: in these conditions my statement becomes absolutely literal).

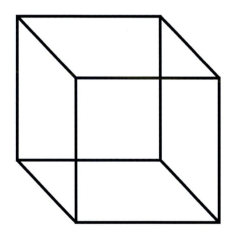

(16.1)

Regarding visual forms, we recall here the well-known young–old woman that was often object of Wittgenstein's reflections, and the fact that one of the most important schools of scientific psychology of the twentieth century takes its name from "form" (*Gestalt*), an observable entity depending on a myriad of phenomenological conditions, that it is completely impossible to explain from a naïvely physicalistic point of view, except by way of vague analogies. Nor shall we find any support for primary qualities in Democritus' and Galileo's sense in those forms revealed through touch: there is a whole literature on the "illusions" of tactile perception, which begins with the discovery, maybe by Aristotle, of certain peculiar alterations of spatial relations in the objects explored with crossed fingers. It is astonishing that many scholars, across the centuries, have believed that tactile exploration of the external world is able to remove the ambiguity of visual tricks.

Primary qualities and secondary qualities, as facts accessible to observation, present analogous complexities in their genesis (under the eyes of the observer), in their internal mechanics, in their sensitivity to influences from the perceived environment, and to strategies of observation. Were Hume to visit our laboratories (but also had he visited Wundt's at the end of the nineteenth century) he would be quite satisfied, and would be tempted to say the deplorable sentence, "I told you so!"

We can affirm with certainty, then, that as much colours, sounds, tastes, etc. as the motion, form, weight, and the position of objects in the space of our ineluctable experience, depend on many conditions that at first are not easy to imagine, tending as we do to oversimplify the appearances of the objects that make up the ordinary ascertainable world, because we aim to act in it swiftly and appropriately.

Normally we have in our heads simulacra of objects, schemes of events, shadows of the qualities of things, stereotyped models of facts and happenings, which enable us to speak appropriately about everything and to plan movements and actions. They are very efficient summaries whose formation follows a ruthless principle of least action (the fewest possible articulations, the fewest possible functional dependences, the least variability, etc.), restricted only by failures to negotiate the things in the world. When we think we are reasoning about objects, we are really reasoning about ghosts of things. For the only way to think about them is not to recall them to the mind, but to construct logical networks while observing them attentively, and to introduce systematic variations in their constitution and in our explorative act.

When I prepare a cup of coffee it is completely useless for me to pose problems concerning the tactile and visual three-dimensionality of the cup, the constancy of its form through its perspective transformations, the paradox of the warm hand and of the cold hand that dunked in the water makes one feel the water cold to one side and warm to the other, the spatial localization of the sputter that the coffee pot makes when it comes to the boil, or the slight quivering of the objects seen through the hot air above the coffee maker. I manipulate more or less distractedly a summary of cup and of coffee and of coffee maker to get to the end of the operation. Only if I put aside my momentary aims and I begin to observe my objects, to pose problems about what I see or touch or that burns, and to look for answers in the observations and conjectures about it that I really have to do with their reality.

In the universe of those summaries it is not difficult to position the primary qualities on one side, following Galileo's beautiful description, and the secondary on the other, with clearly distinct ontological characteristics (and such representations can be very useful for thousands of purposes). But when we move from the summaries to the works, that is the things, all the observable qualities become interwoven, which creates plenty of problems and confuses the distinctions to the point of forcing us, little by little and by way of a sequence of tricks thought up and put to work, to transform our kitchen, or our bedroom into a laboratory. The lab is after all an absolutely normal place in which certain things have been prepared and modified in order to answer to questions. Therefore, we agree with Hume in his critique of the distinction. But the problem remains.

Even after the distinction has been abolished, certain features of things continue to appear much more primary than others. Cancelled on the ontological level, the distinction returns on the phenomenological one, precisely in the field of those observations and tests that had destroyed it.

If I slowly circle around my table, carefully observing it, its colour doesn't change under my eyes: but the reflections of its surface vary with my movement, and certain shadows that earlier fell on a certain part of it now are in a different position. The visible qualities of its surface relating to the lightness, darkness, light and shadow, both change and don't change at the same time: the colour itself, the paint, remains constant, while the other elements undergo transformations related to my position.

Yet that which remains completely constant is the form of the table, its massiveness, the block of material distributed in this specific way, its size and the relation between its dimensions: for all that I go around and around it, I cannot observe any important variation in that.

I will limit myself to ascertaining this, but already this ascertaining reconstitutes the distinction between primary and secondary qualities. "You will see that there is something in this", wrote Berkeley, "if you recall the distinction you made between moderate heat and intense heat, allowing one a real existence outside the mind while denying it to the other" (Berkeley 1977, *Three Dialogues*, I, p. 174). There are complexes of qualities that in a certain way safeguard the stability of the world, others that show themselves to be more yielding or relativizable. At the same time, I can think that "beyond" them there are also the true primary qualities, the ultimate cause of my sensations; or I can think that those qualities don't exist at all, and the whole world is made up of sensations and nothing else; and finally, I can think that the true primary qualities, excepting imaginations, are truly those structures more permanently observable that form at every moment the scenery of the world, the state of motion or rest of objects, and so on. Drawing upon now outdated language, we can truly say that position in space, the solidity and the motion of objects, are *lived* as primary qualities of the furniture of experience. The distinction, expelled through the door, has come back in through the window. A good perceptual psychologist cannot give up distinguishing the levels of the "characteristics of reality" that observable things possess, and so discovers that the classic distinction, instead of being a basis for the explanation of experience, is without doubt the origin of new problems for Experimental Phenomenology.

Now that we have found a place in broad daylight both for primary qualities and for secondary, and precisely because this operation forced us to improve our gaze, it will be not hard to see the need to find a place also for certain other qualities that are observable in things and events, and that are not reducible to the two already well-known categories of qualities.

A certain English-speaking tradition, later revived by the Gestalt psychologists, speaks of "tertiary qualities". If the secondary qualities appear as such because they are less anchored in the outer object than the primary, and somehow perceptibly linked to the observers and to their modes of observing, tertiary qualities seem to find their roots in the most inner resonating chambers of the sensing subject, even though they too appear spatially located in external things. Once[7] the Prague psychologist Max Wertheimer said: "black is gloomy even before being black." Tertiary qualities are strongly present in the bits of world with which we have to deal, even if it is not so easy to define their nature and to find their basis.

If black is gloomy, red is lively. The shadow of a great green tree is soothing and relaxing. A diminished-seventh chord is sharp and anxious. A slow and rising gesture is hieratic. Here we aren't limiting ourselves to arbitrarily bestowing stereotyped adjectives to mere facts; in those facts there are truly characteristics that magnetically attract those adjectives, and those characteristics are not of a verbal or associative nature, but perceptual ingredients present within the facts themselves. Those ingredients emerge from facts in immediate evidence as soon as those facts are removed from the limbo of evocations realized in words to become embodied in flesh and blood within the field of our observation. "Each thing says what it is", wrote Kurt Koffka, ". . . a fruit says 'eat me'; the water says 'drink me'; the thunder says 'fear me'; and a woman says 'love me'." (Koffka, 1935).

And J.J. Gibson comments: "These values are vivid and essential features of the experience itself. Koffka did not believe [and Gibson was Koffka's former student] that a meaning of this sort could be explained as a pale context of memory images or an unconscious set of response tendencies . . . the handle 'wants to be grasped' and things 'tell us what to do with them'." (Gibson 1979, p. 138). Tertiary qualities range from the low sexual arousal engendered by effective pornography to Morgenstein's airy verse: "Seagulls by their looks suggest that Emma is their name" (*Die Moewen sehen alle aus, als ob sie Emma hiessen*) (1963, p. 85).[8]

Naturally, an explanation for these shivers of meaning present within things immediately comes to mind: everything arises by dint of associations. The fact that a smell is sometimes able vividly to evoke a distant episode of our life, or that a phone number makes us think of a pleasant voice – or the fact that we learnt through difficult memorization a foreign language and now we are able to enjoy the expressivity of its words as if the sound were the natural bearer of meaning – easily induces us to believe in the following explanatory stereotype: every characteristic of objects that is not reducible to the raw play of sensorial stimuli (whatever that means) is the fruit of association. I see red, and I associate it with the liveliness of a woman who fifty years ago wore a dress of that colour; I hear the diminished seventh chord and I remember its tormenting and horrifying role in the narrated events of such and such an opera; the green reminds me of that tree under which I used to fall asleep when I was a child; a slow and rising gesture reminds me of a moment of the Mass celebrated by the parish priest of my village, seen from the height of the organ loft; and so on.

Of course this kind of stereotype doesn't explain anything, as would expect, because we are dealing with a stereotype. That sometimes one thing comes to mind because of another is an obvious fact, but it is just a fact, not an explanation of anything. This doesn't mean of course that every quality encountered in things is there where we are able to catch sight of it because of some association. Maybe we don't need to have taken many punches in the face to make our head jerk back when a body of a certain consistency approaches our nose very fast. Certainly we don't need to have had many sexual experiences to suddenly discover, during adolescence or thereabouts, how the charm of female schoolmates is delicately traced along the shape of their limbs and in their gestures. It is also worth asking ourselves whether the hysterical features of the diminished seventh chord can be attached to it just because that set of notes, by pure chance, was introduced as commentary to those upsetting scenes; and then by association it became that chord that it is and is officially acknowledged as such in musical semantics.

But it is also possible to think that the chord in question is made just that way as a matter of acoustics: instead of offering itself to be heard as a "devil in music" (*diabolus in musica*; what a name for the augmented fourth!) woven more than once through the minor thirds, the bunch of notes sounds as a whole like scratching metal: and it is precisely because of this feature, which is not in the least associative, that it perfectly suits as a commentary for something horrifying, just as a long perfect fifth serves to give rise to a stable and cold transparency. Maybe red is chosen because it is lively, and is used to make clothes for the summer holidays, and not the other way round.

Some years ago in a shop in Trieste a very young small yellow parrot was sold. It had been born in captivity and fed with the foods that the same shop sells pre-packaged for captive parrots. The life experiences of that animal were presumably in conformity with the events of its environment, a not very eventful corner of the shop inhabited by some other parrots of the same type. It was not allowed to enrich its experience during the journey between the place of origin and its new home, because it was forced to undergo this journey in a small cardboard box equipped with a few holes, moreover placed in a plastic bag.

In its new residence the parrot saw what is normally to be seen in a large kitchen from a spacious cage hanging a metre and a half from the ground. I don't know how many associations the parrot had formed on the empirical bases that I have described. They must have been limited to a very small number.

After three or four years living in that place of observation the parrot was subjected to an unusual experience. One day the owner of the house bought a live lobster and, when he was about to boil it, as the recipe requires, thought to bring it closer, holding one of its main appendages with two fingers, to the cage of the unlucky bird. Which, as soon as it saw the other animal frantically moving its free appendages in all directions, had from this sight such a great panic that it repeatedly and violently pounded its head and other parts of its body against the cage to the point of losing some big feathers from its beautiful tail. It was in visible terror, in which I was directly implicated. The parrot didn't know tales of horrible and evil animals with many appendages, nor had it been attacked by big spiders, one supposes. Of course it is a good thing that its ancestors, whenever they lived, feared self-propelled things made up of a central form with moving appendages around it. I think it highly unlikely for any animal to regard with equanimity the approach of a creature with waving appendages sticking out in all directions. Directors of horror movies know really well how to make use of these kind of appendages, and their shadows too.

Obviously, I have presented a rather curious case. But it is in cases like these that the thesis of association becomes noticeably weak. On the other hand, these very cases force us to meditate on the immediateness of perceptual properties of events that lend themselves to being described as "terrifying" (or, according to the case, "very sweet"); these are properties located in the object, and so located in the same place within perceptual space as the other properties, both primary and secondary, of the object in question.

It is important to emphasize this last point. It is true that terror lives within us, when we are gripped by it; our bodily schema is directly affected by it: the chest is so constricted as to make breathing difficult, a shudder runs across the skin ("My hair stands on end") and the throat tightens. But it is equally true that the object that is the cause of the terror is *itself* terrifying: its features are immediately seen as the direct cause for our agitation; we would like that very object, and not another one, removed from our environment to feel relief. Sometimes the tertiary quality is only in the object, and our feelings, on the contrary, are at the opposite extreme. Let's suppose we go to a nice and really cheerful party with friends and I am in a really bad mood, a mix of depression, sadness and irritation. We cannot help seeing the jollity and the euphoria, not only on their faces and in their gestures, but even in the disposition of the objects in the room and in the play of the lights and the shadows, in the vivacity of the scene in its context. All of that could even increase our sadness, our bad mood; sometimes the happiness of others can have a taste of evil provocation.

Our ability to read the true features of that widespread lightheartedness in that environment and in the people does not depend on our mood; tertiary qualities do not have their origin there. We don't project our inner anxiety onto the colours of the world: if that happiness is annoying to us it is exactly because we see it as happiness.

We have talked about these considerations at such length to prepare readers for Gibson's thesis, which is as extreme in the objectivistic direction as good common sense is inclined to be through-and-through subjectivist. Gibson says in very certain terms that information contained in reflected light, which is to say in the beam of luminous rays that reaches the eyes of viewers brings with it tertiary qualities, which he prefers to call "*affordances*".[9] According to Plutarch, Favorinus said the same thing: "The images come to us unceasingly from all directions, detaching themselves from movables, from clothes, from trees, and above all from living beings . . . and not only present the similarities of form with the body of which they retain the imprint . . . but also hold and bear within themselves the appearances of the motion of the soul . . . and of dispositions and passions . . ." (Diels-Kranz 1985, 68A77). The affordances are in the *experienced* objects just like colour, shape, motion and sound. They are definitely not projections of moods or targets of associations.

In all likelihood, a randomly selected child would agree with Gibson, which goes some way to show the plausibility of the idea. The goodness of the jam is in the jam jar, mysteriously mixed with its exciting colour, and with its appealing and attractive consistency; when you put the spoon in your mouth you have the proof that the goodness is right there, and it is hard to find a proof more evident than this. It is difficult to give any proof that the goodness in the jam is *not* in the jam. In the same way, the property of "able-to-hide-me" is precisely there, in that soft corner between the sofa and the armchair, where a bit of carpet also covers the floor: in the layout of that room, it is really easy to see that behind there is the perfect place to hide. Every object at knee-height is "for sitting"; many tellings-off are necessary to teach a child to distinguish the objects on which it is allowed to sit from those on which it is not, within the universe of "sittability". Every flat surface that is wide enough and not too sloping or too crowded by obstacles is walkable; and when the flat surface is well levelled, very wide and without obstacles, it must be crossed at a run. A child discovers the back door of a house that it has never seen before, it opens it, outside there is a wide field; it takes two steps beyond the door and immediately starts to run. It is the field that makes it run. Every tapered protrusion is a handle; we have to forbid those that should not be considered such.

And it is definitely not true that an adult doesn't see all of that; the adult perfectly understands children who are showing in an unmistakable way by their behaviour their objectivistic and realistic philosophy. It is only that the adult, invited to speak about that which we have been calling here tertiary qualities (a label for a semantic field that is perhaps rather wider than that occupied by Gibson's affordances, as we shall see), answers producing a fog of clarifications. He "knows" that that is not the way it is: the corner behind the sofa doesn't say "hide yourself here", it is a section of space like any other; it is mere inference that makes us afraid of silent shadows in the night, which in themselves are not really scary; certain musical sounds appear shrill to us because of the fact that sometimes we scratched a pot with a nail or a blackboard with some bad chalk; Zita's smile puts us in a good mood because we know that when we have smiled we usually felt a pleasant feeling toward others inside us; the illuminated Christmas tree gives happiness because behind it there is a very long tradition full of ancestral meanings, check the Encyclopedia. Grown-ups reject their child's reading of the world, as they would that of the dog or of the cat, and try to replace it with a suite of supplementary knowledge that projects itself on mere facts that are physically ascertainable, knowledge founded in equal measure on good common sense and the bad scientific popularization. The cultural trash can, above all that of psychology, is full of associations, past experience, conscious or unconscious inferences, probability calculations, hypotheses of object and projections.

Gibson created outrage asserting that, given a certain animal in a certain environment, affordances are not in its head but in the various bits that make up its environment. And yet this idea guided our behaviour in the world for a remarkable length of time at the beginning of our lives, and actually continues to guide our behaviour every time that it is genuinely oriented towards the world that is out there, not filtered through learned, theoretical images. "An important fact about the affordances of the environment is that they are in a sense objective, real, and physical, unlike values and meanings, which are often supposed to be subjective, phenomenal and mental. But, actually, an affordance is neither an objective property nor a subjective property; or it is both if you like. An affordance cuts across the dichotomy of subjective-objective and helps us to understand its inadequacy. It is equally a fact of the environment and a fact of behaviour. It is both physical and psychical, yet neither. An affordance points both ways, to the environment and to the observer" (Gibson 1979, p. 129).

The height of the knee varies from an adult to a child: so the "sittability" of objects – that property, already visible from a distance, of their physical structure that makes the possibility to sit tangible for the observer wholly without mediation – is different for a child and for an adult; this is where reference to the observer comes in: it is a connection to his or her proportions, to his or her physical structure to combine in some specific way with the physical structure of the objects that furnish the space of existence. The reference to the observer is not "mental" or "psychic" or "subjective": it exists in a banal way in the spatiotemporal connection between two things, that is, the observer and the object. This is a minimal ecosystem out of which, in general, raising questions about the properties of objects in relation to an observer becomes impossible. And this, simply because of the "contradiction that doesn't allow it" and not because of some deep reason that requires objects to depend on the subject.

Gibson continues (ibid., p. 129): "The niche for a certain species should not be confused with what some animal psychologists have called the phenomenal environment of the species." I think this is a clear reference to Koffka, his mentor and, at the same time, to J. von Uexkuell, theoretician of the subjective worlds of animal species. "This can be taken erroneously to be the 'private world,' or the world of 'consciousness'. The behaviour of observers depends on their perception of the environment, surely enough, but this does not mean that their behaviour depends on a so-called private or subjective or conscious environment. The organism depends on its environment for its life, but the environment does not depend on the organism for its existence."

The dichotomy between subjective and objective is thus "cut across". There is no way that organisms can produce worlds of private sensorial experiences around themselves, distortions of the environmental world somehow organized outside them; rather, the innumerable relations that unite the innumerable objects spread in the world are brought into focus, seen all together as if from an ideal, external perspective: among these objects some are "observers" (not owners of a private world, but, so to say, optically tied by defined relations with the other objects), and the relations that hold between these and the other objects explain how these last are bearers of affordances for the first ones. Affordances are undeniably in the object, given an observer in relation to it; they are information that travels from the object to the observer, but their ontological place is there. The seagulls *are* Emma, and the black is gloomy even before being black.

In any case, even assuming a radically subjectivist position, we would have to reach the same conclusion. Let us put ourselves in Bishop Berkeley's shoes: do we want to believe that everything is subjective, that everything is a creation of the subject, that *"esse est percipi"*? If all of this is true – if we are consistent with *"esse est percipi"* – and if, looking at things, we perceive the presence of expressive characteristics there where they are, expressive characteristics are precisely there. If it seems to us that the red is lively, it is lively. If uncertainty appears in the flight of an insect, it is in the flight of the insect. If anxiety is heard in the diminished seventh chord, it is exactly there, in that bunch of sounds.

A consistent objectivism and a subjectivism taken to the limit lead to the same conclusion about the place of expressive characteristics in the world. Only intermediate positions set this natural theoretical arrangement oscillating, with the risk that it will never be able to come to a halt. Nevertheless, we don't want to lure the reader toward one, the other, or some other possible conclusion, at least not in this paper. For our purposes, all we need is to make plausible the thesis according to which the affordances, the tertiary qualities, the expressive characters (what – in short – falls outside every terminology chosen with more or less accuracy within this discourse) are there where they are and are not mere applications of the mind to the facts directly given in experience.

In the wake of a long tradition of research that in a large part is described in K. Bühler's excellent book *Ausdruckstheorie* (*The Psychology of Expression*), Gibson also inserts his way of seeing things regarding the perception of the other person, exactly like Favorinus. Every object within the environment is a bearer of specific affordances, but above all man, first among animals. The tertiary qualities of the human figure, of the face, of the gesture, stand out very clearly, in terms of intensity and complexity, from all the other observables in the environment. Gibson is confident in holding that even these extremely complex characteristics are subject to laws, and therefore are investigable in the terms of an ecological optics, and of experimental analysis of the visual environment. The less recent literature offers to the scholar's curiosity thousands of analyses of facial expressions (experimental investigation began around the middle of the nineteenth century, but observations about that are as old as the world) and the study of human gestures continues down to the most recent developments in ethology. But what matters in Gibson's theoretical framework – and within certain limits in the framework that, apart from Gibson, we want to sketch in this work – is the fact that affordances of the human figure, for all that they are absolutely exceptional among others ("the alter . . . is an object, although it is not merely an object, and we do right to speak of he or she instead of it"; Gibson 1979, p. 135), they, like the others, can be studied in terms of their visual constitution, irrespective of any assumptions about the eventual content of other people's minds and about what we might think we know about it. With a view to presenting this way of attacking the problem in an intuitive manner, one need only think about a fact: the wax museum has always been a perfect setting for an uncanny tale. Wax sculptures are wax sculptures, but they have perfect human features, and in this alone there is enough to unsettle anyone. One might say that in such a story there is always the suspicion that a real criminal is passing himself off among the blood-stained mannequins on show, and that the suspense of reading derives wholly from this suspicion. I don't think so: let us try to imagine a bet, the classic one to spend a night in a room of that kind of museum, with the total and signed guarantee that nobody will go to hide among those figures. You are now there, the sunset has sent its last greeting beyond the glass of the windows and you have nothing to do but wait. If you are honest, you must admit that this won't be the same as spending a night in a library or in a hardware store. Faces are faces, even if they are "empty skulls" (in Homer's recurrent expression), limbs are limbs, even if stuck in a conventional gesture (and I would be almost sure that, as the shadows grow, that stillness will be betrayed by imperceptible movements, so great is the power of the effigy). Your gaze will look for support in some reassuring chest, in the chandelier firmly hooked to the ceiling.

The affordance "face-endowed-with-expression" is so powerful that it suddenly jumps out from a minimum of observable cues. I have often invited my students to describe the sign that I had just drawn on the blackboard, that is, a circle:

(16.2)

and then to tell me what they saw after a later addition, a small circle inside the area already drawn, thus:

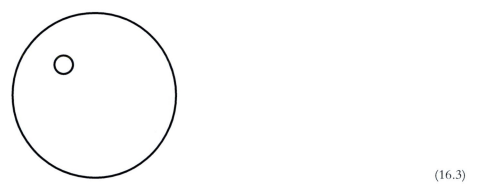

(16.3)

finally, after another addition . . .

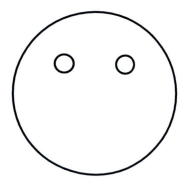

(16.4)

As I draw this last small circle on the blackboard, I can usually hear from behind my back the typical clamour of a class in whispered excitement: "Oh!", "Ah!". It is impossible not to suddenly recognize a face. It could even be a geometry class, but it is impossible for a face not to emerge. Then I have invited some pupil to repeat more than once the experiment in different places of the blackboard, after having erased my three circles to clean the board, and I have challenged him or her to try to draw more perfectly identical faces. But no matter how good the student's ability is, and no matter how hard he or she tries, no two specimens look alike, and not only because of evident mistakes of drawing, but because the facial *expressions* are always markedly different even if the geometrical difference is very slight. Only perfect reproduction, done with ruler and compasses, can achieve two equal faces. All that is needed is that the circles of the eyes are less distant, or one bigger than the other, or placed further down, closer to the centre of the bigger circle, or slightly compressed and maybe with the axes differently aligned, and the face passes from the amazed to the puzzled to the attentive to the foolish. So, at the third circle the face suddenly forms itself, and just a shred is enough to make it change expression. Imagine what the thousands of features of a real face, or of a face painted by an artist, can say to an observer!

The same game can be played with even simpler geometric means. A triangle can be the face and simple lines the eyes. The introduction of some kind of nose (a short line, two small dots) makes the play of expressions even more complicated (Figure 16.5). If we feel like supporting the theory of projection, I would really like to know what the devil we can be projecting upon such poor material, and why we see such definite expressions considering that the paucity of the material would allow all sorts of ambiguity.

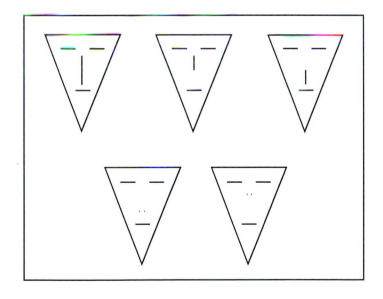

(16.5)

Drawn signs, bound by certain spatial relations, really are expressive, they bear upon themselves an emergent superstructure, an easily recognizable germ of expressivity. Examples like these show that there is a operational spectrum that we can trace between a true, living face endowed with expression and the minimal schema able to emerge as sad, happy or foolish, passing through the portrait, the sketch, the caricature.

It should be noted that what we have called "emergent superstructure" doesn't rest upon the basic elements (lines, small circles, etc.) considered as geometrical entities measurable with ruler and compasses. In the world of immediate experience even the most elementary structures enjoy properties that cannot be reduced to those measurements that are so useful when we want to determine their physical properties. Tertiary qualities do not rest upon the primary, if these later are understood as Galileo understood them; rather, they rest upon the primary qualities as we defined them in these pages after discussing Galileo, and after considering Hume's criticisms. In this universe of the discourse the two segments A-B and A'-B'.

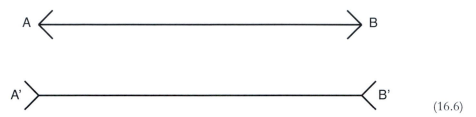

(16.6)

do *not* have the same length, even if the ruler says the opposite. Likewise, the two segments A-B and A'-B' in this other figure

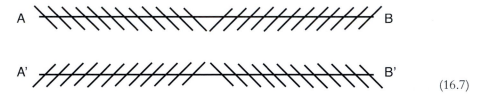

(16.7)

are curved, even if the ruler says that they are not. Tertiary qualities rest upon this level of reality, which is the reality directly shown by observable things, measurement aside.

An example: let us consider three schematic faces with three different kinds of looks, one straight and the other two crossed-eyes, one with a convergent walleye and the other with a divergent walleye (Figure 16.8). Inspecting these three faces, it is not difficult to realize that the three expressions visibly depend on the position that the small dot occupies on the horizontal lines that make up the eyes.

But do these expressions depend on the *metric* position of the dot in respect to the extremities of the line-eye? We shall see that it is not so.

FIGURE 16.8 Do the expressions of these faces depend on the position of the small dot on the line that serves as eye?

FIGURE 16.9 Do the expression of these faces depend on the *real* position of the small dot that serves as the eye, or rather on the *apparent* position that it acquires due to the Müller-Lyer illusion?

Indeed: let us compare the three drawing of Figure 16.9 – another three faces – with those of Figure 16.8 and let us try to couple them to these by means of quick comparisons passing the gaze up and down from one figure to the other in all the necessary combinations for a good comparison; bearing in mind that this comparison concerns the similarity in the "way of seeing" appropriate to each of the figure's faces.

The comparison is possible, maybe even easy, despite the presence in these latter faces of certain appendages placed at the extremities of the line-eye. Here, too, there is the walleye who crosses his eyes, the one who splays them and the one who looks straight ahead. But if you make the appropriate measurements, you'll see – from geometric point of view – that here the small dot is always at the halfway point of the line-eye. (Compasses and the ruler actually don't measure the observable properties of objects, but only systems of coherent relations following a certain logic, which fall in general outside of the observational plane; only occasionally do they emerge in visible, or more generally sensible, evidence.)

Within the concrete geometry of vision, the appendages placed at the ends of the line-eye move the dot from the middle along the line-eye; and they move it in the direction given by the tip of the arrow:

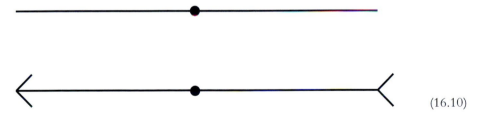

(16.10)

This peculiarity of primary organization, which cannot be discussed here in detail, assigns the expression to the schematic faces.

Taking stock, whether the dot is moved from its central position by the added appendages or by being drawn here and not there has no importance at all: in both cases it doesn't appear in the central position. And this is what matters. (Of course, the compasses would disagree with our description; but so much the worse for the compasses, because here we are in the realm of the observable, in which – unlike the realm of geometry – it may not be that the compasses are always right.)

I wanted to discuss these examples at certain length because they lead us to the following conclusion: it is primary qualities' mode of appearance that sustains tertiary qualities; the elementary ingredients visible in the figures are those on which the physiognomic character, the affordance, is based. Not the ingredients defined through physical, indirect measurements, not the so called "stimuli".

The reader, at this point, might be led to conclude: so it is a matter of appearances founded on appearances, this seems to be the lesson. Since physiognomic expressive features of these simple figures composed by a few signs are appearances (and they can't be anything else, given that we are not considering real faces, with intentions and emotions inside the head), and can be made to depend even on optical illusions, as we have seen, and hence on certain other special appearances, we must conclude that in these games the hidden mechanism is that of a hierarchy of curious *trompe-l'oeil*.

It would be useless to try to combat this conclusion if the basic metaphysics of my interlocutor is dualistic: he calls reality that set of entities that he thinks lie beyond the immediate data of experience, that is, the physical, anatomical and physiological body and perhaps the mental contents enclosed in the neural bundle of another person, not the reflection of that body in his eyes, nor, much less, the image that he has of it, nor worse still, a schema of that image. To him it is clear and obvious that the topics discussed above concern appearances founded on appearances. All that my interlocutor encounters around himself is appearance. There is no remedy for this.

If however my interlocutor is open to non-traditional solutions, or is naïvely realist (this last, a theoretical position that is anything but naïve) he or she will see things in a less confusing light. After all, "optical illusions" are not illusions. First of all because, if it is true that in the future the physiology of the central nervous system will be able to explain all these phenomena of vision, then it is true that these illusions are just so many physical states of our brain: physical states that, indeed, a adequate physics of the brain will be able to define, control and reproduce. And a physical state of the brain it is not an illusion, but a fact. Secondly, they are not illusions but facts, because every observer can witness them, and they vary under the eyes of the observer with the variation of certain well-defined and enumerable circumstances of observability. They are not only observable by more than one observer (together or separately) but their inner properties, their varying with the variation of certain conditions, are repeatable at will any time that somebody wants to have fun with them. When interobservability and the repeatability occur together, the so-called "illusions" (and German authors usually write "*die soggenanten Täuschungen*": the so-called illusions) are in good order relative to the methodology of scientific research, and must be received among the facts – the myriad of facts on which we invent the cosmic order – that explain other facts and wait for their part to be explained in the same way: "*Namque aliud ex alio clarescet. . . ita res accendent lumina rebus*".[10] Therefore, it must be said: that kind of observable event that goes under the name of "expressivity" is directly founded on the constellation of the observable events that identify its position in space, and so depends on them and it is localized there where they are. They, in turn, have the properties that they exhibit to direct inspection, not necessarily those that would result from scrutiny and indirect measurements. For the benefit of psychologists: the physiognomical qualities depend on the primary, phenomenally explicit structure, not on the so-called "stimuli". The constellation of elementary ingredients explains the nature of the global impression. At this point another counter-argument can be sensed in the air: why waste time with such impoverished and schematic objects? We are interested in real faces, the expressions of living and acting people, the affordances that guide our concrete lives, interpersonal relations, loves, flights, apprehensions, authorities.

We could answer, perfectly coherently, that even starting from the schema made up of three objects it is possible to reach that real face that looks at us intently or maybe maliciously. Innumerable enrichments and changes can be woven together with the paucity of the original schema, and when we have also brought it into three dimensions, with colour and movement, who will be able to guarantee that it is not a face? How else could we know its intentions?

But it is not enough to say this. In general, we would like to learn concrete things from psychology rather than subtle sophisms: it would be nice to know how we can lure others' attention, how it is possible to enslave people or induce them to do what we would like (for better or for worse), or come to understand how we are truly made-up in the deepest levels of our identity, those that emerge only rarely with very barbed and painful points; or simply we would like to know how to sleep better. In contrast, we know everything or almost everything about how adjacent colours influence each other, or about the limits we run into in inserting too many subordinate clauses or too many "not"s in the sentence we are writing, or about the memorization of random numbers, or about the recognizability of a melody played at the extreme limits of the audible, up there where we only hear painful whistles.

An epistemological vengeance – which I cannot view, however, with complete aversion – wants the interesting things, or those regarded as such by most people, to be difficult or impossible to study with the desired rigour. And it wants them, even when they are engaged with the most sophisticated quantitative and non-quantitative methods, to permit us to have conclusions that are always open to the doubt, while the small and very small things lead us to certainties, albeit, even here, not without difficulty.

Labs are populated by elementary facts and by questions that demand too much. Somebody would like to know how to bend the will of somebody else with the gaze, or to transmit thoughts, or to perform operations in the style of *Clockwork Orange* (I had a young coworker possessed by similar obsessions; I lost contact with him, and I only know that he now successfully trades in behavioural therapy); then, with the passage of time, such a person discovers that it is better than nothing to be able to clarify how many subordinate clauses can be subjected to a main clause without the sentence's becoming a blur, or how much a colour changes when we make fuzzy the edge of the surface on which it is homogeneously extended.

I'm grateful to nature for its complexity. It inflicts frustrations on anyone who would like to make knowledge pragmatic, to know in order to be able to do, to have a compass for sailing among people. Nature grants a consolation to those disappointed by such endeavours, and sometimes allows the chastened hidden persuader to discover how difficult it is to hang up a painting perfectly straight in a room with a sloping roof and non-orthogonal walls. This is at least a real problem, one that forces us to reflect more on those relations that hold the world up than on psychic muddles, which are the object of ordinary manipulability.

Nature profusely rewards those who, right from the start, are curious about the shining truths nestled in the details, and are therefore necessarily indifferent to the specks of tarry dust of the big pragmatics that occupy every interstice between one thing and another, between one person and the next, transforming those shining truths into a wrecker's tools apt to keep tottering the insecure balance of a stupid ordinary daily routine.

Notes

1 Diels, H., & Kranz, W. *Die Fragmente der Vorsokratiker* (Zurich: Weidmann, 1985), 68B9 [quoted from Freeman, K. (Ed) (1957). *Ancilla to the Pre-Socratic Philosophers*. Cambridge, MA: Harvard University Press, at p. 93].

2 Galen, On the elements according to Hippocrates. In H. Diels, & W. Kranz. *Die Fragmente der Vorsokratiker*. Zurich: Weidmann, 1985, 68A49 [quoted from Taylor, C.C.W. (1999). *The Atomists: Leucippus and Democritus*. Toronto, ON, Canada: University of Toronto Press, at p. 144].A

3 Aristotle, *Physics*, 188a22.

4 Galilei, G. (1953). Il Saggiatore. In F. Flora (ed.), *Opere di Galileo Galilei*. Milan, Italy: Ricciardi, p. 311 [Eng. trans. Stillman Drake]

5 Loc. cit.: *"[B]en sento tirarmi dalla necessità, subito che concepisco una materia o sostanza corporea, a concepire insieme ch'ella è terminata e figurate"*.

6 Hume, D. (1748) *An Enquiry Concerning Human Understanding*, XII, I (ed.) T.L. Beauchamp, 2000, Oxford: Oxford University Press, pp. 115–6.

7 Or, perhaps, "once upon a time": though a good number of Wertheimer's followers have attributed this observation to him, it does not seem to appear in his writings.

8 It would seem that every single seagull should be called Emma. Morgenstern, C. (1963). The Seagulls [1932]. In *The Gallows Songs: Christian Morgenstern's Galgenlieder, A Selection* (trans. Max Knight). Berkeley, CA: University of California Press.

9 By his own admission, the word "affordance" is Gibson's own coining, deriving from the German *Aufforderungscharakter*, invitation-character, but embracing also repulsion, used by Kurt Lewin to pick out the positive and negative values that characterize objects in the environment and that guide our behaviour.

10 Lucretius, De Rerum Natura, I, 1115–1117: "For one thing will become clear by another . . . so clearly with truths kindle light for truths" (trans. W.H.D. Rouse) Cambridge MA: Loeb, 1924 rev. 2nd edn. M.F. Smith, 1982.

References

Berkeley, G. (1979). *Three Dialogues between Hylas and Philonous* (1713) in *Works* (9 vol.) A.A. Luce and T.E. Jessop (Eds), 1948-57, vol. II, London: Nelson.

Brown, J.F. (1931). The visual perception of velocity. *Psychologische Forschung, 14* (1), 199-232.

Buhler, K. (1978). *Teoria dell'espressione. Il sistema alla luce della storia*. Rome: Armando. (Original title: *Ausdruckstheorie. Das System an der Geschichte aufgezeigt*. Jena: Fischer (1933))

Diels, H., and Kranz, W. (1903) *Die Fragmente der Vorsokratiker*, ananstatic reprint, Zurich: Weidman, 1985

Gibson, J. J. (1979). *The Ecological Approach to Visual Perception*. Boston: Houghton Mifflin.

Koffka, K. (1935). *Principles of Gestalt Psychology*. New York: Harcourt, Brace and Company. (The page reference is to p. 7 of the English version, though Bozzi did not supply it.)

Morgenstern, C. (1963). The Seagulls [1932]. In *The Gallows Songs: Christian Morgenstern's Galgenlieder. A Selection* (trans. Max Knight). Berkeley, CA: University of California Press.

COMMENTS ON TERTIARY QUALITIES

Ian Verstegen and Carlo Maria Fossaluzza

"Tertiary qualities" was first published as the third essay in Bozzi's book of 1990, *Fisica Ingenua* [*Naïve Physics*]. After having introduced the overall topic of the book and discussed "violins", he turns to a classic topic for Gestalt psychologists: the so-called "tertiary qualities". However, Bozzi addresses the topic afresh, and specifically in light of James J. Gibson's theory of affordances which had just been translated into Italian the year before by Bozzi's friend, Riccardo Luccio, with whom he had written an Introduction. Bozzi's approach is light and humorous but also deep, passing along the history of western philosophy. For those familiar with Italian psychology, one can recognize veiled references to scientists and problems occupying perception research at the time.

Naïve Physics is a free-standing book, following the collection of essays from the previous year, *Fenomenologia Sperimentale* [*Experimental Phenomenology*], and so can be considered the mature manifesto of Bozzi's thought. Pairing "tertiary qualities" with "naïve physics" is significant because it expresses Bozzi's worldview of the essentially expressive and meaningful qualities of both the physical and human world. It has become a sort of Bible for the new Italian realism (e.g., Kanizsa, 1991).

"Tertiary qualities" were introduced into philosophy by Samuel Alexander (1920), and the name expresses their tenuous relationship to reality as even more subjective than secondary qualities such as colour. However, the term was used by the Gestaltists (Wertheimer, Koffka, Köhler) as a handy reference to expressive qualities, which Wolfgang Köhler (1947, pp. 173–178) also called "Ehrenfels qualities". However, for Italians like Bozzi, the most recent authoritative discussion of the problem would have been found in Wolfgang Metzger's *Psychologie* (2nd edition 1954) published in Italian in 1971 and translated by another of Bozzi's friends, Giovanni Bruno Vicario. Indeed, within the Gestalt tradition research continues, now sometimes influenced by Bozzi himself (Argenton, 2005; Lindauer, 2013). As noted, Bozzi differs in dealing with Gibson's ecological theory, as we shall see in a moment.

Bozzi begins his historical survey with the pre-Socratics to show how persistently the problem of the objectivity of qualities has been for western philosophy. He shows that already in Democritus the skeptical conclusion had been stated: "we know nothing accurately in reality". Galileo is cited for his clear exposition of the problem, which anticipated our modern distinction by stating that the only things that are subject-independent are primary qualities like body, position and numerousness, while the rest depend on the subject. For Bozzi, David Hume merely radicalizes Galileo's doubts to extend backward to the primary qualities themselves, making explicit Bishop Berkeley's idealism.

Here, Bozzi is in complete agreement that the relativity of perception is confirmed in the psychology laboratory. In this, he seems to be displaying a traditional commitment of Gestalt theory, to divorce phenomenal experience from transcendent objects in a critical realism (Bozzi, 1969; Köhler, 1938, 1947). Such a move would also be akin to Edmund Husserl's phenomenological epoché (ἐποχή) a suspension of judgment (Husserl, 1913). Indeed, Bozzi's discussion of the wax works shows that he bases the idea of animacy of an object solely on phenomenal grounds. However, it is clear that Bozzi wants to affirm a more realist stance than this. He sets out a series of discussions of association and innatism as a basis for understanding expression.

It is at this point that Bozzi begins his discussion of Gibson. Bozzi both recognizes the extremity of Gibson's position yet also shows it much sympathy. For Bozzi, a tertiary quality is "a label for a semantic field that is perhaps rather wider than that occupied by Gibson's affordances". Where Gibson writes of physical environments, Bozzi adds classical Gestalt ideas like that cited by Wertheimer, "black is gloomy even before being black". Bozzi concludes, "Affordances are undeniably in the object, given an observer in relation to it; they are information that travels from the object to the observer, but their ontological place is there . . . and black is gloomy even before being black."

In this statement, Bozzi maintains a fruitful openness toward Gibson's theorising. However, according to the critical realism with which some aspects of Bozzi's thinking has affinities, the difference between a physical environment and the expressive qualities of a colour might be regarded as substantial. This is a challenging tension that invites further reflection.

We are left with a few questions. Bozzi does not wish to decide the metaphysical issue but he does state that this is a question of ontological not phenomenological geography. He calls himself "incorrigibly realist" but the only alternatives he seems to think are on offer are dualism and solipsism. He also says that naïve realism is not naïve, but perhaps there is a form of direct realism that does not conflate percept and object. At times, he speaks like Galileo's more realist contemporaries who held that primary qualities cause secondary qualities – an attractive position today (Hatfield, 2009) – but it is only hinted at.

Whatever the case, readers will be engaged by Bozzi's irreverent and wise treatment.

References

Alexander, S. (1920). *Space, Time, and Deity: the Gifford Lectures at Glasgow, 1916–1918*. London: Macmillan.

Argenton, A. (2005). Il nero è lugubre prima ancora di essere nero [Black is gloomy before being black]. In L. Pizzo Russo (ed.). *Rudolf Arnheim. Arte e percezione visiva* [*Rudolf Arnheim. Art and Visual Perception*] (pp. 99–118). Palermo, Italy: Aesthetica Preprint.

Bozzi, P. (1969). Presentazione. In W. Köhler, *Il posto del valore in un mondo di fatti* [*The Place of Value in a World of Facts*]. Florence, Italy: Giunti.

Bozzi, P. (1990). *Fisica ingenua* [*Naïve Physics*]. Milan, Italy: Garzanti.

Hatfield, G. (2009). *Perception and Cognition: Essays in the Philosophy of Psychology*. New York: Oxford University Press.

Husserl, E. (1913). *Ideen zu einer reinen Phänomenologie und phänomenologischen Philosophie. Erstes Buch: Allgemeine Einführung in die reine Phänomenologie*. Halle, Germanyu: Niemeyer.

Kanizsa, G. (1991). *Vedere e pensare* [*Seeing and Thinking*]. Bologna, Italy: il Mulino.

Köhler, W. (1938). *The Place of Value in a World of Facts*. New York: Liveright.

Köhler, W. (1947). *Gestalt Psychology*. New York: Liveright.

Lindauer, (2013). *The Expressiveness of Perceptual Experience: Physiognomy Reconsidered*. Amsterdam: Benjamins.

Metzger, W. (1971). *I fondamenti della psicologia della Gestalt* [*The Foundations of Gestalt Psychology*] (Italian translation of Metzger's book *Psychologie* (1954) by G.B. Vicario). Florence, Italy: Giunti-Barbèra.

AFTERTHOUGHTS

17

EXPERIMENTAL PHENOMENOLOGY

A historical profile

1.

Those who have attempted to trace the evolution of Gestalt theory or who have had occasion to examine its origins, are unanimous in indicating an experimental study by Max Wertheimer (1880–1943) as marking its beginnings.[1] The subject-matter and approach of Wertheimer's study had none of the features typical of a manifesto for a new line of thought, such as those displayed, for example, by the article *Psychology as the Behaviorists View It* that was published by John B. Watson (1878–1958) just one year later than Wertheimer's and that inaugurated the behaviourist movement.

Instead of setting out an epistemological programme, Wertheimer conducted wide-ranging and complex experimental inquiry into a specific type of apparent motion: stroboscopic movement. This was a phenomenon that scientists had been aware of for almost a century, and it was the basis of perception of cinematographic images. Wertheimer's experiments demolished almost all of scientific psychology's previously held tenets. Admittedly, he attacked only theories of perception, which were then based on the two pivotal ideas of "sensation" (the atom or minimum unit of sensory perception) and "association" (the associative intervention of thought, memory or imagination on the material of sensations). It is also true, however, that he thus struck at the roots of the general ideas presupposed by any form of elementarism or summativism and, indeed, at the methodological assumption – which at the time encompassed almost every area of psychology – that it was possible to break every complex event of human experience down into simple parts without thereby losing what today is called information about its inner laws.

Was this a novel idea? In the 1930s, a number of scholars compared the Gestalt revolution to that accomplished by Einstein in physics. Others, however, and among them the leading historian of psychology, Edwin G. Boring, did not regard it as anything particularly new. Nevertheless, following Wertheimer's study, an extraordinary amount of empirical research – and an unprecedented amount of experimentation in controlled conditions – converged on his theory. And it was a theory that, in its turn, generated a very large number indeed of new discoveries, mainly in the field of perception but also as regards other cognitive activities and in social psychology. Even today, Wertheimer's approach still has great heuristic potential in psychological research.

In Boring's view, some aspects of Gestalt theory had roots that penetrated deeply into the history of Western culture. Several psychological theories of the nineteenth century had already modelled concepts that resembled those that would subsequently be employed by the Gestaltists, and Gestalt theory itself comprised a philosophy of knowledge that was fully aware of its philosophical, epistemological and scientific antecedents. Accordingly, it is necessary at the outset to mention certain ideas that, in the history of Western culture, anticipated some of the central notions formulated by the Gestalt movement.

2.

For the sake of brevity, I shall restrict my discussion to two themes. First I shall examine the whole/part relationship, which plays a crucial role in Gestalt theory both in its studies of perception and in those on memory and thought, and which the Gestaltists also used as an interpretative tool in their numerous experiments conducted in the area of social psychology. The whole possesses inner properties that are no longer apparent in the parts into which it is subsequently broken down, and that cannot be inferred from item-by-item inspection of these parts (the slogan "The whole is something more than the sum of the parts" inadequately conveys the idea). The whole is not the totality of consciousness but the structure often possessed by specific events in ongoing experience.

Second, I shall discuss the primacy of the phenomenological method in experimental design and in the construction of explanatory models: that is, the Gestaltists' constant appeal to the forms of immediate experience, to the qualitative structure of the events of everyday experience, accompanied by the temporary "bracketing" of what we know − or believe we know − from the other scientific disciplines or from psychology itself and which might hamper our capacity to conduct ingenuous observation of phenomena.

These are themes already to be found in Plato and Aristotle. In the *Theaetetus* (204 a), Plato poses the question: "Or do you wish to say that also the whole is made up of parts, although it is a single idea and differs from all its parts?" − a question that calls for the answer "no" − after having shown that "the syllable is not the letters, but rather some sort of single idea born from them, with a form unique to itself and different from the letters" (203 c).

In various passages in *Metaphysics*, Aristotle addresses the theme of the inner cohesion of the units of experience, arguing that the strongest unit is characterised by "continuity". There may, however, be increasingly weaker units, such as a bundle of wood lashed together with a cord, pieces of wood simply in contact with each other, and so on.

As far as phenomenological evidence is concerned, Plato's endeavour to "save the phenomena" is well known, and so too is Aristotle's dictum that "to touch with the hand and describe, this is truth".

Interesting examples of phenomenological analysis and observations on the relationship between the whole and the parts are to be found in Descartes, Malebranche and Condillac, and also in the English empiricists (notably in Locke, who distinguishes sharply between summative aggregates and structures in which the organisation of the parts gives rise to a coherent whole) − their programmatic sensism and elementarism notwithstanding. Nicholas Pastore's book *Selective History of Theories of Visual Perception*[2] provides an excellent account of these matters.

However, the history of the ideas relevant to understanding of Gestalt theory, understood as a twentieth-century scientific and philosophical programme (and, in this sense, still under way in certain cultural areas of Europe, Japan and the United States) began with Kant.

I shall devote the first part of my exposition (until Section 5) to certain aspects of the philosophical thought and specifically psychological theory which, from Kant until the early years of the twentieth century, highlighted the shortcomings of the method that broke facts analytically down into elements – although it was a method that led to numerous advances in the natural sciences (chemistry, for example) – and that emphasised instead the organic character and the objective structuredness, of many mental experiences and of the experience itself of the outside world.

The second part of the essay (sections 6 and 7) will examine the foundation of the Gestalt movement, its falsificatory and polemical phase, followed by the open-minded research and theoretical enthusiasm which culminated in the systemisation set out in Koffka's *Principles*.[3]

The third part will conduct a survey of the works that, once the philosophical debate over the foundations of the theory had died away, extended Gestalt principles to broader areas of psychological research, as far indeed as psychopathology and aesthetics.

As already indicated, the most systematic anticipation of Gestalt theory is to be found in Kant. His restoration of the entire problem of knowledge to the realm of phenomena; his theorising of an organising function of subjectivity in the constitution of objects (*realitas phaenomenon*) without thereby over-emphasising the relativity of the particular subjects; and finally – at variance with these premises – his constant assertion of a noumenon lying behind phenomena to which none of the characteristics constitutive of the world of experience can be attributed without committing a gross theoretical error: all these made Kant one of the philosophers most frequently cited by Gestaltist texts. There is, of course, a fundamental difference between the two positions: the noumenon, or transcendent thing-in-itself, was for certain Gestaltists (Köhler, Metzger) the world studied by physics, while the only interpretation of mathematical physics was, for Kant, the world of phenomena. However, this difference may be not so much a divergence as a semantic shift due to the profound changes that physics has undergone in the last two centuries.

Kant's *oeuvre*, moreover, abounds with extremely subtle phenomenological analyses. By way of example we may take the following: if I observe a house before me, I explore it with acts of observation which follow each other in time and are spread out in space; if the house were nothing but these sensations, its parts would be phenomenally successive in time. But the house *qua* phenomenon is the object of this exploration; it is simultaneous in its parts, it exists previously to the acts of observation and it is independent of them. This is said not of the house as a thing-in-itself but of the house as a phenomenon-in-itself. The perceptual structure possesses an autonomy pre-established with respect to the observer, and it is extraneous to the flux of momentary sensations. This passage from the *Critique of Pure Reason* already draws a sharp distinction between the phenomenal objects 'encountered' and the momentary properties of the visual field; a distinction that is crucial to understanding of the Gestalt phenomenology of visual perception.

In the *Critique of Judgment*, the whole/part relationship is treated thus: "we may also conceive of an intellect which, not being discursive like ours, but intuitive, moves (. . .) from intuition of a whole as such to the particular, that is, from the whole to the parts".[4] Consequently we must admit "the possibility of the parts (according to their nature and their connection) as dependent on a whole (. . .) so that the representation of a whole contains the principles of the possibility of its form and of the connection thereto of the parts".[5]

Some lines from this paragraph are quoted by Goethe in a posthumously published philosophical fragment. Goethe was, if one may say so, highly Gestaltist both in his experimental research into colours and in his philosophical-scientific speculations. Although obviously less systematic than Kant, he was nevertheless an empirical researcher of considerable imagination and talent. The cornerstone of Goethe's epistemology is the immediacy of the outside world as given by perception: "It is not the senses that deceive but the judgment (. . .) man in himself, insofar as he makes use of his healthy senses, is the greatest and most exact physical instrument that there can be".[6] Another key idea in Goethe's investigation of chromatic phenomena is that it is extremely difficult to see phenomena in their authentic nature, in their true constitution, because our eyes are clouded by theories, by the abuse of mathematical schematisations, by language itself. A third central component of Goethe's theory is the notion that there is continuity between laboratory research and the world observed in its free state, because it is possible to find ever richer situations starting from simple experiments, and to construct a factual continuum which comprises every level of complexity without omitting the "original phenomenon" (the law identified by means of experiments).

A striking feature of Goethe's theory of colour – although it is one both widely criticised and criticisable – is his insistence that colours are not pure chromatic shades but aspects of material structures endowed, besides chroma, with coarseness or brightness, hardness or softness (a theory which would be later experimentally corroborated by David Katz (1884–1943)): indeed, he once wrote: "might it not be that colour does not belong to sight?".[7] A part of *Farbenlehre* is devoted to study of the expressiveness of colour, which Goethe calls "sensible and moral action". Although this component of his research was not conducted using experimental method, it is rich with subtle insight, especially as regards the combinations of colours capable of generating impressions and affective states.

3.

As we know, to Goethe's detriment there is the fact that he waged a tenacious and (in terms of physics) unfounded polemic against Newton's optics. But there was another factor that undoubtedly helped to prevent the philosophical framework of his theory and the fecundity of his empirical findings from entering the mainstream of scientific research in the decades that followed publication of *Farbenlehre* in 1810: this factor was the birth of psychophysics.

In psychology, psychophysics was the exact opposite of the assumption that the unit of analysis – that is, the subject-matter – of scientific inquiry is the complex organisations of experience. Psychophysics was based on the principle that every complex structure of visual, acoustic, tactile, kinesthetic, and so on, experience had to be broken down into its elementary parts or minimal components (a sound, a colour, a weight), and that empirical research began once this decomposition into isolated elements had been accomplished. It was thus possible to have a sensation of sound insulated against the influence of other possible factors and given that the sound can vary in pitch, timbre and intensity, these three sensory parameters could be applied with great precision to variations – measured by physical instruments – in the frequency, in the spectral make-up of the wave, and in the amplitude of the oscillations of a vibrating body (stimulus). Those wishing to study colours had first to dismantle the ingenious juxtapositions that interested Goethe and to draw a map of all possible variations in each individual colour observed. This map had borders that merged into nothingness because there are stimuli too weak to be noticed, physical impressions on the sense organs incapable of producing sensations. These borders represented the absolute threshold of the perceptible.

If we conceive the world of experience as an infinite collection of sensations, in David Hume's fine description, and the surrounding physical world as an infinite galaxy of stimuli, and if moreover we conceive of every sensation as standing in a one-to-one relation with a specific stimulus and varying in accordance with it, then the study of experience becomes just an analysis of the relations between stimuli and sensations. These relations were formalised in Weber-Fechner's law, which is the basis of psychophysics. Of course, if this scientific programme was to achieve the results it desired, it had to accept *in toto* the chapter in J. S. Mill's *Logic* (1843) that recommended the decomposition of complex phenomena into their elements. It was no coincidence that psychophysics was born in the very same years that British philosophy was codifying the rules of a new associationistic empiricism. The founders of scientific psychology worked for decades on this programme. The vast corpus of analyses produced by Hermann von Helmholtz[8] was entirely based on these presuppositions; to the extent that, with impeccable consistency, whenever Helmholtz came across sensations in his experiments that did not fit the straitjacket of psychophysical laws – that is, sensations that could not be explained in terms of stimulation – he accounted for these facts by resorting to an "unconscious judgment" involving an unwitting memory of past experience or tacit forms of mental calculation able to modify sensations and render them more functional to the identification of external physical objects.

However, these facts proved to be so numerous that the sensations of psychophysics came to be the exception rather than the rule, and the intervention of the higher faculties, or of Helmholtz's "unconscious judgment", was invariably cited as an explanation when the segments of sensory experience being considered, such as the objects of everyday experience or routinely occurring events, possessed a certain degree of complexity. If an object moved away in space, it was the mind that calculated its motion on the basis of the progressive reduction of its retinal projection; if a white sheet of paper was still white at sunset, it was again the mind that remembered its colour at midday and attributed this colour to the paper, and so on.

The deviant behaviour of complex objects with respect to the dictates of psychophysical laws compelled the theory to set off in a fresh direction; and it was this exigency that guided the efforts of the precursors of Gestalt theory.

4.

From the 1880s onwards, numerous mainly German authors carried out experimental research in specific areas or conducted thorough revisions of their philosophical postulates, or worked on both of these tasks simultaneously. They thus developed a viewpoint (or a range of viewpoints) in sharp contrast with the tenets of psychophysics, and they indeed contemplated recasting the discipline on a more convincing basis.

Not coincidentally, the first of them, Ewald Hering (1834–1918), drew directly on the theory of colours developed by Goethe, who had been the first to attempt a classification of chromatic hues based on the oppositions yellow/blue, red/green, etc. Like Goethe, Hering did not attempt to formulate a physical theory of the genesis of colours (following Helmholtz); he started instead from the phenomenon of complementarity, that is, from the fact that prolonged fixation on red generates a green after-image, and vice versa, and that blue likewise generated yellow, and vice versa, as well as the fact that when set against the background of a small grey field each of these colours induces its complementary colour within it. Hering was also interested in the interactions among chromatic areas and in the chromatic changes brought about, not by stimuli, but by the perceptual setting of a particular area. His book *Zur Lehre vom Lichtsinne* (1872) describes numerous strictly phenomenological experiments conducted on complex chromatic structures without the use of psychophysical methods. A distinction is proposed between the colours of things and the ambient light which, from a strictly sensationalist point of view, is nonsensical. Moreover, Hering argued in several of his writings that phenomenological inquiry is physiological in nature because the law of a mental state is the law of a physiological process; which was one way of enunciating what W. Köhler would later call the "postulate of isomorphism".

While Hering was constructing his phenomenological physiology, Franz Brentano (1829–1917) published his book that would be so influential, in various ways, on twentieth-century culture: *Psychologie vom empirischen Standpunkte* (1874). Brentano was not an experimentalist, although he was well versed in the psychophysical literature and in the works of Helmholtz and Wundt. Brentano's "empirical point of view" was founded on direct observation of phenomena, insofar as they are immediately given in experience and ostensible to other observers. His criticism of psychophysics was based on the fact that sensations do not depend solely on the intensity of the stimulus; they also depend on at least the attitude of the subject and on the context in which they are observed. To ascertain this fact it is not necessary to conduct experiments, since mere observation suffices, bearing in mind that the phenomena of perception are "true in themselves". Brentano pushed this argument so far as to contend that perceptual facts, and colours especially, are not psychic facts but immediately physical ones to which the consciousness is directed via intentional acts. *Psychophysical measurements are in reality "physical-physical":* The subject-matter of an empirical psychology is intentionality, and the act, and the dynamics of this act, can be grasped by introspection. He had no misgivings concerning introspective methods because in the act every psychic state is exactly as it appears. Brentano borrowed from Hamilton – who in the mid-years of the century had already advanced an number of interesting phenomenological ideas in British philosophy – the expression "subjectively subjective" in order to describe this aspect of experience *ex parte subjecti*. This sphere comprises, besides sentiments, memories, intentions or will, also sensations; but the object of all of them are the complex things denoted by the term "physical phenomena": "As examples of physical phenomena we may cite: a colour, a shape, a landscape that I see; a chord that I hear; the heat, the cold that I feel; the odour that I smell". It is the task of phenomenology to identify the border or "watershed" between these two realms. The object does not lie beyond the subject but at its limit.

Even more radical were the views set out by Ernst Mach (1838–1916) in his book *Beiträge zur Analyse der Empfindungen* of 1886 and subsequently developed in *Erkenntnis und Irrtum* (1905). What I have called the "watershed" between the subject and the object becomes the ambit of the only reality amenable to scientific inquiry: the order of the sensations on the basis of which, by means of two complex networks of logical relations both coupled to this same empirical material (i.e. sensory experience), it is possible to construct physics on the one hand, and psychology on the other. Physics is constructed – and this is the relatively easier task – by positing systems of relations among sensations which empirically manifest themselves independently of the presence of an observer endowed with a body and mental states. Psychology was born as an attempt to take account also of these latter complexes of sensations, which constitute approximately the "self". The "self" does not have substantial reality, nor does it have clear-cut boundaries; it is instead constituted moment by moment in the overall field of experience as a special portion of it, an aggregate of sensations endowed with specific relationships with those that form the world of physics. We shall see below the extent to which this conception of the self was absorbed into Gestalt theory.

To be sure, Mach was the originator of the concept of "structure" (although this term was not part of his normal vocabulary) in the sense in which it came to play a fundamental role in the Gestaltists' system. Chapter 6 of *Analyse* examines two cases that were decisive in the formulation of this concept. Consider a letter of the alphabet drawn in black on a white background, and the same letter drawn in white on a black background (or the letter could equally be blue on a red background, green on a yellow background, and so on). The identity of the form is immediately recognised, even though all the colour sensations have changed. The form is independent of the matter of the local sensations; it is a structure, precisely, although Mach calls it a "sensation of space". Take these two shapes:

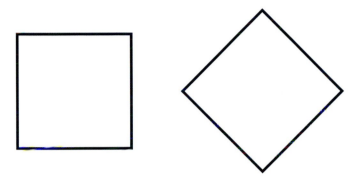

FIGURE 17.1 These are geometrically congruent but optically entirely different shapes. The first is a square, the second is what later authors called a "diamantoid". The abstract geometric relations are the same in the two cases, but the structure changes with the variation in the concrete relations (optical, physiological) between the figure and the surrounding space. Two different distributions of sensations may have the same structure; and two similar distributions of sensations may have different structures. The structure, therefore, is something independent of sensations. Although Mach treats it as a special case of sensation, the theoretical leap has been made: terminology apart, there are objects of vision that are not reducible to sensations as the psychophysicists defined them.

In Chapter 10, Mach states that sensations are so closely interwoven in the complex objects of direct experience that it is only by intentional analytical effort can we separate them and consider them in themselves. But the analysis of music that Mach conducts in Chapter 13 gives a concrete demonstration that this analytical effort is constrained within very narrow limits: it is the structure, that is to say the system of relations, that governs the parts.

A brief digression is necessary at this point. A history of the theoretical antecedents of Gestalt psychology should contain a chapter devoted to the development of musical theory, especially in the eighteenth-century treatises. The progressive codification of the rules of composition, and of contrapuntal composition especially, led musicians to the discovery of numerous laws of the structuring of sound material; laws based on the shared and un-mentioned (because obvious) assumption that the "whole" has properties that are not present in the "parts", the individual sounds.

The vertical structures of sounds — that is, of chords — plainly possess perceptual and expressive properties that are not present in the notes that form them; and every note, while remaining materially the same, changes function as the notes of the chord to which it belongs change. As the succession of chords proceeds horizontally, it must be constructed according to the principle of the "good conduct of the parts", which enables the individual voices to be kept separate. This "good conduct" is based on the Gestalt law of proximity, which we shall meet later in discussing Wertheimer. All the most significant psychologists in the Gestalt school were, moreover, good or excellent musicians who were genuinely interested in musical theory.

Returning to Mach: he demonstrated the existence of a sensation of equality of rhythm with the same technique that he had used previously in analysis of visual shapes: the presentation of two sequences of entirely different notes but possessing the same rhythmic structure. It is therefore not sound sensations that constitute rhythm. Similar considerations concerning simultaneous combinations of sounds enabled Mach to enunciate what later became better known as the "von Ehrenfels principle": a melody is the same melody if it is executed starting from any note but respecting the order of the intervals and the duration of the sounds. The example is absolutely decisive and it falsifies *a priori* any attempt to relate the properties of the whole to the qualities of the elements into which it can be analysed. In fact, the same melody can be executed — and be recognised as the same melody — in two different tonalities chosen so that no note present in the first appears in the second.

In 1890 Christian von Ehrenfels (1859–1932) conducted a wide-ranging discussion of these sensation-independent forms — starting from the case of the transposability of melodies — in his essay *Uber Gestaltqualitäiten* (1890). It was this text that gave currency to the term "Gestalt" in scientific psychology. Von Ehrenfels work was substantially a logical analysis of facts such as those used by Mach which distinguished between sensory ingredients (*Fundamente, Grundlagen*) and the qualities of the whole irreducible to them (*Gestalten*), the latter being classified into temporal structures (for example, melodies) and non-temporal ones (for example, chords or patterns). Von Ehrenfels's essay opened the way for the distinction between structures in the strict sense and expressive properties founded on structures, while it chided Mach for continuing to call such complex objects "sensations".

Von Ehrenfels was a pupil of Alexius Meinong (1853–1920) at Graz. Meinong developed the topic of the formal qualities in two important works: *Zur Psychologie der Komplexionen und Relationen* (1891) and *Über Gegenstände höherer Ordnung und deren Verhaltnis zur inneren Wahrnehmung* (1899). Experience consists of *inferiora* and *superiora*, founding objects and founded objects — which is to say, sensations and structures. The latter are tied to the former by logical necessity, in the sense that they cannot exist without their relative *inferiora*. Accordingly, in Meinong's view, the whole depends on the parts; but it should be added that the joint presence of the *inferiora* in consciousness is not sufficient to give rise to *superiora;* there must simultaneously be a consciousness of their joint presence. Meinong did not accept von Ehrenfels's thesis of the sensory nature of complex forms: relations subsist, sensations exist. However, they both appear in full simultaneity and concreteness. This point becomes clearer if one bears in mind that Meinong's aim was to construct a theory of all the objects that can be experienced and thought, both real and unreal, possible and impossible, and all of them hierarchised by founding relationships. In some way the formal qualities, based on sensations, are the first step towards ideas. Meinong developed this theory between 1904 and 1910, the year in which *Gegenstandtheorie* was published.

The superior intervention of the subject who organises the material of the senses into higher-order objects, and thereby contaminates the sensations of ideality, was investigated empirically by Vittorio Benussi (1878–1927) and Stephan Witasek (1870–1915). Benussi sought to define the act of production which generates what he called the "a-sensory" *(aussinnliche)* structure founded on the *inferiora* by studying configurations in which a change in the observer's stance modifies the organisation of the parts. Of course, this does not happen in melodies, but it may occur in certain cases of structural ambiguities, in the subjective grouping of dots, and even in the reduction through practice of the intensity of certain optical illusions, although Witasek, using very simple melodies, tried to demonstrate their non-sensory nature.

Between 1883 and 1890 two volumes of Carl Stumpf's (1848–1936) *Tonpsychologie* (1883; 1890) were published. A pupil of Brentano and Lotze, Stumpf had already made his mark with an essay in which he argued that extension and colour are properties intrinsic to the perceptual system and able to organise themselves independently of experience. He was an accomplished musician, and it was on musical grounds that he launched a forthright attack against classical psychophysics. He derived a rigorous and productive phenomenological framework from Brentano which enabled him to replace the fragile physicalist theory developed by Helmholtz to explain the consonance and dissonance between musical notes. Stumpf's crucial discovery was that people without musical education, and so not trained in the analysis of sounds, hear pairs of consonant notes presented together as if they were one single sound, whereas on listening to dissonant bichords they are entirely aware that the simultaneously present sounds are two in number. It is very difficult for an octave to be recognised as two simultaneous sounds, and a fifth or a fourth is often taken to be a single sound. But a seventh or a second is readily apprehended as an aggregate of two notes, while a third – in Stumpf's statistics – occupies an intermediate position. The explanation of consonance thus shifts from a physical cause (the beats for Helmholtz) to a phenomenological condition (the "fusion" or indiscernibility of sounds tied by numerically simple frequency relationships).

The influence of Brentano's teaching is certainly apparent in Stumpf's musical psychology, but it is strikingly evident in his two works published in 1907, *Erscheinungen und psychische Funktionen* (1907) and *Zur Einteilung der Wissenschaften* (1907), which addressed themes drawn from Brentano under almost identical titles. The objects of psychology are psychic functions analysed introspectively, but psychology has its necessary propaedeutic in phenomenology – a science no more psychological than physical – whose subject-matter is the world of the things of immediate experience, the condition and outcome of the aggregative functions. Stumpf placed great emphasis on the independence of the properly psychic functions from phenomenal objects by citing cases of empirical evidence in which the function changes without the phenomenon undergoing alteration, or the phenomenon changes without involving the function. The independence of the external world from the subject accordingly finds its phenomenological foundation.

5.

The first years of the twentieth century saw the publication of the *Logische Untersuchungen* (1900–01) by Edmund Husserl (1859–1938).

The work was dedicated to Carl Stumpf, and one of the authors cited in it was Brentano, under whom Husserl had studied. Husserl's aim in the *Logische Untersuchungen* was to give an anti-psychologistic foundation of logic and the theory of knowledge. It should therefore fall outside the line of historical development from Locke to Gestalt theory expounded here. However, experimental psychology in general is anti-psychologistic, although Husserl himself was largely unaware of the fact.

Husserl tended to identify psychology with the theories of Wundt, who, after setting up the first laboratory of psychology (at Leipzig in 1879), dominated the academic scene of the time. Following J.S. Mill, Wundt recommended the breakdown of every experience into elementary sensations or, more broadly, "mental elements". Husserl's notion of "psychologism" may be applied directly only to this manner of proceeding. It should be borne in mind, however, that much of European and American psychology at the turn of the century was of Wundtian derivation. Husserl therefore had a very broad target to attack.

It is impossible here to dwell at length on the analyses of the structure of experience that abound in the *Logische Untersuchungen*. Already in *Philosophie der Arithmetik* (1891), Husserl had based the apprehension of multiplicity on a concept similar to that of *Gestaltqualität* formulated by Mach and von Ehrenfels. In a commentary on Stumpf in *Logische Untersuchungen*, he analysed the functional dependency among the qualities constitutive of an object as evidenced, for example, by the fact that the colour of an object may change with its shape, or the timbre of a sound with variation in its intensity, although cases might arise in which this dependency did not occur. The entire work is traversed by a covert discussion with Stumpf and Brentano that surfaces in the appendix to the second volume: whether or not we call the objects of the intentional acts "physical", they have the same evidence that Brentano attributed to our inner states. Thus: "inner perception and outer perception, to the extent that these terms are used in their natural sense, have exactly the same character from the gnoseological point of view";[9] and "I perceive that anguish squeezes my throat, a tooth causes me pain, sorrow torments my heart in the same sense that I perceive that the wind shakes the trees or that this box is square and is dark in colour".[10] Husserl's subsequent works although they seem to have exerted very little influence on the Gestaltists' theoretical work – are extremely rich in observations that might belong to a scientific and experimental psychology inspired by Wertheimer, although Husserl's prose style grew increasingly impenetrable, and the philosophical implications of his new language tended more towards a noumenology than towards an empirically verifiable phenomenology.

It is worth pointing out that a phenomenology of immediate experience was also outlined by Charles Sanders Peirce (1839–1914) in numerous notes written between 1895 and 1910. Peirce repeatedly recommended that logical constructs or natural prejudices should not rely on the observation of objects. His *phaneron* was the "complete set of everything that is in some way and in some sense present to the mind, irrespectively of whether it corresponds to some reality or not"[11], but mention of the word "mind" does not imply any form of mentalism, despite the fact that it normally carries "a psychological connotation which I intend carefully to exclude".[12] Phenomenology, according to Peirce, "examines direct experience by combining the minutest accuracy with the most broad generalization" and it pits itself "against the reasoning according to which facts *should* be such and such", because its task is the "simple and honest observation of appearance".[13]

Although Peirce's theories were not taken up, in those same years – that is, the first decade of this century – numerous scholars more or less consciously adopted phenomenological methods in their inquiries into perception and thought processes: most notably Georg Elias Müller and Freidrich Schumann, who identified the problem of unity in the visual field and indicated spatial proximity as an organising factor (besides proximity, Müller listed similarity, e.g. identity of colour, and continuity of direction, which we shall meet later when discussing Wertheimer). David Katz resumed one of Goethe's favourite themes and conducted numerous experiments to demonstrate that colours have various modes of appearance:[14] for example the epiphanic colours, which are perceived as surfaces; the diaphanic colours, which appear penetrable to the gaze (fog); the volumetric colours (a turbid liquid), which are perceived as properties internal to the substance of a three-dimensional body; colours that admit to transparency; and so on. These are phenomenological structures that cannot be explained in terms of the physical properties of the light that strikes the eyes – which is subject to only three variables (frequency, amplitude and spectral composition) – but only in terms of the context in which a given colour is present.

At Würzburg, throughout the whole of the first decade of the century, under the supervision of Oswald Külpe (1862–1915) and later Karl Bühler (1879- 1963) numerous researchers conducted phenomenological analyses of thought processes in the form of controlled introspection.

The method – which consisted in the minute description of events occurring in the mind some instants before the subject answered a detailed question, or solved a simple logical problem – was fiercely criticised by Wundt as non-scientific. Nevertheless, replication of these experiments in the conditions described by the original researchers yields very similar results, showing that it is indeed possible to observe thought in its act of genesis and development, and to capture its emotive concomitants (uncertainty, stress, sudden lapses), as well as, sometimes, the images that accompany it (although, according to the Würzburg school, these do not perform an important role). Moreover, the fundamentally important work on thought that Wertheimer wrote some decades later invited its readers to perform the same sorts of experiment in order to test the reliability of his theory empirically.

6.

The essay that Wertheimer published in 1912, and which I mentioned at the outset, is not only an exhaustive account of the conditions and forms of stroboscopic movement, it is also the text that, from an epistemological point of view, inaugurated the first phase of Gestalt theory, which I shall call "falsificatory". In 1910 Wertheimer met Wolfgang Köhler (1887–1967) and Kurt Koffka (1886–1941) at Schumann's laboratory in Frankfurt: Köhler had been a pupil of Stumpf, while Koffka was from Würzburg. They were the first to see Wertheimer's experiments and to act as his experimental subjects. From their discussions the theoretical framework of Gestalt psychology came into being. Enthusiasm for the new theory inevitably bred controversy, and falsificationism was the epistemological guise that the polemic took on. One year after publication of Wertheimer's research, Köhler's theoretical work Uber unbemerkte Empfindungen und Urteilstäuschungen (1913) appeared as the first explicit and rigorous theorisation of the principle of falsifiability.

Wertheimer's main observations can be summarised as follows: if two lights are projected onto a screen, with a short distance between them, with a temporal interval of varying magnitude between the moment when the first light is switched off (*a*) and the second is switched on (*b*), we may see different things: if the interval of darkness is less than 30 ms we see the two lights as switching on and off almost simultaneously; if the interval is longer than approximately 60 ms, we see a single light moving from one position to the other, like an object travelling along a highly visible path; if the interval is extended even further, we again perceive two distinct lights, each of them briefly moving towards the position of the other. But with any further extension of the time interval, *a* and *b* alternately occupy each other's positions, while movement in the pure state occurs between them: a movement without an object in motion, the clear and distinct perception of motion in itself, what Wertheimer called movement(ϕ. Only when the time interval is longer than 200 ms, or more, will *a* and *b* appear consecutively in their positions, with no trace of motion in the space between them. Thus, merely by adjusting the time interval, we obtain two facts that are phenomenologically irrefutable (with the external support of Peirce, the Brentano-Stumpf-Husserl tradition taught *esse est percipi*) and of exceptional theoretical importance: two objects in a *static* position become *one* object in *movement;* and the movement may detach itself from the object and present itself as pure phenomenon. It is extremely difficult to go beyond a phenomenon such as this in search of the elementary sensations of which it is constituted. The movement is *a primum* non-analysable, and it may provide the point of departure for analysis of further problems.

Movement in perception is an axiom to be posited in order to yield further logical developments. But the psychology of sensations had contended that stroboscopic movement is seen because the subject unwittingly moves his or her eyes from one spot to another when light *a* is switched off and light *b* appears. Wertheimer placed *a* to the right and *b* to the left, but just below them *a'* to the left and *b'* to the right, and then switched the lights simultaneously on and off. Thus, while *a* moved towards the right, *a'* moved towards the left; but the eye cannot move in two directions at once. Therefore the thesis was false. The psychology of sensations had also claimed that stroboscopic movement was not really seen; it was thought, or imagined so vividly that it seemed almost real. Wertheimer arranged for an optimal stroboscopic movement (with 60 ms of interval) to be projected over the real movement of a light source. The apparent movement was more real than the real one. The phenomenological method thus confounded the most deeply held tenets of the doctrine of the sensations.

When Wertheimer's essay was published, Köhler was at work on his article on the unnoticed sensations and errors of judgment. The article carried forward a rather acrimonious polemic against his master Stumpf and against the remaining sensationalistic elements in his theory of perception. The current interpretation of perceptual facts, Köhler argued, ran as follows: the physical stimuli that affect the peripheral sense organs generate sensations which vary with the stimulus according to psychophysical laws: as soon as the sensations are formed (and before they are felt; that is, before they become true sensations), judgments in the unconscious sphere of the mind re-order them and transform them in accordance with what we know of the outside world, or in accordance with certain "schemes of calculation" (Helmholtz). This operation of the unconscious judgments on the unnoticed sensations means that we see true objects before us, rather than patches of colour; but a certain inertia or blindness of the mechanisms of judgment means that we also see deceptive things like optical illusions.

Köhler's arguments against this thesis ran as follows:

a)   To be sure, there exist examples of sensations connected one-to-one to stimuli, and they vary with variations in them. These examples are constructed in the laboratory so that every action on sensations that is not reducible to variation in the stimuli is rigorously excluded. By restricting the field of facts to experiments of this kind the psychophysical hypothesis of the constancy of the stimulus/sensation ratio can never be refuted.

b)   Let us take a case in which things do not add up from a psychophysical point of view: an optical illusion in which two psychophysical lengths appear to be different. With effort and a great deal of practice we may finally see them as equal – that is, "as they really are" – except that when our effort ceases they revert to what they were before. Why do we not say, at this second moment, that we see them "as they really are"? Because from the outset we have accepted the hypothesis of stimulus/sensation constancy as a general theory of the sensations.

c)   When we encounter cases that contradict the hypothesis of this constancy, we say that they stem from an "illusion due to the judgment". But this explanation is advanced only when the constancy hypothesis is contradicted by the facts; and moreover we are by no means aware of having this judgment in mind. An effectively thought judgment that is able to modify sensations would offer at least a foothold for research, but unconscious judgment cannot give it any concrete indications.

The conclusions are evident and immediate: the classical theory of the sensations–perceptions is not falsifiable. There is no fact, not even an entirely imaginary one, that it cannot explain. In every imaginable case, indeed, either the perception matches the stimulus and the explanation is psychophysical, or the perception is at variance with the stimulus and the auxiliary hypothesis of the unconscious judgment intervenes. "The auxiliary hypotheses, precisely because of their logical nature, bury faith in observation: specifically, faith in the facts that are the object of psychology, and the pleasure of observation, the taste for progress".[15]

In this way the new phenomenology no longer took the form of the descriptive recognition of immediacy (Brentano, Stumpf) but of recognition of the facts of direct experience that, by virtue of their structure, falsify general theses and explanations comprising mechanisms irreducible to experience itself. For a theory to be true it must foresee which facts should not come about. That is to say, it is not a theory if it explains every possible and imaginable fact. Only in 1934 would Karl Popper write that "an empirical system should be refutable by experience",[16] thereby familiarising philosophers by compelling analysis with this basic principle of scientific inquiry.

If viewed in the light of Köhler's epistemological proposal, Wertheimer's study of apparent movement marked the beginning of a new experimental psychology. The dismantling of theories by citing facts incompatible with whatever can be deduced from them became the pre-eminent style of researchers with a Gestaltist training.

In the same years, moreover, and outside the Wertheimer-Köhler-Koffka group, Edgar Rubin working in Göttingen discovered the first phenomenological laws of the figure/background, articulation. The perceptual field is made up of objects detached from their background because of the shape of chromatically differentiated areas, not because of the individual sensations of colour into which the field can be decomposed. The entire organisation of experience rests on this structure.

If a loop is drawn on a homogeneous surface, one sees that the area within the loop has a visibly different character from the area lying outside it: its colour and grain make it a "thing" *(Dingcharakter)*, while the remaining area does not stop at its boundaries but passes behind it. If a piece of paper is divided into two equal parts, one black and one white, with a straight border between them, it appears to be the juxtaposition of two surfaces. But if the border is curved to make, for example, the white part convex, it becomes a figure against a black background. In a figure like the following:

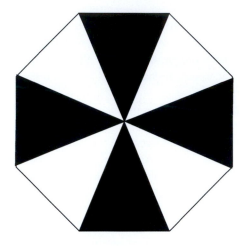

(17.2)

It is possible to see a black cross with horizontal and vertical arms, or a white cross set at 45°. Prolonged fixation on the figure enables the eye to pass from one perceptual pattern to the other. In this passage, all the roles of the parts are reversed. Whereas at first the black cross was figure, with the white between its arms as the background which also extended behind the cross, and the character of "thing" concentrated in the black areas, now it is the black that appears as background and the white becomes more compact.

At the moment of the inversion, the margins dividing the white from the black change their function. They at first limit the black, leaving the white free to expand behind the cross; then they limit the white, with a black octagon lying behind. Therefore, where there are figures, the margins perform a unilateral function.

The shift in the unilateral function may give rise to different figures, as in the following example:

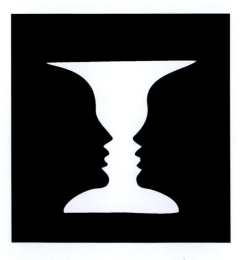

(17.3)

All this happens while the sensations – defined as the close correlates of the stimulus – remain the same. Indeed, the concept of sensation has no role to play in this analysis.

Moreover, the figures are remembered more readily than the backgrounds, and they arouse richer associations of ideas.

These results were published in 1915 in Danish, in 1921 in German, in a book entitled *Visuell wahrgenommene Figuren*.

In the year 1915, Köhler was living in Tenerife, where he had been trapped by the outbreak of the First World War. During this period he devoted himself to the study of intelligence in anthropoid apes. In his work with chimpanzees he conducted lengthy analysis of their behaviour in learning and problem-solving situations. Although the chimpanzees were caged, their movements were unimpeded (the animals were therefore not confined by laboratory equipment that restrained them in accordance with the researcher's experimental design), and the problems set them involved various ways of obtaining a banana. In these conditions, the animals revealed themselves to be highly ingenious. They were able to pile boxes on top of each other when the banana was hanging from the roof, or to find a thread tied to a banana outside the cage but with one end just inside it, or to fit two sticks together and make a longer one when the banana was too far away to be reached with only one stick.

But the real theme of the inquiry was the following: animal behaviour had already brought to light the fact that the solution to a problem consists in the improvised restructuring of the individual parts of the perceptual field. Thought has something in common with perception. Just as the eye suddenly sees the two profiles in the above illustration after first having seen the goblet, so in representation of the objects present in the surrounding field, the intuition may abruptly arise of the relationship between the two short sticks that can be made into one long one, on the one hand, and the goal to be achieved on the other. Even more so when solving the problem is made easier by arranging the sticks in a line, thereby providing a perceptual prompt for the subject to fit them together.

The act of grasping the relations among facts and thus solving the problem was called *Einsicht* – "insight" (intuition, restructuring act) in English – and it became the cornerstone of Gestalt psychology of thought. This body of research was published in 1917 under the title *The Mentality of Apes*. In that same year, Wertheimer was probably already making notes for a study of the psychology of logic, in which the notion of insight was to throw new light on the problem of syllogistic proof. He had in fact promised the study for Stumpf's seventieth birthday. Although from a formal point of view the syllogism is a concealed deduction, as J.S. Mill had pointed out, there are cases in which the conclusion takes the form of a discovery – that is, cases in which the restructuring of the meaning of the premises produces the "insight" of the conclusion, the evidence for its necessity.

The years of First World War, the period in which the foundations of Gestalt theory were laid, saw another theoretical contribution of major importance: Koffka's polemic against Benussi, and in general against the Graz school. The aim of Koffka's arguments was to demolish the idea of "production" which, as we have seen, took the elements of sensory origin (sensations) and shaped them into experiences of a-sensory origin, true Gestalten, structures in which the whole is more than the sum of the parts. Koffka's clarification – which is a model of the logical analysis of a theory – gave a new and definitive form to the Gestaltist idea of Gestalten. These do not arise from a combination of sense data, since they exist as objects of immediate experience from the outset. Hence the problem of their genesis is a false problem. Nor does the question of their correspondence or non-correspondence with the stimulus arise: given a constellation of stimuli, the structure of the object emerges just as it is, without being mediated by sensations. The sensations of psychophysics laboratories are simply what is obtained by decomposing the object. And it is this that should form the basis of a new physiology of the brain.

These theoretical assumptions gave rise to a substantial body of empirical research conducted both by the three founders of the school and by the various researchers who joined them.

Thus 1921 saw publication of the first fascicle of *Psychologische Forschung* (Psychological Research), a journal that gathered and published the research and debate generated by the new theory.

7.

During the life of *Psychologische Forschung*, which ceased publication in 1938 as a result of Nazi persecution, Gestalt psychology extended the bounds of its inquiry beyond the phenomenology of perception to encompass the problems of thought, memory, emotional dynamics, social psychology and even psychopathology.

However, before considering these matters, mention should be made of an essay on natural philosophy that Köhler published in 1920. Entitled *Die Physische Gestalten in Ruhe und im stationären Zustand*, this essay won Köhler appointment to the professorial chair vacated by Stumpf. His discussion centred on the properties of suitably selected physical systems, and on their theoretical applicability in interpretation of certain classes of perceptual facts. The dynamic self-distribution of electrical charges on a semi-conductor, and more in general the properties of electrical and magnetic fields, illustrate in physics the peculiarities of the perceptual forms that Koffka had demonstrated to Benussi: once the appropriate conditions obtain, the structure is instantly realised, and it is the whole of this structure that determines the local properties of the field. If from a semiconductor of a particular shape, and with a certain distribution of electrostatic charges on its surface, some of these charges are eliminated, those that remain redistribute themselves immediately and re-establish the overall pattern of the field.

In addition to these examples, Köhler lists numerous others taken from the mechanics of liquids and rigid bodies. Different physical patterns can be placed in relationship to the same perceptual structure. The permanence of a stable configuration in the visual and auditory field can be likened to the behaviour of an isolated physical system in stable equilibrium, but also to a stationary system in which a dynamic process takes place continuously over time (such as the constant flow of a liquid in a cylindrical tube); or to an oscillating stationary process in which the dynamic properties of the system recur cyclically over time (such as vibrating chords or pendulums).

The relationship between figure and background, for example, can be interpreted as a surge of potential in a homogeneous conductor. Assuming the region of the conductor, which here represents the *figure* (in Rubin's sense), to be considerably smaller than that of the *background*, there will be an average density of energy internal to the region of the figure that is proportionally greater than the energy distributed across the remaining region. Indeed, the same quantity of energy is concentrated into a smaller space in the *figure*. It is not difficult, writes Köhler, to set this fact in relation to the salience possessed phenomenologically by the *figure* with respect to the background.

As his discussion proceeds, Köhler devotes four pages to an attack on universal interactionism.[17] This attack should be mentioned because it rests on an entirely distorted interpretation of Gestalt theory.

A straightforward philosophical adjustment to the arguments set out so far yields the idea that "everything depends on everything" and that, in psychology, only the totality of consciousness is able to explain individual events. From a Gestalt point of view this is an entirely erroneous assumption. The field of experience is made up of a myriad isolated systems, each of which is Gestalt in the sense explained above, but all of which are independent of all the others, just as "the world of physics is sharply divided into physical systems, to which alone natural laws apply".[18] If universal interactionism were true, research would be in principle impossible: it would be impossible to control the variables of a phenomenon if the entire universe changed whenever one of them was altered. Experience is made up of definite things, and research investigates finite objects: it is precisely for this reason that it achieves results. With this specification Köhler rejects both the psychologistic holism of Felix Krueger – which is often erroneously cited as an example of Gestaltism – and the thesis of "ubiquitous relations" (omnipresent functional dependencies) propounded by William James.

The appearance of *Psychologische Forschung* coincided with an essay by Koffka on the basic concepts of Gestalt theory[19] aimed at the American scientific community, which was at that time almost entirely dominated by behaviourism. The origins of the theory in Brentano and Stumpf is evident from the outset in Koffka's definition of the world of perception by negation. The world of perception is not what we represent to ourselves, nor is it what we think of objects, nor is it a content of the imagination; when these psychic activities have been removed, it is the objective residue of direct experience. "When I speak of perception (. . .) my intention is not to speak of a specific psychic function (. . .) and I wish to use the term 'perception' in a sense which excludes any theoretical prejudice",[20] in particular the prejudice that contrapposes perceptions to sensations as a more refined product of the mind.

A year later, *Psychologische Forschung* published Wertheimer's study of the formation of units in the perceptual field.[21] The figure/background category had already been absorbed into phenomenological inquiry from the researches of Rubin. But on the basis of what cohesion factors do objects, already segregated by the background, aggregate themselves into units? A number of dots against a background are not simply dots; rather, they form patterns. They aggregate themselves spontaneously and naturally, although with effort it is possible to see them as connected in different patterns. These latter, however, are short-lived and, as soon as our effort slackens, they yield to the rules of spontaneous aggregation. Consider this simple fact:

● ● ● ● ● ● ● ● ● ●   (17.4)

This is a "row" of dots. The distance between them is now altered as follows:

● ●   ● ●   ● ●   ● ●   ● ●   (17.5)

This is a "row of pairs" of dots. The space visible between one point and the next is the factor that organises them into units (a pair is in its fashion a unit).

But distance is not the only unifying factor. This can be shown by arranging a certain number of objects at regular intervals, but so that two similar objects stand next to each other, in the following order:

● ● ○ ○ ● ● ○ ○ ● ●   (17.6)

Here too we have a pattern of pairs, but this time it is one based on a relationship of similarity. The observer is able to form his or her own pattern at will when the two factors conflict with each other:

● ○   ○ ●   ● ○   ○ ●   ● ○   (17.7)

Here we can see either pairs based on proximity or pairs based on similarity. But this subjective structuring by the observer is momentary, for the objective factors are always stronger.

The factor of the continuity of direction prevails over that of proximity. In the following figure all the dots of segment C are more distant from the dots of segment A than those of segment B. And yet A and C form a single line while B maintains its independence.

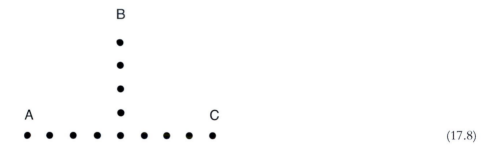

(17.8)

The factor of closure is even stronger than that of continuity in certain conditions, as shown by this example:

(17.9)

There is also a factor of "good form". In the following example we may, in theory, see three enclosed and somehow coordinated areas. Instead, however, we see the overlapping of two squares: two symmetrical objects rather than three irregular polygons.

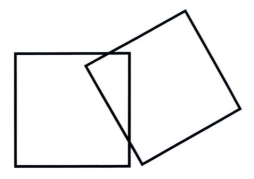

(17.10)

    Past experience may also be influential, albeit relatively rarely, in the organisation of perceptual material into units.

    For instance, experience of the Roman alphabet greatly helps one to see the letters M and W superimposed in the following pattern, because continuity of direction and closure are factors which prevail over the weak action of past experience:

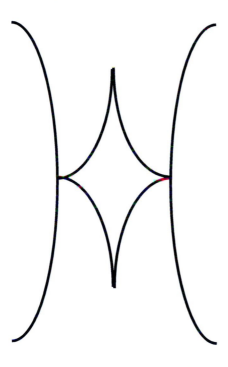

(17.11)

    As already mentioned, some of these factors had been identified years earlier by G.E. Müller, the teacher of Katz and Rubin. However, it was Wertheimer's achievement to realize that the factors of unitary organisation (i) have differing force; (ii) can be made to conflict and give rise to weak units; (iii) can be made to act in synergy to produce strong units; and (iv) allow a conceptual distinction to be drawn between the "natural parts" and the "arbitrary parts" of a given whole or Gestalt.

    Every object of experience can be segmented in scores of different ways. If we make a hole in a piece of black cardboard, we can view the world through it piece by piece just as it, the world, really is. This device and others like it were called "reduction screens", and they were used to obtain true sensations without interference by the context. But objects in their entirety really possess parts, which are the elements discernible in their constitution, hierarchised in some manner and tied together by relationships that depend on the configuration of the whole. Using only the laws of "figure/background" configuration and Wertheimer's factors it is possible to explain most of perceptual experience, or in any case to conceive of it in a problematically new manner.

Still in 1922, Freidrich Wulf applied the concept of "good form" to memory in a series of experiments which demonstrated the mnestic evolution of less regular patterns into more regular ones. Between 1918 and 1922 Adhamar Gold, Kurt Goldstein and Wilhelm Fuchs tested new ideas in the pathology of vision, finding that the structural (or Gestaltic) aspects of perceptual phenomena tend to emerge with specific forms in cases of both brain damage and retinal trauma, sometimes with the effect of compensating for the lost functions.

1922 was also the year in which Kurt Lewin (1890–1947) joined the Gestalt school and published a wide-ranging study, from the point of view of the philosophy of science, on the concept of "genesis" in physics, biology and the theory of evolution which, in certain respects, was apparently an extension of Köhler's theory of physical forms to the biological sphere. Thanks to these contributions (and to a study by Lewin of the concepts of scientific law and experimentation in psychology), Köhler and Lewin came into contact with members of the Berlin neo-positivist circle, which was officially constituted in 1928 but had already been in operation for a number of years on the initiative in particular of Hans Reichenbach and Carl Gustav Hempel. They were active members of the circle until it was dissolved in 1933 when the Nazis came to power. In that year Lewin was in America, where he would remain.

Lewin had contributed studies on acoustic perception to *Psychologische Forschung* since 1922. In 1926 the journal published two essays of fundamental importance: *Vorbemerkungen über seelischen Kräfte und die Struktur der Seele* and *Vorsatz, Wille und Bedürfnis*, two chapters of a single essay on theoretical psychology. Lewin began by developing a theme already treated by Köhler in *Die Physische Gestalten:* the proposition "every thing is connected with every other" is generally false, and it is so in the case of the mind as well. Recognition of this, however, is not prejudicial to a unitary concept of the mind itself. In reality, the mind is a set of more or less independent, and sometimes entirely independent, systems. Not in the sense that the mind comprises diverse and simultaneous psychic faculties, like memory, thought or perception – whose forms of interaction and collaboration should indeed be studied – but in the sense that it is the diverse psychic experiences, in the act in which they originate and in their simultaneity, that constitute autonomous and closely integrated blocks: complex indivisible "Gestalten", like thinking about the solution to a problem, suddenly remembering something, noticing that it is too hot, realizing that there are books and a picture before our eyes. Two psychological events influence each other if they belong to the same system, but they will not influence each other at all, or only weakly, if they belong to different systems. Should this latter happen, however, it will generate a new system. The unity of the mind is simply the entire field of the coexistence of such systems and of the forces that dynamically regulate them. Performing some coordinated and non-chaotic activity presupposes the independence of systems and the possibility of excluding most of the other psychic tensions simultaneously present. In developing this theme, Lewin introduced the concept of tendency towards equilibrium, of vector (the directed thrust which often occurs in locomotion through the environment), and of "boundary among psychic systems".

These conceptual tools made it possible to devise a research programme on the psychology of affective states that was pursued in the following nine years by numerous collaborators. Above all, however, taken together they formed the theoretical basis for a new experimental social psychology that was perhaps the most enduring contribution of Gestalt psychology to the human sciences.

8.

Just as the psychic factors (memories, representations, sensations, etc.) disappear from Lewin's theory to be replaced by the plurality of the systems of experience into which the field of direct experience is segmented, so in a work by Erich von Hornbostel,[22] the prejudice of the "five senses" is eliminated, in this case to be replaced by the objects of experience in their complex inter-sensory integration: "movement can be seen, heard, touched";[23] sounds can be coloured; the same adjective can be used for tactile, visual and acoustic qualities. The five senses are an abstraction; facts are sensorially multi-dimensional. Similar views were expressed in a book by Cesare Musatti.[24] By radicalising some of the theses propounded by the school of Meinong – Musatti had studied with Benussi – he took the world of the objects of experience as his starting point for the conceptual elaboration of various structurings of reality: on the one hand towards the outside, i.e. towards physics and the natural sciences, and on the other towards the inside, i.e. towards phenomenology and psychology. At the basis of a system of fictions lies the "objectuality" of the immediate datum.

In 1929, Köhler published a book[25] that imposed some sort of order on the by-now broad debate over the principles of Gestalt theory. Experimental research had accumulated in *Psychologische Forschung* and in other more traditional journals, while critical reactions came mainly from American behaviourist circles (Koffka had been appointed to a professorship at Smith College in 1927). Much of European psychology was still working on associationist and Wundtian presuppositions, not without resentment at a certain arrogance that had typified the Gestaltist style from the outset. Köhler's book is characterised by its highly systematic organisation and its polemical thrust. It is still the finest exposition of Gestaltism ever written. Köhler begins by showing that there is a close affinity between associationism and behaviourism: in both, the method of empirical inquiry presupposes fragmentation of the situations of experience into their presumed elementary components, which in both theories take the form of simple mechanical relationships: stimulus/sensation, stimulus/ response. He then shows that the sphere of reality from which behaviourism draws its "facts" – facts that in his philosophy must be objective and non-mental, because the mind is private and whatever is private cannot be the subject-matter of science – is the same sphere as that in which phenomenal events occur. If behaviourism were consistent in its rejection of the phenomenal world, it would lose all its empirical data and all the areas in which its measurements are made. Köhler's third step is to show with examples how premature measurement distorts the structure of the facts, which should be taken in their qualitative immediacy because this generates problems – just as happened at the beginning of physics and astronomy, when the most fundamental problems of those sciences arose precisely from the qualitative analysis of phenomena.

Having eliminated the mechanistic interpretation of psychological facts, Köhler proposes a dynamic theory that no longer comprises chains of cause and effect but, instead, conditions that take on various combinations according to the complex phenomenon assumed as the object of inquiry. Experimental analysis of the conditions of the phenomenon (almost always) leads to the discovery that it can be interpreted as a field phenomenon. That is to say, a logic is used that displays close similarities with the logic that describes electromagnetic fields, the gravitational field, and so on. Accordingly, the association itself is a structure and not a simple connection. If we try to memorise a pair of semantically very different words, their mechanical repetition is less help to us than an overall image incorporating both of them, even if it is somewhat odd (lake/sugar: a sugar cube melting in a lake; railway/elephant: an elephant walking along a railway track).

Of course, the psychophysical relationship plays an important role in the theory. But it is recast in totally new terms. Although there is a space-time of physics, it is not that of phenomenology, that is, of direct experience. We never have direct dealings with the objects of physics, which exist in their own space-time. The objects of physics include that particularly complex system that is the central nervous system. Our every dealing with something is the result of the activity of the brain; therefore the brain is extraneous to every experience. The link between the totality of our experiences and the brain is constituted by the fact that they coincide with *one part* of the brain's activity (which is a physical- chemical and electrical activity) and by the further fact that the form assumed by the laws of our phenomenological experiences is that form assumed by the logic of the concomitant cerebral processes (isomorphism). If, when experimenting on phenomena, we find that a given fact depends on three variables combined in a certain way, then there is a process within the brain – perhaps one of those that Köhler described in *Die Physische Gestalten* (1920) – whose realisation depends on at least three conditions, each of which representing, at the level of nervous activity, the variable as manipulated in the ongoing experience. The "postulate of isomorphism" assumes isomorphism between the logical form of the experiential organisation and the logical form of the physical (biochemical, electrical, etc.) process taking place in the central nervous system.

The fact that there are independent systems in experience shows there are independent systems in the brain; the fact that there are functional dependencies in experience shows that there are functional dependencies in the brain. The reality of the functional dependencies that knit the subject and the environment together demonstrate the falsity of the theories derived from Hume's empiricism, for phenomenal causality exists and indeed guides our behaviour as regards the external environment. The "insight" or immediate intuition of dependency relationships is pre-categorial because it is a given which determines behaviour even before the mind becomes aware of the structure of a situation; but it is also a logical category of explanatory thought imposed on the description of states of affairs.

Memory is based on the understanding of relationships; the problem of other minds can be dealt with by eliminating every metaphysical prejudice and analysing the field of experience in terms of expressiveness: tone of voice, facial or gestural mimicry, the environmental and cognitive context, together constitute the phenomenological conditions of the act of comprehension. Köhler argues that the universe of common sense and natural language contains not only all the problems but also many of the productive and rigorous conceptual tools of psychology.

As I said, Koffka moved to the United States in 1927. The headlong rush of events combined with racial persecution also forced Wertheimer to New York in 1933. After wavering between Germany and America, Lewin too immigrated to the United States in 1935, followed by Köhler, who took up an appointment at Swarthmore College after he had made his life in Germany unbearable by launching public attacks against the regime. The entire leadership of the Gestalt movement thus found itself in a cultural environment very distant from the tormented theoretical premises in Europe from which they had drawn their problems, ideas and intellectual style. One of Wertheimer and Köhler's pupils, Karl Duncker, certainly one of the most outstanding minds in the school, was unable to cope with such a radical transplant and committed suicide at the age of thirty-seven. Duncker was the author of the study *Zur Psychologie des produktiver Denkens* (1935). Much of his book is devoted to analysis of the thought processes that lead to the solution of mathematical problems. Duncker's description of ongoing thought enables him to distinguish between nonsensical errors and productive errors, which are amenable to correction, and to isolate those particular cases of "insight" that tie conclusions to premises, both logically and factually. Duncker highlights the affinity that ties the causal relationship to logical implication, and he identifies the conditions under which thought passes from partial understanding to "total insight" or evidence. This is therefore analysis of the logical force that confers ineluctability to every salient step in a proof. Duncker himself stresses the continuity of his investigations with the line of thought developed by Hume, Kant, Husserl and Wertheimer.

In 1935 Koffka's great treatise *Principles of Gestalt Psychology* was published. The "Bible" of all the work thus far accomplished by the Gestaltists, this is a book in which Koffka's theoretical discussion and innovative ideas are interwoven with minute description of a myriad experiments conducted by the Gestaltists and with reinterpretations of experiments in the classical tradition. The first part of the book deals with perception, but an unusually large amount of space is devoted to analysis of memory, of the self and of action. Central to Koffka's theory is the distinction between the geographical environment and the behavioural environment. The former is the set of properties of the external world describable using the language of physics and the natural sciences; the latter is the phenomenological universe in which subjects operate as they move, reflect, remember, recognize, evaluate and construct sensory knowledge; the universe, that is, in which facts are not simply facts but elements of an overall conceptual organisation that confers meaning on its substructures from above (the distinctive feature of *Principles* is its avowedly anti-positivist epistemological stance). However, rather than create a dualism, this distinction is used to sustain a physicalist monism in which the central nervous system performs a role of total mediation, on the one hand identifying itself – in strictest accordance with Köhler's postulate of isomorphism – with a subject's field of experience at a given moment, and, on the other, ensuring interpretation of the macroscopic properties of the surrounding physical world in terms of what is biologically important about them. One of the most interesting features of Koffka's physicalism is his theory of mnestic traces, by which are meant those states of the brain that guarantee our contacts with the past. This theory satisfies the requirements of a physical interpretation of the permanence of states over time simultaneously with those of compatibility with the psychological facts that emerge from studies of the evolution and transformations of memory. Despite the marked unevenness and occasional obscurity of Koffka's treatise, it can nevertheless be regarded as the most outstanding effort to systematise the psychological content of Gestalt philosophy.

Another form of physicalist monism – which was perhaps even more influential in America than Koffka's *Principles* – was that developed by Egon Brunswik, an unorthodox Gestaltist who reintroduced sensations into the theory of perception. In a celebrated article written for the *Encyclopaedia of Unified Science*,[26] Brunswik envisaged the unification of physics and psychology and proposed a probabilistic interpretation of the laws of perception.

9.

However, Gestalt theory's most profound influence on American scientific culture was exerted by the work of Kurt Lewin, not so much in the field of general psychology as in the social sciences, especially in microsociology. Lewin's theories had been well known in the United States since the early 1930s. One year after Koffka's *Principles*, he published a book[27] in which his project of 1926 was developed into a system. Unfortunately, Lewin's reference to the topology of mathematics is highly debatable, if not downright erroneous.

One should read the book bearing in mind that what Lewin calls topology is in fact a graphic language of his own invention able to represent the experience of a given person at a given moment (or by means of more complex depictions, in several successive instants of a "story") and articulated into specific relationships with the phenomenally external environment and specific internal states (affective, cognitive, etc.) hierarchised into systems and subsystems. Inner states and external events are represented by areas. These areas are separated by barriers of greater or lesser permeability, and they are connected by vectors which represent forces with varying degrees of intensity. Areas may carry positive or negative valences which indicate sources of attraction or repulsion.

Koffka's "environment of behaviour" can be thus represented in a language of its own whose terms can be written so that some sort of calculation can be made. A diagram by Lewin represents the life-space of a person P in an environment A at a given moment. Behaviour (i.e. change in the relations internal to the diagram) is a function of the structure of P and A. Since the field – the state of affairs depicted by the diagram – is always considered in a given instant, it must be conceived as a sort of absolute present, in which the past is the presence of the past in the present (e.g. memories) and the future is the set of projects and possibilities currently imagined, here and now. This principle obliges Lewin to distinguish between historical causality and systematic causality. Every behaviour is subject to systematic causality, that is, the pattern of forces present in the field at a given moment, but the structure of the field can only be explained by the factors that have led events, and hence forces, to take on that particular pattern. Dynamic psychology, especially as social psychology and the psychology of small groups, should therefore be framed as the in-depth analysis of the individual case, and not as the statistical balance-sheet of a collection of cases reduced to quantitative data. The method of psychology should therefore be Galilean, Lewin stressed in a celebrated essay, not Aristotelian and therefore classificatory.

Lewin's theory produced a large quantity of research. Mention should be made in particular of *Psychology and the Social Order* (1936) by John F. Brown, which extended Lewin's topological interpretation to macrosociological and mass phenomena. The Marxist slant of Brown's work prevented it from achieving the success that it warranted, but it contains still extremely topical analysis of power relationships in the liberal democracies, and of fascist and communist dictatorships. In 1940 Brown published another book, *The Psycho-Dynamics of Abnormal Behavior*, in which he applied Lewin's concepts and logic to psychoanalysis, psychopathology and psychiatry with rare skill of systematisation.

Of the few Gestaltists who remained in Germany, mention should be made of Edwin Rausch and Wolfgang Metzger (1899–1979). Most notable of Rausch's many works is *Uber Summativität und Nichtsummativität* (1937), the first mathematical treatise on the concept of Gestalt as a structure that does not result from the sum of its parts. Of Metzger's output worth citing is his book *Psychologie*, published in 1941. Just as Koffka's *Principles* had been an encyclopaedia of Gestaltist experimental research prior to 1935, so *Psychologie* was the encyclopaedia of the philosophical problems connected with those researches and theories. Metzger was probably the most Kantian of the Gestaltists: the key chapters in his book are those on the appearance of "reality" and on causality. Metzger proposed a stratification of various realities in experience, ranging from the inescapable reality of the material objects that populate our life-space to the reality of the imagination, of the void and of nothingness, each of them founded on its own conditions and capable of exerting specific effects. He analysed causality with a wealth of examples taken from everyday experience which, in a sharply anti-Humean conceptualisation, he regarded as prefiguring the formal structures of epistemology. Metzger took on the difficult task of keeping the Gestaltist tradition alive in Hitler's Germany, first at Frankfurt and then, from 1942 onwards, at Munster.

Another important book of 1940 was *Organizing and Memorizing* by George Katona (who had studied with Müller at Göttingen, where he converted from associationism to Gestaltism), in which a series of ingenious experiments showed that, as Aristotle had said, "the memories that come to depend on a principle produce themselves in a readier and more beautiful manner". According to Katona, there are in fact two memories: one for the learning of random items (syllables or telephone numbers) and one, which functions Gestaltically, based on structural understanding of the material (theorems, logical games, connections among facts) and which enables the transfer of what has been learnt to other materials.

The end of the Second World War meant that publication of three outstanding works was now possible: *Productive Thinking* by Wertheimer (posthumously), *La perception de la causalité* by Albert Michotte, and *Phénomenologie de la perception* by Maurice Merleau-Ponty.[28]

It was Wertheimer's intention that his book should introduce a project for a new logic that took account of the real progress of thought from the problem to its solution via successive restructurings of the cognitive material, and therefore of its logical form. Wertheimer's fundamental category was "good sense", the ability to see into (in-sight, *ein-sicht*) structures and grasp their inner architecture. It is one thing to find the sum of $1+2+3+4+5+6+7+8+9$ by adding up all the numbers (a blind and necessarily summative procedure to the structure); it is quite another to see – almost visually – that the first number plus the last number in the series makes ten, and that also the second number plus the penultimate one, the third plus the antepenultimate one, and so on, make ten, which is always the double of the central number in the series. Adding up the numbers in this case means taking the central term in the series and multiplying it by the number of terms: the result is immediate and the procedure is elegant. This happens because our eye has "X-rayed" the logical structure of the problem and seen through to its skeleton. Wertheimer's book contains numerous examples of this kind, all of them discussed in detail.

Michotte's book showed, by means of scores of experiments, that there is a direct perception of mechanical causality and that this obeys laws. The perceptual analysis of a structure (an object A moves until it reaches an object B already present in the field, object B immediately moves in its turn, less rapidly than A but along the same trajectory: what one sees is A striking B and pushing it onwards; from this paradigmatic situation numerous variations, causal and other, can be obtained) reveals that certain elementary concepts of mechanics, like those of "force", "impact", "mass", are already present in perception of the physical environment.

Merleau-Ponty's book sought to achieve a philosophical synthesis between Husserl's later reflections and the theoretical and empirical matters investigated by the Gestaltists, thereby amalgamating two perspectives – after they had followed very different routes – which had shared a great deal in common at the beginning of the century.

The most important works written by Gestaltist psychologists in the 1950s were concerned less with perception than with other areas of psychology. Although a considerable amount of good quality research into visual perception was still being conducted in Germany, Italy, Japan and Sweden (Uppsala), no attempt was made at theoretical innovation and there was no enthusiasm for the daring conceptions that had characterised the decades between the wars. Truly innovative works were written by Fritz Heider on interpersonal relations,[29] a book long in the gestation, which attempted to provide a logical formalisation of the sympathy and repulsion relationships between two people who share, or do not share, a liking for a particular object; a book by Solomon Asch[30] which summarised numerous experiments in social psychology, some of them carried out by Asch himself, designed to illustrate the effects of group pressure on an individual or a minority, or to show that the prestige of the source of a message affects its interpretation; a book by Rudolf Arnheim applying the knowledge about perception accumulated by the Gestalt psychologists during almost half a century of research to painting and the visual arts, opening new avenues for art criticism and general aesthetics.[31]

The bulky volume by Wolfgang Metzger, *Gesetze des Sehens* (1975), was the last significant work written in the spirit of Wertheimer. Metzger's book was an encyclopaedia of visual perception running to almost seven hundred pages; its first edition of 1936 ran to fewer than two hundred. The theoretical framework remained the same, but experimental research had proliferated during the forty years between the two dates. This state of affairs is perhaps the deep-lying cause of the declining fortunes of Gestalt theory in contemporary psychology.

Since 1979 a new German journal, *Gestalt Psychology*, has reopened debate on the fundamental themes of the Gestalt tradition, attracting the interest of a good number of scholars in Europe and America.

Notes

1 Wertheimer, 1912.
2 Pastore, 1971.
3 Koffka, 1935.
4 Kant, 2001, Part Two, II, § 77.
5 Ibid.
6 Goethe 1830, aphorisms, 59, 367.
7 Goethe 1830, aphorism 168.
8 Cf. Helmholtz 1867; 1863.
9 Husserl, 1900–01, at p. 231.
10 Husserl, 1900–01, at p. 232.
11 Buchler, 1956, at p. 75.
12 Buchler, 1956, at pp. 74–75.
13 Buchler, 1956, at p. 75.
14 Katz, 1911.
15 Köhler, 1913, at p. 80.
16 Popper, 1934.
17 Köhler, 1920, at p. 157–160.
18 Köhler, 1920, at p. 158.
19 Koffka, 1922.
20 Koffka, 1922, at p. 532.
21 Wertheimer, 1923.

22 Von Hornbostel, 1925.
23 Von Hornbostel, 1925, at p. 82.
24 Musatti, 1926.
25 Köhler, 1929.
26 Brunswik, 1952.
27 Lewin, 1936.
28 Wertheimer, 1959; Michotte, 1945; Merleau-Ponty, 1945.
29 Heider, 1958.
30 Asch, 1952.
31 Arnheim, 1954.

References

Arnheim, R. (1954). *Art and Visual Perception*. Berkeley, CA: University of California Press.

Asch, S. (1952). *Social Psychology*. New York: Prentice-Hall.

Brentano, F. (1874). *Psychologie vom Empirischen Standpunkte*. Leipzig, Germany: Duncker & Humblot.

Brown, J. F. (1936). *Psychology and the Social Order*. New York: McGraw-Hill.

Brown, J. F. (1940). *The Psychodynamics of Abnormal Behavior*. New York: McGraw-Hill.

Brunswik, E. (1952). The conceptual framework of psychology. In *Encyclopaedia of Unified Science* (pp. 1–10). Chicago: The University of Chicago Press.

Buchler, J., (ed.) (1956). *The Philosophy of Peirce, Selected Writings*. London: Routledge & Kegan Paul.

Duncker, K. (1935). *Zur Psychologie des Produktiven Denkens*. Berlin: Springer.

Ehrenfels von, Ch. (1890). Uber Gestaltqualitaten. *Vierteljahrsschrift fur Wissenschaftliche Philosophie*, *14*, 242–292.

Goethe, J.W. (1930). *Werke*, vol. 3. Tübingen, Germany: Cotta.

Heider, F. (1958). *Psychology of Interpersonal Relations*. New York: John Wiley and Sons (reprinted Hillsdale, N.J.: Lawrence Erlbaum Associates, 1983).

Helmholtz, H. (1863). *Die Lehre von den Tonempfindungen als Physiologische Grundlage für die Theorie der Musik*. Braunschweig, Germany: Vieweg und Sohn.

Helmholtz, H. (1867). *Handbuch der Physiologischen Optik*. Hamburg und Leipzig: Voss.

Hering, E. (1905). *Grundzilge der Lehre vom Lichtsinn*. Berlin: Springer.

Hornbostel von, E. M. (1925). Die Einheit der Sinn [The Unity of the Senses]. *Melos, Zeitschrift für Musik*, *4*, 290–297.

Husserl, E. (1891). *Philosophie der Arithmetik*. Halle, Germany: Niemeyer.

Husserl, E. (1900–1). *Logische Untersuchungen*. Halle, Germany: Niemeyer.

Kant, I. (ed 2001). *Critique of the Power of Judgment* (1790), (ed. and trans. P. Guyer). Cambridge, UK: Cambridge University Press.

Katona, G. (1940). *Organizing and Memorizing*. New York: Columbia University Press.

Katz, D. (1911). Die Erscheinungsweise der Farben und ihre Beeinflussung durch die individuelle Erfahrung. *Zeitschrift für Psychologie*, *7*, 6–31.

Koffka, K. (1922). Perception. An Introduction to the Gestalt Theory. *Psychologische Bullettin*, *19*, 531–585.

Koffka, K. (1935). *Principles of Gestalt Psychology*. New York: Harcourt, Brace, & World.

Köhler, W. (1913). Uber unbemerkte Empfindungen und Urteilstauschungen. *Zeitschrift für Psychologie*, *66*, 51–89.

Köhler, W. (1920). Die Physischen Gestalten in Ruhe und im Stationären Zustand. Eine Naturphilosophische Untersuchung (Eng. trans. "Physical Gestalten" in Ellis, W. D. (ed.). *A Source Book of Gestalt Psychology*, pp. 17–54. London: Routledge & Kegan Paul, 1938).

Köhler, W. (1925). *The Mentality of Apes*. New York: Harcourt, Brace & Co.

Köhler, W. (1929). *Gestalt Psychology*. New York: Liveright.

Lewin, K. (1926a). Untersuchungen zur handlungs und affektpsychologie. I. Vorbemerkungen über die psychischen kräfte und ueber die struktur der Seele. *Psychologische Forschung*, *7*, 294–329.

Lewin, K. (1926b). Untersuchungen zur Handlungs und Affektpsychologie. II. Vorsatz, Wille und Bediirfnis. *Psychologische Forschung, 7,* 330–385.

Lewin, K. (1936). *Principles of Topological Psychology.* New York: McGraw Hill.

Mach, E. (1885). *Beitriige zur Analyse der Empfindungen.* Jena, Germany: Fischer.

Mach, E. (1905). *Erkenntnis und Irrtum. Skizzen zur Psychologie der Forschung.* Leipzig, Germany: Barth.

Meinong, A. (1899). Uber Gegenstände höherer Ordnung und deren Verhaltnis zur inneren Wahrnehmung. *Zeitschrift fiir Psychologie und Physiologie der Sinnesorgane, 21,* 182–272.

Meinong, A. (1891). Zur Psychologie der Komplexionen und Relationen. *Zeitschrift fur Psychologie und Physiologie der Sinnesorgane, 2,* 245–65.

Meinong, A. (1904). *Abhandlungen zur Erkenntnistheorie und Gegenstandstheorie.* Leipzig, Germany: Barth.

Metzger, W. (1941). *Psychologie: die Entwicklung ihrer Grundannahmen seit der Einfuehrung des Experiments.* Dresden und Leipzig, Germany: Steinkopff; (rev. Darmstadt 1963, 3rd edn.).

Metzger, W. (1936). *Gesetze des Sehens.* Frankfurt, Germany: W. Kramer. Trans. as *Laws of Seeing* (2006) by L. Spillmann, M. Wertheimer and S. Lehar. Cambridge, MA: the MIT Press.

Merleau-Ponty, M. (1945). *Phénomenologie de la Perception.* Paris: Gallimard.

Michotte, A. (1954). *La Perception de Ia Causalité.* Louvain, Belgium: Editions de I'Institut Superieur de Philosophie.

Mill, J.S. (1843). *A System of Logic: Ratiocinative and Inductive.* London: Longmans.

Musatti, C. (1926). *Analisi del Concetto di Realtà Empirica.* Citta di Castello, Italy: II Solco.

Pastore, N. (1971). *Selective History of Theories of Visual Perception 1650–1950.* New York: Oxford University Press.

Popper, K.R. (1934). *The Logic of Scientific Discovery.* London: Hutchinson.

Rausch, E. (1937). Über Summativität und nichtsummativität. *Psychologische Forschung, 21,* 209–289.

Rubin, E. (1921). *Visuell Wahrgenommene Figuren. Studien in Psychologischen Analyse.* Copenhagen: Gyldenalske.

Stumpf, C. (1883/1890). *Tonpsychologie* (2 vols). Leipzig, Germany: Hirzel.

Stumpf, C. (1907a). Erscheinungen und psychische Funktionen. *Abhandlungen der Preußische Akademie der Wissenschaften, phil-hist. Klasse 4,* 40ff.

Stumpf, C. (1907b). Zur Einteilung der Wissenschaften. *Abhandlungen der Preußische Akademie der Wissenschaften, phil- hist. Klasse 5,* 97ff.

Wertheimer, M. (1912). Experimentelle Studien über das Sehen von Bewegung. *Zeitschrift für Psychologie, 61,* 161–265.

Wertheimer, M. (1923). *Untersuchungen zur Lehre von der Gestalt II, Psycologische Forschung, 4,* 301-350. Partial English translation in Ellis, W. (1938). *A Source Book of Gestalt Psychology,* pp. 71–88). London: Routledge & Kegan Paul [Editors' note: a complete English translation is available in Spillmann, L. (ed.): Max Wertheimer. P*erceived Motion and Figural Organization.* MIT Press, Cambridge, MA 2012]

Wertheimer, M. (1945). *Productive Thinking.* New York: Harper & Row.

Wertheimer, M. (1959). *Productive Thinking* (enlarged edition). New York: Harper & Row.

COMMENTS ON EXPERIMENTAL PHENOMENOLOGY: A HISTORICAL PROFILE

Alan Costall

> The trouble with men [who have] passed away is . . . that they continue to speak, but when questioned they answer no more.
>
> (Vicario, 1994, p. 134)

Phenomenology and "the constancy hypothesis"

I first came to know Paolo Bozzi in 1984, on a visit to Trieste to meet Gaetano Kanizsa. Trieste was an important centre for research in Experimental Phenomenology when almost all other centres, most notably Louvain, had long become inactive. We soon found we shared an enthusiasm for the work of Michotte, but also for James Gibson, whose own approach drew upon Gestalt psychology, thanks to his close contacts with Koffka, Heider, and also Lewin in the USA. I have warm memories of the conversations we had, mainly in the long established sub-department of the Institute of Psychology, "Al Collio" (a local *trattoria*). Paolo and I kept in touch over the years, and he arranged for two of his last doctoral students, Giulia Parovel and Michele Sinico, to come to work with me for an extended period.

My knowledge of Paolo Bozzi's writings is confined to those available in English. He gave me a reprint of his chapter, *Experimental phenomenology: a historical profile*, when it was first published. It is lucid and scholarly, and the English is perfect. I have recommended it to many students, and it was my suggestion for it to be included in the present volume.

Paolo Bozzi challenges the myth that Gestalt theory appeared "without trace" in 1912 with the publication of Wertheimer's experimental studies of movement perception, and convincingly traces this line of thought back to Goethe and Kant, and even to Plato and Aristotle. He also clarifies the subject of "holism" in relation to Gestalt theory, and examines the use of the phenomenological method in experimental design.

I have to admit that it was only on reading the chapter again for this commentary that I noticed that, despite its title's reference to "Experimental Phenomenology" Paolo Bozzi is mainly writing about "the evolution of Gestalt theory" (Bozzi, 1999; Ch. 17 in the present anthology, p. 19). But are "Experimental Phenomenology" and "Gestalt theory" the same thing?

The phenomenological method was concisely set out by Köhler in his book, *Gestalt Psychology*, and the following text is probably the best known statement of this approach:

> There seems to be a single starting point for psychology, exactly as for all other sciences: the world as we find it, naïvely and uncritically. (Köhler, 1929/1959, p. 7)

However, the *choice* of this method of unbiased seeing – *"unbefangenes Sehen"* (Klüver, 1930, p. 427) – was far from naïve. It was a resolute attempt to resist the uncritical importation into psychology of theoretical assumptions mainly developed with reference to the physical sciences, most notably, sensationalism and mechanism.

As Paolo Bozzi explains, the Gestalt psychologists were not against analysis as such (see also Henle, 1985, p. 103). Instead, they were arguing that the units of analysis should be identified on the basis of careful phenomenological study through the systematic variation of the conditions under which the "essence" of a "phenomenon", such as perceived transparency or perceived causality, is conserved (see Buytendijk, 1987, pp. 39–40). The choice of units should not be based on prejudices, not even *scientifically* sanctioned prejudices.

Very few treatments of the Gestalt psychologists, including the present chapter, discuss their wider political and ethical concerns (but see Leichtman, 1979; Ash, 1995). Bozzi's chapter does do justice to their research on memory, thinking, and social psychology. However, the main field of their research was, of course, visual perception, and it was directed against "the constancy hypothesis" or "mosaic theory". This hypothesis is a condensation of several physicalist assumptions, not least those deriving from the histological approach of sensory physiology (Katz, 1989, p. 76):

> perception is based upon elementary "atoms" of sensation, there are corresponding elementary "atoms" of stimulation confined not only spatially but also temporally, the elementary sensations are bound together by a process of association, there is a simple, one-to-one "mechanical" relation between stimulation and sensation.

The constancy hypothesis was the foundation of the research in classical psychophysics. The experiments were a "fix":

> To be sure, there exist examples of sensations connected univocally to stimuli, and they vary with variations in them. These examples are constructed in the laboratory so that every action on sensations not reducible to variation in the stimuli is rigorously excluded. By restricting the field of facts to experiments of this kind *the psychophysical hypothesis of the constancy of the stimulus/sensation ratio can never be refuted*. (Bozzi, 1999; Ch. 17 in the present anthology, p. 33; emphasis added)

Such experiments were stipulative rather than truly empirical: they were studies of the researchers' own theoretical *definition* of the subject under investigation. Unfortunately, this kind of self-enclosure continues. A good deal of current experimental research, most blatantly in the field of "Theory of Mind" (Leudar & Costall, 2009), embodies the dualistic and intellectualistic assumptions upon which it is based.

One outcome of the deployment of the phenomenological method within perceptual research is rather ironic. By the 1950s, the constancy hypothesis was widely agreed to have been *reinstated*, thanks to this results of this method. The hypothesis was now founded on a *molar* rather than atomistic definition of both stimulus and response (see Hochberg, 1957). Gibson's early work on *"perceptual* psychophysics" (e.g. Gibson 1950, 1959) was a prominent example. Although he rejected the atomism of traditional "sensory psychophysics," he also claimed a one-to-one relation between "higher-order" variables of stimulation (e.g. texture gradients) and the corresponding perceptual responses.

In his later work, however, Gibson emphatically rejected the stimulus-response formula, insisting, instead, that information is obtained, not imposed, and also shifting his emphasis from perception to the primacy of *action* (Gibson, 1979). So it is extremely odd that he continues to be characterised as a pure stimulus-response theorist, or even a bottom-up theorist (bottom-*down* would be more to the point!).

Gibson's early work was explicitly phenomenological, not least in relation to his fundamental contrast between the unbounded "visual world" and a delimited "visual field" (Gibson, 1950). In his later writings, this commitment to phenomenology was no longer explicit, and it was also limited as a result of his mistaken attempt to "objectify" his central concepts of information and affordances. Nevertheless, in, for example, his discussion of proprioception − "our awareness of being in the world" − he still included some powerful phenomenological insights (Gibson, 1979, p. 239).

Gestalt psychology and Experimental Phenomenology

As Robert Woodworth nicely joked, Gestalt psychology, despite its emphasis upon holism, "is really made up of individuals" (Woodworth, 1943, p. 107). In the early days, Köhler, Koffka, and Wertheimer ("the Berlin Gestaltists") presented a unified front, with Wertheimer as the acknowledged leader. However, there are many other highly significant figures who are also identified in the textbooks as Gestalt psychologists, including David Katz, Albert Michotte, and Edgar Rubin. The various individuals connected with Gestaltism may have all shared a commitment to a phenomenological method, but there are several key issues on which they also agreed or disagreed.

Gestalt qualities and sensationalism. First of all, there was an important divergence concerning the implications of the existence of Gestalt qualities: whether the existence of such qualities entails the complete rejection of sensationalism, or, instead, just the need to postulate *additional* non-sensory elements founded upon the elementary sensations (e.g. von Ehrenfels and Benussi). The Berlin Gestaltists emphatically rejected sensationalism, yet continued to regard the proximal stimulus as a "mosaic" (Koffka, 1935, p. 75). After all, the very idea of "perceptual organization" itself implies the pre-existence of primitive and incoherent material in need of a subsequent process of organisation! This was one of Gibson's major objections to Gestalt theory. (For an excellent discussion of perceptual structure in relation to Koffka, Heider, and Gibson, see Heft, 2001, pp. 225 et seq.)

Gestalt psychology and everyday life. Although the Gestaltists were highly critical of the artificiality of experimental research in psychology, much of their own research was itself based on highly schematic "displays" whose connection to the everyday world was often far from obvious. There were notable exceptions. David Katz not only "had a genius for seeing problems in everyday phenomena" (R.D. Macleod, cited in Krueger, 1989, p. 4), but also stayed close to those everyday phenomena, as in work on the appearance of colour:

Where do we encounter colours? First of all they are certainly to be observed in objects. A paper is white, a leaf is green, coal is black (. . .). Then further: The sky is grey, the water has a green shimmer, and the air is full of beams of light. (. . .) Experiences of colour in their natural unbroken meaningfulness arise out of the need for a practical orientation towards the colour-qualities of the surrounding world. (. . .) It would be a kind of psychological perversion . . . to cast these cases aside, and, instead, begin [our] study with colour-phenomena which the colour specialist has been able to produce only under the highly artificial conditions of the laboratory. Most people depart from this world without ever having had a chance to look into an expensive spectroscope, and without ever having observed an after-image as anything other than something momentarily wrong with the eye" (Katz 1935, pp. 3–4; emphasis added).

So, another relevant distinction to be made between the diverse individuals who comprised "Gestaltism" concerns the extent to which (a) they derived their problems from the lived world, and (b) also stayed close to that world in the actual conduct of their research.

Invariants. In modern psychology and social theory, relativism is taken to imply the depths of subjectivism. And yet physics long ago confronted the issue of relativity, and come out, as it were, on the other side. The special theory of relativity within physics is really a theory of *invariance.* The exact connection between the development of the concept of invariance within physics and perceptual theory is still unclear, but the existence of a logical and also historical connection is in no doubt (Costall, Sinico, and Parovel, 2003; Bohm, 1965). As I see it, the concept of perceptual invariants as a basis for perceptual constancies is one of the most important contributions of Gestalt psychology. Perceptual *constancy* is only possible precisely because perception is *relative!* Yet the concept of invariance figured differently, and perhaps sometimes not at all, within the work of the individual Gestaltists.

Form and meaning. Another point of disagreement concerns the focus on "form". Gestalt qualities are often discussed in terms of "the psychology of form" (the standard translation of Gestalt psychology in French is *psychologie de la Forme*). "Form" would include shape, and perhaps colour, in relation to vision, and melody, say, in relation to hearing.

By the 1920's, Michotte was already arguing that that this emphasis upon form – and even *perception* – was mistaken:

It is futile to study perception "in itself." Instead, it should be treated as a "phase of action" in relation to the motor and intellectual activity of the individual. (. . .) The problem of meaning, therefore, ultimately has priority over form. One might wrongly conclude that, in principle, meaning has nothing to do with perception, because, as has been long [wrongly] assumed, all meaning is an extrinsic addition to the data provided by perception. (Michotte, 1991, p. 34).

Michotte was concerned with what he called "functional relations," such as the causal relations between objects, and also their uses. But many other researchers concerned with the perception of form were also emphasizing the importance of "meanings" intrinsic to perception, including not only "affordances" but also expressive qualities.

Perception and cognition. A further important issue concerns the relation between perception and "the higher-mental functions". As Paul Guillaume explained:

> ... once we rule out the role of the intellect in organizing "sensations", then the question of the relation between the realms of the sensory and the intellectual must be posed once more, but in different terms. (Guillaume, 1937, p. 213; my translation)

Sometimes, as in the case of Köhler and Wertheimer, principles derived from research on vision were generalised to thinking and problem solving, as with the concept of "insight". In contrast, Michotte, for example, argued for a discontinuity between perceiving and reflective thought, drawing attention to those occasions when, as at a conjuring show, we simply cannot *believe* what we are seeing (see Thinès, Costall, and Butterworth, 1991/2015).

Speculative biophysics. A fundamental point of contention concerned the value of the kind of analogies that Köhler first came to draw between psychological and both physiological and physical processes. As Bartlett (1930) complained to Michotte that "I can't in the least see why it is necessary to force into Gestalt psychology all this speculative biophysics."

In 1930, Klüver drew a distinction between Gestalt psychology, with its physicalist analogies, and "work on Gestaltqualitäten". According to Klüver (1930, p. 431) those adopting a "strictly psychological approach" included: von Ehrenfels, Höfler, Meinong, Cornelius, Witasek, Benussi, Marty, Mach, Stout, Titchener, Lipps, Bühler, Stumpf, Schumann, and Gelb. David Katz should certainly be added to this list. As a reviewer of his classic text on colour observed (though hardly approvingly): "The author ... warns the reader against physical and physiological modes of thought; indeed the word 'wave-length' occurs twice only, an achievement in a book called *The World of Colour*" (Lythgoe, 1935, p. 259)![1]

Gestalt psychology and Experimental Phenomenology. So are the terms "Gestalt psychology" and "Experimental Phenomenology" interchangeable? As I have tried to explain, there were several important points on which the various individuals who have been labelled as "Gestalt psychologists" could take "sides", and not least about the autonomy of psychology from physics and physiology, and a thorough-going commitment to the phenomenological project. For this reason, I think a distinction between "Gestalt psychology" and "Experimental Phenomenology" remains valuable. So I suggest that "Experimental Phenomenology" be regarded as the more generic term, and "Gestalt psychology" as one of its well-intentioned, but ultimately misguided, manifestations.

Re-enchanting the world

Gestalt psychology arose as a protest against a scientific world that had no room for problems of meaning and value, thus no room for the most urgent problems of human beings (Henle, 1985, p. 101).

Gestalt psychology, as it is usually presented in the textbooks, is *no* more than the sum of its parts – the principles of perceptual organisation + the figure-ground relation + the postulate of isomorphism (and so on). But Gestalt psychology was a radical reaction to the scientism of traditional physical science, and its disenchantment of the world. As such, it was closely related to the Romantic Movement, the crucial difference being that Gestaltism was a reaction from *within* science itself.

Traditional science was *anti*-empirical in two senses. In relation to psychology, it did not do justice to the facts of human experience, but simply imposed its own assumptions about what those facts *must* be. Second, and most fundamentally, it radically subjectivised experience in its attempt to promote an ideal of an "objective world" that *excluded* the human subject. The consequence has been the doctrine of two separate worlds. The "subjective world" became the repository for all those qualities – colour, meaning, value – that could find no place in the so-called "physical world", *the world as theorised by physicists*.

In turn, this dualism of the objective and subjective has had two major consequences. The first is that the very idea of a science of psychology becomes a contradiction in terms, in that its very *subject* has been *excluded* from the established scientific ontology. The second consequence is even more serious. This *dualism* of the subjective and the objective under-mines the *empirical* basis for science in general. As Paolo Bozzi (1999; Ch. 17 in the present anthology, pp. 42–43) points out, Köhler was well aware of this serious problem, at least in relation to the objectivist program of *behaviourism*. And, remarkably, even Watson himself was aware of this problem! Despite all his bluster, he could never bring himself to exclude consciousness from his accounts of how science itself is *done* (Costall, 2012).

The experimental phenomenologists were intent on both re-enchanting the world, and de-subjectifying experience. Yet, they remained largely trapped in the Kantian dualism to which Paolo Bozzi importantly draws our attention – the dualism of *nuomenon* (the transcendent thing-in-itself) and *phenomenon* (see Bozzi, 1999; Ch. 17 in the present anthology, p. 21). Contrasts between, for example, phenomenal and physical causality (Michotte), or behavioural and geographical environment (Koffka), reflect that same dualism.

Köhler's biophysical "postulate of isomorphism" was supposed to "knit" together the realms of noumena and phenomena (Bozzi, 1991, p. 44). But I could never understand how this was supposed to work, given that the "physical world", as taken for granted by Köhler, is devoid of *meaning*, if not form (see also Bozzi, 1994). A much more promising alternative is to explore the nature of the "*immanent* order in which we can participate" (Buytendijk, 1947, p. 27; emphasis added), something along the lines of Gibson's project of an ecological psychology. But, most of all, we have to keep *physicalism* firmly in its place:

> Science takes on this task and, under the guidance of its own methodological norms, constructs its universe by means of a complex continuing process of idealization and mathematization. The resulting universe is the product of a methodological procedure (. . .) which must never be mistaken for reality itself. *Reality is, and always remains, the life-world, no matter how vast the possibilities of systematization and prediction that have been opened up by the development of science of the Galilean style.* (Gurwitsch, 1978, p. 88; emphasis added).

Note

1   According to Spiegelberg (1972, p. 42), "Katz was the Göttingen psychologist with whom Husserl's influence went deepest and remained most lasting."

References

Ash, M. G. (1995). *Gestalt Psychology in German Culture 1890–1967: Holism and the Quest for Objectivity*. Cambridge, UK: Cambridge University Press.
Bartlett, F. C. (1930). Letter to Albert Michotte, Cambridge, 29 December, 1930.
Bohm, D. (1965). *The Special Theory of Relativity*. New York: W.A. Benjamin.

Bozzi, P. (1994). What is still living and what has died in the Gestalt approach to the analysis of perception. In S. Levialdi, C. E. Bernardelli (Eds.), *Representation: Relationship Between Language and Image*. London: World Scientific. [Chapter 18 in the present anthology].

Buytendijk, F.J.J. (1947). Address in *Jubilé Albert Michotte*, pp. 22–28. Louvain: Editions de l'Institut Supérieur de Philosophie.

Buytendijk, F.J.J. (1987). Husserl's phenomenology and its significance for contemporary psychology. In J.J. Kockelmans (ed.), *Phenomenological Psychology: The Dutch school* (pp. 31–44). Dordrecht, NL: Martinus Nijhoff Publishers.

Costall, A. (2012). Introspection and the myth of methodological behaviourism. In J.W. Clegg (ed.), *Self Observation in the Social Sciences*, pp. 67–80. New Brunswick, NY: Transaction.

Costall, A., Sinico, M., and Parovel, G., (2003). The concept of 'invariants' and the problem of perceptual constancy. *Rivista di Estetica, n.s., 24*(3), 49–53.

Gibson, J. J. (1950). *The Perception of the Visual World*. Boston: Houghton Mifflin.

Gibson, J.J. (1979). *The Ecological Approach to Visual Perception*. Boston: Houghton Mifflin.

Gibson, J.J. (1959). Perception as a function of stimulation. In S. Koch (ed.), *Psychology: A Study of a Science*, Vol. l, pp. 456–501. New York: McGraw-Hill.

Guillaume, P. (1937). *La psychologie de la forme*. Paris: Flammarion.

Gurwitsch, A. (1978). Galilean physics in the light of Husserl's phenomenology. In T. Luckman (ed.), *Phenomenology and Sociology*, pp. 71–89. London: Penguin.

Heft, H. (2001). *Ecological Psychology in Context: James Gibson, Roger Barker, and the legacy of William James's radical empiricism*. Mahwah, NJ: Lawrence Erlbaum Associates.

Henle, M. (1985). Rediscovering Gestalt psychology. In S. Koch and D.E. Leary (Eds.), *A Century of Psychology as Science*, pp. 100–120. New York: McGraw-Hill.

Hochberg,J. (1957). Effects of the Gestalt revolution. *Psychological Review, 64*, 78–84.

Katz, D. (1935). *The World of Colour*. (Trans. R.B. MacLeod and C.W. Fox) London: Kegan Paul.

Katz, D. (1989). *The World of Touch*. (ed. and trans. Lester E. Krueger) Hillsdale, NJ: Lawrence Erlbaum.

Klüver, H. (1930). Supplement: Contemporary German psychology. In G. Murphy. *Historical Introduction to Modern Psychology (*pp. 417–455) (2nd edn. revised). New York: Harcourt Brace.

Koffka, K. (1935). *Principles of Gestalt Psychology*. New York: Harcourt, Brace, & World.

Köhler, W. (1929/1959). *Gestalt Psychology*. New York: Liveright.

Krueger, L. (1989). Editor's introduction. In D. Katz (1989). *The World of Touch*, 1–21. Hillsdale, NJ: Lawrence Erlbaum.

Leichtman, M. (1979). Gestalt theory and the revolt against positivism. In A.R. Buss (ed.), *Psychology in Social Context*, pp. 47–69. New York: Irvington.

Leudar, I., and Costall, A. (Eds.) (2009). *Against Theory of Mind*. London: Palgrave Macmillan.

Lythgoe, R.J. (1935). Review of The World of Colour by David Katz. *British Journal of Medical Psychology, 15*, 259.

Michotte, A. (1954/1991). Autobiography of Professor A. Michotte van den Berck. In G. Thinès, A. Costall, and G. Butterworth (Eds.), *Michottte's Experimental Phenomenology of Perception* (pp. 24–49). [First published in French in 1954.]

Spiegelberg, H. (1972). *Phenomenology in Psychology and Psychiatry*. Evanston: Northwestern University Press.

Thinès, G., Costall, A., and Butterworth, G.E. (1991). *Michotte's Experimental Phenomenology of Perception*. Hillsdale, NJ: Erlbaum. (re-edited by Routledge, 2015).

Vicario, G.B. (1994). Gaetano Kanizsa: The scientist and the man. *Japanese Psychological Research, 36*, 126–137.

Wertheimer, M. (1912). *Experimentelle Studien über das Sehen von Bewegung. Zeitschrift für Psychologie, 61*, 161–265.

Woodworth, R.S. (1943). *Contemporary Schools of Psychology* (3rd edn). London: Methuen.

18

WHAT IS STILL LIVING AND WHAT HAS DIED OF THE GESTALT APPROACH TO THE ANALYSIS OF PERCEPTION

If other speakers were here in my place some would say that everything in the Gestalt approach is dead, while others would claim that nothing has died, but perhaps a majority would declare that it is in one sense dead and in another sense alive, which is not at all what I want to say. The fact is that the death is rather recent and that before the inheritance can be fairly divided up there will have to be many court cases with many lawyers submitting their documents, and many claimants making their voices heard.

What I want to offer here is, first, a very brief historical overview of the Gestalt Theory, because, today in the 1990s, it may have been forgotten by some; followed by a brief list of the salient points, some of the fundamental notions that underlie this theory; and a summing up that answers the title question.

I.   The Gestalt movement is generally regarded as having originated in a study carried out by von Ehrenfels, the findings of which were published in Graz in 1890. This study concerned the perception of melodies and, in modern terms, it might be considered as the first study of "melodic contours". This learned article, wholly in prose and making use of complicated theories, explained that a melody remained perfectly recognisable even after all its notes had been altered, so long as the relationships among them remained unaltered, thus suggesting that the object of perception is not the sensorial elements but systems of relationships holding among those sensorial elements.

Nevertheless, very few Gestaltists regarded von Ehrenfels's research as their forerunner. It should be pointed out that the Gestalt movement began at a moment of great cultural upheaval in the period immediately preceding the First World War, after Wilhelm Wundt, after William James, after American structuralism, and, therefore, after a great amount of research had already been carried out. Max Wertheimer was a native of Prague and a Jew, who, like Koffka, had studied music, physics and philosophy; though he was at the time unknown, he one day introduced himself to two young professors in Frankfurt, Köhler and Koffka. What he showed them were certain strange phenomena that he had obtained by means of a toy, a stroboscope, which was capable of producing various types of apparent cinematographic movements (a succession of static images perceived as a sequence of continuous movements). He had varied exposure times, the forms of the objects and the light intensities, and thereby discovered many things. The two professors were impressed, proclaiming his findings miraculous, and they elected Wertheimer as their cultural "leader". This was how Wertheimer became the emblem of the Gestalt theory, even though in his lifetime he published only about twenty articles (a further ten as well as a booklet of notes and essays were published posthumously by his son). Although they wrote copious tomes and carried out thousands of hours of research in all parts of Europe and America, Koffka and Köhler always very honestly credited Wertheimer as their master.

In 1929 Köhler produced a synthetic exposition of the Gestalt theory (*Gestalt Psychology*); later on, in 1935 Koffka actually wrote a manual about the theory of form (*Principles of Gestalt Psychology*). Meanwhile hundreds of scholars were working assiduously, producing new and previously unknown visual phenomena, and publishing their findings in the *Psychologische Forschung* a journal that acted as the progressive record of all the Gestalt discoveries as they emerged from the laboratory. Some of the contributing scholars were geniuses. Of these let me mention Rausch (Frankfurt University), who attempted and achieved an extremely complex and in part successful mathematical generalisation of the Gestalt theories; Michotte (Louvain), who while being neither a Gestaltist nor a sympathiser of the Gestalt theory, discovered the phenomenon of causality in perception and studied the question systematically; Metzger who, risking being considered a friend of Nazism (which he was not, I knew him quite well), remained in Germany in order to keep the journal alive, continued his experiments and published a gigantic treatise on the theory of vision (*Gesetze des Sehens*, 1936).

As proof that this research movement is not extinct, although its initial exponents are dead, we may recall that the latest edition of the volume just mentioned above dates from 1974[1], and that, here in Italy, Gaetano Kanizsa published an awe–inspiring number of findings under the title *Grammatica del Vedere* in 1980[2] and that a few weeks ago he brought out another 350-page book entitled *Vedere e Pensare* containing findings from further experimental research[3]. The death of Gestaltism, if it has occurred, has led to the birth of Cognitivism or rather of a number of Cognitivisms, which have replaced or refuted parts of the Gestalt theories. The progress made by neurophysiology has also contributed to this pattern of things. We shall see later on what remains of the original theory.

II.   Now let us take a brief look at the basic ideas. The psychology of the Gestalt school is one of the least fully grasped, even by those who think they know and understand the Gestalt theory well. The Gestalt theory never maintained that the whole is greater than the sum of the parts; and it never said that everything depends on everything; on the contrary, a whole (admittedly difficult) chapter in one of Köhler's books demonstrates beyond any doubt that if everything depended upon everything that would only lead to chaos; certain things may depend upon certain others but not upon the totality in some metaphysical sense. This is typical of the way in which the theory is caricatured to death.

The concepts actually employed by the first generation of Gestaltists are not simple because these men were well versed in classical physics and were up to date with the physiology of their time. That is why it was difficult to catch them out. One of their technical concepts was that of "distal stimulus"; a second that of "proximal stimulus"; a third that of "peripheral stimulus". Then there were the notions of "silent organisation" below the threshold of experience (Köhler, 1929, p. 371) and of "manifest organisation" of the phenomenal field. The famous concept of "isomorphism" was articulated in a series of conceptual guidelines regarding what we might call Gestalt phenomenal analysis. Thus we have the concepts of "*prägnanz*", the minimal principle, and references to the electro-magnetic field etc.

Now I shall continue my discussion in a rather unscientific manner, because, at times, making use of one's imagination, employing an almost visual kind of imagination, allows us to grasp the substance of things better. What is meant by the "distal stimulus" the Gestaltists speak of? Imagine a metal cube suspended in an empty room; this is a possible distal stimulus for vision. To describe the distal stimulus means to describe the material objects that populate our experiences by means of descriptive and measuring procedures that elementary physics allows us to apply to those objects. The cube will have a weight, a shape, a size, its faces will be square, and its sides can be measured. The distal stimulus is a list of properties regarding objects in the space and time of physics defined in terms of physical measurements. It is not within perception because perception is the last step in a sequence (the psycho-physical chain) that starts from an object.

What is a "proximal stimulus"? In the case of vision, it is the projection onto the back of the eye of the properties of the cube that are represented or representable in terms of the rays that, of all the infinite rays that are dispersed in a thousand directions, are reflected by the cube and manage to pass through our pupil and, having been duly inverted, reach the back of the eye. However the proximal stimulus is not an event within the sensitive tissues of the eye, but a cross-section of this "optical flow" an instant before it arrives at the retina. It is the projectional description of the distal stimulus at a certain point in space.

"Peripheral stimulation", on the other hand, is the sum of the processes that take place within the retina when this "optical flow" reaches it. Here the Gestaltists introduce the first erroneous idea. For, in line with the histology of the time, they attributed very little importance to the lateral connections within the retina while giving great importance to the single photo-sensitive units, which led them to coin the expression "retinal mosaic". On this account, the "optical flow" that reaches the eye from a distance, from the observed physical object or from the distal stimulus, is split up into many tiny individual facets corresponding to the photo-sensitive cells, each capable only of transmitting in electrical code along the optic nerve the properties of the luminous rays that struck them. On the other hand, present-day psychophysiology is capable of revealing much that was then unknown. And what is revealed is a huge gap in the Gestalt theory of "silent organisation", which was defined as the sum of these supposed processes occurring behind the retina, identifying them as cerebral events of which we are totally unaware. The Gestaltists imagined, without having any operational evidence whatsoever to support this idea, namely that certain brain processes are capable of transforming the sensorial mosaic (in the visual case, the retinal mosaic) into what we effectively see (that is, into perception). Although they had rather vague ideas about the physical nature of this silent organisation, the Gestaltists entertained unshakeable dogmas regarding its fundamental properties.

Among his other accomplishments, Köhler was very well versed in physics and had received acknowledgement from Max Planck, who had also expressed his enthusiasm for the Gestalt theory. One of the first essays Köhler wrote on what was later to be called field theory, was a book on physics entitled *Physical Forms in Static and Almost Static States*[4]. Here he examined electrostatic phenomena, the self-distribution of electric charges upon semiconductors, the flow of liquids through increasingly complex systems of tubes, and the fundamental properties of the membranes that permit osmosis. By means of the study of all these topics he began, quite indirectly, formulating ideas concerning the workings of the brain; not because he practised neuroanatomy, but because, due to the way the stimulus mosaics transformed themselves into actual perception, the only solution appeared to be that of invoking the Gestalt properties of physics, especially of electric and electro-magnetic fields. After studying this "silent organisation" dictated by these electric-magnetic fields, by osmotic processes and other things, Köhler turned to "evident organisation", visible organisation, which represented another level within the framework of physics. Between these two levels of organisation, we can fit the concept of "isomorphism".

In Köhler's view, the properties we study in analysing our perceptions in highly simplified situations are the properties of the underlying physical processes, going on in the brain, inside the skull, which correspond one-to-one to the phenomena of sight or hearing. Thus, if in studying a visual phenomenon, we discover that it varies with the variation of three conditions, then there will be a physical process in the head that varies in three important respects (whether these be electrical, chemical or osmotic processes we do not know). The rule that expresses the functional connections of the visual phenomenon is the rule governing what happens in the brain at that moment. As a consequence of this commitment, it seemed appropriate to go beyond the brain and take the objects of perception as they are in everyday experience, in the unsophisticated experience measured in psychophysical laboratories, in the experience of which the poet, the painter, and certainly (in that period) the cinemato-graphic technician speak (it is clear that cinema has played an important role as stimulant in the creation of these ideas).

Thus, first of all, it is important to discover the general properties of the objects of everyday perception. It will not have escaped the notice of those who have read the recent literature on the psychology of perception that all this sounds like a prelude to Gibson, to the ecological view. But Gibson is the very opposite of the Gestaltists. He was a junior colleague of Kurt Koffka, one of the three great Gestaltists of the first generation. From Koffka he learnt above all that there is not much to be gained, for example, from studying the sensations obtained in the laboratory to determine where the threshold of a red dot on a black ground lies; we must study the objects of experience in their complexity. Gibson gives the same indication when setting out his ecological view, which is not subjective but realistic. However he gives a definition of stimulus wholly different from that of the Gestaltists. Among other things, Gibson denies the existence of processes of any kind, while the Gestaltists filled their theories with all sorts of conscious and unconscious physical and physiological processes. One concept that the Gestaltists introduced into numerous fields was that of "*prägnanz*" or "good form". Many people associate the Gestalt Theory with the theory of "good form". This also is a widespread misapprehension and needs to be corrected. The original idea of "good form" was simply that when the stimuli under observation are of a rather high level of complexity and contain, at an elementary level, what is needed to form a regular structure, it is more probable that the eye will perceive this structure rather than other structures which, *in theory*, might arise from the same stimuli. The importance of this concept has been over-emphasised, although it does work within certain limits.

Other perceptual processes may be interpreted in terms of minimum principle, as in Wertheimer's famous laws concerning proximity, similarity, continuity of direction, closure, concepts that are taught in the very first pages of psychology manuals.

Far more important is the fact that the Gestaltists emphasised how, as well as having tendencies, as well as *prägnanz*, as well as obeying the minimum principle etc., perceptual events are always the vehicles of "expressive" or "tertiary" qualities, that is they always convey meaning. There is a sentence attributed to Wertheimer, which he never actually wrote, but that his friends always quoted and that runs "black is gloomy even before being black". Most of the Gestaltists who knew Wertheimer and Koffka and who, like Arnheim, later applied Gestalt theory to the visual arts, greatly exploited this trend, which permits one to explore, at a very basic level, the purely aesthetic properties of perceptible structures. A sound or a face may be aggressive, a melody like a dish may be sweet, a thing may provoke fear or attraction. This is true not only of extremely complex objects like human faces or dances, but even, as Kandinsky demonstrated, of very elementary signs like for example a dot within a rectangle or a comma placed at the edge of a picture.

These are, roughly speaking, the most important elements of the theory and we can list them as follows: distal stimulus, proximal stimulus, peripheral stimulus, silent organisation, evident organisation, isomorphism between silent organisation and the immediate datum of experience, experience as minimal perceptual organisation of its elementary constituents, and meaning.

III.   The greatest blow to the Gestalt theory came from the physiology of the brain which has not only failed to prove any of the things the Gestaltists had predicted but has actually come up with completely different findings. Those who study the brain seriously, either from a functional point of view like the physiologists, or from an anatomical point of view, like my good friend Valentino Braitenberg, simply have not found the things predicted by the Gestaltists. They do not exist. It is as simple as that.

The Gestalt theory cannot be falsified in the sense Popper required, because in the Gestaltist community it is impossible to say what kind of results would force one to give the theory up. The explanations of the Gestaltists, like agile cats, always fall on their feet because of the ways that the peripheral stimulus depends on the proximal stimulus and then silent organisation comes into play so that what one sees either does or does not correspond to the stimulation: if it does correspond, there is nothing to explain; if it does not then there are always "processes". But given that the processes are not known, one cannot say when silent organisation is at work or when the eye sees according to classic psycho-physics. Therefore this approach, like Popper's molecular proposition: "either it will rain tomorrow or it will not" is always true but does not tell us about tomorrow's weather. In the same way the optical illusions studied so much by the Gestaltists are cases where silent organisation is present. But in those cases where there are no illusions the eye sees according to stimuli; so the eye sees either "according to stimuli or not according to stimuli". This is another case of a molecular proposition which is always true, a pure tautology.

There is a second fatal point in the Gestalt theory which is common, however, to many of the cognitivists and to brain science: isomorphism is all very well, but after a while it becomes something of a "virtus dormitiva". Molière in his *Malade Imaginaire* included an interesting scene of an examination at the Medical Faculty in Paris. There is a young man who wishes to become a doctor who is being questioned by the professor of pharmacology who asks him "Why does opium make one sleep?" He replies, "Quia in eo est virtus dormitiva" (Because it has the dormitive virtue). So the professor replies "Bene est" (Very good). The student goes on to show how good he really is adding "Cuius est natura sensus assopire" (The nature of which makes one fall asleep). Thus we have the so-called "model" and the "theory". Brain scientists usually do more or less the same, as did the Gestaltists (and it is not to be excluded that many others might do so too). The brain expert says, "When two lights alternate at a certain pace and at a varying intensity so that I see movement, there must be a certain process at work". If you ask him "But why do I see that movement?", he will reply "Because we have a mechanism in our brain that permits us to do so". The lay person may be amazed and may believe that the brain expert has explained something. The truth is that he has explained nothing and the lay person returns home duped. Humans and animals perceive causal relationships because a process taking place in the cortex perceives causal relationships. But what conditions does this process obey? It obeys this speed, that time etc. as seen during our psychological experiments. A real case of "virtus dormitiva".

Then, to tell the truth, there is also the question of fashion. It can go out of fashion to speak in a certain manner; yet, very often it is fashionable to reformulate the very same concepts using new words. This permanence of old concepts that flow through new words gives the sensation of change, and so people are happy and life goes on. In psychology journals today many old Gestaltist theories are wrapped in new words and sold as original ideas.

But what is still living? I think that there are many things still alive that posterity may inherit and exploit to the full.

I would like to begin with the following concept. Despite being so vulnerable to criticisms, some of which, such as those we have reviewed, are decisive objections, how can this theory have also produced so much research concerning new aspects in the field of perception? When I say "new" I mean in the sense of "discovery", that is things never noticed previously but which turn out to be true when put to the test even today. It is an unbelievable crop; there must be as many as 700 to 900 discoveries presented by the Gestaltists in the *Psychologische Forschung* regarding the perception of colour, of motion, of the third dimension, regarding the configuration of space, the sense of the passage of time, the fundamental relationships upon which many basic physical concepts are based (fall, causality, impact, etc). Any attempt on my part to give you an idea of all this would fail due to the immensity of the results obtained. Something is out of joint: so many products from such a faulty theory.

The fact is that the theory of form contains an implicit postulate that must be made explicit, namely, in the world of vision, we know little or nothing. Not in the sense that we do not know what the brain does in transferring incoming data into the world of visual perception (which is in itself a great mystery, though our knowledge is increasing little by little), but in the banal sense that we do not even know what the visual world to be explained by means of the brain is actually like; therefore, let us focus instead on the explanandum *per se*, of which neurophysiology, informatics etc. are meant to be the "explanantia".

Here is an experiment to carry out while you are in a car at night on a motorway. You are sitting in your car, driving, and everything is as usual: as you travel forward, the cat's eyes come up to meet you; you see road signs and you pay attention to them as they come closer to you so that you can read what is written on them; you notice a bend; you stop at a petrol station; and in the end you leave the motorway. What is there to be explained? You have perceived the road, the horizontal and vertical road indications; that's it. No, this is not true! Look carefully at what happens to the line that divides the road into carriageways when it disappears under the bonnet of your car, while you are moving forward. You will discover that when it is about to disappear under the bonnet, it suddenly lengthens. This is called the "Dallenbach effect" and was made known by Dallenbach in the 1930s in the USA. Now look at the cat's eyes that come towards you as you move ahead: very well, you see them coming up to meet you. If you raise your eyes to look in the rear-view mirror, you will see them peripherally in the visual field. Now they no longer come up to meet you; they simply move laterally, going out of sight to your left and your right. Now look back at the road and you will see them again moving towards you. Go back to look at them peripherally and you will see again that they move away from each other, laterally. When you arrive at the exit of the motorway, you will see luminous blocks lengthening and shortening. But that's not true! The lower section is always illuminated while the upper section flashes so that you see something emerging and disappearing. This is called "Polarized Gamma Movement" and was discovered by Kanizsa about twenty years ago.[5] In actual fact, everyone sees something emerging and then returning inwards. Again, if you drive at a constant speed in daylight, the billboards will approach you from afar; they "come closer" you might say. This is the law of "perspective constancy", which some people explain by saying that we have a mechanism in our brain that uses unconscious judgements (which do not exist) or other miraculous things to make us see the billboards come closer. But look carefully at them: when they are at a distance of about fifteen or ten meters they no longer approach you but explode laterally, they open up.

All these things become clear if we know how to observe when driving along the motorway. In the world of vision there are many more things than we notice in normal life.

Now one might think that a complete list of all these things has already been drawn up. As a matter of fact, though, it has not. What I'm emphasising is that our knowledge covers only about 10% of the properties present in the world that surrounds us and that the remaining 90% has still to be discovered. If we do not seek, we shall not find. These are the kind of facts that physiology will have to explain, and not a simplified perceptual world that simply does not exist. This more complex world is what has to be explained by informatics or by the different branches of the neurological sciences, because this is the real world of vision, not that impoverished and approximate world that we carry in our heads as our image of visual reality.

Another important notion, in my opinion, is that of "percept-percept coupling" which is the basis of all experimentation regarding vision. The fact that in immediate experiences within the field of perception one risks making this kind of discovery every other moment depends on the fact that one thing inevitably implies something else. This is "percept-percept coupling". Imagine you have a red circle on a grey background and that the circle has clear contours. You will see a red of a certain degree of intensity. Now, keeping the luminous radiations from the stimulus invariant, if you blur the contours of this circle somewhat, then all the colour of the circle, including that within the circle, will become paler, whitish. If we change one aspect of the world another is also modified. The modification of the second is strictly implied by that of the first: $x = f(y)$ but at times $x = f(y, z, w \ldots)$.

There is a story about a dying peasant who leaves his field to his children and tells them that there is treasure in it. So the children begin to dig and dig and dig. They find nothing, but the field becomes amazingly fertile. Many years later when they die they meet their father in Heaven. The first thing they say to him is, "You said there was treasure but we dug and dug without finding anything". The old ghost replies, "Yes you did, you turned a piece of land into fertile ground thanks to your having dug in depth".

This is the type of work that must be done in the direction indicated by Gestalt Psychology. I mean: changing its concepts, freeing it from physiological superstitions (above all avoiding the creation of new ones), purifying its logic, rendering it refutable, but preserving its method for the analysis of phenomena and perfecting it in all possible ways, so as to reduce the unknown 90% to which I referred above. Otherwise, with our present day physiological inventions and informatics we risk presenting a world of perception that does not exist.

Notes

1 Editors' note: The first English translation of Metzger's *Laws of Seeing*, by Lothar Spillmann, appeared with MIT Press in 2009.

2 Editors' note: *Organization in Vision: Essays on Gestalt Perception* first appeared in English with Praeger, Santa Barbara CA, 1979.

3 Editor's note: Kanizsa, G. (1991). *Vedere e pensare* [*Seeing and Thinking*]. Bologna, Italy: il Mulino.

4 Kohler, W. (1920). *Die physischen Gestalten in Ruhe und im stationären Zustand: eine naturphilosophische Untersuchung*. Braunschweig, Germany: Friedr, Vieweg & Sohn (https://archive.org/details/diephysis chenges00kh).

5 Kanizsa, G. (1978). The polarization of gamma movement. *Italian Journal of Psychology*, *5*(3), 265–285. (Editors' note: the device Bozzi describes is no longer in use on Italian roads, but the effect of a vertical movement is easy to imagine.)

COMMENTS ON WHAT IS STILL LIVING AND WHAT HAS DIED OF THE GESTALT APPROACH TO THE ANALYSIS OF PERCEPTION

Johan Wagemans

It is a funny coincidence that Ivana Bianchi invited me to write a commentary on Bozzi's essay on what is still living and what has died in the Gestalt approach to perception, when I was writing a similar book chapter, entitled "How much of Gestalt theory has survived a century of neuroscience?" (Wagemans, 2014). Together with a dozen international scholars, I had just published two extensive review papers on the empirical and theoretical achievements of Gestalt psychology for perception research (Wagemans et al., 2012a, 2012b) and I had just finished writing a book chapter on the historical and conceptual roots of the Gestalt tradition regarding perceptual organization (Wagemans, 2015). And yet, I was struck by the new insights I gained from reading Paolo Bozzi's chapter. I must admit that I do not always agree with his views, but they are definitely original and insightful. In this brief commentary, I will summarise what I regard as the essence of the chapter and then expand a bit on the main implications for scientists today.

After a brief historical overview of Gestalt theory, Bozzi first discusses some of the core notions of this theory and then gets to the question formulated in the title.

Bozzi presents a coherent version of Gestalt theory, essentially emphasizing so-called "silent organization processes" that bridge the gap between peripheral stimulation and visible organisation. Although the distinction between the distal stimulus – a list of properties regarding objects in space and time defined in terms of physical measurements (basically, the objects out there in the world) – and the proximal stimulus – a cross-section of the optic flow an instant before it arrives at the retina (basically, the retinal image) – is well known, the concept of "peripheral stimulation" is much less recognised. Bozzi (1994; Ch.18 in the present anthology, p. 1) defines it as "the sum of the processes that take place within the retina when the optical flow reaches it" and he criticises the Gestaltists for regarding it merely as a retinal mosaic – the activity of separate photo-sensitive units – and disregarding the important role of lateral connections within the retina. Because of this, they attributed great importance to the silent organisation – the sum of the processes supposed to occur behind the retina, cerebral events of which we are totally unaware, transforming the retinal mosaic into what we see. The silent organisation was then "explained" by invoking electric and electromagnetic fields. More generally, an isomorphism was postulated between the silent and manifest (or evident or visible) organisation (for further discussion of isomorphism, see Luccio, 2010).

While Bozzi discusses the essence of Gestalt theory as he views it (which is a quite original view, by the way), he also highlights three misunderstandings about Gestalt theory. First, Gestalt theory never maintained that the whole is *greater than* the sum of the parts (indeed, they maintained that the whole is *different from* the sum of the parts). Second, according to Bozzi, it is a mistake to associate Gestalt theory with the theory of "good form" or "Prägnanz". Although it is true that the visual system has a preference for perceiving regular structures when the stimuli allow it, the principle works only within certain limits and its importance has generally been overemphasised. Third, and more important than Prägnanz, the Gestaltists emphasised that perceptual events are always vehicles of "expressive" or "tertiary" qualities, that is, they always convey meaning. This tendency, which has often been neglected, permits one to explore the purely aesthetic properties of perceptible structures.

In the final part of his essay, Bozzi gets to the question of what is still living and what has died in the Gestalt approach to perception. Let us start with the positive aspects of the evaluation. What is still living, according to Bozzi, are as many as 700 to 900 empirical discoveries the Gestaltists presented in their journal *Psychologische Forschung* – discoveries in the sense of new facts about perception that had never been noticed previously, but which turn out to be true when put to test even today. I agree with this: These historical papers, mainly from the 1920s and 1930s, continue to be a rich source of inspiration for current vision scientists but unfortunately many of these are not well known to contemporary readers, partly because they still have not been translated into English (except for the top 5% or so). There are still many gems to be discovered by new generations of scholars.

Regarding the theoretical contribution, Bozzi is much more critical. The Gestaltist "explanation" of the "silent organization" in terms of electric and electromagnetic fields has not been confirmed by modern neuroscience. Physiologists and anatomists simply have not found the things predicted by the Gestaltists: "They do not exist. It is as simple as that" (Bozzi, 1994; p. 411 in the present anthology). I personally do not think it is as simple as that. As argued elsewhere (Wagemans, 2014), the experiments by Lashley, Sperry and others, which have been presented as a devastating blow to Köhler's field theory, were not as clear-cut and decisive, and much of the decline of global-field theories was also due to the rise of the single-neuron doctrine following Hubel and Wiesel's Nobel Prize winning work. Moreover, the recent surge of interest in complex adaptive systems and cortical dynamics, as well as the empirical evidence for phenomena such as synchronisation, coherence intervals, and travelling waves (e.g., Alexander et al., 2013; Nikolaev et al., 2010), can all be regarded as a revival of the existence and importance of global-level cortical phenomena, albeit of a kind different from those envisaged by Köhler.

What is probably worse is that "Gestalt theory cannot be falsified in the sense Popper required, because (. . .) it is impossible to say what kind of results would force one to give the theory up" (Bozzi, 1994; p. 412 in the present anthology). In a nutshell, one cannot falsify claims about perception, which sometimes follows classic psychophysics ("according to stimuli") and sometimes does not, invoking processes involved in silent organisation, as in the case of visual illusions. Another fatal flaw, which Gestalt theory shares with cognitive science and brain science according to Bozzi, is that isomorphism becomes something of a "virtus dormitiva" when one postulates a mechanism for everything that perception is able to do. I must admit that such a tendency exists in much of the literature on computational models or neurophysiological mechanisms underlying various perceptual phenomena. Many of these models or theories are post-hoc constructions of the kind that appear to explain things by postulating an entity that does this thing, rather than building it up from established, empirically corroborated or theoretically justified "first principles". Bozzi points out (rightly so, I believe) that there is something strange going on here ("something out of joint"), namely that so many empirical discoveries were produced from such a faulty theory.

When analysing where Gestalt theory, as well as contemporary vision science, has gone wrong, Bozzi (1994; p. 413 in the present anthology) makes a bold claim: ". . . in the world of vision, we know little or nothing (. . .) in the banal sense that we do not even know what the visual world to be explained by means of the brain is actually like". As a recommendation, he adds: ". . . let us focus instead on the explanandum *per se*, of which neurophysiology, informatics etc. are meant to be the explanantia" (1994; p. 414 in the present anthology). What he means by that is then clarified by some examples, and this is the part that was the biggest discovery for me. What he means is an analysis of our hidden percepts, not the phenomenal world we are usually conscious of in terms of objects, scenes, and events around us, but the continuously changing sensations that are much more closely related to the peripheral stimulation than to the manifest organisation. I think what Bozzi recommends is to ask experienced observers to distance themselves from the normal transparent percepts, but to focus instead on the medium through which these percepts are constructed, that is, the sensations that are actually taking place in parts of our visual field, before they are organised into coherent wholes, before they are interpreted in terms of their distal causes, before they are given meaning in terms of the things we know about the world. The silent organisation is then described by Bozzi in terms of percept-percept couplings – the fact that one organisation or interpretation immediately gives rise to another, the fact that these intermediate-level percepts are all coupled together (for further discussion, see Savardi and Bianchi, 2002).

I did not realise this before but I believe this is what Bozzi's Experimental Phenomenology (Bozzi, 1989) is about. Unfortunately, Bozzi's full-blown exposition (Bozzi, 1989) has still not been translated in English, though the present anthology gives at least a flavour of what he was aiming at. If my interpretation of his recommendation is correct, I should add that this is quite distinct from the kind of Experimental Phenomenology that Wertheimer (1922) had in mind when he argued that research had to proceed "from above downward" ("*von oben nach unten*") instead of "from below upward" ("von unten nach oben"). Indeed, Wertheimer argued that a description of phenomenal experience in terms of the units people naturally perceive is needed because the more basic sensations are often no longer accessible for analysis in cases where the holistic tendencies are so strong that they change the given (the building blocks for perception) in many ways. What Bozzi argues for, seems to be the opposite: to go beyond everyday perception and try to analyse the snapshots and components of peripheral stimulation before they are organised and interpreted as caused by distal objects, scenes, and events.

Is it possible that Paolo Bozzi (1930–2003) was theoretically closer to Vittorio Benussi (1878–1927), the most important researcher of Alexius Meinong's "Gegenstandstheorie", who brought the Graz school of Gestalt psychology to Italy, than his older colleagues in Padova and Trieste, Fabio Metelli (1907–1987) and Gaetano Kanizsa (1913–1993), who were more strongly influenced by Cesare Musatti (1897–1989)? Is it possible that this closer affinity to the Graz school followed from Bozzi's interest in auditory perceptual organisation (e.g., streaming), which must have led him naturally to Christian von Ehrenfels's monograph "Ueber Gestaltqualitäten" (1890)? Not knowing the history of Italian Gestalt psychology well enough (see Verstegen, 2000; Zanforlin, 2004), I can only speculate about the reasons and the influences, but the emphasis on sensations on which perception is constructed is very much in line with the Graz school of Gestalt psychology and in contrast with the Berlin school's emphasis on the foundational nature of Gestalten as organised wholes that are not built from more elementary sensations (cf. Wertheimer, Köhler, Koffka). For further discussion of the differences between the Gestalt schools of thought, see Albertazzi (2015), Verstegen (2000) and Wagemans (2015).

In closing, let me reflect on the possibility that experienced observers can analyse their fleeting sensations before these are influenced by their conscious experiences of objects, scenes, and events. One idea has been that artists, because they have to render their visual impressions on a 2D canvas, would be able to see their retinal images as they are, before perceptual constancies and visual illusions come into play, but the empirical evidence for this possibility is weak at best (e.g., Ostrofsky, Kozbelt, and Seidel, 2012; Perdreau and Cavanagh, 2011). Perhaps with a lot of training, some visual psychophysicists, like Paolo Bozzi himself, are capable of this in some circumstances, but even then I wonder how useful the information provided by this method will be, if one is unable to show how these primitive sensations are turned into more coherent organisations and more meaningful interpretations. Because of their fleeting nature and because of the inherent inaccessibility of most of the intermediate-level representations, such a theory will probably remain elusive. Indeed, a thorough analysis of the literature on lightness and form perception by Alan Gilchrist (2015) has demonstrated rather convincingly that the evidence for the very existence of "raw sensations" is virtually non-existent. He even goes as far as to conclude that raw sensations fall into the same category as the concept of phlogiston. (Like Bozzi, Gilchrist is also known for his bold claims.)

For myself, I am still undecided. I am open to the possibility that there are two fundamentally different kinds of Gestalts. First, those that develop from sensations into perceptions, with an emphasis on bottom-up processes, which might be analysable in Bozzi's way of Experimental Phenomenology ("*von unten nach oben*"), because the Gestalt qualities are added along the way, as proposed by the Graz school. Second, those that immediately give rise to strong Gestalts, as proposed by the Berlin school, probably with a great deal of top-down involvement, where the building blocks are no longer accessible for conscious analysis, and the phenomenal experience must therefore be described by Wertheimer's way of Experimental Phenomenology ("*von oben nach unten*"). Only by doing more work in the Gestalt tradition will we be able to provide sufficient empirical grounds to decide about the plausibility of this conjecture. No matter what comes out of this endeavor, the analysis and proper description of visual representations and experiences will deliver the proper explananda for vision science and provide essential information also for those who do not work in the Gestalt tradition. Let us hope that the present collection of Bozzi's writings helps to inspire the young generations of vision scientists, who are in need of new theoretical impetus, to engage in this work.

References

Albertazzi, L. (2015). Philosophical background: Phenomenology. In J. Wagemans (ed.), *Oxford Handbook of Perceptual Organization*, pp. 21–31. Oxford, UK: Oxford University Press.

Alexander, D. M., Jurica, P., Trengove, C., Nikolaev, A. R., Gepshtein, S., Zvyagintsev, M., Mathiak, K., Schulze-Bonhage, A., Ruescher, J., Ball, T., and van Leeuwen, C. (2013). Traveling waves and trial averaging: The nature of single-trial and averaged brain responses in large-scale cortical signals. *Neuroimage, 73*, 95–112.

Bozzi, P. (1989). *Fenomenologia sperimentale* [*Experimental Phenomenology*]. Bologna, Italy: il Mulino.

Gilchrist, A. (2015). Theoretical approaches to lightness and perception. *Perception, 44*, 339–358.

Luccio, R. (2010). Anent isomorphism and its ambiguities: From Wertheimer to Köhler and back to Spinoza. *Gestalt Theory, 32*(3), 219–262.

Nikolaev, A. R., Gepshtein, S., Gong, P., and van Leeuwen, C. (2010). Duration of coherence intervals in electrical brain activity in perceptual organization. *Cerebral Cortex, 20*, 365–382.

Ostrofsky, J., Kozbelt, A., and Seidel, A. (2012). Perceptual constancies and visual selection as predictors of realistic drawing skill. *Psychology of Aesthetics, Creativity, and the Arts, 6*(2), 124–136.

Perdreau, F., & Cavanagh, P. (2011). Do artists see their retinas? *Frontiers in Human Neuroscience, 5.* (171), 1–10.

Savardi, U. and Bianchi, I. (2012). Coupling Epstein's and Bozzi's "percept-percept coupling". *Gestalt Theory, 34*(2), 191–200.

Verstegen, I. (2000). Gestalt psychology in Italy. *Journal of the History of the Behavioral Sciences, 36*(1), 31–42.

Wagemans, J. (2014). How much of Gestalt theory has survived a century of neuroscience? In A. Geremek, M. Greenlee, and S. Magnussen (Eds), *Perception Beyond Gestalt: Progress in Vision Research*, pp. 9–21. New York: Psychology Press.

Wagemans, J. (2015). Historical and conceptual background: Gestalt theory. In: J. Wagemans (ed.), *Oxford Handbook of Perceptual Organization*, pp. 3–20. Oxford: Oxford University Press.

Wagemans, J., Elder, J. H., Kubovy, M., Palmer, S. E., Peterson, M. A., Singh, M., and von der Heydt, R. (2012a). A century of Gestalt psychology in visual perception: I. Perceptual grouping and figure-ground organization. *Psychological Bulletin, 138*(6), 1172–1217.

Wagemans, J., Feldman, J., Gepshtein, S., Kimchi, R., Pomerantz, J. R., van der Helm, P., and van Leeuwen, C. (2012b). A century of Gestalt psychology in visual perception: II. Conceptual and theoretical foundations. *Psychological Bulletin, 138*(6), 1218–1252.

Wertheimer, M. (1922). Untersuchungen zur Lehre von der Gestalt, I: Prinzipielle Bemerkungen. *Psychologische Forschung, 1*, 47–58. (Translated extract reprinted as "The general theoretical situation." In W. D. Ellis (ed.), (1938). *A Source Book of Gestalt Psychology*, pp. 12–16. London: Routledge & Kegan Paul Ltd.)

Zanforlin, M. (2004). Gestalt theory in Italy: Is it still alive? *Gestalt Theory, 26*(4), 293–305.

INDEX

Note. Never part with good money for a non-fiction book without an index – even a quirky one. As an index is of most use to someone who has already at least dipped into the book in hand, and who is looking to re-find what has stuck in mind, we have tried to pick up the more characteristic of Bozzi's distinctions/associations, bugbears and turns of thought and phrase.